SO-AZJ-138

THESE UNITED STATES
The Questions of Our Past

Concise Edition · Volume II: Since 1865

Second Edition

Irwin Unger

New York University

Prentice
Hall

Upper Saddle River, New Jersey 07458

Library of Congress Cataloging-in-Publication Data

The Library of Congress has catalogued the one volume edition as follows:

UNGER, IRWIN.
    These United States: the questions of our past / Irwin Unger. —Combined concise ed.,
2nd ed.
        p.   cm.
    Includes index.
    ISBN 0-13-097805-1
    1. United States—History. I. Title.
E178.1.U54 2003
973—dc21
                                                                    2002029291
                                                                          CIP

Editorial director: Charlyce Jones Owen
Senior acquisitions editor: Charles Cavaliere
Associate editor: Emsal Hasan
Editorial assistant: Adrienne Paul
Production editor: Judy Winthrop
Project liaison: Louise Rothman
Prepress and manufacturing manager: Nick Sklitsis
Prepress and manufacturing buyer: Sherry Lewis
Marketing director: Beth Mejia
Marketing manager: Claire Bitting
Cover design: Kiwi Design
Cover art: Women's march 1913, Library of Congress.

© 2003, 1999 by Prentice-Hall, Inc.
A division of Pearson Education
Upper Saddle River, New Jersey 07458

This book was set in 10.5/12 Berkeley Book by ICC and was
printed and bound by Courier-Stoughton.
The cover was printed by Phoenix Color Corp.

Printed in the United States of America
10 9 8 7 6 5 4 3 2 1

Photo credits begin on page A48 and constitute a continuation from the
copyright page.

ISBN 0-13-097804-3

Pearson Education Ltd., *London*
Pearson Education Australia PTY, Limited, *Sydney*
Pearson Education Singapore, Pte. Ltd.
Pearson Education North Asia Ltd, *Hong Kong*
Pearson Education Canada, Ltd., *Toronto*
Pearson Education de Mexico, S.A. de C.V.
Pearson Education—Japan, *Tokyo*
Pearson Education Malaysia, Pte. Ltd.
Pearson Education, *Upper Saddle River, New Jersey*

To   *Rita and Mickey, Libby and Arnie,*
     Phyllis and Jerry, and Norma and David
     —once more

BRIEF TABLE OF CONTENTS

CONTENTS

MAPS

ABOUT THE AUTHOR

Pulitzer Prize winning historian Irwin Unger has been teaching American history for over forty years on both coasts. Born and largely educated in New York, he has lived in California, Virginia, and Washington State. He is married to Debi Unger and they have five children, now all safely past their college years. Professor Unger formerly taught at California State University at Long Beach, the University of California at Davis, and New York University. He is now professor emeritus.

Professor Unger's professional interests have ranged widely within American history. He has written on Reconstruction, the Progressive Era, and on the 1960s. His first book, *The Greenback Era*, won a Pulitzer Prize in 1965. Since then he has written *The Movement: The New Left* and (with Debi Unger) *The Vulnerable Years, Turning Point: 1968, The Best of Intentions* (about the Great Society), and *LBJ: A Life*. He and Debi Unger are now working on a biography of the Guggenheim family.

PREFACE

This is the second edition of *These United States: Concise Edition*. Like its predecessor, it is a compact version of *These United States: The Questions of Our Past* and is designed to present all the essentials of the larger work in a briefer format to facilitate readability and reduce the price of the work to the student.

The condensing process has not, I believe, sacrificed essential material. Rather, redundant examples, overextended treatments, and marginal topics have been eliminated, a process that drew on reviewers' and adopters' evaluations. And to constrain costs, we have also reduced the number of illustrations and maps and removed the "Portraits" from the main body of the text and placed them in a separate booklet.

In most significant ways the books' plan remains the same, however. First, unlike virtually every other introductory text, it still has a single author and speaks in a single voice. I hope readers will agree that a book by a single individual has inherent advantages over one composed by a committee. Second, each chapter is still organized around a significant question, each designed to challenge students with the complexity of the past and compel them to evaluate critically different viewpoints. This plan, I believe, makes the learning of history a quest, an exploration, rather than the mere absorption of facts. Yet, at the same time, "the facts" are made available. *These United States* provides the ample "coverage" of standard texts.

The word "standard" here does not mean old-fashioned. Though *These United States* discusses political, diplomatic, and military events, it also deals extensively with social, cultural, and economic matters. It concerns itself not only with "events," moreover, but also with people, currents, and themes. It is not old-fashioned in another way: it expands the "canon" to include those who have traditionally been excluded from the American past and seeks to embrace the enormous diversity of the American people. The reader will find in *These United States* women as well as men; people of color as well as those of European extraction, youths as well as adults; the poor as well as the rich; artists, writers, and musicians as well as politicians, generals, and diplomats.

In this newest version of the work, I have added sections on various aspects of social history, particularly on slavery, on the Salem witch trials, and on daily life. I have also extended the story through the events of 2000 and 2001, including the World Trade Center and Pentagon attacks, the war on terrorism, and the collapse of the "bubble" economy of the 1990s.

I hope that, like its precursors, this edition meets with favor among faculty and students and serves both as a successful teaching instrument and an absorbing introduction to the American past.

Irwin Unger
Department of History, Emeritus
New York University

ACKNOWLEDGMENTS

Every author incurs debts in writing or revising a book such as this. I have been the beneficiary of particularly generous help and advice and I would like to acknowledge it here.

My thanks to my editor Charles Cavaliere and associate editor Emsal Hasan. Susan Alkana's editorial advice and services were invaluable during the early and mid-phase of the revisions. I should also like to thank Charlyce Jones Owen for her valuable supervisory help, Claire Bitting for her marketing skills, and Judy Winthrop for her expertise as production editor. A number of my fellow academics were generous enough to read and evaluate the manuscript for this Concise Edition. They include William M. Leary, University of Georgia; Michael Haridopolos, Brevard Community College; Stephen L. Hardin, The Victoria College; David G. Hogan, Heidelberg College. Thank you also to the reviewers of this edition: James A. Page of Collin County Community College (TX); Kurt W. Peterson of Judson College; Thomas A. Kinney of Case Western Reserve. My thanks also to the scholars and teachers who evaluated earlier editions: James F. Hilgenburg, Jr., of Glenville State College; Johanna Hume of Alvin Community College; Robert G. Fricke of West Valley College; Steve Schuster of Brookhaven College; Kenny Brown of the University of Central Oklahoma; Paul Lucas of Indiana University; and last, but assuredly not least, Irving Katz, also of Indiana University. Though I did not invariably follow their advice, I always took it seriously.

■ ANCILLARY INSTRUCTIONAL MATERIALS ■

These United States Concise Edition comes with an extensive package of ancillary materials.

For the Instructor

Test Item File this section contains multiple-choice questions, essay questions, identification questions, and matching questions.

Instructor's Manual with tests includes chapter summaries, learning objectives, suggestions for lecture topics, essay or classroom discussion topics, and suggestions for projects or term papers.

Prentice Hall and Penguin Bundle Program Prentice Hall and Penguin are pleased to provide adopters of *These United States* with an opportunity to receive significant discounts when orders for *These United States* are bundled together with Penguin titles in American history. Please contact your local Prentice Hall representative for details.

History Central provides invaluable support resources for instructors and supplies interactive learning materials for classroom use. Features include PowerPoint™Slides, Instructor Resource Manuals, Maps in U.S. History, Document Library, and Interactive Maps. Please contact your local Prentice Hall representative for details.

Prentice Hall Custom Test, available in Windows, DOS, and Macintosh formats, provides questions from the printed test item file for generating multiple versions of tests.

For the Students

Study Guides, Volumes I and II, include commentary, definitions, identifications, map exercises, short-answer exercises, and essay questions.

Historical Documents and Portraits have been extracted from the unabridged version of the text and compiled as a separate supplement for students, available at no charge when shrinkwrapped (at the instructor's request) to the text. The Historical Portraits consist of biographical information about a representative figure from each chapter, while the Historical Documents are excerpts from primary-source readings.

16

RECONSTRUCTION

What Went Wrong?

1863	Lincoln announces his ten-percent plan for reconstruction
1863–65	Arkansas and Louisiana accept Lincoln's conditions, but Congress does not readmit them to the Union
1864	Lincoln vetoes Congress's Wade-Davis Reconstruction Bill
1865	Johnson succeeds Lincoln; The Freedmen's Bureau overrides Johnson's veto of the Civil Rights Act; Johnson announces his Reconstruction plan; All-white southern legislatures begin to pass Black Codes; The Thirteenth Amendment
1866	Congress adopts the Fourteenth Amendment, but it is not ratified until 1868; The Ku Klux Klan is formed; Tennessee is readmitted to the Union
1867	Congress passes the first of four Reconstruction Acts; Tenure of Office Act; Johnson suspends Secretary of War Edwin Stanton
1868	Johnson is impeached by the House and acquitted in the Senate; Arkansas, North Carolina, South Carolina, Alabama, Florida, and Louisiana are readmitted to the Union; Ulysses S. Grant elected president
1869	Woman suffrage associations are organized in response to women's disappointment with the Fourteenth Amendment
1870	Virginia, Mississippi, Texas, and Georgia are readmitted to the Union
1870, 1871	Congress passes Force Bills
1875	Blacks are guaranteed access to public places by Congress; Mississippi redeemers successfully oust black and white Republican officeholders
1876	Presidential election between Rutherford B. Hayes and Samuel J. Tilden
1877	Compromise of 1877: Hayes is chosen as president, and all remaining federal troops are withdrawn from the South
By 1880	The share-crop system of agriculture is well established in the South

Almost no one has had anything good to say about Reconstruction, the process by which the South was restored to the Union and the nation returned to peacetime pursuits and relations. Contemporaries judged it a monumental failure. To most southern whites it seemed a time when Dixie was subjected to a cruel northern occupation and civilization itself was buried under an avalanche of barbarism. For the freedmen—as the former slaves were called—the period started with bright promise but ended in bitter disappointment, with most blacks still on the bottom rung of society. Contemporary Northerners, too, generally deplored Reconstruction. They had hoped it would remake the South on the national model. But it had not, and most were relieved when the last federal troops withdrew in 1877 and the white South once more governed itself.

Nor have later Americans generally thought well of Reconstruction. A half century ago most historians accused the Republicans who controlled Reconstruction after the Civil War of being blinded by vindictiveness and botching the job. Scholars of the next generation rejected this view, but believed the chance to modernize and liberalize southern society had been missed because the North had neither the will nor the conviction to take the bold steps needed. Recently some younger historians have declared that by failing to guarantee the political rights of the freedmen and provide them with land, the North sold out the black people, leaving them little better off than before the Civil War.

Obviously, then, from many points of view, Reconstruction has seemed a failure. What went wrong? And were the results as bad as most critics have believed?

■ THE LEGACY OF WAR ■

A month after Appomattox, Whitelaw Reid, a correspondent for the Republican *Cincinnati Gazette,* went south to see what the war had done to Dixie. Reid was struck by the devastation he encountered. Hanover Junction, near Richmond, he reported, "presented little but standing chimneys and the debris of destroyed buildings. Along the [rail]road a pile of smoky brick and mortar seemed a regularly recognized sign of what had once been a depot." Not a train platform or water tank had been left, he wrote, and efforts to get the road in running order were often the only improvements visible for miles. Interior South Carolina, despoiled by General Sherman's army, "looked for many miles like a broad black streak of ruin and desolation." In the Shenandoah Valley of Virginia between Winchester and Harrisonburg, scarcely a horse, pig, chicken, or cow remained alive. Southern cities, too, were devastated. Columbia, capital of South Carolina, was a blackened wasteland with not a store standing in the business district. Atlanta, Richmond, Selma, and other southern towns were also ravaged. All told, over $1 billion of the South's physical capital had been reduced to ashes or twisted wreckage.

Human losses were appalling. Of the South's white male population of 2.5 million in 1860, a quarter of a million (10 percent) had died of battle wounds or disease. Most of these were young men who represented the region's most vigorous and creative human resource. Of those who survived, some were maimed and many were worn out emotionally.

The South's economic institutions were also shattered. Its banking structure, based on now-worthless Confederate bonds, had collapsed. Personal savings had been wiped out when Confederate currency lost all its value. Even more crushing, the region's labor system was in ruins. Slavery as an economic institution

THE FALL OF RICHMOND V.ª ON THE NIGHT OF APRIL 2.ⁿᵈ 1865.

Richmond, Virginia, the Confederate capital, being abandoned by the Jefferson Davis government in the last days of the war.

was dead, but no one knew what to replace it with. Many blacks remained on the farms and plantations and continued to plant, cultivate, and harvest. But many others—whether to test their new found freedom, hunt for long-lost relatives, or just to take their first holiday—wandered the roads or fled to the towns, abandoning the land on which the South's economy was based.

The war had also left behind damaging resentments. After struggling for independence against the "tyrannical government in Washington" and "northern dominance" for four years, white southerners could not help feeling apprehensive, angry, and disappointed. Now, even more than in 1860, a weak South would be oppressed by the North, its arrogance reinforced by victory. Northerners, for their part, would not easily forget the sacrifices and losses they had suffered in putting down what they considered the illegal and unwarranted rebellion; nor would they easily forgive the "atrocities" committed by the Confederacy. At Andersonville, Georgia, for example, during July 1864, 31,000 Union prisoners had been confined in a sixteen-acre stockade, protected from the weather only by tents and fed on scanty rations. As many as 3,000 prisoners had died in a month, a rate of 100 a day. To the northern public the Confederate prison officials, and especially the camp commandant, Captain Henry Wirz, seemed beasts who must be punished.

The American people, then, faced a gigantic task of physical, political, and psychological restoration. By the usual measure, the period of revival, or Reconstruction, lasted for some twelve years, until 1877. It was a time of upheaval and controversy, as well as new beginnings. In its own day the problems associated with Reconstruction dominated the political and intellectual life of the country, and they have fascinated and repelled Americans ever since.

■ ISSUES AND ATTITUDES ■

During the years of Reconstruction all Americans agreed that racial and political readjustments were necessary. But what changes should be made and how to make them deeply divided contemporaries, North and South, black and white, Republican and Democrat. People's views tended to cluster around five major positions: Radical Republican, northern conservative, southern conservative, southern Unionist, and southern freedman.

Radical Republicans. The group we call Radical Republican, though never very large, was influential especially in the "upper North." Successors to the hard liners who had pushed Lincoln to pursue the war more vigorously and attack slavery more forcefully, they believed that the defeated South must be made to recognize its errors, and forced to acknowledge that now it could no longer decide its own fate. Southerners could avoid northern wrath and show they deserved to be readmitted as citizens of the United States in a number of ways. At the very least, they must reject their former leaders and choose new ones who had not been connected with the Confederacy. They must take oaths of loyalty to the United States. They must reject all attempts to repay the Confederate debt incurred in an unjust cause. Most important of all, they must accept the fact that the former slaves were now free and must be treated as the political equals of whites.

Many former slaves, they felt, had worked and fought for the Union, and the nation must now help them through the difficult transition to full freedom. As to how this end could best be accomplished, not all Radicals agreed. A few held that it would be necessary for the freedmen to get land so they could support themselves independently. But at the very minimum they must be given the right to vote and, during the early stages of the change, must be protected against privation and exploitation. No doubt they would be grateful for the efforts of their Republican friends in defeating the slave power, destroying slavery, and defending them against those who do not accept the new situation. This gratitude would undoubtedly incline them to vote Republican. But that was all to the good. The Republican party was the great hope of the nation. It was the party of freedom and economic progress and not afraid to use government to encourage that progress. In a word, it was the party that had, since its founding, proved that it was the best embodiment of both the nation's moral and practical sense.

Northern Conservatives. Northern conservatives were generally recruited from the prewar Democratic party. Most had opposed secession and supported the war, but now that it was over and secession defeated, the country, they held, must forget the past. Let southerners—white southerners, that is—determine their own fate. It was in the best American tradition, they believed, to let local communities decide their own future without undue interference from the national government. The nation must confirm this great principle of local self-determination, and let the South back into the Union on its own terms.

The victorious North must not force black suffrage or social equality down the throats of the former Confederates. Almost all white Americans, they noted, believed that "Negroes" were ill-equipped to exercise the rights of citizens. The Radicals insisted on giving them the vote only because they wanted to secure continued control of the national government and guarantee the predominance of the values and goals of the Northeast, the nation's commercial-industrial region, against the very different interests and goals of the country's agricultural West and South. It was clearly hypocritical of the supposed champions of the freedmen, they noted, to be so timid in supporting Negro suffrage in the northern states, where such a stand was politically unpopular and where there were too few blacks to add to their voting strength. The country must reject such hypocrisy and restore peace and tranquility as quickly and completely as possible.

Southern Conservatives.   White southern conservatives could not condemn the "lost cause." It was a noble cause and it had brought out the best in the southern people. The South must never forget the sacrifice and heroism of the gallant men in gray. Perhaps secession was a mistake, but that would never diminish the grandeur of the Confederate struggle.

But it was obviously necessary now to get back to the business of daily living. The South must be allowed to resume its traditional political relations with the rest of the states. It must be free to determine its own fate with a minimum of conditions. Above all, it must be permitted to steer its own course on race relations. The "carpetbaggers" who were descending from the North looking for easy money, and the southern renegade "scalawags" willing to betray their own people for the sake of power, were self-serving and contemptible. They did not understand or refused to accept southern traditions.

Some changes had to be allowed. The South must recognize that blacks were no longer slaves and white southerners must make certain concessions to their private rights. But at least in the public realm these must be limited by their capacities. Above all, they must not be permitted to exercise political power. They were not the equal of whites. They could be duped and deceived by their professed "friends" into supporting the Republican party, but actually their interests would be best served by those who had always been the leaders of southern society and who remained the blacks' natural protectors.

Southern Unionists.   Another group who played a significant role in the debate over Reconstruction were Southern Unionists, who had rejected secession and often been persecuted in the Confederacy. They were, after 1865, at long last free to speak their minds. Now that the secessionists had been defeated, they felt they deserved recognition and favor. Unfortunately the ex-rebels were still in the majority. They said they had accepted the new circumstances of the South, but many of them had not, and the Unionists remained in a vulnerable position. At the very least it was necessary that they be protected by their northern friends against hostile unreconciled rebels. Moreover, they should be rewarded for their loyalty to the Union with an important place in the new order.

Southern Freedmen.   Southern freedmen (though of course they included freed women) believed that they deserved all the rights and privileges of free people as expressed in the Declaration of Independence. They had contributed to Union victory in war and had earned, they felt, the right to be treated as equals. They were also the largest group in the South truly loyal to the Union. Southern whites, with some exceptions, could not be trusted. They were unreconciled to defeat, and if the North failed to protect the freedmen and guarantee their rights as free men and women, these ex-Confederates would once more seize power and nullify the Union victory. The federal government, then, must continue for an indefinite period to take an active role in the process of southern Reconstruction.

Most did not expect white southerners to treat them as social equals; but they felt that they must have equality before the law and full civil rights, including, of course, the right to vote. They must also have economic independence, which meant not only the right to sell their labor in the open market but also their own land. Thousands of the South's best acres, abandoned by disloyal owners during the war, were controlled either by the Freedmen's Bureau or by the army. Giving the freedmen this land would enable them to secure their independence and prevent them from being kept in permanently subordinate positions. They also craved access to education. Literacy was an important tool for achieving economic independence. If the cost of a public school system meant that southern state taxes must rise, so be it.

Several of these positions overlapped. But it would clearly be difficult to reconcile those people who wanted to return to prewar conditions as quickly as possible and those who hoped to make social transformation a requirement for readmitting the South to the Union. In the next dozen years there would be fierce battles between the contending parties, some almost as passionate as the war itself.

■ PRESIDENTIAL RECONSTRUCTION ■

Even before Lee's surrender in 1865 the Lincoln administration confronted the problem of how to govern the conquered territory and subdued people. In 1862 the president appointed military governors for those parts of four Confederate states under federal control. But while military administrators might suffice for a while, they ran counter to the American tradition of civilian rule and could only be considered a temporary resolution of the problem.

Lincoln's Ten-Percent Plan.   Lincoln sought to keep in his own hands the process of restoring southern self-rule and normalizing the South's relations with the rest of the country. He believed this would be more efficient, but he also inevitably preferred guiding the final stage of reuniting the Union himself. The president favored a lenient process, one that would not create too many hurdles to the South's readmission to the Union, impose severe punishment on white southerners, or require unrealistic changes of heart. He agreed, however, that any scheme had to guarantee the South's acceptance of slavery's demise.

Lincoln waited almost a year from the time of the Emancipation Proclamation to announce his plan for reconstruction. Issued on December 8, 1863, his Proclamation of Amnesty and Reconstruction, usually called the Ten-Percent Plan, offered full pardon and full restoration of all rights to white southerners who pledged future loyalty to the Union and accepted the abolition of slavery. Excluded from the pardon and restoration were high-ranking Confederate political and military leaders. When loyal southerners in any rebel state equaled at least ten percent of the number of voters in the 1860 elections, this group could convene and establish a new state government to supersede the old. The new constitution adopted must abolish slavery, but it could also temporarily accept laws for the freed slaves "consistent . . . with their present condition as a laboring, landless, and homeless class." The state governments that met these conditions would be entitled to admission to the Union and to representation in Congress.

The Ten-Percent Plan did not please several important groups. Blacks and their allies condemned it for ignoring black suffrage and saying nothing about civil rights for the freedmen. Radical Republicans deplored the easy requirements for amnesty of former rebels. Rather, they said, the government should impose an "ironclad oath" on southerners, requiring them to declare that they had never willingly helped the Confederacy. Under the president's scheme far too many Confederate collaborators would be restored to full rights.

The differences between the president and Congress came to a head in early 1864 when Louisiana applied for readmission under terms close to Lincoln's blueprint. The state's March 1864 constitutional convention produced a new frame of government establishing a minimum wage and nine-hour day on all public works, adopting a progressive income tax, and creating a system of free public education. The delegates, however, also rejected black suffrage despite the president's suggestion that the vote be given to "some of the colored people . . . as for instance, the very intelligent, and especially those who have fought gallantly in our ranks."

The exclusion of all blacks from suffrage angered the Radicals in Congress. In July 1864 they adopted the Wade-Davis Manifesto, which proposed postponing the reconstruction process until a majority of a given state's white males had pledged to support the United States Constitution. At that point, elections would be held for a state constitutional convention with only those who had taken the Ironclad Oath permitted to vote. In addition, though it stopped short of requiring black suffrage, Wade-Davis proposed that the freed slaves be guaranteed equality before the law. Lincoln feared that the measure would force him to repudiate the Louisiana government and so pocket-vetoed it. But, he said in mock innocence, he had no objection if other southern states chose Wade-Davis rather than his own plan. Despite the disagreement with Congress, by the time of Appomattox Unionist governments recognized by Lincoln were operating in Louisiana, Arkansas, and Tennessee.

Johnson Takes Charge.   Lincoln's assassination profoundly altered the course of political reconstruction. Had he lived, his popularity, prestige, and flexibility might have induced Congress to accept major portions of his plan. Yet Congress resented the war-swollen powers of the president and would certainly have insisted on playing a major role in restoring the Union regardless. It seems unlikely that either side would have gotten its own way entirely. Lincoln's successor had to confront this inevitable struggle with Congress without the martyred president's skills and popularity.

Like Lincoln, Johnson was an ambitious, self-made man from southern yeoman stock. He was not a Republican and had been put on the Union party national ticket in 1864 to attract War Democrats. He did not share the nationalist principles of the Republicans. Rather, he was a defender of local power, even states' rights. Nor did he share the antislavery views of many Republicans. He despised his state's privileged planter class and considered secession a plot to perpetuate the elite's power, but at the same time, he had little respect for blacks. A fierce democrat when it came to the rich and powerful, he drew the equality line at the white race.

Johnson lacked Lincoln's winning personal qualities. Lincoln was confident in his own abilities. Johnson suffered from severe self-doubts, a weakness that made him susceptible to flattery. Lincoln was gregarious. Johnson was a loner with few friends or close advisers. Lincoln was flexible, a natural compromiser. Johnson was a rigid man who could be cajoled out of a position, but when defied directly, refused to budge. This stubbornness, in turn, often drove potential allies into the waiting arms of Radical Republicans. The president's characteristics became apparent only gradually, however. At first the Radical Republicans, tired of dealing with the wily Lincoln, had rejoiced at Johnson's succession. As military governor of Tennessee during the war he had declared that "treason . . . must be made infamous and traitors . . . punished," and they concluded that he would be harder on the South than his predecessor.

During his first eight months in office Congress was not in session and the president had a relatively free hand in formulating Reconstruction policy. Johnson formally announced his Reconstruction plan in two proclamations issued on May 29, 1865. The first offered pardon and amnesty to participants in the rebellion who pledged loyalty to the Union and support for the end of slavery. All who took the oath would have returned to them all property confiscated by the Union government during the war, except for slaves. Exempted from this blanket pardoning process were fourteen classes of Southerners who were required to apply individually for pardons from the president. These included most high Confederate officials and owners of taxable property worth

An idealized portrait of Andrew Johnson. His photographs show a coarser-featured man, an image more in keeping with his actual origins and early life.

more than $20,000. This last proviso reflected Johnson's southern yeoman prejudice against the old planter class as the source of disunion and secession.

The second proclamation designated William Holden as provisional governor of North Carolina and directed him to call a convention to amend the state's existing constitution so as to create a "republican form of government." Voters would be restricted to those who had taken the oath of allegiance; they would not include ex-slaves or any blacks. Johnson soon extended the same process to six other southern states while also recognizing the new governments of Louisiana, Arkansas, and Tennessee, three states Lincoln had already accepted back into the Union. Johnson made it clear that he expected the conventions to accept the abolition of slavery and pledge not to repay any public debts incurred in the Confederate cause. He also asked them to consider giving voting rights to a few educated and property-holding blacks in order to "disarm" those clamoring for full civil rights for ex-slaves. Otherwise they could decide for themselves what sort of government and laws they would adopt.

In the next few months Johnson chose provisional governors from among each unreconstructed state's "loyalists" to manage the process he had prescribed. He often turned to members of the old Whig elite. These men typically had been skeptical of secession but had gone with their states when the decision to leave the Union was made. Few favored any changes in the undemocratic and unprogressive systems of the prewar era; none supported civil equality for blacks. The governors wielded broad patronage power and, during their months in office, used it to win the support of the Old South's planter and merchant class regardless of their Unionism or willingness to accept a new social and political order.

Meanwhile, each of the unreconstructed states held elections for a convention and adopted new state constitutions. Each acknowledged the end of slavery and all, except stubborn South Carolina, pledged to repudiate its Confederate debts. No state conceded blacks the vote, however, though several revised their formulas for representation to favor the white small farmer counties over the plantation regions. Soon afterward, they held statewide elections for permanent governors and other officials and chose state legislators and congressional delegates.

During the summer and fall of 1865, conservative white southerners had reason to feel reassured that, despite Johnson's tough talk about disunionists and his disdain for the planters, the president did not intend to disturb their region's social and political systems. In August he overruled Freedmen's Bureau Commissioner Oliver Howard's Circular 13 setting aside forty-acre tracts of land for the freedmen to farm and ordered the return of land confiscated during the war from disloyal southerners. He also yielded to southern demands for removing black troops, whose presence whites considered a "painful humiliation" and a force for undermining plantation labor discipline. At the same time the president scattered pardons wholesale to those who applied to him directly. By 1866 he had given out almost 7,000 of these. Whatever his initial response to the old planter elite, the president had become the protector of the South's old social order.

The Johnson Governments.　During the months the "Johnson governments" operated without restraint from Washington, their deeds strengthened the Radicals and destroyed any possibility that Congress would accept the president's Reconstruction policy.

Several actions especially offended northern Republicans. In the elections for new state and federal officials southern voters selected few real Unionists. Chosen to represent the former Confederate states in the upcoming Congress were four Confederate generals, five Confederate colonels, six Confederate Cabinet officers, fifty-eight former Confederate Congressmen, and Alexander H. Stephens, vice president of the Confederate States of America. Many of the newly elected state officials were also tainted with secession. It was natural for white southerners to turn to former secessionists for their leaders. But this blatant display of Confederate sympathies outraged many Northerners.

The new state legislatures compounded the offense. Despite the president's recommendations, several refused to ratify the Thirteenth Amendment, passed by Congress in January 1865, that placed the abolition of slavery on a sound constitutional basis. Mississippi and South Carolina also refused to repudiate their wartime state debts. None of the Johnson governments allowed even a handful of blacks to vote. But worst of all, each of them enacted a set of laws to govern race relations (the Black Codes) that jarred Union sensibilities.

These codes did extend to the freedmen several rights of normal citizens. They legalized marriages between blacks, including earlier slave-era relationships; permitted ex-slaves to buy, own, sell, and otherwise transfer property; and gave the freedmen the right to appear, plead, and testify in court in cases involving fellow blacks. But the codes also sought to relegate the ex-slaves permanent to second-class legal, economic, and political status. Under the Black Codes, black southerners could not offer their labor freely on the market. Mississippi required black workers to produce each January a written document showing they had a contract to work for the coming year. Laborers who left their jobs before a contract expired forfeited any wages already earned and could be arrested. "Vagrants"—defined as the idle, disorderly, and those who "misspend what they earn"—could face fines or forced plantation labor. The South Carolina code demanded a stiff annual tax for blacks working as anything other than farmers or servants. In Florida, blacks who broke labor contracts could be whipped, sold into indenture for up to one year, or placed in the pillory. In several states blacks were forbidden to bear arms, were subject to more severe punishment for given offenses than whites, and could not live or buy property in specified locations. Most states prohibited interracial marriage. Most rankling of all were apprenticeship laws, which allowed the courts to "bind out" black minors to employers for a period of time without their own consent or that of their parents. These seemed thinly disguised attempts to reinstate slavery.

Blacks eloquently protested the codes. One black man wrote the Freedmen's Bureau: "I think very hard of the former owners for Trying to keep my Blood when I kno that Slavery is dead." A black Union veteran exclaimed: "If you call this Freedom, what do you call Slavery!" Inevitably many Northerners considered the president's version of Reconstruction deplorable. Wendell Phillips prophetically noted that without the right to vote, blacks in the South would be consigned to "a century of serfdom." But nothing so offended Northern opinion as the Black Codes. The Republican Chicago Tribune declared that the people of the North would turn one of the worst offending states, Mississippi, into a "frog pond" before they would allow its Black Code "to disgrace one foot of soil in which the bones of our soldiers sleep and over which the flag of freedom waves." Another critic called the codes "an outrage against civilization." Meanwhile, northern congressmen were receiving almost daily reports from white southern Unionists that the former secessionists were crowing about how they once again had the upper hand and would make life difficult for their opponents. Simultaneously, northern travelers in Dixie recounted unpleasant experiences with unreconstructed "rebels." Hotels and restaurants often refused them service and individual southerners insulted them.

One of the real advances afforded by the emancipation was the legal recognition of black marriages. After 1865 black men and women seized the opportunity to solemnize relationships begun under slavery or to contract new ones. Officiating at this wedding is a chaplain from the Freedmen's Bureau.

The outrage over the Johnson governments' policies and the Black Codes should not deceive us about the extent of racial liberalism in the nation at large. Northern Democrats were often blatant racists who had no scruples against appealing to the voters' prejudices and resisted every attempt to confer the franchise on blacks. Republicans, generally, were less bigoted and, in any case, believed that the freedmen's votes were needed to keep former rebels from regaining power in the South. But even many Republicans were reluctant to accord black Americans the full rights of citizenship, at least where they themselves lived. In the fall of 1865 three northern states—Connecticut, Wisconsin, and Minnesota—placed constitutional amendments on their ballots to allow the handful of black males within their borders to vote. A substantial minority of Republican voters opposed the changes, and together with the Democrats, helped defeat the black franchise in all three. In effect then, a majority of all white voters opposed letting blacks vote and this reality inevitably tempered the radical ardor of Republican politicians in districts where elections were closely contested.

■ CONGRESS TAKES OVER ■

By the time the Thirty-Ninth Congress assembled on December 4, 1865, the Republican majority was determined to take over the process of southern reconstruction to assure that rebels would not get their way. Its first act was to reject the Congressional delegations sent by the Johnson governments to Washington. Prompted by the Radicals, the Clerk of the House, Edward McPherson, skipped the names of the newly elected southern congressmen as he called the roll. Immediately after, the two houses established a Joint Committee on Reconstruction to look into conditions in the South and consider whether any former Confederate states were entitled to representation. Consisting of fifteen Senators and Representatives, three of them Democrats, their views stretched across the political spectrum, although the "too ultra" Radical Charles Sumner was deliberately excluded.

Despite his policies, Johnson had still not completely alienated the Republican moderates and they listened to his conciliatory annual message with respect. For a time the Republican congressional centrists took charge. This changed abruptly when moderate Lyman Trumbull of Illinois introduced a bill to extend the life of the Freedmen's Bureau and broaden its authority.

Established in March 1865, just before the war ended, the bureau aided refugees, both white and black, found employment for freedmen, and supplied transportation home for those displaced by the war. It had established hospitals and schools and drawn up guidelines for bringing ex-slaves into the free labor market. In enlarging the bureau's scope, the Trumbull bill gave Congress the additional power to protect freedmen against discrimination, including the right to punish state officials denying blacks their civil rights, and authorized it to build and run schools for the ex-slaves. It was generally considered a moderate measure.

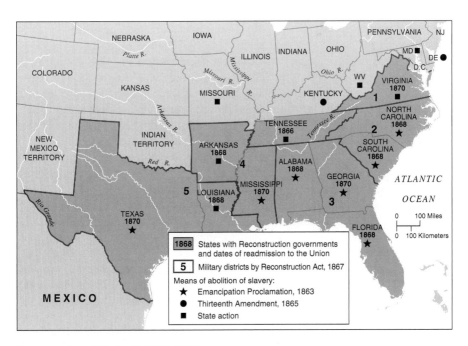

Reconstruction of the South, 1865–1877

The Civil Rights bill of 1865, on the other hand, was far-reaching in scope. It declared all persons born in the United States, including blacks (but not Indians), citizens, and specified their rights regardless of race. These included the right to make contracts, bring lawsuits, and enjoy the "full and equal benefit of all laws and proceedings for the security of person and property." To ensure that no state denied citizens these rights, it authorized federal district attorneys and marshals, as well as the Freedmen's Bureau, to sue in the federal courts. In many ways the law foreshadowed the civil rights measures of the mid-twentieth century.

Johnson refused to sign either bill. The Freedmen's Bureau, he said in his veto message, was a vast patronage boondoggle that would create a horde of bureaucrats to oppress ordinary citizens. Moreover, it violated the Constitution; never before had the federal government been called on to provide economic relief to individuals. The president soon after attacked the Civil Rights bill as another unwarranted extension of federal power. The bill was a "stride toward centralization and the concentration of all legislative powers in the national Government."

In the end Congress was unable to muster the two thirds needed to pass the Freedmen's Bureau bill, though it managed to override the Civil Rights veto. The fight over the Freedmen's Bureau destroyed the hope of moderates that Johnson could be trusted with Reconstruction. It was the opening round of a struggle that lasted until the end of Johnson's term, with each new battle driving more and more moderates into the Radical camp.

The Fourteenth Amendment.   While Congress and the president fought for supremacy, the Joint Committee on Reconstruction set to work on its own comprehensive plan to restore Dixie to the Union. Even with the Thirteenth Amendment finally approved by the states and the Civil Rights bill enacted into law, Radicals worried that the rights of black Americans were vulnerable. Certainly, if it proved necessary to rely on the federal courts, they would have little security. Although it was not until April 1866 that the Supreme Court, in the case of Ex Parte Milligan, voided the Lincoln administration's wartime imposition of martial law on civilians in Indiana, the justices already seemed hostile to the Republican philosophy of federal supremacy. What would prevent them from striking down the Civil Rights Act or any other measure that Congress passed to protect the freedmen? With this in mind, the first initiative of the Joint Committee was another amendment to the Constitution to put the principles of the Civil Rights bill beyond the reach of the president, the states, and unfriendly federal judges.

As finally hammered out and submitted to the states for adoption, the Fourteenth Amendment contained four clauses, the first two of which were of major significance.

The original Bill of Rights had limited only the federal government's power over citizens. Now the Constitution would place restraints on the states as well. The first clause defined citizenship to include all those born or naturalized in the United States. It then declared that no state could make or enforce any law that abridged the rights of American citizens, or deprived any person of "life, liberty, or property without due process of law." Nor could any state "deny to any person within its jurisdiction the equal protection of the laws." In effect, individuals could not be executed, imprisoned, or fined by the states except through the normal processes of law with all their constitutionally protected procedures and safeguards, nor could the states treat any individual or class of individuals as inferior to others. Clause one vastly expanded federal power over the states and served in the end many purposes besides ensuring racial justice in the South.

Clause two, concerning suffrage, was not what the most radical of the Republican leaders wanted. Congress might have bluntly declared unconstitutional all political discrimination on racial grounds. Instead it deferred to continuing northern racial prejudice by a series of evasions. Rather than giving the vote outright to all adult male citizens, it merely declared that whenever a state denied any age-qualified male citizen the right to vote, that state's representation in Congress would be reduced proportionately. The South, with its large black population, would now have a strong incentive to grant full voting rights to black males. (Otherwise it would send far fewer representatives to Congress than its total population warranted.) Northern states, however, with few black residents, could continue to deny them suffrage without serious penalty. Not until after the adoption of the Fifteenth Amendment (1870) were "race, color, or previous condition of servitude" completely eliminated as legal grounds for denying adult men the vote, though, to the dismay of women activists women were not admitted to the franchise.*

■ CONGRESSIONAL RECONSTRUCTION ■

To assure adoption of the new constitutional amendment, Congress made its passage by the southern state legislatures a condition of readmission to the Union. But this incentive did not work. By the end of 1866 Texas, South Carolina, Georgia, Florida, North Carolina, Arkansas, and Alabama had all rejected it. In fact, the ratification process dragged even in the North, and not until well into 1867 did the amendment receive the necessary approval by three fourths of the states.

By now the president's abrasive personality and backward-looking views had alienated almost all the Republicans in Congress. But there still remained a nub of conservative Republicans. In April 1866 these leaders joined with moderate Democrats to form the National Union Executive Committee. In August they held a National Union Convention in Philadelphia to form a third party based on sectional reconciliation and immediate return of the southern states to the Union. The highlight of the convention was the affecting ceremony of Massachusetts and South Carolina delegates, representing the two sectional poles, marching into the convention hall in pairs, arm and arm.

---

*The proposed amendment's two minor clauses (1) denied public office to those who had taken oaths of allegiance as state or federal officials and then served in the rebellion; and (2) repudiated any state debt incurred in aid of the Confederate cause.

Though the president gave the National Union movement his blessing, it came to little. For one thing, the conservative forces could not overcome the impression of southern intransigence created by news from the South. In May an angry white mob invaded the black section of Memphis, killing forty-six people. In late July another white mob assaulted delegates to a black suffrage convention in New Orleans. Before federal troops could arrive, the attackers had murdered thirty-seven blacks and three of their white supporters. Here was proof, if any were needed, that the South would never accept the consequences of defeat without northern coercion.

Despite poor prospects, the president campaigned aggressively for the National Union movement in the 1866 off-year elections. Against the advice of friends, he set out on a "swing around the circle," giving speeches attacking the Radicals as the country's real traitors, defending the South as loyal, justifying his generous pardoning policy, and even offering his life to save the Union and the Constitution. Wherever he went, his critics heckled him unmercifully and goaded him into rash, undignified replies. He probably did his cause more harm than good. Radical Republicans won a decisive victory almost everywhere. The new Congress would retain its three-to-one Republican majority.

But even before the Fortieth Congress convened, the second session of the Thirty-Ninth, its Republican leaders encouraged by the 1866 election mandate, passed the First Reconstruction Act (also called the Reconstruction Act of 1867). By December 1866 Johnson had lost all Republican support and the Radicals felt the time was ripe to replace all the Johnson state governments by a system that would finally express the will of the Union's most progressive forces.

The First Reconstruction Act swept aside the existing state regimes in the former Confederacy and divided the South into five military districts, each under a general who was empowered to use troops if necessary to protect life and property. The military commanders would supervise the choice of delegates to state conventions that would write new constitutions and establish new state governments. All adult males would be eligible for voting for the conventions regardless of race, except those excluded for participating in the rebellion. The new constitutions had to provide for a similar broad electorate for legislature, governor, and other public officials, and required that their work be accepted by a majority of the same, color-blind, pool of voters. When the new constitutions had been so ratified, when Congress had approved them, and when the new state legislatures had ratified the Fourteenth Amendment, the states would then be admitted to the Union and their delegations to Congress seated.

Johnson Impeached.   Radicals feared Johnson would use his appointment authority and general executive powers to frustrate their plans. And before long he did, removing several of the military commanders as too radical and issuing orders to others intended to negate Congress's intentions.

To hedge him in, Congress passed a series of additional measures in 1867. To prevent the president again taking advantage of an interval between congressional sessions, in January it approved a bill that called the new Congress into special session immediately after the old one had expired. In March it passed, over Johnson's veto, the Tenure of Office Act requiring Senate consent for the dismissal of all federal officeholders appointed with Senate approval. A third measure required that all presidential orders to the army be issued through the general of the army. This happened to be Grant, a man who had come to support the Radical Republican position on Reconstruction. At the same time, to goad dilatory southern voters to take steps under the First Reconstruction Act, Congress passed the Second Reconstruction Act. A Third Reconstruction Act in July tightened control by the five military commanders over the provisional governments in the South and sought to broaden the rules excluding ex-Confederates from the Reconstruction process.

For some Radicals these measures seemed insufficient, and in January 1868 they attempted to remove Johnson from office through impeachment. As yet most moderates did not believe there were grounds for such a drastic procedure, however, and the indictment was quashed in committee. But then Johnson handed his opponents their opportunity. In August, during a congressional recess, the president suspended from office Secretary of War Edwin Stanton, a man inherited from Lincoln who supported the Radicals, and appointed Grant as interim secretary. In January 1868 the Senate refused to accept Stanton's dismissal, and Grant, against the wishes of Johnson, stepped down. Defiant, the president once more removed Stanton and replaced him with Lorenzo Thomas. But Stanton, with the urging of congressional Radicals, barricaded himself in his office and refused to leave or to allow Thomas to enter. However ludicrous, the Stanton affair seemed to provide grounds for impeachment that had not existed before. The president, exclaimed one moderate, had "thrown down the gauntlet and says to us plainly as words can speak it: 'Try this issue now betwixt me and you: either you go to the wall or I do'." On February 24, 1868, the House formally voted to impeach the president by a strict party vote of 126 to 47.

The impeachment trial, conducted before the Senate sitting as a court, was the show trial of the century. The major charge against the president was his "unlawful" removal of Stanton. Attorney General Henry Stanbery, the president's counsel, argued that Stanton had been appointed by Lincoln, not Johnson, and so was not covered by the Tenure of Office Act. The law, moreover, was unconstitutional, and it was the right of the president to challenge it to bring it before the courts.

During the six weeks of the trial intense excitement reigned in Washington and the country. Radicals insisted that acquittal would be a victory for rebels and traitors. Democrats, and Johnson's few remaining moderate supporters within Republican ranks, claimed that conviction would mean that Congress had successfully usurped the power of the executive branch. The president's defenders also noted that the man next in line for the presidency was the president pro tempore of the Senate, the truculent Radical, Benjamin Wade.

On May 16, 1868, Johnson was acquitted by one vote. Most historians believe that he should not have been impeached in the first place. There can be no question that he was stubborn and at times boorish, and that he used his executive power to impede Congress. Nor is there much dispute among scholars today that his racial policies were misguided. In a parliamentary system such

In August 1866 President Johnson announced that "peace, order, tranquility, and civil authority now exist . . . in the United States." Dissatisfied with Johnson's idea of peace and order, the House voted his impeachment less than two years later. Here a packed gallery follows the trial of the century.

as Britain's he would have been removed by a legislative vote of "no confidence." But the Founders had deliberately created an independently elected executive with the right to disagree with Congress. It seems unlikely that they intended impeachment to serve as a way to remove an official from office except for breaking the law or for gross incapacity. The Radicals in effect, then, were seeking implicitly to change the Constitution in a vital aspect.

■ RECONSTRUCTION IN THE SOUTH ■

The Election of 1868. Johnson still had almost a year to go before his term ended, but achieved little in the months remaining. During this period he spent much of his time maneuvering for the Democratic presidential nomination. The Democrats did not want him. In the West many preferred George Pendleton of Ohio, a Democratic Senator who favored the "Ohio Idea," a scheme to relieve taxpayers' burdens and stimulate the economy by paying the large federal debt in paper money ("greenbacks"). Eastern Democrats claimed the Ohio Idea would call into question all debts, public and private, shake the financial markets, and set loose the forces of social anarchy. It took twenty-two ballots before Governor Horatio Seymour of New York, a "hard money" man, nosed out

Pendleton. The "soft money" group was able to get the Ohio Idea incorporated into the party platform but, as soon as nominated, Seymour repudiated it.

The Republicans turned, not to their most militant wing, but to the center. The acquittal of Johnson had weakened the Radicals and they could not stop the nomination of Ulysses Grant, the great war hero. General Grant had not opposed the Radicals' policies after 1865 but he was a pragmatist, rather than a zealot, and reassured the moderates. The Republican platform denounced the Ohio Idea as "repudiation" and a "national crime," and defended the civil rights of the freedmen in the South.

The election was remarkably close. In the South, armed and violent whites succeeded in intimidating many blacks from going to the polls. In eleven Georgia counties with black majorities no votes at all were recorded for Grant. But the Republicans did manage to carry all but two states in Dixie thanks to black voters and won most of the North. With 53 percent of the popular vote, Grant won the election.

By the time the new president was inaugurated in March 1869, the governments organized under the congressional reconstruction acts—composed of white and black Republicans and decidedly Radical in temper—had been admitted to the Union, and the Fourteenth Amendment had been incorporated into the Constitution. In a narrow legal sense, Reconstruction was now complete. But, in fact, the situation in the newly restored states remained uncertain and tense.

Economic Recovery. In the South itself, important changes had taken place since April 1865. Damaged southern railroads were quickly rebuilt after Appomattox and the rail system extended to new regions. Much of the needed capital was supplied by investors from the North and from Britain, who anticipated a favorable business climate in the South. The southern state governments, both the Johnson regimes and the ones established under Congress's aegis, also contributed, going heavily into debt to lend money to railroad enterprises. Industry too recovered. Between the 1860s and 1880, southern manufactures increased in value almost 55 percent. In agriculture cotton became even more important after 1865 than before the war. By 1878 the South's cotton output had almost reached its prewar peak. By the 1890s the region was producing twice as many bales as in 1859.

Tenantry and Sharecropping. It was primarily in its social aspects, however, that Reconstruction transformed the southern economy. Before 1861, defenders of slavery had denied that blacks could function in a free labor market. During the war the Treasury Department put this theory to the test in the South Carolina Sea Islands near Port Royal and demonstrated that when ex-slaves were given land and incentives, they made successful farmers. The Port Royal venture collapsed when the Treasury Department failed to transfer land title to the freedmen as it had promised, selling the abandoned Sea Island property to the highest bidder instead.

Efforts to create a class of black farm owners in the South resumed after the war. Thaddeus Stevens and other Radicals in Congress introduced legislation to transfer confiscated rebel estates to newly enfranchised blacks. Only landowning, they believed, could protect blacks against exploitation and keep them from being virtually re-enslaved. The former slaves themselves yearned to become landowners. "We all know that the colored people want land," a South Carolina carpetbagger declared. "Night and day they think and dream of it. It is their all and all." Whitelaw Reid quoted an elderly black man he had met on his trip to the South: "What's de use of bein' free if you don't own land enough to be buried? Might juss as well stay slave all yo days."

Yearnings often became expectations. Many blacks came to believe that the government intended to give them "forty acres and a mule," and they were bitterly disappointed when it proved untrue. In the end, a large black yeomen class failed to appear. Ultimately the Radicals were not so very radical, and their respect for private property rights—even those of ex-rebels—took precedence over their concern for the freedmen. Most were certain that the ballot offered sufficient protection to the freedmen; a social revolution was not needed.

Black southerners might have accumulated some money and purchased land. Southern land prices were low in the 1870s, and a few hundred dollars could have bought a black family a small farm. In 1865 Congress chartered the Freedmen's Bank to support such black self-help efforts. But the bank was poorly managed and could not withstand the financial panic of 1873. When it closed its doors the following year, it took with it over $3 million of hard-won savings from thousands of black depositors. There was still another impediment to freedmen buying land: White southerners believed that if blacks owned land they would not work for white landlords and employers. It is easy to see why they made it difficult for black farmers to buy land even when they could pay cash. Yet despite all the difficulties, by 1880 about a fifth of all black farmers owned their land.

Though only a minority of southern blacks ever became independent farm owners, most continued working the land. For a while after Appomattox they worked for cash wages under contracts supervised by the Freedmen's Bureau. But it was difficult for landlords to find cash in the months following the war. The freedmen, for their part, resented the harshness with which some bureau agents enforced labor contracts against them. Still more unsatisfactory from the freedmen's point of view was the return to gang work and the planters' close supervision of every aspect of their labor and their lives. The system reminded them too much of slavery and seemed a mockery of freedom.

Out of this mutual dissatisfaction with wage-paid farm labor emerged a tenant system that by 1880 had become characteristic of much of the cotton-growing South. Tenantry included whites as well as blacks. Thousands of Confederate privates returned home to become, not successful planters, but tenants on lands owned by former slaveholders. Many were forced into tenantry by high property taxes; others by inability to pay their debts.

Tenantry took many forms. Tenants might pay rent either in cash or in part of the crop. Though the system was not as desirable as ownership, a cash tenant was at least free from constant supervision and sometimes could save enough to buy land for himself. The greater number of tenant farmers, however, especially among the freedmen, were either sharecroppers or share renters. The former contributed only their labor, and in return for use of the land and a house, usually divided the crop equally with the landlord. A share renter could provide his own seed, mule, and plow as well, and usually got three fourths of what he produced. By 1900 three quarters of black farmers were tenant farmers; over 35 percent of white farmers.

Linked to tenantry was the crop-lien system, a credit arrangement by which a storekeeper (who sometimes was the landlord as well) would extend credit to the tenant for supplies during the crop-growing season. When the harvest came and the cotton was sold, the tenant would then repay the debt. Buying on credit was expensive, since it included an interest charge. It also gave dishonest storekeepers a chance to cheat. Tenants who could not meet their debts could not change the merchant they dealt with; they became virtual "debt-peons," tied to him almost like serfs.

The new labor regime that emerged in the South during Reconstruction was an advance over slavery. Some blacks managed to become landowners despite all the difficulties. By 1880 twenty percent of black farmers owned some land, though their holdings were generally smaller and less fertile than those of whites. Most ex-slaves were released from the degradation of close personal supervision by whites. Economically they were better off as sharecroppers than as slaves. Roger Ransom and Richard Sutch conclude that whereas slaves received in food, clothing, housing, and medical attention about 23 percent of what whites received, the freedmen after 1865 obtained a full half of average white income. In addition to these economic advances, blacks were now able to make decisions about their economic lives that they never could before. Almost all decided that black women would no longer work in the fields; like white women, they would stay home and become proper housewives and mothers. Many black children too left the labor market to attend school.

Yet the freedmen's fate represented a missed opportunity for the nation. Many of these gains were a one-time advance, made just after the war. Thereafter, while the country as a whole became richer, black living standards in the South remained stagnant. Indeed, the sharecrop–crop-lien system proved to be an economic trap for the entire lower South. Because they did not own the land, sharecroppers had no incentive to improve it. Landlords, too, had little incentive, for they could only hope to recover a limited portion of the greater output that might come from additional capital investment. Tenantry also tied the South to a one-crop system and prevented diversification. As one sharecropper complained in the 1880s: "We ought to plant less [cotton and tobacco] and more grain and grasses, but how are we to do it; the man who furnishes us with rations at 50 percent interest won't let us; he wants money crops planted." Failure to diversify also produced serious soil exhaustion that could only be offset by expensive additions of fertilizers. Worse still, cotton prices steadily declined for a generation after 1865, pulling down the entire cotton-tied southern rural economy.

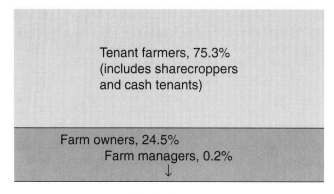

Black Status

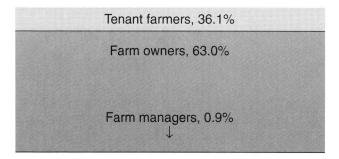

White Status

The status of farm operators in former slave states, 1900

For whatever reasons, the South as a section experienced a relative economic decline. With each year Dixie fell further behind the rest of the nation in almost every measure of material abundance and social well-being: literacy, infant mortality, longevity, health, and per-capita income. By 1890, the section had become America's problem area.

Social and Cultural Change. Despite the imperfect economic adjustment, the end of slavery brought considerable social and cultural gains for black Americans. Black men and women enjoyed a new freedom of movement, which some exercised by going to the cities or departing for more prosperous parts of the country. At the end of Reconstruction several thousand blacks left the lower South and moved north or west. A particularly large movement of "exodusters" to Kansas after 1878 alarmed southern white leaders, who feared that the South might lose its labor force.

The end of slavery freed blacks to express themselves in ways never before possible. Slavery had not destroyed black culture, but it had made it difficult for blacks to demonstrate the full range of their talents and to exercise their organizational abilities. Emancipation released energies previously held in check.

Blacks withdrew from white churches in large numbers and formed their own. These churches gave talented former slaves an opportunity to demonstrate leadership beyond anything previously possible. Unlike politics, which was largely closed to talented black men after 1877, the Protestant ministry continued to provide leadership opportunities.

The end of slavery also expanded educational opportunities for blacks. Before the war slaves had been legally denied education. After 1865 northern educators and philanthropists seized on Dixie as missionary territory to be converted to "civilization." In the months after Appomattox hundreds of Yankee teachers, hoping to uplift a benighted region, went South to establish schools and bring the blessings of literacy. The Freedmen's Bureau also labored to end illiteracy and sought to train blacks in trades. The most permanent impact was achieved by southern self-help. Before long every southern state, under Radical guidance, had made some provision for educating black children. The southern educational system long remained poor and segregated (except for a time in the cosmopolitan city of New Orleans); yet the schools managed to make a dent in ignorance. By 1880 a quarter of all blacks could read and write; twenty years later the figure had risen to half. College training for blacks, nonexistent in the South before 1860, became available as well. Southern state governments founded separate black colleges and universities. Meanwhile, the Freedmen's Bureau and white philanthropists helped charter such black private colleges as Atlanta University in Georgia, Fisk University in Tennessee, and Howard University in Washington, D.C.

Despite the gains, segregation by race became a central fact of life in the South. In 1875 Congress passed a strongly worded Civil Rights Act guaranteeing to all persons, regardless of color, "the full and equal enjoyment of all the accommodations . . . of inns, public conveyances . . . , theaters, and other places of public amusement"; but separation and social inequality persisted; in fact, the separation of the races became more complete than before the war. In most communities, trains, buses, and theaters had white and black sections. In private life the racial spheres were still more exclusive, and blacks almost never entered the homes of white people except as servants. Even southern Radicals seldom treated blacks as social equals.

The Southern Radical Governments.   In many ways, the most serious deficiency of Reconstruction was its failure to create a democratic political culture. Blacks fully participated in the creation and running of the state governments established by the five military commanders under the terms of the Reconstruction Acts. They voted in the elections for state constitutional conventions, served in those conventions, voted in the state elections for state and federal office that followed, and served in these offices. Participation did not mean domination, however. Even where the Republicans were in control, and even in South Carolina and Mississippi, where the black population outnumbered the white, they held only a minority of political offices. The rest were filled by native-born southern whites and northern-born white immigrants to Dixie.

The first colored senator and representatives in the 41st and 42nd Congress of the United States. As a group they acquitted themselves competently.

One of the persistent myths of Reconstruction is that black political officials during the years of Republican rule in the South were unusually corrupt and incompetent. But that was not the case. Among the fifteen black southerners elected to Congress were a number of exceptionally able, honest, and well-educated men. Maine congressman James G. Blaine, who served with many of the black legislators, said of them: "The colored men who took their seats in both Senate and House . . . were as a rule studious, earnest, ambitious men, whose public conduct . . . should be honorable to any race." On the level of state government, black officeholders ranged from excellent to poor. All in all, as legislators and officials, their successes did not fall noticeably behind those of their white colleagues.

Native-born white Republican leaders in the South have also been unduly disparaged. "Scalawags" were denounced by their opponents as "the vilest renegades of the South," as men "who have dishonored the dignity of white blood, and are traitors alike to principle and race." In fact, many were former Unionists and members of the South's prewar Whig business class who were attracted to the Republican party because of its pro-business, pro-growth policies. And they were not the tiny minority of the white population that we would expect if they were merely renegades. In 1872, for example, 20 percent of the South's white voters cast their ballots for Republican candidates.

Nor were the northern whites who participated in the southern Republican state governments the "itinerant adventurers" and "vagrant interlopers" that southern conservatives charged. Called "carpetbaggers," after the cheap carpet-cloth suitcases carried in those years by travelers, many were former Union soldiers who had served in Dixie during the war and come to like it as a place to live. Others were sincere idealists committed to establishing a new social order. Obviously many white southern Republicans—scalawags and carpetbaggers alike—hoped to take personal advantage of new circumstances, but there is no reason to consider them any more venal, corrupt, or self-serving than politicians in general.

On the whole the Radical-dominated southern state governments were remarkably effective and reasonably honest. Of course, measured by the standards of the tight-fisted prewar South, they seemed big spenders. And they did run up large debts. But the new governments took on functions not required of their predecessors. They sought to help railroads and other businesses. They established the South's first state-supported school systems and sharply increased public spending for poor relief, prisons, and state hospitals. Though still far behind the North in providing social services, under Radical rule the South began to catch up with the rest of nineteenth-century America.

The new Radical governments were also more democratic and egalitarian than were the prewar southern state regimes. The constitutions adopted under congressional Reconstruction made many previously appointive offices elective and gave small farmers better representation in the legislatures than before the war. They also extended the vote to white males who did not meet the old property qualifications. The new state governments reduced the number of crimes punishable by death and granted married women more secure control over their property, reforms most northern states had adopted before 1860. They swept away the unequal treatment of black workers that had been incorporated into the Black Codes. Some of the Radical regimes even pursued policies that foreshadowed the modern social welfare state. South Carolina financed medical care for its poor citizens. Alabama paid legal fees for poor defendants. Not for another century would the South—or the nation as a whole—see anything like this again.

Redemption. Regardless of their accomplishments, many white southerners despised the Radical regimes and accused them of corruption. Some were in fact corrupt, but generally no more than was normal in state affairs during those years. Southern conservatives also disliked the reforms they initiated, because they were new, because they seemed to be Yankee-inspired, and because they were expensive. Landlords, in particular, denounced the new programs for raising taxes on real estate, which before the war had been lightly taxed. But above all, conservatives found it difficult to accept the Republican-dominated state governments because they were part of the new racial regime. After 250 years of slavery, the white South found it hard to consider a black person the political equal of a white one.

After 1867 the southern states became arenas for ferocious struggles between the political forces of the new era and those of the old. For a while the Radical governments succeeded in holding onto political office, especially in

When the Freedmen's Bureau set up schools for blacks, former slaves of all ages flocked to them. Wrote Booker T. Washington, "It was a whole race trying to go to school." The Show Hill School, here, abandoned classical education in favor of industrial training, which was deemed more appropriate to black needs.

states where they were most firmly entrenched—Alabama, Mississippi, Texas, Florida, Louisiana, and South Carolina. But in the end they could not match the experience, self-confidence, and ruthlessness of the defenders of bygone times, who hoped to "redeem" the South from "Black Republicanism."

A major weapon of the "redeemers" was the Ku Klux Klan. Formed in 1866 in Tennessee by young Confederate veterans primarily as a social club, the Klan quickly evolved into an antiblack, anti-Radical organization. To intimidate black voters, hooded, mounted Klansmen swooped down at night on isolated cabins, making fearsome noises and firing guns. They also torched black homes, attacked and beat black militiamen, ambushed both white and black Radical leaders, and lynched blacks accused of crimes. During the 1868 presidential campaign Klansmen assassinated an Arkansas congressman, three members of the South Carolina legislature, and several Republican members of state constitutional conventions. Some conservative apologists dismissed the Klan as an organization composed of white riffraff, but in fact, as one Radical newspaper noted, it included "men of property . . . respectable citizens."

At its height in the late 1860s, the Klan's outrages went virtually unchecked. Law enforcement officials felt impotent to deal with the violence. Witnesses of Klan misdeeds were often scared off from testifying against it. In several southern states the Klan created a reign of terror and lawlessness that threatened to undo the entire Reconstruction process. Then in 1870 and 1871 Congress passed three Force Bills, which declared "armed combinations" and Klan terrorist

Secret societies like the Knights of the White Camelia, the Pale Faces, and the Knights of the Ku Klux Klan organized to frustrate Reconstruction. Describing itself as an "institution of Chivalry, Humanity, Mercy, and Patriotism," the Klan violently intimidated blacks.

tactics illegal. The bills gave the president the right to prosecute in federal courts all those who sought to prevent qualified persons from voting. For the first time the federal government had defined certain crimes against individuals as violation of federal law. President Grant invoked the measures in nine South Carolina counties, and soon hundreds of Klansmen were indicted for illegal activities.

The Klan quickly declined, but not the determination of southern conservatives to cow the black population and take control of the South away from Radicals and their supporters. The redeemers abandoned hooded robes, flaming crosses, and night rides, but not other forms of intimidation. In their successful effort in 1875 to redeem Mississippi, conservatives used the powerful weapon of ostracism to force white Republicans to change their party. One who succumbed to their tactics, Colonel James Lusk, told a black fellow Republican: "No white man can live in the South in the future and act with any other than the Democratic party unless he is willing and prepared to live a life of social isolation and remain in political oblivion."

Tougher tactics were often effective against black voters. Blacks who voted Republican were denied jobs or fired from those they had. More stubborn black Republicans were threatened with violence. During the 1875 Mississippi election thousands of white Democrats armed themselves with rifles and shotguns, and then, to make the message clear, entered the names of black Republicans in "dead books." In Vicksburg, Yazoo City, and other Mississippi towns blacks were shot and killed in preelection fights.

In that campaign the Democrats captured the Mississippi legislature and elected the only state official running for statewide office. The Republican governor, Adelburt Ames, faced with impeachment by the new legislature, agreed to resign. Mississippi had been "redeemed." Similar processes took place in other southern states, so that by 1876 only Louisiana, Florida, and South Carolina remained under Republican administrations—and these regimes stayed in power only because they were protected by federal troops.

The End of Reconstruction. Clearly, the redeemers were effective tacticians and organizers. But their success also depended on the weakening commitment of Northerners to Radical rule in the South.

The decline of Northern resolve had several sources. Many honest Republicans came to see the defense of the black man as an excuse for continued domination of their party by its most corrupt wing. Whenever a new scandal was uncovered in the Grant administration, for example—and there would be many—it would be buried under an appeal for Republican unity against the ex-rebels. The process came to be called "waving the bloody shirt." By the middle of the 1870s many Republicans had concluded that abandoning blacks and their friends in the South was better than continuing to uphold the unscrupulous element in their own party.

Fatigue and racism also played their parts. How long, many Northerners asked, could the country invest energy and money to sustain a system that the "best elements" of southern society opposed? The ex-slaves would never make good citizens, and there was no point in continuing the hopeless battle. Such arguments were reinforced by a growing conviction among northern commercial and industrial groups that stability in the South would be better for business than the political agitation that constantly disturbed the nation.

The end came in 1876. In the presidential election of that year the Democrats nominated Samuel J. Tilden of New York, an honest but colorless corporation lawyer. The Republican candidate was Rutherford B. Hayes, the aloof but upright governor of Ohio. The Democratic platform promised to withdraw federal troops from the South and endorsed traditional Democratic low-tariff, small-government positions. The Republicans declared that they would never abandon the black man and would continue to support positive government, a protective tariff, and "sound money."

The election was so close that the results were challenged. The Democrats claimed they had carried New York, New Jersey, Connecticut, Indiana, and the entire South. The Republicans insisted that the votes of Florida, Louisiana, and South Carolina—the still "unredeemed" states—rightfully belonged to them.

Southern black voters after 1865 were alternately courted and coerced by white politicians.
The Democrats found force more necessary than the Republicans did to win black votes.
In this Radical Republican cartoon two Democrats (the one at right looking remarkably like
Jefferson Davis) make no pretense of winning "hearts and minds."

They also challenged one Democratic vote in Oregon, where electors had split between the two candidates. As in 1824, the election was thrown into the House of Representatives. For the next four months the country's political life was in an uproar as the politicians tried to settle the election issue before Inauguration Day in March 1877.

Both sides brought every weapon possible to bear on the dispute—propaganda, legal maneuvering, congressional commissions, and threats of violence. Some historians believe that one hidden issue during the disputed election period was railroads. Southerners, they say, believed that only the Republicans would approve a land grant to the Texas and Pacific Railroad, designed to connect New Orleans and other important southern cities with the Pacific Coast. This reasoning led influential southern leaders, many former Whigs with little love for the Democrats, to seek a bargain with the Republicans. What seems more likely than this "Compromise of 1877" was something less devious: that Southerners merely traded electoral votes for removing federal troops from the South. But whoever is right, soon after Hayes's inauguration as nineteenth president of the United States, the last federal soldiers were withdrawn from Dixie. The redeemers quickly moved in. Reconstruction was over.

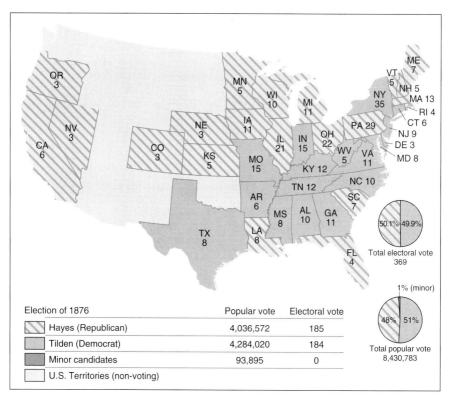

Election of 1876	Popular vote	Electoral vote
Hayes (Republican)	4,036,572	185
Tilden (Democrat)	4,284,020	184
Minor candidates	93,895	0
U.S. Territories (non-voting)		

Total electoral vote
369

1% (minor)

Total popular vote
8,430,783

Presidential Election of 1876

■ CONCLUSIONS ■

Reconstruction was not an unrelieved disaster. During these momentous years southerners repaired the physical devastation of the war and reestablished their states' constitutional relations with the Union. Meanwhile, black southerners were able to create for themselves important new islands of freedom—freedom to move, freedom to create social and cultural institutions of their own, freedom for black women to leave the fields. They also improved their material well-being. As sharecroppers, blacks kept a larger share of the wealth they produced than as slaves. Also on the credit side were the Radical-sponsored Fourteenth and Fifteenth amendments. Once embedded in the Constitution, they would become the bases for a "second Reconstruction" in our own day.

Yet much is dismaying about Reconstruction. Americans of this era failed to meet the great challenges that faced them. Instead of a prosperous black yeomanry, the South would be left with a mass of impoverished semipeons who for generations would be a reproach to America's proud claims of prosperity and equality. Instead of political democracy, Reconstruction would bequeath a legacy of sectional fraud, intimidation, and shameless racial exclusion. Rather than accelerating southern economic growth, Reconstruction would chain the South to a declining staple crop agriculture and leave it ever further behind the rest of the nation.

Who was to blame for this failure? One answer is that Americans were trapped by the past. Deep-seated prejudices and memories of slavery blinded most white southerners (and many Northerners) to the need for racial justice. Traditional individualism and the commitment to self-help obscured the fact that the special circumstances of black dependence resulting from slavery called for imaginative government aid. And there were the accidents of events and personalities. Would Lincoln have seen realities more clearly? Certainly the accession of Andrew Johnson, a stubborn man of limited vision and conventional racial views, did nothing to solve the unique problems of the day. Refusing to recognize the North's need to exact some penance from the defeated South, he needlessly antagonized even moderates and drove them into the Radical camp. The result was a legacy of sectional hatred that poisoned American political life for generations.

Meanwhile, the nation was turning away from the "everlasting southern problem" to what many citizens believed were more important matters. The South and Reconstruction became increasingly remote as the country as a whole experienced a surge of economic expansion that dwarfed anything of the past.

Online Resources

"Finding Precedent: The Impeachment of Andrew Johnson"
http://www.andrewjohnson.com
By examining the impeachment of President Andrew Johnson, this Web site explores the major issues behind the impeachment debate and describes the political factions vying to determine Reconstruction policy. The site employs Reconstruction-era editorials and provides biographical sketches and portraits of many of the key figures involved.

"The Black Codes and Reaction to Reconstruction"
http://chnm.gmu.edu/courses/122/recon/code.html
This site contains the text of the Mississippi Black Code and other Reconstruction policies. The site also chronicles citizens' reactions to these policies through contemporary newspaper editorials, magazine articles, and congressional testimony, and it discusses the impact of these reforms on African Americans.

"Civil War and Reconstruction, 1861–1877: Reconstruction and Rights"
http://lcweb2.loc.gov/ammem/ndlpedu/features/timeline/civilwar/civilwar.html
In addition to a good overview of the Civil War and Reconstruction eras, read transcripts of oral histories from whites who actually experienced Reconstruction in the South. Their stories include eyewitness accounts of racially motivated violence in regard to African-American voting.

Toward Racial Equality: Harper's Weekly Reports on Black America, 1857–1874
http://blackhistory.harpweek.com

This site includes contemporary editorials, illustrations, and advertisements that address the status of African Americans after the Civil War. These primary documents focus specifically on racial violence in both the North and the South, the work of the Freedman's Bureau, and debates on black civil rights.

Reconstruction: A State Divided

http://lsm.crt.state.la.us/cabildo/cabll.htm

Providing an in-depth look at how the Reconstruction policy debate affected one particular place in time, this site offers a window into Reconstruction in the state of Louisiana.

Sharecropping: "After Freedom, We Worked Shares"

http://vi.uh.edu/pages/mintz/45.htm

Illuminating the hardships that African-American sharecroppers faced during the Reconstruction period, this site contains the worlds of Henry Blake, formerly enslaved, who tells about his life as a freed man on the farm.

The Mississippi Black Codes

http://longman.awl.com/history/primarysource_16_1htm

This site has an actual text copy of the harsh black codes from the state of Mississippi. Like those adopted by many state legislatures in the South, these codes bear witness to the legal limitations imposed on African Americans following emancipation.

Railroads and the New South

http://xroads.virginia.edu/~CLASS.am485_98/hall/newsouth.html

This site depicts the history of the New South through the lens of Roanoke, Virginia. It details how the introduction of the railroad affected one town economically, socially, and politically and created a more urban landscape. It is representative of the influences of technology throughout the New South.

"Still Livin' Under the Bonds of Slavery"

http://historymatters.gmu.edu/text/1563a-whitney.html

Download and listen to the audio recording of Minnie Whitney, who describes sharecropping in the late nineteenth century. Hear tales of hard times and oppression as well as agency and self-sufficiency.

17

THE TRIUMPH OF INDUSTRIALISM

What Were the Causes, What Were the Costs?

1862, 1864	Pacific Railroad Acts
1866	The National Labor Union is established
1869	The Knights of Labor is organized
1873	The Slaughterhouse cases; Financial panic; unemployment climbs to 12 percent
1877	The Compromise of 1877: Rutherford B. Hayes elected president; U.S. Supreme Court decides the Granger cases; Socialist Labor party is established
1880	James A. Garfield elected president
1881	Garfield assassinated; Chester A. Arthur becomes president
1882	John D. Rockefeller forms the first trust, but it is dissolved by Ohio courts; Edison's first electric generating station opens in New York; The San Mateo case
1884	Grover Cleveland elected president
1886	Haymarket Riot in Chicago; Samuel Gompers founds the American Federation of Labor (AFL); *Santa Clara Co.* v. *Southern Pacific Railroad*
1888	Benjamin Harrison elected president
1890	Sherman Antitrust Act
1892	Grover Cleveland elected president for the second time; Populist party is established
1893	Sherman Silver Purchase Act is repealed; The American Railway Union is organized by Eugene V. Debs
1894	Pullman strike is ended by federal troops
1895	E.C. Knight case weakens Sherman Antitrust Act
1896	William McKinley elected president
1897	Maximum Freight Rates case
1901	McKinley is assassinated; Theodore Roosevelt becomes president; Eugene V. Debs's Socialist party is founded
1904–12	Socialist party membership increases to 130,000
1913	Federal Reserve System established

In the half-century following the Civil War the United States became the largest and richest industrial nation in the world. As late as 1880 agriculture still created a larger share of income for Americans than any other source. Ten years later its contribution was surpassed by industry, and by 1900 the total value of goods produced by factories and shops in the United States was twice that of goods produced on farms. In the mid-1890s America's output of industrial goods surpassed every other nation's. In 1913 one third of all the world's manufactures came from American factories.

The explosive surge in industry was the major force behind the country's impressive gains in GDP (gross domestic product), the simplest overall measure of economic growth. Between 1865 and 1908 total GDP grew at an average rate of more than 4 percent a year, considerably faster than for most of the period since then. By 1908 total economic output was eight times that of the year Robert E. Lee surrendered at Appomattox. Population was also increasing in this period. Still, at its end, Americans were producing twice the total of goods and services per person each year as at the beginning. Unfortunately, this did not mean that every American was twice as rich on the eve of World War I as he or she—or, more likely, their forebears—had been in 1865. As we will see, the gains were unequally distributed. But the extraordinary performance provided the foundation for broad affluence.

What caused the industrial leap and the economic surge after 1865? Was there some single, predominant factor, or were there a number of separate ones? And was growth essentially cost-free? Or did the American people pay a price for the impressive advance? Let us start with the causes. We shall then consider the costs.

■ CAPTAINS OF INDUSTRY ■

The quality of business leadership is one explanation for the economic advance. According to this view, tycoons such as Andrew Carnegie, John D. Rockefeller, and "Commodore" Vanderbilt were the principal agents.

In fact, it would be difficult to ignore their role in the economic life of this era. Even against the gaudy and boisterous background of the period we call the Gilded Age, these "captains of industry" stand out vividly. In many ways, their image is a negative one. They have been likened to "robber barons" who held the nation for ransom to amass their great fortunes, or seen as heartless employers who cruelly exploited their workers, or attacked as crude and vulgar men who flaunted their wealth and displayed their bad taste. And yet it is also true that in our national mythology they are often given credit for singlehandedly transforming the United States into an industrial giant. What role did they actually play in this process?

A close look at the extraordinary economic achievement of the Gilded Age shows that the great entrepreneurs—the risk-takers, managers, and organizers— were indeed important contributors to the nation's spectacular economic success. Entrepreneurship is a large element in virtually all economic growth. To increase an economy's output, it is not enough to unimaginatively add more materials, labor, and machines to the prevailing economic mix. Growth also requires deploying the initiating, coordinating, and managerial functions to start new firms and expand existing ones. The entrepreneurial skills necessary to detect an important economic need, cut costs, tap new sources of savings, recruit and direct labor, recognize and inspire new talent are not universal. Those societies abundantly endowed with these skills will inevitably advance more rapidly than ones that are not.

Gustavus Swift and the Organizing Function.   To understand the role of entrepreneurship in the economic transformation following the Civil War, let us consider several examples. A good place to start is the meat-packing industry.

Before 1860 most fresh meat came from local butchers. Dressed carcasses spoiled too quickly to come from distant sources, while shipping live animals created large losses in weight. But in the generation following the Civil War, three developments helped transform the business of supplying the public with meat. First, an increasing proportion of Americans came to live in cities, remote from the farms where meat animals were fattened. Second, an expanding rail network made the products of the prairies and plains of the West more accessible to urban consumers. Third, in the 1870s, the railroads introduced refrigerated cars, allowing chilled fresh beef and pork to be shipped long distances without spoilage.

One of the first men to recognize the new possibilities opened for the meat industry was Gustavus Swift. Swift saw the advantages of slaughtering cattle close to the grass and corn of the West and shipping the dressed product to eastern consumers. This would not only eliminate the losses in shipping live cattle; it would allow cheaper centralized processing. Much of the slaughtering could be mechanized. As the industry evolved, it came to employ a "dis-assembly line." As carcasses passed on a moving line they were quickly skinned, dismembered, and prepared for shipping. Labor costs were thereby reduced. The scale of the operations also made for efficiencies. Animal parts that were normally discarded could be sold to make medicines, sausage casings, fertilizers, leather, and other byproducts. (It would be said of the great hog butchers of the late nineteenth century that they used every part of the pig but the squeal.)

Swift sent his first dressed, chilled beef east by refrigerator car in the mid-1870s. Consumers at first resisted the unfamiliar product; local retailers who feared the competition sought to have it legally excluded. But in a few years—joined by other packers, Armour, Cudahy, and Morris—he was shipping millions of pounds of meat annually from his Chicago plants and marketing it through a network of branch houses and agents. In 1875 the Chicago packers slaughtered 250,000 cattle; in 1880, 500,000; in 1890, a million.

Thomas Edison and Technological Innovation.   Swift contributed primarily to improving the organization of an existing industry. Thomas Edison created several whole new branches of manufacture.

We think of Edison today as an inventor of gadgets, and indeed he was. He improved the telephone and the telegraph, and created the motion picture camera, the phonograph, and the incandescent light bulb. Yet he was far more than a tinkerer; he was also a first-rate entrepreneur whose skills launched several giant new businesses.

Edison and his associates met a vital public need. At the beginning of the nineteenth century, Americans worked and played almost entirely during daylight hours and the rhythms of life corresponded closely to the seasonal length of the day. At night city streets were dark. Private homes were often unlighted after daylight except on special occasions. Gaslight arrived during the 1850s, but its use was confined to city streets and to the upper and middle classes of the larger urban centers, where it was economically feasible to install costly pipes and meters.

The new petroleum industry changed this picture. In the 1840s and 1850s, "rock oil" was a substance extracted in small amounts from streams and used as a medicine. Its value as an illuminant was understood, but no one was certain that it could be collected in large enough quantities to be useful for lighting. Then, in 1859 a group of businessmen hired E. L. Drake, a well-driller, to dig for oil in western Pennsylvania. After several weeks Drake struck a major oil pool, proving that there was an abundant supply of the substance underground. Before long, what had been a quack medical remedy became a household necessity. Refined into kerosene, petroleum quickly replaced whale oil lamps and candles as the nation's major source of home lighting.

From the outset, the risk of fire caused problems with kerosene in congested urban centers. By the 1870s electricity seemed the solution. In the form of arc lights, it was already in limited use for illuminating stage productions and city streets, but arc lights were too brilliant and too wasteful of power for private homes. This is where Edison saw his opportunity. If electric light could be produced in small units, it would replace kerosene and gas for home use. Many scientists at the time believed that the feat could not be accomplished, but, at his laboratory in New Jersey, Edison pushed ahead to develop a practical home electric lighting system.

The story as usually told emphasizes Edison's quest for a durable filament for a light bulb. In fact, Edison hoped to develop an entire system similar to gaslighting. This would require a centrally located source of electric power that could serve many lamps, a means to transmit the power efficiently to each lamp, lamps that could be turned on and off without affecting other lamps on the circuit, and finally, a metering arrangement to measure each customer's use of current. Edison had to lure customers from an established workable system to his own, and at the same time make a profit for private investors.

This difficult enterprise aroused Edison's impressive talents as both businessman and inventor. After securing dependable financial backing, he worked out the technical specifications for an efficient and economically feasible lighting system. Once he had developed a usable carbon filament for his glass lamp, he invented a simple metering system that enabled the Edison Company to assess charges against users. In September 1882, he opened a central generating station on Pearl Street near New York City's financial district, where his success would be sure to attract the attention of the nation's money men. During the next few years the Edison Company opened other stations in Boston, Philadelphia, and Chicago. In a few years the nation's cities were alive with light, and urban Americans stayed up later to read, talk, dine, and generally enjoy themselves. A whole way of life had been revolutionized by one man's skill, insight, and enterprise.

Andrew Carnegie and Cost Consciousness.   Careful cost analysis and ruthless cost cutting were the hallmarks of Andrew Carnegie's entrepreneurship.

Carnegie was the classic self-made man. Arriving in the United States with his family in 1848, the thirteen-year-old Scottish lad first worked in a Pittsburgh textile factory replacing broken threads on the spinning spools for $1.20 a week. In the 1850s Carnegie became an assistant to Thomas A. Scott, vice president of the Pennsylvania Railroad. From Scott, Carnegie learned how to deal with a large-scale enterprise and how to save thousands by squeezing pennies.

Carnegie was not an inventor like Edison. He worked with existing technology and processes, but made them show a profit. When he moved from railroading to bridge building and then to iron and steel making during the 1860s, the new Bessemer and open-hearth processes were already being used to make steel. Carnegie adopted the new methods for his Pittsburgh-based Edgar Thomson Works, but he seized on improvements when they appeared, disregarding the costs of scrapping his older but still usable equipment. Carnegie ran his furnaces, hearths, and converters full-blast regardless of replacement costs, and did not let up even when orders tumbled during hard times. He also cut expenses ruthlessly and kept down labor costs by mechanizing as many processes as he could. Carnegie recruited a corps of driving young executives and then held them strictly accountable for every penny spent producing steel. One of these men later said: "You [were] expected always to get it ten cents cheaper the next year or the next month." Within a few years Carnegie and his associates had lowered the price of steel so much that it could be used to replace iron, wood, and stone in construction, thus paving the way for marvels of engineering never before possible.

Of all the so-called robber barons, Carnegie was probably the most civic-minded. Like the others, he fought to keep his employees' wages low, but he also believed that rich men were custodians of wealth for society at large. Before he died, the "Star-spangled Scotsman" gave away much of his immense fortune to charitable institutions, research foundations, endowments for peace and international understanding, and to establish public libraries.

Capital Creation and J. P. Morgan.   Where did the funds to invest in meat-packing plants, power stations, and steel mills come from? Ultimately the source of any money for capital investment must be savings. Swift and Carnegie relied largely on the retained profits of previous and existing enterprises. Many businesspeople, however, were happy to tap the pools of savings set aside by other people.

In the 1880s the American savings rate was about 25 percent, far higher than today. People saved because thrift and prudence were morally approved and because there was no other way to provide for old age, disease, or accident. Rich men and women were particularly able to save because their incomes far exceeded their day-to-day needs. A society with substantial inequalities of wealth and income meant that a large proportion of the public involuntarily contributed to economic growth.

Piling up savings is not enough, however. These savings must be channeled to entrepreneurs who have the will and the skill to use them effectively. When the saver and the investor are the same person—as in the case of Carnegie and Swift—there is little problem. But what if the two are different individuals? It is here that various investment institutions come into play.

One of those institutions was the stock market located on New York's Wall Street, where stocks and other securities issued by corporations and governments had been bought and sold since the late eighteenth century. Those who bought "shares" in a business corporation were part owners of the firm and received a portion of its profits without risking losses beyond the extent of their share purchase (limited liability). This system should have been an effective way for entrepreneurs to raise capital, but its value was seriously undercut by the fact that the stock exchange had become a sort of gambling casino where speculators—"bulls" and "bears"—bought and sold shares, not to gain profits from corporate earnings, but to make killings in "corners," "raids," and other get-rich-quick maneuvers. Prudent people with savings looked aghast at these risky and shady doings and stayed away from the stock market.

A more successful way to channel savings to investors during these years was through the banks. But the nation's banking structure had serious weaknesses. The national banking system, as created by the National Banking Acts of 1863 and 1864, was a major advance over the old state bank system, but it had substantial drawbacks. Banks with federal charters were not allowed to take land as security for loans, a restriction that limited their value for farmers who only had their land to offer as collateral. Nor could they readily increase the country's money supply to take care of seasonal needs or the steady, long-term growth of the economy, since the amount of their paper money issues depended on their holdings of a limited volume of government bonds. Lacking a central bank of last resort that might provide extra funds when needed, the national banking system was also unable to deal effectively with financial panics or other sudden crises.

Despite these flaws the national banks served to bring savers and investors together satisfactorily, at least where smaller amounts of capital were needed. For large-scale capital investment, however, the most effective agent was the investment banker. The need for investment bankers was especially urgent during the Gilded Age, when explosive urban growth and rapidly expanding railroads and industry created an extraordinary demand for capital.

Investment banks did not normally engage in the day-to-day business of commercial banking. Instead, they dealt with large borrowers, either government agencies or industrial and transportation promoters interested in raising large amounts of capital.

Before 1860 a few banking firms had begun to serve as middlemen between the government and savers. During the Civil War Jay Cooke and Company had assumed many of the risks of selling the giant treasury issues of "five-twenty" bonds that had financed the Union army and navy. In the 1870s Cooke became the financial agent of the giant Northern Pacific Railroad. When the public lost confidence in Northern Pacific securities, Cooke and Company went bankrupt, triggering the panic of 1873 and the six years of hard times that followed.

The public's experience in 1873 did little to encourage investor confidence in stocks. But by the 1880s attitudes began to change, largely because of J. P. Morgan. Morgan often said that his chief asset was trust. The public believed that any promotion he orchestrated was apt to succeed. Building on this trust Morgan was able to put together a flock of corporation mergers that combined competing, inefficient, small firms into giants that promoted greater productivity and above all promised managed, tolerable competition. This required inducing hundreds of investors of the constituent firms to accept stock in the new, consolidated firm. Convinced that a Morgan-organized and run company was certain to be profitable, they usually complied.

J. P. Morgan. He had a bulbous red nose—carefully obscured in this portrait. Yet his forceful personality comes through.

Morgan, and the other investment bankers of the day, accustomed prosperous Americans to think of the stock market as a safe place to invest their savings, not merely an arena for risky speculation. By the end of the century the stock exchange had become a vital money market where those with savings came together with those who needed funds to invest in industry. By 1910, billions of dollars of stock were bought and sold annually on Wall Street. Much of this trading remained speculative. But a good deal of it represented the constructive meeting of savers who wanted secure returns and promoters who could put these savings to productive use.

■ THE SPOILERS ■

Clearly the entrepreneurship of Swift, Edison, Carnegie, Morgan, and others like them benefited the American people by providing new or cheaper products or by encouraging investment. Though most nineteenth-century businessmen had limited social sympathies and few scruples against sharp dealing, their efforts helped to increase the income of Americans generally. Not all business leaders, however, were constructive innovators. Some were primarily spoilers who got rich by manipulating finance while cheating investors, bribing politicians, ruining competitors, or rigging prices. Among these spoilers were Jay Gould and John D. Rockefeller.

The Railroads and Jay Gould.   The Civil War slowed the exuberant railroad construction of the 1850s, but after 1865 the country turned with a will to conquering time and distance with rails and locomotives. In 1865 there were about 35,000 miles of track in the United States. By 1890 the country had 167,000 miles of track, and by 1910, when the network was largely complete, America was tied together by 240,000 miles of steel rails.

After 1865, promoters consolidated smaller companies into trunk lines such as the New York Central and the Baltimore and Ohio. Chicago, St. Louis, Kansas City, and Omaha became major rail centers, and from these points other promoters began to push west and south over the rapidly developing prairies. The most spectacular growth, however, was the spread of the transcontinentals. In 1869 construction teams from the Central Pacific, driving east from Sacramento, and from the Union Pacific, driving west from Omaha, met at Promontory Point in northern Utah, completing the first Atlantic–Pacific railroad connection. By 1890 five major railroads crossed the Great Plains, linking the Atlantic to the Pacific Coast.

Railroad efficiency was also vastly increased. Relatively cheap steel rails soon replaced the older iron tracks, allowing the railroads to run larger, more efficient locomotives and cars. Braking problems on these heavier trains were solved with the adoption of George Westinghouse's air brake in the 1880s. Track gauges were standardized in these years so that passengers and freight need not be shifted from one set of cars to another. Meanwhile, George Pullman invented a new passenger car that was an ordinary coach by day but could be converted into a comfortable sleeping car by night.

Scholars have warned against exaggerating the impact of the railroads on the late-nineteenth-century American economy, but most interpreters believe it was immense. Cheap, all-weather transportation accelerated the decline in shipping costs that had begun during the pre-Civil War period, opening vast new regions to economic exploitation. Lower transport costs allowed commodities to be produced in the most efficient locations and by the most efficient firms and then shipped to consumers all over the country. They enabled each region to specialize in what it did best and exchange its products for those of other regions, further lowering consumer costs. The creation of an integrated national market raised the country's total output per capita substantially.

Some of those who helped bring this process about were farseeing, creative individuals who risked their own fortunes in opening new areas to settlement. James J. Hill, for example, the promoter of the Great Northern railroad connecting St. Paul with Puget Sound, built his road without the great federal subsidies behind the other transcontinentals. Many of the railroad promoters of the age were neither as civic-minded nor as creative as Hill. Most notorious of all was Jay Gould.

Gould made a fortune by manipulating railroads' financial structure and leaving them debt-ridden and gutted. In 1867 Gould and his friend James Fisk became directors of the Erie Railroad, supposedly as allies of the New York railroad promoter, Cornelius ("Commodore") Vanderbilt, who hoped to achieve a dominant position in New York City's western traffic by adding the Erie to his New York Central. Vanderbilt began secretly to buy up Erie stock to gain a controlling interest.

The new directors, joined by the notorious speculator Daniel Drew, betrayed Vanderbilt. Drew, especially, was a master of "stock watering," a term borrowed from shady cattle dealing. He and his confederates issued vast amounts of new Erie securities unjustified by any increase in the railroad's earning capacity, and quietly dumped these shares on the market. The unsuspecting Commodore bought and bought, but could not manage to buy enough to gain control of the railroad. Eventually Vanderbilt discovered the deception and sought help from the courts; the Erie ringleaders did the same. For months the two groups fought bitter legal battles, culminating in Gould's wholesale bribery of the New York State legislature to legalize his acts. Gould soon lost interest in the Erie. But the railroad, stuck with millions of shares of watered stock, was never the same. As he turned to new endeavors, Gould jeered, "There ain't nothing more in Erie."

John D. Rockefeller and Monopoly. The career of John D. Rockefeller illustrates another form of business abuse common during these years: monopoly. His manipulations also highlight the permissive legal atmosphere, with rules either unclear or unformulated, characteristic of business operations of the era.

Rockefeller's business stage was the oil-refining industry. After E. L. Drake's successful oil well in western Pennsylvania, the oil industry had boomed, spreading throughout the East and Midwest and even to California. The new sources of supply soon generated spectacular growth in the refining industry, which converted crude oil into kerosene, wax, and lubricants. By the early 1870s the refining companies had begun to concentrate near Cleveland, Ohio, a region close to the eastern oil fields with unusually good transportation connections to the country's major population centers.

The refining industry was risky. For a few thousand dollars anyone could set up a simple plant to produce kerosene. As more and more firms entered the business, profits fell to the vanishing point, and many refineries went bankrupt. The intense competition undoubtedly kept prices low and benefited the consumer, but from the refiners' point of view, the results were disastrous.

Rockefeller's campaign to reduce competition in his own industry was more successful than most. In 1870 he and his partners established the Standard Oil Company of Ohio, which soon became one of the largest refining companies in the country. The technical and managerial skills of the Standard people were important factors in their firm's prosperity. Equally significant, however, was Rockefeller's ability to squeeze cheap rates from the railroads for shipping crude and refined oil. In the 1870s the railroads, too, found themselves in cutthroat competition, slashing rates on competitive lines to stay solvent. Railroad officials tried consolidation of several firms under one controlling firm to reduce competition. They also tried "pools," agreements among several competing roads to divide the traffic according to a set formula and avoid rate cutting. Invariably these agreements broke down when one firm or another found it advantageous to break the pool agreement. Because their legality was at best dubious, these could not be enforced by law.

Taking advantage of the railroads' own fierce competition, Rockefeller arranged to provide large-scale shipments of Standard products by a given railroad in return for rebates that would reduce Standard's shipping charges far below the published rates. So competitive was the refining business that even a small saving on transportation costs could give one producer a vital edge over the others. As a result, Standard Oil grew at the expense of its competitors— many of whom were forced to sell out to their aggressive opponent—and with each spurt of growth the firm further increased its ability to squeeze favorable terms out of the railroad companies.

By 1880 the Standard Oil Company controlled between 90 and 95 percent of the country's refining capacity and 92 percent of the crude oil supply of the Appalachian area, the major oil region at the time. In 1882 Rockefeller and his associates formed the first "trust," a company that owned the securities of subsidiary firms and controlled their operations.

The Ohio courts dissolved Rockefeller's trust on the grounds that it violated the rights of owners of the individual firms and was "a virtual monopoly of the business of producing petroleum . . . to control the price." But the Standard Oil people reorganized under a New Jersey law that legalized a rather similar device, the holding company, enabling a supercompany to own stock in several subordinate firms and so control their operations. Thereafter, Standard's share of the industry declined somewhat, but as late as 1911, when the United States Supreme Court ordered the parent holding company dissolved into thirty separate firms, it was still by far the largest producer of refined oil and crude petroleum in the world.

The post-Civil War business leaders were, then, both wreckers and builders. If all had resembled Jay Gould or John D. Rockefeller, it would be difficult to consider them a positive factor in late-nineteenth-century economic growth. But the Carnegies, the Edisons, the Swifts, and the Morgans assuredly helped speed up the process of transforming America into a rich industrial society.

■ THE INTELLECTUAL FOUNDATION ■

Entrepreneurship was only one component of the economic advances of the Gilded Age. Another was a system of values congenial to material growth. A substantial minority of miners, loggers, construction workers, and factory hands of Gilded Age America were reluctant participants in the era's economic developments. Yet, to a considerable degree, American wage earners and the rest of the American public endorsed private profit, hard work, and economic progress.

In part this support can be explained by the realities of American society. As we shall see, the growing economy, however imperfect, did permit a fair degree of improvement in the economic status and income of average wage earners, and a certain amount of movement up the social ladder for their children. These improvements reinforced the faith of ordinary people in the process. But actual experience was not the whole of it. Faith in the system was buttressed by a mass of ideology, myth, and propaganda that sang the praises—and the inevitability— of the social and economic changes underway.

The Work Ethic. An important cultural accelerator of economic change was the work ethic. In part a residue of Puritan teaching that the elect would reveal themselves by hard work and worldly success, it was reinforced by popular writers, preachers, the schools, and opinion makers generally. The work ethic proclaimed the virtues of reliability, thrift, sobriety, respectability, honesty, and conscientious performance of duties and obligations. These were rewards in themselves, but they also promised other rewards: Those who sowed would inevitably reap. According to the famous *McGuffey Readers,* used by generations of American schoolchildren, "He who would thrive must rise at five; he who has thriven, may lie to seven." Popular biographies and novels made heroes of successful strivers. In the potboiler fiction of William M. Thayer and Horatio Alger, the heroes are usually ambitious poor boys who overcome adversity to achieve social respectability and economic security. Alger's 119 naive formula novels for young people were particularly successful in the Gilded Age. Though obsessed by achievement, in truth Alger's heroes often prosper more by sheer luck than by persistent labor. Yet the ultimate lesson Alger conveyed was that toil was both good in itself and profitable. His heroes are youths who glory in work. Tom

Thatcher is "a sturdy boy of sixteen with bright eyes and smiling, sun-burned face. His shirt sleeves were rolled up, displaying a pair of muscular arms. His hands were brown, and soiled with labor. It was clear that here was no white-handed young aristocrat." Raised on a steady diet of such edifying tales and myths, millions of Americans were prepared to accept the virtues of the contemporary economic system.

The Defense of Inequality. Among its other functions, the work ethic justified unequal rewards, for if hard work was the way to achieve riches, then what divided rich from poor was the quality and intensity of their effort, not birth or good fortune. But there were more direct defenses of the inequalities of wealth as well.

Until close to the end of the century the Protestant ministry often defended the disparities between rich and poor. Henry Ward Beecher told an audience during the 1870s depression: "I do not say that a dollar a day is enough to support . . . a man and five children if a man would insist on smoking and drinking beer. . . . But the man who cannot live on bread and water is not fit to live." In his famous lecture Acres of Diamonds, Baptist minister Russell Conwell delivered the message that material riches were a sign of God's approval, if honestly earned. For the Christian to reject riches was a mistake, for riches allowed the Christian to aid others. During the Gilded Age Conwell gave his standard talk 6,000 times to many thousands of listeners.

The leading writers, academics, and journalists of the day also defended the economic inequalities of the time and praised the competitive spirit of the age. Many of these people drew on the ideas of Adam Smith and other economists of eighteenth- and early-nineteenth-century Britain, who sought to demonstrate how the unrestricted pursuit of private gain by individuals must maximize the profit of all. Through a process Smith called the "invisible hand," free play for personal acquisitive drives would ultimately generate abundance for all. Laissez-faire (hands off) was by far the best policy for government to follow if its goal was economic progress.

After 1865, defenders of inequality could also turn to social Darwinism to make their case. In his monumental 1859 work *Origin of Species,* the English naturalist Charles Darwin had proposed an alternative to the Bible account in Genesis to explain the great diversity of living species. According to Darwin, the fierce competition among living things for limited resources was the cause of diversity. Individuals that were stronger, tougher, fiercer, quicker, more intelligent, or more aggressive—in a word, "fitter"—survived to reproduce. The others died, and their lines, with their distinctive qualities, ceased to exist. In this way small, advantageous differences over many years were encouraged, and gradually, through inheritance, living things diverged in ways that created whole new species. The process seemed "progressive" in that lower gave way to higher, and at the top of the evolutionary ladder was humankind, descended from some common ancestor with the apes.

Social Darwinists claimed that what applied to the biological world also applied to society: Competition and the "survival of the fittest" was the only way to achieve progress. For humankind to advance, competition of all kinds must be allowed a free hand. Every attempt of soft-hearted philanthropists to interfere with the social evolutionary process by curbing the strong and bolstering the weak was shortsighted and regressive. "Let it be understood," wrote Yale professor William Graham Sumner, "that we cannot go outside this alternative: liberty, inequality, survival of the fittest; not liberty, equality, survival of the unfittest."

Given that business leaders often scrambled to create pools and trusts to reduce competition and frequently demanded government aid to protect their profits, it is not clear how sincerely they took laissez-faire or social Darwinist ideas. Yet at times they echoed the slogans of the professors and philosophers. Even Andrew Carnegie, an atypical business tycoon in so many ways, accepted the necessity for inequality on Darwinian grounds. In his famous essay, "The Gospel of Wealth," he startled the reading public by declaring that rich men were only "stewards of wealth" who must give it all back to society. But Carnegie also wrote: "We accept and welcome . . . great inequality of environment; the concentration of business, industrial and commercial, in the hands of a few; and the law of competition between these as being not only beneficial, but essential to the future of the race."

Students of society cannot be certain how ideas such as social Darwinism actually influence human actions and social change. Yet in many cases, at least where such ideas did not fly in the face of clear, first-hand experience, defense of hard work and inequality and propaganda regarding the self-made man were accepted by workers and the middle class, helping to create a disciplined labor force that contributed to economic growth after 1865.

■ THE ROLE OF GOVERNMENT ■

Though the entrepreneurs of this era were certainly instrumental in economic progress, the federal government also stimulated the economy by direct investment, by grants, by tariffs, and by tax policies favorable to savers and investors. Without this help, growth would undoubtedly have been slower.

Government Aid. At times the federal government invested directly in the physical improvements the nation needed, appropriating funds for post offices, docks, and canal locks, and dredged river channels. Each year Congress supported such enterprises by a flock of "rivers and harbors" bills. In 1867 these took $1.2 million from the taxpayers' pockets; by 1895 they cost almost $20 million. Local governments, too—by paving streets, constructing sewers, and building hospitals, schools, reservoirs, and aqueducts—contributed to the country's capital growth.

An especially important federal contribution to Gilded Age economic growth was friendly tax policy. After the 1870s the tariff—in effect a tax on consumers—rose in steps virtually without pause until the twentieth century, providing a wall behind which investors could initiate new industries without fear of more efficient foreign competition. Internal taxes also favored investors.

For most of this period, import duties and excises on tobacco, whiskey, beer, wine, and other items were the main sources of federal funds.

This tax system was quite regressive; that is, it took a larger percentage of the income of the poor than of the rich. Between 1861 and 1872 the federal government imposed an income tax, a progressive tax that rose proportionately with higher income. But this was dropped as part of the postwar retreat from heavy taxation; when it was revived in 1894, it was declared unconstitutional by the Supreme Court. Local governments raised most of their revenues by taxing property, an equally regressive practice. All told, the tax burden fell disproportionately on farmers and people on the lower rungs of the income ladder, constituting a kind of subsidy to business and the rich. The system clearly was not egalitarian. Many would consider it unfair. But by leaving the rich with substantial surpluses to invest in land, securities, or business enterprises, it probably contributed to growth.

Federal subsidies also helped encourage growth. The wartime Morrill Land Grant College Act (1862), which provided public land to endow agricultural colleges, undoubtedly stimulated greater farm productivity after 1865. Federal railroad legislation had even weightier consequences. By 1871, under the terms of the Pacific Railroad Acts (1862 and 1864) and several later railroad land grant measures, the federal government had given private railroad companies over 130 million acres of land in the trans-Mississippi West, about one tenth of the entire public domain. This vast empire included timber, minerals, and some of the most fertile soil on earth. Individual states contributed 49 million additional acres from their public lands. All told, this huge block of real estate—larger than the state of Texas—was a vital source of funds for the railroads.

The wisdom of the railroad land-grant policy has been debated for many years. Some historians call it a giant giveaway that deprived the American people of a large part of their heritage in order to benefit a few. Railroad promoters certainly made money from the land grants beyond their costs of construction, but the government and the public also benefited: The grants accelerated growth of the West, reduced charges for transporting government goods (a requirement written into each of the grants), and enhanced prices of the land retained by the government adjacent to the railroads. Most important, the policy speeded the process of linking the country together by rail. If the railroads had not had land to sell, few private capitalists would have put their money in ventures so risky as railroads thrown across hundreds of miles of empty space, much of it—until the railroads arrived—virtually worthless. Without the land grants, then, economic development would undoubtedly have been slower.

Hands Off. Each of these examples—tariff, taxes, railroad land grants—is an instance of government contributing directly to economic development. But government also helped by refusing to impose restraints on practices business favored, even when such restraints were endorsed by many voters. It was often through the federal courts that this hands-off policy was promoted.

Between 1865 and 1880, federal judges took the position that the states could restrict the exercise of private property rights in order to protect the

Railroads, 1850–1900

health, welfare, or morals of citizens. In the Slaughterhouse cases of 1873, for example, the Supreme Court rejected the contention that the Fourteenth Amendment, which had been passed to safeguard the political rights of black freedmen against state encroachment, also protected the profits and property of individuals and corporations against state regulation. In the Granger cases (notably *Munn v. Illinois*) of 1877, it upheld the right of Illinois to establish maximum rates for storing grain on the grounds that a state, under its legitimate police powers, could regulate any business that embraced "a public interest."

In the 1880s, however, the federal courts began to limit the power of state legislatures to intervene in the operations of business. In the San Mateo (1882) and the Santa Clara (1886) cases—both involving efforts by California to regulate railroad practices—the Supreme Court now asserted that the Fourteenth Amendment did apply to those injured by state economic regulation. Moreover, the amendment's protections applied not just to individuals, but to corporations, which were "persons" under the Constitution. In effect, corporations too could claim that they had been deprived by states of "property" without "due process of law" and appeal for federal protection against regulatory laws. Thereafter, it became more difficult for state legislatures to intrude into the transactions between business and individuals to protect what was perceived as the public interest against the misdeeds of business. *Wabash Railroad v. Illinois*

(1886) struck down an Illinois law prohibiting discrimination between long-haul and short-haul costs in transportation contracts. The decision created a "twilight zone" where the states could not regulate and the federal government had no legal right.

The next year Congress passed the Interstate Commerce Act creating the Interstate Commerce Commission to regulate railroads. Yet it gave the commission, the first regulatory commission in the country, only limited powers. And these were soon diminished by the courts. In the Maximum Freight Rate case (1897), for example, the Supreme Court allowed the Interstate Commerce Commission the right to determine only whether an existing freight rate was reasonable, not to set future rates, and in the E. C. Knight case (1895) it emasculated the monopoly-regulating Sherman Antitrust Act by making it inapplicable to manufacturing businesses.

By 1900, the federal courts had subordinated state regulatory power to federal law and crippled Congress's right to regulate, imposing a hands-off business policy on the nation. The federal government could help business in various ways, as we saw, but it could not limit business for the sake of perceived public need. Later generations would often condemn these policies harshly. But they did create an environment in which those with capital felt confident of high returns with limited risk, undoubtedly accelerating the pace of economic expansion.

■ THE WAGE EARNERS ■

In discussing the triumph of industry after 1865, we have considered causes. What about consequences? For example, how did the laboring men and women fare as the nation accelerated its output, and how did they respond to what they experienced?

If we look only at the cold statistics, the experience of Gilded Age wage earners appears moderately good. Average real wages and annual earnings rose substantially in the half-century following the Civil War. One economist has estimated that hourly wages and earnings of American industrial workers, allowing for changes in the purchasing power of the dollar, increased by 50 percent between 1860 and 1890. Another concludes that during the next twenty-five years the increase was another 37 percent. Even omitting individual improvements in skill and increasing experience, then, industrial workers between 1865 and 1914 almost doubled their real income.

But these statistics tell only part of the story. They are only averages, and so mask a great deal of variation. They also disregard many other aspects of the working person's life in this era of pell-mell economic change.

Social Mobility and Financial Rewards. White males made up the majority of the labor force in this era, and we will consider them first. When they took their first jobs, most received the wages typical of unskilled "laborers." But a majority raised their skill levels over the years, and by their forties or fifties were

Steam-driven trip-hammers stamped out metal parts for reapers and other farm machinery at the McCormick factory in Chicago. Machines like these increased workers' productivity, but they also added immeasurably to the hazards of wage earners' lives.

earning more than thirty years before regardless of the general trend of wage levels. This improvement took place even without a change in the occupation category they began with. But many workers could count on movement out of the occupation where they started the "race of life." The data on occupational mobility among white American working men suggest overall that movement from unskilled to semiskilled and even skilled jobs was not uncommon. A study of Boston in the period 1880–1930 shows that, of those who began as common laborers, between 35 and 40 percent ended up higher on the occupational scale, largely in the better-paid, more prestigious, white-collar group.

We must not exaggerate, however. Horatio Alger and the other myth-makers were defending a system that did not invariably pay off. Mobility and success depended on more than individual effort and merit. We know that the extent of mobility varied, for example, by decade, by ethnic group, and by religious identification. And it was certainly difficult for a poor boy to leap to the very top of the pile. The great tycoons of the Gilded Age were almost all native-born Protestants of colonial stock who received far better educations than did the average American of the day. Their fathers, moreover, were themselves middle class or rich. On the other hand, the popularity of the rags-to-riches myths depended on a substantial number of Americans seeing mobility as a fact of daily life. As the social historian Herbert Gutman has said in a study of late-nineteenth-century mobility in Paterson, New Jersey: "So many successful manufacturers who had begun as workers walked the streets of the city . . . that it [was] not hard to believe that 'hard work' resulted in spectacular material and social improvement."

We must keep in mind, in assessing the fate of Gilded Age working people, that we are dealing with a "segmented" class. Although the average wage in 1900 was $483 a year, carpenters, masons, and other skilled construction workers often earned as much as $1,250 annually. In 1880, when "laborers" were getting an average of $1.32 a day, blacksmiths received $2.31, locomotive engineers $2.15, and machinists $2.45. The wages of federal employees, clerical workers, and western miners were also above the national average. Agricultural workers, even when we take into account that they were commonly fed and housed by their employers, were always poorly paid. In the aptly named "sweated trades" of the big-city garment industry, working people were squeezed hard by their employers—struggling small businessmen who often showed little consideration for those whose wages represented their major cost of production.

One reason for low wages in the garment industry was the presence of many female workers. Very few women in these years received wages comparable to those of adult men. A typical woman's wage was the dollar or two a week earned by female domestics who washed, cooked, sewed, and ironed in middle-class homes; women piece-workers in New York and Chicago garment loft factories received less than a dollar a day. Fortunately, the picture was not as bleak as these figures suggest. Most women eventually married and ceased to be part of the labor market. Yet for the "spinster," the unmarried woman who had to support herself, or the widow with young children, such wages were scandalous.

Black Americans were also paid well below average. Most were sharecroppers in the South, but the few who had left the farms for the mills or factories were almost all relegated to low-paying, dead-end jobs regardless of their education, skills, or talents. Immigrants, too, received lower wages than skilled and native-born white workers, at least until they acquired skills and an adequate command of English.

Living and Working Conditions.　For families at the bottom of the wage pyramid, life was hard. Many wage earners fought a constant battle to maintain a decent living standard and achieve a little comfort. In 1883 the large family of a railroad brakeman in Joliet, Illinois, reportedly ate chiefly bread, molasses, and potatoes. The family's clothes, a contemporary investigator noted, were "ragged" and the children "half-dressed and dirty." A witness before a Senate committee in 1883 described the home of the typical Pennsylvania coal miner as consisting of two rooms, one upstairs and one down. "The houses are built in long rows without paint on the outside," he reported. "The kitchen furniture consists of a stove and some dishes, a few chairs and a table. They have no carpets on the floor. . . ."

Material living conditions improved over the next generation, but despite advances the quality of the wage earner's life remained unsatisfactory from a modern viewpoint. Factory hours dropped from about sixty-six a week in 1850 to sixty in 1890. Between 1860 and 1890 the daily hours worked by nonagricultural workers as a whole declined from eleven to ten. Yet the length of the workday remained a trial for most workers. "I get so exhausted that I can scarcely drag myself home when night comes," exclaimed a woman worker in a Massachusetts mill. A working man knew "nothing but work, eat, and sleep," and was "little better than a horse," declared one Pennsylvania factory employee.

There was often dreary monotony to contend with as well. Much industrial work consisted merely of repetitive, simple manipulations. At one Chicago packing house at the end of the century, five men were needed to handle just the tail of a steer—two to skin it, another two to cut it off, and one to throw it into a box. How could such mindless work provide any satisfaction? One middle-class reformer who tried factory work as an experiment in the 1890s summed up the feelings of most industrial wage earners: "There is for us in our work none of the joy of responsibility, only the dull monotony of grinding toil, with the longing for the signal to quit work, and for our wages at the end of the week."

In some ways "progress" made the worker's life worse, not better. Rapid technological change made many skills obsolete. Although the job market as a whole expanded enormously in this period, skilled hands often found themselves replaced by machines. In the iron industry, for example, Andrew Carnegie pushed relentlessly for new ways to reduce the number of skilled workers in the mills. The mills succeeded in bringing down production costs, but only at a high price to their workers. Some were discharged; many who remained were forced to accept semiskilled or unskilled work, which reduced their income and made their jobs more monotonous. Some employers adopted Taylorism, the ideas of Frederick W. Taylor, an industrial engineer who had developed his theories while trying to increase the efficiency of the workforce at the Midvale Steel Company. Taylor was certain that machine-tenders, like machines, could be made more productive if wasted motion could be eliminated. Workers often charged that Taylorism resulted in speed-ups that made their lives on the job more hectic and difficult.

Industrial work was also unsafe and unhealthy. Thousands died young from silicosis (a lung ailment caused by inhalation of rock dust), tuberculosis, cancer, heart conditions, and other work-induced diseases. Unsafe machinery, mine gases, and explosive, dust-laden air maimed and killed many. Between 1870 and 1910 there were almost 4,000 injuries or deaths at Carnegie's South Works alone. In 1917 the nation's industrial casualty list was 11,000 killed and 1.4 million wounded.

Society did little or nothing to offset the fearful toll. Before 1900, common law held that if a "fellow servant" was responsible for a job injury, the employer was not liable for damages. And even if injury resulted from direct employer neglect or carelessness, injured workers or their families had to sue to receive compensation. Few could take such an expensive course. Some prosperous working people were able to buy private insurance; but when the chief wage earner was killed or lost the ability to hold a job, most families faced a grim future indeed.

In addition, workers had to contend with periodic business downturns. Between 1870 and 1900 there were two serious slumps and several lesser ones. In the first and last of these (1873–1879 and 1893–1897) the proportion of the labor force unemployed ran to over 12 percent, a figure not equaled until the 1930s. During these lean years many working-class families had difficulty keeping a roof over their heads and decent clothes on their backs. Beggars swarmed the streets, and hoboes and tramps rode the freight rails from town to town looking for work.

Averaged out throughout the Gilded Age, unemployment reduced workers' total income only about 7 percent below a full-employment level. But this burden, too, was not equally shared. For older workers, for blacks, for many unskilled immigrants, depressions were especially disastrous. Considered marginal by employers, they were the first to be fired and the last to be rehired. For the least employable members of the labor force, hard times sometimes meant permanent idleness.

Old age also presented economic hazards for working people. There were virtually no pension systems. Men and women who became too old to work usually had little to fall back on if they lacked personal savings. Private charity was often degrading and stingy. Many aging parents were forced to move in with their children. If retired workers presented a less serious burden for society as a whole during this period than today, it was because men and women had more children to support them, and fewer lived to their later, nonworking years.

To understand the circumstances of the American wage earner during the Gilded Age, it is essential, then, to make distinctions. White, male, native-born skilled workers were the nation's "labor-aristocrats"; many lived in decent comfort, owned their own homes, ate well, and enjoyed some comforts, even a few luxuries, though like other workers they were subject to job insecurity and danger and worked long hours. It is difficult to calculate the size of this labor elite, but it probably represented between a third and a half of the total nonfarm labor force. For the other members of the armies of labor—women, blacks, and unskilled, recent immigrants—life was not only precarious but often meager and harsh. The families of the unskilled made up for the primary breadwinner's low wages to some extent by sending everyone to work, young and old, male and female. The prevalence of child labor was one reflection of this need. But this arrangement was a high price to pay for survival. In sum, the lives of the unskilled and semiskilled were not only insecure but also pinched. Life was getting better, but there was still a long way to go before people at the base of the income pyramid could say that America had fulfilled its age-old promise of abundance.

■ WORKING-CLASS PROTEST ■

Horatio Alger and the work ethic notwithstanding, it is not surprising that wage earners felt, and often expressed, discontent. Much protest undoubtedly took the form of angry sounding off to fellow workers, and absenteeism. But workers also expressed themselves in collective ways as well, in the form of trade unionism, political reform, and utopianism.

Trade unionists typically accepted both the capitalist and industrial systems—though sometimes with reservations—and sought higher wages, shorter hours, and better working conditions within them through collective bargaining. If negotiation did not work they were willing to resort to picketing, slowdowns, strikes, and boycotts of employers' goods. The political reformers came in two varieties. The moderates favored separate labor parties to fight for the eight-hour day, workers' compensation laws, safety legislation, and child-labor laws. The militants favored radical parties—socialist or anarchist—that would replace capitalism and private property with some version of the "cooperative common-wealth," either by electoral processes or by violent overthrow. Neither group of political reformers, however, sought to dismantle the system of large-scale industry and return to a simpler form of production. Those who took the third approach to transforming the existing labor system—utopianism—hoped to convert the industrial worker into a small producer.

Before 1860 most trade unions had been local organizations, enrolling workers within a given city. During the prosperous years immediately following the Civil War the national trade union appeared in response to the new coast-to-coast labor market that exposed local wage earners to competition from workers in distant cities. By 1873 there were forty-one national unions with between 300,000 and 400,000 members.

These early post-Civil War years witnessed the rise and fall of the National Labor Union (NLU), the first nationwide labor federation. Formed by Boston machinist Ira Steward in 1866, the NLU at first focused on securing the eight-hour day through state action. Steward believed the eight-hour principle would not only make the worker's job more tolerable, it would also help free workers from the exploitive wage system. Under William Sylvis, Steward's successor, the NLU turned to Greenbackism, a scheme mandating the treasury to issue paper money and lend it to workers. By this means workers could become self-employed small producers in their own right. In 1872 the NLU transformed itself into the National Labor Reform party and nominated Supreme Court Justice David Davis as its presidential candidate.

Depression of the Seventies. The panic of 1873 and the depression that followed made jobs hard to get. Employers, finding that they could hire desperate unemployed men and women willing to accept any terms, became less tolerant of "troublemakers." Union membership nationwide plummetted from about 300,000 in 1873 to some 50,000 in 1878.

The mid-1870s was a time of bitter labor strife. In January 1874 New York City police charged into a crowd of unemployed workers assembled in Tompkins Square to protest hard times, injuring many. The following year was marked by the sensational trial of the so-called Molly Maguires for the murders of coal mine managers in eastern Pennsylvania and for acts of violence against the mine owners' property. Some scholars believe that the sensational evidence against the Mollies, collected by an agent of a private detective agency employed by the owners, was invented so that the principal mine owners could break a miners' union. In any case, when ten Mollies were hanged and another fourteen sent to jail, many middle-class Americans saw their deep suspicions of labor organizations confirmed.

The middle-class public suffered a still-worse shock in 1877 when striking workers turned to violence. After four years of hard times the eastern and midwestern railroads, to preserve their profits, cut their workers' wages and lengthened their hours. In Baltimore the police dispersed angry workers picketing the Baltimore and Ohio Railroad. Soon after, B & O workers seized the railroad's terminal and yards at Martinsburg, West Virginia. The seizures quickly spread to Pittsburgh, Chicago, Buffalo, and points west, involving several major railroads and thousands of workers. For two weeks it looked as if the country was on the verge of a revolution. In Baltimore state militia fired at a mob of workers and youths, killing ten. In Pittsburgh rioters looted stores; burned machine shops, hundreds of freight cars, and the Union Depot; and engaged in a pitched gun battle with militia. Frightened by these signs of "red revolution," governors and local officials called out state troops and deputized volunteers. When the governor of Maryland called for federal troops, President Hayes dispatched several army regiments to protect life and property. By early August the violence had ended, but many conservative Americans were convinced that they had narrowly escaped a complete overthrow of the established order.

The Knights of Labor. With the return of prosperity in 1878–1879, labor unions revived. At the forefront was the Noble Order of the Knights of Labor, a body created in 1869 by a group of Philadelphia tailors led by Uriah S. Stephens.

At first the Knights operated more like a secret lodge or fraternal order than an ordinary trade union. They provided an environment for social activity and offered life insurance, burial plots, and other benefits to compensate for the uncertainties of the wage earners' life. If they had any general labor policy, it was to encourage producers' cooperatives.

In the early 1880s, under the leadership of Terence V. Powderly, the Knights responded to improved times and the enhanced leverage it produced. Abandoning their longer-range reform goals, they confronted employers with wage demands backed by strikes or threats of strikes. In March 1885, the Knights forced Jay Gould's Southwest Railroad to cancel a 10-percent wage cut. On the strength of this victory over the hated Gould, the union attracted throngs of new members. In the next two years membership leaped from a little over 100,000 to almost 730,000.

Here was an opportunity to create a powerful labor movement, but the chance was missed. Powderly and the Knights' other leaders never could decide whether they were organizing a trade union, a lodge, a reform association, or a political pressure group. Nor could they decide whether to recruit black members. Powderly favored organizing black workers, but he denied that he endorsed racial equality and insisted that black members be confined to segregated locals. The Knights could not sustain the momentum of the mid-1880s and soon lost many of its new members.

The final blow to the trade union movement of the era came with the 1886 Haymarket Riot in Chicago. During the spring of that year, McCormick Harvester Company officials had locked out 1,400 members of the Knights of Labor for demanding an eight-hour day and a $2 daily wage. On May 3, when the company tried to bring in "scabs" to replace the union men, the workers attacked the strikebreakers; the police fired on the workers. The McCormick dispute marked the climax of a five-year citywide struggle for the eight-hour day that had deeply disturbed Chicago's labor relations. One element in the inflammable mixture was the anarchists, a group of radicals dedicated to destroying all government, along with private property and the wage system. Though few in number, the anarchists had supporters among the city's large German population. Following the police attack at the McCormick company, August Spies, a leading anarchist, issued a circular in German calling on the city's wage earners to "rise in your might . . . and destroy the hideous monster [of capitalism] that seeks to destroy you." The response of the conservative daily press was equally alarmist and overwrought. "A Wild Mob's Work; Wrought Up to a Frenzy by Anarchist Harangues, They Attack Employees" was the headline in the *Chicago Tribune*.

On the evening of May 4, at the anarchists' call, 3,000 men and women gathered at Haymarket Square on the city's West Side. Many who might have come had been frightened away by Spies's inflammatory words. The meeting was relatively orderly, and the crowd had begun to thin out when the police tried to disperse the small remnant. At this point a bomb exploded among the advancing police. When the smoke cleared, seventy policemen lay wounded. Eventually seven died from the blast.

The forces of law and order reacted blindly. No one ever discovered who threw the bomb, but the public and the authorities blamed the anarchists and, by extension, all "labor agitators," whether radical or not. Hundreds of men were hustled off to jail, and ten anarchists were indicted for conspiracy to commit murder. Seven were sentenced to death after a trial that failed to establish their direct connection with the massacre. In late 1887, four were hanged.

The public outrage at the Chicago bombing shook the entire labor movement. Middle-class people now condemned all unions, even the most moderate and peaceful. To the already weakened Knights, the Haymarket affair was disastrous. Recruiting dried up; timid members quit. The Knights survived for another decade and a half, but after 1886 became a shadow of what it had been at its peak.

American Federation of Labor.   As the Knights sank, the American Federation of Labor (AFL) rose. Established in 1886 by ex-socialists, including Adolph Strasser, Peter J. Maguire, and Samuel Gompers, the AFL concentrated its efforts on native-born workers in the skilled crafts. As its name suggests, the AFL was a federation of unions. Each of the members belonged to the AFL only through his own trade union.

The AFL prospered for several reasons. First, it confined its organizing efforts to skilled workers. These were the most easily organized because they were difficult to replace and so could afford to take risks. The AFL also abandoned utopian goals and avoided politics. Samuel Gompers and his lieutenants, though they had once been socialists, believed that political radicalism was dangerous to the labor movement. Skilled workers, they noted, were profoundly wary of radical politics, and any hint of extremism frightened the middle class. The blow that Haymarket had dealt the Knights of Labor convinced the AFL leaders that direct action, radical or not, was unsafe. Moreover, government intrusion into labor–management relations might be less beneficent than socialists imagined. The authorities might favor measures harmful to labor or seek to impose their decisions on labor disputes.

Gompers, who served as AFL president almost continuously until his death in 1924, endorsed "volunteerism" and "pure and simple" trade unionism as the best policies for the AFL. Unions would improve labor conditions by collective bargaining, resorting to strikes if necessary. Workers would be encouraged to vote for labor's political friends and against its enemies, but beyond that, should avoid political involvement. As for socialism, it was foolish, Gompers declared, to suppose that people could

> . . . go to bed one night under the present system and tomorrow morning wake up with a revolution in full blast, and the next day organize a heaven on earth. That is not the way that progress is made; that is not the way . . . social evolution is brought about. We are solving the problem day after day. As we get an hour's more leisure every day it means millions of golden hours of opportunities to the human family. As we get 25 cents a day wage increase, it means another solution, another problem solved, and brings us nearer the time when a greater degree of social justice and fair dealing will obtain among men.

Joined with this moderate philosophy was a pragmatic program. The AFL fought to extract an eight-hour day from employers along with higher wages and better job conditions. It worked to get employers to recognize the union as the "collective bargaining" agent for their employees. It sought to establish a union shop—that is, get management to hire only union members.

Armed with this philosophy and program, the AFL forged ahead, particularly when prosperity returned after the depression of the mid-1890s. Despite strong opposition by employers, who considered collective bargaining an interference with the rights of private property, the federation made substantial gains. In 1904 it claimed 1.6 million members out of a total of some 2 million union members in the country. By 1914 it had over 2 million workers in its affiliated unions out of 2.7 million union members altogether. A large majority of blue-collar industrial workers, particularly the unskilled, remained outside the protection that unions conferred; so did most black workers and women. But by the eve of World War I, Gompers and the AFL were powers to be reckoned with in national life.

The Socialist Alternative.   The socialism of the late nineteenth century was built on a body of political beliefs and a theory of society that would exert enormous influence over the years. In *Das Kapital* (1867) and other works, Karl Marx, a German social theorist, had asserted the material, or economic, basis of all human interests and actions. Religion, family structure, government, literature, arts, and philosophy reflected each era's fundamental economic institutions. Each era, moreover, was marked by a dominant class. Those were the people who controlled the means of production and so exercised the power and enjoyed the wealth produced by society. In the Middle Ages the dominant class had been the feudal nobility. By the nineteenth century it was the bourgeoisie, the capitalist class.

According to Marxism, by the late nineteenth century, as the capitalist class amassed more and more of society's wealth and power, it would reach a point of crisis. Already, Marx and his disciples noted, capitalist societies were finding themselves with goods that no one would buy and they would soon experience ever more frequent and serious depressions. These crises would further undercut the workers' material circumstances. Eventually the proletariat, or working class, would realize their common interests; abandon the ethnic, cultural, religious, and national differences that had kept them apart; and turn to revolution. The masses would seize the factories, farms, and banks and nationalize the means of production and distribution.

The world would be a far better place after the revolution, insisted the Marxists. Profits formerly skimmed off by the capitalists would be used to benefit the masses. Under the new socialist system there would no longer be exploiter and exploited, powerful and powerless. Instead, there would be only one class, the working class, and within it all would be equal. With the class struggle ended and capitalist "contradictions" eliminated, humanity would prosper as never before under a regime of economic and social justice for all.

Thousands of men and women were inspired by the Marxist vision. It held out hope to the oppressed of a world where they would enjoy the abundance and freedom seemingly reserved for the rich under capitalism. Its promise of a harmonious society after capitalism appealed to intellectuals by offering a substitute for their lost religious faith. It spoke to artists, writers, and romantic rebels by promising an antidote to what they saw as the crude and vulgar world of bourgeois values.

At the turn of the century the Marxists competed with several other socialist groups for the allegiance of wage earners and middle-class dissenters. For a while educated Americans were attracted to the Nationalist clubs organized by the journalist Edward Bellamy who, in *Looking Backward* (1888), described a society in the year 2000 where abundance, cooperation, and leisure had superseded scarcity, competition, and drudgery. Also prominent for a while were the anarchists, whose activities in the Haymarket riot have been mentioned. Members of the so-called Black International (in contrast with the Marxist Red International), they believed that every effort to regiment or coerce human beings was an evil denial of freedom. Anarchists favored rule by voluntary associations of people organized around their jobs. Although noncoercive in their philosophy, the anarchists were anything but gentle in their tactics. In both Europe and America they were notorious for assassinating public officials and throwing bombs to make their antiauthoritarian point.

Prior to the Haymarket bombing the anarchists and socialists had won small working-class followings in the major industrial centers. At first there were several competing socialist groups; but after its founding in 1877, the Socialist Labor party, under the brilliant but abrasive Daniel De Leon, became the chief socialist organization. As we have seen, the public reaction to the Haymarket riot injured trade unionism; it also damaged the various anticapitalist parties, and for several years they languished as little more than debating societies.

The Homestead Strike. A further blow fell on labor in July 1893 in the form of a violent clash at the Carnegie steel plant at Homestead, Pennsylvania, where Carnegie's lieutenant, Henry Clay Frick, had introduced the most modern labor-saving machinery. Claiming that the new equipment would enhance productivity and hence wages for those who worked by the piece, Frick announced that piece rates would be reduced. The Amalgamated Association of Iron and Steel Workers, representing the most skilled men, refused to accept the new arrangement. At the end of June 1892, joined by the unskilled workers, they went on strike and sealed off the plant.

Frick advertised for strikebreakers. To get the new employees to the idle plant, he hired 300 armed Pinkerton agents and sent them in two barges up the Monongahela River, which ran along the edge of the Homestead works. Early on the morning of July 6 the Pinkertons tried to slip by the guards posted by the strikers, but they were detected. The strikers let go with rifles and pistols; the Pinkertons returned the fire until the strikers poured oil on the water and lit it. At this point, rather than face incineration, the Pinkertons surrendered in return for safe conduct. As they departed for the railway station, however, they were badly beaten. All told, five strikers and three Pinkertons died in the savage melee.

Five days later the governor of Pennsylvania sent 8,000 militiamen to the plant and returned it to the company. The Amalgamated then offered to surrender its economic demands in return for recognition of its right to serve as the bargaining agent for the workers. Frick refused. "Under no circumstances will we have any further dealings with the Amalgamated Association," he declared. "This is final." This unyielding attitude, combined with the use of Pinkertons, brought public opinion to the side of the strikers. Though he supported Frick, Carnegie was dismayed by the mayhem and might have forced concessions, but a young anarchist, Alexander Berkman, went to Frick's office and shot and stabbed him repeatedly. Frick survived, but public opinion now turned against the strikers, ending all possibility of compromise.

Depression, Pullman, and Socialist Revival. The depression following the panic of 1893 encouraged further labor violence and gave socialism a renewed impetus. As in the 1870s, unemployment soared and thousands of idle workers tramped the streets looking for work. Employers sought once again to maintain profits and avoid losses by cutting wages. Like all depressions in capitalist societies, that of the 1890s undermined confidence in the system and aroused dissent. By creating a new charismatic leader, Eugene V. Debs, the Pullman strike of 1894 became an important turning point in the history of American socialism.

George Pullman, the inventor of the railroad sleeping car, had established his giant factory outside Chicago and surrounded it with a model community for his employees. With its tree-lined streets, cream-colored brick houses, its gardens and parks, the town of Pullman was a physically attractive place. It was also a repressive place. Pullman insisted on making his town moral, obedient, and profitable. He forbade liquor, spied on his employees, fired workers for running against the candidates he favored for local office, and charged high rents and utility rates. Pullman considered himself a benevolent man, but he acted like a feudal lord.

In the summer of 1893, when orders for new Pullman "palace cars" started to fall off, Pullman began to fire workers and cut wages while refusing to reduce rents and utility rates. To defend themselves, Pullman workers joined the newly organized American Railway Union (ARU) led by a tall, lanky Indianian, Eugene V. Debs. On May 11, 1894, after several unsuccessful attempts to negotiate with Pullman officials, over 3,000 employees walked off the job and asked for ARU support. Debs tried to persuade the Pullman management to negotiate. When his efforts failed, he reluctantly ordered the ARU switchmen to refuse to attach Pullman cars to trains. The railroad officials responded by dismissing the defiant switchmen. The ARU struck back. By July 1 all twenty-four railroads operating out of Chicago, the nation's chief rail hub, had shut down.

Despite their anger, the strikers were restrained and orderly. Yet the shutdown of the country's major transportation system dismayed the middle-class public. Hoping to break the strike and smash the union, the General Managers Association, representing the major railroads entering and leaving Chicago, hired strikebreakers and asked the federal government for aid, claiming that it was Washington's responsibility to guarantee delivery of the mail, which had slowed in many places when the trains ceased to run. In Attorney General Richard Olney the railroad had a friend in government. A hot-tempered former railroad lawyer who despised labor leaders, Olney quickly ordered federal marshals to Chicago. He also convinced a federal judge to issue an injunction that ordered the union to cease the strike or be "in contempt of court." The following day, July 3, over the protests of Illinois governor John P. Altgeld, who denied that there was sufficient disorder to require federal intervention, President Grover Cleveland ordered the entire garrison of Fort Sheridan to the city to prevent violence.

The presence of troops and federal marshals infuriated the strikers, and the railway yards were swept by a wave of shootings and arson. The federal authorities cracked down, arresting Debs and other ARU officials on July 17 for violating the court injunction. Deprived of their leaders, the men gave up and gradually drifted back to work.

Debs went to prison for six months and thereafter turned against capitalism. In 1901 he became a founder of the Socialist Party of America, an organization that would win a larger following than Daniel De Leon's Socialist Labor party. During the remainder of his life, Debs would embody both the best and the worst in American socialism. Generous, humane, and fiery in defense of justice, he was also a stubborn visionary who lacked the ability to manage a party racked by bitter internal disagreements. Despite his failings, under Debs's leadership the Socialist Party of America grew rapidly before World War I, winning the support of many German and Jewish wage earners and even some rural and small-town people in the Midwest. It also attracted a following of authors, ministers, and professional people. Between 1904 and 1912 the party increased its dues-paying membership from 20,000 to 130,000; in 1912 Debs received 900,000 votes, 6 percent of the total, when he ran for president on the Socialist ticket. The party did even better on the local level, electing several congressmen and a half-dozen mayors in cities such as Scranton, Milwaukee, and Syracuse.

Still, the Socialist Party of America never captured the support of a majority of American wage earners and, unlike its counterparts in Europe, never truly challenged the middle-class parties for control of the political system. The most convincing explanation for this failure is that, in contrast to European workers, native-born American wage earners were not class conscious. Well paid by comparison with industrial workers in other lands and just a generation or two off the farm, they expected to prosper and move up the social ladder. Many owned some property and could not accept a philosophy that predicted inevitable class conflict and the increasing misery of wage earners under capitalism. Immigrant workers were not much better as potential recruits for socialism. Most had difficulty enough adjusting to American cities and American industry without making further trouble for themselves, and they avoided "agitators." Despite their initially low status, they too expected to rise socially and economically. All told, the relative prosperity of the United States and people's expectations for improvement were strong antidotes to radical politics. As the German sociologist Werner Sombart noted with some exaggeration at the turn of the century, socialist "utopias" in America inevitably foundered "on the reefs of roast beef and apple pie."

■ CONCLUSIONS ■

As we explore the nation's leap to industrial preeminence a century ago, several factors come into view. Clearly, the skill, intelligence, drive, and even ruthlessness of America's industrial tycoons helped to propel the Republic past its rivals. But the captains of industry could not have created the world's industrial leader alone. Working people, accepting the conventional wisdom of the age, labored hard, believing that success and security would reward their efforts. And without government's substantial contributions, despite the theories of laissez-faire and social Darwinism, progress would have been far slower.

Clearly, many of the men and women who lived through these tumultuous years were ground down by the great economic machine they were helping to build. The pain they experienced was expressed in the violence of the Pullman, Homestead, and the 1877 railway strikes, and in the organized political efforts meant to effect change. Yet we must not exaggerate the extent or depth of discontent among wage earners. Many found their lives satisfactory and, with reason, looked forward to better times. Despite the agitation and the occasional violence, it remains true that most Americans retained their faith in the "system" and refused to accept radical solutions to the problems they faced. This ultimate faith was expressed in the continued vitality of the economy and the mainstream political parties and in the growth of cities and the nation as a whole.

Online Resources

"African American Mosaic—Migrations"
http://www.loc.gov/exhibits/african/intro.html
Maps, illustrations, genealogical charts, and photos depict the African-American quest of the "Exodusters" who migrated West, especially to Kansas, in search of a better life.

"Looking Backward"
http://xroads.virginia.edu/~HYPER/BELLAMY/toc.html
This site provides access to the full text of Edward Bellamy's famed 1888 utopian novel *Looking Backward*.

"The Dramas of Haymarket"
http://www.chicagohistory.org/dramas/overview/main.htm
Produced by the Chicago Historical Society, this site details the events leading up to the Haymarket riot, including the radicalization of many American workers and class tensions in America. The site includes both essays and primary-source material.

"Taylorism and Scientific Management"
http://www.fordham.edu/halsall/mod/1911taylor.html
Read Frederick Taylor's essays in his work, *The Principles of Scientific Management*. These principles of work had a dramatic effect on industry, the way work was performed, and the lives of workers.

Factories and Technology in Industrializing America: Factory Life and Labor in the Southern Mills
http://thehistorynet.com/NationalHistoryDay/teach99/lesson1
Through the words of the workers themselves, this site describes work in the New South textile industry, child labor, the workers' transition from farm to factory, and the impact of industrialization on daily life. While some of the entries discuss work in the early twentieth century, their experiences were similar to those who began work in the mills at the close of the nineteenth century.

Obstacles Faced by African Americans
http://www.pbs.org.wgbh.amex/1900/filmmore/reference/interview/washing_obstaclesfaced.html
This portion of PBS's "The American Experience" website details the status of and challenges faced by African Americans in the areas of education, public accommodations, and voting at the turn of the century.

The Greatest Tyrant in the State of Pennsylvania: A Late Nineteenth-Century Rail Worker Describes Management
http://historymatters.gmu.edu/search.taf?_function=list&_UserReference=938E4E632EAEC9A1BDD099F78_start=1
In the testimony recorded on this Web site, railroad worker Joseph Cahill tells the U.S. House of Representatives about his role in a labor union and management's mistreatment of workers in the late nineteenth century.

18

AGE OF THE CITY

What Did Cities Offer? And to Whom?

1860–1910	American cities, as defined by the Census, increase in number from 392 to 2,220
1871	The Great Chicago Fire
1872	New York's Boss Tweed is indicted and jailed
1878	Asphalt paving introduced in Washington, D.C.
1880	Salvation Army introduced from England; James A. Garfield elected president
1881	Garfield assassinated; Chester A. Arthur becomes president
1882	Chinese Exclusion Act passed in response to organized labor's fear of cheap labor
1884	Grover Cleveland elected president
1888	Benjamin Harrison elected president
1892	Cleveland elected president for the second time
1894	Immigration Restriction League; Coxey's Army marches on Washington to protest unemployment
1896	William McKinley elected president
1897	First subway line is built, in Boston
1899–1904	Mayor Samuel "Golden Rule" Jones institutes municipal ownership of utilities in Toledo
1900–10	Eight million immigrants arrive
1901	McKinley assassinated; Theodore Roosevelt becomes president
1907	Congress appoints Dillingham Commission to investigate immigration
1914	Birth-control advocate Margaret Sanger is forced to leave the country

The city has been a central element in civilization for perhaps 5,000 years. In fact, cities seem to equal civilization, for it has been in urban settings that humanity has produced most of the ideas, artifacts, art, and science that we identify as essential marks of civilized life.

Throughout much of history, however, city dwellers have been a minority; until the years following the Civil War, the United States was no exception to this rule. As late as 1860 only 20 percent of the nation's people were urban. The most heavily urbanized sections of the nation on the eve of the Civil War were the New England and Middle Atlantic areas. Elsewhere, particularly in the West and the South, most Americans continued to live on villages and farms.

The Civil War slowed city growth somewhat, but thereafter it resumed at a rapid clip. Between 1860 and 1910 the number of census-defined "urban places" increased from 392 to over 2,200. In 1860 New York and Philadelphia were the only American cities with more than half a million inhabitants. By 1910 these communities, along with the "prairie colossus," Chicago, had over a million residents each, and five other cities had grown to populations of 500,000. During that fifty-year stretch the urban share of the country's population went from 20 to 46 percent. The Northeast remained the most urban part of the nation in 1910, but urbanization had spread far beyond the areas that had first felt the pull of industry and commerce.

What brought millions of people from the farms of America and from distant regions of the world to the cities of the United States in these years? And how did the millions of new urban dwellers prosper in their new homes?

■ IMMIGRATION ■

One source of soaring urban populations in the half-century following the Civil War was foreign-born newcomers. In the 1880s more than 5 million people entered the United States. The depression of the 1890s reduced the number of immigrants substantially, but between 1900 and 1910 over 8 million more foreigners arrived. Some of these people eventually returned home, either disappointed with America or so successful that they could live well in the "old country" on what they had made here. Yet most immigrants, by far, remained in the United States, and by the end of the century a majority of them made the cities their home.

America's Attractions.   Like previous immigrants, Gilded Age arrivals were moved by both "pushes" and "pulls." The chief "pull" of America for immigrants of this era, as for their predecessors, was economic. Immigrants from every land were attracted by the possibility of improving themselves in some material way; only a minority were drawn by America's reputation for religious and political freedom. Through letters from previous arrivals and from the newspapers and magazines in their native lands, immigrants were remarkably well informed about American economic conditions. During hard times in the United States, such as the mid-1890s, foreigners stayed home. During good times, such as the 1880s and the first decade of the twentieth century, the current of immigrants became a vast flood.

American business actively encouraged immigration in these years. During the 1850s western mining companies had brought in Chinese workers to dig for gold in California and Nevada. In the 1860s the Central Pacific Railroad imported 10,000 Chinese to help construct the first transcontinental line. After its completion many of these laborers remained to build other western railroads and to swell the populations of San Francisco, Sacramento, Denver, and other western towns. In Texas, Arizona, New Mexico, California, and Colorado, railroad employers recruited many Mexicans to work on repair and construction crews. Truck farmers and fruit-growers in the Southwest and on the Pacific Coast recruited other Mexicans to harvest fruit, cotton, lettuce, and tomatoes.

The railroads, endowed with enormous land grants, were also eager for settlers to convert their acreage into cash. The Illinois Central, the Northern Pacific, and other railroads scattered colorful brochures advertising their lands across Europe and established offices in major European cities where railroad representatives offered advice to would-be immigrants and described the favorable terms available to those willing to come. Thousands took the bait.

In 1864 Congress provided business with a means to recruit workers from abroad. Designed to remedy an anticipated labor shortage, the Contract Labor Law authorized employers to hire foreign workers under an agreement that guaranteed passage money, a specified wage, and defined working conditions. The law was not effective. Though only a few hundred skilled workers were brought to the United States under its provisions, trade union pressure induced Congress to repeal it in 1885 (the Foran Act).

A more fruitful source of foreign labor was the padrone system used to recruit Italian labor for eastern mines, factories, and construction projects. Padroni were Italian-American middlemen, frequently connected with small immigrant banking firms, who signed up gangs of Italian laborers in southern Italy at fixed wages and paid for the workers' passage. In the United States the padrone arranged with an American employer to supply workers at a sum that gave him a profit. In the early years, when the United States was still an unfamiliar destination for Italians, the system was useful in providing immigrants with food, board, and advice. The padroni, however, often took advantage of the trusting men they recruited, charging them high prices for what they provided while keeping them in virtual slavery. Fortunately, when the Italian-American community had put down firm roots and would-be immigrants could turn to relatives and friends for advice and help, the system declined.

Though sponsorship and active recruiting contributed to the immigration stream, the great majority of European arrivals needed little incentive to join the booming American economy. Letters from relatives and friends, talks with townspeople back in the old country for a visit, or information supplied by government agencies and shipping companies were enough to draw people by the thousands to embarkation ports to take ship for the United States.

Plummeting prices of ocean fares and the growing speed of ocean travel undoubtedly encouraged immigration. During the 1860s the introduction of large and fast steam vessels with auxiliary sail reduced transatlantic crossing times from as long as three months to as little as ten days. A dozen shipping companies—British, German, Italian, Dutch, and French, as well as American—soon entered the transatlantic trade in people, and their fierce competition quickly brought passenger rates down even more.

The Push: The New Immigrants.   Like the "pull" to America, the "push" from other lands was predominantly economic. Until the 1890s most immigrants came from northern Europe—Britain, Germany, and Scandinavia. In each of these countries agriculture had been hurt by competition from the newer grain-growing regions of Canada, the United States, Argentina, and Australia. Unable to compete with the lower production costs in these new lands, European land-lords introduced machinery and drove out the peasants, thousands of whom sought haven in the United States.

The push from northern Europe soon slackened. Industrialization, plus falling birth rates throughout northern Europe, provided new opportunities for displaced farm people in their own nations' factories and mines. British emigration more and more was deflected to the "dominions"—Canada, Australia, New Zealand, and South Africa.

After 1890 a wave of immigrants from southern and eastern Europe more than offset this north European decline. These so-called New Immigrants were a diverse lot. Many were Slavs—Bohemians, Poles, Ukrainians, Slovaks, Serbs, Croatians, Ruthenians, and Russians—from the Hapsburg Empire (Austria-Hungary) or from Russia, the empire of the Romanov czars. Many came from Europe's south, the largest number from Italy, though there were many Greeks as well. Other eastern Europeans included Hungarians and Rumanians. From the Turkish dominions came Armenians and Syrians. Jews from either Austria-Hungary or imperial Russia formed another large group of New Immigrants. Many of the Slavs and virtually all the Italians were Roman Catholic, and for the first time there were substantial numbers of Orthodox Catholics among the new arrivals.

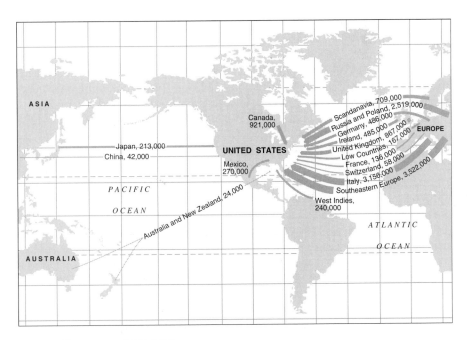

Sources of Immigrants, 1900–1920

Until this time, America had seemed too far away, too alien, and too expensive for these people. Besides, their governments often refused to allow them to leave for fear of reducing their military manpower or their tax rolls. But toward the end of the century Austria, Russia, and Turkey abandoned their opposition to emigration, ocean passage rates and travel time declined sharply, and overseas agricultural competition spread to eastern Europe.

Though the push was largely economic, political and religious factors also played a part in propelling people from the czarist and Ottoman lands across the Atlantic. The czars often treated their non-Russian subjects harshly. After 1870 thousands of German Pietists, who had settled in southern Russia during the eighteenth century, fled when the czars withdrew their privileges. A much larger group of refugees from the czars' domain were Jews who had resided in Russian occupied lands since the Middle Ages. After 1880 a wave of discriminatory laws excluded them from public office, universities, agricultural pursuits, the professions, and other activities. The bigoted Russian government also incited anti-Jewish riots (pogroms) that resulted in hundreds of deaths and the devastation of whole communities. Meanwhile, in the Ottoman Empire, the Turkish government began to brutally persecute its Christian Syrian and Armenian minorities.

These changes, taken together, produced a drastic shift in the source of the immigrant streams from Europe. In 1880 a mere 17,000 immigrants to the United States came from Austria-Hungary; in 1907 there were almost 340,000. Only 5,000 Russian subjects immigrated to America in 1880; in 1907 over 225,000 arrived. In 1880 some 12,000 Italians came to the United States; in 1907, over 285,000.

From Farms to Cities.   The ocean crossing remained unpleasant for poorer immigrants until well into the twentieth century. They usually traveled below decks in "steerage," jammed into large open spaces with hundreds of others. Rough seas produced misery and at times cholera swept the ships, killing scores and so frightening American officials that the federal government imposed quarantines, shutting down all transatlantic immigration for substantial periods.

Most European immigrants came through New York, Boston, New Orleans, Baltimore, or Philadelphia, with New York far in the lead. Before 1892 most New York-bound immigrants passed through Castle Garden, a facility established at the tip of Manhattan Island by New York State officials. In 1892 the federal government assumed responsibility for receiving immigrants and replaced Castle Garden with a new facility at Ellis Island in New York Harbor. Here new immigrants were asked their names, ages, occupations, places of origin, literacy, and financial status. They were also examined by doctors to see that they were not carriers of infectious diseases. At Ellis Island, too, immigrants first made contact with the many societies established by their compatriots to offer advice and services and to keep them out of the hands of swindlers eager to cheat "greenhorns" of their money and possessions.

Once in America, the immigrants had to determine their ultimate destinations. During the 1870s and 1880s thousands of Germans, Scandinavians,

Poles, and Bohemians went to the wheat regions of Minnesota, the Dakotas, Nebraska, and Kansas, where they bought land from the railroads. Then, as the nation shifted from agriculture industry, immigrants were increasingly drawn to the cities and their shops, factories, and construction sites.

Immigrants tended to concentrate in certain industries and occupations by nationality. French Canadians crossed the border from Quebec to the nearby New England textile towns, where they displaced many of the Irish. Jews from Russia and Poland entered the garment industry of New York, Rochester, and Chicago. Italians concentrated in the construction industry; Slavs entered mining and heavy industry; the Portuguese moved into the New England fishing industry.

Nativism. The new pattern of immigration that emerged toward the end of the nineteenth century disturbed many Americans. Some deplored the "New" immigrants' urban concentration, seeing it as a deterrent to their assimilation into American life. Concentrated in tight-knit ghettos, they would be slow to lose their alien ways and become "good Americans." Immigrant organizations themselves were concerned and Jewish and Catholic societies sought to deflect recent arrivals among their co-religionists to rural areas. Many native Americans resented the unfamiliar appearance and ways of the newcomers. The novelist Henry James, while strolling on fashionable Beacon Hill in Boston one Sunday, observed groups of men and women in their best clothes "enjoying their leisure." "No sound of English . . . escaped their lips; the great number spoke some rude form of Italian, the others some outlandish dialect unknown to me. . . . The types and faces bore them out; the people before me were gross aliens to a man, and they were in serene and triumphant possession."

The resentment was not confined to elite, old-stock Americans like James, however. The New Immigrants frequently clashed with the Old Immigrants of the pre-Civil War generation or with their half-assimilated children. In 1877, during the hard times that followed the panic of 1873, Irish-American workers in San Francisco attacked Chinese businesses and the docks of the Pacific Mail Steamship Company, the firm they held responsible for importing the "coolies" from East Asia to undercut their wages. Soon afterward Denis Kearney, a native of Ireland's County Cork, helped organize the Workingmen's Party of California. Kearney denounced the rich railroad and mining magnates of California, but his speeches usually ended with the cry: "And whatever happens, the Chinese must go!"

The anti-Chinese movement in California was not unique. Spokesmen for organized labor elsewhere feared "coolie labor," and indeed any cheap labor, whether from Europe or Asia. Passage of the Foran Act in 1885, repealing the Contract Labor Law of 1864, was, as we noted, largely the result of trade-union pressure. In 1882 lobbying by labor groups induced Congress to pass the Chinese Exclusion Act prohibiting the immigration of Chinese laborers for ten years. Renewed several times, the law was made permanent in 1902. Not until 1943 were foreign-born Chinese allowed to take up legal permanent residence in the United States.

Anti-immigrant sentiment in these years, however, was not solely economic in origin; nativist feelings also had cultural roots. Many native-born Americans were certain that the newest immigrants were inferior to those of the past. They seemed more alien and illiterate. They came, it was said, from more backward lands where democratic institutions were unknown. A larger proportion of them were Catholic or Jewish, and hence further removed than earlier arrivals from the American Protestant tradition. They were responsible for the increased disorder, violence, and vice of the cities. The New Immigrants, moreover, did not intend to stay, the critics said. Many were birds of passage, men without wives or families, who would make their fortunes in America and return to their native lands. They refused to go to the farms, the indictment continued, congregating instead in the big cities, where they retained their foreign ways, turned to crime, and succumbed to insanity, epilepsy, or other nervous or emotional disorders that severely strained local health facilities and raised taxes for real Americans.

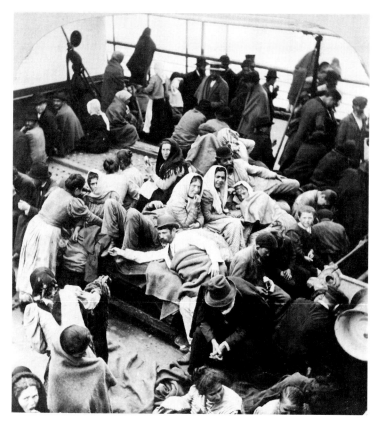

Were poor immigrants a resource? Steel king Andrew Carnegie, himself an immigrant, believed they were. In fact, he estimated that each one was worth $1,500. Immigrants labored in mines and mills, built railroads and bridges, farmed the land, and bought products of the nation's factories.

The hostile response to immigrants was reinforced at the turn of the century by the racist theories of men such as Josiah Strong and Madison Grant, who proclaimed the natural superiority of "Nordics" over darker-haired, darker-eyed white people of southern and eastern Europe. Racist ideology and traditional prejudice against foreigners led in 1907 to the appointment by Congress of the Dillingham Commission to investigate immigration. Its voluminous report confirmed all the common negative stereotypes. The commission described the Old Immigrants as "ideal farmers" and people "imbued with sympathy for our ideals and . . . democratic institutions." By contrast, the more recent arrivals were "different in temperament and civilization from ourselves." Generally speaking, the report endorsed the common view of the inferiority of the New Immigrants and branded them undesirable.

Whatever the reality, many old-stock Americans endorsed nativist organizations dedicated to reducing the flow of immigrants or to limiting their role in American public life. In the 1880s and 1890s, the American Protective Association (APA) demanded that noncitizens be excluded from political office and attacked "the diabolical works of the Roman Catholic church." In 1894 a group of New England bluebloods organized the Immigration Restriction League with a program to impose literacy tests on the new arrivals, many of whom, the League believed, could not pass such a test.

The League failed in its main goals before the 1920s. In 1896, and again in 1913 and 1915, Congress passed measures requiring that all immigrants admitted to the United States be able to read and write either English or their own language. Each time, however, the president in office vetoed the measure. Though many Americans feared the foreign deluge, others opposed restriction. Businessmen resisted cutting off the inexhaustible supply of cheap labor, and the National Association of Manufacturers constantly lobbied against restrictions on immigration. Old-fashioned liberals, who prized America's tradition as a haven for the world's poor and oppressed, also fought efforts to end free immigration. Before the 1920s the doors remained open. Though Congress passed laws excluding immigrants with chronic diseases, those with records as criminals or prostitutes, and those with known anarchist views, drastic limitations on transatlantic immigrants would wait until a later day.

Buckwheats and Hayseeds. City streets and neighborhoods were not only crowded with the foreign-born; they were also thronged with men and women straight off the nation's farms. In the exodus from the nation's farms and villages to Gilded Age cities, there were also both pushes and pulls.

The lure of the city for rural people is a persistent theme in the history of the Western world. Cities were no doubt wicked; they were dangerous. But compared with the sleepy village or farm, the city, with its well-stocked stores, its bustle, its amusements, its street life, and its brilliant lights, was a joy. The novelist Hamlin Garland recalled that everything about Chicago was interesting when he arrived there as a young farm boy: "Nothing was commonplace, nothing ugly." In *The City*, a 1909 play by Clyde Fitch, one character, recently arrived in New York, exclaims: "Who wants to smell new-mown hay, if he can breathe gasoline on Fifth Avenue instead!"

And there were irresistible economic pulls. Thousands of young rural people came to the cities to work as clerks, secretaries, bookkeepers, and salespeople. Farm boys also were drawn to the mills and factories to tend machines, stoke furnaces, and supervise. At his plants in Pennsylvania Andrew Carnegie liked to hire "buckwheats," lads from the nearby countryside. These young men, he believed, made the best workers in the mills. For young Americans with special career interests, the cities were meccas. To talented musicians, artists, writers, actors, or performers of any kind, only the largest cities of the land could provide the training, the experience, and the appreciative audience they needed and craved.

The push also applied to rural youths—"hayseeds" in the vernacular of the day. If the cities were fascinating, the farms and villages often were not. Hamlin Garland wrote about the "sordidness, dullness, triviality, and . . . endless drudgeries" of rural life. In his short story "Up the Coulee" one of his characters complains: "Anything under God's heavens is better'n farmin'."

But even if a farm youth wanted to stay and till the soil, it was often difficult. Farm families were large, and rural fathers could not provide land for all their sons. There was the option of going west, but as we shall see, through much of the late nineteenth century, agriculture was a troubled industry even on the newer western lands. In the Northeast, movement to the cities resembled a mass exodus. With the completion of the transportation network, it became ever more difficult for the old, rocky fields of New England and the Middle Atlantic states to compete with the rich soils of the Great Plains and the prairies. As the census of 1890 showed, the counties in two fifths of Pennsylvania, one fourth of New Jersey, about five sixths of New York, and a very large part of New England had declined in population during the 1880s. Most of these missing people were now living in the region's cities.

■ THE URBAN ENVIRONMENT ■

The Physical Setting. Whether from Italy or Iowa, Austria or Alabama, newcomers found urban life in the Gilded Age replete with problems. American cities in the years immediately following the Civil War were generally harsh, dirty, congested places. City streets were dusty in summer, muddy in winter, and filthy at all times due to the large numbers of horses. Nor was the sky above any better. The soft coal widely used for heating and industrial fuel darkened city air with soot. In the 1890s the ash from its steel and glass factories often brought twilight at midday to Pittsburgh.

Until the end of the century few American cities had adequate public water supplies or decent sewers or street-cleaning services. In 1880 Baltimore, with 330,000 people, had "no sewers to speak of . . . , all chamber slops [being] deposited in cesspools or privy vaults." A newspaper report on Chicago in the same year declared with unusual directness that "the air stinks." Just after the Civil War, Memphis's streets were described as an open sewer.

Newcomers to the city struggled to find decent dwellings at affordable prices. Many were forced to take the dilapidated houses formerly occupied by the middle class, who had fled the growing squalor and congestion of the inner city. Others found rooms in shoddily constructed new buildings. In New York at the end of the century over a million people lived in tenements of five to six stories with shallow air shafts on either side to provide a little light to interior rooms. These structures, called "dumbbell tenements" because of the long, narrow waist where the air shafts were placed, had only one bathroom for every twenty inhabitants. In Chicago, although the Great Fire of 1871 had created new housing opportunities, the city permitted builders to throw up block after block of shanties and ugly two-decker flats for the working class on the burned-over land.

Even before the Civil War the country's largest urban centers had ceased to be "walking cities," in which everything was accessible on foot, and had adopted the horse-drawn "omnibus" and, a little later, the horse-drawn streetcar on rails. After the war many more communities adopted animal power for transportation. Horse-drawn vehicles were faster than walking, but they had many drawbacks. In 1864 a newspaper described a typical streetcar trip as an experience of "martyrdom." Public transportation also compounded the sanitation problem. The thousands of horses trotting the city streets created enormous piles of droppings, and the resulting smells and clouds of flies made summers, particularly, an ordeal for city dwellers.

The Immigrant Adjustment.   Newcomers to the city also faced a harsh and disruptive social environment. Most eastern and southern European immigrants were rural peasants who found the cities alien places. In American cities there were no one-story cottages, but multifloor apartment dwellings. Lighting did not come from candles or an oil lamp; wood logs did not fuel cooking stoves; water did not come from a well. Instead you bought coal from a supplier, or turned on a switch or faucet and paid utility bills to the gas, water, or electric company. In Chicago, Cleveland, or New York, you did not throw your garbage to the pigs; you placed it in refuse cans for the sanitation department. And how different it was to earn a living and get from place to place! Immigrants, in a word, had to abandon the familiar customs and practices of Europe's rural villages and learn to survive in the vast, impersonal metropolis.

Economic problems were the most urgent for immigrants to America's "urban wilderness." Most groups of newcomers included a professional and business class. The Jews in the garment industry not only worked as cutters and sewing machine operators but also owned many of the shops. Italians became building contractors employing Italian workers. Because all groups retained a strong loyalty to the customs, cuisine, and language of their native land, enterprising immigrants with a little capital established restaurants, groceries, theaters, bookstores, and assorted businesses catering to their compatriots. The newcomers also preferred to turn to their own kind for professional help, and immigrant doctors, lawyers, and clergymen found ample demand for their services. By 1914 the typical American city was crowded with street signs in Polish, Italian, Yiddish, Chinese, Spanish, and other languages that advertised the wares of ethnic shopkeepers and the services of ethnic professionals.

Many of the cities' foreign-born remained unskilled or semiskilled workers for most of their lives. Yet in Boston the British and other northern Europeans, as well as the Jews, moved up rather rapidly from unskilled to skilled jobs; some even graduated into the ranks of the business class or the professions. The Irish and Italians, in contrast, lagged behind both native American newcomers to Boston and more mobile immigrant groups. In New York, on the other hand, according to one study, both Jews and Italians moved ahead almost equally fast and both achieved large gains in income and status in a rather short time. In Atlanta immigrants raised their status with remarkable speed, says one scholar, far faster than the city's large black population, a group oppressed by deeply embedded racism.

The crucial factor affecting the immigrants' economic progress apparently was education. Those who were illiterate or who could not speak English were easily exploited. People who had nothing to sell but physical brawn stayed on the bottom rungs of the economic ladder. Immigrants understood the importance of education very well and flocked to night schools where, after a hard day's work, they attempted to learn English and reading and writing. The more enterprising or energetic succeeded. Others failed, defeated by age, bad luck, or personal inadequacy. Those who did not, or could not, acquire a basic education generally remained part of the large mass of urban poor.

Pressures on the Family.   The traditional father-dominated, home-centered rural family changed substantially in the new city environment. On the farms and in the rural villages, whether of America or Europe, fathers worked close to their families. Even in the smaller cities of America this proximity was elusive, and as the urban centers grew, the physical distance between home and work became ever greater. The advent of the horse-drawn streetcar enabled many more prosperous working-class men to commute to their jobs. Although the "streetcar suburbs" provided space for recreation and some of the beauty of the countryside, the long commuting time meant that a man spent longer periods than ever away from his wife and children. With fathers so often absent, young men, in particular, lost close contact with adult role models, and many found the process of adjusting to work and adulthood more difficult than in earlier days.

The gap between generations encouraged by city life was even greater among immigrants than among the native-born. The children of European peasants and laborers encountered very different customs and habits from those their parents had known in the old country. Growing up in the city streets and attending American schools, the "second generation" often developed different values. Girls picked up attitudes that were at odds with strict European views of the proper role for young, unmarried women. Children who knew English and were familiar with American life fared better in the new environment and could use the language more effectively than their parents. Boys often found work when their fathers could not. Adolescence is at best a turbulent time of revolt against parental control; in the cultural clash between foreign-born parents and native-born children, families were frequently shaken to their foundations.

The city not only weakened the structure of the family but also reduced its size. It was expensive to raise children in the city. The cost of shelter in the country was modest. Farmhouses were large and cheap to build. But in the cities working-class families could not afford large apartments and painful overcrowding was common. Nor were children as much of an economic asset in the city as in the country, where they were an important part of the workforce. Working-class urban families were forced to put their children to work at odd jobs. Some city children worked alongside their parents at garment making or some other "sweated" trade conducted in the home. But compulsory education laws and the difficulties of finding wage-paying work for city boys and girls meant that they did not contribute as much to family support as rural children.

The cost of raising a family in the city encouraged family limitation. Fertility rates in the United States had been declining for generations in both towns and countryside. Toward the end of the nineteenth century the constraints of the urban environment provided new incentives to family limitation, and birth rates dropped still further.

The growing trend toward smaller families disturbed social conservatives. Moralists and religious leaders frequently denounced efforts to disseminate birth-control information as sinful. In 1873, at the urging of "purity" crusader Anthony Comstock, Congress classified birth-control information as obscene and excluded it from the mails. Toward the end of the century, however, Margaret Sanger, a visiting nurse on New York's Lower East Side, launched a campaign to provide poor women with scientific birth-control information. Defenders of old-fashioned morality attacked Sanger and denounced the whole family-limitation movement as "race suicide." Sanger persisted but was forced to flee the country in 1914 for publishing her journal *Woman Rebel,* which the authorities considered obscene. She later returned and organized the leading agency of the birth-control movement in the United States, the American Birth Control League.

Margaret Sanger's efforts, initially directed at the slum family, achieved their greatest success among middle-class women and those working-class women most anxious to move into the middle class. The effect on their lives was profound. With fewer children in the family, they were relieved from long years of childbearing and child nurture. Together with new labor-saving devices for the home such as the gas range and hot piped-in water, the decline in family size freed many women from lifelong household drudgery. Some directed their released energies to civic work or self-improvement. Others were enabled to join the labor force in growing numbers. Where previously jobs available to women were largely in domestic service or low-paid factory work, by the 1890s, urban commercial jobs were expanding rapidly, and thousands of middle-class women could become retail salesclerks, bookkeepers, typists, bank tellers, and secretaries. By 1914 city streets were thronged with working women going to and from their jobs in downtown offices and stores.

Family limitation had mixed social consequences. In smaller families children were less often neglected. And with fewer mouths to feed, the family was more prosperous. Children could be allowed to stay in school until they were better prepared for the "race of life." Married women often found their lives more rewarding and the bonds of marriage less confining. But the change in family size also had a darker side. The family as an institution lost some of its cohesion. In 1867, when divorce laws were strict and divorced people often ostracized, only 10,000 divorces were granted in the entire country. By 1907, as a result of divorce-law reforms and the more permissive moral climate, there were 72,000 divorces, a rate over three times as great per capita. Whether viewed as a social calamity or liberation, divorce had become a more widely accepted feature of American life.

Crime, Vice, and Loneliness.   All newcomers to the American Gilded Age city encountered social pathologies. Cities were schools of crime and disorder, with gangs of cardsharps, pickpockets, purse snatchers, and thieves. Then as now, poor people were the major victims of city crime. They were also its chief perpetrators, especially of violent crimes. A city disease, crime was also a way of "making it" in America. Street boys stole from stores, passers-by, and drunks. In Chicago, an observer noted, the newsboys who gathered in the courtyard of the Hearst Building to pick up the evening papers were also petty thieves. Those young men, it seems, usually gambled away what they stole, but other slum dwellers used their illegal gains to get ahead. Crime, in sociologist Daniel Bell's phrase, was a "queer ladder of social mobility" for some of the urban poor.

Prostitution also plagued the cities of this period. The Gilded Age was a particularly prudish era in sexual matters. "Good" women were expected to be indifferent to sex. By itself this attitude might have encouraged prostitution; but in addition the cities attracted multitudes of young women looking for jobs and respectable marriages. Although many achieved their goals, others failed and fell prey to madams, shady saloonkeepers, and others who took them in and led—or forced—them into prostitution. Periodically, reformers and crusaders would close the brothels and chase the prostitutes off the street, but the trade in sexual favors would quickly resume again.

Respectable people deplored the city saloon as a haunt of vice and drunkenness, but it met an urgent urban social need. American cities were lonely places for the thousands of men and women who arrived without family or friends. To offset the isolation of their lives, newcomers to the city joined lodges, church organizations, ethnic societies, and veterans' groups. In the 1890s settlement houses, where the poor could find educational and recreational facilities, helped create community feeling in the city neighborhoods. But the local tavern often served the same purpose. Church leaders and moralists might rail, yet to many isolated men the saloon was a place where they could find companionship for the price of a glass of beer.

The saloon, the settlement house, the fraternal order, and the ethnic society proved inadequate in providing moral and emotional support for city dwellers, especially those without families. Even the churches often failed. Catholics and

Jews were quick to provide for their own religious needs, but Protestants often neglected their less-fortunate members. With their base in older rural America and the prosperous urban middle class, the Protestant denominations frequently found it difficult to understand or cope with the problems of poor city dwellers.

Disturbed by the demoralization in the city centers, in the 1880s Protestant reformers launched the Charity Organization movement. Hundreds of middle-class women became volunteer "friendly visitors" to slum families to advise them how to save, how to use their money, how to dress, and how to keep clean. They made little headway against the vast social ills that afflicted the city poor. The Salvation Army was more successful in aiding the cities' outcasts. Its soup kitchens, shelters, lodging houses, and "rescue missions" in the run-down areas of many cities provided meals and a place to stay for thousands of home-less. The YMCA and YWCA also sought to help. But none of these efforts solved the problems created in the cities by the breakdown of traditional ties to family, neighbors, and other social groups. By the end of the century every city had its "skid row," where lonely men and women lived out narrow hopeless lives amid squalid surroundings.

■ CITY GOVERNMENT ■

Contemporaries might disagree over the social and physical virtues of cities, but few cared to defend their politics. James Bryce, a prominent English observer of Gilded Age America, in fact considered American cities "the worst governed in Christendom."

The critics' chief target was the city machines—political organizations designed to perpetuate a faction or party in office. Each machine was led by a "boss," who might or might not serve as mayor but who, regardless of his official title, dominated the city government. Beneath the boss was a collection of faith-ful aides—the ward or precinct captains ("ward heelers") and various rank-and-file hangers-on—who performed the machine's essential function of mobilizing the vote for its mayoral and city council candidates. The machines kept the loyalty of their retainers by providing them with jobs, often sinecures that paid well but did not require serious effort or any demonstrated competence.

The purpose of the machine was to win and retain office. But for what? Reformers, the champions of "good government," insisted that the machine's only goal was to milk the city treasury or to confer under-the-counter favors on busi-nesspeople and purveyors of vice for the personal gain of its members. The boss and his henchmen, they said, were at heart little more than racketeers. And their methods were no more savory than their goals. Machines, the reformers noted, won the support of voters by wholesale bribery and corruption. They paid the poor $5 or $10 each for their votes; they stuffed ballot boxes with false returns; they brought in "floaters" from other communities to vote in city elections; they illegally naturalized aliens to cast ballots for the machine and against its opponents. In short, as good-government people saw it, the machines were essentially diseased organs that should be cut out of the body politic if city life was to be improved.

The Machines in Action.   The reformers were not entirely fair. The machines were often corrupt, but they performed important functions that could not be handled by the more formal institutions of the day. New York in the 1870s illustrates how they operated and why they became so deeply entrenched.

In the years immediately following the Civil War, the country's largest city was governed by a confused jumble of overlapping agencies. It had a board of aldermen, a board of councilmen, twelve supervisors, and a separate board of education—all with power to make decisions in various spheres without the mayor's approval. The police commissioners were appointed not by the mayor or by any city agency but by the governor of the state, as were the commissioners of Central Park and of the fire department. The system was a "hodgepodge," declared a contemporary critic, that made New York virtually ungovernable.

Into this confusion stepped William Marcy Tweed. Tweed was not the gross, predatory figure depicted in the savage cartoons of reformer Thomas Nast. Neither was he the model of an upright public servant. Tweed and his henchmen bilked the city treasury of millions of dollars collected largely in the form of kickbacks from private contractors who provided the city with supplies and services at rigged prices and then secretly returned some of their take to the machine and its leaders. One estimate puts the total thefts of Tweed's Tammany Hall, the New York City machine, at between $45 million and $200 million.

But Tweed and his henchmen did not take without giving. The Boss made the chaotic, aimless political system of New York respond to the pressing needs of its citizens. Did shippers need improved docks? Tweed would get new powers for the city to build them. Did working people need a rapid transit system? Tweed would see that transit promoters could acquire private property for the right-of-way. Did households need new sewers or a better water supply? Tweed would use his influence in the state capital so that the city could borrow to provide them. Other cities—St. Louis, Philadelphia, San Francisco, Cincinnati—had versions of Tweed.

The machines were not only useful devices for getting new sewers, improved lighting, and transit lines; they were also informal welfare organizations. Official almshouses, orphanages, and hospitals for the insane were dreary and oppressive places avoided by the poor. Churches and private philanthropic organizations could not provide adequately for such large numbers of needy. The machines helped offset the failings of the contemporary "safety net." Because they controlled massive amounts of patronage, they could find jobs for the unemployed in the police department, the fire department, the schools, or the sanitation service. Civil service rules seldom applied to these jobs, and the local ward captains reserved them for their favorites. The machines also supplemented the incomes of the poor—coal during the winter, turkeys at Thanksgiving and Christmas, and free medical services—and fed money into private charities. During his term as state senator, Tweed, though a Protestant, pressured the New York legislature into appropriating funds for the Catholic charities and parochial schools that many of his poor city constituents relied on.

The city machines were also buffers between poor citizens and the law. Much of what was accounted illegal in contemporary American cities was "victimless crime": gambling, drinking on Sunday, "blood" sports such as cock-fighting or bare-knuckled boxing, and sex for money. Not all Americans approved of making these activities illegal, and many continued to engage in them, regardless of the law. When, during a sudden surge of civic virtue, the authorities clamped down on saloons, gambling, or vice, people were arrested for practices that they considered at worst venal sins. Where could they turn for help? The obvious answer was the precinct captain, who could "speak to" the judge. Even better, the machine could quash the spasm of virtue before it developed. City machines were understanding of human weaknesses, as reformers seldom were, and overlooked transgressions that did not unduly disturb public order.

The machines, then, often functioned both as social service organizations and as shields between city people and the barbs of city life. As Tammany leader George Washington Plunkitt explained, a ward captain was always obliging: "He will go to the police courts to put in a good word for the drunks and disorderlies or pay their fines, if a good word is not effective. He will feed the hungry and help bury the dead." Martin Lomasney, a Boston machine leader, explained it more philosophically: "I think that there's got to be in every ward somebody that any bloke can come to—no matter what he's done—and get help. Help, you understand; none of your law and justice, but help."

Goo-Goos. Of course, the machines were not purely altruistic. In return for these services they expected gratitude that could be turned into votes at election time, as well as tolerance of graft and corruption. The public's patience was finite, however. Eventually Tweed, for example, ran up bills that the voters would no longer accept. When a disgruntled former Tammany leader decided to tell all, the commercial and financial leaders of the city, joined by good-government reformers ("goo-goos" to their enemies) and an outraged citizenry, mounted a campaign to cut Tweed down. In 1872 the reformers elected to the mayor's office William F. Havemeyer, a wealthy sugar refiner and one of their own. Tweed was indicted on criminal charges and sent to jail. On his release he was rearrested to stand trial in a civil action to recover the sums he had stolen. He fled to Spain, was returned to New York, and sent to jail again, where he died in disgrace in 1878.

Under Havemeyer the reformers attempted to run the city on economical and honest principles. They cut back on hundreds of patronage positions in the city services departments and eliminated many construction projects. Thousands of workers lost their jobs. With Tweed no longer in Albany to manage the necessary legislation, the state ceased to appropriate money for private and religious charities. Ticket-fixing, "speaking to" judges, and gifts of coal and turkeys also stopped, as did the tolerance for the petty law-bending of working-class life. This moralism and the cuts in patronage and services cost the reformers the support of the poor, and bossism soon returned in the form of "Honest" John Kelley. As leader of Tammany Hall, Kelley was a more scrupulous man than Tweed; but he, too, anchored the machine squarely on the support of the city poor and dispensed favors and services with a ready hand.

The pattern of spendthrift machine followed by tight-fisted reformers and spendthrift machine once again was repeated over and over in American cities during the Gilded Age. The working class often preferred open-handedness to economy, ethical tolerance to the moralism of the reformers. If municipal reform movements before the 1890s were generally short-lived, it was due as much to the reformers' limitations as to any perversity on the part of city voters.

■ A BETTER PLACE TO LIVE ■

Many of the difficulties city dwellers faced after the Civil War were the result of extraordinary growth that outran the capacity of cities to solve their problems. By the 1890s, when the cities finally began to catch up, city life improved.

Physical Improvement.   A measure of progress was the upgrading of the physical environment. The introduction of asphalt in the 1870s made city streets cleaner and safer. It soon became the standard paving material for cities. Waste-disposal problems were also conquered as the years passed. In 1887 Los Angeles, a city without a major river to use for dumping waste, built a sewage treatment plant. Chicago stopped the pollution of Lake Michigan, the source of its drinking water, by reversing the direction of the Chicago River so that it flowed into the Mississippi. In the landlocked Midwest several cities turned to incinerators to dispose of waste. Most of these schemes only postponed the difficulties or imposed them on some other community downstream. But they were better than those that had preceded.

One of the great urban triumphs of the age was the provision of pure water. By the time of the Civil War many cities had systems for piping water into homes. After the war, following the discoveries of Robert Koch and Louis Pasteur that bacteria are powerful disease-causing agents, cities began to filter and chlorinate their water. By the time of World War I (1914), virtually every American city had pure drinking water, and death rates from cholera, typhoid, dysentery, and other water-borne diseases plummeted. Combined with milk pasteurization and other new health measures, these advances drastically reduced urban mortality rates, especially among the young.

New Ideas in Housing and Architecture.   The most intractable urban problem—the lack of adequate housing for the working class—became a concern of philanthropists during the 1870s. In that decade Alfred T. White, a successful Brooklyn businessman and engineer, became convinced that landlords' profits and decent housing for the poor were compatible. Pursuing "philanthropy and 5 percent," he completed his Home Buildings near the Brooklyn waterfront. These attractive structures accommodated forty families in apartments two rooms deep, ensuring good light and ventilation; they included a bathroom for each apartment. White's experiment, unfortunately, failed to revolutionize building practices. Developers continued to throw up jerry-built structures that crammed human beings into dank, dark apartments with few amenities.

Clearly, better design was not enough; but until the 1890s philanthropists had no other approach. Then, as part of the emerging "progressive" mood, reformers began to mobilize the power of government to protect urban citizens against the unrestrained profit motive. In New York, the legislature adopted a series of state tenement laws culminating in the measure of 1901, which outlawed the dumbbell structure and established more stringent minimum housing guidelines. Chicago, too, revised its housing code in 1898 and 1902 to impose higher standards on builders. Still, housing for the poor continued to be overcrowded and squalid.

Architects, philanthropists, and reformers upgraded other urban physical facilities as well. Before the 1890s American cities had few parks and open spaces. Office buildings, city halls, and courthouses were often ugly structures scattered about the downtown areas without plan or order. Above the city streets unsightly tangles of telegraph and telephone wires crisscrossed the sky. Many city streets were blighted by elevated trains that clattered overhead and plunged the ground below into gloom.

Toward the end of the century new attitudes began to alter the cities' appearance and comfort. Inspired by the gleaming neoclassical structures of the White City, erected in Chicago to house the great Columbian Exposition of 1893, architects and urban planners sought to bring aesthetic order and distinction to American cities. During the next generation the City Beautiful Movement induced scores of American cities to build elaborate civic centers of neoclassical buildings to house city agencies. These structures, usually grouped around a large landscaped plaza, provided spacious open areas for urban dwellers in Cleveland, San Francisco, St. Louis, San Diego, and other cities.

The "White City" at the 1893 Chicago World's Fair imitated ancient Rome and inspired countless "civic centers" in American cities.

This period also saw the birth of the skyscraper as a characteristic American architectural expression. The offspring of engineering and economics, the skyscraper conserved downtown land by combining the new technology of steel, which permitted tall structures without space-wasting thick walls, and the electric elevator. Although it started as an engineering innovation, it soon became a distinctive architectural style, worthy of aesthetic consideration.

City Transit.   Transportation also improved as the century approached its end. In the 1870s New York had built its first "el" (short for elevated railway), a commuter steam railroad raised on columns above the city streets. Chicago and other cities had quickly followed suit. The el was fast, but it was also dirty and unsightly. Pedestrians on the street below were subjected to a steady rain of soot and ash, while the el structure created a ribbon of blight along every avenue it traversed.

Help came during the 1870s. The cable car, attached to a moving cable between the rails, was adopted in San Francisco in 1872 to meet the special needs of that hilly city. Then, in the late 1880s, Frank Sprague, a naval engineer and former colleague of Edison's, built the first electric streetcar system in Richmond, Virginia. The Sprague streetcar drew its power from an overhead "trolley" held against a power wire by a spring arrangement. Fast, smooth, and nonpolluting, the electric trolley car was an immediate success. By 1895, some 850 lines were operating, carrying passengers from home to office, stores, factory, and amusement parks. Many longer interurban lines connected towns and cities in a dense network that blanketed the populous East and parts of the metropolitan West. Especially admired was the system of "red cars" whose tracks stretched like spokes

New Yorkers in the 1890s amused themselves at Steeplechase Park in Coney Island. Almost every city in America had its equivalent in this era.

from the central hub of Los Angeles to the surrounding satellite communities of southern California.

The final improvement was the subway, which combined electric traction with an underground right-of-way unobstructed by pedestrians or other traffic. Boston became the first city to acquire an underground transit system when it dug a mile-and-a-half tunnel for its trolleys under its downtown streets in 1897. New York opened the first true underground railroad in the United States in 1904 when it completed the first fifteen-mile stretch of what would eventually become the most extensive subway system in the world. Philadelphia and Chicago, too, acquired subways before World War I.

Schools for Newcomers.   As the country approached the new century, cities also began to cope better with assimilating the mass of newcomers who poured in from every part of the world. The major agency for Americanizing the new arrivals was the city school system.

When we look back at urban schools of the 1890s and beyond, we are struck by their strict discipline, narrow range of subject matter, and limited physical facilities. Nonetheless, they were successful in teaching the basic skills that society needed. By contrast with our own day, the schools in large cities during the early twentieth century often performed better than those in rural or suburban areas.

Americanizing the immigrants and their children was a difficult and impressive accomplishment of the schools. A cultural gap often existed between the children in city classrooms and their teachers. At times the teachers literally did not speak the pupils' language, and textbooks made no concessions to the pupils' cultural backgrounds. Yet many immigrant children overcame this gap. Mary Antin, a young Russian-Jewish immigrant, writing in 1912, told how the Boston schools had made her into a "good American." Mary sat "rigid with attention" as her teacher read the story of the Revolutionary War. As she learned "how the patriots planned the Revolution, and the women gave their sons to die in battle, and the battle led to victory, and the rejoicing people set up the Republic," it dawned on her "what was meant by my country." She, too, was an American citizen, and the insight changed her life. Mary went on to become a successful writer.

Not every immigrant child was so successfully Americanized. Many, finding the schools alien and uncongenial, resisted their influence. Some dissenters believed the schools were taking away the children's sense of their own heritage and leaving them stranded between two cultures. Horace Kallen, a prominent teacher and social philosopher, conceived an alternative approach to the problem of American social and cultural diversity. His "cultural pluralism" celebrated a "democracy of nationalities, co-operating voluntarily and autonomously in the enterprise of [American] self-realization through the perfection of men according to their kind." Kallen hoped men and women of diverse backgrounds could retain their heritages while sharing important common values and attitudes. Few schools in these years heeded his advice, yet they managed on the whole to ease the transition from immigrant to American.

Reform with a Heart.   The schools' contribution toward easing the cities' social problems was supplemented by other agencies. The most comprehensive effort took the form of a new kind of humane political reform.

During the 1870s and 1880s, as we have seen, urban reformers had emphasized economy and efficiency over social justice and had often offended the urban poor. If any group of city politicians was concerned with the well-being of the city masses, it was the bosses who ran the machines. This division—shady politicians with a heart and honest reformers with a balance sheet—did not entirely cease with the advent of the new century. During the Progressive Era that began in the mid-1890s, one group of reformers continued to be more concerned with economy and efficiency than with social justice, as we shall see in Chapter 23.

But there was another thread to the urban reform movement that developed in the 1890s. As public-spirited citizens became aware of the failings of the Gilded Age city and of previous reform philosophies, they began to acquire a more sophisticated understanding of what had to be done. The result was compassionate urban reform and movements for social justice in cities such as Detroit, Cleveland, Toledo, and Milwaukee.

In Detroit, Mayor Hazen Pingree, the agent of the new reform, rode to office as mayor following the indictment of several Democratic aldermen for taking bribes. At first Pingree differed from the traditional reformers more in style than in substance. Although he emphasized reducing "the extravagant rate of taxation," he was not a rigid puritan. He avoided the usual goo-goo attacks on the voters' cultural preferences. In the style of the old ward leaders, he launched his first campaign by a round of drinks with the boys at Baltimore Red's Saloon.

Pingree learned, however, that his constituents also demanded that he acknowledge their economic needs. Pingree soon became their champion against "the interests." He attacked the street-railway monopoly for its high fares and harsh labor policies. During an 1891 street-railway strike, the mayor sided with the strikers against the company. Following the panic of 1893, he initiated a much-publicized "potato-patch" plan under which the city turned over vacant lots to needy families so that they could raise vegetables to help support themselves. The mayor also shifted some of the city's tax burden from Detroit's citizens to the corporations that did business with the city.

Toledo's equivalent of Pingree was the colorful Samuel ("Golden Rule") Jones. Jones began a program of city ownership of water, gas, and electric utilities; put to a popular vote such questions as extending city franchises to private companies; and inaugurated a major expansion of the system of parks, playgrounds, and municipal baths. Like Pingree, Jones refused to go along with the conventional reformers' prejudice against working-class customs, amusements, and presumed vices. He rejected demands that he close the saloons and put drunks in jail. When local ministers asked him to drive prostitutes out of the city, he asked them pointedly: "To where?"

In Milwaukee, too, the city's reformers had been of the traditional goo-goo type. But during the hard times following 1893, when the utility companies tried to raise their rates while refusing to pay local taxes, reformers' attitudes changed. Outraged by the arrogance of the state's utility tycoons, they sought allies among the working class in a concerted attack on privilege. A decade and a half later the Socialists took control of the city from the middle-class reformers when Emil Seidel became mayor and instituted a regime that combined good government and social justice. During the years of Socialist control the city enacted a minimum wage for all city employees and established a permanent committee on unemployment. In addition, Seidel expanded the public concert program, established commissions on tuberculosis and child welfare, and encouraged the use of the public schools for after-hours social, civic, and neighborhood clubs.

■ CONCLUSIONS ■

In the half-century following the Civil War, American cities exerted a powerful pull on the peoples of the world. Glamour, culture, excitement, and, above all, jobs drew millions of rural men and women, foreigners and natives, to the cities of the United States. For a while the deluge overwhelmed many urban services and facilities, making life for the newcomers uncomfortable, unsafe, and unhealthy.

American cities never became paradises. But by the early years of the twentieth century, they were better places to live than they had been fifty years before. Billions of dollars were spent for sewers, streets, aqueducts, and other municipal services, improving the health and comfort of citizens. Electric streetcars and subways brought fast, clean, and relatively comfortable transportation. Best of all, new leadership by people with a strong sense of responsibility toward the voters made government more efficient without sacrificing the values and interests of the great mass of working-class citizens. Many problems remained; in later years much that was gained would be lost. But for a while, around the year 1910, the American city had become an interesting, relatively livable, place. In 1905 the reformer Frederic C. Howe could call the American city "the hope of democracy."

Online Resources

"How the Other Half Lives"
http://www.yale.edu/amstud/inforev/riis/title.html
Explore the world of immigrants in New York in the late nineteenth century by viewing the full text and illustrations of Jacob Riis' work. To see a collection of over a dozen photographs depicting tenement life, see
http://www.masters-of-photography.com/R/riis/riis.html.

"Metropolitan Lives"
http://nmaa-ryder.si.edu/collections/exhibits/metlives/index.html
See the Ashcan artists' scenes of the realism of the city. Informative essays that discuss class relations, immigration, and changing gender norms accompany the paintings.

On the Lower East Side: Observations of Life in Lower Manhattan at the Turn of the Century
http://tenant.net.80/community/LES/contents.html
Articles, documentaries, and first-person accounts found on this site provide rich details of the neighborhoods and living conditions of working-class immigrants in an urban American environment. Learn about their social networks and enduring folkways.

"The Gilded Age and the Titans of Industry"
http://www.pbs.org/wgbh/amex/carnegie/gildedage.html
On PBS's The American Experience Web site, learn about the experience of Americans during the so-called Gilded Age. Timeline features and a picture gallery provide links to a biography of industrialist Andrew Carnegie and photos of the industrialists' New York homes known by many as "Millionaires' Row."

19

THE TRANS-MISSOURI WEST

Another Colony?

1849	Bureau of Indian Affairs formed
1851	Federal government begins negotiating treaties for small Indian reservations in place of the Indian Frontier
1862	The Homestead Act; The Morrill Land Grant College Act
1864	The Chivington Massacre at Sand Creek; Lincoln reelected
1865	Sioux War on the Plains; Lincoln assassinated; Andrew Johnson becomes president
1866	Long drive of cattle, from Texas to railroad sites to expand market to East begins
1867	Federal Peace Commission creates reform policies to assimilate Indians to white civilization; Patrons of Husbandry founded
1868	Ulysses S. Grant elected president
1873	The Timber Culture Act
1876	Custer's Last Stand at Little Big Horn
1877	Rutherford B. Hayes becomes president; The Desert Land Act
1880	James A. Garfield elected president
1881	Garfield assassinated; Chester A. Arthur becomes president
1884	Grover Cleveland elected president
1887	The Dawes Severalty Act designed to make Indians individual landowners; Severe winter destroys cattle boom on the Great Plains
1888	Benjamin Harrison elected president
1890	Massacre at Wounded Knee Creek
1892	Cleveland elected president for the second time
1893	Financial panic begins depression
1896	Presidential election between "goldbugs" and "silverites"; McKinley elected president over Bryan
1901	McKinley assassinated; Theodore Roosevelt becomes president
1902	The National Reclamation (Newlands) Act is passed to develop irrigation
1904	Roosevelt elected president
1905	The California Fruit Growers' Exchange introduces Sunkist products

America has had many "Wests." The colonial West was the forested region just beyond the settled Atlantic coastal plain. On the eve of the American Revolution, the West was the eastern half of the great valley across the Appalachian Mountains. For the generation preceding the Civil War, it was the land between the Mississippi and the Missouri. The "Last West" of 1865 to 1910 was the broad expanse of territory stretching from the Missouri River to the Pacific Ocean.

In the Last West, as on America's previous frontiers, people with a basically European culture came into contact with an unfamiliar human and natural environment. As they adapted to western realities, the settlers often came to resent the power the East held over the country and over their lives. Easterners, they felt, did not understand the country's newest region or its problems; they were only interested in milking the frontier and its people. Many western Americans came to view themselves as inhabitants of a colony, exploited by people who lived hundreds of miles away. Meanwhile, they themselves often callously exploited the land and brutalized its native inhabitants.

To an extent, the Last West was treated as a colony of the East. Western mining companies held their board meetings in New York or Chicago, not in Denver, Butte, or Boise. The great cattle ranches of the Great Plains and Great Basin were often owned by Bostonians, New Yorkers, or even French and British investors. Indian policies and land policies were not made in "the territories"; they were made in Washington, D.C., by people who did not seem to understand either Indians or western needs or wishes. When a cartoonist in the 1890s pictured America straddled by a huge cow grazing on the Great Plains and being milked in New York, westerners knew what he meant.

The men and women who settled the trans-Missouri West would eventually feel almost as alienated from Washington, D.C., Boston, and Chicago as had the white colonists of Massachusetts and Virginia from the England of George III. Howard Lamar, a historian of the West, notes that by 1889 "every territory in the West was calling its federal officials colonial tyrants and comparing its plight to that of the thirteen colonies." Eventually, in alliance with the South, they would rise up in a major political revolt against the urban East.

How did this antagonistic East–West relationship develop? What was the basis for western discontent following the Civil War?

■ SETTLEMENT OF THE LAST WEST ■

The Land.   The Last West was a vast and diverse area of some 1.2 million square miles, approximately two fifths of the entire nation. Its eastern third, the Great Plains, is a level plateau gradually rising toward the west like a table tilted upward at one end. In its eastern portion rainfall in normal years is twenty inches or more, sufficient for grain crops. West of this band a few elevated spots such as the Black Hills of South Dakota catch the moisture-laden winds coming from the Pacific. Elsewhere the rainfall is usually too scanty for ordinary farming. Before the land was settled by whites, the ground was mainly covered with grass—long grass in the more humid eastern parts, short "buffalo" grass in the drier western half. Without trees or hills, the area lacked shelter from constant winds that often brought fierce blizzards in winter and turned grass and grain to dry straw in a few days during blazing hot summers.

As settlers moved west across the Great Plains, 600 miles beyond the Missouri River, they abruptly encountered a great escarpment rising like a wall—the lofty, forested Rocky Mountains. The Rockies form the eastern rim of several shallow but extensive basins. The largest is the Great Basin, which consists of most of present-day Nevada, western Utah, northern Arizona, and the extreme southeast of California. Much of this region is arid. Besides the Colorado, there are few rivers with outlets to the oceans. Before the advent of dams and irrigation, water flowed only briefly, after occasional cloudbursts. Rivers generally petered out into "sinks" or ended in shallow lakes that evaporated during the dry season, leaving behind white alkaline "flats."

The narrow band of the Cascade and Sierra Nevada mountains form the western rim of the harsh basin region. Their eastern slopes are arid, but their western slopes catch the moisture-laden Pacific winds and are heavily forested. Between the Cascade–Sierra range and the coastal hills of Oregon, Washington, and California are several broad valleys: to the north, the valleys of Puget Sound and the Willamette River; to the south, in California, the great Central Valley.

Beyond the coast ranges, a narrow coastal plain, scarcely more than a thin ribbon of beach in many places, borders the Pacific. From San Francisco Bay northward, the climate of the Pacific Coast region resembles that of northwestern Europe, with rainy, relatively warm winters and cool, drier summers. South of San Francisco, the climate is Mediterranean: warm all year with little cloud cover and only sparse winter rains.

The Exploitation Ethic.   In the years following Appomattox, few Americans perceived the virtue of pristine wilderness in itself. Yet in 1872, Congress managed to set aside 2 million acres of northwestern Wyoming as Yellowstone National Park, the first of the nation's national parks. During the discussion of the Yellowstone bill, Ferdinand Hayden, sometimes called father of the national park system, emphasized the value of the region primarily as the site of natural curiosities—"decorations" such as geysers—rather than as a specimen of unspoiled nature.

But with the possible exception of the national parks, most Americans perceived the West as a treasure trove awaiting human exploitation. Eastern entrepreneurs hoped to turn western resources into corporate profits. New settlers were eager to wrest livelihoods as ranchers, farmers, and miners from the new region. For most contemporaries, the West was a great cornucopia of timber, gold, grass, oil, and copper to be skimmed off its surface or extracted from its bowels. These people often resented even minor federal interference with their right to exploit the land. In 1883 Senator John J. Ingalls of Kansas declared "the best thing the Government could do with the Yellowstone National Park" was "to survey it and sell it as other public lands are sold."

Settlement Patterns.   The earliest part of the Last West to be occupied by whites was the Pacific Coast. The fertile soils of the Willamette Valley of Oregon attracted midwestern farmers in the 1840s, and in the 1850s gold brought thousands to California by ship around Cape Horn or overland by wagon train. By 1860 two Pacific Coast states had entered the Union: Oregon with 52,000 people and California with 380,000.

The Great Basin and Rocky Mountain regions were peopled as much from the West as from the East. By the mid-1850s the easy pickings in the Sierra gold streams of California had ended. Gold remained, but it was either buried under many layers of silt or embedded in quartz rock. Ordinary prospectors did not have the capital or expert knowledge to extract the metal from these deposits and were forced to leave gold mining to large corporations. Through the next decades, displaced California miners and prospectors scattered through the Great Basin and Rocky Mountain regions from Mexico to Canada, their bedrolls, shovels, pans, supplies, and rifles piled on a burro or mule, ready to dig again. News, or even rumors, of a strike brought prospectors rushing from all directions to stake claims along reported gold streams. There they would join crowds of men, and a few women, from the East who were new to the game. Many of the gold-seekers were black; many more, especially among the Californians, were Mexican or of mixed Indian–white parentage; and there were many Celestials, as the Chinese were called. As in California, only a few struck it rich. Most of the others soon drifted off in quest of new bonanzas.

The settlement pattern in the Great Plains was more conventional. The Plains population came predominantly from the agricultural Mississippi Valley immediately to the east. These people were farmers and farmers' children seeking lands cheaper than those available in the Midwest. During the 1880s Iowa, Missouri, and the five states of the Old Northwest lost a million of their sons and daughters to the Great Plains region. Joining these ex-midwesterners were immigrants from Ireland, Canada, Germany, and Scandinavia, as well as former black slaves fleeing southern sharecropping.

Plains settlers usually came as individuals or members of family units, but part of the migration was sponsored or even subsidized by outside agencies. In the Great Basin, for example, Mormon missionaries were responsible for drawing thousands from the East and from Europe to Utah and the so-called Mormon Corridor, stretching south from Idaho to Arizona. The transcontinental railroads attracted easterners and Europeans to their lands on the Plains by colorful brochures advertising $4-an-acre land, free seed, and free agricultural advice.

■ NATIVE PEOPLES OF THE LAST WEST ■

To the Indian tribes of the trans-Missouri West, the whites were unwelcome intruders. The Great Plains alone were inhabited by over 125,000 Native Americans in mid-century. About 75,000 of these were former woodland

Indians—including the Blackfoot, Assiniboine, Sioux, Cheyenne, Arapaho, Crow, Shoshone, Pawnee, Kiowa, and Comanche—who had moved into the Great Plains from the East and adopted nomadic ways several hundred years before whites arrived. These tribes shared the region with an almost equal number of Indians of the so-called Five Civilized Tribes (Cherokee, Choctaw, Chickasaw, Creek, and Seminole), who had been transplanted by government order before the Civil War from their traditional lands in the Southeast. In the Oregon region there were some 25,000 Nez Percé, Spokane, Yakima, Cayuse, Chinook, Nisqually, and other peoples. Texas contained 25,000 Lipan, Apache, and Comanche Indians. In California and New Mexico Territory there were 150,000 Native Americans, distributed among the Ute, Pueblo, Navajo, Apache, Paiute, Yuma, Mojave, Modoc, and a flock of smaller coastal tribes, collectively called "Mission Indians," who had been gathered by the Spanish friars into settlements centering around mission churches during the preceding century.

The Western Cultures. These Indians were diverse in their cultures, economies, religion, and political institutions. The Navajo and Apache of the Far Southwest were mostly nomadic hunters, though they practiced some agriculture as well. Along the Rio Grande and its tributaries were the Hopi, Zuñi, and other "Pueblo" peoples, who used irrigation to grow crops and lived in villages of adobe and stone structures that resembled modern apartment houses. The Hopi and Zuñi had repulsed the Spaniards and the Mexicans during the eighteenth and early nineteenth centuries and would fend off American influences, too. Unlike other tribes, they were able to avoid the social and cultural breakdown that contact with whites generally brought.

The Indians of the Northwest—the Oregon–Washington region—included the coastal fishing peoples, who consumed salmon, traveled the sea in canoes of great hollowed-out tree trunks, lived in timber lodges, wore clothing made of pliant inner bark, and engaged in elaborate social ceremonies (potlatches) that involved competitive destruction of physical wealth to establish social status. To their east the Nez Percé lived in brush lodges, wore skin garments, and both fished for salmon and hunted elk, deer, and mountain goats for food.

The Plains Indians were the classic "Indians" of American frontier legend: tall, bronzed, with straight black hair, high cheekbones, and prominent, often curved, noses. At the eastern fringes of the Plains some tribes practiced agriculture. Farther west, where the rainfall diminishes, they were nomadic hunters.

These western Plains Indians were formidable opponents. They traveled light. Their homes were skin-sided teepees that could be folded up in minutes and loaded on a pony to be set up quickly again miles away. Unlike the Indians of the East, people such as these could not be subdued by burning their crops and destroying their villages; they grew no crops, and did not live in settled communities.

The vast buffalo herds provided the Plains Indians with almost everything they needed to survive. They ate buffalo steaks and tongues; they made their clothing and their teepees of buffalo hides; buffalo "chips" (droppings) were their fuel; and buffalo sinews provided their cord and string. The guns and horses they had acquired from Europeans enabled the Plains Indians to increase their range and prosperity, and made them formidable adversaries. By the time the westward-moving Americans encountered the Plains tribes, the Americans' only military advantage was sheer numbers.

Conflicting Views.   Indian and non-Indian societies were separated by a wide cultural gulf. Among whites, the individual took precedence over the group. By contrast, Indians generally subordinated personal ambitions to the tribe's needs and goals, and merged individual identity with that of the collectivity. The tribe came first even in adult–children relationships. As one Indian shaman told a French Jesuit missionary: "You French people love only your own children; but we love the children of our tribe."

Indian attitudes toward the land and resources were also different. The white settlers conceived of the land as a source of wealth, a means to an end. It could be bought, sold, bequeathed, and exploited by an individual owner. Most Indians saw land as part of the sacred, superhuman, world. Men must live in balance with nature. Land was also the collective possession of either tribe, family, or clan. If an individual had any special claim to a piece of land, it was only because he or she used it. Land left idle could be redistributed among other members of the tribe.

The nomadic ways of the western Plains tribes compounded Indian–white differences over real estate. Nomads must wander far and wide in search of food and cannot respect artificial boundaries established by treaties, property deeds, and land laws. Because they exploit the land extensively for hunting and food gathering, rather than intensively for farming, they need vast amounts of space. What seemed to whites an enormous surplus of land was barely enough to provide a Cheyenne or a Sioux tribe with sufficient food.

Federal Government, the Indians, and the Settlers.   In dealing with the Indians, the federal government often showed no more understanding of Indian realities than white settlers who went west. Until 1871 the federal authorities accepted the fiction that the tribes were independent Indian "nations" that, like other sovereign states, could be dealt with through diplomatic negotiations and treaties. This view was useful to white Americans because the disparity in power between the United States and the individual tribes made it possible to impose conditions that favored whites. In exchange for some blankets, food, tools, a few rifles, or a little cash, the Indians were often pressured into surrendering by treaty vast stretches of valuable land. If the government could not extract a favorable agreement from the current Indian leaders, it would find some dissident group to deal with that could be bribed or coerced. But the federal government did not respect the treaties it signed with the Indians as it did those concluded with foreign nations. When local western interests found a treaty inconvenient, they could often induce the government to abrogate it. At times the whole treaty system seemed nothing more than a facade for exploitation. As a governor of Georgia at one point expressed it: "Treaties were expedients by which ignorant, intractable, and savage people were induced without bloodshed to yield up what civilized people had the right to possess. . . ."

Until the 1850s the federal government tried to maintain a permanent Indian frontier beyond the Mississippi where no whites could trespass. But the opening of California and Oregon to settlers soon made a shambles of the plan, and the government replaced it with the "reservation" policy. In place of a solid wall of Indian communities blocking off white settlement and passage westward, the tribes would be concentrated in widely spaced compact tracts. Here, supposedly, they would be protected from white exploiters and taught the ways of agriculture and other "civilized" arts and practices. The reservation policy was accompanied by serious troubles. White settlers on the scene often begrudged the Indians even the reduced areas the treaties gave them, while many of the Indians fiercely resisted the government's efforts to deprive them of their traditional range.

The most important treaties with the Plains tribes were those concluded at Forts Laramie and Atkinson in 1851 and 1853, respectively. Under their terms, the Indians promised to dwell in peace with the whites and with one another forever and to allow whites to build roads through their territory. The treaties also defined precisely the boundaries of each tribe's lands. These boundaries would later become the bases of the Plains reservations.

The Indians and the Civil War. The Civil War converted the Last West into a battleground between Indians and whites and among the Indians themselves. Meanwhile, despite the war, whites continued to enter the region, drawn by a series of gold strikes in the Pacific Northwest, the eastern flank of the Sierra Nevada range, and the foothills of the Rockies.

No group suffered as much from disturbed wartime conditions as the Civilized Tribes of Indian Territory (Oklahoma). Many owned slaves and sympathized with the South. A minority, however, favored the Union. Both groups tried to avoid the white man's quarrels, but failed. At one point Cherokees wearing Union blue slaughtered Cherokees wearing Confederate gray. Several regiments of Creek, Seminole, and Cherokee fought with the Confederate forces at the Battle of Pea Ridge in 1862.

Nor did the remainder of the West escape the bitter turmoil of the war period. In Minnesota seething Sioux discontent with the reservation policy boiled over into a major Indian war that cut a bloody swath through the new state. Meanwhile, in the far Southwest, General James Carleton and Kit Carson, colonel of the New Mexico territorial volunteers, clashed with the restless Navajo and forced them to settle down at Bosque Redondo reservation, a barren region where many died of exposure, disease, and malnutrition. The worst disaster of the wartime Indian "troubles" was the notorious Chivington Massacre in Colorado Territory.

This dark page of Indian–white relations began in the spring of 1864 when Cheyenne chief Black Kettle defied a government order to remove his tribe to a small reservation and began to raid mining camps and attack mail coaches. By the fall the Indians decided that they had done enough damage and sued for

Indian Relations Beyond the Mississippi, 1850–1890

peace. But whites were not satisfied that the culprits had paid the full price for their offenses. Pressed by vindictive Coloradoans, at dawn on November 29 the Third Colorado Volunteers under Colonel J. M. Chivington swooped down on 500 sleeping Cheyenne at Sand Creek. Black Kettle tried to surrender, but the volunteers ignored the Indians' white flag. The soldiers shot and killed 450 Cheyenne, two thirds of them women and children, and scalped and mutilated many. The fearless victors of Sand Creek soon after paraded through the streets of Denver to the cheers of the citizens. "Colorado soldiers have again covered themselves with glory," trumpeted the Denver paper, the *Rocky Mountain News*.

Developing an Indian Policy.   The end of the Civil War marked a watershed in the government's Indian policy. The Republicans who dominated federal policymaking after 1865 were, as we have seen, more strongly committed than their predecessors to racial justice. They were also strong nationalists who believed in the integration of all racial elements into the community. The Chivington Massacre, moreover, had shocked many sensitive men and women and convinced them that major reforms were needed.

These new attitudes opened a major gap between the sections over how to deal with the Native Americans. Easterners were now convinced that a "peace policy" was the best approach to the Indian problem, but recent events only confirmed western convictions that the government in Washington, D.C., was too feeble to suppress the Indian menace. When Senator James R. Doolittle of Wisconsin arrived in Denver in the summer of 1865 to represent the Senate Indian Committee, he quickly learned how wide the East–West disagreement was. At a public meeting in the city's opera house Doolittle attempted to explain the peace position that was now winning approval in the East. Should the Indians, he asked his audience, be firmly placed on reservations and taught to support themselves or should they be exterminated? Doolittle assumed that the question answered itself. But, as he later reported, his rhetorical question was followed by "such a shout as is never heard unless upon some battle field"—"Exterminate them! Exterminate them!"

The new approach also created a rift between civilians and the military. Having seen what force could do against an implacable white enemy, the victorious Union generals saw no reason why it should not be used against a lesser foe, the Indians. The divisions in opinion widened when chief Red Cloud's Cheyenne, Arapaho, and Sioux warriors ambushed a detachment of U.S. troops under Captain William Fetterman in late 1866 near Fort Philip Kearny in Wyoming. Fetterman and his whole force of eighty-two men were killed.

In the end the peace advocates and reformers prevailed. In 1867 Congress established a commission to end violence on the Plains. The commissioners' attitudes typified those of reformers for the next half-century. They wanted peace with the Indians and hoped to see them prosperous and content. But the tribes must surrender their nomadic life, settle down on reservations as farmers, and shift from "barbarism" to "civilization." To help the Indians assimilate white culture, the government would provide schools to teach them English, agriculture, and mechanical skills, and would bring them the blessings of the Christian faith. Until they became self-supporting, they would be supplied with food, blankets, tools, and clothing.

The commissioners met with the Kiowa, Comanche, Cheyenne, and Arapaho in 1867 and, after bribes, threats, and cajolery, induced them to accept reservations in western Oklahoma on lands confiscated from the Civilized Tribes as punishment for their support of the Confederacy. The next year the Sioux signed the Treaty of 1868 at Laramie, Wyoming. In exchange for the government's abandonment of a mining road through their lands and the usual promise of blankets, rations, and other handouts, they agreed to lay down their arms and accept a reservation in western South Dakota. Federal officials extracted similar agreements from the Shoshone, the Bannock of Wyoming and Idaho, and the Navajo and Apache of Arizona and New Mexico.

The peace policy did not work any better than previous strategies. Whites continued to covet Indian lands and encroached on the reservations. The government itself violated its agreements, often failing to come through with the promised food and blankets. The efforts to christianize the Indians offended their religious sensibilities. To make matters worse, the Bureau of Indian Affairs soon became a hotbed of corruption. The commissioner of Indian affairs, a political appointee, was almost always a party hack. He and his agents used money allotted for Indian supplies to line their own pockets. Effective administration of Indian affairs was further undermined by the division of responsibility between civilian officials and the army. In the end, violent confrontation between the army and the Indians continued to be a chronic element in Indian–white relations in the Last West.

The Final Indian Wars.   One of the gravest blows to the Indians' autonomy was the destruction of the great Plains buffalo herds. The slaughter of the buffalo was not a deliberate effort to subdue the Indians. Many animals were killed to supply meat for the crews building the transcontinental railroads that began to cross the Plains soon after the Civil War ended. Others fell to "sportsmen" who came to the Plains to hunt the great beasts for the thrill of it. Eventually, random slaughter gave way to more purposeful and profitable hunting to satisfy the consumer demand for leather and buffalo robes. During the 1870s buffalo hunting became a major Plains industry, and it was soon clear to everyone that the buffalo were on their way to extinction. "From the way the carcasses are strewn over the vast plains," wrote a traveler in these years, "the American bison will soon be numbered among things of the past." He was almost right. By 1883, 13 million animals had been destroyed. When an eastern museum expedition arrived on the Plains that year to obtain specimens for its collection, it found only 200 animals still alive.

The destruction of the buffalo virtually ended the Plains Indians' nomadic ways. The Indians became more dependent than ever on the government for handouts, or else were forced to take up an alien agricultural way of life to support themselves. For a generation more, however, the Indians resisted giving up their traditional life while resentment against the reservation policy festered.

The last years of the nineteenth century were marked by a chain of white provocations against the western Indian tribes. In the mid-1870s, gold prospectors invaded the Sioux reservation in the Black Hills of South Dakota. At first the federal authorities tried to exclude the whites. When the prospectors persisted, the government attempted to buy back or lease Sioux lands containing the gold diggings. The Indians defied the authorities and were declared renegades.

The Sioux turned for leadership to Sitting Bull, a chieftain of imposing appearance and fierce determination. Sitting Bull had only contempt for the Sioux who had accepted life on the reservations. "You are fools to make yourselves slaves to a piece of fat bacon, some hardtack, and a little sugar and coffee," he taunted his weak-willed brothers. Allied with Chief Crazy Horse, he encouraged the rebels and was soon being pursued by soldiers under the command of General Alfred Terry. On June 25, 1876, a detachment of Terry's troops led by the reckless Colonel George Custer walked into a trap at the Little Bighorn River. Sitting Bull's warriors pounced on Custer's men and by the time Terry's remaining forces came to the rescue, Custer and all 264 of his men were dead.

In this vivid portrait of Sitting Bull we can see the determination and strength that led to the United States cavalry's greatest defeat—Custer's disaster at Little Big Horn in 1876.

Though an immense moral victory for the Sioux, Custer's defeat ultimately hurt the Indians' cause. The government sent more soldiers to the Plains and forced the Sioux to surrender much of the Black Hills region to whites. During the next fourteen years almost all the tribes as yet untamed were compelled to accept confinement on the reservations. But discontent continued to seethe. The final pitched battle—though not the last violence—of the 400–year Indian–white war in North America took place in December 1890 at Wounded Knee Creek on the Sioux reservation in South Dakota.

As at times in the past the brutal incursion by whites into Indian territory and Indian life had encouraged a surge of "renewal" among the affected tribes. Among the Plains groups this new mood was spread by a Paiute Indian prophet named Wavoka. Wavoka promised the Indians a paradise where they would be free of the whites and where they would live forever amidst their ancestors in peace and prosperity, without sickness or suffering. This Indian Garden of Eden could be attained by practicing love, hard work, and peace with the whites, and by participating in the Ghost Dance, a ceremony of spiritual renewal emphasizing singing and dancing to the point of trance.

The Ghost Dance religion worried the white authorities, who, despite its professions of peace, saw it as a possible incitement to violence. Their nervousness converted a possibility into a reality. When the commander of the U.S. Seventh Cavalry tried to disarm a group of Sioux at Wounded Knee, someone fired several shots. A bitter hand-to-hand fight ensued. When the Indians broke through the army's line, the troops fired at them with hotchkiss repeating guns, killing at least 150, including many women and children.

The New Reformers.   During the closing years of the century, influential congressmen and their constituents, particularly in the East, were alerted to the Indians' plight and the whites' atrocities by the writings of Helen Hunt Jackson. Her 1881 book, *A Century of Dishonor*, recounted the doleful record of American Indian policy since independence and created a large public in favor of reform. The active Indian reformers of the period were well-meaning men and women who found the western Indians worthy objects of their compassion and social consciences. But like the peace commissioners of 1867, they had little regard for traditional Indian ways and believed assimilation was the solution of the Indian problem.

The reformers' views were incorporated into new legislation. Congress established special Indian schools both on the reservations and off, where Indian children were taught to read and write English and learn trades that presumably would help them prosper on the reservations. The reformers also succeeded in changing the land laws to suit their theories. The Dawes Severalty Act of 1887 gave the president the power to order Indian lands surveyed and divided into 160-acre plots to be allotted to each Indian head of family, with additional amounts for minor children.

The law broke with Indian tradition. Each adult male Indian was to become an individual landowner; the tribe would no longer own the land collectively. Indians would, it was hoped, become independent farmers on the white American model. To help ensure that the Indians would not quickly lose their land to sharpers, it was to be held in trust tax-free for twenty-five years. Individuals who took the allotments would in time become citizens of the United States and no longer be considered members of autonomous Indian "nations." The Dawes Act did not cover the Five Civilized Tribes, but under the Curtis Act of 1898 similar policies were applied to them.

Easterners and westerners generally welcomed the Dawes and Curtis acts, but for different reasons. The humanitarian reformers, with their assimilationist views, called the Dawes Act the "Emancipation Proclamation for the Indian." Westerners rejoiced because the laws reduced tribal holdings and allowed them to acquire additional Indian lands. For the Indians, the results were almost entirely negative. Government agents often prevented them from claiming the best lands for their individual plots. The long-term exemption of Indian lands from local taxation led several states to refuse to provide schools and other services to

Indians, and despite its promises, Congress did not come through with adequate funds to offset this loss.

As agencies of "civilization," too, the acts were failures. The tribes lost their culture and cohesion without many Indians becoming strong, self-sustaining individuals as, presumably, intended. Caught between two cultures, Indians often turned to drink, petty crime, and idleness. Though the twenty-five-year trust period written into the original laws supposedly protected the Indians from confidence men, the laws were amended so often that many Indians lost their property to speculators for a song. Between 1887 and 1934, Indian-owned lands were reduced from 139 million to 47 million acres. Without means or livelihoods, many Indians became charges on the public authorities.

Looking ahead, by the 1920s it had become clear to a number of white Americans that forced assimilation deprived the Indians of their heritage without providing a satisfactory alternative. Working through the American Indian Defense Association, the social reformer John Collier and his supporters demanded that the Dawes policy be replaced. The government should guarantee basic civil rights to Indians, confer limited self-government on the reservations, end paternalism, and encourage the preservation of Indian traditions and culture. Commissioner of Indian affairs after 1933, Collier secured passage of the Wheeler–Howard Act of 1934, which repealed the allotment policy, recognized the right of Indians to organize for "the purposes of local self-government and economic enterprise," and stated that the future goal of Indian education should be to "promote the study of Indian civilization, arts, crafts, skills, and traditions."

Passage of the act did not solve all the Indians' problems or satisfy all their grievances. Yet it could be said that mainstream America was finally beginning to reverse the damaging trends of the past.

■ THE MINING FRONTIER ■

There had been mining and mineral booms before in America—in California during the 1850s, and in the Pennsylvania oil regions a few years later. But none had been so extensive or would leave so deep an imprint on regional social development and on the collective American imagination as the post-Civil War far western mining frontier.

Mining Communities. The late 1850s spillover of prospectors from the California gold streams first reached north into British Columbia. In 1859 the search was deflected to the region around Pike's Peak in western Colorado. In a few months a new town, Denver, appeared in the shadow of the Rocky Mountains. Soon afterward two gold prospectors in northwestern Nevada Territory hit "pay dirt." Their find, called the Comstock Lode after a gabby drifter who claimed to be its discoverer, was one of the richest gold strikes on record. The district became an instant magnet for thousands of California miners, and Virginia City—a settlement of tents, lean-tos, and prefabricated frame structures—rose mushroom-like from the desert in a few weeks.

The Comstock Lode discovery was followed by strikes on the Snake River in northwestern Idaho. In 1863 gold was found at Last Chance Gulch in west-central Montana. The next strike was in the Black Hills of South Dakota during the 1870s. Coeur d'Alene in northern Idaho followed in the early 1880s. This was the last of the major gold rushes in the contiguous forty-eight states. But at the very end of the century fabulous finds would be made in the Canadian Yukon and in Alaska, marking the last episodes of the North American gold mining frontier.

The mining communities that grew up around the strikes have become a vivid part of American legend. They were places of great variety, where every nation, race, and class could be found. The California diggings, reported Louisa Clappe, were "a perambulating picture gallery" where one could hear English, French, Spanish, German, Italian, and many Indian tongues spoken on the streets. They were also violent. The gamblers and hangers-on who followed the gold frontier were often unruly dissolute men and women. But violence and crime also flowed from the refusal of the federal government to provide either laws or law enforcement. The western answer was the vigilance committee, a group of local worthies who, without benefit of legal trial, hunted down and hanged the worst of the troublemakers as an example to the rest.

Slow in providing law enforcement officers for the territories, the federal government was also remiss in responding to demands for statehood in the mining regions. When Congress failed to act on Colorado's statehood petition, settlers in 1859 organized the Territory of Jefferson with an elected governor and legislature. Congress rejected this initiative, and not until 1876, when the community was well beyond the frontier stage, did it admit Colorado to statehood.

Big Business and Mining.   The tent camps and the vigilance committees were only passing phases of the western mining boomtowns. In some cases the next stage was abandonment. In scores of communities, when the richer ores gave out, the miners, storekeepers, and camp followers departed, leaving ghost towns of rusting machinery, decaying buildings, and empty mine shafts. Many mining communities, however, became permanent towns and cities. Denver, Lewiston, Coeur d'Alene, Pueblo, and Butte developed into substantial places with schools, churches, opera houses, and police forces. The mining industry also stimulated the growth of regional supply, shipping, and outfitting centers such as Seattle, Spokane, and Tucson.

The change from raw mining camp to sedate city seldom took place without a major shift in the mining business that sustained the local economy. As in California in an earlier period, after the loose nuggets and flakes had been skimmed off by men panning the streams and washing earth through cradles, gold mining became a heavily capitalized industry that required deep shafts and expensive machinery.

Gold was not the only mineral that drew people and capital to the Last West. The region also was rich in silver, copper, lead, zinc, and other valuable metals. These ores required deep mines, rock crushers, and complex chemical

Creede, Colorado, a silver boom town in the Rockies, sprang up in a canyon so narrow there was only room for one main street. During the flush times of the early 1890s, Creede grew by several hundred people a day; by 1900 it was a virtual ghost town.

processes—operations that depended on heavy infusions of capital, trained mining engineers, technicians and chemists, and a permanent force of wage-earning miners and smelter workers.

The capital needed by the postpioneer mining industry was seldom available from local sources. Much of the costs of sinking shafts and erecting smelters and refineries in the fabulous Comstock Lode district, for example, came from San Francisco capitalists. These men extracted millions in profit from the Comstock lode, and with the proceeds built great mansions on Nob Hill overlooking San Francisco Bay. One Californian who made a fortune in Nevada silver was George Hearst, whose son, William Randolph, would become a powerful New York press lord at the end of the century. In the 1880s Meyer Guggenheim, a lace manufacturer of Philadelphia, began to invest in the Leadville silver district of Colorado and soon became a major economic force in the state and the West. In 1907 one of his sons, Simon Guggenheim, head of the "Smelter Trust," came to Washington as Republican Senator from Colorado. In Montana the copper kings—William A. Clark, Marcus Daly, and Frederick Heinze—built Butte into a major copper-smelting center. Clark represented local capital, but Daly was allied with the Anaconda Copper Company, an eastern corporation with many English investors. Phelps Dodge, a New York firm, owned large copper mines and refineries in Arizona.

Although outside control over local resources would later fan westerners' discontent, the opening of the western mines added enormously to the country's resources. By 1900 the United States was one of the world's largest producers of gold, silver, copper, lead, and zinc. The production of gold and silver would also have immense political repercussions. The flood of gold would facilitate the adoption of the international gold standard in the last half of the century. But at the same time, the even greater proportional increase in silver production would depress its price relative to gold and profoundly disturb the nation's monetary—and political—affairs.

■ THE CATTLE KINGDOM ■

Just east of the mining regions another economic frontier was taking shape. During the two decades that followed the Civil War, cattle raising became the basis of the Great Plains's economy, attracting eastern and even European investors. Even more than the mining frontier, the cattle kingdom would become an American legend.

Longhorns and Long Drives.   The Plains cattle industry originated in the Texas grasslands. Before the Civil War, Mexican ranchers had pastured immense herds of wild, rangy animals there. When Americans entered the south Texas area, they brought new breeds of cattle with them. These mingled with the Spanish-Mexican variety to produce the famed Texas longhorn, a wiry, resourceful creature that could survive winter on the open grasslands by digging through the snow with its sharp hooves to the nutritious dried grass beneath.

The Civil War cut off the Texas cattle industry from its major markets. During these fallow years the cattle ran wild on the Texas grasslands, and by 1866 there were an estimated 5 million head grazing on the Texas plains. Meanwhile, the rest of the country, having depleted its cattle stock to meet the Union army's needs, was starved for beef. In Texas cattle were selling for $4 a head, while in the eastern cities they were worth as much as $40 and $50.

Returning Confederate veterans were soon pondering ways to get Texas attle to eastern consumers. The answer seemed clear. By this time the Missouri Pacific Railroad had reached Sedalia, Missouri, 700 miles north of San Antonio, in the heart of the Texas cattle country. If cattle could be driven on the hoof to the railroad, they could then be shipped east. In March 1866 a group of Texas ranchers and Iowa and Kansas businessmen launched the first of the classic "long drives" of range cattle north to railhead to satisfy the eastern market for beef and hides.

The Texas cattle drives soon became annual affairs. In a standard drive, a half-dozen mounted "cowboys" under a "trail boss" guided each band of a thousand or so unruly longhorns across open country accompanied by "chuckwagons" to carry food and equipment and a "horse wrangler" to care for the mounts. The Sedalia Trail passed through Indian territory where resentful tribesmen often stampeded the herds. Missouri farmers feared that the invading longhorns carried the dread Texas fever and sometimes engaged in shootouts with the Texans. Despite these obstacles, cattle that got through sold for $35 a head in Sedalia, providing a clear profit for the ranchers.

It did not take long for an enterprising businessman to see how the system could be improved. In 1867 a cattle dealer from Illinois, Joseph G. McCoy, established a depot at Abilene in central Kansas along the Kansas-Pacific Railroad. There ranchers could pen their animals and arrange for their sale to eastern buyers. Between 1867 and 1871 some 1.5 million head of Texas cattle were driven to Abilene for shipment east. When the area around Abilene became too densely populated, the drive was deflected farther west to Ellsworth on the Kansas-Pacific line. Later the "cow towns" of Newton and Dodge City were developed along the Santa Fe Railroad.

The Kansas cow towns, like the mining camps, were rowdy places. It was hard to maintain law and order among the transient "cow poke" population. Cowboys were a diverse lot of ex-Confederate and ex-Union soldiers, former slaves, Mexicans, and Indians who rode the range twelve hours a day looking for strays. At spring roundup they worked hard roping and branding the unmarked calves. On the long drives they spent as many as four months in the saddle, keeping the cattle moving and preventing stampedes. The work was dirty, hard, lonely, and unhealthy. No wonder that when paid several months' wages in Dodge City or Abilene at the end of the long drive, cowboys often went on roaring sprees—drinking, gambling, debauching, and sometimes shooting up the town.

Boom and Bust.   As the railroads penetrated farther into the central and northern Plains, thousands of Texas cattle were driven north to stock the newly accessible region. By the early 1870s these regions were covered with ranches.

During the late 1870s and early 1880s, the range cattle industry of Colorado, Wyoming, Montana, Idaho, and the western Dakotas relied on free use of the public land and on weather mild enough for the cattle to graze outdoors on the open range all year. The cattle used the public domain at no cost to the ranchers, who, in effect, were subsidized by the government with free land, grass, and water. All the ranchers had to do was wait as their cattle multiplied and put on weight. In the spring they rounded up their herds and shipped the mature animals east for a good profit.

For a decade the cattle kingdom flourished, sustained by high prices for beef and low cost of production. "Cotton was once crowned king," exulted a contemporary western editor, "but grass is now." The free, adventurous, and individualistic life of the Plains rancher proved a powerful magnet for outsiders. Easterners, like the impetuous young New Yorker, Theodore Roosevelt, bought land on the Plains and became ranchers. So did Europeans, especially Englishmen and Scots. And many outsiders who did not come themselves sent their capital. In 1883 twenty cattle-raising corporations capitalized at $12 million were formed in Wyoming alone.

By 1885 farsighted people began to suspect trouble ahead. Each year the range grass became sparser as more and more cattle grazed the Plains. To prevent personal disaster, ranchers began to fence off areas with barbed wire (invented in 1874) though this was illegal on publicly owned land. They also formed livestock associations to regulate the number of cattle grazed, exclude intruders, and protect the herds against rustlers and wolves. Despite these efforts, by the

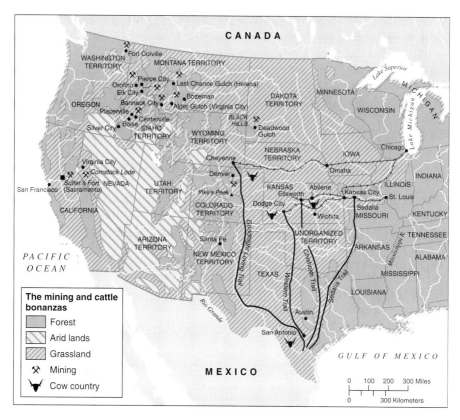

The Cattle Kingdom

mid-1880s the Plains were overstocked. So numerous were cattle shipments that prices began to tumble.

Then nature struck. In 1886 the unusually mild winter weather the northern Plains had enjoyed for a decade abruptly changed. That summer was hot and dry; by fall the cattle, lacking decent forage, were weak. In November the blizzards came. January 1887 was the worst winter month that anyone could remember, with record snows and temperatures dipping at times to seventy degrees below zero. Thousands of cattle were buried alive by the drifts. Others froze to death standing upright. Unable to get to the grass beneath the snow, crazed animals poured into the streets of several Plains towns and tried to eat everything in sight. When the terrible winter ended, hundreds of cattle carcasses were carried down the streams by the spring freshets, bearing with them the fortunes of their owners.

The cattle industry survived on the Plains, but it was never the same. Many of the cattle corporations went bankrupt. Now under the control of local people, the industry was transformed. Even more land than before was fenced in. Ranchers began to raise hay for winter feed and replace the wiry longhorns with Herefords and other breeds that would produce more meat per animal. Some ranchers, recognizing that sheep were hardier than cattle, turned to wool production, though others fought the sheep invasion as a threat. Meanwhile, wheat farmers began to intrude from the east, driving the cattlemen into the more isolated portions of the Plains. The ranching industry survived, but as a smaller, more localized, and more rational industry than during the heyday of the open range.

■ WESTERN LAND POLICIES ■

Cattle ranchers were not the only people to capitalize on liberal federal land policies. Almost all the land in the Last West was public domain, acquired by war, purchase, or treaty. From 1862 to the end of the century, Congress gave away or sold vast amounts of these western lands under inconsistent policies designed to satisfy a variety of interests. In the end the small western farmers who were supposed to benefit from these policies often felt betrayed. By the end of the century many of them were convinced that outside speculators and the government's remoteness from western realities were responsible.

Land Acts of the 1860s. The passage of the 1862 Homestead Act fulfilled the dream of Jeffersonian agrarians by providing that any adult head of family or person over 21 who was a citizen or intended to become a citizen, could acquire, free of cost, 160 acres of surveyed federal land if they resided on the land for five years and "improved" it. In reality, however, only a fraction of the immense public domain ever got into the hands of small farmers free of charge. At the same time it was giving land to bona fide settlers under the Homestead Act, the government was distributing large parcels for other public purposes. The 1862 Morrill Land Grant College Act conferred on each state a portion of the public domain in proportion to its congressional representation to be used for state-run agricultural colleges. Most of the land went to populous eastern and midwestern states, where agriculture was subordinate to industry, and then sold or leased. The railroad land grants of the 1860s and 1870s were another instance of land excluded from homestead entry. In addition the federal government handed out land to encourage the construction of wagon roads and gave away millions of acres to states that entered the Union after 1862. Nor did it cease outright land sales. In 1862 some 84 million acres of federal lands were on the market for customers with cash.

Spokesmen for small farmer groups complained that free homesteads were largely an illusion; much of the best land was available only by cash purchase. And they were right. Between 1862 and 1904 only some 147 million acres of free land passed to farmers under the Homestead Act; in that same period more than 610 million acres were sold.

Acts Tailored to Western Realities. The Homestead Act took no account of the special land problems of the arid Great Plains and Great Basin. The 160-acre allotment was too small for the "dry farming" cultivator on the eastern edge of the Plains; for the rancher who grazed hungry cattle in the drier portions of the region, it was impossible; each animal required 40 acres of grazing land to survive.

Following the Civil War, Congress passed a series of measures to deal with the special land problems of the West. One, the Timber Culture Act of 1873, allowed farmers with 160-acre homesteads to take out papers on another 160 acres of adjacent land if they agreed to plant trees on some portion of it. Trees, contemporaries believed, would encourage rain and so make the plains less arid. In reality, the tree-planting provision was largely ignored; the effect was to give Plains farmers about 10 million additional acres of dry land.

The Desert Land Act of 1877 was also designed to accommodate the land laws to the arid West. Most scholars, however, consider it a giveaway to the cattle companies. Under its provisions lands could be bought for a down payment of 25 cents per acre if the purchaser agreed to irrigate a full section (640 acres) within three years. After meeting the requirement the purchaser could pay an additional dollar per acre and own the whole parcel. Unfortunately, the law allowed purchasers to assign the acreage to others even before they had met the irrigation requirement. Large tracts thus passed to the cattle companies with few public benefits.

The Timber and Stone Act of 1878 also violated the spirit of the Homestead Act. The law applied to lands "unfit for cultivation" and "valuable chiefly for timber or stone." After declaring that the land in question contained no useful minerals, any citizen could buy up to 160 acres at $2.50 an acre. Few small farmers benefited from the law. Instead, through various sorts of fraud, large tracts ended up in the hands of timber companies.

In dealing with the climatic realities of the arid West, federal policy inevitably reflected the knowledge and values of the day. Today we are skeptical of large dams and irrigation systems. They may for a time "make the deserts bloom," but their long-term effects on desert ecology are often disastrous and, in many cases, they produce only temporary benefits. After years of being soaked with alkaline river water, the irrigated soil becomes chemically poisoned and unproductive.

Still, we should not blame our forebears for what they could not know. In the National Reclamation, or Newlands, Act of 1902 the federal government believed it was adding to the West's, and the nation's, wealth. And, in the short run, it was. The law established a reclamation fund from the proceeds of federal land sales in the arid states and territories, to be used for building dams, water channels, and other irrigation facilities in these states. Under the act a score of dams were constructed and thousands of acres were irrigated and reclaimed from the desert. Less successful than the engineering feats were the social results. Many settlers found that they could not pay the government's charges. Much of the land passed to large holders, despite periodic government efforts to provide relief for the hard-pressed small farmers.

■ FARMING IN THE LAST WEST ■

Indians, miners, and cattlemen could all show how imposed eastern policies were inappropriate to western needs. For the Indians, certainly, the mistakes were devastating. But ultimately it was the farmers' grievances that became the most unsettling to the nation.

Plains Agriculture. The Great Plains presented special difficulties for the would-be farmer. In most places rainfall was sparse and new agricultural approaches were required. In some regions pumps, powered by the unobstructed breezes of the flat plains, could tap underground aquifers for water. During the 1880s windmills raised on pylons became a characteristic feature of the Plains landscape. Another solution was "dry farming," a system based on planting seeds far apart and covering plant roots with a dust mulch after each rainfall to preserve moisture. Dry farmers also adopted new drought-resistant grain types, some brought from Russia.

Even in regions of adequate rainfall, transplanted easterners faced difficulties not encountered at home. Given the absence of stone and timber, what could settlers use to fence their fields and build their barns and dwellings? During the 1860s agricultural experts touted hedges as fencing for cultivated fields. But before hedging could come into wide use, barbed wire appeared. A barbed-wire fence required only a few timber uprights; the rest was iron wire, a few rolls of which could enclose hundreds of acres. One contemporary listed the advantages of barbed wire: It "takes no room, exhausts no soil, shades no vegetation, is proof against high winds, makes no snowdrifts, and is both durable and cheap."

To solve the shortages in housing material, early Plains settlers used squares of sod cut from the thick Plains turf. These were piled up to make walls along the edges of deep excavations in the ground that served as basements. The roof of such a house was also sod, placed on brush and cottonwood rafters. Warm in winter and cool in summer, these half-buried structures were also dirty, and during heavy rains leaked badly. Yet they served some families for many years and were even used for schoolhouses and other public buildings. Eventually, when the railroads came, timber from the East and Far West made frame structures possible. In time the houses of the Plains began to resemble those in the Midwest.

The Plains environment presented still other problems. In 1874 swarms of grasshoppers descended on the region from the Dakotas to Texas, consuming grain, vegetables, bark, clothes, and even the handles of plows and pitchforks. During the 1870s and early 1880s, however, rainfall was generally sufficient in the region, and with the confinement of the Indians to reservations and the arrival of the railroads, people flocked to western Kansas, Nebraska, and the Dakotas to grow grain for the East and Europe. Then the late 1880s ushered in a decade of extremely dry conditions. Crops drooped and died, and whatever survived the parching winds was consumed by insects. Farmers and their families fled the

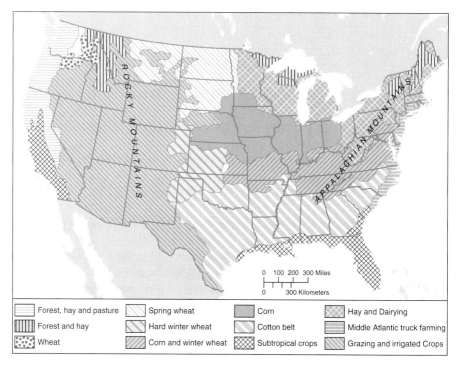

Agricultural Regions of the United States

searing sun during the early 1890s and returned east with the sides of their wagons sardonically inscribed: "In God We Trusted; In Kansas We Busted!"

Yet many farmers persisted and ultimately prospered. Once labor shortages—another chronic problem on the Plains—had been solved by the invention of special harvesting and threshing machines, Plains farming became enormously productive. It was extensive agriculture that cultivated vast acreages using little labor. It focused on wheat, the crop best suited to grasslands and, due to its durability, to production in regions far from consumers. By 1899 the United States was producing over 600 million bushels of wheat a year, much of it from the Great Plains. In 1870 the wheat belt had been centered in the older Midwest. By 1899 Minnesota, North Dakota, South Dakota, and Kansas were among the top five wheat producers.

Pacific Coast Agriculture. As the Plains became the nation's wheat belt the Pacific Coast emerged as the nation's fruit and vegetable belt. Taking advantage of the region's mild climate, Oregon began to supply the San Francisco market with apples, pears, peaches, plums, and grapes. In Washington the arrival of the Northern Pacific Railroad in the 1880s stimulated the production of apples and pears in the state's eastern valleys. Meanwhile, California was developing into a significant specialty agricultural region. Grapes had been grown there long before Americans arrived. By 1900 California produced 19 million gallons of wine, over 80 percent of American output. In the 1870s Brazilian navel oranges were introduced on irrigated fields in southern California. When refrigerated railcars became available in the 1880s, navels picked during the early winter could be shipped all the way to the East Coast. Summer-ripening Valencia oranges, introduced somewhat later, enabled the growers to produce year-round.

The citrus industry at first was plagued by haphazard marketing. Shipments spoiled or got lost; at times the market was glutted, at other times undersupplied. To deal with these problems, in 1893 the growers organized the Southern California Fruit Exchange, which later became the California Fruit Growers' Exchange and marketed its product under the brand name Sunkist. The Exchange brought stability to the industry.

■ FARM DISCONTENT AND WESTERN REVOLT ■

In quantity, acreage, output per person and per acre, the advances of American agriculture were spectacular. Largely because of the mechanized farms of the Great Plains, wheat production tripled between 1860 and 1899. In the older Midwest, states such as Illinois and Iowa shifted from wheat to hogs and cattle, feeding them on the country's huge corn harvests—840 million bushels of corn in 1860, 2.7 billion bushels in 1900. In cotton and livestock the increases were equally dramatic. The nation's farm labor force continued to rise in absolute numbers until 1910, but the increase in farmers was far smaller than the expansion in their output, for new technology, new plant science, the land-grant colleges, and the Department of Agriculture all helped to increase productivity per capita at a rapid pace. The result was that the United States became an agricultural horn of plenty, capable of producing cheap grain, meat, and fiber, not only for its own exploding urban population, but also for much of the industrializing Atlantic world.

Yet another, darker tale competed with this agricultural success story: Post-Civil War American farmers felt oppressed, exploited, and ill-used by the rich and powerful residing in the eastern and midwestern cities.

Farm Problems. According to farm spokespersons, farmers were victimized by bankers and mortgage companies that kept interest rates high and squeezed farmers and other borrowers and debtors through "hard money" policies that restricted the country's money supply and relentlessly forced down prices. The typical American farm, they claimed, was mortgaged to the hilt, and the money-lenders and bankers showed no mercy in foreclosing when the farmer could not pay. The prices of the goods that cultivators bought were kept artificially high by tariffs and business monopoly practices, whereas prices they received for their unprotected crops fell steadily. Middlemen—bankers, millers, grain elevator operators—skimmed off profits, leaving little for farmers. Beyond these economic grievances, spokespersons for "agrarianism" expressed fears that those who "fed them all," the nation's cultivators, were losing influence and the new "money power" was in the driver's seat.

Today, economic historians consider the charges leveled by farm advocates during these last years of the nineteenth century exaggerated. For one thing, they note, farmers did not all fare alike economically. Pacific Coast farmers prospered by adopting fruit and vegetable crops. Prairie farmers of Iowa and Illinois switched from wheat to corn and hogs and made decent profits. East Coast and Great Lakes truck and dairy farmers found profitable markets in the cities.

As for claims of financial oppression, this too may be overstated. Interest rates were higher in the West and South—the country's prime farm areas—than in the Northeast. But this difference can be explained by the shortage of savings in the two staple-crop regions and the higher risks of farming compared to manufacturing or commerce. Nor were American farm borrowers poor peasants turning to moneylenders to stave off starvation. Most of the money that farmers borrowed was for barns, fences, plows, harvesters, and other items needed to increase productivity and income. The loans were, in effect, no different from the loans of any other small businessperson. Nor were the oppressive farm mortgages as universal as the critics claimed. Even in the wheat belt, no more than 39 percent of the farms were burdened with mortgages in 1890, though the figure was higher in Kansas and Nebraska. As for the bankers' wicked urge to foreclose, this was not common. The banks and the mortgage companies that lent farmers money were not interested in acquiring farm acreage; they often extended the repayment terms of loans more than once to avoid having to foreclose.

The claims that falling prices were contrived deliberately by a cabal of bankers and money power monopolists to squeeze the nation's "producers" are equally exaggerated. All prices fell during the generation following the Civil War. This meant the prices the farmers paid as well as those they received. There is no good evidence that the "terms of trade" between the producers of food and fiber and the providers of the services and manufactured goods that they used shifted significantly against the nation's tillers in these years. Moreover, the price declines were not only an American phenomenon; they were common to the entire world. If there was a conspiracy to force down prices, the conspiracy was evidently worldwide in its scope.

Nor is it clear that monetary forces were responsible for the great deflation of the late nineteenth century. This was an era when real costs were going down as a result of new technology and new management techniques. Even the middlemen's real costs declined due to greater efficiency. When, in the 1890s, the Russians sought to make their grain more competitive in the world market, they sent a delegation to the United States to learn how American brokers and grain handlers managed to get the American wheat crop to market at such low cost. Even scholars who believe that late-nineteenth-century price declines can be traced to an excessively slow increase in the money supply doubt that this was deliberately engineered by a cabal of conspirators.

Agrarianism.   And yet we are left with the reality of turbulent farm discontent in the generation following the Civil War. How can we explain it?

First, let us note that the agrarian insurgency of the period was confined primarily to the wheat- and cotton-growing areas. As we noted, dairy farmers, corn-hog farmers, and truck farmers who sold their products to domestic consumers in the fast-growing cities were generally proof against the insurgent appeal. Though their prices declined like all others, they were more stable than many.

Instability, indeed, is one possible answer to the riddle of insurgency in the wheat and cotton belts. Grain and cotton farmers were subject to greater uncertainty than other producers. These cultivators sold their crops in a world market where they competed fiercely with other nations. By the end of the nineteenth century the entire world was knit together in a single market for nonperishable agricultural goods, and prices were established by countless impersonal transactions between buyers and sellers. The system was a tremendous boon to consumers. Everywhere they benefited from the declining cost of food and fabric. But it produced disturbing price fluctuations. A bumper wheat crop in the American Plains could be expected to lower world grain prices. But it might be more than offset by a dearth in, say, Argentina, that would push prices up. And, of course, the reverse might also occur: An American farmer, expecting good prices after a short crop, might be bitterly disappointed if Australia or Ukraine had a bounteous harvest. The net effect was that farmers found themselves on a roller coaster over which they could exercise no control. The villains were actually impersonal market forces, but these were not as satisfactory as flesh-and-blood villains of the sort that farmers saw or heard about every day—the bankers, railroad officials, politicians, and farm machinery manufacturers. In some ways the late-nineteenth-century farmer's plight and response resemble that of many American workers and manufacturers today confronting the globalization of the world economy for industrial goods.

Clearly, American farmers as a group faced difficult problems adjusting to the demands and circumstances of a new industrialized, urbanized era. Besides price instability, one cannot deny the distress of sharecroppers in the South, penalized often by a vicious social and racial system that placed them at the mercy of powerful and privileged planters and landowners. Land in America, moreover, bore a disproportionate share of the national tax burden; personal property and personal income were lightly taxed or entirely tax-exempt. Then there was the legitimate concern for transportation gouging. Though railroad rates generally went down, in noncompetitive areas, usually in the West and South, the railroad managers tried to make up for the "cutthroat" competition on major trunk lines by charging all that the local traffic would bear. Finally, as fuel for farm discontent, agriculture as a way of life had lost standing. More and more the cities had seized on the imaginations of Americans. This explained, in part, the exodus of young people from the rural areas. It also accounted for the increasing references to "rubes," "hayseeds," and "appleknockers" in the metropolitan press. As the nation urbanized, American farmers felt more and more disesteemed and neglected.

Moved by such forces and feelings, post-Civil War farm advocates, playing on resonant Jeffersonian chords, sought to create a social philosophy based on farm distress and rural rights that can best be labeled agrarianism.

Agrarianism exalted the farmer as the only true citizen, the backbone of the nation, the heart of the "producing masses." Agrarians gradually expanded the concept to include the ever-growing number of wage earners, and some sought to construct a farmer–labor alliance of producers, whose plight was said to be shared by the nation as a whole. On the other side, agrarians personalized the enemy as the "money power" or the "bloated middlemen." These "plutocrats," they said, had seized control of the economy and through various hidden financial arrangements had imposed their will on the nation. The United States was fast becoming the land of a rich few and an impoverished, exploited, and powerless many.

Though agrarian advocates sought to universalize their protest, much of their indictment had a sectional edge. Both the Great Plains and the South regarded themselves as colonies in bondage to the "East." It was the East that was the source of credit, and it was eastern moneylenders and bankers who charged the high interest rates the "producing sections" paid. The railroads had their headquarters in Boston, New York, Philadelphia, or Chicago, and it was in these eastern and large midwestern cities that the freight rates that squeezed cotton and wheat farmers were set. Easterners—or Europeans—also owned the land and marketed the crops, the agrarians said. The farm-machinery manufacturers, the barbed-wire producers, and the other industrialists who made the equipment western and southern farmers needed to survive were easterners. Furthermore, the East dominated the major political parties and through them the government. Policies regarding the Indians, finance, money, tariffs, and land were not made by the people of the West and South, who were most directly concerned. They were made by the representatives of the eastern "money interests," who sought only their own gain, or by eastern reformers who did not know the problem first hand.

Whether true or false, whether exaggerated or exact, the agrarian indictment of plutocracy and the East had become a powerful political force by the end of the century. The agrarian reformers were never enemies of private property and the profit system. Their complaint was with the way capitalism had supposedly been rigged in favor of the few and against the many. Their desire was not to end profit and property but to make sure that the benefits of both were more widely distributed among the masses of the people.

■ THE GRANGERS ■

In the early 1870s restless farmers flocked to local "Granges" of the Patrons of Husbandry, a fraternal order founded in 1876. At first the Granges were primarily social and educational organizations. Farm life was isolated and lonely, and farmers and their wives welcomed the chance to socialize and listen to lectures at the local Grange hall. The Granges soon became politically active. Joining with eastern merchants and businesspeople who also disliked the railroads' high and often arbitrary freight charges, in farm belt states including Illinois, Iowa, Wisconsin, and Minnesota, the Grangers were able to enact railroad and grain elevator regulatory laws.

The Patrons were also active in various cooperative ventures to improve the economic standing of farmers. In several midwestern states Grange agents negotiated purchases of large quantities of supplies from merchants or manufacturers at special low prices. In 1872 a group of merchants formed Montgomery Ward and Company for the specific purpose of dealing with the Grangers. Efforts to produce farm machinery cooperatively failed, however; the managers of Grange manufacturing enterprises lacked experience and were unable to meet the aggressive competition of established private firms.

The Alliances.   By the late 1870s the Grange had ceased to be anything more than a social-educational organization, but by this time a more militant force had appeared.

The Alliance movement began in the mid-1870s when small rancher-farmers in central Texas organized a secret club to catch horse thieves, collect stray cattle, and fight the large ranchers who ignored the rights of their smaller neighbors. The organization soon spread to the rest of the state and grew in strength and ambition. In 1886 the Texas Alliance, borrowing ideas from the Greenback party of 1884, adopted a platform of opposition to landholding by foreigners, for stiff taxes on railroads, and for abundant paper money. Under Charles W. Macune the Alliance expanded into a regional Southern Alliance that incorporated the Arkansas Wheel and a large Colored Alliance composed of black tenant farmers and sharecroppers. By 1890 the Southern Alliance had a million members. Farm discontent in the prairies and Great Plains led to similar efforts. By 1890 the Northwest Alliance, organized a decade earlier, had spread to fifteen states, with particularly heavy concentration of membership in Kansas, Nebraska, the Dakotas, and Minnesota.

Toward the end of the 1880s the Alliances began to emphasize politics rather than cooperatives. Alliance-affiliated candidates won election as either Democrats or Republicans to state legislatures in the South and West. In several states they captured one of the major parties and compelled it to endorse farmers' programs. Alliance-controlled state legislatures enacted some legislation regulating railroads and businesses, but these measures were largely ineffective. Alliance-dominated state governments were frequently led by political novices who were easily out-maneuvered by the seasoned politicians of the regular parties. Frustrated by their initial experiences with politics, Alliance leaders concluded that the fault lay in relying on the Democrats and Republicans. Instead, the farmers should organize their own party, one that would be free of the old-line politicos, who seemed indifferent at heart to the needs of rural people.

■ CONCLUSIONS ■

The development of the last American frontier made an enormous difference in the nation's history. The exploitation of the trans-Missouri West added immense resources to the country's economic base. The cattle and mining frontiers also supplied raw material for American literature and legend. For the American Indian, development of this area was the final defeat in almost three centuries of bitter conflict with people of Old World origins.

The last West was also the focus for the last truly serious threat of sectional disunity. Along with the cotton South, it was indeed in some ways a colony of the Northeast. Eastern money controlled its resources; eastern attitudes affected its Indian policy; eastern politicians decided its political fate. By the end of the century, moreover, western and southern grievances had created a sense of apartness, of distinctiveness, that contributed to a mighty political revolt. This sense was reinforced and given focus by a group of agrarian thinkers who drew their ideas from the Jefferson-Jackson tradition of the early Republic. Scholars may argue over the validity of western grievances or whether western leaders properly identified the causes of their section's difficulties. But there can be no question that by 1890 in the West and the South a powerful wave of discontent was gathering force. Before the new century began, it would sweep over the nation, threatening to push aside long-standing political alignments and shift the country's balance of power.

Online Resources

"We have Got a Good Friend in John Collier: A Taos Pueblo Tries to Seal the Indian New Deal"
http://historymatters.gmu.edu/search.taf?_function=
detail&layout_0uid1-32811&_UserReferA24A66F5FFD82CB6BFDCC596
In a letter to his friend John Collier, Taos Pueblo Indian Antonio Lunan describes his progress in persuading the Indians to accept New Deal federal policy. He describes the Indians' questions and concerns.

Little Bighorn Battlefield Archeology and History
http://www.mwac.gov.libi/
This site provides information about this well-known battle though narratives, a chronology, photos, and artwork. Artifacts from the battlefield lend insights about warfare and the people who waged it.

California Notes: Museum of the City of San Francisco
http://www.sfmuseum.org/hist9/turrillgold.html
Providing detailed explanations of the terminology and technology, this site details the process of gold mining in California in the late 1800s. Links to the San Francisco History Index lead to a collection of sketches and primary-source documents about the excavations and miners.

Photographs of the American West, 1861–1912
http://www.nara.gov/nara/nn/nns/amwest.html
See how people transformed the West into an organization of settlements through this large collection of photographs whose subjects include training-at Indian schools, the first continental railroad, and scenes of life on the homestead.

20

THE GILDED AGE

How "Gilded" Was It?

1851	The YMCA is established in the United States
1858	The National Association of Baseball Players is founded
1859	Darwin's *The Origin of Species* published in England
1870–82	Printing process improves, enabling newspapers to print more news daily; The Associated Press and the United Press are founded; Pulitizer begins yellow journalism in the *New York World*
1870–90	American school of art, led by Winslow Homer
1873	The Coinage Age ("Crime of 73") congress drops silver from coinage system
1875	The Whiskey Ring scandal
1876	American Library Association founded, lobbies for support free public libraries
1877	Rutherford B. Hayes is elected president in Compromise of 1877
1878	The Bland–Allison Act
1879	The United States returns to gold standard
1880s	More than 80 percent of the electorate votes in presidential elections
1880	James Garfield elected president; William Le Baron Jenney designs first skyscraper
1881–82	The Star Route scandals
1881	Garfield is assassinated; Chester A. Arthur becomes president
1883	The Pendleton Act establishes Civil Service Commission; Brooklyn Bridge is completed; Metropolitan Opera House opens
1884	Mark Twain's *Huckleberry Finn* published; Grover Cleveland elected president
1886	*Wabash, St. Louis and Pacific Railway Co. v. Illinois*
1887	The Interstate Commerce Act creates the Interstate Commerce Commission (ICC)
1888	Benjamin Harrison elected president
1890	Sherman Silver Purchase Act; Sherman Antitrust Act; McKinley Tariff Act
1892	People's party (Populist) formed; Grover Cleveland elected president—second time
1893	The Chicago World's Fair; Financial panic leads to depression
1894	The Wilson–Gorman Tariff Act

1895	Stephan Crane's *The Red Badge of Courage* published
1896	First showing of a commercial motion picture in a legitimate theater; William McKinley elected president, defeating William Jennings Bryan
1897	Almost half of federal employees are under Civil Service rules
1900	Theodore Dreiser's *Sister Carrie* published; Tin Pan Alley marks beginning of popular music; Frank Lloyd Wright begins functional modernism in architecture
1903	First World Series
1904	Pragmastist philosopher John Dewey changes educational system; The Henri Ashcan school marks trend toward modernism in painting
1913	Armory exhibition shows Cézanne, Van Gogh, Picasso, Matisse, Duchamp in US
1915	Over 80 percent of all children attend school due to compulsory laws

"Golden ages" are eras of cultural creativity, high ethical ideals, and benevolent political relationships. By contrast the generation following the Civil War has acquired the name the *Gilded age,* referring to a thin veneer of gilt applied to a base metal.

The disparaging label comes from an 1873 novel written by Mark Twain and Charles Dudley Warner. *The Gilded Age* deals with types who came to the top of the social pile in the post-Civil War era. The characters are self-seeking, insincere, corrupt, hypocritical, coarse, materialistic. They seem to epitomize the new era when greed, gain, and good times dominated the nation's political, economic, and cultural life.

Mark Twain and his collaborator were writing primarily about the tawdry, mercenary national politics of the day. Other observers of the post-Civil War years were just as harsh about the cultural scene. In 1874 Edwin L. Godkin, a transplanted Anglo-Irishman who edited the prestigious *Nation,* declared that his adopted country was a "chromo civilization"; like the inexpensive, popular prints of the day (chromolithographs), its colors were gaudy and false.

How "gilded" was the political and cultural life of America in the generation following Appomattox? Did it, perhaps, contain some nuggets of real gold?

■ POLITICS IN THE GILDED AGE ■

American voters during the Gilded Age were passionate political participants. Voter turnouts during these years were enormous. Except in the South, where thousands of black voters were effectively deprived of the right to vote after 1877, a far larger proportion of the eligible voters cast ballots than today. In

1896, for example, the turnout was more than 95 percent in the five states of the Old Northwest.

These citizens were steadfast partisans. In those years, "Independents"—voters without party allegiances—were treated with contempt as people without spirit or commitment. Few voters were willing to accept the label. Obviously Americans considered it important whether one party or the other won. But we must ask why?

Politics as Recreation.   One nontrivial explanation for the public's interest in politics was its entertainment value. Americans of this era enjoyed relatively little leisure time. Besides the Fourth of July and Washington's Birthday, there were few legal holidays. A political rally gave working people one of their few occasions to take time off. Few employers dared say no when an American male citizen asserted his God-given right to hear a political speech. Besides an excuse to avoid work, political rallies were diverting. In the absence of television, motion pictures, and professional athletics (except baseball, already the national game), politics provided lively amusement. One reporter described a Republican political rally in Cambridge City, Indiana, in 1876 as "a spectacle no foreign fiesta could equal." Even though most people could not hear the distant speaker, General Benjamin Harrison, they were perfectly content, for it was "the holiday diversion, the crowds, the bravery of the procession, the music and the fun of the occasion they came chiefly to enjoy."

In part the excitement and fun derived from the closeness of the contests, which, like a tight baseball pennant race, brought out the partisans of both sides in record numbers. Between the 1870s and the late 1890s, neither party could dominate national politics. True, every president during these years except Grover Cleveland was a Republican, but almost all federal elections were close. In 1880 Republican James Garfield defeated his Democratic opponent, Winfield Scott Hancock, by only 7,000 popular votes. Four years later Cleveland, a Democrat, defeated James G. Blaine by under 25,000 votes out of 10 million cast. Only for three short periods during this era did the same party control the presidency and both houses of Congress. In only one midterm national election between 1878 and 1888 inclusively did more than 2 percentage points separate the total Democratic and Republican votes. When, after 1896, the Republicans forged far ahead of their Democratic rivals in presidential races and the excitement declined, voter turnouts dropped off sharply.

Like all exciting and well-patronized spectator sports, Gilded Age politics had to have its stars, its heroes, its villains. Many were colorful characters. There was the magnetic, charming, combative, brilliant, and corrupt "plumed knight," James G. Blaine, Republican senator from Maine. His sworn enemy from New York was Roscoe Conkling, a strutting "turkey-gobbler," who wore yellow shoes, scarlet coat, waistcoat with gold lace, and green trousers. Thomas B. Reed, the 300-pound-speaker of the House, tossed off aphorisms as funny as Mark Twain's: "A statesman is a dead politician"; "One with God is always a majority, but many a martyr has been burned at the stake while the votes were being counted." Men like these alternately delighted and dismayed the voting public and helped sustain the enthusiasm for Gilded Age politics.

Politics as Morality Play.   The metaphor of Gilded Age politics as a sport is useful up to a point. To some Americans, however—the so-called "best men"— politics during these years seemed rather to be a profound moral drama, a contest between good and evil. The evil was personified by the political rogues who had risen to the top after the Civil War and had perverted the once-virtuous republic. The good was personified by men like themselves—disinterested, dedicated, scrupulous, and expert, who wished only the public good and who, if allowed to govern, would restore America to a state of grace.

Almost all the "best men" were young. Many came from the country's most distinguished families: Charles Francis Adams, Jr., and his younger brother, Henry, were the grandsons of one president and great-grandsons of another. Several, however—such as the righteous Carl Schurz and the self-righteous E. L. Godkin—were self-made or foreign-born. Almost all were people of cultivation and refinement. They were never more than a small minority, but they were an influential group. Through the pages of Edwin L. Godkin's *Nation* and other journals of criticism and opinion, their views entered the homes of the educated middle class. The independents became a sort of conscience for the country, and few well-read Americans could entirely resist the feeling that what they supported was virtuous and what they opposed evil.

Corruption.   The "best men" believed that both parties were corrupt, and almost alone among the politically active people of the era, they voted for candidates and platforms rather than parties and gloried in being "independent." Their tone was one of almost constant outrage—an attitude that often amused the general public. One subscriber to the independent *New York Evening Post* noted that she always felt safe with the paper on her doorstep: "It just lay there and growled all night."

However exaggerated or humorless, this indignation had much to feed on. Scandal after scandal marred state and national politics in the Gilded Age. In many states rings of dishonest businessmen allied themselves with corrupt politicians to achieve their private ends. In New York the Erie Ring of Jay Gould and his allies bought and sold legislators like cattle. In Pennsylvania it was said that when Thomas A. Scott, president of the Pennsylvania Railroad, finished his business with the state government, the legislature at Harrisburg adjourned. At the federal level the Whiskey Ring, an alliance of federal officials and distillers, bilked the treasury of millions of dollars in revenue taxes. In 1881–1882 the federal authorities uncovered a gang of Post Office personnel that awarded generous contracts to private parties to deliver mail to remote areas (the "Star Routes") in return for kickbacks.

Corruption spread even to elections. Every year, following some local or national political contest, the newspapers carried long accounts of bribery, ballot box stuffing, illegal voting by aliens, and the use of "floaters," who, to tip a close election, crossed state or county lines to vote illegally. Most of the electoral chicanery took place in the cities, where the foreign-born were often blamed. But in fact, one of the most flagrant instances of chronic electoral dishonesty in this era occurred in Adams County, Ohio, a rural community composed mostly of old-stock Americans where virtually the entire voting population sold their votes to the highest bidder. Given the near-equal strength of parties, it is likely that more than one presidential election was won by voting fraud.

The Spoils System.　Besides outright corruption, the independents also deplored the spoils system, or patronage system, which had emerged during the 1820s and 1830s but came to full flower during the Gilded Age.

The practice grew out of a problem that Americans have never fully solved: how to pay for party government. Many today are still concerned that parties are financed by the rich and the powerful to the detriment of the common public good.

Under the Gilded Age spoils system, parties were in effect financed by the government, largely in the form of job patronage. And vast amounts of patronage were available. Between 1865 and 1891 the federal payroll expanded from 53,000 to 166,000 employees. Even the lowest-paid federal workers earned from two to three times the annual income of privately employed unskilled workers, and they normally spent only eight hours a day at their jobs, in contrast with the ten- to twelve-hour workdays common in private business.

Men and women, not surprisingly, eagerly sought federal employment. Would-be officeholders worked hard for political candidates and expected patronage appointments in return. Once on the job, appointees were willing to contribute further effort and a portion of their salaries ("assessments") to keep their party in office lest a victorious opposition deprive them of their positions.

The system was wasteful and often inefficient. Although government was becoming ever more complex and technical, the spoils system made flattery, party loyalty, and political know-how the sole measures of merit. Moreover, when competent people did gain office, they seldom kept their jobs long enough to learn their duties and perfect their skills. At the beginning of each administration the civil service, and with it the whole federal government, was immobilized while the president sorted out the patronage claims of party supporters all over the country. The spoils system also encouraged outright corruption. Men and women bribed influential politicians to get choice jobs and even advertised in the newspapers their willingness to pay cash to obtain federal employment.

The independents demanded civil service reform that would substitute merit (determined by competitive examination) for party loyalty, and tenure in office for constant replacement. But the spoils system was so deeply rooted in American politics that it was difficult to eradicate. Then, in 1883, after the assassination of President James Garfield by Charles Guiteau, a disappointed office seeker, Congress passed the first federal civil service law, the Pendleton Act. The law forbade the assessment of federal employees, made appointments contingent on examinations, and regularized promotions and linked them to demonstrated competence. Presidents Arthur and Cleveland placed some 20,000 federal jobs on the "classified list" of those covered by the new rules. By 1897, when William McKinley became president, 86,000 employees—almost half the federal civil service—were recruited by examination, promoted by merit, and protected by tenure.

■ THE BASES FOR PARTY AFFILIATION ■

Viewing Gilded Age politics as an exciting game or as a moral drama tells us something about how and why the political system worked. But it does not tell us what distinguished the average Democrat from the average Republican.

The Civil War Legacy. One distinction was attitudes toward the Civil War. The war, its antecedents, its Reconstruction aftermath, and the long memories of these emotion-stirring events helped forge links both of shared affection and of antagonisms that contributed to party identification.

Republican politicians worked hard to keep former Union sympathizers in the Grand Old Party. Republicans leaders regularly "waved the bloody shirt" to appeal to Union veterans and northerners generally. In a typical bloody-shirt tirade, Republican Oliver Morton of Indiana roared: "The Democratic party may be described as a common sewer, and loathsome receptacle, into which is emptied every element of treason North and South, every element of inhumanity and barbarism which has dishonored the age."

Even when they abandoned the black population of the South to the conservative white "redeemers" in the 1870s, Republicans were quick to react when southern mistreatment of blacks became too blatant. As late as 1890 a Republican House of Representatives passed a "force bill" designed to reimpose federal supervision of national elections so that blacks were not totally disfranchised by the southern states. Republicans also furiously denounced Grover Cleveland, the first Democratic president since Buchanan, and forced him to retreat when he threatened to return captured Confederate battle flags to the southern states as a gesture of sectional reconciliation. Black voters, for their part, though not numerous in either section due to disenfranchisement in the South and sparse numbers generally in the North, remembered their champions, Abraham Lincoln and Thaddeus Stevens, and were among the most loyal Republicans in the entire nation.

The Democrats, too, capitalized on Civil War and Reconstruction memories. In the white South, hatred of "Black Republican" emancipation and later Radical Reconstruction policies created a powerful and long-lasting Democratic solidarity. Any white man who voted Republican was branded a traitor to his race by Democratic politicians. By the 1880s, except for a few small dissenting pockets in the former anti-secession mountain regions, it was hard to find a Republican voter in the South. Winning the Democratic nomination for office became tantamount to election.

One key component of the Republican coalition was Union veterans. Not only were they energized by bloody-shirt appeals; they were also shamelessly bribed by Republican administrations. Prodded by the Union veterans' organization, the Grand Army of the Republic (GAR), successive Republican Congresses appropriated millions of dollars in pensions for former Union soldiers and their widows and dependents. By 1899 the total paid annually to these people by the U.S. Treasury amounted to almost $157 million. One scholar has called the Union veteran pension policy the beginning of the social welfare state in America.

Religion, Race, and Nationality. With each passing year the political hold of the Civil War became a little weaker, especially among northern voters. Yet party loyalty remained intense, and only the most extraordinary scandal or the most lackluster candidate could drive the average voter away from his traditional allegiance. What tied the voters to their individual parties so firmly after the Civil War issues had dimmed?

Many historians now believe that ethnic and religious factors forged the tightest bonds of Gilded Age party loyalty. By the 1880s the German, Irish, and Scandinavian immigrants of the 1830–1870 period had put down roots and emerged as an important political force. In addition, there were now many second-generation, American-born children who combined an understanding of the American political system with a continuing loyalty to their ethnic and religious traditions. It is no surprise, then, that in the generation following the Civil War, cultural loyalties and tensions played a special role in political life.

Religion apparently shaped party loyalties more than nationality or ethnic background by themselves. Whatever their national origins, members of the "liturgical" churches, which emphasized "right belief" over personal regeneration, were generally Democrats. The most numerous of the liturgical church groups were the Catholics who, since the days of Jefferson, had found a political refuge in the more "popular" of the two parties. Members of other churches that similarly emphasized ritual and well-defined dogma—Lutherans, Jews, Episcopalians—frequently voted the same way. The Democrats had welcomed the Catholic French, Germans, and Irish who crossed the Atlantic before the Civil War, and had catered to their needs. These needs, in part, had been material and practical, and, as we have seen, the predominantly Democratic machines in the cities helped the immigrants with jobs, handouts, and legal aid.

Both parties played this game, but concessions to cultural differences were more difficult for the Republicans to make. Republicans, like their Whig forebears, shared a latter-day puritanism that generally opposed the cultural and religious values of the liturgical faiths. Both Whigs and Republicans, each in its own day, were drawn heavily from members of evangelical churches that emphasized inner regeneration, personal reformation, and "right behavior." They were mostly native-born Baptists, Methodists, Presbyterians, and Congregationalists; but some were foreign-born Pietists who, like their native-born counterparts, tended to consider politics a vehicle for imposing their moral vision.

In the 1850s evangelicals had helped found the Republican party dedicated to the containment and ultimate extinction of sinful slavery. Through the remainder of the century Republican zeal for public and private virtue was expressed in demands for blue laws and restrictions on the manufacture and sale of liquor and the suppression of "blood" sports such as cockfighting and boxing. Republicans also insisted on strict separation of church and state, since the alternative, they felt, was to allow Catholic ascendency in public institutions.

Catholics, as well as many Lutherans, resented these efforts to restrict their personal freedoms and limit their influence. Unlike evangelicals, they held that what citizens did in their personal lives was no business of the state. They also believed that far too many state-supported institutions, though supposedly nonsectarian, were actually dominated by pietistic Protestants. The Democrats naturally played on these resentments. John ("Bathouse") Coughlin, a Chicago Democrat, warned the voters: "A Republican is a man who wants you t' go t' church every Sunday. A Democrat says if a man wants t' have a glass of beer on Sunday he can have it. Be Democrats unless you want t' be tied t' a church, a schoolhouse, or a Sunday school."

Political puritanism went beyond blue laws and mild expressions of religious intolerance. In the 1880s the antiforeign, anti-Catholic American Protective Association (APA) demanded the exclusion of noncitizens from American political life, attacked "the diabolical works of the Roman Catholic Church," and pledged to fight for the "cause of Protestantism." During the 1890s the APA intruded into several local campaigns as an unacknowledged, but not unrecognized, ally of the Republicans and a champion of "true Americanism" against "aliens" and "papists." However impatient liturgical voters might become at times with their traditional party allegiances, or however tempted to vote for a particularly attractive Republican candidate, such virulent anti-Catholic and antiforeign sentiment confirmed their view "that personal liberty . . . [was] surely only safe with the Democratic party in power."

■ PARTY REALIGNMENTS ■

For fifty years, then, cultural values and memories of the Civil War had forged bonds between the voters and the two major parties. In the 1890s the discontented westerners and southern farmers discussed in Chapter 19 would form a new party, and in the process unintentionally created a new political era dominated by the Republicans.

The Populist Party.   The People's Party of the U.S.A., or Populists, was launched in 1892 by leaders of the Farmers' Alliances (see Chapter 19) and assorted political dissidents at a convention held at Omaha, Nebraska. The preamble to the new party's platform delivered an agrarian message. Wealth concentration and the power of bondholders, usurers, and millionaires had brought the nation to the verge of ruin. "A vast conspiracy against mankind" had been "organized on two continents" and was "rapidly taking possession of the world." The conspirators had reduced the nation's money supply to an amount totally inadequate for its business, and the consequences were "falling prices, the formation of combines and rings, and the impoverishment of the producing class." The two traditional parties had failed the voters and now, in the impending political campaign, they proposed "to drown out the outcries of a plundered people with the uproar of a sham battle over the tariff, so that capitalists, corporations, national banks, rings, trusts, watered stock, the demonetization of silver, and the oppression of the usurers may be lost sight of."

To counter the people's oppressors, the Populists called for "free and unlimited coinage of silver" at a sixteen-to-one ratio with gold, a money supply of at least $50 per capita, a graduated income tax, and a postal savings bank for small savers afraid of private banks. The government should own the railroads and the telephone and telegraph systems and aliens and the railroads should be compelled to give up excess land. Tacked on as a platform afterthought was a section calling for a secret ballot, restrictions on immigration, an eight-hour workday for government workers, the "initiative" and "referendum" as ways of furthering direct democracy, and direct election of the president and United States senators without the intermediaries of the electoral college or the state legislatures.

Several provisions of the 1892 Populist platform foreshadowed the programs of the early-twentieth-century progressives and even the modern social welfare state. Its overall thrust was the desire to make government more responsive to the popular will, limit the power of large corporations, and reduce some of the worst disparities of wealth. At the same time, it did not directly challenge the existing regime of private property. It is not surprising that several leading socialists of the day dismissed the Populists as a "bourgeois party" composed of petty rural capitalists.

In 1892 the Populists faced the difficult task of overcoming traditional party allegiances. The problem was especially difficult in the South, where a third party threatened the unchallenged Democratic dominance established by the Redeemers in the 1870s and maintained by their equally conservative successors, the Bourbons. Still worse, the Populists might open the door to black suffrage, erased so successfully after 1877.

The fears seemed valid. Some southern Populists were eager to gain black votes. In Georgia Tom Watson, a leading Populist, promised black voters that if they stood "shoulder to shoulder" with the Populists, they would have "fair play and fair treatment as men and citizens, irrespective of color." In fact, the Populist commitment to racial equality was limited. Populists in southern state legislatures did not differ noticeably from the Bourbons in their desire to keep blacks "in their place," nor were they particularly sensitive to the special social problems that blacks faced beyond those they shared with poor whites. Yet many white southerners feared the third party endangered white dominion.

In the 1892 presidential election the Populist candidate, James B. Weaver, a former Union general, was an effective campaigner. Unfortunately Weaver's Union record aroused suspicion in the South. On the western Plains the new party did better. In the end the Populist ticket won over 15 percent of the vote in the Deep South and higher percentages in the silver-producing mountain states and parts of the Great Plains. Weaver received over 1 million out of 12 million votes cast, or about 8.5 percent. Cleveland won, but the Populist vote promised— or threatened—much for the future.

Unrest Under Cleveland. Grover Cleveland's second presidential term (1893–1897) was marked by social unrest more threatening than anything the country had seen since the Civil War. In the spring of 1893 the stock market crashed, ushering in a devastating depression. Strikes, labor demonstrations, and riots erupted in many parts of the country as workers struggled desperately to keep their jobs or prevent cuts in pay. This climate of fear and anger set off the Pullman strike of 1894 (described in Chapter 17).

Another manifestation of the hard times was Coxey's Army, a march on Washington of the unemployed in 1894. Led by Jacob S. Coxey, an ex-Greenbacker, the demonstrators sought to dramatize the plight of the jobless and advertise Coxey's plan for a federal works program financed by a paper-money issue of $500 million. The experts of the day ridiculed the idea, and when Coxey's 400 bedraggled men arrived in Washington, federal officials arrested their leaders for trampling the Capitol grass.

The reaction of the Cleveland administration to the distress of the laboring population was at best unimaginative. The president believed that Populist agitation and the government's piling up of silver—required by the Sherman Silver Purchase Act of 1890—had set off the panic and the resulting slump by shaking public confidence in the ability of the government to pay its obligations in gold. And, in fact, hoarders were withdrawing gold from the banks and the treasury and threatening to force the nation off the gold standard. To stop the gold drain and reassure public creditors, Cleveland asked Congress to repeal the Sherman Silver Act. Simultaneously he sought to shore up the treasury's gold reserve by selling bonds to the public for gold coin. The public bought the bonds, but then brought more paper money to the treasury to be redeemed for gold. Gold went in one treasury door and out the other. Ultimately, by getting the international investment bankers to guarantee delivery of foreign gold, Cleveland saved the gold standard, but his tactics only confirmed the belief of millions of southerners and westerners that J. P. Morgan, "Wall Street," and the Rothschilds, the prominent European banking family, owned the country.

Bankruptcies, unemployment, and suspicious dealings with the international financiers form the background of the momentous election of 1896. By 1895 many Americans, especially in the West and South, believed that the United States was fast falling under the sway of the "money power." These sections could not be ignored. In the generation since the Civil War the South had regained some of its self-confidence and the West had become an important force in the nation's economic and political life. In 1889–1890, North Dakota, South Dakota, Montana, Washington, Idaho, and Wyoming had been admitted to the Union, adding to Congress twelve senators who endorsed the West's view of politics and increasing the political power of the silver-mine owners, the chief financial backers of free-silver candidates.

"Bryan! Bryan! Bryan." Despite the Populists, the arena in which the contending forces fought out their differences was the Democratic party. On one side were the Democratic goldbugs, mostly from the Northeast and the Midwest, who believed that civilization itself rode on the gold standard. On the other side were the many western and southern Democrats, who were equally convinced that humanity could survive and prosper only if silver were restored to the currency system. The Republicans also had silver and gold wings, representing western and eastern attitudes, respectively. But the proponents of silver were far stronger among the Democrats.

In June 1896 the Republicans nominated William McKinley of Ohio on a platform pledged to a high tariff, a gold standard (although promising to consider monetizing silver as well if acceptable by international agreement), and an aggressive foreign policy. The gold-standard plank was a bitter disappointment to the Republican silverites, and Senator Henry M. Teller of Colorado and his western friends walked out of the convention.

At the Democratic convention in Chicago the silverites were in the majority. Senator Richard ("Silver Dick") Bland of Missouri was the front-runner as the delegates arrived. But a young ex-congressman from Nebraska, William Jennings Bryan, was also a serious contender. Bryan had spent many months writing letters to influential politicians, speaking before silverite audiences and Democratic groups, and cultivating the Farmers' Alliances to win support for himself and his cause. Rising as the last speaker before the convention voted on whether to endorse a gold-standard or a free-silver platform, he launched into the most influential convention address in American party history.

Bryan sought to make silver the cause of the masses everywhere. In answer to the previous speaker, a defender of gold, he pointed out that the man who worked for wages, the "merchant at the crossroads store," the farmer, and the miner were also "businessmen." All were the same and must be treated the same. But he quickly made clear that the money question inevitably drove a wedge between Americans. "We say not one word against those who live upon the Atlantic Coast, but the hardy pioneers who had braved all the dangers of the wilderness . . . are as deserving of the consideration of their party as any people in this country. . . . It is for these that we speak." He continued:

> You came to tell us that the great cities are in favor of the gold standard; we reply that the great cities rest upon our broad and fertile prairies. Burn down the cities and leave our farms, and the cities will spring up again as if by magic; but destroy our farms and the grass will grow in the streets of every city in the country.

Now followed the soaring conclusion that gave the name "Cross of Gold" to the address. If the gold men insisted on the gold standard, the silverites, supported by the "producing masses" and the "toilers everywhere," would fight them to the end. Pressing his hands to the sides of his head, Bryan thundered: "You shall not press down upon the brow of labor this crown of thorns, you shall not crucify mankind upon a cross of gold." As Bryan finished, he stretched his arms out horizontally, as if crucified himself. For several seconds the crowd was silent, then it burst into frenzied shouts and cheers: "Bryan! Bryan! Bryan!" Amid flying hats and waving handkerchiefs, the delegates lifted the speaker onto their shoulders

Though they criticized Bryan's religious rhetoric, the Republicans had their own pious slogan: "In God we trust, in Bryan we bust." The election's religious flavor is ironic because the issues of 1896 were, ultimately economic. (Courtesy of Library of Congress)

and carried him off the platform. On July 10, 1896, the Democrats chose Bryan as their candidate and Arthur Sewall, a silverite Maine businessman, as his running mate.

The Election of 1896.   At their convention in St. Louis soon after the Democrats had adjourned, the Populists faced a dilemma. Many saw free silver as an exaggerated issue. According to the Populist journalist Henry Demarest Lloyd, silver was the "cowbird" of the insurgent movement. It would deposit its eggs in another bird's nest and when its young were born they would evict the offspring of the original parents. In effect, silver would crowd out the other issues. Bryan, moreover, was a Democrat. To southern Populists especially, the Democrats were the enemy. After fighting the Bourbons for so long, how could they now fuse with them on the candidate at the top of the ticket?

Despite misgivings, delegates to the St. Louis People's Party convention gave Bryan their nomination as president. Unable to support banker Arthur Sewall, however, they selected Georgia's fiery Tom Watson, one of their own, as their vice presidential nominee.

The campaign that followed was one of the bitterest on record. Both major parties split. A large group of conservative Democrats refused to endorse Bryan and organized a separate "gold" Democratic ticket with John M. Palmer of Illinois at its head. "Silver" Republicans endorsed the Democratic candidates, Bryan and Sewall.

Obviously the underdog, Bryan campaigned hard. Consciously or not, he sought to change the foundation of Gilded Age party alignments. Playing on the hard times, he labored to overcome evangelical allegiance to the Republicans by appealing to class and economic interests. With silver, he declared, times would get better, prosperity would return, and wealth inequalities would be reduced. At the same time Bryan appealed to traditional Republicans by speaking the language that Americans of pious Protestant background understood. A devout Protestant himself, raised on the Bible and old-time religion, he saw free silver as more than an economic position; it represented justice and virtue. Gold, on the other hand, was not just the metal of the creditors; it was the source of injustice and oppression. "Every great economic question," Bryan declared as he crisscrossed the country, was "in reality a great moral question." Through the Midwest he called on goldbug sinners to "repent." In the South and on his beloved prairies, the people treated his rallies like great religious camp meetings. The Democratic campaign of 1896 was a moral crusade.

The Republican campaign was a countercrusade. To conservative Americans, Bryan and his forces were dangerous radicals. Postmaster General William L. Wilson declared that the silver leaders were "socialists, anarchists and demagogues of a dangerous type. . . ." A writer to the *New York Times* asserted that "within six months of Bryan's election mobs would be rushing up and down our streets howling for bread." If Bryan tried to make the free-silver cause a moral issue, so did his opponents. The *Chicago Tribune* declared that the gold position was a matter of simple honesty. "It is in no respect a question of politics, but of moral principle. It is taking the commandment, 'Thou Shalt not Steal' . . . , and applying it to the Nation."

The goldbugs had the tremendous advantage of deep pockets. The Republican national chairman, Cleveland industrialist Mark Hanna, was spectacularly effective in convincing the business community to write checks for McKinley and other antisilver candidates. The one important business group that might have contributed to Bryan, the silver-mine owners of the mountain states, proved surprisingly stingy (the price of silver having dropped). To make up for the lack of money, Bryan had only his own fierce energy and dazzling eloquence.

In the end these were not enough. The public perceived the election as the most critical since 1860 and turned out in record numbers. But the consequence was a resounding defeat for Bryan. The Democratic candidate won 6.5 million popular and 176 electoral votes to McKinley's 7.1 million and 271.

The nature of the vote reveals much about the social and sectional tensions of the 1890s. Bryan did not carry a single state in New England, the Middle Atlantic region, and the Old Northwest. On the Pacific Coast he carried only

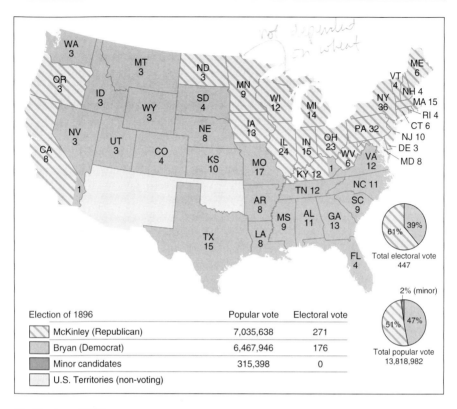

The Election of 1896

Election of 1896	Popular vote	Electoral vote
McKinley (Republican)	7,035,638	271
Bryan (Democrat)	6,467,946	176
Minor candidates	315,398	0
U.S. Territories (non-voting)		

Washington. In the Great Plains he did much better, taking Kansas, Nebraska, South Dakota, and Missouri. Bryan's real support, however, came from the South and the mountain states. In the South traditional Democratic voters gave Bryan the large majorities that Democratic candidates could invariably count on from the former Confederacy. In the mountain states, however, the Bryan sweep represented a major shift, best explained by the Democratic focus on silver.

Despite Bryan's appeal to all "producers," city people voted strongly Republican. Republicans who normally offended Catholic and other liturgical voters were careful this time to emphasize unity and tolerance. "We have always practiced the Golden Rule," declared McKinley: "the best policy is to 'live and let live'." There were also economic factors. Rather than splitting the rich from the poor, the self-employed and professional classes from the wage earners, the threat of free silver forged a bond across class lines. Eastern working men saw no advantage for themselves in cheap money. The Republican promise that a new tariff would bring prosperity and "the full dinner pail" seemed more likely than the millennium promised by Bryan.

Bryan's partisans have charged that the Republicans used coercion to win wage-earner votes for McKinley. And, in fact, many businessmen were panicked by the prospect of free silver and made extravagant statements expressing their fears. But this pressure was probably not decisive. In the end, Bryan and free silver lost because their appeal was confined primarily to southern and western voters.

■ CULTURE IN THE AGE OF THE DYNAMO ■

The nation's political life in the post-Civil War era was not, then, notably golden (except in the financial sense!). What about America's cultural life? Was it equally gilded?

In fact, in the half-century following Appomattox the United States produced a flood of authors, painters, architects, thinkers, and educators who made it one of the vital cultural centers of the Western world. There was also an exuberant and vigorous growth of "low" culture—the song, dance, theater, and amusements of average men and women—that helped make America a cultural beacon to people of other lands.

Literature.   Post-Civil War Americans had an impressive literary heritage to build on. But many of the outstanding figures of the prewar days were dead by 1865. The Boston-Cambridge area continued to be the literary capital of the nation and its major journals of culture, the *Atlantic Monthly* and the *North American Review,* along with the *Nation* and *Harper's Weekly,* published in New York, remained the arbiters of literary taste among the educated elite.

These publications defended the "genteel tradition" in literature. Fiction and poetry, they held, must represent the spiritual, the pure, and the noble, for literature was a moral medium. It should not seek to report life as it actually was, but help to transform it into something nobler and more refined. The poet James Russell Lowell declared that no man should write what he was unwilling for his young daughter to read. Evil existed in the fiction of the genteel authors, of course, but it was without detectable social cause and always, in the end, defeated. Sex was so buried under flowery romanticism that a traveler from another planet who read a genteel novel might not have known that men and women were biologically different.

But even in the 1870s and 1880s these pallid principles were being left behind by writers who insisted on depicting American regional reality with all its coarse vigor and liveliness.

One of the new voices came from the mining camps of California and depicted a way of life that had just recently passed. In 1867 Bret Harte, a transplanted easterner, published a short story "The Luck of Roaring Camp," in the San Francisco-based *Overland Monthly.* It concerned the hard-bitten miners and dance-hall girls of a Sierra mining camp who are, disconcertingly, bequeathed a baby. The plot was less important, however, than the cast of characters; each has a rough exterior and speaks the way people in the mining camps probably did speak. Few are "good" people in the usual sense. It was this quality of apparent authenticity that made the story an instant sensation and turned Harte into a celebrity. In the next few years his other stories about the mining camps, including "The Outcasts of Poker Flat," "The Idyl of Red Gulch," and "Tennessee's Partner," were widely applauded as examples of honesty in literature.

Over the next few decades "regionalism" attracted other authors. Edward Eggleston's books depicted rural Indiana with a sharp eye for local color and a true ear for regional speech. George Washington Cable wrote brilliantly about creole New Orleans. The southern mountain people of the Great Smokies and the Cumberland plateau found their literary portrait painter in Mary Noailles Murfree. Joel Chandler Harris's "Uncle Remus" stories depicted poor Georgia whites and even poorer Georgia blacks. The East, too, had its "local colorists." Sarah Orne Jewett began to write stories of the village and farm people of southern Maine during the 1860s.

The most talented of all the regional authors, one who exceeded them in depth and universality, was Samuel Langhorne Clemens, alias Mark Twain. Mark Twain shared with the local colorists their love of dialect, their focus on rural and small-town "types," their humorous emphasis. But Twain was far more talented than the local colorists. Combining the traditions of the frontier tall tale with an uncanny ear for speech, and at times a sense of the tragic, he became an author of international stature. At the beginning of his career, however, he capitalized on his capacity to make people laugh. In books such as *Innocents Abroad* (1869) and on the lecture circuit, which occupied much of his time and earned him large fees, he told jokes and funny stories and in general seemed to be interested solely in amusing people.

Mark Twain's more serious side became evident in his later books. In three of these he turned to the upper South before the Civil War, describing the joys and the agonies of youth. *Tom Sawyer* (1876) is about a boy growing up in a town very much like Sam Clemens's own Hannibal, Missouri. *Life on the Mississippi* (1883) is a superb nonfiction account of the great days before the Civil War when the steamboat dominated commerce on the South's rivers and the steamboat captain was almost a Renaissance prince. Mark Twain's greatest novel, *Huckleberry Finn* (1885), was a sequel to *Tom Sawyer*. But Huck is a more interesting boy than Tom—less conventional, more genuine, less spoiled by romantic illusion, more spontaneous.

Despite his genius and his willingness at times to choose truth over romantic convention, Mark Twain never fully escaped from the literary conventions of the Gilded Age. Even his best works contain much sentimentality and cheap farce. He eventually turned to vapid historical romance and developed a tendency to flaunt an adolescent melancholy.

As the century progressed, "realism," employing more modern materials, would supersede the older style. Leader of the new genre was William Dean Howells, a midwesterner who edited the Boston-published *Atlantic Monthly*. Though he never fully liberated himself from the prudishness of the day, Howells insisted a novel must by "true to the motives, the impulses, the principles that shape the life of actual men and women." As editor and critic, he welcomed newer talents such as Hamlin Garland, whose bitter stories of western farm life, *Main-Travelled Roads*, appeared in 1891. He also introduced to American readers the realism of Émile Zola in France and Henrik Ibsen in Scandinavia.

As a novelist, Howells practiced what he preached. The hero of *The Rise of Silas Lapham* (1885) was a self-made millionaire manufacturer who finds that his simple western ways cause social difficulties for himself and his family in Boston. The violent Haymarket affair in Chicago awakened Howells's social conscience and in *A Hazard of New Fortunes* (1890), his business characters are less amiable and sympathetic, and his canvas expands to include poor working people, a German-American socialist, and a violent streetcar strike. *A Traveler from Altruria* (1894) and *Through the Eye of the Needle* (1907) raised socialist alternatives to what seemed a dog-eat-dog economic system.

A major American literary figure not easy to classify is Henry James, brother of the philosopher William James. James, acutely aware of the nuances in human relationships, wrote about men and women in comfortable circumstances whose lives revolved about the subtleties of taste, class, and nationality, and crises of personal integrity. The tensions in many of his best works—*The American* (1877), *Portrait of a Lady* (1881), *The Wings of the Dove* (1902), and *The Golden Bowl* (1904)—arise between simple but honest and intelligent Americans, often young women, and sophisticated but corrupt and devious Europeans. James seemed little interested in the vast social changes sweeping the Western world. Yet he escapes the false sentimentality of the genteel authors. His people, though well-bred and worldly, are recognizably real human beings with the complex personalities found in actual life.

By the 1890s a new breed of women authors had made gender an issue in literature. American women had been successful and admired authors as far back as the colonial era. During the early nineteenth century women had dominated the field of the popular novel. After the Civil War women entered the front ranks of literature.

The female local colorists at times expressed the emotions of the "New Woman" beginning to emerge as the century wound down. In Jewett's *A Country Doctor* (1884), one character protests against society's effort to "bury the talent that God has given me." Other women authors went beyond the local colorist genre in expressing the full range of women's yearnings. Among the novelists, Ellen Glasgow, a Virginian, wrote about her native section with special attention to the false gentility of southern womanhood. Edith Wharton, a descendant of New York's old Knickerbocker families, depicted heroines caught between the vulgar new rich and the decaying upper class. But the novelist who best exemplified the New Woman was Kate O'Flaherty Chopin, a widow and mother of six, who despite her own experience—or because of it—raised explicit questions about women's roles as wives, mothers, and lovers. Chopin's novel, *The Awakening* (1899), offended the more prudish critics as "sex fiction" for its focus on women's sexual feelings. The hostile response, including refusal of librarians in her native St. Louis to circulate it, crushed Chopin's spirit.

As the end of the century approached, Howells's mild realism gave way to something more vigorous and more brutal. The realists retained an essentially sunny view of life; the "naturalists" often perceived it as sordid and vicious. In their novels men and women are mere atoms in the grip of forces beyond their control or even understanding. Their endings are generally tragic. Naturalist novels often focused on the emerging industrial-urban order, and even their rural characters are people whose lives are entangled in the vast social changes that characterized the closing years of the nineteenth century.

One young writer who explored the relationship between large social currents and the lives of rural Americans was Hamlin Garland, a "son of the middle border," the prairie region undergoing momentous and jarring change during the 1870s and 1880s. In *Prairie Folks* (1893), Garland told of the bitter failures and intense hardships of rural life, and of farm people crushed both by cruel nature and by even crueler human oppressors. Stephen Crane's *Maggie: A Girl of the Streets* (1893) is about a young woman who is destroyed by the poverty, drunkenness, and crime of her environment. The picture is one of brutality and sordidness so frankly rendered that Crane had to finance its publication himself under a pseudonym. Crane, who died young of tuberculosis, would write one masterpiece, *The Red Badge of Courage* (1895), the story of a young soldier in the Civil War experiencing his first taste of battle.

Theodore Dreiser, an Indianian from a background of poverty, was a crude stylist but a writer of great cumulative power. His characters are often at the mercy of their appetites, their drives, their yearnings. Carrie, of *Sister Carrie* (1900), is an ambitious young woman who uses men, is corrupted by them, and then destroys them in turn as she claws her way up the social ladder. Frank Cowperwood of *The Financier* (1912) and *The Titan* (1914), modeled after business tycoon Charles Yerkes, is an unprincipled big businessman driven by a lust for power who allows nothing and no one to stand in his way; although he triumphs over all his enemies, he is no more master of his destiny than Crane's tragic Maggie.

Other authors of these years who played on the theme of powerful forces molding people include two Californians, Frank Norris and Jack London. In *McTeague* (1899) Norris depicted a simple-minded San Francisco dentist who is gradually overwhelmed by material failure and tragically driven to murder. *The Octopus* (1901) concerns the wheat farmers of California's Central Valley and their struggles with the railroad. London, though an avowed socialist, worshiped the power of the individual, and in adventure books set in Alaska—*The Call of the Wild* (1903), *White Fang* (1905)—as well as in works dealing with driven men—*The Sea Wolf* (1904)—he glorified the superman. Modeled on philosopher Friedrich Nietzsche's "blond beast," these brutal, arrogant, commanding characters, acting like elemental forces, sweep lesser beings aside.

Painting and Architecture.   In two other areas of the arts, painting and architecture, we encounter the same movement from romantic gentility to an attempt to incorporate the emerging twentieth-century world. In both, as in literature, some of the results are lasting and impressive achievements.

American painting during the 1860s and 1870s was dominated by borrowed European romanticism, and Europe of the "Old Masters" remained for many years the measure of good taste. During the 1880s a more distinctively American school appeared. Led by Winslow Homer, John La Farge, and Thomas Eakins, their work was direct and vivid, but its subject matter lacked relevance to the world in which most Americans lived. Not until the beginning of the new century did a group of American painters come to terms with the emerging urban-industrial America.

The core of this group consisted of former newspaper illustrators from the Philadelphia area. Trained to capture events in quick, vivid pen and pencil images, Everett Shinn, George Luks, John Sloan, and William Glackens developed keen eyes for city scenes and city types. In the early 1890s they came under the tutelage of Robert Henri, a teacher at the Pennsylvania Academy of Fine Arts, who had been influenced by the French impressionists. Impressionists relied on the sort of visual shorthand that the eye in real life detects and the mind converts into reality. Toward the end of the decade Henri and his four disciples, one by one, moved to New York, where they were joined by Maurice Prendergast, Arthur B. Davies, and Ernest Lawson.

The Henri circle considered the conventional American painting of the day anemic and feeble, suitable for interior decoration, "merely an adjunct of plush and cut glass," as one of them said. Their own work was vigorous and real. They depicted prize fights, ordinary people waiting for taxis and streetcars, pigeons wheeling over tenement roofs, urban backyards, children at play in city streets, and the New York "el" at rush hour. Their technique often bordered on caricature. People were fat, frumpy, often coarse-looking. The critics attacked their work as harsh and vulgar. Before long the Henri group was being derided as the "Ashcan School." Offended by the tight rein imposed on artists by the conservative National Academy of Design, which excluded them from its prestigious exhibitions, eight Ashcan painters held their own show at the Mac-Beth Gallery in New York in 1908. The show immortalized "the eight" and marked a new era in American painting.

In 1913 the Henri group, and the still more radical Postimpressionists, sponsored a major showing of the best new European and American work at the Sixty-Ninth Regiment Armory in New York. Here for the first time a large number of Americans saw the works of Cézanne, Van Gogh, Picasso, Matisse, and the cubists, who seemed to have abandoned representation entirely. The sensation of the show was Marcel Duchamp's *Nude Descending a Staircase,* a cubist painting that by a succession of overlapping cut-out figures suggested the motion of a woman walking down a flight of stairs. One critic called the Duchamp painting "an explosion in a shingle factory." Another labeled the whole exhibit an exercise in "incomprehensibility combined with symptoms of paresis."

Despite the attacks, the Armory show was a profoundly influential event in American art. The paintings attracted immense crowds wherever they were shown. Most people came to smirk, but many stayed to marvel and appreciate. In all, 235 of the paintings were eventually sold. The market for modern art boomed, and American taste was given a tremendous push toward modernism.

The years immediately following the Civil War found American architecture particularly out of tune with contemporary life. Designers of public buildings were still creating Greek temples or combining elements of so many traditional European styles that no clear label could be given them. Meanwhile, the ordinary middle-class family bought a balloon-frame house constructed of wood uprights and siding stuck together with nails, and decorated, if at all, with wooden "gingerbread" trim.

By the 1880s and 1890s critics began to ask for a finer aesthetic. The plea was answered by a group of young men—including Stanford White, Charles McKim, Daniel Burnham, and William Robert Ware—who had studied in Paris and could reproduce the fine detail of Renaissance and Elizabethan homes and Gothic libraries and churches. But, the carpers asked, in what sense were these American buildings? The first signs of change came in the 1880s when a group of Chicago architects began to look at building in a new way. During this decade the Windy City was caught up in a frenzy of construction, both to restore structures destroyed in the devastating fire of 1871 and to meet the space needs of the nation's fastest-growing metropolis. In the midst of this building boom William Le Baron Jenney designed the first true skyscraper.

In the past, tall buildings had not served commercial purposes. Their walls had to be very thick at the base to bear the enormous weight of the masonry above, thereby reducing the usable space. The many flights of stairs made space at upper floors virtually unrentable. In the new buildings of Jenney, Louis Sullivan, Ernest Flagg, and Cass Gilbert, instead of heavy, weight-bearing walls, thin outer walls of brick or stone veneer were attached to a frame of light, interlocked steel beams. With electricity and fast elevators, such a building could provide convenient, usable space at much lower cost than an equivalent masonry structure. Because the skyscraper could be erected to virtually any height, designers could go up rather than out and so reduce the outlay on expensive downtown real estate.

At first skyscrapers were made to look like overblown Gothic cathedrals. Gradually, however, architects began to insist that a structure's design and appearance honestly reflect its technology and function. In the words of Louis Sullivan, "Over all the coursing sun, form ever follows function, and that is the law." A building should not disguise its use, but proclaim it boldly and honestly. Sullivan's best works were the Schiller Building (1891–1892) in Chicago and St. Louis's Wainwright Building (1890–1891).

Frank Lloyd Wright, Sullivan's pupil, translated his mentor's theories into domestic architecture. Wright made the close relation of form, use, materials, and site the basis for his famous prairie houses—low structures to match the terrain of the flat Midwest. He avoided traditional elements of exterior design and built the homes of local stone and timber that suited their locations. Critics hailed Wright's work as strikingly innovative, yet at first few patrons came to him. Not until the 1920s did his form of architectural modernism begin to attract widespread public acclaim.

Popular Culture. The gradual response of the arts to the realities of the American social and economic scene was matched in popular culture, entertainment, sports, and recreation.

As more and more Americans moved to the cities, they found that the world of play as well as the world of work had changed. In the larger cities space for people seeking physical exercise was often unavailable. As we have seen, few

American cities had preserved open space in their congested centers. Not until the very end of the nineteenth century did cities open playgrounds for children and add sports and exercise programs to school curricula. Insufficient leisure remained a deterrent to sports for a longer time. Most wage earners worked every day except Sunday, and in many cities evangelical Protestant groups imposed blue laws that kept theaters and ball parks closed on the Sabbath. Only gradually as the old century gave way to the new did pressure from Catholics, nonbelievers, working people, and various secular groups force city officials to permit Sunday sports and amusements. Increasingly, sports became incorporated into city life. But most urbanites were caught up in the movement as paid spectators rather than personal participants.

The first of the nineteenth-century sports to be commercialized was baseball. By the 1850s amateur baseball clubs had become common in the cities and towns. Their matches soon attracted spectators, and reports of their encounters began to appear in the newspapers. Before long the teams were erecting high fences around their playing fields and charging spectators for admission to underwrite the cost of equipment, uniforms, and travel to rival communities.

In 1858 promoters organized the National Association of Baseball Players, and in 1869 the Cincinnati Red Stockings began to pay salaries to players. In 1876 the National League of Professional Baseball Clubs—with teams in New York, Philadelphia, Hartford, Boston, Chicago, Louisville, Cincinnati, and St. Louis—superseded the amateur organization. In the next few years more professional teams joined the National League, and in 1901 entrepreneurs organized the American League. In 1903 the champions of each met in the first World Series; the American League's Boston Red Sox beat the National League's Pittsburgh Pirates. Baseball attendance grew rapidly in the early part of the new century, and in the 1913 World Series gate receipts for the five games reached $326,000. In 1908 the song "Take Me Out to the Ball Game" became a popular hit and marked the triumph of baseball as the country's "national" sport.

Football and boxing, though popular, failed to match baseball's audience during these years. Until the 1920s football remained a game played at colleges by amateurs and patronized by upper-middle-class people, often graduates of one of the schools. Yet toward the end of the century college rivalries encouraged active recruiting of players, often poor sons of immigrants. By 1917 critics were charging that the supposedly amateur game had become commercialized with hidden subsidies to players, vulgar hoopla, and expensive stadiums—in addition to excessive violence.

Because of its brutality, boxing carried a stigma as a "blood" sport in these years. Few women and few middle-class men attended matches, and in some cities boxing was forbidden. Yet the sport was popular among working men, especially recent immigrants and second-generation Americans in the big cities. When John L. Sullivan returned to his native Boston after knocking out Jake Kilrain in a harrowing seventy-five-round, bare-knuckle fight in 1889, the city's Irish turned out in force to honor him as an ethnic hero.

Professional sports were relatively democratic. The lists of star players or champions in a particular sport record the growing assimilation and acceptance of newer-stock Americans. At the beginning the names are Anglo-Saxon; by the 1890s they are German and Irish; by 1910 or 1920 they are increasingly Italian, Spanish, and Slavic. Clearly, professional sports provided an escalator upward for each new European group in America.

Most professional sports retained the "color bar," however. Black players were forced to play in segregated black leagues, where salaries were low, equipment poor, and ballparks mere fenced fields. College football was somewhat more open in the North, though when northern teams played rivals in the South, they benched their black players in deference to southern prejudices. The least segregated major spectator sport was prize fighting; in 1908 Jack Johnson, a black man, defeated Tommy Burns, a white Canadian, to become heavyweight champion of the world. But even boxing was not free of prejudice. The white public resented Johnson's reign as champion and yearned for a "white hope" to defeat him. Johnson's marriage to a white woman made him even more unpopular, and when he was defeated by Jess Willard, a white American, the white public cheered.

Music, the theater, the circus, and the amusement park were other ways in which city people in the half-century following the Civil War filled their limited leisure time and softened the sharp edges of their daily lives.

The amusement park was largely the invention of the streetcar companies, which, to encourage weekend business, established resorts on the outskirts of the towns they served. On Sundays city people flocked to these parks to hear concerts, watch balloon ascensions and bicycle races, and patronize the "rides," including the Ferris wheel, the roller coaster, and others. Here Americans ate hamburgers and hot dogs for the first time.

Before World War I "classical" music was the music of an elite, composed— and often performed—by foreigners. Popular music was home grown. During the post-Civil War years, songwriting, composing popular songs to be sold as sheet music and played and sung at the parlor piano, became a successful profession for a score of composers. By 1900 most of the songwriters and their agents were located along New York's Twenty-eighth Street, "Tin Pan Alley." The label soon became the nickname for the lucrative popular music business.

Some of the most successful composers, Gussie Davis for one, were black. An unusually large contingent, including Edward Marks, Monroe Rosenberg, and Irving Berlin, were Jewish. During the 1890s Scott Joplin and other black composers introduced ragtime to a wider public. "Rags" were instrumental pieces written for either piano or band. They combined elements of traditional white music, the syncopation of urban black music, and the street music of the white underclass. In the hands of Joplin, a Texas-born black man with formal musical training, they were often complex, sophisticated works. Joplin wrote thirty-nine rags and was widely imitated by other composers, black and white alike.

Jazz, like ragtime, had roots in the black city ghettos. Its original home was New Orleans, where blacks had long been a vital part of the cultural scene. Black wind musicians played at important public occasions—parades, funerals, and political gatherings—both solemn and joyous. They freely improvised on melodies from traditional French and American marches and popular songs, combining them with ragtime-style syncopation drawn from the black musical experience. Black singers, pianists, and instrumentalists also played in the saloons and brothels of Storyville, the New Orleans red-light district. Here one heard both ragtime and "the blues," a mournful vocal form related to rural black spirituals, but concerned with less uplifting themes: crime, betrayal, sexual passion. It was in Storyville that such inspired performers as Ferdinand ("Jelly Roll") Morton, Louis Armstrong, Joseph ("King") Oliver, and "Ma" Rainey got their start.

When military authorities closed the Storyville brothels in 1917, supposedly to protect servicemen from venereal disease, New Orleans musicians scattered in all directions. Eventually many settled in the emerging black neighborhoods of Chicago, St. Louis, Kansas City, Memphis, and New York, where they played in the nightclubs and speakeasies that Prohibition had spawned. Young white musicians found "Jass" an exciting new form and began to imitate the black players. Their lively new Chicago Style, like the original, relied on improvisation and spontaneity. At its worst, as in the music of Paul Whiteman, the "King of Jazz," white adaptation was a slick, contrived sort of popular music that suited the palates of a middle-class white audience.

Popular music in this period often shared billing with other entertainment on stage. The minstrel show, a form of "review" dating from before the Civil War, featured songs, dances, and comedy routines that exploited black stereotypes and black musical themes. By the 1880s vaudeville had replaced the minstrel show. A typical vaudeville performance consisted of as many as thirty brief acts—dances, comic skits, songs, acrobatics, animal stunts, juggling, magic. Like the minstrel show, it was a showcase for popular songs. It also offered talented young men and women from newer immigrant stock—Jewish, Spanish, Italian, Irish—opportunities to win fame and fortune as performers. The vaudeville show was especially popular among the new urban audiences. Even if they knew no English, they could enjoy a juggler or a magician, and the costumes and music created a glamorous image, briefly transforming their narrow, impoverished world.

The motion picture was even better suited to the growing urban audience. Many of its technical elements emerged from the laboratory of Thomas A. Edison in New Jersey, but at first the great inventor considered it an amusing toy and was happy to license exhibitors to show thirty-second films in penny arcades. The first films were merely scenic views or bits of action. Soon the exhibitors discovered more profit in such racy material as *Taking a Bath, What the Bootblack Saw,* and *Dolorita's Passion Dance.*

The audience for the new medium proved enormous. Live theater was expensive and relied on conventions that sometimes baffled untutored audiences. There was also no language barrier. The early movies were silent and told their simple stories with broad gestures and large images. Once the medium's success was assured, Edison attempted to impose a monopoly by insisting his patent rights be respected and charging movie makers high fees to use his cameras and projectors. He could not stop the tide. Dozens of small picture makers, using equipment of their own make or imported from Europe, were soon shooting films in backyards and makeshift studios. Many were Jewish small businessmen who, excluded from other enterprises, were quick to recognize the potential of the new medium.

There was a similar proliferation of exhibitors. By 1900, hundreds were showing films in empty stores, town halls, school auditoriums, almost any place they could assemble some chairs in a darkened room. These early movie houses, often called "nickelodeons," charged five cents for an eight-minute showing of a humorous, exciting, or exotic incident. Most of these primitive sketches were created on the spur of the moment by directors, camera operators, or other employees of the many small firms formed to provide material for the exhibitors.

This impromptu approach to filmmaking soon gave way to more careful and deliberate efforts. In 1903 Edwin Porter of the Edison company produced *The Great Train Robbery*, which told a story of some complexity, in almost a full reel of film. Soon other firms were imitating Porter. Equipment became better, theaters more permanent and comfortable, and films more impressive artistically. By 1905 producers had established many of the classic film types—western, comedy-romance, crime, travelogue, science fiction.

At first many of the film companies were located in the East, close to the established pool of actors and technicians. But land for studios in the big eastern cities was expensive and the cold and rainy eastern weather often hindered "shooting" outdoors. The East was also close to the Edison "film trust," which pursued a policy of suing every company that did not pay a substantial fee for the privilege of making films. In 1907, to escape the trust and to take advantage of cheap space and sunny climate, William Selig, a Chicago producer, moved his company to southern California. Soon Selig was joined by others. By 1912 the Los Angeles suburb of Hollywood had become the nation's filmmaking capital.

Motion picture viewers eventually came to expect more sophisticated fare than purveyed by the pioneers. After 1910 they could count on D. W. Griffith, working for the Biograph studio. Griffith was the first producer-director who truly understood the new medium and successfully exploited its unique potential. In 1915 he produced, for the then-immense figure of $100,000, *The Birth of a Nation*. Concerned with the tribulations of Reconstruction, the movie was blatantly racist and pro-Ku Klux Klan. Wherever it was shown it aroused fierce opposition among blacks and white liberals, but it was an immense popular success, and from a purely artistic perspective deservedly so. Twelve reels long, it made use of the fadeout, the dissolve, crosscutting, the close-up, and the long-shot. In the special theaters where it was shown, orchestras accompanied the action. However deplorable ideologically, *The Birth of a Nation* set a new standard of artistic and technical excellence for the entire film industry.

Education.   In their various ways, then, the arts, both "high" and "low," responded to the transformation of America from a rural and agricultural society to one dominated by cities and industry. The educational life of the nation between the Civil War and World War I revealed a similar shift.

The greatest change in education in the half-century following 1865 was its sheer expansion. In 1870 about 7 million pupils were enrolled in public day schools; by 1915 there were over 18 million, with another 1.5 million in private schools, mostly Catholic parochial institutions. By 1915 well over 80 percent of all young people were attending classes of some sort. School outlays rose even faster than enrollments, growing to $605 million in 1915, or $31 annually per pupil.

The expansion had many sources. In 1860 few states in the South had systems of public education. During Reconstruction, however, southern states had joined the rest of the country in accepting responsibility for supporting elementary schools. Meanwhile, in the large cities a parallel system of parochial schools sprang up, largely to serve the nation's growing Catholic population. More and more states also made school attendance compulsory. In 1881 nineteen states and territories in the North and West had compulsory attendance laws; by 1898 there were thirty-one. At the same time legislatures raised school-leaving ages and made the school year longer.

These changes added substantially to the taxpayers' bills, but education seemed well worth the cost to this generation of Americans. A larger and more complex economy not only made education easier to pay for; it also made it more essential. Business needed more and more young men and women who could calculate receipts, add figures, write letters, and follow written instructions. Assured of well-paying jobs requiring literacy, the young found staying in school more attractive.

Secondary education particularly benefited from the increased demand for clerical and managerial skills. Before the Civil War, only Massachusetts had a system of high schools supported by public funds. Secondary education elsewhere was the domain of the private "academy." After 1865 several states followed Massachusetts's lead. By 1915 the United States had more than 11,000 public high schools, with over 1.3 million pupils.

Initially the curricula of the public high schools emphasized the same liberal arts and classic languages that were dominant in the private academies. School administrators soon introduced commercial programs, including typing, bookkeeping, and accounting. Latin and Greek gave way to modern foreign languages. Even more "practically" oriented were the vocational classes that began to invade the high schools under the prodding of the National Society for the Promotion of Industrial Education. In 1917 Congress passed the Smith–Hughes Act providing subsidies to the states to underwrite vocational and industrial skills courses for high school students.

During these same years the United States began the transformation that would make it a world leader in college and university education. Before the Civil War the typical American college was a small church-related institution that prepared young men for the ministry or for the learned professions. Most had a few hundred students, a single classroom building, a museum containing stuffed and preserved animals, and a library of a few hundred books, mostly on religion, tucked into some corner. Faculties were small, and many of the professors were ministers who doubled in science and modern languages—if these subjects were taught at all.

After 1865 change came swiftly. The Morrill Land Grant College Act (1862) provided funds for a new class of agricultural and technical colleges, many of which developed into major universities. At the same time vast sums to establish new colleges and universities and revive old ones flowed from the swollen fortunes of post-Civil War business tycoons. During these years Rockefeller, Leland Stanford, Andrew Carnegie, James B. Duke, and others contributed millions to establish new universities or upgrade old ones. Under the guidance of a new breed of college president, curricula altered rapidly to provide students with training in the sciences, modern languages, and the new social sciences, as well as vocational courses such as accounting and engineering. In the 1880s, President Charles W. Eliot of Harvard introduced the elective system, ending the requirement of tightly prescribed courses and allowing students to choose their own programs within broad limits.

Higher education for women also expanded. Before 1860 only a handful of institutions allowed women to take college degrees. After the Civil War women's colleges proliferated and state universities opened their doors to men and women on an equal basis. In the older elite schools—the so-called Ivy League—women were admitted to sister institutions with separate faculties, courses, and buildings. In the state schools they sat in the same classrooms with men, though they used separate dormitories and were subject to stricter rules of decorum.

This period also witnessed the appearance of the research university and the graduate school. Before the Civil War American college faculty were not expected to advance the frontiers of knowledge as part of their duties. Then, in 1876 Johns Hopkins in Baltimore opened on the German model, as a graduate school where the sciences, social sciences, and humanities were treated as scholarly disciplines. The new university taught by the seminar system, where a prominent scholar and a small group of advanced students worked on a common set of problems. The result for the student was published research and the degree of Ph.D. (Doctor of Philosophy).

Hopkins was soon widely imitated. Several new institutions were founded on the same model, while many existing institutions set up graduate schools for training scholars and scientists. In 1900 some 240 Ph.D.s were conferred on American students, and the degree was well on its way to becoming the "union card" of the college teaching profession. Meanwhile, however imperfectly, the best American universities were being transformed into communities of creative men—and some women—dedicated to the quest for new fundamental understanding as well as important practical knowledge.

Other professions followed college teaching from a field for amateurs to one dominated by trained and "credentialed" experts. The trend was fueled by the sheer accumulation of knowledge, which forced each field to divide into ever-narrower specializations. Professionalization was also a consequence of efforts by occupational groups to raise their status and income by restricting entry into the field, usually by credentialing procedures in the name of higher professional standards.

In law and medicine, training through apprenticeship gave way in these years to formal education in law schools and medical schools. In medicine, at first, this led to an enormous proliferation of inferior schools, some mere diploma mills where students acquired M.D. degrees for a fee and perfunctory clinical and course work. In 1910 a report by Abraham Flexner, supported by the Carnegie Foundation, exposed widespread abuses in medical education and led the American Medical Association to push for the closing of inferior schools and the upgrading of others. The effects were drastic. The number of medical graduates dropped from over 5,000 yearly between 1900 and 1906 to about half that number in 1922. Critics charged that the true purpose of the upgrading was to restrict the number of physicians in order to prevent overcompetition. Yet the changes did indeed improve the level of skills among doctors.

Legal training also improved, though the overall effect was less restrictive. During these years more and more universities established law schools with three-year courses of study. At first, students could begin legal training after high school. Gradually, however, the better law schools insisted on college preparation, and in the 1870s Harvard introduced the case method—learning legal principles by studying actual cases decided by the courts.

The process of Professionalization soon spread to many other areas. The usual pattern was for some occupational group, dissatisfied with its income, social status, and prevailing intellectual level, to band together in a professional association. The association then set new standards for education and training and established a degree program to be required of all future entrants into the profession. Another step in many cases was a state-administered examination imposed on those seeking to practice the profession under state license. In this way such diverse groups as teachers, nurses, engineers, accountants, social workers, dentists, pharmacists, optometrists, and others raised themselves to professional status. As in the case of doctors, professionalization improved the level of service for the public, but also increased the cost of those services. A final beneficiary of professionalization was the universities, which acquired crowds of students eager to gain degrees and the training needed to pass professional licensing exams.

The New Journalism. In 1865 newspapers were very different from their counterparts today. For one thing they were smaller, usually only sixteen to twenty pages long. News-gathering facilities were primitive. Foreign news, in the absence of the transatlantic cable (which was not successfully laid until 1866), took weeks to arrive. Domestic news was transmitted by telegraph, but only a few of the very largest urban papers had reporters outside their home cities. For coverage of any American community but their home towns, newspaper editors were forced to copy stories from other newspapers received by "exchange" in the mail.

The newspaper of 1865 had no pictures. The few illustrated weeklies relied on woodcuts or copper engravings, which could not be prepared quickly enough for the daily press. There were also no comic strips, syndicated news columns, food columns, horoscopes, or advice to the lovelorn. Anyone reading an 1860 newspaper today would also be impressed by the relative sedateness of the coverage. Editors reported crimes and disasters, but usually in a sober, matter-of-fact way. Most of their space was filled with political news from Washington, D.C., the state capital, and the local board of aldermen. Reported in enormous detail, these stories are valuable for a political historian today, but may well have induced instant sleep in contemporary readers.

During the next generation new technology improved the gathering, packaging, and distributing of news and transformed the newspaper industry. The new technology came through widely scattered developments. The modern typewriter, capable of printing both upper- and lowercase letters, appeared in the 1870s. A decade later Ottmar Mergenthaler's linotype machine eliminated the need to set type for presses laboriously by hand. Cheap pulp paper came into wide use about the same time, as did processes for fast reproduction of illustrations and photographs. The telephone, invented in the 1870s by Alexander Bell, a Scottish-born teacher of the deaf, was in wide use by the 1890s and proved an invaluable tool for information gathering.

New sorts of news-collecting and news-packaging agencies also facilitated change. In the 1840s a group of New York editors began to pool information and sell it to subscribers. Out of this grew the Associated Press, with information-gathering facilities in major foreign capitals and in many American news centers. The United Press followed in 1882. In 1884, S. S. McClure, an inventive publisher, established "Newspaper Features," providing ready-made syndicated columns, short stories, and a "woman's page" for subscribing papers.

Taking advantage of these changes was a group of aggressive publishers. One of them, Joseph Pulitzer, a Hungarian refugee who arrived in the United States in 1864 with hardly a penny, acquired the ailing *St. Louis Post-Dispatch* in 1878 and made the paper a success. With the money he accumulated he next bought the *New York World*, in the nation's press capital. Pulitzer helped create what critics would call "yellow journalism." The *World* emphasized "human-interest" stories—crime, corruption, disasters, strange reversals, sudden luck, and the like. It printed illustrations showing "X—Where the Body Was Found." Its headlines ran to: "Baptized in Blood" and "Death Rides the Blast." Pulitzer also attracted readers by promotional schemes. In one of these he sent the "girl reporter" Nellie Bly on a world-circling race to beat Jules Verne's fictional hero of *Around the World in Eighty Days*. He was also the first editor to publish a comic strip, R. F. Outcault's "The Yellow Kid," printed in yellow ink. Thereafter Pulitzer's approach to the newspaper business came to be called "yellow journalism."

Pulitzer soon acquired a flock of imitators, including the Scripps brothers, with papers in Detroit, Cleveland, St. Louis, and Cincinnati, and William Randolph Hearst in San Francisco. In 1895 Hearst came to New York, determined to outdo Pulitzer. He introduced his own comic strips, "The Katzenjammer Kids" and "Happy Hooligan," and then stole "The Yellow Kid" from Pulitzer. Before many months his *New York Journal* was engaged in a full-scale circulation war with the *World*, with each editor attempting to out-sensationalize the other. In later years Hearst acquired or established newspapers all over the nation and even set up his own press service. By the early years of the twentieth century he had become the nation's most powerful "press lord," using a formula of sensationalism plus human interest that usually lacked Pulitzer's saving grace of concern for the underdog.

New Ideas and Modes of Thought. In the half-century following the Civil War a substantial group of urban, educated men and women adjusted their thinking to a flood of new ideas, many of them derived ultimately from the theories of the English naturalist Charles Darwin. Darwin's ideas often served as a prop for the social and economic status quo. Yet Darwinism also had a radically dislocating tendency, unsettling old attitudes and ways of thinking about society.

American social thought at the end of the Civil War was "formalistic." Attitudes toward society were often rooted in received wisdom, based on universal principles that changed little over time. To understand the world, to prescribe policies for society, one merely had to reason logically from these first principles. Formalistic thinkers assumed a static, rather than dynamic, reality and held tight to precedent and tradition when considering the lot of humankind. The advent of Darwin, stressing change and flux, seriously challenged this way of thinking. Institutions, like species, were not static; they evolved. Institutions, said these "reform Darwinists," must indeed be encouraged to change so as to maximize human welfare.

One man who found a progressive lesson in Darwinism was the sociologist Lester Ward. A man who had spent many years as a federal civil servant, Ward did not fear government. Society's ultimate goal, he believed, should be "the scientific control of the social forces by the collective mind of society." Similarly, Richard T. Ely used Darwinism to support the idea that government should play a positive role in the economy. Ely endorsed trade unions and believed the state was "an educational and ethical agency whose positive aid is an indispensable condition of human progress."

A still more radical break with the formalism of the past emerged from the fertile mind of the Norwegian-American Thorstein Veblen. Veblen rejected the economic "first principles" associated with the laissez-faire economists. These assumed that people made decisions based on rational self-interest and that their efforts to maximize material advantages explained how the economy operated. In fact, Veblen said, people were more often impelled by inherited drives and historically transmitted cultural values than by the desire to maximize wealth or profit. In *The Theory of the Leisure Class* (1899) Veblen sought to show that the great business magnates of the day were impelled as much by the primitive drives for status and emulation as by rational calculation. In later books he spoke about the "instinct of workmanship" as the wellspring of true economic progress. Veblen's major intellectual contribution, however, was to create a new school of "institutional" economics that substituted the study of economic practices evolving over time for model-making based on supposed first principles.

Legal thinking, too, felt the impact of the evolutionary revolt against formalism. Here the outstanding figure was Oliver Wendell Holmes, Jr., associate justice of the Supreme Court (1902–1932) and one of the great legal minds of his generation. Holmes attacked the idea that the law was a static set of rules struck off by some great intellect in the past or the incontestable collective wisdom of the ages. Such a view, he stated in *The Common Law* (1881), was merely a convenient defense of the past. All law, even law embodied in revered documents such as the federal Constitution, had evolved gradually in response to the needs of particular periods and groups. "The felt necessities of the time, the prevalent moral and political theories, institutions of public policy, avowed or unconscious, even the prejudices which judges share with their fellow men," he declared, "have a good deal more to do than the syllogism in determining the rules by which men should be governed." The law must evolve with the times, said Holmes. When it was out of touch with modern conditions and needs, it merely served as a brake on progress.

In the discipline of history we find the same critical spirit during the years following 1890. American historical studies had emphasized the extent to which characteristic American institutions were planted as "germs" (seeds) by northern European settlers. Thus the New England town meeting and ultimately the nation's democratic legislatures were survivals of ancient German peoples' assemblies. There was no sense in the work of scholars that the American environment had substantially altered those germs. Then in 1893 Frederick Jackson Turner famously informed the American Historical Association that "American democracy was born of no theorist's dream; it was not carried in the *Susan Constant* to Virginia, nor in the *Mayflower* to Plymouth. It came out of the American forest, and it gained new strength each time it touched a new frontier." This was an evolutionary view of American institutions, one that took seriously the three centuries of experience on American soil. Turner eventually developed a theory of change that emphasized the molding effect of the physical environment.

The new spirit of dissent from static and excessively abstract ways of viewing social institutions also affected philosophy, the most abstract area of thought. The new approach was Pragmatism, and its major practitioners were John Dewey and William James.

The pragmatists dealt with the issue of "what is true?" The old view, they noted, held that truth was some ultimate measuring rod to which statements or beliefs corresponded. But this was not so. Truth, in reality, was a quality that changed, evolved, as relationships were viewed from different perspectives or as an idea was employed for different purposes. To the pragmatists, most of the ideas about ultimate realities that had concerned philosophers and thinkers over the centuries simply had no real answers, except formal and inconsequential ones. What men and women needed to know was what difference did it make whether this was true or that was false. The "value" of an idea, then, was not in its truth or falsity in the traditional sense, but in what consequences flowed from believing it or applying it. In a vivid but misunderstood phrase, William James declared that it was "the cash value" of an idea that really counted.

Because true ideas were those that had desirable effects in the world around us, the purpose of thought was not to contemplate eternity but to solve problems and serve as a guide to some practical course of action. In John Dewey's version of pragmatism the model of all truth-seeking was the experimental method of the natural sciences. Social and political ideas could not be tested by rigorous experiments, perhaps, but social and political thinkers, like natural scientists, could ask about the consequences of choosing course "A" as opposed to course "B," and act accordingly.

The pragmatic approach was experimental, practical, relativistic, and evolutionary. To the pragmatists the world was not rigidly laid out and determined. It was, rather, incomplete, ongoing, open, diverse, and turbulent—very much, they said, like the urban-industrial America of the day—and the task of philosophers and other thinkers was to find solutions to the problems of real people in the real world.

As a whole, Pragmatism was a method or approach rather than a fully rounded system with precise prescriptions. Yet in one area, education, Dewey sought to apply his ideas directly. He believed that the education of the day was excessively static, mechanical, and irrelevant to the new society he saw emerging around him. Rather than memorizing by rote, he wanted students to be actively involved in learning. Dewey's disciples, the "progressive" educators, called this kind of teaching "learning by doing." Dewey also believed that teachers should spend less time on books and more on showing students how to get along with one another so that they could ultimately make society less competitive and exploitive. In 1904 Dewey joined the faculty of Teacher's College at Columbia University. There his teachings profoundly influenced an entire generation of professors of education and through them thousands of student teachers who spread the message of progressive education to virtually every school system in the country.

Darwinian ideas were profoundly disturbing to many people. Not all scientists accepted them. But most hostile were traditional Christians, both laypeople and ministers.

In the half-century after the Civil War Christian ideas powerfully affected the way Americans thought about the world and their place in it. Most Christians, but especially Protestants, placed the Bible at the center of their faith as God's revealed word. To the orthodox the account in Genesis of how God created the world and all its creatures in six days and how all humans were descendants of Adam and Eve was literally true. Darwinian ideas challenged the Bible's authority by proposing slow, natural processes for events that Scripture describes as under the immediate guidance of God and as happening in a brief period of time. Evolution also connected humankind to lower creatures in the biological realm. If Darwin was right, the Bible could not be literally true. In itself this conclusion was unthinkable, but its human consequences were also disturbing. If humans were part of the "brute creation," they could not be creatures made in God's own image and set above other living things as the Bible said. Evolution not only contradicted the Bible; it also seemed to strip humans of their unique dignity.

Traditional Christian belief also came under attack as scholars in England, France, and Germany began to examine the Bible as a historical document. Exponents of the so-called Higher Criticism depicted the Holy Scriptures as a work of men living in distinctive historical settings and compiled over generations. It did not represent God's exact words, they said, so much as the thoughts of inspired poets, chroniclers, philosophers, and prophets. As such it was not infallible, nor was it to be taken literally. Though the Higher Criticism originated abroad, it quickly won disciples among the American Protestant clergy and laity.

Many Christians, including clergymen, found it possible to accept both the essential truth of Christian teachings and the views of Darwin. Yet many, especially among the more evangelical Protestant denominations with rural roots, saw Darwin's ideas and the Higher Criticism as deplorable theories that endangered true religion. In 1910, to counter these views, the traditionalists published a pamphlet, the "Fundamentals," that enumerated five points as the irreducible foundation of true Christian faith: the infallibility of the Bible, Jesus's virgin birth, His resurrection, His atonement for humankind, and the inevitability of His second coming. In the following decades those who accepted the "Five Points" would wage a mighty battle to halt the erosion of traditional Protestantism and the growth of the modernism they perceived as false, dangerous to society, and threatening to human salvation.

Religious modernism was often linked to another new current in religious thought: the social gospel. During the 1870s and 1880s many clergymen and laypeople began to believe that Protestantism had retreated too far from the old Puritan zeal to make the world a better place and had lost contact with the urban poor. To ministers such as Washington Gladden, William Bliss, and Walter Rauschenbusch, it appeared that Christianity had failed the poor by emphasizing the problem of personal salvation excessively. To traditional Christians, Gladden explained, religion was "too much a matter between themselves and God." Yet true Christianity was social as much as individual. It required righteous dealings with other people, not merely concern for personal salvation. To the social gospel preachers it seemed essential that the churches take stands on social issues and defend the weak and oppressed from those who exploited them. As early as the 1880s Gladden endorsed trade unions and the right to strike. Bliss, an Episcopal minister influenced by the Christian socialism of England, organized an American society of Christian socialists in 1889. Rauschenbusch denounced the competitive economic system and supported one based on the cooperative ideal.

Social gospel ideas were especially powerful among the Unitarians, Episcopalians, Methodists, and Congregationalists—the denominations that were also most open to the Higher Criticism and new scientific ideas generally. In 1905, thirty-three social gospel-oriented denominations, representing millions of communicants, banded together in the Federal Council of Churches of Christ in America. The council endorsed the abolition of child labor and the adoption of the six-day workweek, workers' compensation for injury, old-age insurance, a living wage for workers, and other social reforms.

■ CONCLUSIONS ■

How tawdry and corrupt, then, was the Gilded Age? The cultural and intellectual life of the United States underwent a colossal transformation in the half-century following the Civil War. On every level, from the heights of academic philosophy to the everyday amusements of ordinary men and women, culture adapted to the new urbanism and to the changes in technology and in political and economic institutions that swept the nation.

Were the cultural adaptations to the new forces cheap and vulgar? Was Gilded Age America a "chromo civilization"? So many changes are involved that it would be difficult under any circumstances to answer these questions. The problem is made worse by the fact that we are seeking to evaluate ideas as well as artistic expression.

In the case of the arts, surely the changes of the period 1865–1915 were "progressive." It is difficult not to applaud the eclipse of insipid literary gentility by robust realism; it is difficult to defend the imitative architectural old guard against the innovative Louis Sullivan and Frank Lloyd Wright. In the area of popular culture, too, the changes of the period were surely advances, ultimately making accessible whole new worlds of enjoyment and knowledge to masses of ordinary people.

Changes in the realm of ideas, however, cannot be seen as a simple matter of progress. The struggle between the progressive thinkers and the formalists, for example, represents merely one round in a battle between competing views of the world, humanity, and God that has been fought in the Western world for hundreds of years. If the formalists were often too rigid, their opponents were often so flexible that they weakened all moral and intellectual guideposts.

The political system, on the other hand, clearly lagged behind. America was often admired for its freedom and democracy, but few at home or abroad believed it enjoyed a government of honest, principled leaders who gave the public what it deserved. In the political realm, the gilt was highly visible.

Meanwhile, as the twentieth century began, a new awareness of neglected needs and higher standards began to stir beneath the surface, inspired in part by the social gospel, reform Darwinism, and the pragmatic philosophers. Before long the nation would embark on a new, transforming political crusade.

Online Resources

"1896: The Presidential Campaign, Cartoons, and Commentary— The Populists"
http://www.iberia.vassar.edu/1896/populists.html
This site provides extensive information about the Populist Party, including explanations about dueling Populist factions, the party's platform, and primary news accounts.

"The Cross of Gold Speech"
http://www.ukans.edu/~kansite/hvn/articles/b_gold.htm

Read the full text of William Jennings Bryan's speech at the 1896 Democratic National Convention in which he attacks the notion of the gold standard.

Northwestern Industrial Army Marches to Join Coxey's Army
http://www.historylink.org/output.CMF?file_ID=2181
The unemployment that plagued men of Coxey's Washington army also stretched to the West Coast. This Web site describes the efforts of men from Seattle, Washington, to join in the demonstrations in the nation's capital.

Money Matters: The American Experience with Money
http://www.frbchi.org/pubs_speech/publications/BOOKLETS/money_matters/money_matters.html
This Web site of the Federal Reserve Bank of Chicago explains the history of money in the United States and sheds light on the late-nineteenth-century debate over silver, gold, and paper currencies.

21

THE AMERICAN EMPIRE

Why Did the United States Look Abroad?

1853–54	Commodore Perry opens American/Japanese trade
1867	Secretary of State Seward negotiates the purchase of Alaska and American control of the Midway Islands
1868	Ulysses S. Grant elected president
1869–70	Grant attempts to annex Santo Domingo
1877	Rutherford B. Hayes becomes president
1878	Coaling station at Pago Pago established
1880	James A. Garfield elected president
1881	Garfield is assassinated; Chester A. Arthur becomes president
1883	Congress appropriates funds to build modern naval vessels
1884	Grover Cleveland elected president
1887	The United States secures a naval base at Pearl Harbor
1888	Benjamin Harrison elected president
1890	The McKinley Tariff Act; Alfred Thayer Mahan's *The Influence of Sea Power upon History* published
1892	Grover Cleveland elected president
1893	American planters organize coup d'état in Hawaii; Frederick Jackson Turner's *The Significance of the Frontier in American History* published
1895	The United States disputes British claims in Venezuela
1896	William McKinley elected president
1898	The *Maine* is sunk in Havana harbor; Congress declares war on Spain; Congress votes to annex Hawaii; Treaty of Paris: Spain surrenders the Philippines, Puerto Rico, and Guam, and frees Cuba
1899–1900	Secretary of State Hay writes the *Open Door Notes*; The Boxer Rebellion
1899–1902	Emilio Aguinaldo leads a guerrilla war against the American occupation of the Philippines
1901	McKinley assassinated; Theodore Roosevelt becomes president; The Platt Amendment affirms American right to intervene in Cuba; The Hay-Pauncefote Treaty allows the United States to build a Central American interocean waterway
1903	Hay-Bunau-Varilla Treaty gives the United States the Canal Zone
1904	Roosevelt states Monroe Doctrine Corollary

In April 1898 Albert Beveridge, a young Indiana Republican soon to go to the United States Senate, spoke to Boston's Middlesex Club on the occasion of former President Grant's birthday. The Spanish-American War had just been declared, and although the fighting had scarcely begun, Beveridge looked ahead to what would follow the expected American victory.

> American factories are making more than the American people can use; American soil is producing more than they can consume. Fate has written our policy for us; the trade of the world must and shall be ours. . . . We shall establish trading posts throughout the world as distributing points for American products. We will cover the ocean with our merchant marine. We will build a navy to the measure of our greatness. Great colonies governing themselves, flying our flag and trading with us, will grow about our posts of trade. Our institutions will follow our flag on the wings of our commerce. And American law, American civilization, and the American flag will plant themselves on shores hitherto bloody and benighted, but by those agencies of God henceforth to be made beautiful and bright.

In this brief burst of oratory Beveridge summarized virtually every motive that contemporaries and later scholars would advance for America's overseas thrust during the generation following the Civil War. The American people needed markets for their surplus manufactures and farm products. They envisioned the glorious Stars and Stripes waving around the globe, with American civilization conferring immense benefits on the "benighted" peoples fortunate enough to fall under United States dominion. All this was to be accomplished by the "agencies of God." Glory, Gold, and God all justified an American empire in 1898—as they had a Spanish empire in 1498 and a British empire in 1598.

The resemblance between historical phenomena spread over 400 years is striking, and it is tempting to assume that not much had changed in the interval. But nineteenth-century Americans were not fifteenth-century Spaniards or sixteenth-century Englishmen. Even if they had the same general self-serving motives for expansion as their predecessors, these were expressed in different ways and present in different proportions. How can we explain America's expansionist impulse during the years immediately preceding our own century?

■ THE BACKGROUND ■

Viewed one way, post-Civil War expansionism seems merely an extension of the American past. For 250 years following the first permanent English settlements along the Atlantic Coast, Americans had pushed steadily westward toward the Pacific. This was not the filling in of an empty continent. The vast interior of North America was occupied by Native Americans who resisted the settlers' thrust and were pushed aside, often brutally. Parts of what later became the United States, moreover, were under the sovereignty of European nations, and Americans used aggressive diplomacy and military force to incorporate these areas into the United States. In this sense, the overseas thrust following 1865 was simply a continuation of what had preceded.

Any theory of post-Civil War expansionism must also consider the immediate international context. Expansionism is an expression of unequal power. As the Western world's advantage in technology and wealth increased during the nineteenth century, the temptation to use that edge grew irresistible. The closing decades of the century witnessed the last burst of European colonialism, until the remotest regions of the Earth were firmly under European control. America in these years surpassed its competitors on every index of wealth; inevitably, this view holds, it felt the same urge as the other western nations to impose its will on others.

And we must consider a common Marxist theory of capitalist imperialism that has long been influential in intellectual circles. Marxists hold that advanced capitalist societies inevitably develop "contradictions" that take the form of insufficient markets for their goods and outlets for their capital at home, and so turn to weaker societies to exploit. Imperialism derives from the capitalist need to stave off crisis and social upheavals.

■ THE BEGINNINGS OF OVERSEAS EXPANSION ■

The story of American overseas expansion does not begin abruptly in 1865. Before the Civil War southern pressures had induced President Franklin Pierce to offer Spain $130 million for the island of Cuba. In the same era American adventurers and soldiers of fortune had fomented revolutions in Central America for the purpose of annexing territory to the United States. In the mid-1850s, an aggressive policy of encouraging foreign trade culminated in the visits of an American naval squadron to Japan under Commodore Matthew Perry, forcing Japan to open its doors to commerce and traditional diplomatic relations with other nations. The Civil War brought these expansionist activities to a sudden halt. But after Appomattox Americans began once again to look with interest toward the surrounding oceans and the lands that dotted and bordered them.

Foreign Policy Under Seward. The man at the forefront of this revived concern with the outside world was William Henry Seward, Andrew Johnson's secretary of state. Seward's interest in American expansion had its practical, strategic side. The nation's difficulties in dealing with the Confederate ships raiding northern commerce during the Civil War had convinced him that the United States must have naval bases and coaling stations scattered around its perimeter to fend off any future naval aggressor. He also had a romantic vision of a benevolent American empire that resembled the Manifest Destiny of the 1840s. In 1867, in a burst of poetry surprising in a man so practical and businesslike, Seward announced:

> Our nation with united interests blest,
> Not content to pose, shall sway the rest;
> Abroad our empire shall no limits know,
> But like the sea in boundless limits flow.

But first Seward had to attend to the problem of European intrusion into the Western Hemisphere. In 1863, while the United States was preoccupied by the Civil War, the French had established a puppet regime in Mexico under Archduke Maximilian of Austria and had sent troops to support him against Mexican patriots led by Benito Juárez. The French occupation of Mexico was a clear challenge to the Monroe Doctrine of 1823, and when the war ended, Seward told Napoleon III, the French emperor, that the United States would no longer tolerate Maximilian's rule in Mexico. Growing opposition at home, the cost of maintaining troops in America, and the threat of the seasoned Union army just across the border induced the French to withdraw their support of the puppet regime in 1867. Shortly thereafter, Maximilian was captured by Juárez's forces and executed.

Seward's success in driving out the French was applauded by both Americans and Mexicans. For once, the Monroe Doctrine had served as an effective shield against European aggression in the Americas. But Americans did not greet Seward's expansionist moves as warmly. Most were either indifferent or stubbornly opposed to empire building. When Seward tried to buy land for a coaling station in Santo Domingo (the Dominican Republic), Congress refused to back him. He also could not get Congress to approve a treaty to purchase the Danish West Indies (now the U.S. Virgin Islands). Critics of the secretary had a field day with these island-shopping trips. A mock advertisement in a New York newspaper ran: "A Few West India Islands Wanted.—Any distressed persons having a few islands to dispose of in the Spanish Main can find a purchaser by applying to Washington D.C. . . ." The only islands that Seward ever managed to acquire were specks of land a thousand miles west of Hawaii: the Midway group. Seward's only major expansionist success was the vast northwestern edge of North America, Alaska.

"Seward's Folly." Alaska, a Russian possession, had been exploited for many years by the Russian-American Company primarily for its furs. By the mid-nineteenth century the fur trade had begun to decline, and the Russian government faced the prospect of having to rescue the company from bankruptcy. The Russians also feared that in a war with Great Britain, they would not be able to protect their distant colony. Unsure of Alaska's defenses and unwilling to support it financially, the czar decided to sell it to the United States.

The American secretary of state was more than willing to talk terms. Seward saw Alaska not only as a base for American naval defense in any Pacific war, but also as a way-station to the Far East and the potential markets of China. But many outspoken Americans were opposed to acquiring a distant, unknown, and apparently worthless chunk of land. Those who had ridiculed Seward's Caribbean interests promptly called his new scheme "Seward's Folly" and the territory itself "Seward's Icebox." A weekly newspaper reported that the benefits of buying Russian America included a bracing climate, a promising ice crop, and cows that gave ice cream instead of milk. At the very least, the $7.2 million that the Russians wanted was a high price for half a million square miles of desolate mountains, icefields, tundra, and scrub forest.

Seward quickly mounted a sales campaign to change his fellow citizens' minds. He secured expert testimonials describing the region's vast natural resources and collected 1803 newspaper attacks on the Louisiana Purchase to show his opponents as timid men without vision or foresight. Aided by Charles Sumner, the influential chairman of the Senate Foreign Relations Committee, he induced the Senate to pass the Alaska annexation treaty. When the House of Representatives balked at appropriating the necessary money, the Russian minister plied the reluctant members with cash. In the end it all worked out. On October 18, 1867, the American flag was raised over the Russian fort at Sitka. Alaska was now American territory.

A Stronger Navy. For almost two decades following Seward's retirement, the American people turned inward. In 1869–1870 the Senate rejected President Grant's attempt to annex all of Santo Domingo, and thereafter the expansionist impulse subsided. During the 1870s and 1880s much of the nation's energy was consumed in filling in the rest of the continent with farms, railroads, mines, factories, and new cities and towns. So remote and unimportant did America's foreign relations appear that as late as 1889 the *New York Sun* could half seriously suggest doing away with the diplomatic service as "a costly humbug and sham" that did "no good to anybody."

Yet even during this low point, there were rumblings of a revived interest in foreign concerns and a new aggressiveness toward the outside world. The new mood manifested itself initially as anxiety about American naval impotence. Of the 1,900 vessels in the fleet in 1880, only 48 could fire a gun. Citizens began to wonder how the country could protect itself against foreign attack. To remedy the problem, in 1883 Congress authorized four new steel coast defense warships, adding the battleships *Texas* and *Maine* to the fleet several years later. Americans breathed a little easier, but still the navy remained primarily a defensive force.

Then, in the 1890s, the United States began to build a high-seas fleet capable of supporting an ambitious foreign policy. The inspiration for the "new navalism" was the writings of Captain Alfred Thayer Mahan, a career naval officer who taught at the Naval War College at Newport, Rhode Island. In *The Influence of Sea Power upon History,* published in 1890, he described how Britain had become the mightiest nation in the world by seizing command of the seas. America must now strive to equal Great Britain or accept eventual decline.

Mahan's popular book convinced many that the country must have a navy second to none. Spurred on by Mahan's ideas, during the 1890s the United States built numerous fast warships with long cruising ranges, capable of meeting an enemy anywhere in the world. By the end of the decade the naval building program had created a high-seas fleet consisting of seventeen steel-hulled battleships, along with six armored cruisers and numerous modern smaller craft.

"Jingo Jim" Blaine. Still, Americans as a whole remained uninterested in foreign concerns. James G. Blaine, secretary of state under James Garfield (1881) and again under Benjamin Harrison (1889–1892), felt differently. Blaine was not a man to sit at his desk and shuffle papers. "Jingo Jim" was particularly interested in Latin America. Like many Americans since Monroe's day, he believed that the United States had a special big-brother role to play in the Western Hemisphere and he advocated stronger ties among the nations of the New World, a policy he referred to as "Pan-Americanism."

Blaine's interest in Latin America combined altruism and economic gain in roughly equal parts. Although the United States bought large quantities of foodstuffs and raw materials from its southern neighbors, Latin America continued to buy most of its manufactured goods from Europe. Blaine hoped to divert the flow of Latin American trade from Europe to the United States, but he feared that improved economic relations would be impossible so long as the Latin American nations continued to squabble constantly among themselves. If the United States could act as a peacemaker and a stabilizing influence in the Western Hemisphere, everyone would benefit. Good deeds would bring good profits.

In 1881 Blaine called an inter-American conference to meet in Washington to further these goals. Before it could assemble, President Garfield was assassinated. Blaine soon resigned as secretary of state, and his successor in the State Department canceled the conference. Blaine got another chance during the second round of his "spirited diplomacy" when he again became secretary of state under President Benjamin Harrison. In October 1889 representatives of seventeen Latin American states convened in Washington at Blaine's invitation. The results, from Blaine's point of view, were mixed. The delegates rejected the secretary's pet project, a Western Hemisphere customs union to increase United States–Latin American trade and curtail trade with Europe. They also turned down his proposal for establishing procedures to handle inter-American disagreements. The conference, however, did establish the Pan American Union as a clearinghouse to distribute information and further hemispheric cooperation.

A New Frontier.   Thus, even during this low point in diplomacy, Americans never completely lost their interest in international affairs. In the last two decades of the century, thoughtful men and women began to reconsider their country's place in the world. During the 1880s and 1890s a sense of crisis seized many middle-class Americans. The nation, it seemed, was threatened with serious instability in the form of Populism, labor unrest, and political radicalism. Why was discontent so rife and what could be done about it? As they struggled for answers, Americans encountered a persistent theme: The United States had run out of physical space.

The most influential spokesman for this idea was the historian Frederick Jackson Turner, who in 1893 announced that the frontier experience was over. For almost three centuries the "West" had provided a constructive outlet for social discontents and had encouraged social and political democracy. Now it was gone, he said, and a vital safety valve had closed. Turner did not propose moving the American frontier overseas, but he raised in the minds of the educated the frightening prospect of growing inequality and social chaos if America could not find some alternative to continental expansion.

The Reverend Josiah Strong made the overseas expansion solution explicit. His views in some ways parallel those of the Marxists. In his popular book *Our Country* (1885) he asserted that since the free land was gone, the United States would soon "approximate European conditions of life," marked by class conflict and gross inequality. To avoid these afflictions, America must leap the oceans and find new frontiers abroad where its civilization would have room to expand. Though Strong's vision combined Protestant missionary zeal and American expansionism, his advocacy of expanded foreign Christian missions was lost in the defense of American destiny.

Strong and Turner used history and sociology to justify expansion; another group of expansionist thinkers relied on science, or pseudo-science. Social Darwinists viewed the competition among nations and peoples as a necessary continuation of the struggle for survival that fueled biological evolution. In this struggle the strong would win and gain dominion over the weak. Imperialism then was condoned by nature. At its most extreme, social Darwinism tipped over into the "scientific" racism of Madison Grant, John Fiske, John W. Burgess, and others who believed in the "natural superiority" of the Nordic and Anglo-Saxon peoples. Grant, who was associated with the Museum of Natural History in New York, used notions of nordic superiority primarily to justify immigration restriction. But other racists insisted that this superiority gave Americans the right to rule "inferior peoples." Anglo-Saxons had always been conquerors, declared philosopher and historian Fiske, and would continue to assert their "sovereignty of the seas" and "their commercial supremacy." Burgess, a professor of political science at Columbia University, taught his students that people of English origin were particularly well suited to the establishment of national states and were destined to impose their political institutions on the rest of the world.

The Foreign Policy Elite. The literate, middle-class Americans who read the works of Turner, Strong, Grant, and the other expansionist thinkers were an important part of the political community. But closer to the process of decision making in foreign affairs was what one scholar has called "the foreign policy elite." This was a small group of people who were seriously, and often personally, concerned with what went on in the outside world. Strategically located in government, journalism, the universities, the professions, and business, they influenced public opinion, Congress, and the State Department out of proportion to their numbers. Undoubtedly their concerns were in part economically derived. But there were also elements of nationalism, cosmopolitanism, and broad cultural and intellectual interest in world affairs. To many of this elite it seemed a shame that the United States, as strong as any of the great European colonial powers, had so far held back. America's restraint, they said, had encouraged Europe to consider it unimportant in international affairs outside the Western Hemisphere. Few European countries, they noted, assigned ambassadors to Washington, being content with ministers or lesser diplomatic representatives. A colonial empire promised to end this inferiority and propel the United States into the ranks of the world powers, where the foreign policy elite believed it belonged.

■ HAWAII AND VENEZUELA ■

Toward the end of the 1880s, then, expansionist sentiment and national assertiveness began to reemerge among the decision makers and the public at large. Early in the 1890s the phrase "Manifest Destiny" began to appear once more in political platforms; in 1893 Congress created the rank of ambassador to replace that of minister in the diplomatic service. Yet for some years Americans' interest in overseas matters would continue to vacillate, as the experience with Hawaii illustrates.

Ambivalence About Expansion.   The strategic value of the Hawaiian Islands had been recognized ever since the English explorer, Captain James Cook, had encountered them in 1778. In the early nineteenth century American merchant ships en route to China often stopped at the beautiful islands for fresh water and supplies. In 1820 the first American missionaries arrived and devoted themselves to bringing their Christian faith to the native Polynesian peoples. Whalers soon came to the island kingdom, and the whaling crews, long without female companionship, helped to undo the missionaries' efforts to change Hawaiian morals. The sons of the missionaries, along with other American settlers attracted to the islands, made sugar-growing rather than soul-saving their chief concern and eventually came to own much of the land. The strong American presence and the strategic location of the island chain inevitably aroused the interest of the United States government. Seward soon added the annexation of Hawaii to his other ambitious schemes. But few Americans were interested and nothing was done at this time. Then, in 1875 the United States agreed to allow Hawaiian sugar, unlike that from other foreign lands, to enter the United States duty free. As a result, the islands' economy soon became dependent on the profitable American market. The Hawaiian government, meanwhile, came under the influence of the American planters and businessmen who had brought prosperity to the kingdom. In 1887 the United States renewed the sugar agreement and received the right to use Pearl Harbor as a naval base.

Suddenly the rosy Hawaiian economic situation changed. The McKinley Tariff of 1890 removed the duty on all sugar entering the United States, thus ending Hawaii's advantage over its competitors in the American market. The islands' economy took a nose dive. Almost simultaneously Queen Liliuokalani succeeded her brother to the Hawaiian throne, determined to restore much of the royal power he had surrendered to American advisers. The new queen was anti-American. Adopting the battle cry "Hawaii for the Hawaiians," she launched a campaign to end all foreign influence in her kingdom. In 1893 she issued a new constitution that disenfranchised all Europeans, except those married to native Hawaiian women, and gave the monarch dictatorial powers.

The Americans in Hawaii promptly organized a "Committee of Safety," staged a coup d'état, and established a provisional government. The American minister to Hawaii, John L. Stevens, used the pretext of protecting American property to deploy marines from the cruiser U.S.S. *Boston* outside the queen's palace. Unable to resist this show of force, the queen abdicated. Stevens then

*Queen Liliuokalani was actually less benevolent
than this picture suggests.*

proclaimed the islands an American protectorate and triumphantly wrote the
State Department: "The Hawaiian pear is now fully ripe and this is the golden
hour for the United States to pluck it." Repeating the process of Texas-Americans
sixty years before, the provisional government leaders soon applied for annexation to the United States.

President Harrison quickly signed an annexation treaty with representatives
of the rebel government. Unfortunately for the annexationists, Grover Cleveland
became president before the Senate could act on the treaty. Upright, principled,
conscientious, Cleveland opposed territorial acquisition and doubted the morality of the American residents' takeover. He withdrew the treaty from the Senate
and sent James H. Blount as his personal representative to the islands to investigate the circumstances of the queen's downfall.

When the Blount report arrived in Washington, it confirmed Cleveland's
worst suspicions. Stevens, it said, had high-handedly interfered in Hawaii's
internal affairs; a large majority of native Hawaiian voters opposed annexation.
For a time, Cleveland considered restoring the queen to her throne. But when

she declared her intention to decapitate the revolutionaries as soon as she regained control, he withdrew his support, allowed the Americans to remain in power, and recognized the provisional government as the legitimate authority of the Republic of Hawaii. But he refused to join the islands legally with the United States. Until its annexation in 1898, Hawaii remained an independent republic controlled by its American residents.

The Monroe Doctrine Reasserted. The Hawaiian affair points up the still-cautious side of American foreign policy. But as the century approached its end the jingoist, aggressive side took hold. This more combative attitude was displayed in the Venezuela incident of 1895. Independent Venezuela and the English colony of British Guiana, on the Caribbean coast of South America, had long disputed their common boundary. From the beginning of this controversy, the Venezuelans had sought American support and had taken pains to depict the British as callous aggressors against a weaker nation.

The American State Department had become suspicious of renewed European interest in Latin America. The Royal Navy had recently landed troops in Nicaragua on the pretext that the British consul had been insulted. The incident, made doubly offensive to Americans by the British admiral's remark that the Monroe Doctrine was a myth, had set off a strong anti-British response in the American press. American anxiety over European colonial ambitions in the Western Hemisphere was reinforced by the desire to prevent British commercial dominance in the large area of the continent drained by the Orinoco River. Matters came to a head in 1894 when the British government refused President Cleveland's offer to arbitrate the dispute.

Early in 1895 Congress passed a resolution denouncing British claims in Venezuela. Secretary of State Richard Olney backed the resolution in a brusque and aggressive letter to the American minister in London. Defending the right of the United States under the Monroe Doctrine to guarantee the independence of Latin American republics, the secretary launched into a blunt declaration of American power that startled the British. "Its infinite resources," he boasted, "combined with its isolated position render [the United States] the master of the situation and practically invulnerable against any or all other powers." Olney concluded by demanding arbitration and insisting that Britain respond before Congress met later in the year. Offended by Olney's tone, the British prime minister, Lord Salisbury, rejected the call for arbitration with a brusqueness almost equal to Olney's. President Cleveland replied that if Britain refused arbitration, the United States would impose a boundary line and defend it with military force if necessary. Amid a wave of anti-British enthusiasm throughout the United States and Latin America, Congress approved Cleveland's plan and quickly appropriated $100,000 for a boundary commission. Anglophobes and jingoes eagerly awaited war with Great Britain.

Fortunately for world peace, sober second thoughts soon took hold on both sides of the Atlantic. By now Britain had begun to fear an aggressive German empire that was challenging British naval supremacy and had recently sided against the British in their dispute with the Boer settlers in South Africa. Rather than take on both the United States and Germany, Lord Salisbury chose to placate the Americans. In the United States a peace faction composed of clergy, business leaders, financiers, and journalists was able to cool down heated tempers. Britain and Venezuela eventually agreed to accept arbitration; but by the time a decision was handed down in 1899, the whole dispute had been virtually forgotten.

■ CUBA LIBRE ■

Cleveland's second administration (1893–1897) marked a transition from an isolationist to a more expansionist attitude toward the world. The shift was triggered by events in Cuba. That rich island, along with Puerto Rico, had remained under Spanish rule long after the rest of Spain's New World empire had disintegrated. The Cubans, however, were dissatisfied with Spanish rule and in 1868 launched an insurrection to gain independence. During the ten-year uprising Cuban rebels, some of them naturalized American citizens, appealed to the United States for help. But despite a number of minor diplomatic brushes with Spain, the United States refused to be drawn in, and the revolt eventually subsided.

Revolution in Cuba. For seventeen years the Cuban revolutionary spirit remained dormant. Then, in the early 1890s, harsh Spanish rule, its effects amplified by a severe crisis in the Cuban sugar industry, goaded the Cubans to revolt once again. The insurrectionists set fire to sugar plantations and cattle ranches in the countryside, hoping that Spain would capitulate if nothing of value was left on the island. Cuban patriots living in the United States organized groups called "juntas" to aid the rebels and provoke trouble between Spain and the United States. The Spanish authorities under General Valeriano Weyler (called "the butcher" in the anti-Spanish press) struck back by rounding up thousands of suspected rebels and sympathizers, including women and children, and confining them in concentration camps. Weyler did not intend mass murder, but unsanitary conditions and rebel interference with the food-supply systems made the concentration areas death camps.

American Sympathies. As in virtually all revolutions and civil wars, both sides were brutal and destructive, yet almost without exception the American people condemned Spain and supported the Cuban rebels. It used to be said that our sympathies were determined by our economic interests in the island. But there is little evidence to support this assertion. In reality, with the depression of 1893–1897 finally coming to an end, involvement in Cuba that might lead to war was the last thing the business community wanted. As relations with Spain worsened, the business press attacked any drastic action that would "impede the march of prosperity and put the country back many years." Farmers were more interventionist. Agricultural spokesmen favored policies to expand overseas markets for American crops, but few favored war with Spain. As for labor, working people usually shared the views of their employers: A war with Spain would depress business and therefore hurt the working class. And yet by April 1898 most Americans—farmers, businesspeople, wage earners, and others—had come to favor intervening in Cuba despite the risk of war with Spain. Why?

Clearly, Americans were moved by age-old sympathies for underdogs and identified the Cuban insurrection with their own struggle for freedom from a European power 120 years before. But traditional attitudes were not enough to push Americans to war. Fortunately for the Cuban rebels, American sympathies were strongly reinforced by the activities of the "yellow press," especially William Randolph Hearst's *New York Journal* and Joseph Pulitzer's *New York World*. During the late 1890s, as we saw, the two press lords fought a bitter circulation war. Truth often took a back seat to profit. Each sought to provide a daily diet of atrocity stories detailing Spanish brutality, for that sold papers. Both were unscrupulous, though Hearst was probably even less principled than his rival. According to one story, when an American artist sent to Cuba to illustrate the insurrection reported that things were quiet, Hearst shot back: "You furnish the pictures and I'll furnish the war."

War Becomes Unavoidable.   Yet war seemed only a remote possibility when William McKinley was inaugurated in March 1897. The new president shared the business community's reluctance to jeopardize returning prosperity and declared in his inaugural address that war must be avoided "until every agency of peace has failed; peace is preferable to war in almost every contingency." But McKinley could not control events. Ordinary public opinion was running against him, and the foreign policy elite considered his course cowardly and unworthy. The chauvinist New Yorker Theodore Roosevelt, for one, believed McKinley was as spineless "as a chocolate éclair." Early in 1898 a key group of congressional Republicans agreed to push the president for a war resolution, promising to join with the Democrats and sponsor one themselves if he did not comply. The religious press, viewing the issue in Cuba as a fight between Cuban virtue and Spanish beastliness, also demanded that the American government intervene to end the atrocious situation.

The Spaniards seemed to be their own worst enemies. In January 1898 the Spanish minister to the United States, Enrique Dupuy de Lôme, a well-meaning but indiscreet grandee, wrote an imprudent letter to a friend in Cuba expressing his contempt for McKinley and admitting that Spain was negotiating in bad faith over a proposed trade treaty with America. A Cuban patriot stole the letter from the desk of the recipient in Havana and sent it to Hearst, who promptly published it in his newspapers. The outraged public demanded that de Lôme be sent home. The minister instantly resigned in hope of mending the situation, but the damage was done. The American people now had even more reason than before to picture the Spaniards as arrogant and deceitful.

De Lôme's blunder was soon followed by an even bigger blow to Spanish–American relations. In January 1898 the American government sent the battleship *Maine* to Havana. The visit was officially "friendly"; the ship was supposedly only there to protect American lives and property following a serious local riot. The captain and the crew of the vessel were treated courteously by Spanish officials in Havana, though the visit naturally aroused some suspicion. Then, on February 15, a tremendous explosion rocked the ship, sending it to the bottom of the harbor with the loss of over 260 lives.

A modern investigation of the sunken ship has confirmed the view that the *Maine* was destroyed by a boiler explosion. But contemporaries disagreed. Spanish authorities disclaimed responsibility for the sinking. American divers at the time concluded that the explosion had come from outside. Regardless of who or what sank the ship, most Americans considered it an act of war. Agreeing with Theodore Roosevelt's theory that the *Maine* had been "sunk by an act of dirty treachery on the part of the Spaniards," they demanded immediate retaliation. Jingoes had a field day. Mass rallies were held all over the country at news of the atrocity. People marched through the streets, chanting, "Remember the *Maine*. To Hell with Spain!" The yellow press, of course, insisted that Spain be punished with all the force of America's might.

McKinley could not resist the growing pressure to intervene. He promptly instructed the American minister in Madrid to demand that the Spanish government grant an armistice to the rebels and end the cruel concentration camp policy. If Spain did not accept these terms by October, the United States would impose a settlement. The Spanish government was caught in a dilemma. Public opinion would be outraged by surrender to the United States; but war seemed

A contemporary artist's horrific vision of what the destruction of the battleship Maine *looked like.*

the certain alternative. For a while it wavered, but finally, on the advice of the pope, it agreed to grant an armistice and abolish the concentration camps.

Spain had given the United States virtually everything it had asked for, but it was not enough to avoid war. American opinion now would not be satisfied with anything less than an independent Cuba—"Cuba Libre." The president was still reluctant to intervene, but he, too, was caught in a dilemma. In Congress the pressure to declare war was becoming irresistible; even if he did not request a declaration of war, there were signs that Congress would go ahead without him. Moreover, if he held back, the Democrats would charge him with weakness and jeopardize his chances of winning reelection in 1900.

On April 11 McKinley sent a war message to Congress. The United States, he said, must protect the lives and property of American citizens and put an end to the "barbarities, bloodshed, starvation, and horrible miseries . . . right at [its] door." Intervention was justified, the president claimed, by the "very serious injury to commerce, trade, and business of our people, and by the wanton destruction of property and devastation of the island." In addition, it was of "utmost importance" to end a disturbance that was a "constant menace to our peace and entails upon this Government an enormous expense."

On April 19 Congress passed four resolutions defining the nation's war policy: (1) Cuba must be free; (2) Spain must withdraw from the island; (3) the president could use the armed forces to obtain these ends; and (4) the United States would not annex Cuba. The commitment to nonannexation—the Teller Amendment—was approved without a dissenting vote. On April 25, 1898, Congress formally declared war on Spain.

■ THE SPANISH-AMERICAN WAR ■

The war with Spain was short and cheap. Few American lives were lost; more soldiers died at "Custer's Last Stand" than from battle wounds in the entire Spanish-American conflict. Moreover, the war was over in a few months and peace concluded by December 1898. As wars go, this one was also a bargain: It cost the United States only $250 million. John Hay, soon to be secretary of state, called it a "splendid little war," and from the point of view of most Americans, the successes of their country's armed forces, particularly the navy, were splendid indeed.

Quick Victory. As assistant secretary of the navy, Theodore Roosevelt had anticipated war with Spain and, acting in the absence of his superior, he had dispatched Commodore George Dewey and the navy's Asiatic squadron to China even before McKinley delivered his war message. With the official war declaration, Dewey sailed for the Philippines, a Spanish possession in the China Sea. Commanding six modern vessels of the new fleet, Dewey attacked and sank the whole Spanish Asiatic squadron in Manila Bay without losing a ship and hardly a man. The navy soon repeated Dewey's Pacific triumph in the Caribbean. In July the main United States naval force in Cuban waters under admiral William T. Sampson sank the Spanish fleet in a brief battle off Santiago. American losses were one sailor killed, one wounded.

The army's performance was considerably less impressive. For years its main job had been to contain and control the Indians in the West. When war came, the War Department had to recruit and train a large number of volunteers, including Roosevelt's band of western cowboys and eastern gentlemen who, along with Roosevelt himself, enlisted as the "Rough Riders." Secretary of War Russell A. Alger botched the job of organizing and supplying the new recruits. Amid incredible confusion, 17,000 ill-equipped soldiers were embarked from Tampa, Florida, and landed near Santiago in southeastern Cuba. After several sharp skirmishes with the Spaniards, including the Rough Riders' famous charge up San Juan Hill, the Americans captured the heights overlooking the city. On July 17, following Sampson's naval victory, the Spanish military commander in Santiago surrendered. Soon after the American army occupied Puerto Rico without opposition.

The Spoils of War. By the end of July the Spanish government was ready to sue for peace. In October delegates from the United States and Spain met in Paris to work out final details. Spain had already agreed to give Cuba its independence and to cede Puerto Rico and the Pacific island of Guam to the United States. The issue that blocked final terms was the fate of the Philippines. Although Dewey had sunk the Spanish Asiatic fleet, he lacked occupation troops and waited offshore for reinforcements before taking Manila, the capital city. Meanwhile, Britain and Germany assembled naval squadrons nearby, ostensibly to protect the interests of their citizens in the Philippines but actually to claim the islands if the United States proved uninterested.

Before the war few Americans paid attention to the Philippines; most did not even know where they were. Now, suddenly, they were up to their ears in international complications over these exotic islands. What should they do with them? Many were disturbed by German designs. Since its unification twenty years before, Germany had become an aggressive colonial power, rummaging around for new properties all over the world. This had seldom disturbed Americans before, but the United States had fought for the islands; the Germans had expended nothing for them. Why allow them to fall into undeserving hands?

And there were also practical matters to consider. Though initially skeptical of war, the business community was now convinced that the islands could serve as a base for trade with China. In July 1898, moved by a new, war-generated expansionist fever, Congress had finally annexed Hawaii. Add the Philippines as well and the United States would have a convenient set of steppingstones across the Pacific to the Asian mainland. As Senator Henry Cabot Lodge noted, controlling the port of Manila would be "the thing which will give us the eastern trade."

There were serious moral considerations as well. Could we rescue Cuba from Spanish tyranny and return the Filipino people to Spain's harsh rule? Besides, what a field for missionary effort the islands promised to be! Ignoring the fact that most Filipinos were already Catholics, McKinley found this opportunity to advance Christian civilization a compelling reason to hold on to the islands. He had been troubled by the fate of the Philippines and its people, he later told a church group, until in answer to his prayers for divine guidance he had suddenly seen what must be done:

> We could not give them back to Spain—that would be cowardly and dishonorable. . . .
> There was nothing left for us to do but take them all and to educate the Filipinos, and
> uplift and civilize them and Christianize them, and by God's grace do the very best by
> them, as our fellowmen for whom Christ also died.

After reaching this convenient inspired and practical conclusion, McKinley told the American negotiators in Paris to insist that the whole island chain be given to the United States as part of the peace agreement. Spain resisted at first, but in exchange for $20 million it surrendered the Philippines, along with Puerto Rico and Guam, and at the same time confirmed Cuban independence.

The Anti-Imperialists.   The Treaty of Paris, especially the provision ceding the Philippines, triggered a storm of protest in the United States. The war had undoubtedly legitimized imperialism, but many opponents of expansion remained unconvinced. Mugwump reformers, along with many intellectuals and clergymen, believed that acquiring colonies was immoral and damaging to American traditions. By searching for colonies, lamented professor Charles Eliot Norton of Harvard, America had "lost her unique position as a potential leader in the progress of civilization" and had "taken her place simply as one of the grasping and selfish nations of the present day." Other anti-imperialists were more angry than sad about the nation's desertion of its ideals. "God damn the United States for its vile conduct in the Philippine Isles," wrote the philosopher William James. If the United States made the islands a colony, it would leave the Filipinos with nothing: we could "destroy their own ideals," he declared, "but we can't give them ours." Many anti-imperialists feared that racial problems would overwhelm the United States if it incorporated the Philippines and parts of the Caribbean into its domain. Could the nation, asked Carl Schurz, absorb territories inhabited by "savages and half-savages" all "animated with the instinct, impulses and passions bred by the tropical sun." If we attempted to do so, "what will become of American labor and the standards of American citizenship?" Banded together as the Anti-Imperialist League, the opponents of colonies tried to block American negotiators from signing the Treaty of Paris. When this effort failed, the league turned its attention to the Senate, where the fight for ratification promised to be long and bitter. In the course of a few months it badgered senators and other politicians to stop the treaty and mailed thousands of propaganda pieces denouncing colonialism.

Ratification of the Treaty of Paris.   In the end the anti-imperialists failed. Under a barrage of cajolery, persuasion, and pressure from McKinley and other administration leaders, almost all Senate Republicans pledged to support the treaty. But Democratic votes, too, were needed for passage and William Jennings Bryan seemed to hold the key to success. Though defeated for president in

1896 and now a private citizen, he continued to exert great influence among fellow Democrats. Bryan was not an imperialist, but he threw his support behind the treaty, believing that ending the war was more important than the details of the settlement. He also naively assumed the United States would give the Philippines its freedom almost immediately. Enough Democrats went along with Bryan to carry the treaty 57 to 27, just one vote more than needed for ratification.

■ IMPERIAL AMERICA ■

Yet this did not end the controversy over expansionism. Bryan still opposed overseas colonies and hoped to make the election of 1900 a referendum favoring return to the country's old, nonimperial ways. But American presidential elections seldom revolve about a single issue. In the end, the election of 1900 turned on silver, reform, prosperity, and the achievements of the first McKinley administration. Bryan's resounding defeat revealed little of what the American public felt about overseas expansion: Even the anti-imperialists split their votes between the two candidates.

Meanwhile, events in the Philippines were demonstrating the dangers and costs of America's new imperial course. Two days before ratification of the Spanish treaty, full-scale fighting broke out between the Filipinos, led by Emilio Aguinaldo, and the forces seeking to impose American sovereignty. Aguinaldo and his followers proclaimed Filipino independence in June 1898 and resisted American annexation. Eventually the United States was forced to fight a full-scale colonial war to put down the Filipino patriots. The "insurrection" required more than 125,000 American troops to quell after a four-year fight that cost 4,000 American lives and many more Filipino. The fighting was often savage with atrocities on both sides. Not until mid-1902 were the army regulars able to capture Aguinaldo and pacify the islands. The Philippines Insurrection was America's first land war in Asia, and like Vietnam in the 1960s, it called into question America's democratic values.

In the years following the United States sought to make amends in the Philippines by introducing land reform, establishing local self-government, and improving educational facilities. In 1902 Congress created a Philippine legislative assembly, though the governor of the islands remained an American. But the ugly war experience was a disturbing one and made Americans all the more uneasy in the role of colonial power.

During the next twenty years the nation vacillated between its liberal and its imperial tendencies. In 1900, under the Foraker Act, Congress authorized limited self-government for Puerto Rico. By the Platt Amendment to the Army Appropriation Bill of 1901, it directed the president to withdraw American forces from Cuba. Yet Cuba was not to be truly free. It could not enter into any treaty that would impair its sovereignty, nor could it contract debts beyond its capacity to pay. Also, the United States might intervene in the island's internal affairs to maintain law and order.

Relations with Latin America.   America's attitude toward its closest neighbors in Latin America during these years was that of a strict, disapproving older brother: It would protect them against outsiders, but they must behave or face American wrath. This policy worried and offended Latin Americans; Yankees considered it necessary for their peace of mind. The United States was the only great power in the Western Hemisphere, and Americans found this situation comfortable. Any hint that a European country was trying to extend its influence into the Western Hemisphere set off immediate alarm bells in Washington.

Sometimes this proprietary attitude operated to the advantage of America's smaller neighbors. Without American protection, a number of the weaker Latin American states would almost certainly have fallen again into the hands of one or another of the great European powers. Yet Latin America undoubtedly paid a high price for this protection. The United States insisted that its own strategic, political, and economic interests came first, and often acted in ways that left a legacy of resentment.

Events in Panama early in the century vividly illustrate this highhanded-ness. During the conflict with Spain the Pacific-based U.S.S. *Oregon* had been forced to sail around Cape Horn to come to the defense of the East Coast, exposed, it was feared, to a possible attack by the Spanish navy. The delay had underscored the advantages of a canal across the narrow isthmus that joined North and South America. With the war over and America the uneasy owner of a new Pacific empire, a canal seemed even more imperative.

Two obstacles blocked the way. The Clayton-Bulwer Treaty, signed with Great Britain in 1850, had denied the United States exclusive control over an isthmian canal. This hurdle was overcome by the 1901 Hay-Pauncefote Treaty with Britain, which gave sole right to the United States to build, control, and fortify a Central American waterway. Location was the second problem. Two routes were possible: one through Nicaragua and one at Panama. Favoring Panama was the enormous labor already expended by the French under Ferdinand de Lesseps, builder of the Suez Canal, who had been hacking their way unsuccess-fully through the fever-ridden jungles and mountains of the isthmus since the 1880s. When the French offered to sell their rights and equipment for $40 million, Congress accepted.

But another difficulty now loomed. Panama was a province of Colombia. Before construction could begin, that nation would have to agree to the arrange-ment. In January 1903 the United States concluded a treaty with Tomás Herrán, the Colombian minister in Washington, giving the South American republic a one-time $10 million payment and $250,000 annually for the rights to build the canal and to lease a canal zone six miles wide along the right-of-way for ninety-nine years. When the treaty reached the Colombian Senate, however, it was defeated. The Colombians had two major objections: The treaty gave the Americans too much power over a portion of their territory; it also failed to give them, rather than the French canal company, the $40 million promised.

President Theodore Roosevelt considered the Colombians' action outrageous. These people, he shouted, were "contemptible little creatures" who were "imper-iling their own future." The United States might have to teach them a lesson for their own good. Equally upset were the agents of the French canal company, who saw the promised $40 million escaping their grasp, and those residents of Panama who looked forward to the prosperity that the canal would bring and feared that it would now be built in Nicaragua.

In the end, the French agents, the Panamanians, and Theodore Roosevelt combined to assure a Panama route. Although they had revolted against Colombia in the past, the Panamanians had never succeeded in gaining their independence. Now, encouraged and financed by the French canal company, they rose once again. Fortunately for the insurgents, the U.S.S. *Nashville,* an American warship, had conveniently arrived just a day before the revolt broke out and was docked at Colón on Panama's Caribbean coast. Inspired by this scarcely disguised support, the rebels quickly overcame the feeble Colombian military forces and in a matter of hours proclaimed an independent Panamanian republic. To no one's surprise, Roosevelt immediately concluded an accord with the new government. For the same financial terms offered Colombia, the United States was granted the right to build a canal through a ten-mile-wide zone where it would exercise "all the rights, power, and authority" it would possess "if it were the sovereign of the territory."

With the political details out of the way, work on the gigantic engineering project began. Using mammoth steam shovels and thousands of black laborers drawn from the Caribbean islands, American engineers chopped their way across the isthmus. Hundreds of lives were lost to yellow fever until Colonel William C. Gorgas wiped out the mosquito-breeding places at Colón and Panama City and eliminated the disease from the country. On August 15, 1914, the interocean canal connecting the Atlantic and Pacific, the dream of three centuries, was formally opened to world shipping.

Roosevelt also acted aggressively elsewhere in Latin America. Many of the smaller Latin American countries, he felt, by defaulting on their debts and failing to control internal political turmoil, were inviting European nations to intervene in the western hemisphere to protect their citizens and their investments. By American reasoning, if the Caribbean and Central American republics expected the United States to defend them against the European powers they could not expect their protector to ignore their misdeeds. In 1904, when several European nations threatened to blockade the Dominican Republic until it paid its debts, Roosevelt decided to lay down the law. In his "corollary" to the Monroe Doctrine, he announced that "chronic wrongdoing" by Latin American countries or political "impotence" that resulted in serious disorder might force the United States to "exercise . . . police power, and compel it to intervene in the offending nation's internal affairs." While the Roosevelt Corollary prevented takeovers by European nations, it also gave the United States an excuse to intrude at will into Latin American affairs.

The Open Door in China. The United States often took advantage of its power to overawe its weaker hemispheric neighbors, but its role in the Far East was, on the whole, more benign. After acquiring Hawaii and the Philippines, the nation eagerly awaited the opening of the supposedly vast China market. It never materialized: In those years the Chinese people neither wanted the major American exports nor could they pay for them. Nevertheless, Americans remained hopeful and were anxious to prevent China from being carved up by Japan and the major European powers into exclusive "spheres of influence" where others could not trade. But American interest in China went beyond trade. Educated Americans were fascinated by China's ancient civilization, art, and customs. Many also considered the Celestial Empire a promising field for Christian missionary effort. The first American missionaries had arrived in China before the Civil War, bringing Western science and learning along with the Protestant faith. However much they deplored Chinese "heathenism," the missionaries deeply sympathized with the long-suffering Chinese people and conveyed their compassionate feelings to pious churchgoers at home. By the end of the nineteenth century millions of Americans considered China an arena for Christian benevolence, not for crass economic and political exploitation.

For many years American policy toward China was marked by this combination of self-interest and compassion. After China's defeat by Japan in the First Sino-Japanese War (1894–1895), the great powers renewed their demands for political and economic concessions. The United States, which had no designs on Chinese territory, feared that the Western nations would completely carve up the decaying empire, destroying Chinese sovereignty while excluding the United States commercially. Encouraged by the British, Secretary of State John Hay in 1899 sent notes to the major colonial powers asking for assurances that they would not demand special trading privileges in China. Most gave Hay evasive answers, but he chose to interpret these as acceptance of his "open door" principle, which rejected exclusive "spheres of influence" and held that all nations must be free to trade throughout China. In 1900, following suppression of the violently antiforeign Chinese Boxers by an international army, the United States converted the principle of economic parity into one of defending the Chinese nation against European annexation. In a circular letter of July 1900 Hay declared that it was "the policy of the United States government" to "bring about . . . peace to China" and to "preserve Chinese territorial and administrative entity. . . ."

The Open Door policy was a perfect mirror of American ambivalence. Unprepared by its history and traditions to take up the burdens and responsibilities of blatant colonialism, the United States sought to protect its share of the Chinese market in some less costly way than political control. At the same time, Americans sincerely sympathized with the Chinese people and sought to preserve Chinese sovereignty. But whatever the motives, the concern of the United States for an independent China would serve on more than one occasion to keep it from being dismembered by the European colonial powers and an expansionist Japan.

■ **CONCLUSIONS** ■

Many elements contributed to the outward thrust of the post-Civil War generation. The impulse that had carried the American people 3,000 miles across the North American continent continued to operate even after the Pacific was reached. Much as the earlier expansion had been fortified by the quest for gain, so the later one was reinforced by the desire for trade and expanded investment opportunities. Altruism, however misguided and arrogant, also influenced America's interest in foreign lands. Americans continued to believe that they had unique gifts—political freedom and material abundance—to offer other peoples. The American role in China, Hawaii, and the Philippines, in particular, expressed this mixture of the crass and the idealistic.

But post-Civil War expansionism also contained new ingredients. The desire to achieve great-power status by collecting colonies on the model of the western European imperialists, augmented the older Manifest Destiny. So did the fear that now that continental expansion had ended, the United States must seek out new territory or cease to prosper and grow. It is not true, as the Marxists believed, that American capitalism could only survive if fed by imperial expansion. But that does not mean that some contemporaries did not believe something that resembles this idea.

The aggressiveness of the American government, particularly toward Latin America, reflected the new mood of big-power assertiveness: Great powers cut a wide swath in their own neighborhoods; they did not allow themselves to be defied by troublesome pygmies. And yet Americans never wore the mantle of imperialism very comfortably. A rich nation of continental proportions, the United States inevitably threw its weight around, but less so than nations that had fewer natural resources and smaller home markets. The United States was also more restricted by its traditional liberal anticolonial values and by its fears that overseas acquisitions could not be incorporated into the Union as equal partners with the older states. In the new century just opening, the world would see many further instances of American forbearance and even generosity toward weaker nations combined with manifestations of self-serving interest, and would be puzzled by the inconsistent course of the Great Republic.

Online Resources

The Age of Imperialism
http://smplanet.com/imperialism/toc.html
Through narrative text, maps, and illustrations, this site lends insight into American expansion into the Pacific as well as involvement in Latin America.

William Jennings Bryan: "The Paralyzing Influence of Imperialism"
http://mtholyoke.edu/acad/intrel/bryan.htm
Offering a negative view of American imperialism, Bryan's speech to the 1900 Democratic Convention contended that American expansionism was against the very nature of a republican democracy.

A War in Perspective: Public Appeals, Memory, and the Spanish-American Conflict
http://www.nypl.org/research/chss/epo/spanexhib/page_2.html
This exhibit site examines the public sentiment about the Spanish-American War from the viewpoints of Cuban, Spanish, and U.S. citizens.

22

PROGRESSIVISM

What Were Its Roots and What Were Its Accomplishments?

1874	Women's Christian Temperance Union established
1890	Jane Addams's Hull House opens in Chicago; National American Woman Suffrage Association is formed in a merger of two older groups
1892	Grover Cleveland elected president
1895	Booker T. Washington's Atlanta Compromise Address
1896	*Plessy* v. *Ferguson* legalizes segregation; William McKinley elected president
1899	The National Consumers' League is formed
1900–06	Governor La Follette of Wisconsin establishes state primaries and taxes railroads
1901	McKinley assassinated; Theodore Roosevelt becomes president
1902	Roosevelt's antitrust campaign begins
1903	Congress establishes the Department of Commerce and Labor and the Bureau of Corporations
1904	Roosevelt elected president
1905	W. E. B. Du Bois launches the Niagara Movement
1905–07	Most states limit or outlaw child labor
1906	Congress passes Hepburn Act, Meat Inspection Act, and Pure Food and Drug Act
1908	William H. Taft elected president; Aldrich-Vreeland Emergency Currency Act
1909	Ballinger-Pinchot controversy; The Payne-Aldrich Tariff; National Association for the Advancement of Colored People (NAACP) founded
1910	The Mann-Elkins Act; The Mann Act
1911	*Standard Oil Co.* v. *United States*
1912	Woodrow Wilson elected president
1913	The Sixteenth and Seventeenth amendments allow a federal income tax and direct election of senators; The Federal Reserve Act; Underwood Tariff
1914	The Federal Trade Commission Act; The Clayton Antitrust Act; World War I begins in Europe
1916	Wilson sponsors the Federal Farm Loan Act, the Kern-McGillicuddy Act for federal employees, and the Keating-Owen Act limiting child labor

"Slowly, as the new century began its first decade," wrote editor William Allen White from the vantage of 1946, "I saw the Great Light. Around me in that day scores of young leaders in American politics and public affairs were seeing what I saw, feeling what I felt. . . . All over the land in a score of states and more, young men in both parties were taking leadership by attacking things as they were in that day."

White's "Great Light" was the urge to change American society that historians have called the Progressive movement. In the years between the beginning of the new century and America's entrance into World War I, men and women of all national backgrounds and all classes felt the yearning to improve life for themselves and for their fellow citizens. They did not join any one organization; they had no single leader, no neat, well-defined set of goals. Their support of change was not always unselfish. Most groups—whether intellectuals, professionals, wage earners, or farmers—understandably placed their own concerns first or believed their own concerns were truly everybody's. Nevertheless, many progressives displayed broad social sympathies, encompassing many groups besides their own.

The new views first appeared in the cities during the 1890s. A little later they came to the statehouses. Finally, about 1904 or 1905, they arrived in Washington, D.C. When they did, they were given the name "Progressivism," and they helped transform the nation. How can we explain this sudden passion for reform? What made so many people conclude that things had to change? What did the reformers want, and what did they accomplish?

■ UNCERTAINTIES ■

Fear of Bigness. If any single concern united the forces of reform during the opening years of the twentieth century, it was the fear of inflated, uncontrolled private economic power. The sense of being at the mercy of great aggregations of private wealth and privilege was not new; it was as old as the republic and had never ceased to affect political perceptions. In each of the early instances— whether Jeffersonian, Jacksonian, or Populist—the opposition to "monopolists" had come predominantly from small producers such as farmers, independent artisans, and small manufacturers. That was inevitable; until late in the nineteenth century most Americans had belonged to one of these occupational groups. By the 1880s and 1890s the nation had spawned a large class of urban wage earners, salaried professionals, and white-collar workers, but by and large they had refused to join the populistic movements of the period; it had been the small farmers of the South and West who had formed the backbone of the People's Party and the free-silver movement.

Progressivism, the new, early-twentieth-century attack on concentrated power and wealth, originated in, and found its chief support among, groups that Populism and Bryanism had failed to ignite. Rural Americans would consider themselves progressives in these years, but the movement would be led by middle-class urbanites widely supported by the city working class. What had happened in one short decade to change the perception of millions of city dwellers, blue collar and middle class?

The Growth of Trusts.   One answer is that the shift of attitude was sparked by the acceleration of business consolidation during the closing years of the nineteenth century. In the generation following the Civil War the nation's economic integration was brought to swift completion by the final wave of railroad building. As the cost of shipping goods to distant customers declined, local markets evolved into regional markets and then into national markets. Firms grew larger as they sought to serve growing numbers of customers, many now living in the burgeoning cities. For a time business competition intensified. And for a time prices dropped. However beneficial to consumers, this regime did not please producers and, as we saw, they tried to stabilize market shares and prices through pools, trusts, mergers, and other arrangements to avoid "cutthroat" competition.

Late-nineteenth-century business consolidation came in two bursts. The first began in the 1870s and culminated in the formation of the Standard Oil Company. It was this round that had spurred the anxiety of the Grangers and the Alliances. It ended abruptly with the panic of 1893 and the depression that followed. Then, beginning in 1896, the merger movement revived, primarily among industries that catered to the exploding urban market. As midwifed by J. P. Morgan and other investment bankers, this second merger wave came to a grand climax between 1898 and 1902. In those five years 2,500 large firms combined into huge ones. In 1901 the process reached its peak with the formation of United States Steel, the world's first billion-dollar corporation.

Americans watched the consolidation process with apprehension. Trusts seemed to be everywhere. In 1904 financial analyst John Moody counted 318 trusts, with total capital of over $7.2 billion, "covering every line of productive industry in the United States."

The New Urban Consumers.   Almost all Americans deplored the trend toward ever-greater concentrations of private economic power. But to urbanites the trusts appeared particularly threatening. Many city people remained producers who turned out manufactured goods in small or large shops. But many others were now white-collar workers—professionals, clerks, accountants, office workers—whose connections with a physical product were indirect at best. To an increasing extent urban Americans, especially those of the middle class, viewed themselves more as consumers than producers.

When most Americans were farmers they had been able to supply many of their own needs. They had slaughtered their own hogs and cattle, raised their own fruits and vegetables, and produced their own eggs and milk. Even urban folk had been less dependent on others in the simpler days before 1900. They had been closer to the country suppliers of their needs, and these needs had been less complicated. Through most of the nineteenth century average Americans had burned wood from their own woodlots in their stoves, read by candlelight or firelight, communicated with their friends face to face, gone to work on foot, and doctored themselves with nostrums from their own gardens or from a local medical practitioner. In all these matters they had relied on themselves or on someone they knew well personally.

For city dwellers in 1900 this self-reliance was a thing of the past. The food they consumed, for instance, was now supplied by remote corporations—meat-packers, canners, millers, and other food processors whose products could not be trusted. Dishonest meat packers, for example, could and did doctor spoiled beef to make it appear fresh. Firms disguised lard and suet as butter and packed turnips in syrup to be sold as canned peaches or pears.

Nor was this all. City dwellers now relied on public utilities to light their houses, fuel their stoves, and transport them from their homes to their offices and shops. But the gas and lighting companies had legal monopolies through franchises and could squeeze customers as they pleased. The traction companies that ran the streetcars and elevated railroads corrupted city officials to secure exclusive charters, and then provided poor and expensive service to riders.

Personal health care too now often depended on others. When ill, city dwellers often counted on over-the-counter "patent medicines"—bottled or packaged concoctions they saw advertised in the newspapers and magazines. These were generally useless and sometimes harmful potions, fortified with al-cohol or even opium. Nevertheless, the drug companies claimed their value for every disease known, and for several invented by the patent medicine purveyors themselves.

In short, urban consumers were at the mercy of others and were vulnerable to deception and exploitation without precedent. As the economist Richard Ely expressed it in 1905: "Under our present manner of living, how many of my vital interests must I entrust to others! Nowadays the water main is my well, the trolley car is my carriage, the banker's safe is my stocking, and the policeman's billy is my fist."

Dependence and deception were bad enough, but consumers of this period also faced remorselessly rising prices. For a whole generation after 1897 the na-tion escaped major depressions such as those of the 1870s and 1890s. But the income gains that Americans made in these years were partly offset by the steady inflation that reversed the trend of the previous decades. Beginning about 1902, consumer prices started a steady climb that did not end until the early 1930s. Deflation following the Civil War had hurt farmers and other producers; now inflation hurt consumers. Everyone who went to the corner grocery store or butcher or who paid a utility bill or bought a load of coal soon became painfully aware of the new trend. Who was responsible for the "high cost of living"? The answer seemed inescapable to many: the monopolies.

The new consumerism was a particularly effective political glue. As one journalist pointed out in 1913: "In America to-day the unifying . . . force is the common interest of the citizen as a consumer of wealth. . . ." The producers were "highly differentiated," but "all men, women, and children who buy shoes (except only the shoe manufacturer) are interested in cheap, good shoes."

Because consumers were "overwhelmingly superior in numbers than producers," consumer consciousness, this writer was certain, formed the basis for a political revolt of vast proportions that the politicians would not fail to note.

Besides their exposed position as consumers, urban people also confronted the special hazards of the city environment. Large cities provided men and women with more opportunities to learn, grow, and amuse themselves. But for wage earners they were also places where crime, vice, loneliness, and poverty flourished. In the 1870s and 1880s, as we have seen, the city poor had often turned to the political machines to protect them against the hard edges of urban life; by the 1890s many had come to believe that urban reform might be in their interests. The urban middle class, meanwhile, saw city government as inefficient and wasteful. Why could it not cities be run like businesses, though obviously ones dedicated to the public interest, rather than profit? Dissatisfaction with city government further fueled the desire for progressive reform.

Farmers, Blacks, and Women.   The addition of urbanites to the ranks of the nation's uneasy and discontented citizens may well have been the crucial trigger to Progressivism. But farmers still faced many difficult problems. Railroad officials and farm machinery manufacturers remained arrogant and arbitrary. Credit for farmers was still in short supply. Country life continued to fall behind city life in its amenities. The voice of dissatisfied rural Americans would at times imbue Progressivism with a strong agrarian tinge reminiscent of Populism.

In these years many women, especially urban middle-class women, found their lives constrained in ways that no longer seemed acceptable. By now there were thousands of women high school and college graduates, but there were still only limited professional outlets for their talents and energies. As late as 1910 women in only Wyoming, Colorado, Utah, and Idaho could vote; several other states had rejected referenda to establish woman suffrage. Many educated women with unused talents and energies joined women's clubs and spent their time discussing art, high culture, and great ideas. Women were active in church affairs. A few middle-class or wealthy women also did "charity work" among the poor. Yet as the new century opened, many talented women felt that society was not properly using their skills and brains, and it made them receptive to social and political change.

Black Americans, too, found much to complain of as the new century dawned. In the South blacks were deprived of voting rights either by intimidation or by ingenious legal dodges. All through Dixie, where in 1900 two thirds of the country's 10 million black citizens still lived, the system of legal segregation prevailed. In many ways, in fact, southern "Jim Crow" was more powerfully entrenched as the twentieth century began than at the end of Reconstruction. Worst of all was the brutal regime of lynchings. Each year blacks accused of criminal offenses were taken from local jails and hanged, burned, or maimed by white mobs unwilling to wait for the slow processes of law. From 1920 to 1920 there were on average 75 lynchings a year, mostly in the South. Blacks were better treated in the North. Few were lynched; they could vote in national and local elections. But unofficial segregation, especially in housing, and discrimination in jobs, college admissions, and professional education were commonplace. And even northern African Americans did not fully escape violence. In Springfield, Illinois, in 1908 a white mob went on a rampage, attacking blacks and destroying black business property. Order had to be restored by 5,000 state militia.

Until now most of the black community had accepted the leadership of educator Booker T. Washington. Born a slave in 1856, Washington had risen to prominence in the 1890s as a protégé of southern whites. White philanthropists had sent him to Hampton Institute in Virginia, one of the few all-black institutions of higher education. In 1881 they chose him to head a school for black youths at Tuskegee, Alabama. Washington made Tuskegee into a flourishing institution emphasizing industrial education, modeled on the work-ethic, self-help principles of Hampton. In 1895 he achieved national prominence with an electrifying address at the Atlanta Cotton States Exposition. Speaking to a white audience, he proposed that blacks accept disenfranchisement and racial segregation in exchange for the right to advance economically and be secure in their persons and property. This so-called Atlanta Compromise immediately impressed influential white southerners. Opposed equally to disorder and black equality, they saw it as a formula for a peaceful status quo. Thereafter the white establishment made Washington the "spokesman" for his race and the quasi-official dispenser of white philanthropy and political patronage to blacks.

Washington's Atlanta Compromise acquiesced in segregation and appeared to encourage black passivity in the face of mistreatment. But in truth, while projecting a public image of meekness, behind the scenes Washington quietly fought segregation, lynching, and debt peonage. When President Theodore Roosevelt gave dishonorable discharges in 1906 to three companies of black soldiers for refusing to identify the leaders of a riot in Brownsville, Texas, Washington went to the White House to intercede for the wronged men, though without success.

At all events, as the twentieth century began, a new generation of college-educated black urban leaders appeared, determined to make white Americans grant black citizens their constitutional and God-given rights.

Some historians have seen Progressivism as a predominantly middle-class movement. Yet it is clear that it recruited recent immigrants, factory workers, and slum dwellers as well. In fact, for a time almost all Americans came to consider themselves progressives in some sense. Progressivism by about 1910 was definitely "in the air," a fact that helps to explain its complexity and its seeming inconsistencies. No coalition so large could have been all of a piece or definable in a single sentence.

■ THE OPINION MAKERS ■

The Progressive movement owed much to the anti-formalistic intellectual currents that had appeared in the last decades of the nineteenth century. Many of the new thinkers—including Oliver Wendell Holmes, Jr., John Dewey, and

Charles Beard—were also reformers. It was through their intellectual challenges to the social pieties of the day, however, rather than their personal activities that they made their contribution to change.

The Muckrakers.   A group of talented editors, journalists, and essayists known as the muckrakers contributed more directly to the new reform movement by focusing the public's fears and discontent.

The muckrakers aimed dazzling spotlights into every dark cranny of American political and social life to reveal existing abuses. They owed their name to Theodore Roosevelt, who often sympathized with their aims but considered their passion for uncovering dirt and wrongdoing excessive. TR likened them to a morose character in John Bunyan's "Pilgrim's Progress" who "continued to rake to himself the filth of the floor" even when offered a "celestial crown."

The hard-hitting published exposé was not invented in the Progressive Era. Yet it was not until after 1900—when lower printing costs, the new mass audience educated by the public high schools, and the capacity to produce magazines in vast numbers all came together—that true exposé journalism appeared.

Samuel S. McClure, a shrewd and ebullient Irishman, was the first publisher to take advantage of the new opportunity. His instinct for profitable journalism was sound, if at times disconcerting. He would have paid well, one wit observed, for a "snappy life of Christ." McClure did not consciously intend to create a new kind of journalism; he wanted to sell magazines. But his practice of hiring talented writers and reporters to investigate various aspects of American life produced a journalistic revolution. In October 1902 *McClure's* carried an article by a young Californian, Lincoln Steffens, describing the efforts of a young district attorney to prosecute the corrupt St. Louis Democratic machine. The November issue carried the first installment of a series by journalist Ida Tarbell exposing the monopolistic practices of the Standard Oil Company. Early in 1903 Ray Stannard Baker's article on unfair labor practices appeared. The public took notice of these articles, and McClure was soon selling more magazines than he had ever believed possible. Other publishers, observing their rival's success, rushed to hire men and women with a talent for uncovering wrongdoing and writing about it in a colorful and exciting way.

What followed was the greatest outpouring of exposé journalism in American history. Eventually the muckrakers probed into every national abuse: uncontrolled sale of patent medicines; the shady doings of stock market manipulators; businessmen's efforts to corrupt legislatures, city councils, and Congress; the harsh treatment of labor; the disgusting and unsanitary conditions in the meatpacking industry; the profiteering of the "beef trust"; the exploitation of child workers; the savage treatment of defenseless young women by purveyors of vice; the behind-the-scenes effort of the "money trust" to manipulate the entire American economy. Some of the muckrakers' output does not stand up to careful rechecking. But it touched the contemporary public's exposed nerves, confirmed its uneasiness, and gave direction to its unfocused fears.

■ PROGRESSIVISM ENTERS POLITICS ■

The Cult of Efficiency in City Government. The first expressions of progressivism appeared at the local level. In the cities the "reform with a heart" that emerged in the 1890s (discussed in Chapter 18) was one aspect of the new political mood. Later, a group of city reformers emerged with somewhat different goals and a different clientele. Most of these were professionals—engineers, lawyers, doctors, teachers, journalists—who believed that cities were much like large business firms and could be run effectively if subject to scientific management principles. Their motto, and their god, was efficiency.

This "cult of efficiency" reflected the growing prestige of science and technology in these years. In the view of the efficiency reformers there was no Democratic or Republican way to clean the streets or provide police protection or pure water. City government, accordingly, should be headed by nonpartisan "managers" or "commissioners" who would run them on scientific and business principles designed to provide good value for the taxpayers' money.

In the 1890s the new city reformers organized the National Municipal Reform League and formulated a model city charter, which they hoped cities and state legislatures would adopt. Their first actual success came in 1901 when Galveston, Texas—following a catastrophic hurricane—adopted the commission plan. City government was turned over to a board of five commissioners chosen on a nonpartisan basis and at-large, rather than by wards, to eliminate old-fashioned politics from the selection process. The board combined the role of mayor and city council in one body. By merging functions and by eliminating partisan politics, the commissioners could run city government like an efficient business. Still another idea was the city manager scheme first adopted in Staunton, Virginia, in 1908. City managers were professionals selected by an elected city council and paid to manage the city much as a corporation might hire an executive to run the firm. By the 1920s several dozen cities, usually small or middle-sized, had adopted one or the other of the new municipal government schemes.

The Social Progressives. The Progressive movement reached beyond city hall, down into the neighborhoods and slums. There men and women dedicated to changing the urban environment established networks of neighborhood voluntary associations designed to improve the lives of the poor. These "social" progressives formed the most militant wing of the Progressive movement. Many were inspired by the social gospel of Walter Rauschenbusch or the Christian socialism of Washington Gladden. They were for the most part recruited from among the idealistic young people who poured from the secondary schools and colleges in the last years of the nineteenth century. Particularly prominent among them were young college women who sought to use their skills, education, and energies for something more fulfilling than the self-improvement of women's clubs. Many of these young people became voluntary charity workers or took up the new profession of "social work." An especially dedicated contingent went to live in settlement houses in the noisome slums that dominated the cities' centers.

Settlement houses were places where slum children could go for recreation and entertainment; where mothers could learn about nutrition, scientific child care, and household management; and where fathers could learn vocational skills, improve their English, prepare for citizenship, and discuss city or community problems. Beginning with the Neighborhood Guild on New York's Lower East Side and Hull House in Chicago, settlements sprang up during the 1890s in all the major cities. Hull House, under the leadership of Jane Addams, and New York's Henry Street Settlement, run by Lillian Wald, were the most prominent, but there were scores of others in every large city.

Most of the people who used the settlements were European immigrants and their children, but the settlement workers were also concerned with the problems of black city dwellers. Frances Kellor of New York's College Settlement helped organize the National League for the Protection of Negro Women after she discovered how young black farm women were lured to the cities by promises of good jobs and then harshly exploited by employers or forced into prostitution. Another white social worker, Mary White Ovington, established a settlement in a New York black slum. The settlements soon became springboards of social reform. In Chicago Jane Addams and her Hull House colleagues worked for the election of reform politicians who dared to challenge the machines. Addams also supported improved tenement housing and better educational and recreational opportunities for the urban working class. She and her counterparts in other communities regularly joined in citywide efforts to eliminate vice and reduce crime.

Women's clubs too became sources of reform in neighborhoods and cities. The clubs were especially active in the fight for honest city government, but middle-class women also took up consumers' issues and worked to help the urban poor. In 1899 a group of upper-middle-class women established the National Consumer's League, which threatened boycotts of employers who did not adhere to fair employment practices. The league also labored to improve community health through licensing of food vendors, and supported measures to protect urban consumers against retail fraud.

Progressivism in the States.   Only so much could be accomplished on the neighborhood or city level, however, and in the end the reformers had to turn to the state legislatures to achieve their goals. Until the 1890s state governments all too often had been little more than junior partners of large business corporations. Legislators often accepted money from businesspeople and did their bidding without concern for the public interest. For years reformers had denounced the "unholy alliance" of state government and big business characteristic of the Gilded Age. Their voices went unheeded. Then the panic of 1893 exposed many of the flaws in the country's economy and pointed up the dangers of unregulated economic power as never before.

The revelation came with particular force to the people of Wisconsin, a state dominated by a Republican machine that had always worked hand-in-glove with the major corporations. The depression of 1893–1897 severely jolted Wisconsin's economy. By the winter of 1893–1894 more than a third of the state's wage earners were unemployed. Meanwhile, the hard-pressed utility firms refused to pay their taxes and raised their rates to city consumers to offset declining revenue. To make matters worse, the distress of the unemployed and consumers was accompanied by revelations that a clique of bankers had been embezzling funds from depositors and stockholders.

No Wisconsinite better understood the growing public outrage than the ambitious young Republican lawyer Robert M. La Follette. As governor after 1900 La Follette made Wisconsin the nation's "laboratory" for progressive lawmaking. His first reform measure was a state "primary" system that allowed the voters to bypass the party bosses and nominate their own candidates for state office. He next pushed through a railroad tax that shifted some of the burden of supporting government from farmers and wage earners to the previously untaxed railroad corporations and their stockholders. He later supported a state railroad commission to regulate the rates that the railroads could charge.

In 1902 La Follette ran for reelection. In his first successful campaign he had stressed his Republicanism, albeit a reform variety. This time he appealed for nonpartisan support and got it. Virtually all Wisconsin citizens, not just Republicans, by now feared the power of the "interests." The sense of insecurity in the face of irresponsible wealth cut across ethnic lines, and many Catholic voters abandoned their earlier allegiance to the Democratic party to vote for the reformer. La Follette's resounding reelection victory helped eclipse the old party politics of the Gilded Age.

Wisconsin continued to be a center of progressive reform even after "Battle Bob" went to Washington as United States Senator. Under his successors, the state adopted two new instruments of "direct democracy." The first, the initiative, was a procedure enabling voters to introduce legislation without waiting for legislators to do so. The referendum allowed voters to accept or reject, by a direct ballot, certain laws passed by the legislature. Progressives hoped that these innovations would allow the voters to bypass or overrule legislatures controlled by powerful economic interests and gain a greater say in the political process. The state also established a public utility commission to protect consumers against gouging by gas companies and power and light companies. Working closely with social scientists from the University of Wisconsin, successive state administrations enacted a workers' compensation act for injured or disabled wage earners and a state income tax to make wealthier citizens bear a larger part of the community's tax load. They established a board of public affairs to protect vital natural resources from corporate exploiters. All told, under the "Wisconsin Idea," ordinary citizens would be protected against the hazards of an exploitive business-dominated economy through the agency of a benevolent and responsive state government.

The Wisconsin experiment captured the attention of millions of Americans. Other states soon adopted Wisconsin's program. Much of the new legislation was designed to protect citizens in general. A good deal of it was aimed specifically at weaker groups in society. Beginning with Illinois in 1899, for example, many states established special courts for juvenile offenders. Between 1905 and 1907 two thirds of the states enacted laws limiting the hours of child labor or outlawing paid labor for young children. Both juvenile offenders reform, and child labor restrictions were part of a larger "child saving" movement, which also included the goals of making widely available germ-free milk and play facilities. Working women, too, were increasingly surrounded by state regulations intended to prevent employer exploitation and abuse. The states also limited the working hours of men employed in exhausting or hazardous occupations such as baking and mining. More and more states joined Wisconsin in adopting workers' compensation insurance schemes, though, in part, this was at the behest of business firms increasingly beset by lawsuits instigated by injured workers. As an expression of the most advanced social vision there was even talk of publicly funded health and unemployment insurance.

Southern Progressivism. In 1912 Robert La Follette remarked that he "did not know of any progressive sentiment of any progressive legislation in the South." But he was wrong. Beginning early in the century, progressive southern governors launched attacks against railroads, utility companies, insurance firms, and other business groups that seemed to be exploiting the region and its citizens. In Alabama Braxton Bragg Comer, a wealthy Birmingham manufacturer, banker, and landowner, expanded the authority of the state railroad commission and reduced passenger and freight rates. In Arkansas, Attorney General Jeff Davis initiated scores of suits against insurance companies, tobacco firms, and oil companies, charging them with unfair, monopolistic practices and price-fixing.

Southern progressives were often openly anti-Yankee, aiming their sharpest barbs at "Wall Street" and "foreign"—that is, northeastern—corporations, which were accused of sucking profits out of the region while giving back nothing in return. At times skeptical southern progressives twitted their colleagues for reluctance to attack such home-grown abuses as child labor, when doing so might discourage the growth of local industry. But the South had its advanced social reformers, too. The Southern Sociological Congress—composed of ministers, urban humanitarians, and middle-class clubwomen—worked to improve the lot of the region's children, the handicapped, consumers, and prisoners. The congress could claim credit for only a small amount of advanced social legislation, but it brought together men and women of like mind and helped to create the "southern liberal" type, whose efforts would help transform the region in later years.

Black Americans. The Sociological Congress worked to improve race relations, but by and large southern progressivism was "for whites only." A number of prominent southern politicians—James K. Vardaman and Theodore G. Bilbo of Mississippi, for example—managed to combine sympathy for white yeomen farmers exploited by corporations with a violent antiblack rhetoric that poisoned the racial atmosphere. Even southern primary laws often injured black southerners. Arguing that the conservative southern Bourbons used the black vote to reinforce privilege, southern progressives often excluded blacks from the primaries.

Meanwhile, as progressive laws poured from southern state legislatures, the "Jim Crow" system, which kept the races strictly segregated, expanded into every corner of the region's daily life. Blacks and a few white liberals tried to check the process through legal action. But the Supreme Court ruling in the landmark *Plessy* v. *Ferguson* (1896) decision that segregation did not violate the equal protection clause of the Fourteenth Amendment as long as the facilities provided each race were equal in quality, frustrated their efforts. Far worse, lynching continued and even grew as a savage weapon of terror to keep southern blacks in "their place."

A new generation of African-American leaders blamed black acquiescence for the South's continued oppression of its black citizens. To a new group of urban black intellectuals Booker T. Washington's willingness to surrender fundamental constitutional rights and to consent to permanent second-class citizenship came to seem intolerable. Led by the Boston editor William Monroe Trotter, T. Thomas Fortune of the *New York Age,* by the Jacksonville minister J. Milton Waldron, and, most prominently, by W. E. B. Du Bois, they launched a movement to make blacks equal citizens of the republic.

An early advocate of black liberation from white economic and cultural domination, the Massachusetts-born Du Bois insisted that black Americans must run their own businesses, provide their own professional services, write their own books, and create their own art. In 1903, in *The Souls of Black Folk*, he attacked Washington as a man who had "practically accepted the alleged inferiority of the Negro," and urged prominent black Americans to cease flattering the white South and to speak out on the race issue.

In 1905 Du Bois and Trotter convened a meeting at Fort Erie, Ontario, near Niagara Falls, to raise a militant voice against black oppression. The convention issued a manifesto demanding true manhood suffrage, the end of racial discrimination, the freedom of blacks to criticize American society, and free access for blacks to liberal education as well as to vocational training. Incorporated as the Niagara Movement, the group continued to meet annually for several years to defend black rights and demand that white America practice its professed principles of equality.

In 1909 the Niagara Movement militants merged with a group of white progressives, including Oswald Garrison Villard, Jane Addams, Clarence Darrow, William Dean Howells, and John Dewey, to establish the National Association for the Advancement of Colored People (NAACP). The NAACP quickly came to the forefront of the battle to defend the legal and constitutional rights of blacks wherever they were threatened or denied. By 1914 the NAACP had 6,000 members, mostly middle-class blacks in the cities. However small at first, the modern movement for racial equality was now underway.

Women Progressives.   Women were among the most active workers for social reform before and during the Progressive Era. Nowhere were they more effective than in the cause of temperance.

Throughout his long life (1868–1963), W. E. B. Du Bois's thinking anticipated developments in black positions on race. The first black to receive a Ph.D. from Harvard, he helped start the Niagara Movement and then the NAACP, advocated Pan-Africanism, lost faith in integration, became a Communist, supported Black Power, and finally moved to Africa.

The battle to end the social and moral evil of drunkenness had engaged the attention of American women for many years. In 1874 female reformers organized the Women's Christian Temperance Union (WCTU), which allied itself after 1900 with the predominantly male Anti-Saloon League. Together the two organizations propagandized in the schools and churches against alcohol and lobbied for state laws outlawing the production, sale, and consumption of beer, wine, and whiskey. In later years the temperance movement would often be associated with social and political conservatism, but in the early years of the twentieth century temperance reformers like Frances Willard and Anna Shaw were champions of child-labor laws and other progressive legislation.

No cause, however, engaged the energies of women reformers so completely as the issue of suffrage for women themselves. For decades women suffragists had been struggling for the right to vote. But most men—and many women—dismissed women suffrage as a violation of nature and a threat to the family. The battle proved long and hard. During the Gilded Age, Susan B. Anthony and Elizabeth Cady Stanton, both pre-Civil War suffrage leaders, working through the National Woman Suffrage Association, scored some successes in the West.

By 1896 Wyoming, Utah, Colorado, and Idaho had granted women the vote. Meanwhile, a more conservative group, including Lucy Stone and Julia Ward Howe, had formed the American Woman Suffrage Association. In 1890 the two organizations merged under the presidency of Stanton as the National American Woman Suffrage Association (NAWSA).

To NAWSA's left was a cluster of "social feminists" who insisted that true gender equality depended on deep changes in women's relations with men, on shifts in the economy, and on alteration of the traditional family. Charlotte Perkins Gilman argued in *Women and Economics* (1898) that women's subordinate economic role had stunted their personalities and damaged their effectiveness as wives and mothers. Crystal Eastman, an active suffragist, also advocated sexual emancipation of women and free dissemination of birth-control information and devices. In 1914, Eastman and Alice Paul, a young Quaker activist, organized the Congressional Union to agitate for a suffrage amendment to the Constitution in place of a state-by-state approach. The new militants adopted the flamboyant protest tactics of English suffragists, which included mass marches, chaining themselves to lampposts, and prison fasts when arrested. In the elections of 1914 and 1916, Paul's group (organized as the National Women's Party in 1916) campaigned to punish the Democrats, the party in power, for failure to support a suffrage amendment.

■ PROGRESSIVISM GOES NATIONAL ■

Progressivism was at first largely a local political phenomenon. Until about 1900 all was quiet along the Potomac.

In 1898, four months after his much-publicized charge up San Juan Hill in the war with Spain, Theodore Roosevelt was elected governor of New York. Although he had been the hand-picked candidate of Thomas C. Platt, the state's Republican boss, as governor Roosevelt appointed honest men to office and supported bills to tax public utilities. Unhappy with his choice, and anxious to get him out of New York, Platt maneuvered Roosevelt into accepting second place on the 1900 Republican ticket with William McKinley. McKinley and Roosevelt won a landslide victory in 1900 over Democrats William Jennings Bryan and Adlai Stevenson. On September 6, 1901, while on a visit to the Pan-American Exposition in Buffalo, McKinley was shot by Leon Czolgosz, a demented anarchist. The president died a week later. Suddenly, at forty-two, Roosevelt found himself the youngest man yet to occupy the presidential office.

The new president was a remarkable person. A graduate of elite Groton School and Harvard College, TR was a highly literate man whose histories, *The Naval War of 1812* and *Winning of the West,* though bellicose, can still be read with profit today. He was also a man of frenetic action who forced even the most distinguished guests at his Long Island home, and later at the White House itself, to join him on jogs about the countryside while he shouted his views of politics, art, and economics. Though capable of dashing off reviews, speeches, books, and articles, and holding his own with distinguished scholars, he also enjoyed living with the cowboys of western Dakota and spent long, happy months in the wilds of three continents hunting, exploring, and collecting zoological specimens. TR had a juvenile streak that often led him to snap judgments. One distinguished foreign observer remarked to an American friend: "You know your president is really six." An intense nationalist, Roosevelt identified the United States with virtue and tended to see non-"Anglo-Saxons" as inherently inferior. Despite his failings—or perhaps partly because of them—Roosevelt charmed and delighted the American public, and his personal appeal would rub off on the programs he supported.

Roosevelt's First Term.   The conservative Republican "Old Guard" did not trust Roosevelt. When his name was first proposed for vice president on the 1900 Republican ticket, Senator Marcus (Mark) Hanna warned that if the governor received the nomination, only one life would stand between the country and a "madman." Yet as president TR at first adopted a moderate course. In his first annual message to Congress he recommended a cabinet-level department of commerce and labor to protect labor's rights and to publicize inflated corporate earnings, stronger measures to protect the country's forests and conserve its natural resources, and increased power for the feeble Interstate Commerce Commission to help guarantee fair treatment to shippers.

Congress eventually gave TR much of what he asked for. In 1902 it passed the Newlands Act, which set aside money from federal land sales in the arid West for dams and canals to irrigate the land (see Chapter 19). In 1903 it established the Department of Commerce and Labor, incorporating a Bureau of Corporations empowered to subpoena information from industry that could then be used for antitrust suits under the Sherman Antitrust Act. That same year Congress passed the Elkins Act outlawing rebates to favored shippers and giving the federal courts the power to issue injunctions ordering railroads to desist from practices that benefited some shippers at the expense of others.

Despite these advances, reform-minded observers considered Roosevelt's initial legislative performance timid. In his executive capacity, however, he proved bolder and startled the nation in 1902 by ordering Attorney General Philander Knox to file suit against the Northern Securities Holding Company for violating the Sherman Antitrust Act.

The Northern Securities Company, put together by J. P. Morgan, James J. Hill, E. H. Harriman, and the Rockefellers, merged most of the railroads in the northwestern corner of the nation into one giant firm. If ever a business trust promised to "restrain trade" and impose an economic stranglehold on millions, this was it. Now, after twelve years, the Sherman Antitrust Act, gutted by the Supreme Court, was finally to be used for its intended purpose. Soon after, Knox also indicted Swift and Company, the Chicago meat-packers, for conspiring with its competitors to fix prices for beef and pork.

The liberal press and the growing contingent of reform-minded citizens hailed the antitrust suits with delight. Morgan, however, was dismayed by the Northern Securities indictment. How could the president act in such an arbitrary way? The uncrowned king of Wall Street did not see himself as a mere private citizen subject to ordinary law, and he told the president: "If we have done anything wrong send your man to my man to fix it up." Roosevelt was not swayed and the suit proceeded to a successful conclusion in 1904, when the Supreme Court ordered the dissolution of the Northern Securities Company.

The Northern Securities case, the Swift suit, and later suits against Standard Oil and the American Tobacco Company gave TR the reputation of being a "trustbuster" and an uncompromising foe of big business. Actually, Roosevelt distinguished between "good trusts" and "bad trusts." The first, though they dominated a given industry, obeyed the law and did not use their power to squeeze the consuming public; the latter exercised no such restraint. "Bad trusts" should be punished, but "good trusts" should be left alone because large firms were more efficient than small ones. Besides, TR felt, the country could not stop the processes of corporate growth. Instead, it could "regulate and control them," to prevent misuse of corporation power. In fact, though he rejected Morgan's overtures, TR was not adamantly opposed to negotiations with big business. In 1905, for example, he struck a bargain with Elbert Gary, board chairman of giant U.S. Steel. If Gary cooperated with a federal investigation of his company's practices, then any wrongdoing detected would be reported to him to correct before the government commenced a suit.

Clearly TR was at most a qualified opponent of big business. He was an equally qualified friend of organized labor. Like most middle-class Americans of the day, the president feared socialism and at times confused it with trade union activity. Yet far more than most of his predecessors, TR believed that unions had a legitimate place as agencies to protect wage earners.

Roosevelt demonstrated his sympathetic attitude early in his first term. In May 1902, after months of arguing with the coal mine owners in eastern Pennsylvania over higher wages, union recognition, and an eight-hour day, members of the United Mine Workers, led by John Mitchell, walked off their jobs. The anthracite coal they produced was the major source of heating fuel along much of the Atlantic Coast. If the strike dragged on through the summer and fall, there would be no coal for winter and millions of householders would suffer. Yet for months the mine owners arrogantly refused to negotiate. In reply to critics, George F. Baer, spokesman for the owners, haughtily declared that the "rights and interests of the laboring man will be protected and cared for not by labor agitators but by the Christian men to whom God has given control of the property rights of the country."

Roosevelt and a majority of the voters were offended by the owners' arrogance and indifference to the public's welfare. In early October, as winter approached, Roosevelt invited the union leaders and the mine operators to the capital to discuss a settlement. At an all-day conference Mitchell declared his willingness to negotiate with the owners directly or to abide by the decision of a presidential arbitration commission—if the owners also agreed to accept its decision. The owners refused to budge. Their spokesman denounced Mitchell personally and demanded that the president use federal troops to end the strike.

Outraged by the stubbornness of the operators and their discourtesy toward Mitchell, Roosevelt threatened to seize the mines and run them as federal property. Faced with the president's determination, the mine owners finally yielded. At another White House conference, representatives of the miners and the operators agreed to a settlement. The men would go back to work; and a five-man commission consisting of an army engineer, a mining engineer, a business-man, a federal judge, and an "eminent sociologist" would be appointed by the president to arbitrate differences. The eminent sociologist Roosevelt selected was a union leader: E. E. Clark of the Brotherhood of Railroad Conductors, a novel choice for the day. The commission granted the miners their wage increase and some reduction in hours, but not union recognition. It was at best a mixed result, but to many Americans it was, as TR described it, a "square deal." The settlement established an important new precedent: From now on, the national government would be a factor to reckon with in disputes between capital and labor that vitally affected consumer interests.

The New Nationalism.   With a Square Deal for all Americans as his rallying cry, Roosevelt ran for reelection in 1904. Tired of two defeats in succession under Bryan's banner, the Democrats nominated the conservative New York judge Alton B. Parker to oppose him. The change did not help them. TR won an impressive victory with 56 percent of the popular vote.

Roosevelt soon moved significantly to the left, responding to the changing mood of the American people, as well as to his growing political confidence now that he had been elected president in his own right. By this time a contingent of Republican progressives, including La Follette, Senators Albert Cummins of Iowa, Albert Beveridge of Indiana, Moses Clapp of Minnesota, Joseph Bristow of Kansas, and William E. Borah of Idaho, had arrived in Washington, D.C., from the states where they had long been active in local reform movements. In later years they would be joined by other Republican progressives such as Hiram Johnson of California and George Norris of Nebraska. In addition, an increasing number of Democrats, caught up like their rivals in the surge of reform zeal, were prepared to support legislation to protect the public against "the interests." The opposition promised to be formidable, however. The Republican stand-pat Old Guard—led by Senators Nelson W. Aldrich, Orville Platt, and John C. Spooner—were still powerful and would fiercely resist every attempt to alter the status quo.

Despite the stand-patters, during his second term Roosevelt was able to get some notable progressive legislation on the books. In 1906 he induced Congress to pass the Hepburn Act, for the first time giving a government agency—the Interstate Commerce Commission, in this case—the power to set rates for a private business. The bill allowed the commission to inspect the books of interstate railroads before setting rates and outlawed the practice of issuing free passes with which the railroads had bribed politicians. The bill was not a complete victory for the reformers. The railroads, through Aldrich, succeeded in inserting a provision giving the courts power to overturn commission-set rates. Nevertheless, the law was an important addition to the federal arsenal against business abuses.

Pure Food and Drug Legislation.   Two other important regulatory measures passed in 1906 provided direct federal protection to consumers. For years reformers had attacked irresponsible meat-packers and food processors. In the government itself Dr. Harvey Wiley, chief of the Department of Agriculture's Bureau of Chemistry, had long warred against the patent medicine quacks and demanded that drug preparations be labeled to show their contents. Wiley supplied most of the data for "The Great American Fraud," a sensational muckraking article on the drug companies by Samuel Hopkins Adams, published in *Collier's* in 1905. An even more effective brief for consumer protection came in 1906, when Upton Sinclair published his lurid novel *The Jungle*. Sinclair's description of the filth of the Chicago meat-packing plants, of men falling into the lard vats and being rendered into cooking fat, and of packers injecting spoiled meat with chemicals to improve its appearance and then selling it to city saloons for their free lunch counters revolted the public and turned the stomach of the president himself.

After checking Sinclair's charges, TR threw his support behind a meat inspection bill then in Congress. Although the bad reputation of American beef had hurt their sales abroad, the meat-packers resisted the bill's passage strenuously. Only when the president warned them that he would publish the results of his own investigation of Sinclair's charges did they yield, though not without extracting concessions. The bill that Roosevelt signed into law as the Meat Inspection Act on June 30, 1906, provided for government supervision of sanitary practices in meat-packing plants, but the cost of the inspection would be borne by the treasury. On the same day, the years of agitation for drug regulation also bore fruit when TR approved the Pure Food and Drug Act requiring that the contents of food and drug preparations be described on their labels. Now at least the public could tell what it was getting when it bought "Brown's Iron Bitters" or "Horsford's Acid Phosphate."

Conservation.   Progressives strongly favored policies to protect and conserve the nation's natural resources and endowment.

Their efforts appealed to a wide range of citizens. Lovers of nature considered the unspoiled wilderness a delight in itself, one capable of renewing the soul and the spirit. Led by Scottish-born naturalist John Muir and groups such as the Sierra Club of California, these "preservationists" insisted that the country's natural heritage be protected against any sort of defilement and preserved intact. Another group—the "conservationists"—was more pragmatic in its goals. Led by Chief Forester Gifford Pinchot, a Pennsylvanian trained in forestry and land management, they worshiped efficiency and sought the "best use" of resources. Best-use conservationists of the Pinchot variety believed the natural endowment must be exploited, but exploited rationally, scientifically, so that it would remain available to future generations. They noted the destruction of the buffalo, the disappearance of the enormous Great Lakes forests, the erosion of the soil everywhere, and the neglect of usable resources, and called for scientific resource management. At times the preservationists and the conservationists fought one another, but they also cooperated to battle the great lumber and mining companies, which they accused of putting profit ahead of the nation's long-term interests. At times, too, they found themselves at odds with ranchers and other western groups that resented eastern attempts to interfere with the traditional free-wheeling way they exploited the land.

Both preservationists and conservationists embodied the growing realization, as the nineteenth century closed, that the country's last frontier was rapidly filling in. As we saw, the emerging new sense of finite unspoiled space inspired creation of Yellowstone National Park in 1872. Yellowstone would be the precedent for setting aside other tracts of exceptionally scenic land as permanent recreation areas. In 1890, after strenuous efforts by Muir and other preservationists, Congress created Yosemite National Park in California, embracing one of the most beautiful natural spots in North America. Eventually the United States would create a national park system unequaled in the world. And the conservationist–preservationist impulse to protect resources from exploitation went beyond scenic sites. In 1891, the Forest Reserve Act withdrew acreage in federally owned forests from the public domain and exempted them from private purchase.

As an authority on wildlife and a lover of the outdoors, Roosevelt naturally championed the conservation movement. Closer to Gifford Pinchot than to John Muir, he approved such "best-use" projects as the 1902 Newlands Act. In 1905 he transferred the government's forest reserves from the Department of the Interior to the Department of Agriculture, where Chief Forester Pinchot could supervise their management. Two years later he and Pinchot saved millions of additional acres of public-domain forest and several important power sites from western timber companies by placing them in the forest reserves or designating them as ranger stations. In 1908 the president called a National Conservation Conference of forty-four state governors and hundreds of experts to consider resource-management problems.

The Panic of 1907.   Although the economy generally was healthy during the Progressive Era, in 1907 the country only narrowly averted a serious depression when a major New York bank closed its doors, setting off a wave of panicky deposit withdrawals from other banks. If matters had taken their usual course, the panic would have spread to the stock market and, in the absence of a central bank, would have tripped off a major depression. Fortunately, the combined action of the treasury, which deposited $35 million of the government's surplus in various private banks, and large loans by J. P. Morgan and other private bankers to troubled financial institutions, stopped the panic in its tracks. A business downturn did follow, but it was both brief and shallow.

Morgan and the treasury had saved the day; but in the wake of the scare, Congress considered what could be done to avoid future panics. In 1908 it passed the Aldrich-Vreeland Emergency Currency Act, making $500 million in new currency available to certain national banks that deposited bonds with the treasury, and establishing a congressional commission to investigate the deficiencies in the country's banking system and to recommend changes.

Taft's Misfortunes. Theodore Roosevelt left the White House in March 1909 convinced that William Howard Taft, his hand-picked successor, would carry on in his progressive steps. He had reason to be confident. The ponderous, 350-pound Taft—a former federal jurist, Commissioner of the Philippines, and secretary of war—had campaigned in 1908 on his predecessor's record. With the popular Teddy behind him, Taft defeated William Jennings Bryan, once again the Democratic candidate.

Affable, well-liked, but indolent, Taft did not really want to be president. His was a judicial rather than an executive temperament. At one point he said that if he could be made a common pleas judge in Hamilton County, Ohio, he would be content to remain there all his life. His obesity hampered him. He ate gargantuan meals and then fell asleep at the table even with guests present. It made him a figure of derision.

Taft was pledged to continue TR's progressive policies, but at heart he was a conservative. He and his attorney general, George W. Wickersham, would be reasonably energetic in enforcing the Sherman Antitrust Act, for it was the law of the land. Indeed, Taft brought more suits against trusts than either Roosevelt or Wilson, Taft's progressive successor. But he was at best a timid reformer who refused to dramatize his policies or rally public opinion in their favor. When opposed by the party's Old Guard, Taft usually retreated.

TR chooses his successor. Carrying the mountainous William Howard Taft on his shoulder this way would have been quite a feat!

Roosevelt had scarcely left office to go big-game hunting in Africa when the new president managed to alienate the progressives in his own party, turning them into fierce opponents. Taft's problems with the Republican "insurgents" began when, in fulfillment of a campaign pledge, he asked Congress to consider lowering tariffs. By 1909 tariff revision seemed long overdue. With brief and minor exceptions, taxes on foreign imports had risen steadily since the Civil War. Reformers charged they had been costly to the American consumer. The Dingley Tariff of 1897 had pushed import duties to their highest level in history and had inflated the price of everything the public wore, ate, and used. Indeed, some critics insisted that the Dingley Tariff explained the rising prices that Americans had been experiencing since the turn of the century. To make matters worse, they said, the high tariff was the "mother of trusts," encouraging the great industrial combinations that further gouged the public.

Prompted by the party's recent campaign pledge and the president's request, in 1909 the Republican House of Representatives passed a tariff revision bill sponsored by Sereno E. Payne, cutting rates sharply. This bill ran afoul of Rhode Island's Nelson Aldrich when it came to the Senate. A businessman himself as well as a stand-patter, Aldrich threw out most of the House bill's lowered schedules. Taft was appalled by the Payne-Aldrich bill, but he left the fight against it to the Senate Republican progressives.

Day after day, during the hot Washington summer, La Follette, Beveridge, Dolliver, Clapp, and other midwestern Republican progressives attacked the Payne-Aldrich bill. Taking up each of the schedules in turn, they showed how the Senate version would raise costs to the consumer and benefit only the trusts. The Aldrich measure, La Follette declared, would encourage monopoly, and with competition gone the results would be "shoddy in everything we wear and adulteration in everything we eat." Beveridge acknowledged that the country had to protect wage earners and manufacturers, but "a just and equal consideration . . . [must] be shown the consuming public."

The insurgents' fight was futile; the Aldrich rates prevailed. The results might have been different if the president had intervened, but Taft refused to use his influence to defeat the measure. When it came to his desk with the Aldrich changes intact, he signed it into law. Soon afterward he called it "the best tariff measure the Republican party has ever passed."

The president's response shocked progressives. The midwestern Republican insurgents considered Taft's performance a repudiation of TR's policies and betrayal of the party's promises to the public. In short order the reformers found new cause for dismay in the president's handling of conservation policies.

Taft's secretary of the interior was Richard A. Ballinger, a Seattle attorney with close ties to western mining and lumbering interests. As secretary, Ballinger restored lands to commercial exploitation that Roosevelt had removed from entry, interfered with the Reclamation Service, and cancelled an agreement giving the Forest Service control over forest preserves on Indian lands. In each of these actions he clashed with Pinchot, who was still Chief Forester and who, somewhat self-righteously, considered himself the special guardian of the public against selfish business interests.

The argument between Ballinger and Pinchot came to a head when government-owned coal lands in Alaska were transferred to a Morgan-Guggenheim syndicate. Pinchot considered this a blatant giveaway of public resources and accused Ballinger of being in cahoots with the despoilers of the public domain. Rather than confining his criticism to memos to the president, he made speeches all over the country attacking his department chief. He also leaked information to the newspapers pillorying Ballinger, and by inference condemning Taft himself. Eventually Pinchot clashed head-on with the president, who fired him while retaining Ballinger. Pinchot was now a progressive martyr, and his treatment another reason to distrust Taft.

The insurgent Republicans also clashed with Taft over congressional reorganization. They had long feuded with the Republican Speaker of the House, the profane, hard-drinking "Uncle Joe" Cannon, a man fiercely opposed to progressive legislation. Soon after Pinchot's dismissal, Cannon began to deprive the party rebels of committee chairmanships they had earned by seniority. The insurgent Republicans resolved to break his power and turned to the president for support. Taft disliked Cannon but declined to help the insurgents, claiming that the speaker was too deeply entrenched to be ousted. The rebels refused to give up. At the opening of the March 1910 congressional session, led by George Norris, a young progressive Republican from Nebraska, they joined with anti-Cannon Democrats to strip the speaker of his power to appoint members to the all-important House Rules Committee and deprived him of his own place on it.

By mid-1910, then, Taft had thoroughly alienated the progressive, largely midwestern wing of his party. In truth, the president's record on progressive measures was not all bad. He supported the Mann-Elkins Act (1910), which gave the Interstate Commerce Commission the power to suspend railroad-initiated rate changes if they seemed excessive and also authorized government supervision of telephone, wireless, and telegraph companies. That same year he endorsed a "postal savings" scheme to allow small savers, often victimized by private bank failures, to place their money in the safekeeping of the federal post office. He also threw his considerable weight behind the Sixteenth Amendment to the constitution, which authorized a federal income tax, and signed the Mann Act (1910), which prohibited the interstate transportation of women for purposes of prostitution. Yet on most of these issues Taft so equivocated that he received little credit from the insurgents. Perhaps worst of all, in their eyes, the lethargic, dull chief executive was not the dynamic, joyous, charismatic TR. One progressive publication put its dismay in verse:

> Teddy, come home and blow your horn,
> The sheep's in the meadow, the cow's in the corn.
> The boy you left to tend the sheep, is under the
> haystack fast asleep.

Republican Split. The progressive Republican leaders rapidly deserted Taft. In May 1910 Pinchot met with Roosevelt in Europe, as he was returning from Africa, and filled his ears with news of Taft's transgressions. By the time TR arrived back in the United States, his cordial feelings for his protégé had decidedly cooled. The last straw was the administration's revelation, in the course of an antitrust suit, that during the 1907 panic Roosevelt had allowed U.S. Steel to buy the Tennessee Coal and Iron Company without protest, though the purchase enhanced the firm's monopoly position in steel. Roosevelt believed that the move had been justified to restore business confidence when it was badly shaken, but the leak made him appear a tool of Morgan. He deeply resented the administration's effort to smear him.

Besides his growing doubts about Taft's political wisdom and loyalty, TR simply could not abandon politics. In 1910 he was only fifty-two and still overflowing with energy. Permanent retirement seemed unthinkable. He had served only one elected term, even though he had been president for almost eight years, so tradition did not bar his reelection. Under the barrage of the anti-Taft insurgents, Roosevelt quickly warmed to the idea of opposing the president for the 1912 Republican nomination.

By this time Herbert Croly's book *The Promise of American Life* (1909) had crystallized the activist view of the government's role that he had played with for some years. In a speech at Osawatomie, Kansas, in August 1910, TR used Croly's phrase, "the New Nationalism," to describe a federal government that, rather than forbidding combinations or attempting to break them up, would seek to "control them in the interest of the public." This New Nationalism would also place the well-being of the public ahead of property rights. "Every man," TR told his Kansas audience, "holds his property subject to the general right of the community to regulate its use to whatever degree the public welfare may require." Here was an endorsement of government paternalism and control beyond anything previously espoused by a major-party candidate. It distanced Roosevelt still further from the president.

Not all Republican progressives favored Roosevelt. Many, especially in the Midwest, preferred Wisconsin's La Follette. In January 1911 the midwesterners had organized the National Republican Progressive League to advance progressive ideas and promote La Follette's candidacy. Roosevelt refused to join. For a while the two men jockeyed for leadership of the party's progressive wing, but then, unable to compete with TR's broad national appeal, La Follette dropped out of the race.

Throughout the spring of 1912 Roosevelt and Taft battled for Republican convention delegates. TR won in the states, mainly western, that used the new presidential primaries to choose convention delegates. Taft swept the states in the South and East where tightly controlled conventions, dominated by party regulars, made the delegate choice. At the national convention in Chicago the Republican National Committee, controlled by the Taft men, refused the Roosevelt partisans' claim to a large block of disputed convention seats, giving almost all to Taft. The Roosevelt delegates walked out, leaving the convention firmly in the president's hands.

But Roosevelt and his friends were not through. Early in August, 2,000 men and women, many of them social workers, settlement house leaders, and state and local reformers, assembled in Chicago to organize the Progressive party and nominate Roosevelt for president. The delegates selected Hiram W. Johnson of California as their vice presidential candidate. The platform of the Progressive party—or Bull Moose party, as it was called after TR's remark that he felt as energetic as a bull moose—was the most radical ever proposed by a major party, foreshadowing almost all of the modern American social welfare state. Taking many of the emerging progressive ideas and carrying them several steps further, the platform endorsed popular election of United States senators; presidential primaries; the initiative, referendum, and recall in federal matters; women's suffrage; the recall (by citizens' petitions) of state court decisions; tariff reduction; a commission to regulate interstate industry as well as interstate commerce; a more stringent pure food and drug law; old age pensions; minimum wage and maximum hours laws; and the prohibition of child labor. The closing words of TR's acceptance speech conveyed the crusading mood of the new party. "Our cause," the candidate thundered, "is based on the eternal principles of righteousness, and even though we who now lead for the first time fail, in the end the cause itself will triumph. . . . We stand at Armageddon and we battle for the Lord."

The Election of 1912.   Meanwhile, the Democrats had nominated Woodrow Wilson, former president of Princeton University and, most recently, progressive governor of New Jersey. The son of a Presbyterian minister from Virginia, Wilson was a slender, scholarly man who joined stubborn self-righteousness with an eloquence unequaled since Lincoln and a vision of human potential unmatched since Jefferson. In 1910 the New Jersey Democratic bosses had selected him as a figurehead candidate for governor, but he had gone on after the election to repudiate his sponsors and make an impressive record as a strong, liberal leader who brought staunchly conservative New Jersey into the progressive era. At the 1912 Democratic convention in Baltimore, with Bryan's support, Wilson defeated Speaker of the House, Missouri's Champ Clark, in a grueling forty-six ballots.

During the next few months the country experienced the liveliest presidential battle since 1896. The contest was really between Roosevelt and Wilson, with Taft lagging badly from the beginning. During the weeks of campaigning the conflicting ideologies of the two front-runners were thrown into sharp relief. TR trumpeted the message of the New Nationalism: Bigness as such was not bad; it only became bad when it injured the public and the national interest. Government could, and should, regulate private economic interests. Government also had a responsibility to protect citizens in many other aspects of daily life and reduce life's uncertainties and hazards. Wilson, a man from the Jeffersonian tradition of limited government, fought back with his New Freedom, much of it inspired by the liberal Boston lawyer Louis D. Brandeis. The New Nationalism was "big-brother government," Wilson charged. "You will find," he told a Buffalo audience of working men, "that the programme of the new party legalizes monopolies and systematically subordinates workingmen to them and to plans made by the Government. . . ." Like the Bull Moosers, Wilson believed that concentrated private economic power was a danger to the American public; he differed from them in holding that the way to salvation lay in breaking up

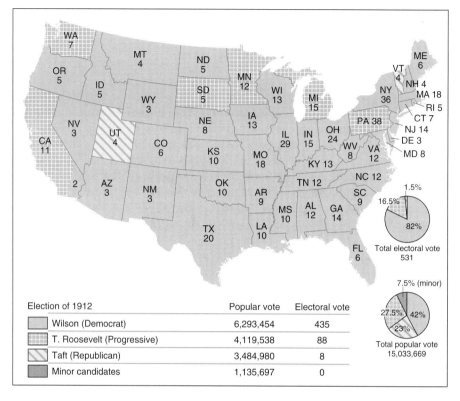

Election of 1912		Popular vote	Electoral vote
	Wilson (Democrat)	6,293,454	435
	T. Roosevelt (Progressive)	4,119,538	88
	Taft (Republican)	3,484,980	8
	Minor candidates	1,135,697	0

The Election of 1912

these monopolies by vigorous antitrust action. TR's response to the New Freedom was blunt: It was "rural toryism," he declared, more suitable for a simpler age than for the twentieth-century world.

Wilson won the election by a plurality. The public loved Teddy, but many progressives were suspicious of his newfound radicalism, especially since he had allowed a Morgan partner, George Perkins, to play an important role in the campaign as fund-raiser and organizer. In the end TR received the votes largely of the Republican progressives; Taft, of the Republican stand-pat core. Wilson, on the other hand, won the votes of both Democratic progressives and traditional conservative Democrats. (Eugene V. Debs took 900,000 votes for the Socialists.) For the first time since 1897 a Democrat would occupy the White House, but only because a third party had split the opposition.

■ THE WILSON ADMINISTRATION ■

The New Freedom in Action.   Woodrow Wilson proved to be a strong president. Disregarding the precedent established by Jefferson in 1801, he appeared before Congress in person to read his first annual message. Wilson's first major concern was the tariff, which, he reminded Congress, had long fostered mono-polies and exposed the consuming public to oppressive prices. The structure of "privilege" and "artificial advantage" must be destroyed and American busi-nesses compelled to compete with their rivals in the rest of the world. Wilson was determined to do what Taft had failed to achieve in 1909.

The fruit of the president's efforts was the 1913 Underwood Tariff. This measure substantially lowered the nation's tariff walls for the first time since the Civil War. To make up for the expected loss of federal revenue, Congress took advantage of the recently adopted Sixteenth Amendment and included a grad-uated income tax in the legislation. Lobbyists for manufacturing and other special-interest groups resisted passage of the tariff bill, but Wilson fought back. Lashing out at the "industrious and insidious" lobbyists, he accused them of seeking to "create an artificial opinion and to overcome the interests of the pub-lic" for their own selfish ends. His counterattack jarred the Senate, and the bill passed.

Wilson's next important achievement was the Federal Reserve Act. The na-tional Banking Acts of the Civil War Era had failed to create a central bank to regulate the supply of money and credit and extend help to hard-pressed local commercial banks in time of crisis. Nor had the national banking system pro-vided a flexible currency that could expand to meet the needs of the economy during peak periods and then contract during quiet months. Farmers con-demned the system for forbidding federally chartered banks to lend on land, the only security for loans that they generally possessed. Yet agrarians feared a sys-tem that would be centralized in New York City and tightly controlled by Wall Street.

As finally passed in 1913, the Federal Reserve Act was a compromise between the centralizers and agrarians, the supporters of government rule and those who favored private control. It created twelve district banks, whose direc-tors were chosen by both private bankers and the government. The entire system was placed under the weak overall supervision of a central Federal Reserve Board in Washington, D.C. The district banks would hold the reserves of member banks—the commercial banks that did the day-to-day business of the nation. By lending money to member banks at low interest rates, or alternately by limiting such loans by charging high interest rates (through the "rediscount" process), the district banks could regulate credit and the money supply to suit the economy's seasonal needs and head off financial crises. The new system also allowed mem-ber banks to lend on farm mortgages. Despite the serious failings that time would reveal, the new system seemed a great improvement over the old.

The third major item on Wilson's first-term agenda was antitrust legislation to fulfill his campaign promise to break up the monopolies. Over the years the government's antitrust drive had been blunted by the federal courts. Most recently, in its 1911 "rule of reason" decision (*Standard Oil* v. *United States*), the Supreme Court had declared that only "unreasonable" restraints on interstate commerce were illegal; from now on an instance of monopoly must be blatant to be subject to antitrust prosecution. But that was not all. For over a decade the federal courts had been treating labor unions as "combinations in restraint of trade," and hence subject to antitrust prosecution. They had even issued injunctions (as in the 1894 Pullman strike) compelling unions to cease strikes and boycotts or face federal contempt-of-court charges. In the hands of the courts the Sherman Antitrust Act had become a union-busting weapon.

To protect organized labor's rights, help consumers, and get around the courts' limitations on antitrust actions, Wilson proposed two new measures. The first established the Federal Trade Commission (1914) to replace Roosevelt's Bureau of Corporations. The FTC was given powers to procure data from corporations and issue cease-and-desist orders against abuses such as mislabeling, adulteration of products, trade boycotts, and combinations to fix wholesale prices. The new commission would be the public's watchdog against the trusts. The second measure, the Clayton Antitrust Act (1914), strengthened the Sherman Antitrust Act by prohibiting firms from charging one price to one customer and a different price to another when such discrimination tended to foster monopoly, and forbidding contracts that required buyers not to do business with sellers' competitors. It also declared illegal most "interlocking directorates," a device by which one group of corporate directors headed several firms simultaneously. Similarly, a corporation was prohibited from acquiring stock in other corporations when the transaction threatened to reduce competition. A final provision— called by AFL president Samuel Gompers "labor's Magna Carta"—declared both labor unions and farmers' cooperatives exempt from the antitrust laws and limited the right of federal courts to issue injunctions in labor disputes.

Another important change during Wilson's first months in office—one that was a general progressive initiative rather than Wilson's alone—was the adoption of the Seventeenth Amendment to the Constitution (1913). Henceforth all United States senators would be elected by direct vote of the people in each state rather than by the state legislators. No longer, the reformers felt, would the Senate be a bastion of conservatism that could ignore public opinion and protect the big corporations.

Wilson's Failings.   Despite the president's legislative successes, his first few years disappointed some of the most advanced progressives. He declined to support women's suffrage and at first refused to fight for a child-labor law. Nor was he as fierce an opponent of trusts as he had promised to be during the campaign. Like TR before him, he bargained with big corporations, agreeing not to prosecute them for combining to restrain trade if they would modify their behavior in some acceptable way.

But the most conspicuous defect of Wilson's first administration was its attitudes toward black Americans. The new president was a Virginian by birth and had lived much of his early life in the South. His party, moreover, was strongly southern in its makeup, and many of his closest advisers were white southerners. The new administration had few ties to the black community. Once in office, it abruptly cut off much of the political patronage that the Republicans had conferred on black supporters. In addition, one by one, federal departments and agencies in Washington began to segregate their remaining black workers, imposing on the federal government the Jim Crow system that permeated the

South. Eventually, following loud protests from black leaders and their white progressive allies, the president tried to undo some of the damage. But it was too late. By the end of his administration the nation's capital had become a full-blown southern city in its racial practices.

Wilson Shifts Left. Wilson's first three years in office produced mixed results from the progressive perspective. After passage of the Clayton Act of 1914, the president appeared to lose interest in pushing further progressive legislation. Then, as the 1916 election approached, his reformist enthusiasm revived.

The change was politically expedient. Wilson had won in 1912 because the Republicans had been split between Taft and Roosevelt. By 1916 TR had returned to the GOP of his youth, virtually killing the Bull Moose party. To win reelection, Wilson concluded, he would have to attract former Bull Moosers, and this meant moving to the left. Hitherto his New Freedom brand of reform had avoided the social legislation that required expansion of federal authority. Now Wilson shifted ground.

To further aid farmers, he pushed the Federal Farm Loan Act of 1916, which established twelve Federal Farm Loan banks to lend money at low rates to farmers who joined certain farm loan associations. A bolder innovation was the Keating-Owen Act (1916), which prohibited interstate traffic in goods manufactured by the labor of children under sixteen years of age, and was intended to end child labor. The president also pushed the Kern-McGillicuddy Compensation Act (1916) providing workers' compensation for injured federal employees, and the Adamson Act (1916) establishing an eight-hour day and time-and-a-half overtime pay for railroad workers. Though these new laws applied to only limited groups of employees, they represented a long step toward federal regulation of the labor market.

One additional move rounded out Wilson's shift to the left in 1916: the nomination of his friend Louis D. Brandeis as Supreme Court justice. For years Brandeis had been one of the best-known labor lawyers in the country. His work in establishing arbitration procedures in the New York garment industry had been hailed as a model approach to labor–capital relations. In 1908, in the case *Muller v. Oregon,* Brandeis had mustered arguments drawn from sociology to demonstrate that long work hours were detrimental to the health of women and seriously injured society as a whole. The "Brandeis brief" had convinced the court and saved the Oregon law. It established an important precedent for defending future social legislation.

The nomination of Brandeis raised a storm. The Supreme Court in 1916 had only one progressive member, Oliver Wendell Holmes, Jr., and the nation's liberals cheered the prospect of Brandeis joining him. But conservatives, including ex-president Taft and the American Bar Association, fought the nomination with every ounce of their strength. Running through much of the opposition was a barely disguised streak of anti-Semitism. Despite the powerful opposition, Wilson fought hard for his friend and adviser, pulling all the strings he could. His success earned him additional gratitude from progressives of both parties.

Despite the list of accomplishments, by late summer of 1916 the Progressive movement had largely run its course. By now the public's attention had shifted from domestic issues to the question of war or peace. In a few months the country would embark on a crusade to make the whole world safe for the kind of liberal society that the progressives had been trying for a decade or more to construct at home. In the process the domestic reform impulse would lose its spark.

■ CONCLUSIONS ■

Between 1890 and 1917 more and more Americans became uneasy over unrestrained private power. As the nation became ever more tightly knit together, giant corporations had become essential to provide the products people needed for a comfortable life. Meanwhile, growing numbers living in the cities became dependent on large firms for virtually everything they consumed. Seeking to protect themselves, urban Americans of all classes adopted a new political outlook, one that resembled views earlier held by rural reformers such as the Populists and the free-silver Democrats.

The progressives took much from Populism. Their primary enemy was similar—the trusts, the monopolies—and they borrowed the familiar rhetoric of an earlier rural age when they attacked "the interests." Especially in Wilson's New Freedom, we find echoes of Jefferson and Jackson in attitudes and ideas. Progressives also revived the Populist concern for direct democracy to bypass corrupt legislatures. Yet the addition of urban people to the reform cause altered its quality. Progressivism was more sophisticated than Populism. Borrowing from the liberal social Darwinists and the new efficiency-oriented professionals, progressives abandoned monetary cure-alls and developed new ideas of direct government action to solve social ills. Inevitably they focused on city problems and on wage earners, though rural grievances were not ignored. Especially in its New Nationalism guise, which emphasized a powerful regulatory federal government, progressivism foreshadowed to future reform in a complex urban society.

Progressivism was not a complete success even in its own terms. It did not end the dangers inherent in a society with large inequalities of wealth and power; it did not end the insecurity that afflicted many Americans. It would remain to a later generation to tackle these problems again, with somewhat greater success.

Progressivism had inherent limitations. The prophets of efficiency clearly had a restricted vision of a better society. Nor were progressives as a whole free of the racial and ethnic prejudice that marked their predecessors. Today, moreover, many would question their faith in the efficacy of federal and state paternalism. Nevertheless, the reformers of 1900–1917 were the first generation to grapple with the problems of an urbanized nation. For all their failings, they laid the foundation for much of the reform that would follow.

Online Resources

"Racial Prejudice"
http://www.iberia.vassar.edu/1896/prejudice.html
This informative Web site includes many primary-source documents that speak to racial issues in the New South period. These documents include the full text of a public address by Booker T. Washington, African American and white responses to African-American' quest for civil rights, and links to African-American pamphlets published from 1880–1920.

"The Triangle Shirtwaist Factory Fire"
http://www.ilr.cornell.edu/trianglefire/
This rich and informative site details this now-infamous workplace disaster. Through the use of an interpretative introductory essay, photographs, oral histories of survivors, and contemporary newspaper accounts, this source explains the impact of the industrial accident on workplace safety reform.

"The Evolution of the Conservation Movement"
http://memory.loc.gov/ammem/amrvhtml/conshome.html
Explore this area of progressive reform through timelines that link to important documents in conservation history, such as Teddy Roosevelt's addresses on the subject and Acts of Congress.

"The Urban Log Cabin"
http://www.wnet.org/tenement/logcabin.html
See what living conditions were like in a 1915 tenement house. This site describes the many conditions progressives were battling, including overcrowding, poor sanitary conditions, and disease.

"How the NAACP Began"
http://www.i/stu.edu/RSO/NAACP/history.htm
http://www.naacp.org/history.asp
These sites offer a copy of Mary White Ovington's history of the organization as originally printed in 1914. As a former executive secretary and chairperson of the organization, Ovington outlined in the document the NAACP's original platform, acts of civil injustices against blacks, and the role of W. E. B. DuBois.

Child Labor in America, 1908–1912
http://www.historyplace.com/unitedstates/childlabor/index.html
Showcasing the photographs of Lewis Hine, this site shows the realities of children at work in mines and textile mills and on city streets. Used to help encourage social reform, Hine's original captions accompany his photographs.

In the Shadow of the IWW
http://www.reuther.wayne.edu/iww.html
Visit this site to explore the IWW, one of the Progressive Era's most radical labor unions. Featuring the union platform, IWW illustrations, and the lyrics to the union's organizing songs, this site chronicles the creation and downfall of the union.

23

WORLD WAR I

Idealism, National Interest, or Neutral Rights?

1914	American marines occupy Veracruz, Mexico; World War I begins in Europe; Wilson calls for American neutrality
1915	Marines occupy Haiti; Germany declares a war zone around the British Isles; U-boats sink the *Falaba*, the *Lusitania*, and the *Arabic*, all with loss of American lives; Wilson initiates the preparedness program to enlarge the army and the navy
1916	Wilson orders General John Pershing and 6,000 troops to Mexico to capture Pancho Villa; Colonel Edward House promises American intervention if deadlock on Western Front continues; U-boat sinks the *Sussex* with resulting American injuries; Germany suspends submarine warfare; Wilson reelected on "He kept us out of war" platform; Marines occupy the Dominican Republic
1917	Germany resumes submarine warfare and the United States severs diplomatic relations; British intelligence intercepts the Zimmermann telegram; Wilson orders the arming of American merchant ships; The Russian Revolution; Congress declares war on Germany; the War Industries Board, the War Labor Board, and the Committee of Public Information manage the war effort at home; Congress passes the Espionage Act
1918	The Sedition Act; Postmaster General Albert Burleson excludes publications critical of the war from the mails; The Justice Department indicts socialist leaders Eugene Debs and Victor Berger on charges of advocating draft evasion; Wilson announces his Fourteen Points; Germany collapses and armistice ends the war
1919	Peace conference at Versailles; League of Nations incorporated into treaty
1919–20	Congress rejects the Versailles Treaty
1920	The states ratify the Nineteenth Amendment providing for women's suffrage; Warren G. Harding elected president; Harding signs separate peace treaty with Germany in lieu of Versailles Treaty

As Americans read their newspapers over morning coffee on June 29, 1914, many wondered "Where is Sarajevo?" The day before, in that remote Balkan town in present-day Bosnia, a fanatical Serbian nationalist had shot and killed

Archduke Francis Ferdinand, heir to the Austro-Hungarian throne. Few people could have anticipated how their lives and those of millions of others would be affected by the archduke's murder in that unruly corner of southeastern Europe.

Within six weeks the major European powers were at war. Tied together by a bewildering tangle of alliances and agreements, both public and secret, all the large nations of Europe were quickly drawn into the dispute, with France, Russia, and Great Britain (the Allies) on one side, and Germany and Austria-Hungary (the Central Powers) on the other. Before many months Japan and Italy had joined the Allies; and the Ottoman Empire (Turkey) and Bulgaria had allied themselves with the Central Powers. By the end of 1914, using the most lethal weapons that twentieth-century technology could devise, enormous armies, navies, and air fleets grappled in ferocious combat in Europe and around the world.

President Wilson quickly declared that Americans must be "neutral in fact as well as in name during these days that are to try men's souls." We must "be impartial in thought as well as in action, must put a curb on our sentiments as well as upon every transaction that might be construed as a preference of one party to the struggle before another." Thirty-one months later the same man would appear before a joint session of Congress to ask for a declaration of war against the Central Powers.

What had happened in those months to bring the peaceful and self-satisfied republic into this "most terrible of wars"? Why did the United States and its people not heed the president's early advice and remain neutral both "in thought" and "in action"?

■ WILSON AND THE WORLD ORDER ■

To understand American involvement in World War I, we must consider Wilson's view of America's place in the world. Some progressives—internationalists such as Theodore Roosevelt and Albert J. Beveridge—believed the United States must play a vigorous role in world affairs and serve as a force for honorable behavior among nations. Isolationists, within the progressive group, such as Senators Robert La Follette of Wisconsin and Hiram W. Johnson of California, feared that United States involvement in concerns beyond its borders would interfere with reform at home. Neither doubted that enlightened, liberal capitalism was the most benevolent social system in the world.

Wilson's foreign-policy views fluctuated between these poles. At times he seemed to believe progressive democracy was for domestic consumption only. On other occasions he acted as if it was for export as well. In addition, his attitudes were infused with an intense moralism. To complicate matters further, like every national leader, he had to consider first his country's vital interests and defend them against any threatening power. To satisfy all these differing imperatives Wilson walked a tightrope, and his resulting unsteadiness and hesitation led to charges of inconsistency and even hypocrisy.

Moral Diplomacy.   Wilson chose William Jennings Bryan as his first secretary of state. Bryan had worked long in the cause of peace and shared Wilson's view that America must serve as the world's "moral inspiration." In 1913 and 1914 he negotiated conciliation treaties with twenty-one nations, binding the parties to submit all international disputes to permanent investigating commissions and to forgo armed force until the commission had completed its report.

A similar idealism infused other aspects of Wilson's early diplomacy. Both Bryan and his chief opposed using the American government to serve the interests of American businesses abroad. Under Taft, Wilson's predecessor, the United States had supported the participation of American bankers in a multinational consortium to build railroads in China. Feeling that the arrangement might undermine China's fragile sovereignty, Bryan withdrew the government's support. Wilson and Bryan also induced Congress to repeal a 1912 law that had exempted American coastal vessels from paying tolls on the Panama Canal, a law that violated the Hay-Pauncefote Treaty and its promise of equal treatment for all nations using the canal.

But Wilson never forgot the country's "vital interests"; where they seemed at stake, and where the risks appeared small, he was sometimes insensitive to moral considerations. In the Caribbean, which the United States considered an American lake, Wilson and his chief lieutenant proved as overbearing as Roosevelt. In 1913 Bryan negotiated a treaty with Nicaragua giving that small nation $3 million for exclusive American rights to construct a second Atlantic–Pacific canal. The Bryan-Chamorro agreement, not ratified until 1916, made the strategically located Central American republic a virtual satellite of the United States, with little control over its own international economic relations. In 1915 and 1916 the United States intervened militarily in Haiti and the Dominican Republic—in the first to put down disorder, in the second to prevent the European powers, especially Germany, from landing troops to protect their citizens and collect unpaid debts. In each of these cases Wilson believed that he was merely holding America's less scrupulous neighbors to universal standards of order and honesty. To outsiders, the United States seemed to be imposing its will on countries too weak to resist the American giant.

Mexico.   In Mexico the United States managed to combine blatant self-interest and idealism in a particularly confusing way. For a generation following 1880 Mexico was ruled by strongman Porfirio Díaz. Díaz had encouraged foreign investment in Mexican mines, oil wells, and railroads; by 1913 American businesses had poured over a billion dollars into his country. Though this infusion of capital helped the middle class, ordinary Mexicans remained as poor, illiterate, and oppressed as in Montezuma's day.

In 1911 Díaz's enemies among the country's liberal intellectuals toppled him from power and made Francisco Madero president. Madero tried to effect sweeping democratic reforms and restore constitutional liberties denied by Díaz. His policies aroused the hostility of the Mexican landed aristocracy, the army, and the Catholic Church. Two years later Victoriano Huerta, Madero's chief military adviser, seized power and had Madero murdered.

Great Britain, Germany, and France had already officially recognized Huerta when Wilson took office. Many Americans, including businesspeople with investments in Mexico, advised Wilson to follow suit. He refused. Despite the tradition of nations, including the United States, recognizing established governments no matter how they gained power or what their internal policies were, in Wilson's eyes Huerta was a "butcher." Instead of according diplomatic recognition to the Huerta government, Wilson proclaimed a new policy toward revolutionary regimes in Latin America: The United States would not recognize any new government unless it was "supported at every turn by . . . orderly processes . . . based upon law, not upon arbitrary or irregular force."

Wilson sought to isolate the new Mexican tyrant by pressuring the British into withdrawing their recognition. He also stationed American naval vessels off Mexico's major ports to stop arms shipments to Huerta while allowing arms to reach his enemies. Eventually, he hoped, Huerta might be pushed out by some champion of liberal rule such as Venustiano Carranza, an associate of Madero who had raised the banner of revolt in the northern part of the country.

Wilson's policies led to trouble. In April 1914 crewmen of an American naval vessel were arrested by a Huertista officer when they went ashore at Tampico. Although they were soon released, the American naval commander, Admiral Henry Mayo, demanded that the Mexican officer be punished and that the commander of the port give the American flag a twenty-one-gun salute as a sign of respect. The Mexican commandant apologized and promised disciplinary action against his subordinate, but refused the salute.

The incident now seems trivial, but Wilson made it an issue of principle. Appearing before Congress, he asked for authority to compel the Mexicans to show respect for American rights. At this point, a German vessel began to land arms for Huerta at Veracruz. To prevent this, Admiral Mayo shelled the city and ordered it occupied by marines. In the fighting that followed, over a hundred Mexicans lost their lives.

In explaining the Veracruz disaster, the president maintained that he meant only the best for the Mexican people and hoped to see them establish a new order based on "human liberty and human rights." The Mexicans would have to equalize the condition of rich and poor and keep foreign corporations from exerting excessive power and influence. This worthy prescription for Mexico's future ignored its heritage of bitter class antagonism and ideological conflict, and assumed that fundamental social change in such a nation might be effected as peaceably and amicably as progressive legislative reform in the United States. Still more imperceptive was the president's conclusion that the United States had the right to prescribe for Mexico at all. The Veracruz incident illustrated how American intrusion, even in a good cause, could produce damaging consequences for its intended beneficiary.

Meanwhile, the Veracruz attack had outraged all patriotic Mexicans, raised Huerta's stock among his own people, and cast the United States in the role of a brutal aggressor. It looked as if the Wilson administration would now be forced into the folly of war with Mexico. The president was rescued from this fate when Argentina, Brazil, and Chile offered to mediate. In May 1914 the United States,

WOODROW WILSON, THE SCHOOL TEACHER.

A minister's son and a historian, Wilson had been president of Princeton University. As president of the United States, he continued to lecture and preach. Here, symbolically, he instructs a rather skeptical Mexico in the principles of true democracy.

Mexico, and the so-called "ABC powers" met at Niagara Falls, Canada, and thrashed out a compromise that averted war.

But war with Mexico soon threatened again. Unable to resist the growing pressure at home and abroad, Huerta finally resigned, and control in Mexico City passed to Carranza. Once in office, however, Carranza was challenged by Francisco ("Pancho") Villa. Hoping to goad the United States into some overt action against Mexico that would unite the Mexican people against the "gringos" and help his chances to seize power, Villa ordered his men to attack American citizens both in Mexico and across the border.

American indignation quickly reached a new peak. Whatever they felt following Tampico and Veracruz, virtually all Americans now agreed that the United States must take strong action. In March 1916, after 35 Americans had been murdered by Villista soldiers on both sides of the border, Wilson ordered General John J. Pershing to cross into Mexico with 6,000 troops. The wily Villa eluded the American army, however, while drawing it deeper and deeper into Mexican territory.

Carranza had reluctantly given the Americans permission to enter Mexico to capture Villa. But he soon came to regard the American penetration as a virtual invasion. War was averted at the last minute only when Wilson, realizing that the United States had far more pressing concerns in Europe, ordered Pershing to return to Texas. The president then sent Ambassador Henry Fletcher to Mexico and formally recognized the Carranza administration.

With this move Wilson ended the threat of war with Mexico. Though his bungling caused anti-American feeling to run high in Mexico for years, his support for Carranza and his newfound determination to avoid war despite sharp provocations allowed the revolutionaries to establish control. The Mexican situation revealed the principal elements of the Wilson foreign policy: moralism, self-interest, missionary interventionism, and a deep reluctance to make war. These contradictory urges would also be apparent in the American approach to the war in Europe.

■ NEUTRALITY AND PUBLIC OPINION ■

Wilson's call for neutrality in August 1914 had summoned a loud "amen" from the American public. Americans had a traditional distaste for the complicated alliances formed among the European nation-states and almost no one wanted to become directly entangled in Europe's quarrels. Moreover, war promised to arouse conflicting sympathies and create domestic social tensions and unrest.

Americans Take Sides.   Yet how could Americans remove themselves from European concerns as the president hoped? Millions of citizens had been born in one or another of the belligerent nations and found they could not escape the emotional commitments of their heritage. Recent arrivals from England, Scotland, and Wales retained their affection for Britain and hoped to see it remain mistress of the seas. On the other side, the large German-American population still had strong attachments to the "Fatherland." The picture was complicated by the immigrants from Austria-Hungary and Russia, sprawling empires containing millions of Poles, Czechs, South Slavs, Finns, Jews, and many other groups denied their national aspirations or actively persecuted. Irish-Americans further complicated this tangle of responses; many hated Britain as their homeland's centuries-long oppressor and hoped that England's troubles could be turned to Ireland's advantage.

Old-stock Americans looked askance at the continued attachment of immigrants to their native lands and accused the "hyphenates" of putting European concerns ahead of America's. Yet even they took sides. Aside from a small group of intellectuals who respected German culture and scholarship or disliked the pervasive English influence on American life, most old-stock Americans were pro-Ally. Such people read the classics of English literature and admired English law and parliamentary institutions. Many of them tended to feel affection for France as well, remembering with gratitude French aid during the Revolution, and fascinated with French fashions, food, and thought.

Beyond these considerations, however, England and France were tied to the United States by a common bond of democracy and rule of law. This natural sympathy was to some extent offset by the revulsion Americans felt toward tyrannical and backward czarist Russia, but Russia was very remote and seemed, at most, a junior partner of the western Allies. Meanwhile, Germany's conservatism, militarism, and arrogance confirmed American preferences. A nation dominated by Prussian militarism since its unification in 1871, Germany had allowed its imperial ambitions to swell to gigantic proportions under Kaiser Wilhelm II. Since 1898 American military and naval leaders had become increasingly worried about a German threat to the Western Hemisphere. As recently as 1910 the Navy General Board had estimated that Germany was probably America's most dangerous potential enemy. Opinion makers and the foreign policy elite shared the fear of German aggressiveness and power, and many other citizens could not help feeling that Germany's defeat would benefit America and democratic principles everywhere.

All told, a majority of Americans were pro-Ally from the outset. At no time would intervention to help Germany be a conceivable option. The best that the Central Powers could expect was American neutrality. From the beginning, however, the British and French had reason to hope that the United States could be turned into an active ally, willing to supply arms and even men to help them defeat their opponents.

The Propaganda War.   Both sides sought to sway American opinion, the Allies for intervention, the Central Powers for neutrality. They were soon waging a fierce propaganda battle in which truth often took a back seat to expediency.

In the passionate struggle for America's mind, the Germans labored under serious handicaps. The British and French controlled the transatlantic cables, which transmitted European news to the American press, leaving the Germans with only the still-primitive wireless for getting their message out. The Central Powers were also inept. German war propaganda emphasized hate and destruction—an approach that often aroused more revulsion than sympathy abroad. Some of the most effective Allied efforts to win American approval consisted of reprinting German hate propaganda against Britain and France.

German deeds offended American opinion even more than German words. Germany opened its military campaign on the Western Front in 1914 by invading little Belgium, thereby violating an international agreement of long standing. The German chancellor then contemptuously referred to the agreement as a "scrap of paper." When patriotic Belgians challenged the invaders, the German authorities retaliated by executing Belgian civilians and by burning the old university town of Louvain.

If the Germans were clumsy, the Allies were adroit. The British in particular spoke the language of Americans, literally and figuratively. Instinctively, they knew how to arouse American sympathies for their cause and to make their enemy seem bestial. They were quick to blow up German atrocities to enormous proportions. In 1915 the British government issued an official report signed by James Bryce, a distinguished historian and respected former British ambassador to Washington, which concluded that under the German occupation "murder, lust, and pillage prevailed . . . on a scale unparalleled in any war between civilized nations in the last three centuries." Many of the atrocity stories were unfounded; others were grossly exaggerated. Nevertheless, the Bryce Report convinced many Americans that the Germans were savage "Huns" who deserved the condemnation of the entire civilized world.

The Wilson Administration's Partisanship.   In some ways the Allies' strongest supporter in America was the president himself, despite his appeal for neutrality. Ever since his early career, when he wrote *Congressional Government,* praising the English parliamentary system, Wilson had been an Anglophile. As president he felt close to the leaders of the Liberal party in England, whose program of social welfare in the years immediately preceding the war had closely paralleled his own. The president tried to be neutral, but his true feelings often showed through his reserve. At one point he told the British ambassador that everything he loved most in the world depended on Allied victory. He remarked at another point to his private secretary that "England is fighting our fight. . . . I will not take any action to embarrass England when she is fighting for her life and the life of the world."

In addition, Wilson and his closest advisers, Colonel Edward M. House and later Robert Lansing, took the threat of German expansionism seriously and looked to Britain and France to check the German emperor's ambitions. Ever since the Spanish-American War, when Britain alone among the European powers had supported the United States against Spain, makers of American foreign policy had regarded England as a bulwark against the ambitions of expansionist Germany. This feeling remained a major, though unspoken, cornerstone of American foreign policy from the late 1890s onward and would influence American policymakers after August 1914.

■ NEUTRAL RIGHTS ■

Despite the pro-Ally bias of the American people and their government, the United States could have avoided the war if not for neutral rights. Once more, as during the Napoleonic Wars a century before, the United States found itself the major neutral power in a world divided into two warring camps, each determined to defeat the other no matter what the cost to bystanders. This country insisted that the European belligerents observe the rights traditionally due neutral nations in wartime. Under these rules, vessels owned by neutrals had the right to carry unmolested all goods except contraband. Contraband normally meant arms and munitions, with commodities such as food, textiles, and naval stores explicitly excluded. Neutrals also had the right to trade freely with all belligerents, although their ships might be legitimately intercepted and turned back by an effective surface blockade maintained outside a belligerent port. If a neutral merchant or passenger ship was stopped by such a blockade, however, the blockading power was responsible for the safety of the passengers and crew of the detained vessel.

Wilson, in his characteristic way, gave the longstanding American policy of defending neutral rights a new moral emphasis. The right of neutral citizens to go wherever they pleased, sell whatever they pleased, to whomever they pleased, subject only to the recognized rules of war, he said, was more than a legal abstraction or a matter of profit. What was at stake was the fundamental structure of the international order. This structure must be based on well-defined inviolable rules, which in turn must be derived from the basic principles of respect for human life and fair treatment of all peoples and nations.

Still, no matter how pro-British or how determined he was to guarantee American rights, for many months following the outbreak of the war, Wilson saw no reason to intrude into European affairs. By remaining neutral, America might exert a strong moral force to end the fighting quickly and then help establish new relations among nations based on disarmament, arbitration, and international justice. A neutral America, Wilson declared, would be "fit and free to do what is honest and disinterested and truly serviceable for the peace of the world."

Allied Violations of American Rights.   From the beginning, both the British and the Germans disregarded American "rights" in international trade. The British extended the definition of contraband to include almost everything that might be useful to German survival. They stopped American vessels and forced them to go to British ports for thorough and time-consuming searches. They planted mines in the North Sea, endangering all neutral ships routed through the area. They set up blacklists of American firms suspected of trading with Germany through other neutral nations, and threatened these firms with the loss of English business.

The United States possessed the power to retaliate against the British and force them to relent. Soon after the war broke out, the British and the French had placed immense orders with American firms for arms, grain, cotton, and other supplies. In the beginning the Allies paid cash; but when cash ran low, they requested loans from American bankers. Secretary of State Bryan at first considered credits to the Allies a breach of neutrality and refused to sanction them. Gradually he retreated, and in October 1914 Wilson informed National City Bank and the Morgan Company that he would not oppose bankers' credits to finance Allied war orders. By early 1917 Americans had lent Great Britain over $1 billion and France $300 million more.

Had Wilson wished, he might have discouraged loans or asked Congress to embargo munitions to belligerents unless the Allies complied with American demands. He justified his failure to use this powerful weapon of coercion—one employed by Thomas Jefferson in 1807—on the grounds that neutralizing the Allied advantage of control of the shipping lanes to Europe would be equivalent to helping the Central Powers. But it is difficult to avoid the conclusion that the president was less willing to enforce neutral rights against the Allies than against their enemies.

There were strong reasons other than pro-Ally feelings for discriminating between British and German violations of American rights, however. England avoided injuring too many American interests simultaneously for fear that a general outcry would force retaliation. The English were also careful to blunt the edge of their actions. When placing cotton on the contraband list produced a loud protest from southern cotton growers, for example, the British agreed to buy enough cotton to make up for the lost German-Austrian market. But the most compelling reason for distinguishing between the Allies and the Central Powers was that Allied policies toward neutrals hurt only their pocketbooks; German policies took lives.

Submarine Warfare.   The chief German naval weapon against the Allies was the U-boat (*Unterseeboot*), a submarine armed with torpedoes and one small deck gun. U-boats could creep up on their targets unseen and sink them without warning. But because they were small and thin-skinned, they could not risk surfacing to warn of their intentions, to search for contraband, or to care for civilians aboard the vessels they attacked. German U-boats could strangle England, which relied on overseas sources for vital food and munitions, but only by "unrestricted" U-boat warfare—attacking all shipping, naval or merchant, enemy or neutral, found in the waters off the British Isles, thereby endangering civilians and deeply offending international opinion.

Chancellor Theobald von Bethmann-Hollweg and a few other German leaders foresaw that a "shoot-on-sight" U-boat policy would lead to serious problems with the United States. Nevertheless, in February 1915 the German government announced that it would authorize its submarines to sink without warning all ships found within a large war zone surrounding the British Isles.

The American State Department immediately denounced these "unprecedented" tactics and declared that the German government would be held to "a strict accountability" for any action that injured Americans or their property. The Berlin authorities were unmoved. A month later a German submarine sank the British passenger liner *Falaba,* killing an American citizen. Bryan urged the president to forbid Americans to travel in the war zones, at least on belligerent ships; but Wilson refused on the grounds that to do so would surrender a valid American right. A far worse tragedy took place in May when the British luxury liner *Lusitania* was sunk off the Irish coast by a German submarine, with a loss of 1,198 lives, 128 of them American. Before the vessel left New York, the German authorities had advised Americans to avoid belligerent ships, but the actual attack had come totally without warning.

The sinking of an unarmed passenger liner, with such wholesale destruction of life, profoundly shocked Americans. "From the Department of State," the *New York Times* trumpeted, "there must go to the imperial Government in Berlin a demand that the Germans shall no longer make war like savages drunk with blood." For days afterward American press editorials denounced the attack as "criminal," "bestial," "uncivilized," and "barbarous." "Condemnation of the act," the *Literary Digest* summarized, "seems to be limited only by the restrictions of the English language."

For a time there was some loose talk of war with Germany. But the public was not ready to plunge into the European bloodbath, and most Americans concluded that strong words would be sufficient. On May 13 Wilson dispatched a note to the German government demanding the Germans apologize for the brutal act and renounce future attacks on merchant and passenger vessels. The United States would hold it responsible for any infringement of American rights on the high seas. The Germans expressed regret for the American dead, but defended the sinking as an act of "self-defense" because the *Lusitania* had carried arms that would have been used against German soldiers. In a second, stiffer note, Wilson insisted that the Germans give up unrestricted submarine warfare entirely. A third note threatened to sever diplomatic relations if another passenger ship was attacked.

Bryan considered the second *Lusitania* note a threat of war against Germany. He resigned in protest. Wilson replaced him with Robert Lansing, a man of a very different stripe, who believed that German victory "would mean the over-throw of democracy . . . , the suppression of individual liberty, the setting up of evil ambitions . . . , and the turning back of the hands of human progress two centuries." Lansing's leadership of the State Department strengthened the pro-Ally groups in the government and undoubtedly helped steer the country into war.

The conflict with Germany remained unresolved when the Germans struck again in mid-August 1915, sinking the *Arabic*, another unarmed British passenger liner, and killing two Americans. The sinking brought to a climax the battle between the cautious Chancellor Bethmann-Hollweg and the German admirals, who wanted to continue unrestricted submarine warfare. This time the German emperor sided with the moderates and assured the American State Department that his navy would stop attacking passenger ships without warning and in the future would provide for the safety of passengers and crews. The German government suspended submarine warfare against passenger vessels.

The War Spirit Rises.   The Arabic pledge prevented a break in diplomatic relations with Germany, but it did not fully comply with Wilson's demands. The German government had not agreed to exempt neutral cargo vessels from attack and had not apologized for the *Lusitania* sinking. It also had not offered reparations for lost American lives.

While these grievances festered, Americans were treated to new demonstrations of seemingly outrageous German behavior. Shortly after the *Arabic* sinking, an American Secret Service agent picked up a briefcase carelessly left by a man on the Sixth Avenue el in New York. The contents revealed that its owner, Dr. Heinrich F. Albert, was head of a widespread covert German operation in the United States to influence American opinion and sabotage munitions factories and shipyards producing war matériel for the Allies. At almost the same time, the British released captured documents that disclosed German-Austrian plans to foment labor stoppages at American armament plants. Soon afterward the United States accused two German diplomatic attachés of spying and sent them home; another German agent was indicted for blowing up a bridge; and still others were held responsible for various unexplained explosions and accidents in American factories and war plants.

The sensational revelations of German undercover activities deeply antagonized the American public. Bombings and espionage brought the terrible war to America's shores. By mid-1915 many citizens had begun to fear that the nation could not avoid entering the fight.

The changing public mood manifested itself in a "preparedness" movement to rearm the United States for any eventuality. Some preparedness advocates believed that if the country was strong militarily, it would not have to fight. But many thought war with Germany unavoidable, or even desirable, and wanted to ensure that when it came, the country could fight effectively. The most militant leader of the preparedness-interventionist group was former president Theodore Roosevelt, who toured the country calling Wilson "yellow" for holding back on rearmament and for not taking a stronger line against the Germans. At one point, in his typically intemperate way, TR recommended that if war came, peace advocate Senator Robert La Follette should be hanged forthwith.

A strong peace contingent, however, resisted the preparedness movement. The peace advocates included Quakers and members of other traditional "peace churches," and many progressives who believed that domestic reform would be forgotten if the country became embroiled in war. Women progressives were particularly prominent in the peace movement. War represented the male principle of physical force, asserted Harriot Stanton Blatch, and would be ended only when the "mother viewpoint" prevailed in international diplomacy. Socialists were even more strongly opposed to the preparedness campaign and intervention than progressives. The war in Europe, they held, was a battle between rival capitalist imperialists. Its outcome was only of marginal interest to the world's working class.

At first Wilson was skeptical of the preparedness movement, but his growing anger at Germany and belief that preparedness was politically popular soon changed his mind. In mid-summer 1915 the president finally asked his naval and military advisers to draw up plans for an enlarged army and navy. On the basis of these proposals, in November he recommended that Congress approve a $500 million naval building program and expand the army to 400,000 men.

Even as he readied the nation for the possibility of war, however, Wilson struggled to avoid it. In early 1915 he had sent Colonel House to Europe to try to bring the belligerents together around the peace table. House was ignored. In January 1916 Wilson sent the colonel back to Europe for the same purpose, determined this time that if either side refused to parley, the United States would use its "utmost moral force" to compel the reluctant party to accept compromise terms that would include disarmament and a world peacekeeping organization. Once again, House accomplished little. The warring nations wanted no part of peace except on their own terms. Despite the stubbornness of both Allied and German leaders, House made some startling promises to Britain and France that exceeded the president's instructions. If the 1916 Allied effort to break the military deadlock on the Western Front failed, and if Germany appeared to be winning, the United States, House told the British and French leaders, would intervene to prevent Allied defeat.

The Sussex Pledge. German–American relations took a turn for the better early in February 1916 when the Kaiser's government finally expressed regret for the sinking of the *Lusitania* and offered to pay an indemnity for lost lives. But the pendulum soon shifted once more when a U-boat torpedoed the unarmed French steamer *Sussex,* injuring a number of Americans.

Wilson shot off a note to the German government declaring that unless it ceased all attacks on cargo and passenger ships, the United States would immediately break off diplomatic relations. With the moderates still in control, the German government gave the so-called Sussex pledge: It would abandon its practice of shoot-on-sight in all cases except those involving enemy warships. The pledge was qualified, however. The Germans would honor it only if the United States compelled the Allies to abide by the rules of international law. Wilson accepted the Sussex pledge, knowing that it would be impossible to force the Allies to comply with Germany's conditions. But peace was preserved for the moment at least.

For some time following the Sussex pledge, the Germans acted in exemplary fashion. Meanwhile the British seemed determined to arouse the wrath of the American public. They seized American packages and parcels sent abroad by mail to look for contraband, opened and read letters to and from America, and refused to allow American shipowners to use British coaling facilities unless they submitted to British inspection. They also brutally suppressed the Easter Rebellion in Ireland. The execution of the Irish rebels appalled Americans and seriously damaged Britain's image as a defender of democracy. War talk ebbed as Americans had second thoughts about the Allied cause.

The Election of 1916. For the next few months public interest in foreign affairs was eclipsed by the excitement of a presidential election. In 1916, with the Progressive party virtually dead, Wilson faced a single opponent, Supreme Court Justice Charles Evans Hughes, an attractive candidate who had established a solid reputation during two terms as progressive Republican governor of New York. Despite Hughes's appeal, Wilson was reelected. The president's success in part derived from his late turn to the left, as discussed in Chapter 22. But even more, the campaign outcome turned on the issue of war and peace.

Hughes had the difficult task of holding together a party with a substantial number of pro-Ally interventionists and a large number of German-American supporters. A poor speaker, he seemed to waver on the issues to please every segment of the voting public. The Democrats were more forthright. "He kept us out of war" was their campaign slogan. A Democratic ad in the New York Times reminded voters:

> You are working;
> —*Not Fighting!*
>
> Alive and Happy;
>
> —*Not Cannon Fodder!*
> Wilson and Peace with Honor?
>
> or
>
> *Hughes with Roosevelt, and War?*

The election was close. Hughes carried the Northeast and much of the Midwest. Wilson took the South, the mountain states, and most of the Pacific Coast. Because of slow returns from California, not until the Friday following the Tuesday balloting was Wilson assured of four more years in the White House.

The Road to War. Wilson's reelection was a vote for peace. However sympathetic to the Allies, most Americans still wanted very much to keep out of the war. In the wake of his victory Wilson decided to make one last effort to force both sides to hammer out a compromise settlement. Late in December 1916 he sent notes to the belligerents asking them to state their war aims and offering again to mediate. He warned both sides that only a "peace without victory" would last. Any other "would leave a sting, a resentment, a bitter memory upon which terms of peace would rest . . . only as upon quicksand." The president's words were prophetic, but neither side was willing to stop the fighting and talk terms.

German–American relations now moved swiftly toward a final crisis. By the end of 1916 the military stalemate in Western Europe was becoming intolerable to the German leaders. Continued frustration weakened the moderates in Berlin and strengthened the military. At a momentous conference in January 1917 the aggressive generals told Kaiser Wilhelm that because the United States was already providing the Allies with as much war matériel and financial aid as it could, it would make little difference if it formally joined the enemy. Moreover, Germany was now so well supplied with U-boats that if the submarine captains were not required to observe the rules imposed by neutral opinion, they could deliver a knockout blow to the Allies in short order. The generals' analysis was convincing: Germany chose unlimited submarine warfare.

On January 31, 1917, the German ambassador in Washington informed Secretary of State Lansing that Germany would direct its U-boats to sink without warning all ships, both neutral and enemy, found in the eastern Mediterranean and in the waters surrounding Great Britain, France, and Italy. The new German order repudiated the Sussex pledge. True to his promise, Wilson severed diplomatic relations with Germany. Most Americans, even many of Wilson's former critics, supported his decision. Volunteers began to show up at army enlistment centers.

Wilson still hoped to avoid hostilities, and refused Lansing and House's advice to prepare for war. While he deliberated, rallies all over the country demanded American forbearance and further negotiations before taking the final step. Much of the president's and the public's remaining doubt was dispelled by the revelation of a secret note from the German foreign secretary, Arthur Zimmermann, to the German minister in Mexico proposing that if the United States and Germany came to blows, Mexico ally itself with Germany and help persuade Japan to switch its allegiance to the Central Powers. In the event of German victory, Mexico would be rewarded with its lost territory in Texas, New Mexico, and Arizona. Intercepted by British intelligence, the "Zimmermann telegram" pushed Wilson over the line. The day following the receipt of the incriminating document he asked Congress for authority to arm American merchant ships and employ "any other instrumentalities or methods" to protect American interests on the high seas. When the isolationists in the Senate, led by La Follette and George W. Norris of Nebraska, threatened to talk the measure to death, Wilson released the telegram to a shocked and furious public. Carried along by a wave of public indignation, the House gave Wilson the power he wanted. But the Senate isolationists blocked action despite Wilson's condemnation of them as a "little group of willful men, representing no opinion but their own."

On March 9 Wilson announced that he was arming American merchant vessels under his authority as commander-in-chief. Public outrage against Germany reached a new pitch when soon after three American merchant ships were sunk by submarines, with heavy loss of life. In the minds of many Americans, final doubts about the Allied cause evaporated when a liberal uprising in Russia overthrew the autocratic government of the czar. Now if the United States joined the Allies, it would be able in good conscience to claim it was fighting on the side of democracy.

Wilson's War Message. On the evening of April 2, 1917, the president appeared before a joint session of Congress to ask for a declaration of war. German contempt for American rights and American lives, displayed by brutal, unrestricted U-boat war, left no other course, he said. But there were higher moral considerations than self-defense. The United States would be fighting for all people, for the "vindication of right, of human right" against "autocratic governments backed by organized force." As the American people faced the months of "fiery trial and sacrifice" ahead, they would not forget that they were struggling for

> the things which we have always carried nearest our hearts—for democracy, for the right of those who submit to authority to have a voice in their own Governments, for the rights and liberties of small nations, for a universal dominion of rights by a concert of free peoples as shall bring peace and safety to all nations and make the world at last free.

The Senate passed the war declaration on April 4. House approval followed on April 6.

■ THE WAR ■

America was finally in! In London, Rome, and Paris, crowds cheered the news and drank toasts to the United States and its great president. Sagging Allied spirits soared. At home most socialists and a number of midwestern isolationists still opposed the war. Senator Norris charged that the war's sole cause was greed and that Americans would be "sacrificing millions of . . . [their] countrymen's lives in order that other countrymen may coin their lifeblood into money." Many German-Americans, Irish-Americans, and a small minority of intellectuals remained skeptical of the Allied cause. But on the whole the American people embraced the war wholeheartedly and accepted the sacrifices it required.

Combat.   Now, the nation's resources had to be mobilized. Americans had not expected at first to send large numbers of men to the fighting fronts, but it soon became clear that the Allies could not fight on without American troops. The liberal Russian Revolution of March 1917 had been followed by the Bolshevik Revolution of October 1917. The Bolsheviks soon concluded peace with the Germans, freeing the German troops fighting Russia to move to the Western Front. Only American forces could offset the surge in German strength in France.

The first military draft since the Civil War provided the needed manpower. It worked surprisingly well. Scrupulously administered by local civilian draft boards, it did not arouse the feeling of class favoritism that had appeared fifty years before. With its help the army grew from 200,000 to 4 million men. Draftees were sent to thirty-two training camps and were quickly transformed into soldiers.

Over 2 million American troops eventually went to France, and 1.4 million of them saw action on the front lines. The lot of American "doughboys" on the Western Front was as miserable as that of their European counterparts. They faced mud, rain, cold, vermin, and constant fear of death. They huddled in the trenches while fierce artillery bombardments shook the earth for days at a time. They "went over the top" in savage assaults on the enemy's positions, sacrificing their lives for a few hundred yards of ground. About 50,000 died in combat; an equal number succumbed to disease.

The American navy, under Admiral William S. Sims, escorted troop and supply vessels to France and, in cooperation with the British, helped end the U-boat threat. For every American soldier it brought safely to the fighting front,

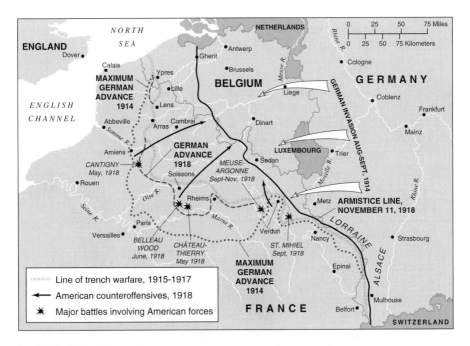

World War I: The Western Front

the navy had to guarantee the arrival of fifty pounds of supplies and equipment daily. Ultimately millions of tons of food, munitions, vehicles, medicines, clothing, guns, horses, and fuel were ferried from American ports to Le Havre, Bordeaux, Calais, Brest, and Boulogne, with minimal loss from U-boats.

"Over There."   American troops made a major difference in the war's outcome. The American Expeditionary Force (AEF) under the command of General John J. Pershing saw little fighting before early spring 1918. In March 1918 the Germans, strengthened by the armies brought west from defeated Russia, attacked on a broad front, engaging the Americans in May and June around the town of Chateau-Thierry and at Belleau Wood, fifty miles from Paris. In September the American First Army, some 500,000 strong, pushed back a German salient at Saint-Mihiel. Between late September and the armistice, 1.2 million Americans were committed in the Meuse-Argonne campaign around Verdun.

■ THE WAR EFFORT AT HOME ■

Mobilization.   This enormous military and logistical effort was made possible by the effective mobilization of economic and emotional resources at home. The war cost the United States $33 billion, including $9 billion of loans to the Allies. About a quarter of this huge sum was raised by taxes. The war taxes were highly progressive, taking up to 75 percent of the largest incomes. Inheritance taxes of 25 percent, an excess-profits tax of 65 percent, and a variety of excise taxes also helped spread the burden throughout the population. The rest of the money came from banks and from campaigns to sell Liberty Bonds, which not only provided needed funds, but also helped whip up enthusiasm for the war effort.

The billions, however, had to be effectively deployed. For this purpose the Wilson administration borrowed a page from the New Nationalism progressives by setting up a cluster of new federal agencies. In 1917 the administration created the War Industries Board (WIB) to mobilize the country's productive resources. Under Financier Bernard Baruch the WIB-established production priorities instituted measures to save rubber, copper, and steel and establish fair prices for raw materials. To conserve fuel used for lighting, the government instituted daylight saving time. Agriculture, too, got a "czar" in the person of Herbert Hoover, a millionaire mining engineer of Quaker background. Hundreds of government groups intruded into the private economy to expedite production and conserve raw materials. By the end of the war these administrative bodies were exerting many new powers and had achieved extraordinary control over the economy. They also anticipated a number of governmental structures and measures of the New Deal and provided precedents for the mobilization effort of World War II.

Food production burgeoned under the direction of Food Administrator Herbert Hoover, who had supervised food relief to ravaged Belgium earlier in the war. Americans voluntarily observed "wheatless" and "meatless" days in a remarkably effective campaign to conserve food. The Food Administration guaranteed an attractive price for the entire 1917 wheat crop, causing a dramatic jump in the number of acres planted with wheat. Vegetable gardens appeared everywhere, and exotic meats such as horse and rabbit were introduced into the wartime diet. Hoover launched a campaign for Americans to conserve food that included catchy slogans: "Don't Let Your Horse Be More Patriotic Than You Are—Eat a Dish of Oatmeal"; "Serve Beans by All Means." The Food Administration was a great success, and it helped boost Hoover's popularity after the war.

The War Industries Board, headed by Baruch, performed relatively well after a slow start. American arms and clothing factories equipped the American doughboy better than any other soldier in the world. American shipyards struggled, not always successfully, with the crucial task of replacing Allied vessels sunk by U-boats. The board built new production facilities and converted existing ones for war purposes, developed new sources of raw materials, served as purchasing agent for the Allies, standardized thousands of items, and established strict economic priorities. Despite the immense effort American industry failed to provide all the equipment that the armed forces needed. American pilots would be forced to fly British or French fighter and reconnaissance planes. Much of the AEF's artillery consisted of French "seventy-fives."

Montgomery Flagg, a popular illustrator of the day, produced this saccharine poster urging boys and girls in 1917 to help the American war effort by saving money.

Meanwhile, the United States Railroad Administration took tight control of the country's rail transportation, now called on to carry millions more passengers and tons of freight than in peacetime. The administration combined railways into regional units, limited unnecessary passenger travel, standardized rates and schedules, and gave priority to munitions and war matériel over nonessential goods.

Harry A. Garfield became a virtual dictator over the nation's fuel supply. When a coal shortage immobilized thirty-seven munitions ships in New York harbor during the bitterly cold winter of 1917–1918, he closed down all civilian manufacturing plants to release their coal for the ships' use.

The war overstimulated the economy. Unemployment melted away, and men and women were soon working long hours at good pay. But despite high taxes and the Liberty and Victory Loans that drained off much excess purchasing power, prices rose sharply and offset many of the workers' gains. It soon became apparent that labor would have to be regulated, along with other sectors of the economy, to ensure uninterrupted work, prevent strikes for higher wages, and provide the highest priority for war industry. To attain these goals, Wilson created the War Labor Policies Board. By granting recognition to labor unions and establishing generally favorable working conditions for wage earners, the board purchased labor peace during the war. It prohibited strikes, but it also forced management to negotiate with the unions. Under these policies the AFL and other unions expanded their membership to over 4 million, a 50 percent increase over 1914.

Women and the War.   One firm principle of the War Labor Policies Board was that women should have equal pay for equal work in war industries. High wages, encouraged by wartime labor shortages and labor board policies, soon drew thousands of women into the labor force. Thousands also went "over there" to France with the doughboys, working as ambulance drivers and nurses and representing organizations such as the Salvation Army and Red Cross. The war accustomed many American women to working outside the home and accelerated their economic independence.

The war gave a massive push to the women's suffrage movement. During the 1916 presidential election Alice Paul and her new National Woman's Party (NWP) attacked Wilson and the Democrats for failure to act on the suffrage issue. Meanwhile, using gentler means, Carrie Catt of the National American Woman Suffrage Association managed to convert the president himself to the women's suffrage cause.

Still, Congress and much of the male public resisted. The suffragists appealed to the nation's conscience with slogans like "Democracy Begins at Home," and advertised the giant contributions women were making to the war effort. Alice Paul and her group picketed the White House. When District of Columbia officials carted the picketers off to jail they became martyrs whose treatment aroused sympathy for their cause. Eventually, even Wilson relented, feeling women had earned the right to vote. "The services of women during the supreme crisis," he noted in 1918, "have been of the most signal usefulness and distinction; it is high time that part of our debt should be acknowledged."

At last, in January 1918, the House of Representatives, anxious to further national unity during wartime, passed the women's suffrage amendment (the Nineteenth) to the Constitution by precisely the two-thirds' majority needed. The Senate took another year and a half to approve the amendment, and not until August 1920 was it ratified by three fourths of the states. But without the impetus of war, women would have been forced to wait longer for the right to vote.

Black Americans and the War.   Blacks also made economic gains during 1917–18. With millions of men in the armed forces and European immigration at an all-time low, the supply of civilian labor tightened just when the economy needed labor most. To meet the shortage, employers were forced to lower their barriers to black workers. Thousands of black men and women were soon leaving southern farms for the high wages of the northern war plants. Most came to the large industrial cities. Chicago's black population leaped from 44,000 in 1910 to 110,000 in 1920. Cleveland's grew from 8,000 to 34,000. But thousands more took jobs in the coal mines and the railroads.

The war did not seriously disturb the racial status quo in the United States. Segregation continued in America wherever it had existed before, including the armed services. The 367,000 blacks in the military forces were kept apart from whites and largely led by white officers. The black migration north, meanwhile, created serious tensions between new black arrivals and people who felt challenged or displaced. In 1917 thirty-eight blacks lost their lives in lynchings; the following year the number rose to fifty-eight. In East Saint Louis a race riot triggered by employment of blacks in a factory producing war matériel resulted in the death of at least forty blacks. The Germans sought to take propaganda advantage of racial tensions in the United States. They kept close track of racial incidents and urged black Americans to refuse to help the country that permitted these atrocities. Black Americans did not respond. Indeed, they were among the most patriotic groups in the nation. But the threat of disunity goaded Wilson into denouncing lynching and mob violence.

The Propaganda War.   To lead the propaganda war, the government created the Committee on Public Information (CPI) and chose George Creel, a progressive journalist with a gift for storytelling and platform oratory, to head it. Creel mobilized thousands of people in the arts, advertising, and motion pictures to "advertise America." Some of the most talented painters and graphic artists in the country designed Liberty Loan and recruiting posters. An army of lecturers, called "Four-Minute Men," delivered pithy patriotic talks all across the country on subjects like "Maintaining Morals and Morale," "Why We Are Fighting," and "The Meaning of America." "There was no part of the great war machinery that we did not touch," Creel wrote after the war, "no medium of appeal that we did not employ . . . to make our own people and all other peoples of the world understand the causes that compelled America to take up arms."

Civil Liberties during the War.   Creel's campaign was immensely effective in whipping up enthusiasm for the war and Wilson's goal of making the world "safe for democracy." War fervor also unleashed a wave of intolerance against those who did not show the proper patriotic spirit or who harbored pacifist or socialist attitudes.

Quick to sense the new superpatriotic mood, Congress passed the Espionage Act and the Trading-with-the-Enemy Act in 1917. The first imposed severe penalties on persons found guilty of obstructing military recruitment, aiding the enemy, or encouraging anyone to be disloyal or insubordinate or to refuse duty in the armed forces. Under it the postmaster general could exclude from the mails any material he deemed treasonable or seditious. The Trading-with-the-Enemy Act authorized the government to confiscate and run German-owned businesses and to censor international communications and the foreign-language press. In 1918 Congress passed the Sedition Act, declaring "disloyal" or "seditious" all talk against the war and making the use of "profane, scurrilous, or abusive language" about the Constitution, the flag, or the armed forces a crime.

Wilson had warned that war might bring intolerance and repression, and it did, with administration officials often at the forefront of the hysteria. Attorney general Thomas Gregory fanned the flames of intolerance with his assertion that opponents of the war should expect no mercy "from an outraged people and an avenging government." Postmaster General Albert S. Burleson excluded from the mails publications opposed to the war. The federal courts also failed to bolster the right to dissent. In *Schenck v. The United States* the Supreme Court upheld the conviction of a man for mailing circulars that urged draftees to refuse military induction. In war, said Justice Oliver Wendell Holmes, Jr., speaking for the majority of the Court, such material posed a "clear and present danger" to the nation and therefore could by law be suppressed. In 1918 the Justice Department indicted and secured the convictions of Eugene V. Debs and Victor L. Berger, two Socialist party leaders, on the charge of encouraging draft evasion. Kate O'Hare, a socialist firebrand, went to federal prison for a speech claiming that "the women of the United States are nothing more than brood sows, to raise children to get into the army and be made into fertilizer."

Local officials joined the repressive chorus and fined and imprisoned those who spoke out against the war. Meanwhile, vigilante groups and self-appointed "patriots" intimidated supposed subversives and "slackers" who failed to don their country's uniform. In the Pacific Northwest their target was often the Industrial Workers of the World (IWW), a radical labor group with a strong following among western miners and loggers.

One of the war's casualties was ethnic tolerance. Many schools and colleges suspended the teaching of German. Bigots renamed sauerkraut "liberty cabbage" and German measles "liberty measles." Superpatriots attacked their German-American neighbors. One group of Jingos even thought it desirable to change the names of American cities borrowed from Germany, such as Berlin, Frankfort, and Potsdam, to Anglo-Saxon names.

■ MAKING THE PEACE ■

On November 1 the American army broke the German line of defense. Beaten on the battlefield and on the verge of collapse at home, the Germans began talking of peace.

The Fourteen Points. The Central Powers' defeat was in part military. But it also stemmed from deteriorating morale. By late 1918 the overstretched German will to resist had been seriously undermined by expectations of a generous peace as laid out in Wilson's Fourteen Points. Announced in a January 1918 speech while the fighting was still at an indecisive stage, the Fourteen Points was a blueprint for the postwar world. Wilson addressed several immediate, war-connected issues: Germany must abandon all occupied territories in France, Russia, and Belgium; Austria must surrender territorial gains in the Balkans; all nations must agree to respect neutral rights on the high seas. The American president also sought to remedy the fundamental causes of the war still raging: Armaments must be sharply reduced to prevent future destabilizing arms races; Serbia should be given access to the sea; the repressed aspirations for nationhood among the peoples of the Turkish, Austrian, and German empires should be satisfied; Italy's frontiers should be altered to incorporate Italian-speaking people living outside its existing borders; the conflicting colonial claims of the great powers must be adjusted with due regard to the rights of the colonial populations themselves.

On a more abstract level, Wilson proposed to remake the international order so that future disputes among nations could be kept from deteriorating into war. The president was here expressing American liberal idealism and, critics would say, American naiveté. He denounced "private international understandings" and demanded in their place "open covenants of peace, openly arrived at." He called for "the removal, as far as possible," of all international economic barriers and the establishment of "equality of trade conditions among all the nations consenting to the peace." The most visionary "point" of the fourteen was "a general association of nations . . . for the purpose of affording mutual guarantees of political independence and territorial integrity to great and small states alike." Wilson concluded with an assurance to the Germans that the United States did not desire their destruction or humiliation. America would welcome them into the family of "peace-loving nations" if they demonstrated their clear desire for peace by overruling the "military party and the men whose creed is imperial domination."

Central Powers' spokesmen initially derided the Fourteen Points as propaganda and almost a year more of fighting and dying would follow. Then, following the 1918 German military failure on the Western Front, Wilson's hopeful and generous terms pushed Germany over the line to peace. That fall events moved swiftly. On October 27 the Austrians notified Wilson that they would be willing to conclude a separate peace. The next day the sailors of the German Imperial Navy mutinied at their base in Kiel when ordered to sail for a desperate showdown battle against the British fleet. The revolt soon spread to other German garrisons and towns. On November 9 the German kaiser abdicated and went into exile; Germany was proclaimed a republic. By this time German officials had already agreed to surrender terms at Compiègne in northern France. These incorporated much of the Fourteen Points but also imposed on Germany punitive reparations for war damages. On November 11 at 11 a.m. the guns fell silent; World War I, the Great War, was over.

Versailles.   On January 18, 1919, the victorious Allied leaders met at Versailles, near Paris, to determine the shape of the peace. Wilson was there in person. Although widely criticized for his precedent-shattering decision to leave the United States while in office, the president insisted that only his physical presence could ensure that the victors would accept a just and secure peace.

Wilson was received like a savior in Europe. Wherever he went, enormous crowds turned out to cheer him. In Paris 2 million people lining the Champs-Elysées rained flowers and bouquets as he drove down the boulevard in his open automobile. The people of Europe were honoring not only the man; Wilson represented American idealism and the possibility of a more decent and democratic world system. Even the defeated Germans seemed willing to entrust their future to his hands.

But while the common people of Europe applauded the president, his chief Allied colleagues—Georges Clemenceau of France, David Lloyd George of Britain, and Vittorio Orlando of Italy—remained skeptical. To these unsentimental men Wilsonian idealism was all very well to shore up faltering Allied morale and weaken the German will to fight, but it seemed impractical as the basis for an international settlement. The major Allied powers wanted Germany condemned as a war criminal, totally disarmed, and forced to pay stiff indemnities that could be used to rebuild the devastated Allied economies. France, in particular, feared the might of a restored Germany and demanded guarantees that the attack of 1914 would not be repeated. The European Allies were also determined not to surrender any of their gains, including the German colonies that they had seized during the war. Finally, they were suspicious of the principle of self-determination. Could the confused patchwork of nationalities in eastern Europe really be sorted out into functioning nations? Reinforcing all anxieties and doubts was the specter of Russian Bolshevism hovering over a continent devastated by war and shaken by the breakup of old empires. As the victorious Allied leaders conferred amid the splendors of Louis XIV's palace at Versailles, it seemed vital to move quickly or face Bolshevik-inspired revolutions throughout eastern and central Europe.

Wilson soon discovered that he could not force the European powers to accept his Fourteen Points without drastic modification. The French refused to consider any provision that threatened their quest for secure borders. The British would not hear of the "freedom of the seas" that might challenge Britain's naval supremacy. Several of the European Allies wanted a slice of the overseas German empire, and they all wanted the German aggressor punished and forced to pay financial compensation for their losses. The president was not happy with the changes his colleagues demanded, but he went along with most of them, convinced that his "general association of nations" would eventually right many of the injustices of the peace settlement.

The terms of the resulting treaty were a severe disappointment to idealists all over the world. The agreement allowed many German-speaking peoples to be absorbed into the newly created nations of Poland and Czechoslovakia. Italy acquired the German-speaking Tyrol. The German possessions in Africa and Asia were greedily parceled out among the European Allies. And, disastrously, Germany was forced to accept complete responsibility for the war—"war guilt," it was called—to disarm completely and pay reparations (ultimately set at $33 billion) to the victors. Unmentioned in the treaty were Wilson's idealistic calls for world disarmament, tariff reductions, and freedom of the seas.

Throughout the Versailles deliberations Wilson worked tirelessly for the League of Nations, the provision he considered the cornerstone of his peace proposals. As finally hammered out, the League would consist of a general assembly of all member nations, with an executive council to consist of the United States, the British Empire, France, Italy, Japan, and four other countries to be elected by the assembly. These bodies would listen to disputes among member nations and dispense international justice. The League's decisions could be enforced by economic sanctions against the international wrongdoers and, if necessary, by the use of military forces contributed by member nations. In addition, the League would help adjust minor disputes between citizens of different countries through a permanent International Court and seek to improve world social standards through an International Bureau of Labor.

As Wilson labored at Versailles during the winter of 1919, his support at home eroded. Before leaving for Europe he had asked the American public to vote for his party in the 1918 congressional elections as a mandate for his policies. When the voters gave the Republicans control of the Senate, his enemies claimed that they had repudiated the president's leadership. Wilson had further antagonized his political opponents by appointing only one Republican to the peace commission that accompanied him to Paris, although treaty ratification in the Senate would require the support of both parties.

Now, as news of the treaty's provisions filtered back to the United States, his opponents took sharp aim at its specific proposals. Irish-Americans were soon attacking the failure of the treaty to further the cause of Irish freedom from Britain. Italian-Americans complained because Italy had not been awarded the Adriatic city of Fiume (now Rijeka). German-Americans denounced the war-guilt clause that made their ancestral land a self-confessed criminal nation. Jingoes and superpatriots claimed that the treaty would compromise American sovereignty. Isolationists insisted that the League would entangle the United States in affairs abroad in which it had no true interest.

After two months of hard negotiating at Versailles, Wilson returned briefly to the United States to discover that the still-uncompleted treaty had come under withering fire. Thirty-seven senators, led by Henry Cabot Lodge of Massachusetts, had signed a "round robin" declaring that they would not vote for the treaty without amendment. Lodge and his fellow dissenters feared the loss of American autonomy under the League. Lodge himself also personally despised Wilson. "I never thought I could hate a man as I hate Wilson," he once said. The treaty had enough No votes to defeat it; clearly, a bitter battle was in prospect.

The president returned to Europe for further negotiations certain that the American people, if not the Senate, shared his vision of a new world order. To accommodate his critics, however, he had the League Covenant modified to allow any member nation to withdraw from the organization and to refuse colonial trusteeships if it so wished. The League would also keep hands off member nations' domestic tariff and immigration policies and avoid intruding into regional security arrangements such as the Monroe Doctrine. The treaty, incorporating the revised League Covenant, was ratified by the delegates in the Hall of Mirrors at Versailles on June 28, 1919. Soon afterward Wilson departed for home to fight for its ratification.

The Battle for the League.   Scores of newspapers, many labor leaders, and representatives of farm and women's organizations—much of the old progressive coalition—supported Wilson's League, fearing that the peace would otherwise prove fragile. Wilson counted on people like these to get the treaty through the balky Senate. But by this time Senator Lodge had developed a clever strategy to defeat it. He would not oppose it directly but would demand a series of "reservations." (Reservations, unlike amendments, would not have to be approved by other League members.) Most of these would be moderate enough to attract support from a number of fence-sitting senators. But Lodge foresaw that Wilson and his supporters would reject them. If he maneuvered adeptly, Lodge believed, he might get its own supporters to defeat the treaty in the Senate.

First, Lodge called hearings that consumed many weeks. By the time the interested parties had finished their wordy testimony, the protreaty public had begun to lose interest. Wilson fought back. Although thoroughly exhausted by the arduous negotiations in France, he decided to take his case directly to the American people. For three weeks the tired president toured the country, speaking before large audiences in support of his work at Versailles. Soon after a speech at Pueblo, Colorado, Wilson collapsed and had to cancel the remainder of his trip. Following his return to Washington, he suffered a severe stroke that partially paralyzed him. For months he was unable to work, and during this period his wife and the cabinet took over most of the duties of the presidential office. Though Wilson's strength gradually returned, he never fully recovered, and he remained irritable and quick to take offense. The illness exaggerated Wilson's stubbornness and heightened his belief in his cause.

The president's illness proved fatal for the treaty. By the time he returned to Washington, Senator Lodge had appended fourteen "reservations" to the Versailles agreement. These actually altered the document only in detail. But the obstinate Wilson believed they "emasculated" his work, and he insisted that his supporters vote against the modified treaty. They did. At the same time the isolationists refused to accept the original treaty. It looked as if the agreement hammered out at Versailles was finished.

The treaty and the League were not yet dead, however. Under public pressure the Senate was forced to reconsider its decision. In March 1920 the modified treaty was once more put to a vote. Wilson again proved unyielding. "Either," he declared, "we should enter the league fearlessly, accepting the responsibility and not fearing the role of leadership which we now enjoy, contributing our efforts towards establishing a just and permanent peace, or we should retire as gracefully as possibly from the great concert of powers by which the world was saved." Wilson's supporters were loyal to him again, but they did his cause a fatal disservice by helping to defeat the treaty for the last time.

The ailing Wilson sought to make the 1920 presidential election a referendum on the League. It was a wasted effort, for the public was tired of war and progressivism and great crusades at home and abroad. Campaigning for "normalcy," the Republican candidate Warren G. Harding won by a landslide of seven million votes over his opponent, enabling the isolationists to claim that the American people had repudiated internationalism. The new Harding administration eventually signed a separate peace treaty with Germany officially ending the hostilities, but the United States never entered the League of Nations.

■ CONCLUSIONS ■

The outcome of World War I was profoundly disillusioning to those Americans who shared Wilson's view of their country as a missionary nation ordained to carry the blessings of liberal democracy to every part of the world. Most citizens, however, were not deeply committed internationalists, and after 1918 were happy to return to the business of their daily lives. They might agree with Wilson that the world deserved a better international order, but far more than the idealist in the White House, they had supported the war as the only way to punish the nation that had brutally violated American "rights" as a neutral and murdered Americans on the high seas. Both the ordinary citizen's modest goal of fending off a savage attacker who used barbarous U-boat warfare to gain his ends and the president's more exalted vision of a "new world" were needed to bring the United States into the great conflict. But the simple defeat of Germany was enough to satisfy the average American, and Wilson's hopes remained unfulfilled. America, having entered the war from a position of self-proclaimed moral authority, was forced to recognize that there were limits to what could be accomplished with great wealth and missionary zeal. The unworkable settlement reached at Versailles, the failure of the League of Nations, and the resurgent American isolationism that followed World War I—all these contributed to the causes of World War II, an even more colossal tragedy.

By 1919 progressivism, which had dominated the first two decades of the twentieth century, was in deep shadow. The battle to defeat Germany had consumed the emotions that had helped fuel the crusade against injustice and unregulated private power. At home wartime intolerance had broken up the broad progressive coalition by pitting American against American. In the prewar decades the issues of trust control, more responsive government, consumer protection, and social justice had united Americans. Now the nation was about to enter an era when cultural issues and prejudices would deeply divide them from one another.

Online Resources

"War Message of World War I"
http://www.lib.byu.edu/~rdh/wwi/1917/wilswarm.html
The speech featured on this site was delivered to Congress by President Woodrow Wilson on February 3, 1917. In it, he severed diplomatic relations with Germany, drawing America into the Great War.

"World War I Document Archive"
http://www.lib.byu.edu/~rdh/wwi/
This archive consists of official primary documents such as conventions and treaties concerning World War I. Also, the site contains personal stories of men and women who were involved with the war.

Sow the Seeds of Victory! Posters from the Food Administration during World War I
http://www.nara.gov/education/cc/foodww1.html
In an appeal to the public's sense of voluntarism and because of the need for rationing food for the war effort, the U.S. Food Administration produced posters to meet their goals. This site, which features five of these posters, also explains other government methods of food rationing during the conflict.

The Influenza Epidemic of 1918
http://www.pbs.org/wgbh/amex/influenza/filmmore/index.html
This portion of PBS's "The American Experience" Web site examines the influenza pandemic of 1918 and its social, psychological, and scientific effects in America. Read how the virus outbreak influenced life in Boston and San Francisco.

Sir, I will Thank You with All My Heart: Seven Letters from the Great Migration
http://historymatters.gmu.edu/text/541b-Letters.html
Millions of southern African Americans sought defense jobs in the North with the beginning of American involvement in World War I. This collection of letters, addressed to the editors of a national black newspaper and written by black men seeking such work, speaks to their desire for nonagricultural employment and for social and economic justice.

24

THE TWENTIES

Happy Adolescence or Decade of Stress?

1913	Henry Ford introduces the moving assembly line in his automobile plant
1916	Wilson is reelected president; The Federal Highways Act
1917	The Eighteenth Amendment provides for national Prohibition
1919	The Volstead Act enforces Prohibition; Steelworkers strike unsuccessfully for union recognition; Attorney General Palmer breaks miners' strike; Race riot in Chicago
1920	Palmer orders Department of Justice agents to jail 4,000 aliens suspected of radical activities; Warren Harding elected president; Pittsburgh station begins commercial radio broadcasting
1920–21	Postwar recession
1920–29	Unemployment and low profits beset the New England textile industry, coal mining, railroads, and agriculture; 1.2 million leave farms for cities
1921	The Sacco and Vanzetti trial; The American Plan is designed by the National Association of Manufacturers to resist unions; The Immigration Act establishes national quotas for first time
1921–23	Congress exempts farmers' cooperatives from antitrust laws and regulates middlemen's rates
1921–31	Treasury Secretary Andrew Mellon shifts the tax burden from the rich to the middle class
1922	The Fordney-McCumber Act raises tariff rates
1923	Harding dies; Calvin Coolidge becomes president; The Teapot Dome scandal
1924	Coolidge elected president; The Johnson-Reed Immigration Act establishes stricter immigration quotas
1925	Scopes trial; Ku Klux Klan membership reaches 3 million
1927	Sacco and Vanzetti executed; Charles Lindbergh makes first transatlantic solo flight; Marcus Garvey, black leader of Back to Africa movement, is deported
1928	Herbert Hoover elected president
1929	Southern mill owners defeat United Textile Workers' union drive; Automobile production reaches five times that of 1915; National Origins Act further limits immigration; The stock market crashes ushering in the Great Depression
1930	Union membership falls to 3.6 million, down from a high of 5 million in 1920

To many of the men and women who reached adulthood after Versailles, the 1920s would seem a wonderful time of vitality, zany creativity, and bounding affluence. Novelist F. Scott Fitzgerald called the twenties "an age of miracles, . . . an age of art," when world leadership "passed to America." It was "the greatest gaudiest spree in history." Joseph Wood Krutch, one of the decade's bright young men, later recalled that he and his fellow journalists and critics "were . . . fundamentally optimistic, . . . gay crusaders. . . . The future was bright and the present was good fun at least." Many of the serious scholars of the day also liked the new era. "We are approaching equality of prosperity more rapidly than most people realize," declared Harvard economist Thomas N. Carver in 1925.

Contemporary judgment was not all on one side, however. The novelist Sinclair Lewis considered the nation's heart hollow and sick. H. L. Mencken, a persistent critic of American life, thought only a tiny minority escaped the sham and stupidity of daily life in twenties America. After months spent in Muncie, Indiana, during 1924 interviewing citizens and investigating social conditions, sociologists Robert and Helen Lynd, New York sophisticates and social liberals, concluded that "Middletown's" people had failed to adjust to rapidly changing technology. Change had produced serious "friction spots" that people tried to relieve with boosterism and police repression.

What were the 1920s really like? Was it an era of happy adolescence when Americans, released from puritanical restraints and blessed with newfound abundance, responded creatively and joyously to a new world? Or was it a period of friction, repression, and painful adjustment covered over with a thin glittering veneer?

■ THE SWING TO THE POLITICAL RIGHT ■

One way to view the twenties is as a time when diversity replaced unity. During the Progressive Era Americans were in general harmony on the big issues. As we have noted, they shared a fear of big business and joined the crusade to check irresponsible power and protect the "common man." World War I projected this crusading mood out to the rest of the world and reinforced the voluntary unity of the preceding decade and a half with overheated patriotism. But the war also exhausted the national zeal to right wrongs and opened ideological and cultural fissures. With the armistice the consensus came apart. Americans lost their sense of a common foe and abandoned their concern for social justice. In its place they substituted pursuit of the good life as each individual defined that term.

The Retreat to Privatism.   The new mood of privatism affected politics first. By 1919 many progressive reformers were tired and disillusioned. Much of the great progressive crusade, it seemed, had ended in triviality. Journalist Walter Weyl of the *New Republic* despaired that the person "who aspired to overturn society, ends by fighting . . . for the inclusion of certain books" in a village library. Walter Lippmann, Weyl's colleague, summed up the new attitudes, and poetically expressed his own waning political faith: "The people are tired," he wrote, "tired of noise, tired of politics, tired of inconvenience, tired of greatness, and longing for a place where the world is quiet and where all trouble seems dead leaves, and spent waves riot in doubtful dreams of dreams."

Progressivism did not entirely disappear, however. Its concern for efficiency in business and government survived in Herbert Hoover's Commerce Department, which worked to eliminate wasteful practices in private industry and government practice. In New York Governor Alfred E. Smith successfully continued many progressive welfare programs. And the conservation ideal, well represented by Horace Albright, superintendent of Yellowstone National Park, remained before the public's mind. In Congress meanwhile some fifty representatives and senators from the Midwest and South, the "farm bloc," regularly fought big-business domination of political life and senators George Norris and Robert La Follette continued to demand that government protect the weak from the rich and powerful. But most of this dissent lacked a broad vision, and in the case of the farm bloc, too often was a defense of narrow agricultural interests against urban ones. These survivals were at best a remnant of the once-pervasive progressive impulse.

Isolationism, which had been in eclipse since the 1890s, once again became the dominant public sentiment in foreign policy. The country did not cut its ties with the rest of the world. On the contrary, during the 1920s, under presidents Harding, Coolidge, and Hoover, the government aggressively fostered outlets for American goods and capital abroad. Meanwhile, the State Department sought to promote international stability in the Western Hemisphere by landing marines in several small Latin American countries to put down disorders and protect American lives and property. This intervention did not last. Gradually, under the leadership of secretaries of state Charles Evans Hughes and Frank Kellogg, the nation backed away from intruding in Latin America's domestic affairs.

A more significant sign of isolationism, however, was the response to Europe and collective security. The United States never joined the League of Nations and, after long dickering, rejected membership in the League's Court of International Justice. The nation's one stab at collective international peace efforts was the Kellogg-Briand Pact of 1928 to "outlaw war," jointly initiated by France and the United States and signed by scores of nations. The pact provided no penalties for violators and was little more than a pious expression of hope. Meanwhile, Americans alienated our former allies, Britain, France, Belgium and other nations, by insisting that they pay us back for money lent in fighting the common enemy.

Harding's Presidency.   The swing in political mood was best expressed by Senator Warren G. Harding of Ohio. Speaking to a Boston audience early in 1920, before his election as president, the senator declared that the nation needed "not heroism, but healing, not nostrums but normalcy, not revolution, but restoration, not agitation but adjustment, not surgery but serenity, not the dramatic but the dispassionate, not experiment but equipoise, not submergence in international duty but sustainment in triumphant nationality." It is difficult to say precisely what Harding meant by these alliterative pairings, but the general drift was clear: Americans wished to retreat to a quieter, less demanding, more private world. And Harding was right about the public mood. Americans indeed wanted "normalcy."

Harding reflected the best and the worst of postwar America. He was amiable, kind, and neighborly, as befitted a small-town newspaper editor. But he also was provincial and morally shoddy, bringing illegal liquor and a mistress into the White House while president. His good cheer and easy-going ways suited the public mood, however, and in 1920, against Democrats James Cox of Ohio and Franklin Roosevelt of New York, Harding and his running mate, Calvin Coolidge of Massachusetts, scored the most sweeping victory in a presidential election to that time.

Harding was an indifferent president. He did select for his cabinet talented men such as Charles Evans Hughes, the 1916 Republican presidential candidate, and Herbert Hoover, wartime food czar and administrator of Belgian war relief. He also successfully carried out the public mandate to reconcile government and business interests. During his administration, Washington became the friend and ally of business. The president himself supported the Fordney-McCumber Tariff (1922), which raised import duties far above those of the Underwood Tariff of 1913, and pushed for a bill to subsidize the American merchant marine, which, now that the war was over, could not compete with the merchant fleets of other nations.

Though government–business reconciliation was probably desirable after 1918, the administration tilted too far in giving capital its way. Secretary of the Treasury Andrew Mellon, a rich Pittsburgh industrialist, saw the high taxes imposed to finance the war as hampering enterprise, and he persuaded Congress to eliminate the wartime excess-profits tax and reduce income tax rates at the upper levels while leaving those at the bottom untouched. Between 1920 and 1929 Mellon won further victories for his drive to shift more of the tax burden from high-income earners to the middle and wage-earning classes.

Many of Harding's appointments were deplorable. As attorney general, he chose his old crony Harry M. Daugherty, a man of loose principles who distributed government favors with a free hand. The "Ohio gang" presided over by Daugherty's close friend Jesse Smith dispensed Justice Department pardons and paroles, granted businessmen immunity from antitrust prosecution, and bestowed government appointments on any who would pay the price. To head the Veterans' Bureau, the president selected Charles R. Forbes, whom he had met while on vacation and liked. Forbes sold off veterans' hospitals' supposedly surplus blankets, sheets, and medical supplies for a song—and a kickback. Worst of all, perhaps, was Albert B. Fall, secretary of the interior. Soon after taking office, Fall got the secretary of the navy to turn over the government's naval oil reserves to the Interior Department. Then, disregarding the public's interests, Fall promptly leased the Elk Hills (California) oil reserve to Edward L. Doheny of the Pan-American Petroleum Company and the Teapot Dome (Wyoming) reserves to Harry F. Sinclair. In exchange Doheny "lent" Fall $100,000 in cash; Sinclair gave Fall's son-in-law $200,000 in government bonds.

Harding was probably unaware of the Teapot Dome frauds and the other unsavory doings of his subordinates. In subsequent months, Fall would be convicted of accepting bribes, and Forbes would be sent to prison. The president, however, would never learn about these events. In June 1923 he had set out on a speaking tour of the West Coast and Alaska. In San Francisco, on the way home, he suffered a stroke and died in his hotel bed.

Coolidge Does Little.   Calvin Coolidge, who now became president, was as inward and dour as Harding had been outgoing and friendly. As governor of Massachusetts he had done little to attract attention outside the state and seemed merely another regional politician. Then, in September 1919, when the Boston police went on strike, leaving the city exposed to unchecked crime and chaos, Governor Coolidge captured national notice by declaring that there was "no right to strike against the public safety by anybody, anywhere, anytime." These blunt words expressed the public's own growing impatience with labor unrest and won Coolidge the Republican vice presidential nomination the following year.

As president, Coolidge restored the public's faith in the honesty of the executive branch. He appointed two outstanding attorneys as prosecutors of the government's case against the Teapot Dome culprits, thus bypassing Daugherty, the corrupt attorney general. He soon replaced Daugherty with the distinguished former dean of the Columbia University Law School, Harlan Fiske Stone. The White House itself, hitherto the scene of hard-drinking, poker-playing cronyism, became a more dignified place with Coolidge and his charming and cultivated wife, Grace, as its occupants.

Otherwise Coolidge slept away most of his five years in office. During his term the watchword of government was "do nothing." The administration avoided new programs to achieve a balanced budget and reduce the national debt. This inaction pleased business, but it ignored pressing social and physical needs of the country. The nation acquired a major new road system and hundreds of new schools, courthouses, and other public facilities; but the burden of constructing them was thrown largely on the states. Farmers found the new president a disappointment. Hoping for substantial assistance from the government to help them out of economic difficulties brought about by the contraction of war-inflated agricultural prices, they were dismayed when Coolidge twice vetoed congressional farm assistance plans.

But to be fair, Coolidge did suit the public mood. On balance, most Americans liked what they saw: dignity in the White House and a president who knew when to let well enough alone. When Coolidge ran for president in his own right in 1924, he won by a large majority over the combined votes for La Follette on the Progressive Farmer–Labor ticket and Democrat John W. Davis, a conservative corporation attorney from New York.

■ "NEW ERA" PROSPERITY ■

Republican electoral success in the twenties was assured by the country's booming economy. By 1925 the United States was producing a flood of commodities beyond anyone's dreams, and most Americans could see little reason to challenge the party that stood watch over this affluent "New Era."

In fact, the decade opened with a brief depression. Government spending during the war had produced a boom that poured money into the pockets of millions of Americans. For a year following the armistice, good times continued and eased the return of 4 million men to the civilian economy. The bubble burst in 1920. As Europe recovered and restored its devastated fields and factories, its reliance on American exports declined. At the same time American consumers, appalled by sky-high prices, held off buying. Down came prices with a resounding crash, a collapse that particularly hurt farmers.

The hard times soon passed, however, and the economy surged. Growth of total GNP reached an average of 7 percent a year between 1922 and 1927. By 1923 unemployment was only about 3 percent of the labor force. Total national product in 1929 would be 75 percent higher than in 1909. The income of the average American was a third higher in 1929 than in the last prewar years.

The Consumer Durables Revolution.   The great economic expansion of the middle and late 1920s was in part stimulated by readily available credit. Interest rates remained low through the decade. Thousands of citizens could and did borrow money to invest in factories and productive machinery, buy houses, and acquire expensive goods "on the installment plan." Foreigners borrowed extensively from American bankers, and the borrowed dollars soon came back to pay for imported American automobiles, electrical equipment, petroleum, wheat, and corn.

More fundamental than cheap credit was a major structural change in the economy. Between 1910 and 1920 average family income reached the point where many Americans had substantial amounts of discretionary income (that is, money left over after buying necessities, such as food, clothing, and shelter). For the first time, a relatively large number of consumers could afford services and goods that had always been beyond their reach. Many middle- and working-class women could now buy silk, or at least rayon, stockings and pay for the services of beauty parlors and hairdressers. Middle-class families could "eat out" more often, go to the movies, and hire household help. Most important, American consumers could now buy expensive "durables" like radios, vacuum cleaners, washing machines, electric irons, refrigerators, and, above all, automobiles. In 1929 automobile production was five times greater than it had been fourteen years earlier, and there were over 23 million registered passenger cars. This development in consumption patterns has been called a "consumer durables revolution."

The total impact of these new markets was immense. Demand for consumer durables called forth billions of dollars of investment in new factories and offices, creating jobs and income for building contractors, architects, electricians, bricklayers, and a host of people directly involved in construction. The indirect

Cities had known traffic jams in the age of the horse and wagon. But they got much worse—and spread to the suburbs as well—after the automobile became supreme in the 1920s.

effects, especially of the automobile, were also immense. Cars needed roads. Until the 1920s the typical American highway was a dirt track leading from the farm to the local railroad depot. Now the states, aided by matching federal outlays under the Federal Highway Act of 1916, poured billions into new, hard-surfaced, all-weather roads. At the end of the 1920s the nation had an un-equaled network of 275,000 miles of asphalt and concrete intercity two-lane highways.

Investment in roads was only the beginning. To meet the needs of auto-mobile manufacturers and users, capital poured into the steel, rubber, glass, and petroleum-producing industries. The automobile also gave birth to a new gener-ation of suburban communities now made accessible to city wage earners by the family car and the paved highway. Within ten years new "automobile suburbs" grew up in a ring beyond the streetcar suburbs of an earlier period. There was a downside, undoubtedly, of this surge in automobile ownership and use. It was in many ways the first phase of the major problems of pollution and suburban sprawl that would worsen in our own day. But clearly it spurred the economy.

Growing industrial efficiency also fueled the economic boom. In 1913 Henry Ford had introduced the moving assembly line in his Detroit automobile plant. During the war the need for speed to supply the fighting fronts and offset labor shortages led to greater reliance on mass-production techniques using standardized, interchangeable parts. Meanwhile, the principles of Frederick W. Taylor, which reduced management to a precise "science," spread to more and more industrial concerns. All these elements combined to increase labor productivity dramatically. By one estimate, the amount of labor time needed for a given unit of industrial output shrank 21 percent between 1920 and 1929.

Business and Labor.   Still another cause—as well as effect—of prosperity was the new public attitude toward private enterprise. Americans had far greater respect for business and businesspeople during the 1920s than during the Progressive Era. At times their good opinion approached reverence. "The man who builds a factory builds a temple," intoned President Coolidge, and "the man who works there worships there." In a 1925–1926 bestseller *The Man Nobody Knows,* an advertising executive could find no better way to convey the glory of Jesus than by describing him as a first-rate entrepreneur who "picked up twelve men from the bottom ranks of business and forged them into an organization that conquered the world." The clergy itself was saturated with business values. Typical sermon titles of the 1920s included "Christ: From Manger to Throne," "Public Worship Increases Your Efficiency," and "Business Success and Religion Go Together." Preachers were admonished by parishioners and church superiors to "preach the gospel and advertise."

This pro-business attitude inevitably hurt organized labor. Without public support, the unions suffered a succession of defeats when they attempted to organize sectors of industrial labor. In 1919, the Steelworkers lost a major strike to gain union recognition from the large steel firms. In 1929, mill owners defeated the efforts of the United Textile Workers to unionize southern cotton workers. Encouraged by the changed environment, American business, under the auspices of the National Association of Manufacturers, adopted the "American Plan" to roll back trade unionism. Businessmen were encouraged to use labor spies to ferret out and report on union activities, to hire strikebreakers if unions tried to shut them down, and to spread propaganda among their employees to discourage union organizing.

An unfriendly federal government and biased federal courts also contributed to labor's declining fortunes. The steel strikers lost in 1919 in part because Attorney General A. Mitchell Palmer dispatched federal troops to the United States Steel plant at Gary, Indiana, to protect strikebreakers. Shortly thereafter Palmer broke a mine workers' strike. In 1922 Attorney General Daugherty had a federal judge issue an injunction against idle railroad shopworkers, forcing them back to work. Under Chief Justice William Howard Taft, the former president, the Supreme Court gutted the provision of the Clayton Act exempting unions from antitrust prosecution and made it possible once again for employers to attack union activities as illegal restraints of trade.

The figures reflect these changes. In 1920, as a result of wartime expansion, the number of union members had reached over 5 million—almost 20 percent of all nonagricultural workers. It soon dropped to 3.6 million, hovering around this figure for the remainder of the decade while the labor force grew rapidly. By 1930 scarcely 10 percent of nonfarm workers belonged to unions.

The Depressed Industries. The boom of 1923–1929 was wide and deep enough to validate the conservative, pro-business values of the day. But prosperity was by no means universal. Unemployment remained high and wages low in several chronically sick industries. Miners of soft coal experienced hard times throughout the decade. The railroad industry was depressed, and the railroad companies laid off many workers. Cotton manufacturing also failed to benefit from overall prosperity. To survive in the face of stiff competition, many textile companies moved from New England to the southern Piedmont region of Virginia, the Carolinas, and Georgia, where labor and land were cheap and where they could put up new mills with the latest and most efficient equipment. The southern mill communities were often squalid places. Upton Sinclair reported that at Marion, South Carolina, most mill workers' homes lacked running water or toilets. Old newspapers served as wallpaper.

The most seriously depressed of all economic sectors was the most competitive one: agriculture. In 1925 there were still 6.5 million American farms, and growers of wheat and cotton faced millions of foreign competitors as well. During the war farmers had borrowed heavily to buy more land and upgrade their equipment to take advantage of high wartime prices. Farm prices dropped sharply at the end of 1920, leaving farmers with large interest payments but less income. During the remainder of the decade farmers continued to confront low prices and large debts.

Farmers adapted to the agricultural depression in different ways. During the 1920s over 1.2 million people abandoned agriculture, most of them to go to the cities and their growing suburbs. The black migration out of the rural South became a flood, though new opportunities in northern manufacturing was as much an incentive to move as depressed conditions in the cotton fields. Farmers also turned to politics, as they had in the past. But except for La Follette's short-lived effort in 1924 to create a farmer–labor alliance, they relied on pressure-group politics rather than third parties. The congressional farm bloc extracted legislation from Congress to ease agricultural credit, exempt farmers' cooperatives from antitrust prosecution, and regulate the rates various middlemen charged. Their major program, however, the McNary-Haugen plan, stalled. This scheme obligated the federal government to buy domestic farm surpluses at prices that would guarantee growers a good income and then sell them abroad at the lower world price, with the loss made up from a small fee paid by each farmer. Twice Congress approved the McNary-Haugen Farm Relief Bill and twice Coolidge vetoed the measure as favoring a special class of citizens and unduly interfering with free markets. Though the scheme never passed, it familiarized Americans with the idea of farm price supports, which a more experimental decade would later enact into law.

■ OLD AND NEW AMERICA ■

During the 1920s, then, the United States was not exempt from economic difficulties and class antagonisms. Yet organized opposition to the class and economic arrangements of society remained weak. Support for the Socialist party dwindled as working- and middle-class citizens lost interest in radical action. In 1928 Norman Thomas, the Socialist party's presidential candidate, received only 267,000 votes; William Z. Foster, of the new Communist party, only 49,000.

Still, the 1920s were scarcely harmonious. Americans fought bitterly over many issues, but they were primarily social and cultural rather than political or economic. As in other periods of relative prosperity, the questions that divided citizens involved religion, ethnicity, race, culture, and styles of life.

As we look at the twenties we can identify two broad divisions of opinion, separated by a deep cultural chasm. On one side were the forces of New America. New America was urban, and professed to be urbane. It was also modernist and free thinking in religion and was apt to be liberal or, occasionally, radical in politics. It was also culturally liberal. At the level of the "man-in-the-street" this often meant "fun-loving" hedonism. Among the better educated it was associated with avant-garde or modernist taste in the arts. New America accepted freer sexual standards and was "wet"—that is, it considered drinking a matter better left to private conscience than government regulation. On the issue of alcohol, though not necessarily on the others, New America found itself allied with urban Catholics.

Old America, by contrast, was rural or small town and proud of its simplicity and family-centered values. In religion it was Protestant, and often fundamentalist. Its politics tended to be conservative and strongly Republican in the North. It rejected the freer sexual practices of New America. Old America considered drinking both a social evil and a sin that should be discouraged by the authorities.

Old America and New America were both loose clusters that at no point had any formal embodiment in a single organization. And yet, to a surprising degree, these two sets of attitudes can be found consistently ranged against each other in the passionate cultural war that raged throughout the twenties.

Wets Versus Drys.   Prohibition was a major cultural battlefield of the decade. During the Gilded Age, the Women's Christian Temperance Union (WCTU) and the Anti-Saloon League had launched a crusade against "demon rum." Early in the new century progressives took up the cause of restricting liquor to suppress a social evil. By 1915 fifteen states in the South, Midwest, and Far West had prohibited the production and sale of alcoholic beverages. In truth, not all rural Americans were drys. In the rural South, especially, there was a venerable tradition of illegal distilling—and consumption—of "moonshine." Yet it was the big cities in the industrialized states where the resistance to prohibition was most formidable. These were home to many New Americans—Catholics, sophisticates, and social liberals—who considered it tyrannical for the state to dictate what a person could or could not drink. Other enemies were the brewers and distillers, loudly seconded by the saloonkeepers and proprietors of hotels and restaurants, who stood to lose business, if not their very livelihoods, if Americans were not permitted their beer, wine, and whiskey.

World War I gave the campaign for national prohibition an enormous boost. Temperance organizations proclaimed that brewing and distilling consumed badly needed grain. They played on the public's concern for the morals of the young men drafted into the army and took advantage of the fact that many brewers were of German origin. In 1917 Congress passed the Eighteenth Amendment, outlawing the manufacture, sale, and transportation of intoxicating liquors one year after its adoption. In January 1920, after state confirmation, national Prohibition went into effect.

The Volstead Act of 1919 implemented the Eighteenth Amendment by declaring illegal any beverage containing more than 0.5 percent alcohol and establishing a Prohibition Bureau for enforcing the law. But at no time during the Prohibition Era did Congress ever give the bureau enough money to do its job. Nor were city and state authorities particularly willing to spend money to enforce the federal measure. Some states passed their own "baby Volstead acts," but their enforcement, too, was generally poorly funded and weak. Americans continued to drink.

Poor enforcement was as much a symptom as a cause of Americans' continuing homage to John Barleycorn. Many of those who supported Prohibition did so only for the sake of appearances or to guarantee someone else's good behavior. In a famous quip humorist Will Rogers remarked that the people of one thoroughly dry state would "hold faithful and steadfast to Prohibition as long as the voters [could] stagger to the polls." In fact, by adding an element of the forbidden to the usual attractions of drinking, Prohibition made alcohol consumption appealing to new classes of people. In former days the "better" people seldom consumed hard liquor. Now whiskey, rum, and gin became a significant part of urban middle-class life. Alcohol consumption overall apparently declined during the 1920s and with it such diseases as cirrhosis and alcoholic psychosis as well as arrests for public drunkenness. But the "noble experiment" also replaced the tea party with the cocktail party as a social diversion and a mark of distinction between the urban sophisticate and the puritanical, small-town "rube."

It has been said that whenever a community forbids a practice that many favor, it encourages disregard for law in general. This formula held true in the 1920s. The United States might forbid the manufacture and sale of intoxicants, but Canadians, Mexicans, and Europeans did not. Alcohol transported by truck across the borders or landed clandestinely by boat on the beaches produced huge profits for rumrunners. Once in the country, its distribution and sale were taken over by bootleggers, who were also happy to furnish customers with "moonshine," "white lightning," "bathtub gin," and other potent—and often dangerous—native American concoctions.

Prohibition, along with the fast automobile and the Thompson submachine gun, helped create modern-day organized crime. To accommodate the thousands of citizens who were willing to pay to drink, enterprising and ruthless men organized liquor distribution networks that rivaled major legitimate business enterprises in their complexity and efficiency. Just as successful businessmen often diversified, successful bootleggers, organized into "families" under strong and brutal leaders, extended their operations into prostitution, gambling, and the "protection" racket.

The "mobs" brought new violence to the cities. When one gang tried to invade another's territory, the result was often warfare that left scores dead. In the 1929 St. Valentine's Day massacre, for example, six members of Bugs Moran's North Side gang were gunned down by unknown rivals in a Chicago garage while waiting for a shipment of bootleg liquor. Periodically, crusading district attorneys, goaded by the newspapers or citizens' groups, cracked down on the gangsters. But indictments and convictions were hard to get. Members of rival mobs refused to testify against their opponents; honest citizens were intimidated; officials, judges, and juries were bought off. Al Capone, the Chicago gang lord, foiled every attempt to bring him to justice and was only convicted when Eliot Ness of the U.S. Justice Department's special squad of "untouchables" found evidence against him of income tax evasion.

Throughout the 1920s millions of citizens continued to consider Prohibition a "noble experiment" worth supporting for the sake of national health and social order and to purify the country's morals. The "drys" agitated constantly to increase appropriations for Volstead Act enforcement; the Anti-Saloon League maintained lobbyists in Washington and the state capitals to ensure that lawmakers did not relax their vigilance. No group endorsed the noble experiment as vigorously as the Protestant clergy, especially those of the conservative evangelical denominations. Nevertheless, by the end of the decade the dry forces were losing ground, and each day more and more people came to believe that the noble experiment had failed.

Xenophobia.   During the war, as we saw, superpatriotism and xenophobia had tarnished the nation's liberal record on civil liberties and ethnic tolerance. Antiforeign tensions grew after the armistice as Europeans sought to escape the devastation of their homelands by fleeing to the United States. European immigration quadrupled between 1919 and 1920 and almost doubled again in 1921.

The new wave of foreigners threatened Old America. The immigrants were largely Catholic and Jewish and hence religiously alien. They were also certain to be "wet" since neither Catholics nor Jews generally considered drinking sinful.

"Red Scare."   Some of the new arrivals were also radicals—or so many Old Americans believed. Ever since the war and the Bolshevik Revolution, the public had worried about radicals and revolution. This anxiety was magnified soon after the armistice by a wave of politically motivated bombings. In early 1919 a series of bomb-laden packages arrived at the homes of public figures despised by the left. When opened by unsuspecting recipients they exploded, causing serious injuries. That April a clerk at the New York post office, alerted by the bombings, spotted sixteen suspicious packages about to be mailed to prominent people. Charles Kaplan notified his superiors; when opened, the packages indeed contained "infernal devices." In June a series of bombings ripped the homes of judges and public officials in cities across the country. The worst in its effects was the enormous explosion that detonated outside the home of Attorney General

A. Mitchell Palmer in Washington on the night of June 2. The blast shattered the windows and destroyed the porch. One who came to the Palmers' aid was assistant secretary of the navy, Franklin Roosevelt, who lived across the street.

Palmer and the public blamed the violence on alien extremists, and they were probably right, though their response was clearly disproportionate. In January 1920 Department of Justice agents rounded up 6,000 men and women, mostly eastern European aliens, on suspicion of radical activities, and threw them into unsanitary, overcrowded cells. There they were kept for weeks without explicit charges placed against them. Despite Palmer's assertion that a radical uprising was imminent, the police discovered no explosives and only three handguns among the hapless radicals. Eventually the courts released most of the prisoners.

Even after Palmer's term, fear of Bolshevism remained a central component of antiforeign feeling among traditional Americans, as evidenced by the ordeal of Nicola Sacco and Bartolomeo Vanzetti. These Italian-born anarchists were convicted in 1921 of having robbed and murdered a shoe factory paymaster and his guard in South Braintree, Massachusetts. Scholars still disagree over whether the two men were guilty of the crime, but it is clear that judge Webster Thayer, who officiated at their trial and presided over a number of the review hearings, was strongly prejudiced against foreigners and radicals. And he was not alone. To many Old Americans the men were aliens, both in their "race" and their views.

The liberal community, however, rallied around the two Italian radicals. Led by Walter Lippmann and Felix Frankfurter, liberals and intellectuals turned the defense of Sacco and Vanzetti into a crusade for free speech and common justice. Meetings, petitions, lobbying, and civil disobedience were deployed to drum up support for retrial or pardon of the two prisoners. The issue so deeply divided public opinion that one Sacco–Vanzetti supporter, the novelist John Dos Passos, described the opposing sides as "two nations." The liberals succeeded in getting the case reconsidered several times. But on August 22, 1927, after final appeals for clemency were rejected, both men were electrocuted. Whatever most Americans believed, to the political left, in both America and around the world, their execution seemed judicial murder.

The Door Is Closed. The antiforeign feeling propelled a drive for immigration restriction. It would be unfair to dismiss the arguments for restriction as mere bigotry. The United States could not have continued an open-door policy on immigration indefinitely. Yet the restriction legislation clearly reflected ethnic prejudice and political hysteria. In 1921, as a preliminary, Congress limited for a one-year period the number of new arrivals of each nationality to 3 percent of that group present in the country in 1910. In 1924 it passed the Johnson-Reed Immigration Act limiting total immigration to 154,000 persons annually and assigning national quotas that strongly favored northern and western over southern and eastern Europe. Italy, Poland, and Russia—the major sources of recent immigrants—were left with ludicrously small quotas.

The 1921 law and the Johnson-Reed Act ended the three centuries of free European immigration that had marked American history. It also enshrined into law the prejudices of native-born Old America against persons who, by their mere presence, seemed to be endangering the customs, habits, and beliefs of the United States.

Black Achievement.   The growing assertiveness of blacks disturbed much of Old America. During the war thousands of black soldiers had served their country in France, where they had encountered a racially more liberal society than their own. When they returned home, some sought to defy the segregation and bigotry of their own country and, in the South, became targets of violence. In 1919 alone, ten black veterans were lynched in southern states, several while still in uniform. Less dramatic, but far more important, thousands of southern blacks left for the North, continuing the wartime exodus. By 1930 Chicago would have over 230,000 black residents; New York, over 327,000; Philadelphia, over 219,000; and Detroit, over 120,000.

Few blacks who came north found jobs beyond unskilled or semiskilled labor. The typical black worker in the North during the 1920s was a factory worker or a day laborer. In increasing numbers black women replaced Irish and German women as domestics in middle-class urban homes.

The mass movement of rural blacks to northern slums caused painful social problems. Black families experienced many of the same strains as the immigrant families of the recent past. Children, once physically close to parents, now lost touch as fathers and mothers went to work away from the home. Poverty in the northern city seemed worse at times than in the rural South, where a family could at least raise part of its food and was spared many city costs. The black migration to northern cities brought racial tensions in its wake. Many whites resented and feared the new arrivals and fought to exclude them from their neighborhoods. In Chicago racial antagonisms built during the summer of 1919 and exploded in a furious race riot in late July when a black teenager, swimming off a Lake Michigan beach that whites considered their preserve, was stoned and drowned. Within hours gangs of white and black youths were battling one another and beating innocent bystanders. For thirteen days the city was torn by riot, arson, and vandalism, with the authorities unable to stop the destruction. When the casualties were finally counted, the death toll stood at almost 40, with over 500 injured.

Despite the troubles and difficulties, some blacks found new opportunities in northern cities. Sociologist and historian W. E. B. Du Bois, poet and critic James Weldon Johnson, and painter Henry Ossawa Tanner already had established reputations in professional circles. But the black achievements of the 1920s outshone anything earlier. Harlem, in upper Manhattan, became a black Athens where poets, writers, painters, musicians, and intellectuals gathered from all over the country and from other parts of the world. Among the Harlem Renaissance writers were Claude McKay, a Jamaican, who wrote eloquently and bitterly about the repression of blacks; Jean Toomer, an author of realistic stories about black life; and Countee Cullen, a master of delicate lyric poetry. Most impressive of all was Langston Hughes, a poet, novelist, and short-story writer of rare power who could employ humor as well as satire and argument to defend his race and express its hopes.

The 1920s was also an era when black musicians began to attract the attention of white Americans. Although they seldom gave it a second thought, whenever a white "flapper" and her "lounge lizard" boyfriend danced the Charleston or Black Bottom, they were affirming the vitality of black musical creativity in the 1920s. This was the decade when jazz broke out of the black community and began to find an appreciative audience around the world. Within the black community itself, great performing artists like the trumpeter Louis Armstrong, trombonist Kid Ory, and the powerful blues singer Bessie Smith were immensely popular. Their records sold millions of copies among the "cliff-dwellers" of Harlem, Chicago's South Side, and the other developing urban black neighborhoods.

Marcus Garvey. The new urban environment was fertile soil for a Back-to-Africa movement led by Marcus Garvey, a native of Jamaica, who came to New York in 1916 to establish a branch of his Universal Negro Improvement Association. Garvey appealed especially to working-class urban blacks, who did not feel at home in the NAACP, the middle-class black defense organization. He told blacks to be proud of their race; everything black, he declared, was admirable and beautiful. Because America was unalterably racist, blacks should return to Africa and there erect a new empire befitting their potential. The black middle class considered these ideas unsound; but among the urban immigrants from the rural South, Garvey's message was electrifying. Many joined the movement to become knights of the Nile, dukes of the Niger and Uganda, and members of the Black Eagle Flying Corps or the Universal Black Cross Nurses.

Federal officials accused Garvey of mail fraud. Tried by a liberal white judge who was a member of the rival NAACP, he was sentenced to five years in jail and died in obscurity in 1940. Despite his failure, he had blazed a black separatist trail that other black leaders would follow over a generation later.

The Sexual Revolution. Sexual behavior was yet another issue that divided the two Americas. No matter how fiercely traditionalists might protest, the nation's sexual values were changing, especially among the young.

Women were at the forefront of this transformation, yet while they were leading the revolt against traditional sexual taboos, they were losing their political punch. Once the battle for female suffrage was won, the women's rights movement began to retreat. The League of Women Voters succeeded the National American Woman Suffrage Association, but failed to arouse the same enthusiasm for expanded economic opportunity for women as it had for suffrage. Alice Paul's more militant National Woman's party, with an equal rights amendment to the Constitution as its major goal, survived into the 1920s, but with only 8,000 members it had little influence.

But having won the right to vote, women activists and dissenters now challenged the status quo in the social realm. Young urban, middle-class women began to demand in ever-larger numbers that they be treated as adult individuals, not as overgrown children or fragile dolls. In the 1920s respectable wives, mothers, and daughters began to smoke, a habit that till then had been confined to men or to women of ill-repute. They also began to drink as never before. The new cocktail party introduced a feminine element to social drinking, previously an all-male preserve. However, dubious for health, the changes marked a new level of feminine independence.

More shocking was the new female sexual assertiveness. For women who reached their late teens or twenties between 1919 and 1929, sex was not so obviously linked to marriage and children as it had been for their mothers. Influenced by a popularized version of Sigmund Freud's theories concerning the emotional dangers of sexual repression, many young women began to insist that they were as entitled as men to the pleasures of physical love and the free choice of sexual partners. The incidence of premarital sex increased sharply, especially among well-educated women. Adultery also became more common. Even when young women did not "go all the way," they were far more relaxed in their social relations with men than before. Young women of respectable families "petted"; they refused to be chaperoned; they danced "cheek-to-cheek."

The "flapper," as the liberated young woman of the 1920s was called, also insisted on greater freedom in her dress and appearance. In contrast to the "womanly" long skirt, sweeping picture hat, rounded bosom, tight natural waist, and petticoats of the past, her skirt was cut off at the knee to reveal a long stretch of silk- or rayon-stockinged leg. Her waistline was high, her bosom flat-tened, her underclothes minimal, her cloche hat brimless. In 1913 a typical woman's outfit consumed nineteen and a half yards of cloth. In 1925 it required a scant seven. Hair, previously grown long and worn down the back or pinned up, was cut short and "bobbed" or "shingled." To offset the tomboy effect of her dress and reassert her femininity, the flapper painted her face as respectable women never had before.

Older people, particularly those of traditional America, predictably deplored the new trends in dress and behavior among the female young. Smoking by women was the "beginning of the end," according to one male social critic. Dr. Francis Clark of the Christian Endeavor Society denounced modern dances as "impure, polluting, corrupting, debasing." One clergyman proclaimed: "We get our [dress] styles from New York, New York from Paris, and Paris from Hell." Legislators joined the disapproving chorus. In 1921 the Utah legislature consid-ered a bill to fine or imprison any woman whose skirts were higher than three inches above the ankle.

The Media Assault on the Small Town.   In explaining the erosion of the tra-ditional sexual code, moralists often pointed to the debasing effects of the media. Novels like Walter Fabian's *Flaming Youth* (1923), F. Scott Fitzgerald's *This Side of Paradise* (1920), and Floyd Dells' *Moon-Calf* (1920) glorified the pursuit of pleasure by the young. Early in the decade Hollywood produced a flood of films with such suggestive titles as *Up in Mabel's Room, A Shocking Night, Sinners in Silk,* and *Her Purchase Price.* One producer described his films as replete with "neckers, petters, white kisses, red kisses, pleasure-mad daughters, sensation-seeking mothers . . . the truth-bold, naked, sensational." Though this was pretty tame compared to recent "X-rated" films, it brought down the wrath of the

UNE, 1922   35

The S MART S ET

Edited by
George Jean Nathan
and
H. L. Mencken.

"The Diamond as Big as the Ritz"
By F. Scott Fitzgerald

A 1922 cover of George Jean Nathan and H. L. Mencken's "The Smart Set" featuring a story by F. Scott Fitzgerald. It touches on a set of famous twenties cultural icons: jazz music and flappers.

moralists and censors. To avoid legal repression, the movie industry in 1922 chose a "czar"—Warren Harding's postmaster general, Will H. Hays—to lay down guidelines of taste and decorum. The Hays Office rules ended the rash of cheap exploitation movies. Critics charged that they also lowered the intellectual and artistic level of Hollywood films to that suitable for a sheltered child of twelve. In 1930 the movie industry adopted a "production code" to guarantee that motion pictures would not offend the most prudish tastes.

The moralists undoubtedly exaggerated the social impact of the movies. But they were not entirely wrong. Popular media helped undermine the values and culture of Old America even when they did not directly attack them. Good roads and the automobile had reduced the isolation of America's farms and small towns. Now the movies brought to the smallest communities an image of sophisticated urban life that appealed intensely to American youth. Young people learned what passed for romantic technique among worldly men and women. "It was directly through the movies that I learned to kiss a girl on her ears, neck, and cheeks, as well as her mouth," wrote one young man. After long exposure to the fantasies of Hollywood, one small-town girl told a social researcher that her "daydreams . . . consist of clothes, ideas on furnishings, and manners." Such young people were not easily induced to accept the sexual taboos, dress customs, and social values of their small town and rural communities.

Radio, too, challenged small-town values. The basic technology of radio was invented before World War I, but the medium did not come into its own until 1920, when Station KDKA in Pittsburgh began to broadcast commercially. In 1927 General Electric, Westinghouse, and the Radio Corporation of America joined to create the first radio network, the National Broadcasting Company. The Columbia Broadcasting Company came the next year. By 1929 over 10 million American families owned receiving sets. Radio broadcasting was not placed under government control, as in most of Europe. Instead, it became a private industry dependent on advertising for revenue. In 1927 the federal government did intrude to assign station wavelengths to avoid chaos, but it did little to compel broadcasters to serve the public. Advertisers who paid the stations' bills and naturally wished to attract the largest audiences were far more inclined to sponsor "Roxy and His Gang" or "Amos 'n Andy" than serious intellectual or political discussion or the Metropolitan Opera.

But if commercial broadcasting failed to promote serious discourse or elevate public taste, it exposed listeners to a high level of professionalism that did much to unintentionally undermine the confidence and morale of village America. How could a community amateur hour outdo the "Ipana Troubadours"? How could the local high school dance band compete with Paul Whiteman, coming "live from New York"?

Rebel Artists.   Nor was the decade free from more direct assaults on traditional cultural values. The big cities, especially New York, were the havens of sophisticates who projected a barely disguised contempt for rural, small-town America. The bohemians of the shabby-chic apartments and refurbished townhouses of Greenwich Village in lower Manhattan felt themselves escapees from small-town culture. They expressed their new freedom through hard-drinking, free sex lives, socialism, and devotion to the avant-garde in the arts and in thought.

The bohemians of the twenties considered American culture hopelessly provincial. Europe, with its greater intellectual and artistic depth, seemed far more interesting. Many of the decade's writers, including Ernest Hemingway, F. Scott Fitzgerald, Edna St. Vincent Millay, and Gertrude Stein, felt so alienated that they left the country, most to live in Paris for long periods.

Some who stayed, as well as a few who left, wrote novels that ridiculed and condemned the life of the American small town. Sinclair Lewis's *Main Street* (1920) recounts the story of a young woman who moves to Gopher Prairie, a typical small town. There she resolves to reform her neighbors' tastes, values, and politics, but is instead defeated by their ignorance and materialism. Sherwood Anderson's *Winesburg, Ohio* (1919) depicts the small-mindedness, hypocrisy, and secret vice that Anderson believed afflicted provincial Americans.

American writers and intellectuals ridiculed not only the small towns but also the entire culture of Old America. H. L. Mencken, the acid-tongued social critic of the *Baltimore Evening Sun,* turned his guns on almost everything in his native land and shocked traditional Americans by his irreverence, elitism, and attacks on established beliefs. Mencken reserved his sharpest barbs for the "booboisie," the crass and puritanical middle class he claimed inhabited the country's heartland. Sinclair Lewis followed *Main Street* with *Babbitt* (1922), a novel about a businessman in a middle-sized midwestern city whose material success and irrepressible boosterism masked deep doubt about his own worth. Its hero's name gave a new word for conformity to the English language. Another powerful indictment of the nation's materialism was *An American Tragedy* (1925) by Theodore Dreiser, a tale of the corrupting effect of ambition for wealth and position on a weak young man.

F. Scott Fitzgerald was a more subtle denigrator of America's false values. Fitzgerald was alternately attracted and repelled by the life of the American upper bourgeoisie in the 1920s. He never lost his fascination for the rich and their doings, but in *The Great Gatsby* (1925) he brilliantly depicted the dry rot at the heart of America's business civilization in the person of Jay Gatsby, a man who destroys himself in pursuit of wealth and glamor.

A representative young man of the "Lost Generation," who had fought in World War I and had returned to find "all Gods dead, all wars fought, all faiths shaken," Ernest Hemingway was another mordant critic of American civilization. In *The Sun Also Rises* (1926) he portrays a group of young Americans wandering through Europe seeking a substitute for the ideals of the past that now seemed hollow and insincere. In this first book and such later works as *A Farewell to Arms* (1929), in muscular, unadorned prose, Hemingway depicts characters struggling against the hypocrisies of the world and forced to find heroism and authenticity in their private lives.

Drama also became a vehicle of protest against the conventionality of the decade. Eugene O'Neill, the most important figure of the "little theater" movement, was the first American playwright of international distinction. O'Neill and the stage designers, producers, and other writers connected with the Provincetown Players, sought to make the American theater into a vehicle for expressing serious ideas. With such productions as Elmer Rice's *The Adding Machine* (1923), satirizing the emptiness of modern commercial life, and O'Neill's *Desire Under the Elms* (1924), debunking American puritanism, the little theater groups looked critically at American life.

■ CONFRONTATION ■

Old America watched with pain, frustration, and anger the influx of immigrants, the new assertiveness of blacks, the frivolous and "immoral" behavior of the young, the rise of organized crime, and the ridicule and naysaying of the writers and intellectuals. The "intellectuals and liberals," declared one defender of the old ways, had "betrayed Americanism" and created "confusion in thought and opinion, a groping and hesitancy about national affairs and private life alike." Old America seized on every sign that all was not lost. The successful solo flight of Charles Lindbergh to Paris in 1927 touched off a wave of hero worship unequaled since Washington's day. "Lindy," the tall, clean-cut, blond young American from the Midwest, demonstrated that something survived of the noble past. His achievement, noted one social critic, showed "that we are not rotten at the core, but morally sound and sweet and good!" Old America fought back against modernity, setting off a series of confrontations that alternately disturbed and fascinated the nation.

The Klan Reborn.   At its most angry and extreme, Old America's counterattack took the form of a revived Ku Klux Klan. The Klan of Reconstruction days lived on in the South's collective memory as the heroic savior of white culture and the bulwark against "ignorant" blacks and their villainous carpetbagger allies. This view was reinforced and widely disseminated by a popular historical novel, *The Clansman,* published in 1905 by Thomas Dixon. In 1915 the novel became the basis for D.W. Griffith's groundbreaking film "The Birth of a Nation."

The movie stirred the imagination of William Simmons, an Atlanta Methodist preacher and professional organizer of fraternal orders and lodges. Soon after seeing it, he set about establishing a new "high class order for men of intelligence and character," which he named after its Reconstruction predecessor. The war's superpatriotism and intolerance helped swell the new Klan's ranks to several thousand, all dedicated to defending white Protestant America against blacks, aliens, and dissenters. After 1918, with the help of Edward Young Clarke and Elizabeth Tyler, two skilled publicists, Simmons capitalized on the pervasive postwar anxiety over social change to recruit members for his new organization.

The Klan represented the most extreme fringe of traditional, white, native-born America. Utterly devoted to white supremacy, it condemned Catholics and Jews as aliens, under obligation in the first case to the pope and in the second to an international anti-Christian conspiracy. The Klan also became the defender of traditional public morals. It endorsed Prohibition and denounced the illegal liquor traffic; it attacked prostitution and sexual laxity; it warned wife beaters and criminals to cease their nefarious doings; it stood for "100 percent Americanism" and opposed all radical ideology.

During the 1920s the Klan became a political force in the rural parts of the nation, especially in the South, Midwest, and Far West. It even penetrated the big cities, where it appealed to white Protestants recently arrived from rural areas, who felt lost amid the social and ethnic diversity that surrounded them. The "Invisible Empire" entered politics in many states and cities. At one time it virtually controlled the governments of Indiana and Oregon. Denver and Dallas fell under its sway; in Denver it succeeded in defeating the reelection bid of the famous liberal judge, Ben Lindsey.

By 1925 there were 3 million Klansmen, and their presence was felt almost everywhere. Daytime Klan parades of sheeted, robed men, and nighttime rallies under immense fiery crosses became common in many American communities. Some Klansmen, no doubt, were well-meaning if misguided men who sincerely believed they were upholding decency and traditional values. Others joined the Klan because it was economically or politically expedient. Yet many lawless and viciously racist people hid behind Klan regalia to commit crimes against blacks, supposed radicals or social deviants, and Jews and Catholics. Intimidation, boycotts, tar and feathering, and even murder were all part of the Klan arsenal.

Outraged by Klan atrocities, various Catholic, Jewish, black, and liberal groups fought back. Many big-city newspapers, led by the *New York World,* denounced it. Even many conservative Protestants, frightened by its divisive influence on the nation, resisted the Klan.

This counterassault was aided by the hypocrisy of Klan leaders. Thousands of dollars poured into Klan coffers, but much of the money stuck to the fingers of Klan officials. Even more damaging were instances of sexual laxity by several prominent Klan leaders. For an organization that denounced the ethical slackness of the times and appointed itself the guardian of community morals, the financial and carnal weaknesses of its own leaders were damaging blows. By 1930 the Klan was practically dead. But in later years, when social tensions once more intensified, it would again become a vehicle for hate, intolerance, and mindless superpatriotism.

The Klan fight was only one of many battles pitting Old and New Americans against each other. Two others were the Scopes trial in Dayton, Tennessee, in 1925, and the presidential election of 1928.

The Scopes Trial. During the 1920s education became a major battleground between conservative fundamentalists and liberal modernists. Religious conservatives held that the schools had to be kept from purveying skepticism and irreligion; modernists held that teachers had to be free to teach the latest theories of science, wherever they led. Inevitably, the teaching of Darwinism and evolution ignited a furious battle between the Old and the New America.

The confrontation came to a head in 1925 when the Tennessee legislature passed the Butler Law, which made the teaching of Darwin's theory of evolution illegal in state-supported public schools and colleges. In the small town of Dayton, John Scopes, a young high school teacher, agreed to challenge the law at the suggestion of a group of young local rebels. Several days later, after lecturing to his class from a textbook that included a section on evolution, Scopes was arrested.

The response of outsiders to Scopes's arrest was startling. The venerable William Jennings Bryan volunteered to help the prosecutor protect traditional America from the theory that humanity had evolved from lower forms of life. The American Civil Liberties Union (ACLU), an organization dedicated to free speech, had looked forward to a test case on the Butler law; when the prominent liberal lawyer Clarence Darrow volunteered to defend Scopes, the ACLU joined him in the defense. All the major news services set up shop in sleepy Dayton. Curiosity seekers and hundreds of local farmers poured into the town. The square in front of the courthouse became a bustling fair with hawkers of soft drinks, souvenirs, fans, books, and religious tracts everywhere.

Scopes's guilt was not in question; he had violated the letter of the law. But Darrow and the ACLU were more interested in attacking what they saw as the irrationality and ignorance of traditional America than in establishing their client's legal innocence. At one point Darrow declared that his purpose was to "show up Fundamentalism . . . to prevent bigots and ignoramuses from controlling the educational system of the United States." Enraged at the attack, Bryan responded that his purpose was to "protect the word of God against the greatest atheist and agnostic in the United States."

Neither side came off well in the encounter. Bryan appeared as grossly misinformed about modern science; Darrow showed himself to be a cocky smart aleck. The trial ended in a draw. The jury found Scopes guilty and fined him $100, but the state supreme court later threw out the verdict on a technicality. The law remained on the books, and its violator went free. The legal results were anticlimactic, but the Scopes trial proved a setback to traditional religion and provided a window into the forces contending for America's cultural soul.

The Election of 1928.   More momentous for the country was the 1928 presidential election. The contestants were Secretary of Commerce Herbert Hoover and Alfred E. Smith, the Democratic governor of New York.

The two men seemed complete opposites. Smith was an extrovert who loved clubhouse politics and enjoyed the company of men and women from all walks of life. Hoover was a painfully shy man who seldom evoked warm personal affection. Smith was a natty dresser who made his trademark the striped suit and the brown derby that had been high fashion in his youth. Hoover's clothes were always well cut and black. Smith's formal education was minimal. Hoover was a mining engineer, a graduate of Stanford University, and a world traveler. Most important of all, Smith's origins were urban, Irish-Catholic, and wet. Hoover was a Quaker from the tiny hamlet of West Branch, Iowa, who believed Prohibition was "a great social and economic experiment, noble in motive and far-reaching in purpose."

Smith was a controversial figure to many Americans. Good government voters had reservations about his Tammany Hall affiliations. Drys deplored his stand on liquor and the Volstead Act. Snobs winced at his imperfect English pronunciation and education. Rural voters questioned his knowledge of farm problems. Westerners doubted he cared about their section. But among traditional voters it was his Catholicism that awakened the most misgivings. Sophisticated critics charged that Catholics did not accept American traditions such as the separation of church and state and did not support secular public education. At the lowest level there was the Klan's unthinking prejudice against Catholicism as a perversion of Gospel Christianity and an evil international conspiracy. One Vermonter expressed the anti-Smith position succinctly when he prayed that "the good Lord and the Southland [might] keep us safe from the rule of the Wet, Tammany, Roman Catholic Booze Gang."

In fact, no Democrat could have won in 1928. Most Americans agreed that the country had never been so prosperous, and during the campaign, while some Republicans attacked Smith's religion and his personal attributes, others played up the blessings of good times. "Given a chance to go forward with the policies of the last eight years," Hoover intoned in his acceptance speech, "we shall with the help of God be in sight of the day when poverty will be banished from this nation." Elect the "Great Engineer," Republican campaign slogans declared, and there would be a "chicken in every pot and two cars in every garage." Good times, added to the fear of Catholicism, made the Republican ticket unbeatable in November 1928.

Nevertheless, the Democratic candidate won wide support in the cities. If thousands in the South and the rural West and North voted against him because of his Catholicism, thousands of others in the northern cities voted for him for the same reason. In some Irish and Italian election districts in New York City, Smith received 97 or 98 percent of the total vote! If one views the campaign in the context of American party history from the Civil War to the present, Smith's candidacy marks a point where the urban immigrant vote, which had been loosened from its nineteenth-century Democratic moorings by World War I and Republican New Era prosperity, became more strongly fastened to the Democrats than ever before. Hoover carried 40 of the 48 states, with 444 electoral votes and over 21 million popular votes, to Smith's 87 electoral votes and 15 million popular ones. For the first time since Reconstruction, Texas, Florida, North Carolina, Tennessee, and Virginia went Republican. On the face of it, it was a Democratic disaster. In reality, it was the beginning of a great resurgence that would soon make the Democrats the party of the normal American majority.

■ CONCLUSIONS ■

In his inaugural address Herbert Hoover told the American people that the years ahead were "bright with hope." He was expressing the optimism that many Americans felt, and he and they apparently had good reason for their sunny expectations.

The decade was a period of unusual achievement. For the middle class and upper levels of American wage earners, it was a breakthrough into a new affluence. It was also a time of expanding freedom for women, young people, and intellectuals, and it was a creative age in the arts.

But the decade had a darker side. It was a time of contraction for farmers and of severe material limits for the semiskilled and unskilled. But above all it was also a decade of bitter cultural and social strife. Between 1919 and 1929 an older, rural, traditional, native, fundamentalist America collided with a newer, urban, modernist, foreign-born, non-Protestant America. The Klan, immigration restriction, Prohibition, political intolerance, and organized crime were all ugly manifestations of that cultural clash.

And now a new force was about to intrude into the cultural battleground. Seven months into Hoover's term the stock market collapsed, altering the lives of millions of Americans and the course of the nation's history.

Online Resources

"The Red Scare"
http://newman.baruch.cuny.edu/digital/redscare/
This site consists of some 300 images, including political cartoons, that depict Americans' distrust of immigrants and radicals following World War I.

"Talking History"
http://www.albany.edu/talkinghistory/archive/goinnorth.ram
Beginning with part 2 of "Goin' North, Great Tales of the Great Migration," hear African Americans talk through audio files about their experiences in going to Philadelphia for jobs during World War I. (This is an audio file and requires the common audio player feature.)

"The 1920s: Society, Fads, and Daily Life"
http://www.louisville.edu/~kprayb01/1920s-Society-1.html#A1
This site chronicles the changing popular culture of the 1920s in areas such as fashion, entertainment, and language.

"Prosperity and Thrift: The Coolidge Era and the Consumer Economy, 1921–1929"
http://memory.loc.gov/ammem/coolhtml/coolhome.html
This site is a compilation of numerous primary sources—from mass advertising and presidential addresses to short films. It tracks the nation's transition to a consumer society and examines the role of the government in that change. It also discusses life for those who did not enjoy the emerging fruits of the economy.

"Famous Trials in American History. Tennessee vs. John Scopes: The Monkey Trial"
http://www.law.umkc.edu/faculty/projects/ftrials/scopes/scopes.htm
This site details the famous legal battle, which testifies to the challenges to tradition that were prevalent in the 1920s. The site includes eyewitness accounts, excerpts from the trial, photographs, and more.

"Harlem: Mecca of the New Negro"
http://etext.lib.virginia.edu/harlem/index.html
The e-text of the historical 1925 *Survey Graphic,* a journal of social work, featured on this site is an example of one of the first attempts to understand the social, cultural, and political significance of the Harlem community in New York.

25

THE NEW DEAL

Too Far or Not Far Enough?

1929	Depression begins with financial panic on Wall Street; President Hoover increases federal spending on current projects but avoids deficit spending
1930	4 million Americans are unemployed; Hawley-Smoot Tariff
1932–35	Drought makes Great Plains a dust bowl
1932	Congress establishes the Reconstruction Finance Corporation (RFC); Dispersal of the Bonus Army; Franklin D. Roosevelt elected president
1933–35	First New Deal
1933	Roosevelt orders a four-day bank holiday; New Deal legislation and agencies: Emergency Banking Act, Agricultural Adjustment Act (AAA), National Industrial Recovery Act (NIRA), Public Works Administration (PWA), National Recovery Administration (NRA), Home Owners Loan Corporation (HOLC), Federal Emergency Relief Act, Civilian Conservation Corps (CCC), Federal Deposit Insurance Corporation (FDIC), Tennessee Valley Authority (TVA), Civil Works Administration (CWA)
1934	Securities and Exchange Commission established; Conservative Democrats and wealthy Republicans form the anti-Roosevelt Liberty League
1935–38	Second New Deal
1935	Legislation: Emergency Relief Act, National Labor Relations (Wagner) Act, Social Security Act, Public Utility Holding Company Act, Revenue (Wealth Tax) Act, Banking Act, Frazier-Lemke Farm Mortgage Moratorium Act, Resettlement Administration Act, Rural Electrification Act; The Supreme Court strikes down the NIRA; Committee on Industrial Organizations (CIO) formed; The Supreme Court invalidates the AAA; Huey Long is assassinated; Benny Goodman organizes his own orchestra
1936	Roosevelt reelected president; Soil Conservation and Domestic Allotment Act
1937	Roosevelt's attempt to pack the Supreme Court; General Motors Corporation and United States Steel recognize unions as the bargaining agents for their employees; Chicago police kill ten while breaking up a strike against Republic Steel; The Farm Security Administration established; Wagner-Steagall Housing Act
1938	Agricultural Adjustment Act; Food, Drug, and Cosmetic Act; Fair Labor Standards Act

The New Deal, that wide-ranging political response to the massive social and economic crisis of the 1930s, has always been controversial. Contemporary conservatives called it "socialistic" and denounced it for destroying fundamental American liberties. Contemporary radicals condemned it for preserving America's capitalist institutions and the inequalities of wealth and power that went with them. Critics from both ends of the political spectrum continue to attack it today. According to conservative scholars, the New Deal delayed recovery from the Great Depression by frightening the business class that might have invested and restored economic momentum. Recently, they have attacked it as the source of the bloated federal presence in American life and the author of the demoralizing welfare state. At the other end of the political scale, historian Barton J. Bernstein critically notes that the "liberal reformers of the New Deal . . . conserved the protected American corporate capitalism. . . . There was no significant redistribution of power in American society, only limited recognition of other organized groups, seldom of unorganized people."

Was the New Deal's role in American life positive or negative? Did it fall short of the goals it set for itself? Were its goals too limited? Did it really create as many problems for our society as it solved? To answer these questions we must look at the difficulties the nation faced during the Great Depression, and for this purpose we must turn back to the closing months of the New Era.

■ BOOM AND BUST ■

American capitalism had a dazzling year in 1929. By almost every measure the economy had never performed so well. Automobile production reached almost 4.5 million units, 800,000 more than in 1928; steel production climbed to 5 million tons above the year before. Manufacturing output as a whole reached an all-time peak. Late in the summer the stock market soared to a historic high, with shares in American corporations selling for prices never before attained. When economists got around to figuring out the gross national product for 1929, they would put it at over $104 billion, or $857 for every man, woman, and child—25 percent higher than a decade before.

Life for millions of Americans seemed good as the 1920s drew to a close. Over 20 million of the nation's 30 million families had automobiles. Radios were prized possessions in over 10 million households; many people were beginning to acquire electric washing machines and refrigerators. Almost half of all American families owned their own homes, and over two thirds had electric power—twice the proportion of the previous decade. Never before had so many enjoyed so much. Few Americans doubted that 1929 was a charmed year.

Abruptly, the spell broke. In the weeks following Labor Day, the stock market plunged, paused, and then plunged again. On Thursday, October 24, a record-breaking 13 million shares changed hands at prices so sharply deflated that $9 billion in investment values were wiped out in that single day. Thousands of investors and speculators scrambled to sell stocks for whatever they could get. On October 29, 16 million shares were sold, with prices down an average of 40 points.

For the next two and a half years the 1920s "bull market" deflated. At times there were rallies, but they were short-lived. By July 1932 stock prices had reached bottom at a fraction of their former value and would take years to recover. During the long slide over $70 billion of investments and paper wealth were wiped out, $616 for every person in the country!

Causes of the Depression. Americans have often blamed the stock market collapse for their plight during the 1930s. The blame was not entirely misplaced. The Crash wiped out billions in paper wealth and replaced the buoyant optimism of the New Era with caution. It badly frightened the people who made the economy's decisions to invest. By 1932 gross private domestic investment had sunk to one ninth the 1929 amount. Although far fewer Americans proportionately than in recent times then owned stock, the Crash also destroyed the confidence of consumers, who tightened their belts and delayed buying. If the blind optimism of stock market investors during the New Era had helped cause the Crash, the equally blind pessimism following it undoubtedly prolonged the Great Depression.

The stock market tumble, however, was only the most visible cause of the economic collapse. The 1920s had been a time of economic growth, but that growth had depended on an unstable balance of factors. New markets for automobiles, radios, refrigerators, and other durables had induced businesses to invest vast sums to expand production. In addition, governments had poured more billions into roads, bridges, and other capital improvements, while private citizens, now able to rely on the family automobile for quick transportation to city jobs, bought homes in the burgeoning suburbs. Pushed by the consumer durables surge, construction, steel, cement, petroleum, rubber, and scores of other industries boomed, creating jobs and income for millions of urban Americans. Most people came to see the new affluence as normal and to assume that it would never end.

But they were wrong, of course. The end of the surge was inevitable. With 50 percent of the nation's income going to only 20 percent of its families, the market for expensive consumer durables, though wider than in the past, was limited. When all those who could afford the new car or the new radio had satisfied their needs, demand had to decline. By 1927 or 1928 these effects were already being felt and manufacturers were beginning to cut production and lay off workers. A spiral was now set in motion: Fewer new orders for goods led to fewer jobs; in turn, the unemployed could not buy what the factories produced, and so orders further declined. Overall, the massive push to invest, which had fed the economy since World War I, had lost its momentum.

The international economy also contributed to the decline. The burdens of war debts and tariff barriers were becoming harder to bear as the decade neared its end. England and France had emerged from World War I owing enormous debts to America. To pay they needed to export their own goods to the United

States. But, as we have seen, this country raised tariffs during the 1920s, making it increasingly difficult to sell foreign goods to Americans. The $33 billion indemnity imposed on Germany by the postwar Allied Reparations Commission could potentially make up the Allied payments gap with America. But the Germans could not pay it, and in two successive stages (the Dawes Plan, 1924, and the Young Plan, 1929) the payments were pared down and stretched out. For a while, large-scale lending by American banks took up the slack, enabling the former Allies to buy American goods on credit. Indeed, American banks invested heavily in nations around the world, helping to fuel the worldwide 1920s boom. By 1928, however, the bankers were beginning to have second thoughts about foreign loans. The whole shaky structure of foreign trade was now in jeopardy.

The Great Depression. The collapse of the stock market triggered an avalanche of disaster. Credit became tight, and interest rates soared. The Federal Reserve Board could have eased the situation by lowering interest rates, but foolishly took no action. To save themselves, banks cut off credit to businesses and foreign borrowers. All trade slowed, but foreign commerce, which had been sustained by constant infusions of American credit, was especially hard hit.

To sustain their exports and reduce their imports, many nations imposed strict foreign trade barriers and raised tariffs. The world's trading nations had used a currency exchange system pegged to the price of gold that had encouraged international trade and investment. Now, many abandoned the gold standard, allowing the values of goods and currencies to fluctuate wildly and further disturbing international commerce. Under the combined blows of trade restrictions and currency instability, commerce among the world's nations declined precipitously. By mid-1930 the Great Depression had become virtually worldwide.

Meanwhile, the domestic banking system faced collapse. As the economy worsened, frightened depositors rushed to withdraw their savings. Bank after bank failed as "runs" forced even solvent institutions into bankruptcy. In November 1930 alone a total of 256 banks with deposits of $180 million closed their doors. Most severely affected in this round were the financial institutions of the farm areas, where bank failures had been numerous even in the 1920s.

The decline of consumption was a key factor in worsening and prolonging the Depression. The collapse of the bull market frightened consumers of luxury goods, whose sense of well-being depended on their paper profits and wealth. But even ordinary consumers, who had not "played the market" during the twenties, turned timid after the Crash and ceased to make their indispensable contribution to the economy. Here the nation's very affluence hurt it. In former times, when most consumers' income went for necessities, they had limited choices whether to spend or not when times turned bad. But in this rich era they could put off vacation trips and decide not to buy new radios, cars, or refrigerators. The most durable of all durable goods—houses—could be deferred the longest, and new housing sales dropped off disastrously.

Deferring purchases and investment at first was largely voluntary, but it soon became inescapable. As unsold inventories built up in stores and showrooms, retailers reduced their orders to manufacturers and suppliers. They in turn lowered their investment goals, cut back on production, slashed wages, and fired employees. Unemployment shot up. By the end of 1930 over 4 million men and women were out of work. Many more were working part-time or for sharply reduced wages. Families whose breadwinners lost their jobs in turn cut their budgets to the bone. Total demand now declined still further, establishing a vicious downward spiral of economic deflation.

If commodity prices had fallen as far and as fast as consumer income, goods might have continued to move, and workers might have kept their jobs. In areas where there were many competitive producers prices did fall. Between 1929 and 1933 agricultural prices dropped 56 percent, while output remained virtually the same. The plunge was unfortunate for farmers, but it kept farm production and farm employment high and prevented widespread hunger. In segments of the economy where competition was limited, however, prices stayed high. Automobiles remained expensive—about $600 for the average vehicle both in 1929 and in 1932. Because most people could not buy cars, production—and employment—fell. By 1932 automobile output had dropped to 25 percent of the 1929 figure, and the number of automobile workers had declined to under 40 percent of the 1929 total.

The Human Toll.   The Great Depression was a human disaster of colossal proportions. Despair spread through every part of the country and penetrated every walk of life. By the winter of 1932–1933 a quarter of those Americans willing to work were without jobs. The plight of blue-collar wage earners, who had few resources to cushion them against adversity, was the worst. Millions of factory hands and construction workers tramped the streets looking for jobs or waited in lines for handouts from charity organizations. But hard times did not respect class lines. Small business owners went bankrupt as their customers dwindled. Lawyers had fewer clients; doctors and dentists discovered that their patients put eating before health care. The sharp decline in building and construction left architects without commissions.

Private agencies were not equipped to handle the thousands of destitute families who applied for help. Nor could state and local governments provide sufficient relief. During the Depression three states and hundreds of municipalities went bankrupt trying to cope with widespread want at a time when tax revenues were declining sharply. Few, if any, Americans died of starvation during these appalling years. But many went hungry, and doctors saw thousands of cases of malnutrition.

What did the unemployed do to survive? When a family's savings had been exhausted, day-to-day survival became precarious. Families borrowed money from pawnbrokers, from friends, or against insurance policies, until no one would lend anymore. As in past periods of hard times, many jobless young men and women became "hobos," traveling by freight train, dodging railroad police, begging, or working at odd jobs. Some of the unemployed set up small, undercapitalized stores. Others sold apples on the streets. These pathetic efforts became symbols of pluck and determination, but they seldom succeeded.

The Great Cash and ensuing Great Depression spared neither working-class nor middle-class people, though clearly the former suffered more absolute deprivation. The Depression's near universality made it an exceptionally potent political force.

One of the most urgent problems of the unemployed was housing. Many families could not pay their rent or their mortgage and were evicted from their homes. A common sight on city streets was the "dispossessed" family sitting disconsolately on their streetside furniture, not knowing where to go. (A joke that made the rounds in 1933 was a version of an old classic. Bill asks Mike: "Who was that lady I saw you with last night at the sidewalk café?" Mike replies: "That was no lady; that was my wife. And that was no sidewalk café; that was my apartment furniture.") Thousands of Americans moved in with friends or relatives. On the outskirts of every large city the unemployed and their families took shelter in squatters' settlements thrown together from loose boards, packing crates, tin sheets, and cardboard. For the first time migration from country to city was reversed as young adults returned in droves to the rural homestead where at least there was enough food.

The Special Plight of Black Americans. Among the most unfortunate victims of the Great Depression were many of the nation's 12.5 million blacks. In the North, where black Americans had only recently found a toehold in industry, they were often the first to lose their jobs when employers cut back their work-force. In April 1931 some 35 percent of the black workers in Philadelphia were unemployed, compared with 24 percent of white wage earners. In the South the economic crisis provided a new basis for white bigotry. In Houston black and Mexican-American relief applicants were regularly turned down by officials. In Atlanta in 1930, a group of Klanlike "Black Shirts" paraded downtown carrying banners inscribed "Niggers, back to the cotton fields—city jobs are for white folks." But things were no better in the cotton fields. In 1931 the price of cotton slumped to 4.6 cents a pound, the lowest since 1894. Early that year a Red Cross worker in a rural cotton-growing area of Arkansas found that more than half the homes he visited did not have enough food to last forty-eight hours.

Women and Families.   Women, of course, shared the fate of their families, but the Depression imposed special burdens as well. With so many male "breadwinners" without work, employers, public and private, often sought to discourage women from taking jobs. There were also new male competitors for jobs formerly considered "women's work," such as elementary school teaching. Yet the Depression, if anything, increased the proportion of women, even married women, who joined the labor market. As the wages for men fell and as male family heads lost their jobs, more women looked for and found work. By the end of the Depression there were 25 percent more women working than in the late 1920s.

Family life was inevitably affected by the hard times. On the one hand divorce rates declined; it was simply too expensive to break up established male–female relationships. Better a less-than-perfect marriage than alimony, child support, and the rest. (Though there were many informal marriage breakups in the form of desertion.) On the other hand birth rates plummeted. Children were costly to raise and, in an urban society, could not be put to work for their families at an early age as on the farm in previous eras.

Life Goes on.   Yet a majority of Americans continued to work and to provide their families with the necessities of life. They even managed to enjoy them-selves. During the winter of 1929–1930 a craze for miniature golf took hold, and by the summer of 1930 thousands of Americans were tapping golf balls through little tunnels and over tiny bridges. By 1930 radio had produced its first superstars: Freeman F. Gosden and Charles J. Correll, both whites, who amused listeners with their comic stereotypes of the uneducated but shrewd black char-acters Amos 'n Andy. The theater flourished as well. In the fall of 1931 the big Broadway hit was *Of Thee I Sing,* a musical spoof of American politics. Through the worst years of the Depression, Hollywood continued to prosper. During the 1930s, 85 million Americans went to the nation's 17,000 movie houses each week to seek escape from the drabness and worries of their lives.

Popular music, too, helped people, especially the young, get through the hard days. New Orleans-type jazz had gone into eclipse with the end of good times. By the early 1930s black arrangers, including Edward ("Duke") Ellington, Fletcher Henderson, and Sy Oliver, had adapted jazz to the big-band format. Then, in 1935, clarinetist Benny Goodman created a sensation with a new sort of big-band dance music, called "swing." Thousands were soon dancing the Lindy Hop, the Suzie-Q, and the Big Apple to the arrangements of Tommy Dorsey, Glenn Miller, and Count Basie, as well as of Goodman, the "King of Swing," himself. In 1938 swing became a part of "culture" when the Goodman band gave a sensational concert at New York's Carnegie Hall.

■ HOOVER AND THE DEPRESSION ■

Viewing the 1930s from the present, the reaction of the federal government to the economic disaster seems inexplicably limited and slow. We must recognize that it took months before anyone could assess how serious the damage was. There was, moreover, a strong conviction that government could, or should, play only a limited role in financial crises and that self-righting forces would soon assert themselves.

Federal Inaction. Though Hoover had never been an extreme believer in laissez-faire, he and his administration initially rejected an active interventionist role in the economy. Secretary of the Treasury Andrew Mellon proposed doing nothing whatsoever and allowing the downturn to bottom out by itself. "Liquidate labor," Mellon advised, "liquidate the farmers, liquidate real estate. It will purge the rottenness out of the system. . . . Values will be adjusted and enterprising people will pick up the wreck from less competent people." The president, however, was never as committed to inaction as his treasury secretary. In November 1929 Hoover called a series of conferences of business and labor leaders and local government officials to consider the economic crisis. At his urging they pledged to maintain wages, desist from strikes, and continue the existing level of investment and local public works spending. Simultaneously, Hoover went to great pains to project optimism. The "fundamental business of the country," he told the public several days after the Crash, "is on a sound and prosperous basis."

As the dreary months passed, voluntary efforts to maintain spending, employment, and investment levels became grossly inadequate. The obvious solution was a public works program to get the unemployed back on the job and put money into the hands of consumers and investors. Hoover did increase the federal government's planned outlays for public projects, and because federal tax revenues had dropped sharply, he could not avoid a budget deficit in doing so. But he refused to allow the government to borrow money to finance public works, because he believed it would compete with weakened private industry for limited investment funds. Actually, with business prospects so shaky, there was no need for the president to worry about the government's outbidding private industry for limited capital.

Hoover was even more reluctant to use federal funds to relieve human misery than to stimulate recovery. For a man who had served as relief administrator for Europe during and immediately following World War I, he seemed strangely insensitive to his fellow citizens' misfortunes. It was dangerous to make people dependent on federal handouts, he argued; aid to the unemployed must come from voluntary organizations and local governments, not from Washington. Hoover's view disregarded realities. Private religious and charitable organizations could not come close to meeting the needs of the vast army of the unemployed; cities, counties, and states found themselves, as their revenues declined, overwhelmed by demands for social relief. Only the federal government could deal with a disaster that deprived millions of the nation's families of their fundamental means of support.

Hoover's Programs.　The president never endorsed direct federal outlays for relief, but gradually he came to see that something more than pep talks was needed to check the economic slide. To help restore the international economy, in 1931 he proposed a one-year moratorium on German reparations and the intergovernmental debts of the former Allies. This was a wise, if limited, move. But Hoover was inconsistent. The previous year, against the advice of the country's best economists, he had accepted a traditional Republican solution to economic difficulties and signed the Hawley-Smoot Tariff Act, which raised the already high American protective wall and further weakened international trade.

By late 1931 Hoover finally recognized that the federal government must intervene directly in the domestic economy to get the country moving again. In his State of the Union message to Congress that year, he proposed establishing an agency to lend federal funds to business to restore confidence, encourage growth, and increase employment. In compliance, Congress created the Reconstruction Finance Corporation (RFC) in 1932 and gave it a $500 million appropriation with authority to borrow $1.5 billion more. It could lend these funds to faltering banks, railroads, savings and loan associations, and industrial firms. In addition, the president signed into law measures providing new capital to federal land banks, liberalizing the credit-granting powers of the Federal Reserve System, and establishing home-loan banks to refinance home mortgages.

Hoover's liberal opponents labeled his program, particularly the RFC, a "breadline for big business" that only indirectly touched the predicament of ordinary men and women. To be fair to Hoover, his moves—though tardy and insufficient—were steps in the right direction. But the president got little credit from the public for more vigorous actions in the last two years of his administration. Herbert Hoover lacked the popular touch. Characteristically, through the worst years of his term, he continued to wear formal clothes when dining at the White House, even when he and his wife were eating alone. As the economic clouds became ever darker, the president's popularity plummeted. Soon people were referring to empty pockets turned inside out as "Hoover flags," shantytowns on the outskirts of cities as "Hoovervilles," and newspapers wrapped around the body for warmth as "Hoover blankets."

The Bonus Expeditionary Force.　Most difficult to forgive, in the public's estimate, was the president's treatment of the Bonus Army. World War I veterans were among the "forgotten men" of the Depression. In 1924 Congress had authorized a "delayed bonus" for veterans, to be paid in 1945. In 1931, over

Hoover's veto, Congress liberalized the law to allow former doughboys to borrow immediately up to 50 percent of the amount ultimately due them. This money was quickly spent, and veterans wondered why they should wait for the rest of it. In June 1932 several thousand veterans, calling themselves the Bonus Expeditionary Force (BEF), arrived in Washington, D.C., to demand immediate payment of the remainder of the bonus.

The veterans camped out in tents and shacks at Anacostia Flats, a vacant area on the edge of the city. They asked to see the president, but he refused to have anything to do with them. When Congress rejected a new bonus bill, 15,000 veterans resolved to "stay till 1945." The men, many of whom had brought their wives and children, were orderly and sober. Most were prepared to wait patiently for Congress to act. As the congressional session drew to a close, however, tensions mounted. Though reluctant to involve the federal government in what he considered a local police problem, Hoover called in the army when the District of Columbia officials asked for federal help.

The troops evicted the veterans from some abandoned buildings in the city and then, despite Hoover's orders, General Douglas MacArthur ordered his men onto Anacostia Flats. Firing tear gas in every direction, the soldiers put the tents and the shanties to the torch and drove the BEF out of the camp with bayonets and sabers. Over a hundred people were injured in the melee, and two infants died of tear-gas inhalation.

The scene at Anacostia shocked many Americans. Men who had served their nation bravely had been treated like dangerous revolutionaries. Hoover's standing, already low, dropped still further. The president was not responsible for ordering the attack; but he had refused to see the BEF leaders and he shared the blame for the outcome.

Hoover Defeated. The Bonus Army was not the only episode of confrontation during the first years of the Depression. In mid-1932 desperate midwestern farmers organized a "farm holiday" movement that stopped shipments of food to cities, halted the forced sale of farms whose impoverished owners had fallen behind in tax payments, and dumped underpriced milk into gutters. In parts of the country, meanwhile, hungry men looted stores and food delivery trucks. Early 1932 saw 3,000 unemployed men march on Henry Ford's River Rouge plant to demand jobs. Police used tear gas to stop them and then opened fire with revolvers and a machine gun, killing four.

Still more ominous to conservatives was rising public interest in socialism as a solution to the crisis. Big business, which had claimed so much credit for good times, now bore the brunt of the public's wrath when times turned bad, and angry voices began to denounce capitalism as a cruel fraud against humanity. In September 1932 the Marxist journal *New Masses* published a symposium in which prominent intellectuals Edmund Wilson, Clifton Fadiman, Sherwood Anderson, Upton Sinclair, and others declared that socialism alone could save the country. Two months later the Socialist party candidate for the presidency, Norman Thomas, received 880,000 votes, the largest Socialist vote since 1920.

There is no way of telling how much change in the existing social order Americans might have demanded if the nation had been forced to endure four more years of Hoover. Despair might have pushed Americans into communism or into a right-wing dictatorship such as emerged in central Europe in response to similar pressures. Fortunately, the two-party system provided orderly constitutional ways to express the public's anguish.

In the congressional elections of 1930 the Democrats came close to winning control of both the House and Senate. At this point they did not offer drastic ideological or programmatic alternatives to the Republicans. Many Democrats, in fact, were as conservative as Hoover. Yet as the party out of power, they could not be held responsible for the economic debacle. In the end the public got more than it expected.

By early 1931 the Democratic presidential front-runner was Franklin D. Roosevelt, the governor of New York. An only child born to comfort in Hyde Park, New York, Roosevelt had developed the confidence and poise that came with an assured position in society and the love of a doting mother. Though from an upper-class family, he was a Democrat who had supported Wilson for president. In 1913 he became assistant secretary of the navy, and in 1920 he received the vice presidential nomination of his party. During the 1920s he contracted polio, and for the rest of his life was unable to walk or stand without assistance. Though he failed to recover his mobility, the experience confirmed FDR's sense that any obstacle could be overcome with enough determination. Encouraged by his strong-willed wife, Eleanor, he refused to give up politics. In 1928 he ran for governor of New York and was elected, although Smith, the party's presidential candidate, went down to defeat.

In 1930 Roosevelt was reelected governor in a landslide. During his second term, as the Depression spread, he proved to be a vigorous and compassionate leader who used his power to alleviate the plight of the state's unemployed. Surrounded by astute political managers, and a proven vote-getter in the nation's then most populous state, FDR won the 1932 Democratic presidential nomination handily. In a lackluster convention, the Republicans renominated Hoover without opposition.

The campaign was not an inspiring one. Neither party platform was especially bold or innovative. Nevertheless, Roosevelt promised increased aid to the unemployed and endorsed government involvement in electric power generation, national resource planning, and federal regulation of utilities and the stock market. The Democrats also favored the repeal of Prohibition. Hoover warned that Roosevelt's election would worsen the country's economic plight; but everywhere he went, he was greeted with hoots, catcalls, and hostile demonstrators accusing him of killing veterans or of personally causing the country's economic problems. He soon became his party's worst liability, a man exuding gloom from every pore. On election day, as expected, Roosevelt and the Democrats were swept in with 23 million votes to Hoover's 16 million. FDR captured 282 counties that had never gone Democratic before. Both House and Senate also went overwhelmingly for the Democrats.

■ FDR'S NEW DEAL ■

In the four months between the election and Roosevelt's inauguration, the economy plunged to new lows. During the early weeks of 1933 virtually every bank in the country stopped paying its depositors or tottered on the edge of doing so. To stave off legal bankruptcy, by March 4 the governors of thirty-eight states had been forced to declare "holidays," allowing the banks to close their doors rather than acknowledge insolvency. By the eve of the inauguration it seemed that the whole financial structure on which American capitalism rested was about to crumble.

During these dismal lame duck weeks, President Hoover tried to enlist Roosevelt's cooperation on emergency measures. The president-elect listened to Hoover's suggestions but, unwilling to tie his hands, refused to commit himself and his administration to anything specific.

The First Hundred Days.   Roosevelt's inaugural address of March 4 set the tone for the early months of what would be called the New Deal. He proposed federal public works measures, legislation to redistribute population from the cities to the country, to raise the prices of agricultural products, to end home and farm mortgage foreclosure, to cut costs at all levels of government, to improve and make more efficient relief measures, and finally, to tighten federal regulation of banking and stock speculation. His specific proposals were less important than his tone and manner, however. In a resonant voice the president told the American people that "fear itself" was the chief danger and that if they submitted to sacrifice and discipline, all would be well. If necessary he was prepared to ask for broad emergency powers similar to those he would need if the nation were facing a foreign invasion.

The response to the address was remarkable. In the succeeding days the White House received a half million letters and telegrams from people who were cheered by the president"s words. "It was the finest thing this side of heaven," wrote one citizen. "It seemed to give the people, as well as myself, a new hold on life," exclaimed another. Actually, Roosevelt had not moved much beyond his campaign proposals, but he had conveyed some of his own jaunty optimism and given people the feeling that there was now a strong hand at the helm.

Yet Roosevelt had few specific remedies in hand. Although influenced by the progressivism of his youth, he was not a brilliant economist or a man with a clear-cut set of principles to guide him. At times these deficiencies would create confusion and lead to serious mistakes. But FDR had some impressive assets, notably his open-mindedness and willingness to experiment. "Take a method and try it," he advised. "If it fails, admit it frankly and try another." And he had gathered around him a talented array of advisers, a so-called Brain Trust— drawn from the universities, from law, and from the social work profession— who could supply him with the ideas he himself lacked.

The new president's first move, on March 5, was to order the nation's banks closed. The four-day federal bank holiday was accompanied by an order that, in effect, took the country off the gold standard. Four days later, acting with the enthusiasm it had never shown Hoover, Congress passed the Emergency Banking Act, confirming the bank closings and providing for an orderly reopening of those that proved sound. The administration's bold action reassured the American people, who expressed their confidence in the president when the banks reopened by redepositing the cash they had earlier withdrawn in panic.

The bank holiday was the first shot of a whirlwind hundred-day war on defeatism, despair, and decline such as Americans had never witnessed before. The assault was marked by confusion and contradiction and did not end the Depression. But it did check the decline and restore a sense of forward motion to the American people.

The AAA (1933) was the New Deal's major effort to deal with the acute farm crisis. Farmers would be encouraged to reduce their output or acreage of seven basic commodities by a fee from the proceeds of a special tax levied on food processors (millers, meat-packers, canners, and so on). Scarcity would check the price slide and ultimately raise farm income. The parallel National Industrial Recovery Act (NIRA) was designed to further industrial recovery. It established the National Recovery Administration (NRA) with the power to negotiate codes of "fair competition" with representatives of the nation's major industries. These codes would set prices and assign production quotas to individual firms. Though the authors of the law added language expressing concern over creating monopolies that might squeeze consumers, in reality the measure represented a suspension of antitrust principles. Labor, too, was handed a gift. Section 7(a) of the NIRA required that every code provide for collective bargaining for labor and comply with presidential guidelines for minimum pay rates and maximum working hours. Tacked on to the NIRA as Title II was a provision establishing a Public Works Administration (PWA) with a $3.3 billion budget to undertake large-scale public construction projects.

The two major recovery measures fell far short of their goals. By the time the AAA went into effect in the spring of 1933, southern farmers and sharecroppers had already planted many acres of cotton, and in the corn belt millions of sows had produced their annual litters. To keep this supply of fiber and food from coming to market and further weakening prices, the Department of Agriculture had to persuade cotton growers to uproot a quarter of their crop. In September 1933 it induced farmers to destroy 6 million pigs. Some of the pork was given to people on relief. Nevertheless, the wholesale destruction of commodities at a time when people were hungry and ill-clothed seemed irrational to many Americans. More serious was an unanticipated social effect. Reducing cotton production squeezed sharecroppers off the land. Those who remained, both black and white, were often deprived by landlords of the federal cash due them.

Despite the AAA's failings, during the two years following its passage, farm income more than doubled. Some of the gains represented direct payments to farmers for cutting production; some came from the higher prices that reduced output encouraged. But the AAA was responsible for only a part of the advance. Higher wheat prices, for example, owed as much to the severe drought that parched the Great Plains between 1932 and 1935 as to government programs.

The drought turned a vast area stretching from Texas to the Dakotas into a "dust bowl," where the skies were obscured by blowing topsoil and crops withered. Meanwhile, thousands of tenant farmers in Oklahoma and Arkansas were uprooted. Imprecisely called "Okies," many became "gasoline gypsies" and set off in jalopies for the warmth, jobs, and presumed easy living of southern California. The sharp drop in wheat production added substantially to the impact of the AAA wheat program. When the federal judiciary declared the tax on food processors unconstitutional, the AAA's major crop-reduction features were reincorporated into a new law, the Soil Conservation and Domestic Allotment Act (1936).

Unlike the AAA, the NIRA was almost a complete disappointment. The flamboyant NRA administrator, General Hugh S. Johnson, had hoped to use the PWA to beef up demand by putting people to work. But Roosevelt handed over the agency to Secretary of the Interior Harold Ickes, depriving Johnson of one of his tools for success. Working with what he had, Johnson bullied the nation's largest industries into writing codes of fair practices that included mandatory collective bargaining for employees and limitations on child labor. In return for these, however, the NRA authorized price-fixing and output limitations and allowed big business to adopt policies that injured small firms.

But the greatest disappointment of the NIRA was that it failed to revive industry. The government gave its program a symbol—a blue eagle—and a slogan—"We Do Out Part." Blue eagle parades wound through the downtowns of a score of cities; blue eagle stickers were plastered over store fronts and factory windows. For a time the ballyhoo boosted investor confidence and consumer morale and probably kept the Depression from worsening. But the agency established no effective machinery for restarting silent mills and factories, and industrial production remained stalled. When in May 1935 the Supreme Court struck down the code-making sections of the NIRA as unconstitutional, few people, even in the administration, mourned the agency's passing.

Fiscal Stimulus.   It is easy to see today why the two major recovery measures failed. In addition to their unfortunate side effects, they did little to increase investment rates or consumer spending. Under the circumstances of the day, only the government, by spending on a large scale, could have given the economy the stimulus it needed.

The treasury under Roosevelt did spend more money than it took in. The RFC gave money to the banks to help them expand their loans. The Home Owners Loan Corporation (HOLC) dispensed billions of dollars to savings and loan associations to refinance mortgages. The PWA, which survived the Supreme Court's invalidation of the NIRA, poured millions into major federal works projects. Between 1933 and 1939 the agency built 70 percent of the nation's new schools and 65 percent of its new city halls, sewage plants, and courthouses. It was responsible for more than a third of all the new hospitals. It funded university libraries, the Lincoln Tunnel connecting New York and New Jersey, the causeway linking the Florida Keys to the mainland, and many other outstanding construction projects.

Whatever his critics charged, however, Roosevelt was never a deliberate "big spender." He believed that a little "pump priming" by government could be useful, but he worried about running the treasury consistently in the red. Federal spending exceeded federal income in every year of the New Deal, but the deficits were always incidental to relief; they were never part of a deliberate program. Nor were they ever large enough to spark a complete recovery. Few in the Roosevelt administration had read the works of the apostle of deliberate deficit spending, English economist John Maynard Keynes, though Marriner Eccles, a Utah banker who headed the Federal Reserve Board, was an instinctive Keynesian.

Relief.   By far the largest outpouring of federal funds throughout the New Deal Era went to jobs and relief for the unemployed. Although conservative in fiscal matters, FDR, unlike Hoover, put the welfare of ordinary men and women before a balanced budget.

As part of the First Hundred Days, Congress established the Civilian Conservation Corps (CCC). The corps took 2.5 million idle young men on relief rolls and put them to work on public lands at $30 a month planting trees, building forest ranger stations, clearing branches, and restoring historic battlefields. Congress also created the Federal Emergency Relief Administration (FERA) and appropriated $500 million for local and state relief agencies to distribute to the unemployed. Administering the program was a fast-talking, poker-playing young social worker, Harry L. Hopkins, who believed that jobs, rather than outright charity, were needed to restore individual morale and self-respect. In late 1933 Hopkins persuaded Roosevelt to establish the Civil Works Administration (CWA) with funds drawn from FERA and the PWA to put the unemployed directly on the federal payroll. By mid-January 1934 the CWA was providing 4 million men and women with a steady paycheck averaging $15 a week. But the president worried that it was too expensive and would create a permanent class of government dependents. By summer Roosevelt had shut down the program and returned relief to the local governments.

It did not remain there for very long, for the local authorities simply did not have the means to carry the burden. In January 1935 Roosevelt asked Congress for $5 billion to support other work relief programs. The men would be employed on various government projects at wages higher than the straight dole under FERA, but lower than the amount paid by CWA. Congress responded to the president's request and made the largest single appropriation in the nation's history. Secretary Ickes wanted it devoted to long-term projects under his PWA. Hopkins wanted it for short-term projects like those of his CWA. In the end Roosevelt allotted most of the money to a new agency, the Works Progress Administration (WPA), under Hopkins's direction.

For the remainder of the Depression, the WPA was the major distributor of government funds to the unemployed and an important stimulant to the economy. Government spending, however incidental, pushed up the GNP and cut into unemployment. By 1935 the number of jobless had declined from almost 13 million, or 24.9 percent of the labor force, to 10.6 million, a little over 20 percent of those seeking work.

The WPA under Harry Hopkins sought to rescue people in the arts, as well as other Americans, from idleness during the Depression. Moses Soyer here, in Artists on WPA, depicts a room full of WPA painters using their skills and earning some money in the process. (Courtesy of Art Resource, NY)

The relief programs cannot be measured solely by their statistical consequences, however. True, much of the WPA outlay went to make-work projects. But Hopkins was an imaginative man who saw that artists, writers, intellectuals, and performers were also victims of the economic collapse. Under his direction the WPA sponsored programs to put these people to work enriching community life, while preserving their own skills. Hundreds of musicians were paid to perform in school auditoriums and community halls. Artists were hired to paint murals for the new federal courthouses and post offices built with PWA funds. Writers were set to work compiling state guidebooks. Many talented writers— including Saul Bellow, Ralph Ellison, Richard Wright, and Arthur Miller—owed their starts to the Federal Writers Project or the Federal Theater Project under the WPA. The WPA also established a National Youth Administration to give part-time work to college and high school students to enable them to complete their studies.

Reform and Innovation.   The president had promised reform and innovation along with relief and recovery, and he came through on his promises. A series of New Deal measures sought to end stock market abuses by placing the management of Wall Street under the new Securities and Exchange Commission (SEC). The banking system was made more secure and stable by creation of the Federal Deposit Insurance Corporation (FDIC) to insure depositors' accounts and prevent the sort of panic withdrawals that had almost destroyed the banking system following the Crash.

The most original program of the First Hundred Days was the Tennessee Valley Authority (TVA). In May 1933 FDR secured congressional approval of the TVA, a resource-management project long advocated by Senator George Norris of Nebraska and other conservationists who were dismayed at the physical and social deterioration of the potentially rich Tennessee River valley and the waste of its precious water resources. The agency was given the authority to build dams, manufacture fertilizer, undertake soil conservation and reforestation measures, and join with local authorities within the seven-state valley in various social improvement projects. Between 1933 and 1944 the authority built nine major dams, bringing low-cost lighting and power to valley homes and farms and providing new recreational facilities on the man-made lakes created. Cheap power attracted large industries to the region, especially during World War II. Together with reforestation and soil conservation, inexpensive electricity helped reverse the valley's long decline, turning it into one of the more prosperous parts of the South.

For all its benefits the TVA represented an old-fashioned sort of conservation. From a modern ecological point of view its virtues seem limited. Its disruption of the natural environment and its focus on maximizing energy use would not get high marks today. In fact, it is doubtful if the project could have passed the environmental impact tests imposed on new developments in the twenty-first century. But for decades the TVA would be cited as a triumph of the New Deal at its best.

■ FRIENDS AND ENEMIES ■

The early months of the New Deal were a tumultuous time. The public wavered between fear and hope, still stunned by the economic catastrophe but encouraged by the new surge of energy in the nation's capital. Congress gave Roosevelt almost everything he wanted without looking too closely at the cost or questioning the wisdom of his proposals. As the months passed, however, opposition mounted at both ends of the political spectrum, and by 1935 Roosevelt and the New Deal were beset by critics and enemies.

Thunder on the Right.   Despite the new legislation to regulate and constrain the banks and Wall Street, FDR was not a foe of business. Many of his advisers were conservative men who endorsed business–government cooperation. Their views had been incorporated into the NIRA. Unfortunately for FDR, once the worst of the economic crisis had passed and businesspeople lost their fear of total collapse, many began to accuse the New Deal of unwarranted interference with the economy, fiscal irresponsibility, and socialist leanings. In August 1934 a group of conservative Democrats and executives of Du Pont, General Motors, and other large corporations organized the Liberty League to fight the "further aggrandizement of an ever-spreading governmental bureaucracy."

At the same time a more formidable conservative challenge came from the Supreme Court. Composed of men whose average age was over seventy, the Court was dominated by some of the most tradition-bound lawyers in the American bar. On May 27, 1935, in the Schechter case, it struck down the NIRA on the grounds that it unconstitutionally conferred legislative power on the executive branch. Shortly after, in *United States* v. *Butler,* the Court invalidated the AAA on the grounds that the processing tax to pay farmers was primarily a means to regulate production and exceeded Congress's powers under the Constitution. If the principles of the AAA were allowed to stand, federal taxing power could be used to regulate industry throughout the United States.

The Attack of the Left.   Roosevelt also came under attack from the political left. Most Americans retained their faith in private property and a market economy during the Depression years, but an influential segment of intellectuals, artists, journalists, academics, and trade union leaders came to believe that the only hope for America lay in a socialist state. The apparent success of the Soviet "experiment" clinched the argument. While capitalism was reeling in the United States, the Soviet economy seemed to be forging ahead under Joseph Stalin's bold Five-Year Plans. Capitalism appeared to be in its death throes while Soviet socialism had, some said, solved the problems of growth, unemployment, and economic inequality.

American Marxists attacked the New Deal as too little, too late. The Socialist party leader, Norman Thomas, at first was friendly to Roosevelt. By 1935, however, the socialists were denouncing the New Deal as "the greatest fraud among all the utopias." Whether right or wrong, the American socialists were at least their own masters. In 1934 Earl Browder, head of the Communist Party of the United States, called the New Deal "a program of hunger, fascization, and imperialist war." When, after 1935, the Soviet Union sought a policy of cooperation with the western democracies to stop Hitler and Nazi Germany, Browder and his colleagues ceased their attacks. Under a new "United Front" policy, the New Deal and Roosevelt became acceptable.

The Neopopulists.   The Socialists and Communists were at most an annoyance to Roosevelt. The real political challenge from the left came from a collection of neopopulists in the dissenting tradition of the West and South.

Closest to the Populist heritage was Senator Huey Long, the Louisiana "Kingfish." An earthy man who wore pink suits, called fellow officeholders "dime-a-dozen punks," and conducted public business in pajamas and a silk bathrobe, Long was also a shrewd politician who knew that the times cried out for a savior. As governor of Louisiana during the late twenties he had raised taxes on the state's corporations and used the money to build bridges, hospitals, mental institutions, and schools. Long had employed any weapon at hand to carry out his program, including physical intimidation, political blackmail, and kidnaping. His opponents considered him a dictator.

In 1932 Long came to Washington as a Democratic senator. He had supported Roosevelt during the election, but within six months he had turned against him and the new Deal. In part the argument between Long and Roosevelt was a clash between two strong and ambitious men. But they also disagreed ideologically. The Kingfish wanted to "share the wealth" by taxing away all large incomes and fortunes and giving every citizen a lump sum gift of $5,000 and a guaranteed income of $2,000 a year. Long's proposal to make "every man a king" appealed to millions of ordinary people, but Roosevelt, as many others, considered him a rabble-rousing demagogue and one of the most dangerous men in America. The Senator and the administration were soon at war.

Another outspoken critic of the New Deal was Father Charles E. Coughlin, a Catholic priest from Royal Oak, Michigan. Coughlin's radio broadcasts of sermons and commentary had begun in the late 1920s, and by 1933 the golden-voiced "radio priest" had an audience of millions. Like Long, he first supported the New Deal, but turned against FDR when the president refused to endorse inflationary measures to end the Depression. In late 1934 Coughlin formed the National Union for Social Justice, a pressure group advocating silver inflation and the nationalization of power, oil, light, and natural gas companies, and ultimately the seizure of the banks as well. At various times he was denounced by Catholic prelates for his rhetorical excesses, especially his anti-Semitism; but secure in the support of his own bishop, he continued to attack Roosevelt and those he called the "money-lenders."

A third populist challenge came from an aging California physician, Francis E. Townsend. A generous man with a tender heart, Townsend was outraged by the lack of public concern for the elderly victims of the Depression. To rescue them and aid the distressed nation generally, he proposed that all persons over sixty be given pensions of $200 a month on condition that they retire from their jobs and "spend the money as they get it." The scheme, he declared, would simultaneously remove thousands of older workers from the overcrowded job market and inject millions of dollars of fresh purchasing power into the economy.

The Townsend Plan quickly won a following among older people and was incorporated into a bill introduced in Congress in early 1935. Critics attacked the measure as unworkable and unfair to the great majority of Americans under sixty. Many of its opponents were conservatives who saw the plan as socialistic, but Frances Perkins, FDR's secretary of labor, also derided it as a crackpot scheme. The *Townsend Weekly*, the doctor's editorial voice, soon responded with an angry attack on the administration.

The Roosevelt Coalition.   Fortunately for Roosevelt, he had also won many friends. By 1935 millions of Americans had reason to thank the New Deal and the Democratic party for their help. Artists, writers, and musicians were grateful for the opportunity under the WPA to do productive work and maintain their skills and talents. Young people were grateful for the subsidy from the National Youth Administration that allowed them to stay in school and prepare for careers. Middle-class homeowners sang Roosevelt's praises for sparing them the humiliation of eviction from their homes through a timely HOLC loan. Unemployed factory workers could thank the president for the relief payments that kept them from hunger. Farmers welcomed cash under AAA and its replacements. For many millions of citizens, the federal government for the first time seriously touched their lives and the contact seemed protective and benign.

Black Americans were especially grateful to Roosevelt and his party. Not since Reconstruction had black Americans received as good a shake from their government as now. Not that the administration's policies were ideal in racial terms: The AAA programs, as administered, had hurt black sharecroppers and Roosevelt, needing southern votes in Congress, was unwilling to attack the racial caste system of the South. A federal antilynching bill he endorsed was filibustered to death in the Senate. Nonetheless, blacks shared in WPA programs; the National Youth Administration helped many hundreds of young black men and women. When the New Deal adopted a slum-clearance program, blacks would become prominent beneficiaries of the new public housing. New Dealers, moreover, were often solicitous of black pride. Eleanor Roosevelt and Secretary Harold Ickes, particularly, accorded recognition to talented black men and women, supported black aspirations, and sought to further the cause of civil rights. When the Daughters of the American Revolution refused to allow the distinguished black contralto Marian Anderson to sing at Washington's Constitution Hall, Secretary Ickes invited her to use the steps of the Lincoln Memorial for an open-air concert. Black Americans appreciated the benefits of the New Deal and ignored its deficiencies. Many broke their traditional Republican ties and shifted their votes to the Democratic column.

By late 1935 organized labor had also joined the Roosevelt camp. During the 1920s, as we saw, the unions had declined in power and numbers. After 1924 leadership of the labor movement rested in the conservative hands of William Green, Samuel Gompers's successor as head of the American Federation of Labor. Green did little to counteract the decline in union membership and influence; nor was he interested in bringing the millions of new industrial wage earners into organized labor's house. There were a few industrial unions in the nation—the feeble United Mine Workers under the unpredictable John L. Lewis and two unions of garment workers under Sidney Hillman and David Dubinsky. But these were exceptional. Unlike skilled craftspeople, most factory workers and miners were unorganized.

Then came the NIRA and its Section 7a, authorizing collective bargaining in industries that adopted NIRA fair-practice codes. The administration to enforce the NIRA labor provision pursued a vigorous policy of encouraging labor unions and collective bargaining. Before long thousands of workers, inspired by labor organizers' claim that "the president wants you to unionize," were flocking into both old and new labor organizations, glad to oblige the president and certain that he wished them well. Roosevelt was at first indifferent to organized labor. But many prominent New Dealers, particularly Senator Robert F. Wagner of New York and Secretary of Labor Frances Perkins (the first woman cabinet member), were strongly pro-union. Whether he deserved it or not, FDR would come to be seen as the champion of the working man and woman against their enemies the "bosses" and the "economic royalists."

■ THE SOCIAL WELFARE STATE ■

The first New Deal had been devoted largely to recovery and relief. Of the two goals, only the second had met with any large measure of success. In 1935 growing opposition, particularly from the neopopulists, and the sense that the New Deal had stalled, pushed Roosevelt into a new program to weaken the power of big business, equalize opportunity, and increase economic security. In a burst of energy known as the Second Hundred Days, or the Second New Deal, the administration transformed the nation by creating the modern social welfare state.

The stimulus for the new tack may have been immediate problems, but the inspiration was derived from the reform impulse of the early twentieth century. The Second New Deal elevated the progressive social welfare programs, largely confined to the states before 1917 to the national level. Now the federal government would not only complete the job of subduing the "vested interests" but also make Washington the guardian of the weak and unfortunate and the source of security for all Americans.

In June 1935 the president sent Congress a list of "must" legislation consisting of four crucial items: a social security bill, a measure to replace the collective bargaining provision of the defunct NIRA, a banking regulation proposal, and a new income tax with rates that rose sharply as income increased. In addition, he demanded that Congress pass several important secondary measures to expand social and economic benefits for various segments of the nation.

Labor's New Charter. Over the next few months FDR got most of what he asked for. In July Congress passed the National Labor Relations Act (also called the Wagner Act, after its chief sponsor, Senator Robert Wagner of New York), establishing a permanent National Labor Relations Board with the authority to supervise elections to determine whether workers in an industry wanted union representation. The union, if approved, would become the legal collective bargaining agent for its members, whether employers liked it or not.

The Wagner Act would prove a powerful weapon in the struggle to organize the nation's industrial workers. But many obstacles remained. For years employers had successfully used labor spies, strikebreakers, strong-arm methods, and legal injunctions to defeat unionization in the mines and factories, and they were certain to fight back now. Nor could the industrial union organizers expect much help from the AFL, whose leaders considered the growth of industrial unionism a threat to their own power and were contemptuous of the semiskilled workers of immigrant stock who labored in the factories and mines. When, at the 1935 annual AFL convention, president William Green and his friends refused to support the principle of industrial unionism, dissenters Sidney Hillman, David Dubinsky, and John L. Lewis set up the Committee for Industrial Organization. In 1938, under the name Congress of Industrial Organizations (CIO), it became a separate and competing national labor federation.

The steel industry was the first target of CIO organizers. Several of the smaller steel firms resisted unionization. On Memorial Day 1937, outside Republic Steel, strikers and the police clashed violently, leaving several strikers dead and many injured. The giant of the industry, United States Steel, however, quickly capitulated, signing an agreement with the steelworkers in March 1937 recognizing the union as their collective bargaining agent. The automobile industry was tougher, but it, too, yielded. In February 1937, after a series of dramatic sit-down strikes in which workers refused to leave the plants until their demands were met, General Motors surrendered and recognized the United Automobile Workers. Ford Motor Company, under the fiercely individualistic Henry Ford, held out for many more months, using hoodlums and spies to help break the union drive. But in 1940 Ford, too, capitulated. By the eve of World War II the entire auto industry had been unionized.

By 1941, as a result of the Wagner Act and the doggedness of Lewis, Hillman, and other leaders of industrial labor, the number of men and women belonging to unions had swelled to a record 8.4 million—23 percent of the nonfarm labor force. It would not be easy for the politicians to ignore labor representatives again. The successful organizing of industrial labor seemed to be a power shift as dramatic as any that had taken place since the Civil War.

Social Security.   The next installment of Second Hundred Days "must" legislation had consequences that were even more far-reaching than the Wagner Act. Advanced progressives had long championed a system of social security for the unemployed, the handicapped, the sick, and the aged. Other nations had adopted such schemes, but in the United States health costs, job loss, and retirement uncertainties were problems left to the individual or to private charities to solve. The Social Security Act of 1935 established a system of unemployment insurance under the joint administration of the states and the federal government, financed by a payroll tax levied on employers. It set up a pension scheme for retired people over sixty-five and their survivors to be paid for by a tax levied equally on both employers and employees. Finally, it provided federal funds to the states to aid the destitute blind and provide support for delinquent, crippled, dependent and homeless children, and for establishing public health and maternity care programs, and vocational rehabilitation services.

The United States had finally joined the ranks of the other advanced industrial nations in providing economic security for its citizens. But it was at best a qualified commitment. Roosevelt backed off including a comprehensive health insurance scheme in his Social Security package when the American Medical Association, speaking for the nation's doctors, attacked it as "socialized medicine" that would damage the doctor–patient relationship and make the medical system heavy with bureaucracy. And even within its limited scope the original Social Security legislation was imperfect. The old-age pension plan as enacted excluded farm workers and the self-employed, for example. The sums provided were often skimpy. A later generation would plug some of the gaps and beef up the amounts but would also allow the aid-to-dependent-children provision to become a dole for a permanent class of healthy adult "welfare" clients unwilling to take care of themselves.

Additional "Must" Legislation.   Still other legislation of the Second Hundred Days fulfilled or reinforced old progressive promises. The Public Utility Holding Company Act gave the federal government control over interstate transmission of electricity and gas. It also conferred on the new Security and Exchange Commission power over monopolistic corporate holding companies. The Wealth Tax Act increased estate and gift tax rates and imposed stiffer levies on high-income recipients. The final "must" law was the Banking Act of 1935, which strengthened the federal government's control over the Federal Reserve System and gave the hitherto weak Federal Reserve Board a more effective voice in the management of the country's monetary affairs.

Several measures of the Second New Deal were designed specifically to improve the quality of rural life. In May 1935 Congress established a Rural Electrification Administration (REA). In a few years this agency brought electricity to millions of the nation's farms, created large new markets for electrical appliances, and dramatically changed the lives of farm families. The Soil Conservation and Domestic Allotment Act of 1936 rescued the crop-limitation features of the AAA by paying farmers not to grow "soil-depleting" crops. The Frazier-Lemke Farm Mortgage Moratorium Act extended farm mortgages for three years to save hard-pressed farmers from foreclosures.

Conservatives often criticized New Dealers as "planners," a term equivalent among some critics to "socialists." In reality, besides the Tennessee Valley thority, the Resettlement Administration (RA) was one of the few deliberate New Deal attempts at social planning, in this case to eliminate the chronic problem of rural poverty. Established by Roosevelt as part of Federal Emergency Relief Administration, the RA sought to move farmers from unfertile, "submarginal" land where they lived at bare subsistence levels to farms where they could support themselves in modest comfort. The federal government would provide subsistence farmers with better acreage, low-cost loans, and expert advice. Under Rexford Tugwell, one of Roosevelt's liberal brain trusters, the underfunded agency succeeded only in relocating some 4,000 poor farmers and sharecroppers. The RA's successor, the Farm Security Administration (established by the 1937 Bankhead-Jones Farm Tenancy Act), took on the special task of converting tenant farmers into farm owners. It, too, was starved for money and made little dent in the problem of rural poverty.

■ END OF THE NEW DEAL ■

By the end of the Second Hundred Days the 1936 presidential campaign was well underway. Roosevelt easily won his party's renomination. The Republicans turned to Governor Alfred M. Landon of Kansas, a modest, likable man with progressive leanings. To the left of the Democrats—or to the right, some insisted—was the Union party, whose nominee, William Lemke of North Dakota, was a farmer-laborite in the Populist tradition. In all likelihood Huey Long would have headed the third-party ticket had he not been assassinated by one of his many Louisiana enemies in September 1935.

The campaign outcome was never really in doubt. By now a new political coalition had formed around Roosevelt, composed not only of the Democratic party's traditional southern whites, Catholics, and urban ethnics, but also of blacks, Mexican-Americans, intellectuals, organized labor, and a big slice of the Protestant lower middle class. Many of these voters were beneficiaries of New Deal programs. But they also revered FDR as a man and a leader. Millions listened to his "fireside chats" on the radio and felt that their government cared.

Conservatives called Roosevelt a dictator who had seized unheard-of powers over every aspect of American life. They denounced the "bloated" federal bureaucracy and warned that "big government" would soon dominate every other institution. They were not entirely wrong. No president had ever achieved such power over the economy and over so many people's lives. The combination of big government and a vigorous leader who had a rare rapport with the people focused more attention on Washington, D.C., than ever before.

Whatever drawbacks time would disclose in this arrangement, in 1936 only a minority of Americans took the conservatives' warnings seriously. In November the voters turned out in record numbers and expressed their enthusiastic support of the Democrats. Roosevelt carried every state in the union except rock-ribbed Republican Maine and Vermont and won the most impressive popular mandate in American political history: almost 28 million votes to Landon's 17 million. In the congressional contest the results were equally lopsided. When the new Congress convened, the Democratic side of the House was so crowded that many of the new Democrats were forced to sit with the opposition.

In his second inaugural address Roosevelt promised to extend New Deal social and economic programs to meet the needs of the "one third of a nation" that was "ill-housed, ill-clad, ill-nourished." It was a call for a new burst of reform, and he secured a part of what he wanted. In September 1937 the National Housing Act (Wagner-Steagall Act) initiated a generation of federal slum clearance and public housing projects for the urban poor. The Agricultural Adjustment Act of 1938, without the unconstitutional processing tax, restored the crop-limitation provisions of the first AAA and made farm price supports a permanent feature of the American economy. The Food, Drug, and Cosmetic Act of June 1938 strengthened the consumer-protection features of the progressives' Pure Food and Drug Act of 1906. The Fair Labor Standards Act established for the first time a federally mandated minimum hourly wage and a maximum workweek for millions of workers in occupations involved in interstate commerce. But the Fair Labor Standards Act was the last important piece of New Deal legislation. Thereafter New Deal initiatives ceased. The effort to overhaul America and promote recovery had run out of steam.

Given Roosevelt's overwhelming vote of confidence in 1936 and the top-heavy Democratic majority in Congress in 1937 and 1938, this outcome is startling. Yet it is understandable if we consider where the nation was at this point. Despite every New Deal effort, the economy had failed to make a complete recovery. In 1937, though the nation's output forged ahead, unemployment remained at 14.3 percent of the labor force. Growth, moreover, had been accompanied by sharp price rises. Fearing inflation, in June Roosevelt cut back sharply on federal spending, throwing the economy into an unexpected tailspin. By the following year unemployment was back to 19 percent of the workforce. Roosevelt checked the descent by quickly increasing relief and other outlays, but it was clear to everyone that the country had not solved its chronic unemployment problem.

The persistence of hard times undoubtedly damaged New Deal zest and morale. Nothing seemed to work—or work well—and the administration seemed to have no new ideas. FDR's inability to get the economy going again injured his prestige within his own party. Divisions between northern liberals and southern conservatives, which had been papered over by the mutual concern for recovery, now broke through. Within months of the November electoral victory, the Democrats were in disarray, squabbling with one another and uncertain which way to turn.

At this point Roosevelt launched an ill-considered attack on the Supreme Court. FDR saw the Court as a bastion of judicial conservatism. It had struck down the AAA and the NIRA and had declared unconstitutional the Frazier-Lemke Act as well as several other New Deal measures. Roosevelt feared that it would wipe from the books the major social legislation of 1935–1936.

The justices were almost all elderly men, and Roosevelt might have allowed resignations and deaths to change the Court's profile. Instead, in February 1937 he asked Congress for the power to name up to six new judges, one for each incumbent who refused to resign after reaching seventy years of age. This scheme to "pack the Court" with more liberal judges stirred up a storm. Predictably, conservatives saw it as an attempt to subvert the Constitution. But even liberals balked at the proposal to undermine the Court's independence. When the "nine old men," perhaps intimidated by the president's stand, unexpectedly sustained several crucial pieces of New Deal legislation and several liberal state laws, the Court-packing bill's congressional support melted away. In late July the Senate sent the bill back to the Judiciary Committee, where it quietly died. The president had suffered a major legislative defeat, almost his first, and the blow to his prestige was damaging. Thereafter, as confidence in Roosevelt's leadership waned, southern Democrats would increasingly side with conservative Republicans against their own party's leader.

The loss of support was also expressed by the public at the polls. In the 1938 congressional elections, hoping to strengthen the liberal contingent in Congress, Roosevelt urged Democrats to defeat conservatives in the party congressional primaries. Many voters, resenting interference in local politics, ignored the president's wishes. In the elections the Democrats lost eighty-one seats in the House and eight in the Senate. Losses in midterm national elections are not unusual for the party in power, and in any case the 1936 Democratic congressional majority was too lopsided to last. Nevertheless, it was clear that many citizens had lost confidence in the man and the party they had turned to save the country. In the turbulent years that followed, Roosevelt continued to be admired as the country's savior; but for all intents and purposes the New Deal was incapable of further innovation.

■ CONCLUSIONS ■

The New Deal did not usher in a revolution of the scope of the Russian upheaval of 1917, for example. The United States remained a capitalist nation after 1938. But it would be capitalist with a difference. In the words of economist John Maynard Keynes, Roosevelt had made himself "the trustee" for all those who sought "to mend the evil of our condition by reasoned experiment within the framework of the existing social system." Never again would Americans be completely exposed to the uncertainties of a freewheeling economy qualified only in favor of business. The government's ability to restore full employment by massive deficit spending was still unproved. But after 1939 it would be difficult for any president to insist that the business cycle had to work itself out no matter what the human cost.

Even more important, the New Deal created permanent safeguards against another collapse and against private insecurity. Perhaps a more rigorous system of progressive taxation and a better-funded and more sustained social welfare program might have created a more egalitarian system. But that FDR could have achieved a socialist society, as some later critics have implied—even assuming that this goal was desirable—is doubtful. Public fear in 1933 gave Roosevelt a broad mandate for change and experiment. Yet few Americans would have supported anything so much against the national grain as federal ownership of industry and the banks. And if, in panic, the voters had endorsed such measures, they certainly would have regretted and reversed their action once they had regained their confidence.

In reality, only a small minority of Roosevelt's aides were radicals, and in the end his New Deal preserved capitalism and private property. It did so by reviving hope, providing the nation with a sense of forward motion, and preventing mass misery. In retrospect, it is easy to see that the New Deal was precisely what the majority of Americans wanted.

In the process of creating the modern social welfare state, there were undoubtedly losses as well as gains. Federal power and executive authority were both greatly expanded. Few, except the hidebound conservatives who opposed virtually every New Deal measure, could see the dangers in this change as the 1930s came to an end. Only time would reveal to what extent FDR had encouraged an "imperial presidency." But there can be no doubt that by his programs and his awesome charisma he had helped expand federal and presidential power to the detriment of local and congressional autonomy.

Meanwhile, as the 1940s loomed, the country began to turn its attention to the threatening events taking place beyond its shores.

Online Resources

"The History of Mexican Americans in California: Revolution to Depression"
http://www.cr.nps.gov/history/online_books/5views/5views5c.htm
Explore the subject of immigration from Mexico to America. Through this site, learn about Mexican-Americans' lives in the barrios in California and their struggle for a better life through mutual aid and work.

"The Great Depression"
http://xroads.virginia.edu/g/1930s/PRINT/newdeal/intro3.html
This in-depth site examines all facets of the economic crisis, from its causes to the reactions in the United States and form the government to the populace.

"Fireside Chats of Franklin D. Roosevelt"
http://www.mhric.org/fdr/fdr.html
Learn about FDR's New Deal programs much like many Americans did in the late 1930s through these radio addresses known as fireside chats. Read transcripts of these broadcasts that spanned from 1933–1944.

"Labor Unions During the Great Depression and the New Deal"
http://memory.loc.gov/ammem/ndlpedu/features/timeline/depwwii/depwar.html
In addition to an overview of the status of labor unions during the era, this site provides documents and interviews from Americans who belonged to these unions. The site discusses the importance of the New Deal to unionization and to workers' lives and also contains union songs and chants that reflect this period of unionization.

"TVA: Electricity for All"
http://newdeal.feri.org/tva/index.htm
On this site, read the Tennessee Valley Authority Act, explore letters from the field that tell of the social and environmental impact of the expansive federal project, and learn about rural electrification.

New Deal Network Library
http://newdeal.feri.org/library/index.htm
This site offers a first-hand glimpse into the world of the Great Depression and the New Deal era with more than 4,000 photographs online.

The Great Flint Sitdown
http://www.reuther.wayne.edu/exhibits/sitdown.html
This online exhibit provides just one example of the strength of labor unions during the New Deal era with its discussion of the UAW strike in Flint, Michigan. See photos of strikers in action, and read a compelling narrative of the strike.

26

WORLD WAR II

Blunder, or Decision in the National Interest?

1904	Japan defeats Russia, takes control of Korea and Manchuria
1908	Root-Takahira Agreement
1921–22	Washington Conference; Benito Mussolini rises to power in Italy, imposing Fascist regime
1928	Kellogg-Briand Pact
1931–32	Japan reoccupies Manchuria
1932	Franklin D. Roosevelt elected president
1933	Adolf Hitler ends Weimar Republic and becomes German chancellor, imposing Nazi rule
1936	Hitler occupies the Rhineland; FDR reelected
1937–38	Japan invades China
1938	Hitler annexes Austria; Munich Pact cedes Czechoslovakia's Sudetenland to Germany
1939	Germany occupies the remainder of Czechoslovakia; The Soviet Union and Germany sign a nonaggression pact; Germany invades Poland; Great Britain and France declare war on Germany
1940	Germany conquers Norway, Denmark, Belgium, Luxembourg, Holland, and France; Japan, Italy, and Germany sign a military and economic agreement forming the Axis alliance; FDR reelected
1941	Lend-Lease Act; Germany invades the Soviet Union; Roosevelt and Churchill issue Atlantic Charter; Japan bombs Pearl Harbor; United States declares war on Japan; Germany and Italy declare war on United States; Manhattan Project begins; Fair Employment Practices Act; Hitler begins extermination of Jews
1942	Roosevelt orders the War Department to confine Japanese-Americans on West Coast; Battle of Midway checks Japanese Pacific advance; Women's Army and Navy corps (WACS, WAVES) established
1943	Allies defeat the German Afrika Korps, invade Sicily; Soviets stop Germans at Stalingrad; "Big Three" in Teheran; MacArthur and Nimitz close in on Pacific islands; California and Detroit race riots
1944	Normandy invasion; Japanese launch first kamikaze attacks; FDR reelected

| 1945 | Yalta Conference; MacArthur recaptures Philippines; Germany defeated; FDR dies; Harry S. Truman becomes president; Atomic bombing of Hiroshima and Nagasaki; Soviets declare war on Japan; Japan surrenders |

December 7, 1941, dawned partly cloudy over the Hawaiian island of Oahu, 2,200 miles southwest of San Francisco. At Pearl Harbor, base of the United States Pacific Fleet, eight battleships, nine cruisers, twenty destroyers, and forty-nine other naval vessels lay at their berths or in dry dock. It was Sunday, and many of the sailors were on weekend liberty. At the airfields, Army Air Corps planes were parked in tight clusters, almost wing to wing, on the runways to prevent possible sabotage. The air crews were mostly away or asleep in the barracks.

Suddenly at 7:55 a.m. Pearl Harbor erupted in flames as tons of explosives, released by Japanese torpedo planes and bombers, slammed into the American ships tied up at Battleship Row. At the military airfields American planes became sitting ducks for the attackers. Only forty American pursuit planes rose to challenge the enemy. Meanwhile, several Japanese midget submarines, having sneaked through the harbor's protective net, were launching torpedoes at every target in sight. Two hours later, when the attack ended, much of America's naval and air power in the Pacific had been destroyed. In that brief, hellish interval 2,400 American sailors, marines, soldiers, airmen, and civilians died; 8 battleships were sunk or badly damaged; and 183 planes were lost. Fortunately the aircraft carrier force had been at sea and so had escaped intact. Still, it was the worst naval disaster in American history.

On December 8, shortly after noon Eastern Standard Time, President Roosevelt appeared before a joint session of Congress to ask for a declaration of war against Japan. The country, he declared, would never forget that the Japanese had attacked while their emissaries were in Washington talking peace. December 7 was a date that would "live in infamy." With only one dissenting vote, Congress declared war against Japan. On December 11 Germany, Japan's Axis ally, declared war against the United States; Italy, the third Axis power, immediately followed. The crowded and tragic events of four days had finally brought the United States into World War II, the greatest war in history.

How did the country arrive at this tragic point? In the weeks and months following Pearl Harbor, few Americans doubted that they had any choice but to defend themselves against a treacherous attack. The war stilled the discordant voices that for three years or more had debated war or peace. But after 1945 Americans resumed the argument. A majority saw Pearl Harbor as the logical culmination of Axis plans to enslave all free peoples. A minority concluded that the United States had blundered into an unnecessary war or had even been pushed into it by scheming men. Some accused Franklin Roosevelt of deception to achieve his misconceived interventionist ends.

Who was right? Was American entrance into war a mistake that might have, and should have, been avoided? Or was it the only way the United States could have protected itself and its vital interests against a pack of dangerous predators intent on destroying democracy and freedom?

■ SEEDS OF CONFLICT ■

The Japanese attack and the great war that followed were the culmination of events that began as much as a century earlier and involved the relations of one half of the industrialized world with the other.

Friction with Japan. American interests in the Far East dated from late in the eighteenth century when China became an important United States trading partner and an object of philanthropic and missionary concern. American–Japanese relations commenced in the 1850s when Captain Matthew Perry of the United States Navy forced the Japanese to abandon their traditional isolation and open trade relations with the West. Perry's visit propelled Japan into the modern world. To fend off Western domination the Japanese were soon imitating not only the West's parliamentary institutions, universal education, and industrialization but also its aggressive nationalism and imperialism. In 1895 Japan wrenched Korea from China. In 1904 it challenged czarist Russia over China's loosely attached northern provinces and defeated the Russian giant in a brief and bloody war.

In the early twentieth century American–Japanese relations were often bumpy. The United States supported the Japanese against the Russians in 1904–1905. But when President Theodore Roosevelt helped bring the Russo-Japanese War to an end by compromise, the Japanese blamed the United States for depriving them of the gains they considered their due. Matters worsened two years later when the San Francisco Board of Education placed Japanese-American students in segregated schools. A proud people, the Japanese were outraged by this action that implied inferiority. Theodore Roosevelt patched things up with the so-called Gentlemen's Agreement: The school board would cancel its order, and the Japanese government would not issue any more passports to would-be immigrants to the United States. The issue was superficially settled, but by this time feelings between the two nations had been rubbed raw. In succeeding years there would be talk, particularly in the Hearst newspapers, of the "yellow peril" in the Far East.

In the next few years Japanese and American interests would frequently clash in Asia. In the 1908 Root-Takahira Agreement, Japan accepted the American position that China must remain independent and retain its territorial integrity. But resentments continued to fester. Japan coveted the natural resources of China and Southeast Asia. Japanese nationalists were certain that the United States and the other Western powers—"have" nations with abundant resources either at home or within their empires—were trying to keep Japan—a "have-not" nation, without oil, coal, rubber, iron, and copper—from becoming the great power it deserved to be.

Japan took advantage of Europe's preoccupation at home during World War I to present China with the so-called Twenty-One Demands (1915). Negating the

Root-Takahira Agreement, these would have reduced China to a Japanese protectorate. American protest forced the Japanese to back off. The Washington Armament Conference of 1921–1922 further constrained Japan. Called by Secretary Hughes to help stabilize international relations in the Far East, the conference resulted in the Four Power Treaty by which France, the United States, England, and Japan pledged to respect one another's possessions in the Pacific. A Nine Power Treaty signed by the same four powers and four smaller European nations plus China promised to respect Chinese territorial integrity and the Open Door principle.

For a while Japanese ambitions diminished, and relations with the United States improved. At the end of the 1920s, however, Japanese militarists and extreme nationalists came to power in Tokyo and launched a more aggressive policy toward China. In 1931–1932 the militarists provoked an "incident" with China and seized its rich northern province of Manchuria, converting it into a puppet kingdom, renamed Manchukuo. The United States viewed Japan's aggression against its weaker neighbor as a violation of Japan's international agreements. But distracted by the Depression and unwilling to take action stronger than the American public would then support, Washington limited itself to diplomatic protests. In January 1932 Secretary of State Henry L. Stimson, reasserting John Hay's Open Door policy of a generation before, announced that the United States would not recognize any act that impaired the "territorial and administrative integrity of the Republic of China."

The Stimson Doctrine did not deter the Japanese military leaders. Early in 1932 Japanese army units clashed with Chinese troops in Shanghai, and during the fighting thousands of Chinese civilians were killed. In 1937, following a shooting incident at the Marco Polo Bridge near Peking, the Japanese began a piecemeal occupation of the Chinese Republic. Before long their armies had seized major Chinese cities and torn large chunks of the republic from the control of Chiang Kai-shek, leader of the Kuomintang, China's ruling party. In 1938 the Japanese announced a "new order" in the Far East based on thinly disguised Japanese domination of the whole region.

The Rise of Fascism in Europe.   Meanwhile, an even more dangerous group of aggressors had appeared in Europe. In Italy, where bitter conflict between Communists and conservatives and the losses of World War I had undermined the parliamentary system, Benito Mussolini seized power in 1922 in the name of law and order. "Il Duce" and his Fascists brutally eliminated their opponents, established a centralized totalitarian regime, and unveiled an aggressive foreign policy. In 1935 Fascist Italy attacked Ethiopia, one of the few still-independent African nations, and brutally conquered it. The moving plea to the League of Nations of Ethiopia's emperor, Haile Selassie, brought economic sanctions against Italy. But weakly supported by member nations and the United States, these did not deter Mussolini.

Authoritarian governments resembling Fascist Italy's spread through eastern and southern Europe following the collapse of the international economy in the early 1930s. The boundaries drawn by Wilson and his colleagues had created several small nations out of the ruins of Austria-Hungary and the Russian empire; few of these had democratic traditions or the social institutions to support parliamentary government. By the early 1930s Hungary, Poland, Yugoslavia, and the Baltic states, along with Bulgaria, Romania, Albania, and Greece, all had authoritarian regimes. Many of the new states were not viable economically or politically, and their weaknesses would be a permanent temptation to their greedy, more powerful neighbors.

Most dangerous of all, the post-World War I settlement failed to create a stable German democracy. By blaming Germany for the war, imposing vast indemnities on the German economy, and forcing the German nation to disarm, the Versailles treaty left a legacy of intense bitterness. German nationalists held the democratic Weimar Republic, successor to Kaiser Wilhelm II's imperial regime, responsible for the degrading treaty and never became reconciled to it. Despite these problems, for a few years in the late 1920s the German people experienced a period of prosperity and cultural creativity under their new democratic government. When the bottom fell out of the world economy in 1929, however, the inability of the Weimar regime to stop Germany's downward economic spiral destroyed the public's fragile confidence. Right-wing and Communist groups quickly took advantage of the situation to attack democracy. By 1930 Weimar's enemies, on both the extreme left and the extreme right, were engaged in a life-or-death struggle to see who could destroy the democratic republic first and impose its own ideology, Communist or Fascist, on the German nation.

The victor in the competition was Adolf Hitler, a fanatical right-wing German nationalist whose National Socialist (Nazi) party proclaimed its intention to repudiate Versailles and the galling military restraints and financial burdens it had imposed on Germany. The new "Third Reich" would restore German pride and German might. Like Italy's Fascists, the Nazis glorified the state and expressed contempt for democracy and parliamentary institutions.

Indeed, Hitler's hatred of liberal values went beyond even Mussolini's. The Nazis were rabid racists who carried ideas of Nordic supremacy to a chilling conclusion: All other peoples were inferior beings who must bow to the *Herrenvolk*, the superrace of northern Europe. In Hitler's view the Jews, especially, were malign beings who were responsible for most of Germany's calamities, including the defeat in 1918. Elevated to Chancellor in 1933, Hitler promised the German people that he would punish the Jews, destroy the Communists, repudiate Versailles, and make Germany the most powerful nation in Europe once more.

Few Americans had paid much attention to events in Germany before 1933, but Hitler and the Nazis could not be ignored. Once in control of the German state, Hitler renounced the armaments limitations of the Versailles treaty and began to rearm Germany. He quickly swept away parliamentary government and either assassinated his democratic and leftist opponents or threw them into concentration camps. Finally, he deprived Germany's Jewish population of all their civil rights and sent thousands of the nation's most talented scientists, writers, musicians, doctors, and scholars fleeing as refugees to western Europe and the United States.

From the outset Hitler scarcely concealed his lust for European dominance. In 1936 he reoccupied the Rhineland, which had been demilitarized by the Versailles treaty. That same year he and Mussolini concluded an alliance of mutual support (the Rome-Berlin Axis). In 1937 the two dictators intervened in the civil war in Spain, siding with the Fascist strongman Francisco Franco against the coalition of liberals, socialists, Communists, and anarchists (the Loyalists) who supported the Spanish Republic. In 1938 Hitler began his campaign to reincorporate all German-speaking territories in Europe into "Greater Germany" by annexing Austria. Hitler's next target was Czechoslovakia, a democratic republic formed from parts of the Austro-Hungarian Empire, which contained several million Germans within its Sudetenland region.

Not all Americans saw fascism-nazism as a serious danger. Some Catholics and conservatives, for example, preferred Hitler's client, Franco, to the Spanish Loyalists. Small numbers of Italian-Americans and German-Americans endorsed the dictators of their mother countries. There was even a small group of intellectuals who believed that Nazism represented the "wave of the future." Yet undoubtedly the great majority of Americans deplored and feared what they saw taking place in central and southern Europe.

Nazi Germany clearly threatened the balance of power in Europe. Yet England and France, traumatized by their enormous human and financial losses in World War I and weakened by the worldwide Depression, were reluctant to take a strong stand against the German threat. When, in early 1938, Hitler demanded that Czechoslovakia turn over the Sudetenland to Germany, the Czechs asked Britain and France for support. British Prime Minister Neville Chamberlain and French Premier Édouard Daladier refused. Believing they could successfully appease the Germans, they agreed, at a conference with the German dictator at Munich in September 1938, to support Hitler's demands on the Czechs. Unable to confront Germany alone, the Czechs were forced to surrender the Sudetenland to preserve the rest of the republic.

Chamberlain returned home from Munich convinced that appeasement would work and that the Munich Pact would bring "peace in our time." It did not. In March 1939, despite the Munich agreement, German forces occupied the rest of now defenseless Czechoslovakia and set up a puppet regime. Hitler soon made territorial demands on Germany's large eastern neighbor, Poland. By this time only the near-blind could believe that Hitler and Mussolini did not pose a serious threat to the peace and stability of Europe. In April 1939 Britain and France signed a mutual assistance pact with Poland, promising to come to its aid if attacked.

Roosevelt and the Interventionists. Though most Americans deplored the rise of the dictators, they did not agree on the implications for the United States. Liberals and leftists saw the rising tide of authoritarianism as a danger to free government everywhere. Even many middle-of-the road Americans feared that German, Italian, and Japanese expansionism would throw the world into turmoil. After the fall of Czechoslovakia, Americans were forced to confront the possibility that the aggressors could be stopped only by force.

Yet few Americans wished to see the United States become directly involved in Europe's troubles. By the late 1930s isolationism had hardened into an ideology that denied American vital interests abroad and insisted that, in the past, Americans had been duped into foreign wars by munitions manufacturers, bankers, and other cunning, self-serving manipulators. Between 1934 and 1936 isolationist views were reinforced by the Senate Munitions Investigating Committee hearings probing the origins of World War I. The committee, chaired by Senator Gerald P. Nye, concluded that those who profited from munitions manufacture had encouraged United States intervention. In the wake of the Nye Committee hearings, Congress passed a series of Neutrality Acts requiring the president in the event of war to embargo arms shipments to belligerents, forbid American citizens to sail on belligerent ships, and deny bankers the right to extend credit to the warring powers. By avoiding the entangling policies of 1914–1917, they believed, the United States could stay out of any future war. By 1937, according to an opinion poll, 94 percent of the American people favored nonintervention abroad regardless of who the combatants were or how just their cause.

From the outset President Roosevelt was more interventionist than most Americans. FDR believed in America's responsibility as a great power to cooperate with other nations to achieve a stable world order. During the 1920s he moved with the drift of American public opinion to isolationism, but the rise of the dictators quickly revived his internationalist convictions. At what moment Roosevelt and his advisers concluded that the dictators must be stopped at all cost is unclear. As early as 1933 he tried to induce Congress to prohibit the sale of arms to aggressor nations. In 1935, in the interest of world security, he asked Congress to approve admitting the United States to the World Court. Congress, dominated by isolationists, rejected both schemes.

Frustrated in Europe, Roosevelt worked to strengthen the United States against "the aggressors" by establishing closer ties with Latin America. His Good Neighbor Policy, built on the earlier initiatives of his Republican predecessors, was designed to create "hemispheric solidarity." During his first term of office FDR renounced the Platt Amendment, which had allowed the United States to intervene in Cuban affairs. At two Latin American conferences in 1933 and 1936, the United States reinforced the pledge (given in the 1928 Clark Memorandum) to cease intervening in the affairs of Central and South America. Before long the United States had removed its last troop contingents from Caribbean nations. The Good Neighbor policy would pay dividends: When war came, almost all the Latin American countries would support the United States against its enemies.

During his second term, as the international situation darkened, the president turned to face the aggressors directly. In 1937, following Japan's attack on China, he denounced "international lawlessness" and proposed that nations contributing to "international anarchy" be "quarantined"—isolated and walled off by the rest of the world. By this time the president clearly considered Germany, Italy, and Japan potentially dangerous adversaries; in private conversations he referred to them as the "three bandit nations."

In the emerging international crisis, ideology inevitably influenced Roosevelt's views. The totalitarian and militaristic regimes of Germany, Italy, and Japan represented everything a liberal democrat despised: repression, racism, and brutality. The president, moreover, was surrounded by advisers who saw Hitler as embodying every primitive, irrational, reactionary current in Western society. But there were also more self-interested motives at play. Ever since the late nineteenth century the United States had relied on the Western European nations, especially Britain, to impose stability in the world outside the Americas. With England and France threatened by Germany, and the Japanese on the rampage in the western Pacific, the president feared for the safety of the United States. What would happen if Britain and France could not check Hitler? A triumphant Germany to the east, allied with a triumphant Japan to the west, would leave the United States a besieged outpost in the middle of a hostile and dangerous world.

By this time most Americans shared FDR's opinion of the dictators. A Gallup poll, following Germany's occupation of Czechoslovakia, showed that 65 percent of Americans endorsed a boycott of Germany and Italy, and 55 percent wanted the Neutrality Acts revised to aid the democracies. But there seemed little need for direct American involvment. If war were to erupt, Britain and France would surely prevail, but in any case, safe behind its ocean moats, the American fortress could hold out indefinitely against the dictators.

■ THE EROSION OF AMERICAN NEUTRALITY ■

American complacency would be put to the test in the fall of 1939. On September 1, after signing a nonaggression pact with the Soviet Union's Joseph Stalin, his former archenemy, Hitler attacked Poland. Two days later Britain and France, fulfilling their pledge to Poland, declared war on Germany. World War II had begun.

On September 3 Roosevelt delivered a fireside chat to the American people. Like Wilson in 1914, he promised to expend "every effort" to avoid war. Consciously diverging from his predecessor, however, he refused to ask Americans to "remain neutral in thought" as well. As required by the neutrality legislation, he forbade the export of arms to the belligerents. But on September 21 he called a special session of Congress to ask for repeal of the arms embargo.

Roosevelt kept out of sight while others carried the burden of getting repeal through Congress. Meanwhile, behind the scenes he used his patronage to bring fellow Democrats into line. The strategy worked. On October 27, by a vote of 63 to 30, the Senate replaced the arms embargo with a "cash-and-carry" policy that permitted the British and French to buy war matériel as long as they paid cash and transported their purchases in their own ships. A week later the House accepted the revision, 243 to 181.

Hitler Conquers Europe.   Had the war against Hitler gone well for the Allies, the United States could have remained aloof. It went badly. Poland fell to the German invaders in five weeks. For several months thereafter an ominous quiet hung over Europe. During the "phony war," as isolationists contemptuously called this period, nothing suggested that the major European powers were locked in a life-or-death struggle. Then on April 9, 1940, the German army struck at Norway and Denmark. Denmark fell virtually without a shot; Norway was quickly subdued. On May 10 German armored units smashed across the borders into Belgium, Luxembourg, and Holland aiming for France. In a week German armored columns were sweeping toward Paris.

The British and French armies were quickly overwhelmed by the fast-moving German tank columns supported by terrifying Stuka dive bombers. The German *Blitzkrieg* destroyed French military resistance in a few weeks. By the end of May the British forces in France were pinned against the English Channel near Dunkirk by a tightening ring of German troops and artillery. They were able to hold the German tanks at bay long enough for an armada of small ships to rescue the entrapped forces from the flaming beaches, but most of their equipment had to be left behind. On June 10 Paris surrendered and Italy entered the war as Germany's ally. On June 22, with more than half their country in German hands, the French, now led by Marshal Henri Philippe Pétain, an arch conservative enemy of the French Third Republic, signed an armistice with the Germans that allowed the invaders to occupy the whole northern half of the country and the Atlantic coast. A few Frenchmen rallied around the free French leader, Charles de Gaulle, who established a London-based government-in-exile. The Free French and the Pétain government, located at Vichy, were soon battling for control of the French overseas empire.

Hitler had conquered Norway, Denmark, Luxembourg, France, Belgium, and Holland and had almost destroyed the power of mighty Britain. In a few weeks he had achieved what his imperial predecessor, Wilhelm II, had been unable to do in four years of war. Americans were stunned by the rush of catastrophic events, and for the first time a substantial minority began to talk of war as inevitable. Roosevelt's reaction to the Nazi triumph was swift in coming. In mid-May he asked Congress for vast sums for rearmament, including funds for 50,000 planes a year and a "two-ocean navy." By October Congress had appropriated $17 billion to strengthen the nation's neglected defenses. In September it would authorize peacetime compulsory military service for the first time in American history. On October 16, 1940, some 6.5 million young men registered for the draft and soon went off to training camps to become soldiers.

Meanwhile, the Germans had launched an all-out air campaign to soften England up for invasion (Battle of Britain). During the summer of 1940 German aircraft bombarded and strafed the British Isles in daylight until the losses exacted by the gallant but badly stretched Royal Air Force made these raids too costly. In early September the *Luftwaffe* began night raids that set London and other English cities ablaze. The British people held on. Sustaining them were the words of their eloquent prime minister, Winston Churchill, who had succeeded Chamberlain after the Allied defeat in Norway. A master of English prose, Churchill declared that if the British Empire lasted a thousand years, men would say: "This was their finest hour." He promised victory though the cost would be "blood, toil, tears, and sweat."

Britain's brave struggle aroused the admiration of virtually all Americans. In 1940–1941 news from Europe for the first time was relayed instantaneously to the United States by short-wave radio, creating a sense of participation impossible in an earlier day. From London Americans heard Edward R. Murrow of CBS and other American correspondents describe the Nazi air attacks while sounds of air-raid sirens, anti-aircraft guns, and exploding bombs filled the background. As they listened, most Americans found it impossible not to feel that they themselves were cowering under the storm of German bombs.

Roosevelt's Third Term. By mid-1940 few Americans doubted that Britain's plight was desperate, and many believed that their country was on Hitler's list. In the spring, supporters of England—mostly eastern liberals—organized the Committee to Defend America by Aiding the Allies, with the old Kansas progressive, William Allen White, as head. That fall a Gallup poll showed that half the voters were willing to help England "even at the risk of getting into war." Yet the isolationist voice remained powerful and insistent. In early September 1940 a group of isolationists organized the America First Committee, composed of philosophical isolationists and conservatives with a fringe of Anglophobes, Roosevelt haters, and pro-Nazi anti-Semites. For the next year the two groups waged a bitter war for the minds of the American people.

Meanwhile, the country found itself in the middle of another presidential campaign. After keeping everyone guessing for months, FDR concluded that the survival of liberal policies and the nation's safety during the international crisis required his strong hand at the helm. Having effectively eliminated all potential party rivals, he left the Democrats with no choice but to break with the two-term tradition and nominate him for a third time.

The 1940 Republican nominee was Wendell Willkie, a utility magnate from Indiana whose sincerity and boyish charm appealed to younger, less conservative Republicans. Fortunately for the country's unity, Willkie proved to be as much of an interventionist as Roosevelt. He denounced the president's gift of fifty overage destroyers to England in exchange for bases in British North American possessions (September 3) as "the most dictatorial and arbitrary act of any President in the history of the United States." But on the whole, the two candidates were careful to avoid arguing over foreign policy. Toward the end of the campaign, however, Roosevelt uttered some words that would later make his friends cringe. "I have said this before," he told a Boston audience in October, "but I shall say it again and again and again: Your boys are not going to be sent into any foreign wars." FDR would have been elected in any case; in the midst of the grave world crisis Americans were not inclined to exchange the veteran leader for a novice. But the promise helped. On election day Roosevelt carried 38 states to Willkie's 10 and won a popular majority of 27.2 million votes to his opponent's 22.3 million.

Lend-Lease. During the next full year of peace Roosevelt maneuvered the country ever closer to war. A month following the election Churchill laid out Britain's plight in stark outline to the president in a private letter. He warned that the well-being of the American people was "bound up with the survival and independence of the British Commonwealth of Nations." British sea power protected the United States and the Americas against their enemies. But it was spread very thin and might collapse entirely if the Pétain government at Vichy turned over the French navy to the Nazis. Nor was this all. In the Far East Japan was taking advantage of French, Dutch, and British weakness and inability to protect their Asian possessions by expanding its power and influence. Britain did not require American manpower, said Churchill, but it did need to guarantee that American supplies could get through the tightening German submarine blockade. He pleaded for American naval assistance and for an end to the cash-and-carry system. Cash-and-carry was better than the embargo, but Britain was running out of money and more direct help was needed if it was to survive as a bulwark against the Nazi scourge.

Churchill's letter played effectively on Roosevelt's deepest fears. Soon afterward in a fireside chat, the president prepared the ground for his new aid scheme by warning the public of the critical danger to civilization posed by the Axis powers and explaining the need for the United States to become the "arsenal of democracy." In January 1941 he submitted a "lend-lease" bill to Congress authorizing the president to "lend" military equipment to any country "whose defense the President deems vital to the defense of the United States" and providing $7 billion for the purpose, the largest single appropriation in the nation's history.

The bill immediately came under withering attack. Isolationist Senator Burton K. Wheeler of Montana called lend-lease the "New Deal's Triple A foreign policy" that would "plow under every fourth American boy." The *Chicago Tribune* called it "a bill for the destruction of the American Republic . . . [and] a brief for an unlimited dictatorship . . . with power to make war and alliances forever." Administration officials retorted that Britain faced invasion within three months and without such aid would be defeated. If the British navy were destroyed or seized, the United States would be in serious danger.

Both sides had a point. Wheeler's remarks were grossly unfair and the *Tribune's* attack was as much an anti-New Deal tirade as a legitimate defense of the Constitution. But in later years many Americans would come to regret the erosion of congressional control over foreign policy that began under FDR. Yet the president was not consciously attempting to usurp power; he and his advisers were expressing their honest fears. And most informed citizens supported them. After a furious battle the congressional isolationists were defeated. On March 11 Roosevelt signed the lend-lease bill into law. In a few weeks the $7 billion of war matériel that Congress had authorized began flowing to Britain.

United States Aid Increases.   The additional American aid had little immediate effect. During the spring of 1941 Americans gasped as Germany and Italy smashed the Yugoslavs and Greeks in the Balkans and forced the British to retreat almost to the Nile in North Africa. Britain was also losing the vital Battle of the Atlantic, as German submarines sent vast quantities of American munitions and supplies to the bottom of the ocean. Could nothing be done to stop the Axis?

In Washington, Roosevelt moved cautiously to provide further aid to Britain. On April 9 he concluded an agreement putting Greenland, a Danish colony, under United States protection, thereby extending American naval patrols partway to Britain. His advisers urged him to use the United States Navy to convoy arms all the way to Britain, but the president held back. On May 13 he agreed to shift part of the Pacific Fleet to the Atlantic. On May 27 he announced an unlimited national emergency giving him expanded powers over the economy. In June he issued an executive order freezing Axis assets in the United States and placing German and Italian ships in American ports under federal control. Each action brought the nation a little closer to outright belligerency, but still the president was reluctant to throw the country's full weight behind Britain. He believed war must come but felt unable to start it himself. In mid-May he told Secretary of the Treasury Henry Morgenthau, Jr.: "I am waiting to be pushed into the situation."

Hitler carefully avoided a showdown with America, for he had other things in mind. Four thousand miles from Washington, on the plains of eastern Europe, German and Soviet troops faced one another along an extended common border that ran through what had once been the independent republic of Poland. For almost two years the two countries had maintained an uneasy marriage of convenience. Then, on June 22, 1941, in fulfillment of his long-cherished ambition to destroy communism and expand German power eastward, the Nazi dictator sent his tanks, aircraft, and troops hurtling toward the heart of the Soviet Union.

In London and Washington the Nazi attack provoked a quick response. The British and Americans could have ignored Russia's plight. Many people in both countries considered it little better than Nazi Germany. Yet neither the British nor the American government hesitated very long in offering help to the Russians. Two days after the German attack, Roosevelt promised aid to the Soviet Union. In the fall a British-American mission traveled to Moscow to determine Soviet war needs. Soon afterward the United States pledged $1 billion in lend-lease matériel to the embattled Russians; by the end of the war American aid would grow to $11 billion in value.

Although he welcomed Russia as a new ally against Hitler, Roosevelt could not lose sight of Britain and the Atlantic. In July he sent troops to occupy Iceland and announced that the American navy would escort British-bound supplies as far east as that strategic island. The following month the president met Churchill on a ship off Newfoundland. Out of that meeting came the Atlantic Charter linking Britain and America in a common set of war goals. This document affirmed and expanded upon the Wilsonian ideals of self-determination for all people, freer international trade, cooperative efforts for world prosperity, freedom of the seas, disarmament, and "freedom from fear and want."

Bit by bit, Roosevelt was pushing the United States toward a direct confrontation with Germany. He did not confide his plans to the American people, and that lack of candor has troubled even his firmest admirers. Yet the president was not seeking power or personal glory. FDR was certain that the fate of civilization depended on Hitler's defeat. But he feared taking a divided people into war and was still convinced that the enemy must act first.

By the fall of 1941 events seemed to be moving the way FDR hoped. Soon after his return from Newfoundland, a German U-boat commander off the coast of Iceland, believing his vessel to be under British attack, launched two torpedoes at the United States destroyer *Greer,* which had been tracking the submarine and radioing its location to the British. The *Greer* returned the fire. Roosevelt (neglecting to mention that the *Greer* had been engaged in unneutral activities) called the incident an act of "piracy legally and morally," adding that from now on American naval vessels would "shoot on sight" at any German submarine found between Iceland and North America. On October 9, 1941, he asked Congress to modify the Neutrality Acts further to permit the arming of American merchant vessels. Early in November, after the Germans had torpedoed the destroyer *Kearney* and sunk the U.S.S. *Reuben James* with heavy loss of life, Congress authorized the arming of American merchant vessels and removed restrictions on their carrying cargoes to belligerent ports.

By mid-November the United States was in a virtual naval war with the Germans. Yet a substantial minority of the American people still hoped to avoid full-scale military intervention. As recently as August the House had voted to extend the draft period an additional eighteen months by a margin of only a single vote. Isolationist sentiment in Congress was powerful enough to prevent easy passage of the modifications of the Neutrality Acts. In the Senate the president's majority was only 50 to 37; in the House, 212 to 194.

The continuing strength of isolationism troubled Roosevelt. What if the Germans avoided further serious incidents? How could Americans be brought, united, to the point of war? The problem stumped the president. As his friend and biographer Robert Sherwood later wrote: "He had no tricks left. . . . The bag from which he had pulled so many rabbits was empty." Fate—and the Japanese— would soon solve the problem for the president and the undecided nation.

Miscalculations in the East.   Roosevelt and his advisers misunderstood and underestimated the Japanese. Convinced that without the resources of Manchuria, China, and the East Indies, it could not survive as a great power, Japan had a deep commitment to its expansionist policies. It would not be easy to get the Japanese to back down in China, or the Far East generally, without the use of military force. In addition, the American government did not take Japan seriously as a military opponent. Americans knew that Japanese industry was capable of producing the shoddy trinkets and gewgaws that flooded the five-and-dime stores of the day, but doubted that it could produce modern weapons in quantity.

Until the fall of France, the United States, over the protest of China's many American friends, supplied much of the steel and petroleum to supply Japan's war machine. Then, when the Japanese began to pressure the Vichy French for bases in Indochina and threatened the Dutch in the oil-rich East Indies, the American government imposed licensing requirements on the export of American oil and scrap metal and forbade the export of aviation gasoline. These moves goaded the Japanese into seeking allies elsewhere. In September 1940 Japan signed an agreement with Italy and Germany, converting the Rome-Berlin

Axis into the Rome-Berlin-Tokyo Axis. The agreement pledged the three nations to support one another's plans to establish a "new order" in Europe and a "Greater East Asia" in the Far East. If any one of them was attacked by a fourth power—with which it was not then already at war—the others would go to its aid. The Soviet Union, which the Japanese feared, was specifically exempted from this provision, making it clear that it was aimed at the United States. In effect, if the United States attacked either Japan or one of the European Axis nations, it would find itself with a two-ocean war. The American government responded to this threat by prohibiting the export of scrap iron and steel outside the Western Hemisphere.

As yet, however, neither the Americans nor the Japanese were prepared for a showdown. In March 1941 the moderate government of Prince Fumimaro Konoye opened conversations with Secretary of State Hull in Washington to prevent an irreparable break between the two countries. The Japanese were willing to make minor concessions but not, as Hull demanded, to evacuate China. As the talks dragged on, the Japanese, who already controlled northern Indochina, moved to seize the rest of the French colony. In July 1941 Japan forced the Vichy government to grant it bases in southern Indochina, close to the East Indies and British Malaya. Shortly thereafter, Roosevelt ordered all Japanese assets in the United States frozen, virtually ending trade between the two nations. This move was quickly followed by the order of the governor of the Dutch East Indies embargoing Dutch oil to Japan.

By showing Japan how dependent it was on foreign sources of raw material, the Americans and Dutch hoped to give the Japanese pause. Their moves had the opposite effect. During the remaining months of peace two groups of Japanese leaders—the military chiefs on one hand and the royal family on the other—battled over what policy to pursue toward the United States. The army generals were confident they could defeat the United States in any war. The admirals hoped that a massive surprise blow would so damage American naval power that the United States would be forced to give Japan a free hand in East Asia. If Japan did not act soon, the American oil embargo would cripple the Japanese war machine. Prince Konoye and Emperor Hirohito opposed this aggressive course except as a last resort.

In August, Konoye proposed a meeting with President Roosevelt to iron out Japanese–American differences. Secretary Hull distrusted the Japanese, however, and the meeting was never held. But the American government was not anxious for a showdown, and for a while strung Prince Konoye along. In October, his credibility with his own people damaged by American delays, Konoye resigned in favor of the more militant war minister, Hideki Tojo.

Tojo was determined to break the deadlock between the two nations or attack. On November 5 the Japanese government decided to adopt the admirals' policy unless the United States and Great Britain halted their aid to the Chinese and allowed Japan access to oil and other vital raw materials from America and Southeast Asia. In return, Japan would agree to withdraw its troops from the French possessions when the war with China was over and would eventually leave China itself. On November 25 Admiral Isoroku Yamamoto ordered the navy strike force to put to sea, subject to last-minute recall. The United States refused to accept the final Japanese terms. America could not, Hull believed, end its aid to Chiang Kai-shek; we were too firmly committed to a stable Chinese republic to desert him. Moreover, the Japanese could not be trusted to evacuate China.

The American government had broken the top-secret Japanese "purple cipher" code by this time and knew from intercepted messages that unless a settlement with the United States was soon reached, Japan would launch an attack against American or British-Dutch forces somewhere in the Pacific. The American government assumed that the blow would land in Southeast Asia and alerted military commanders in Hawaii and the Philippines. On the morning of December 7, Washington time, Army Chief of Staff General George C. Marshall sent radiograms to military commanders in San Francisco, the Canal Zone, Hawaii, and the Philippines, warning of an imminent attack. Electrical interference delayed the radio message to Hawaii, and it had to be sent by cable. By the time it arrived at the Western Union office in Honolulu, the bombs were falling over Pearl Harbor.

As we saw, on December 8 the United States declared war on Japan. Three days later the Germans and Italians ended American uncertainty regarding the European conflict by declaring war on the United States. The titanic struggle over intervention was finally over: A united American people were now heart and soul in the crusade to stop Hitler and the other aggressors.

■ THE HOME FRONT ■

Mobilization.   World War II was the most costly war in American history. Between December 1941 and the Japanese surrender in the late summer of 1945, the war effort cost the treasury almost $300 billion. Sixteen million men and women served in the armed forces. Of these, almost 300,000 died in combat; another 700,000 were wounded.

The government, as we saw, had begun raising a military force before Pearl Harbor. Late in 1940 the first peacetime draftees were inducted into service. After induction the new GI—so called because of his "government issue" uniform and gear—was shipped off to a training camp for eight weeks or more of "basic training," followed by either advanced infantry training or, if qualified, instruction in some specialty. The voluntary branches of the service—Navy, Marine Corps, Coast Guard, and Army Air Corps—conducted similar training operations.

Most young Americans found it difficult to adjust to the armed forces. They were fed well, and the transformation of many once-skinny adolescents into well-muscled young men amazed their families and friends when they returned home on their first leave. But they did not like military discipline and despised the hard, dirty jobs of obstacle-course running, calisthenics, bivouacking, and marching—not to speak of KP (kitchen police) and guard duty. The War and Navy departments tried to make the hardships acceptable by providing libraries, movies, and religious services. Church and volunteer organizations sponsored camp dances to which young women were invited. Yet complaints about the military's stupidities and foul-ups became the mark of the wartime citizen-soldier; SNAFU, an acronym usually politely translated as "situation normal, all fouled up," was added to the American vocabulary. Nevertheless, as time would show, American youths would make fine soldiers when well led.

Racism on the Home Front. Pearl Harbor was a tremendous shock to American confidence. For days after the frightening news from Hawaii, Americans peered anxiously at the skies, expecting to see bombers overhead with Japan's rising-sun emblem on their wings. In the early weeks following December 7 there were air-raid scares in several cities.

The fears were aggravated by an unbroken string of Japanese victories that followed the initial Pearl Harbor attack. On the West Coast something close to panic seized Americans in these early weeks. Jittery citizens, certain that the resident Japanese-American population was a potential "fifth column," demanded their removal from the exposed Pacific Coast. Fear was reinforced by racism and greed. Long the targets of bigotry, the Japanese were envied for their economic success. Many whites coveted their property, much of it rich farmland.

For a time Washington officials resisted the pressure for relocation by West Coast congressmen and state officials. But they soon yielded. On February 19, 1942, Roosevelt signed an executive order allowing the War Department to "prescribe military areas . . . from which any or all persons may be excluded." Within weeks thousands of Issei (immigrant Japanese) and Nisei (their American-born children) were forced to sell their homes, businesses, and farms, often at a fraction of their true value, and move to detention centers in isolated areas of inland states such as Utah, Arizona, and Arkansas.

Though these centers were a far cry from the concentration camps of Nazi Europe, they were a disgrace to American democratic principles. Despite harsh living conditions, most of the imprisoned people survived the war; remarkably, many of them retained their loyalty toward the United States.

By comparison, the government treated other enemy nationals generously. Italians and Germans, even those not citizens, were left alone. Leaders of the pro-Nazi German-American Bund, along with a handful of native-born Fascists, were indicted under the antisubversive Smith Act of 1940, which imposed tighter controls over aliens and made it a crime for any person or group to teach the overthrow of the government by violent means. But the extreme anti-Germanism that characterized World War I did not surface. Nor did the antiradicalism that flourished during the earlier war. The Communist party, which had denounced Roosevelt as a warmonger during 1940 and early 1941, hailed him as a hero after the Soviet Union was attacked by Hitler. During the war itself American Communists were among the most fervent patriots. Combined with the heroic struggle of the Russian people against Hitler, this enthusiasm deflected antiradical excesses.

Of course, the war did not turn the country into a tolerant social paradise. In June 1943 some young Mexican-Americans (Chicanos), wearing characteristic "zoot suits"—flashy outfits with broad-shouldered jackets, tightly pegged trousers, and wide-brimmed flat hats—attacked U.S. sailors on liberty in Los Angeles. The sailors retaliated by beating up every zoot-suiter they could find. It was, *Time* magazine said, "the ugliest brand of mob action" in California "since the coolie riots of the 1870s." Hundreds were injured before the violence ended.

Black Americans. Blacks, too, fell victim to wartime social stresses. War brought a mixture of good and bad to black Americans, much as it had in 1917–1918. During the peacetime arms buildup, defense contractors had resisted hiring black workers. When A. Philip Randolph, president of the all-black Brotherhood of Sleeping Car Porters, threatened in May 1941 to organize a mass march on Washington to protest this exclusion, Roosevelt established the Fair Employment Practices Committee (FEPC). Thereafter, the FEPC and the pressure of urgent war orders forced open the employment doors to black Americans. Black men and women by the thousands soon found jobs in the tank factories of Detroit, the steel mills of Pittsburgh, the shipyards of Puget Sound, and the aircraft factories of southern California, Texas, and Kansas.

Economic opportunities for blacks during the war was not equaled by advances in other areas of American life, however. More black soldiers than ever before became commissioned officers, and for the first time blacks were admitted to the Marine Corps and to the navy at ranks higher than mess boy. But through most of the war black servicemen were kept in segregated military units. Their obvious second-class status injured black military morale. In the South and at army camps in the North, serious tensions developed between black servicemen and neighboring white civilians. In Detroit, where thousands of blacks and newly arrived southern whites lived and worked side by side, racial friction set off a bloody race riot in mid-1943 that left 30 people dead, 800 injured, and over $2 million in property destroyed.

Despite their mistreatment, black Americans were loyal and patriotic. Hitler's virulent racism, of course, was particularly repulsive to black Americans; but many of them might have been attracted to the Japanese who were nonwhites fighting the white European nations. A tiny minority did find the Japanese cause appealing; the overwhelming majority, however, supported the war effort. Like other Americans, black citizens bought bonds, worked in war plants, and collected scrap metal and rubber. Thousands of black troops fought in Europe and the Pacific, albeit in segregated units. In Italy the all-black Ninety-Ninth Fighter Squadron achieved a distinguished record in air combat against the German *Luftwaffe*.

Despite their overall patriotism, black leaders put the nation on notice that it could not indefinitely treat African Americans as it had in the past. The watchword was the "Double V"—"victory over our enemies at home and victory over our enemies on the battlefields abroad." Yet ultimately, they recognized, black Americans would have to fight for their own civil rights. As Walter White, head of the NAACP, declared, the majority of black soldiers would "return home determined to use these efforts [fighting the Axis] to the utmost."

Pressures on Women and Families.   The war was hard on American families. Married men had been exempted from the peacetime draft; but in 1943 even fathers were inducted. The wartime industrial boom also strained family relations. Whole families from the Northeast and Midwest moved to remote parts of the nation to work in war plants, but sometimes male workers left their wives and children behind to move in with parents or other relations. Between 1940 and 1945 the number of families headed by a married woman with her husband absent rose from 770,000 to almost 3 million.

Young wives and mothers made the best of a bad situation, but the best was often not very good. Women were lonely and sought out one another's company. Some inevitably found other male companionship, and marriages broke up. More than a few GIs received "Dear John" letters telling them that other men had taken their place.

Many young women found military service attractive. In 1942 Congress authorized the Women's Auxiliary Army Corps (the WACS, after "auxiliary" was dropped from the title), and later established the WAVES, the navy equivalent. In all, a quarter of a million young women donned military uniforms and served in noncombatant jobs at home and overseas.

Many women took jobs in the civilian sector to keep busy, to supplement their incomes, or to help the war effort. "Rosie the Riveter," in overalls and cap,

Woman war workers made up for the manpower shortage during World War II.

became a familiar figure in every American industrial community. The nation valued her, but working mothers compounded the problems caused by absent fathers. Children often did not get proper care. During the war juvenile delinquency leaped. In San Diego, a major aircraft-manufacturing center and naval base, 55 percent more boys were charged with crimes in 1945 than in the previous year; the arrest rate for girls climbed 355 percent.

The pressures on families were particularly severe where there was a heavy concentration of war industry. Housing inevitably was in short supply and families had to live in trailers or Quonset huts. Schools were forced to hold double sessions. The government provided money for education in "war-impacted" areas, but it was not enough to improve conditions created by the influx of new people.

To a degree, all civilians paid a price for the war. After Pearl Harbor the government drastically cut automobile production and housing construction. It soon began to ration rubber tires and later restricted gasoline consumption. Metals, deflected into war production, were replaced by wood or plastic. Rationing of meat, sugar, coffee, butter, and cooking fats began in 1942. Rationing of clothing began at about the same time. The housing, gasoline, and rubber shortages produced hardships, but the food and clothing restrictions were relatively easy to accept. Consumers often discovered that they had ration "points" for more items than they either needed or could afford. Compared with the bitter experiences of Britain or Russia, life in wartime America remained easy.

The Wartime Economy.   The war gave an immense boost to the homefront economy. By 1941 lend-lease and defense spending had reduced unemployment to less than 10 percent of the civilian labor force, the lowest figure since 1930. By 1943 it was down to a miniscule 1.9 percent. By 1943 the country enjoyed a per capita GNP some 70 percent higher than in the "miracle" year 1929. Even when purely military items are subtracted, Americans were better off economically by the middle of the war than in the most prosperous peacetime era. In essence, by forcing the government to forsake a balanced budget, the war made up for lagging private consumption and investment. The Depression was over!

Everyone welcomed the return of prosperity, but a new danger, inflation, soon appeared. The public had billions of extra dollars to spend, but relatively little to spend it on. The absence of expensive consumer durables such as automobiles, household appliances, and new homes put great added pressure on the prices of those goods that were available. To deal with this imbalance of commodities and cash, the government raised taxes drastically. Beginning with the first "defense" budgets in 1940, Congress lowered the personal income tax exemption, raised tax rates sharply, and established the excess-profits tax for business firms. In June 1943 the treasury began withholding income taxes from paychecks. Forty-four percent of the cost of the war was paid with tax money; for the first time most working Americans paid income taxes.

To further reduce the danger of inflation, the government, as in World War I, issued war bonds. In September 1942 the treasury launched its first war-bond

BUY THAT INVASION BOND!

An artist depicts the 1944 Allied invasion of Normandy for a war-bond drive. The casualties are difficult to find, an omission typical of wartime propaganda.

drive with a massive advertising campaign in print and on radio. The most effective support for these drives came from Hollywood stars, who were credited with selling bonds worth $834 million in the first drive alone.

Neither taxes nor bond sales were sufficient to skim off all the excess purchasing power, and prices soon began to rise. Then in 1942 Congress established the Office of Price Administration (OPA) and the War Production Board, with the power to ration scarce raw materials, set wage rates, and fix wholesale and retail commodity prices, rents, and other charges. From April 1943 to August 1945 retail prices rose only 4.2 percent, a remarkably low figure for wartime.

Arsenal of Democracy. The most important role of the American homefront was to supply the fighting front. The role was magnificently performed; American industrial might proved to be a decisive factor in victory. Under a succession of "dollar-a-year" men called in from private industry to run various superagencies, war production soared despite bottlenecks, labor and raw material shortages, strikes, and union disputes. Between 1940 and 1945 United States factories turned out 300,000 aircraft, 5,425 merchant ships, 72,000 naval vessels, 87,000 tanks, 2.5 million trucks, 372,000 artillery pieces, and 44 billion rounds of small-arms ammunition. Far more than in 1917–1918, the country met all its military needs, and beyond that truly became, as Roosevelt had promised, the arsenal of democracy.

■ THE FIGHTING FRONTS ■

The months immediately following Pearl Harbor were a time of disastrous American and Allied military retreat. In quick succession, the Japanese captured Singapore, Hong Kong, the Dutch East Indies, and Burma. In May 1942, after a long siege of the Bataan Peninsula and Corregidor Island, in the Philippines, they compelled the surrender of a combined force of Americans and Filipinos. Before the final collapse, however, the navy rescued the American commander, General Douglas MacArthur, and brought him to Australia to lead the defense and reconquest of the South Pacific. Despite these critical Pacific losses, Roosevelt and his advisers, believing Hitler the more dangerous enemy, accepted the policy, strongly favored by the British, of Europe first. The war against Japan would be a holding operation until American factories and training camps had provided enough arms and men to deal with Hitler and the Japanese simultaneously.

The British favored an attack on Germany either through Africa or through Europe's "soft underbelly," the Mediterranean. But Roosevelt and Chief of Staff Marshall preferred a direct thrust across the English Channel into France and

Japanese empire in 1933 □ Maximum area of Japanese control □ Neutral nations
◄- - - Japanese advances □ Allied nations ✱ Naval battles

World War II: Japanese Advances, 1941–1942

the heart of German-occupied Europe. In the end British and American strategies were combined, but the decision spread Allied strength too thinly and probably lengthened the war.

Early in 1942 the first American GIs arrived in Britain, the vanguard of millions of American soldiers and airmen who came for the delayed cross-Channel attack. At the end of the year the United States and Britain undertook Operation Torch, an invasion of North Africa that pitted Allied troops against combined German and Italian forces commanded by General Erwin Rommel.

Meanwhile, the Allies were slowly winning the vital battle against the U-boats in the Atlantic. America's entrance into the war provided German submarine commanders with easy pickings, and during 1942 millions of tons of Allied shipping went to the bottom. By 1943 new techniques using destroyers, aircraft, and innovative submarine-detection equipment cut losses to enemy submarines drastically while the sheer productivity of American shipyards began to offset losses.

The year 1942 was the darkest of the war, but also marked the turning of the tide. On May 7–8 American carrier planes stopped the Japanese advance toward Australia by sinking a Japanese aircraft carrier and damaging two others at the Battle of the Coral Sea. A month later, alerted to enemy plans by code-breakers, they inflicted a stunning defeat on the Imperial Navy at the Battle of Midway, sinking 4 Japanese carriers and shooting down 275 enemy aircraft. Midway shifted the balance of naval strength in the Pacific permanently to the United States. In August American marines, soldiers, and naval forces invaded the Japanese base on Guadalcanal Island, opening a three-year "island-hopping" counteroffensive against the Pacific enemy. The struggle on Guadalcanal, and in the waters surrounding it, proved bitter and costly. Not until early February did the Japanese abandon their efforts to hold on.

In Europe the Germans were equally tenacious. By 1942 the Hitler regime had enslaved millions of people, from France in the west to Russia in the east. Its treatment of virtually all these people was bestial, but none were subjected to the horrors experienced by the millions of Jews who had fallen into Nazi hands in Poland, western Europe, and the Soviet Union. Hitler considered the Jews subhuman and marked them for total extermination. Many were shipped to slave-labor camps where they were worked to death. In late 1941 the Nazis launched the "final solution to the Jewish problem": the mass slaughter of all of Europe's Jews—men, women, and children. By the time the war ended, almost 6 million Jews—along with hundreds of thousands of Russians, Poles, Gypsies, and other "inferior beings"—had been shot, hanged, tortured, starved, or gassed to death in such camps as Auschwitz, Treblinka, and Majdanek. This monstrous event—the Holocaust—is one of the most appalling atrocities in human history.

Wartime Diplomacy. The United Nations war effort required complex interactions among countries allied as much by necessity as by admiration and shared values. Relations among the Western Allies were relatively good. Roosevelt did not get along with the touchy Free French leader de Gaulle. But overall Britain and the Commonwealth countries (Canada, South Africa, Australia, and

New Zealand) cooperated closely with the United States. With its vast man-power and industrial output, America was clearly the senior partner. If the British resented that seniority, they recognized its inevitability.

Generally speaking, relations with China were good, too. Roosevelt believed that under Chiang Kai-shek China had the makings of a great power, once freed of the Japanese yoke. In 1942 he and Churchill agreed to abandon the remaining special privileges their nations' citizens held in China. In November 1943, at Cairo, the two Western allies and China agreed to exact "unconditional surrender" peace terms from Japan and resolved to return to the Chinese Manchuria, Formosa (Taiwan), and the Pescadores, which Japan had wrenched from them in past years.

Relations between the Western partners and the Soviet Union were not as cordial. In 1943 the Russians dissolved the Comintern, the central body of the revolution-provoking international Communist movement, as a gesture of friendship with the West. Yet Stalin remained suspicious of Britain and the United States, and they of him. Though Hitler's invasion of Russia temporarily papered over East–West differences, the war itself created grounds for mutual distrust. Stalin suspected that Roosevelt and Churchill would be content to see the Soviet Union and Nazi Germany destroy each other on the Eastern Front. Starting in late 1941, he repeatedly demanded that Britain and America open a second front in Western Europe to relieve the pressure on Soviet troops and the Soviet people. Aware of German military prowess, the Allies insisted on sufficient planning and build-up, and the delay became a sore point with the Soviet Union.

Still, suspicion did not prevent cooperation. In October 1943 Secretary of State Hull, British Foreign Secretary Sir Anthony Eden, and Vyacheslav M. Molotov, the Soviet foreign minister, met in Moscow to discuss wartime problems and consider postwar reconstruction. The ministers agreed to establish a European Advisory Commission to formulate policy for Germany after victory and to set up a world organization to maintain international peace. One problem they could not solve was the postwar fate of Poland. Britain and the United States were committed to returning the Polish government-in-exile, then in London, to power when the war ended. The Soviet Union preferred a pro-communist government friendlier to itself. The issue was not settled at the Moscow meeting and continued to fester; but as a token of good faith, Stalin promised to join the war against Japan as soon as Germany was defeated. At Teheran, Iran, a month later, Churchill, Roosevelt, and Stalin met personally to confirm the results at Moscow and plan joint military operations against the common foe.

The Defeat of Germany.   By the time of the Teheran meeting, Soviet fortunes had begun to improve. The initial German offensive against Russia had carried Hitler's armies to the gates of Moscow by September 1941. In the course of their eastward drive the Germans killed, captured, or wounded some 2.5 million Soviet troops, virtually wiped out the Soviet air force and tank corps, destroyed enormous quantities of war matériel, and laid waste hundreds of Russian cities. At first many Soviet citizens, despising the communist regime, had welcomed the Germans. But the Nazis imposed a reign of utter brutality on the Russian people that left them no choice but resistance, turning the struggle into the "Great Patriotic War."

During the winter of 1941–1942 Soviet forces counterattacked, forcing the Germans to retreat at a few points. In the spring the German offensive eastward resumed, and by fall Hitler's armies had penetrated to Stalingrad, on the Volga River, and Maikop, deep into the Caucasus. During this critical period of the war vast British and American air fleets based in England dropped tons of bombs on Germany and German-occupied territories. These raids devastated the civilian population of Germany but did little to relieve pressure on the Russians or impair the German war effort.

The turning point of the European war came in February 1943 when the Russians trapped thousands of German troops in a vast pocket near Stalingrad on the Volga and forced them to surrender. In August the renewed German

World War II: Closing the Ring, 1942–1945

eastern offensive was stopped dead by the Soviet armies and then reversed. Meanwhile, in the spring of 1943, in North Africa, the combined British and American forces led by generals George S. Patton and Bernard Montgomery, under the overall command of General Dwight D. Eisenhower, dealt the final blow to Rommel's Afrika Korps. Rommel escaped to fight again, but on May 13 some 250,000 Axis troops surrendered to the British and Americans. In early July the Allies invaded Sicily. The king of Italy soon announced the resignation of Mussolini and negotiated the surrender of Italy. Mussolini was rescued by German troops and placed at the head of a puppet Italian regime. Meanwhile, British and American troops had invaded the Italian boot across the Straits of Massina and at Salerno, only to encounter fierce and effective opposition from the entrenched Germans, who retreated slowly northward while inflicting heavy casualties on the Allies.

In 1944 Germany began to crumble. In January the Russians freed Leningrad, their second city, from a devastating two-and-a-half-year siege and began their major westward drive toward the heart of the Reich. By February they had crossed the 1939 Polish-Russian frontier. In Italy the stalled Allied advance resumed, and on June 4 the American Fifth Army liberated Rome; in August the British marched into Florence.

By this time Eisenhower had launched Operation Overlord, the long-awaited second front in France. The cross-Channel attack began before dawn on the morning of June 6, when a colossal armada of Allied warships, transports, landing craft, and massive artificial ports approached the French coast in Normandy. Overhead, the Allied air forces dropped thousands of paratroopers at strategic points across northern France. After several days of ferocious fighting, the beachheads were secured. For six weeks the Germans were able to contain the Allies in a shallow pocket in Normandy. Then, at the end of July, the American Third Army under George Patton, the swashbuckling tank commander, began a swift drive east toward Germany. On August 15 the United States Seventh Army landed on the French Mediterranean coast and advanced north to attack the Germans from behind. On August 25 the Free French Second Armored Division liberated Paris.

The end of Hitler's empire was in sight. In October American troops crossed onto German soil. The Germans rallied briefly in December in a desperate counterattack at the Battle of the Bulge in the snowy Ardennes Forest that stopped the allied advance. The Americans had to be rescued by George Patton's Third Army shifting direction, but in March 1945 American armies crossed the Rhine in force and dashed eastward. Meanwhile, the Russians, too, had crossed into Germany. On April 22, 1945, they reached Berlin. Rather than face defeat, Hitler committed suicide in his underground Berlin bunker. On April 25 American and Russian troops met at Torgau on the Elbe. On May 7 the German military commander accepted unconditional surrender at Allied headquarters. The war in Europe was over.

Yalta.   In February 1945, as Germany's collapse neared, Stalin, Churchill, and Roosevelt met once again, this time at Yalta in the Soviet Crimea. Out of their deliberations emerged a set of important agreements that helped mold the post-war world.

In their public pronouncements the three leaders agreed to cooperate militarily until Germany's unconditional surrender and then to establish four occupation zones in the defeated nation, one for each of the major powers plus France. These would remain under military control until a final peace settlement with Germany down the road. They agreed to root out Nazism from Germany so that its people could eventually join the community of peaceful nations. They announced that they would meet in San Francisco in April 1945 to draw up the charter for a "United Nations" world organization that would replace the League of Nations. In the countries liberated from the Nazi yoke, provisional governments would be established composed of all "democratic elements" to be chosen by free elections. The future Polish government, they declared, would be made up largely of the pro-Soviet provisional government established at Lublin, rather than the London-based, pro-Western government-in-exile. Poland's postwar boundaries would be shifted westward at the expense of Germany. The Soviets would annex parts of prewar Polish territory in the east, and in Yugoslavia, the pro-Soviet guerrilla leader, Josef Tito, would lead the future provisional government.

"The Big Three" met for the last time at Yalta in February 1945. There they discussed the United Nations and the partition of Germany, boundaries and political arrangements in eastern Europe. Two months later, Roosevelt, already looking frail, died.

The secret clauses, not revealed until later, included an agreement on mutual repatriation of Soviet and American prisoners of war recaptured by the respective UN armies, a voting formula for the Big Four nations in the UN Security Council to come after the San Francisco meeting, and, most important of all to the Americans, an agreement by the Soviet Union to declare war on Japan "in two or three months after Germany . . . surrendered." In return for helping Britain and the United States to defeat Japan, the USSR would receive from Japan the Kurile Islands and the southern half of Sakhalin Island off the Siberian coast. In addition, it would be assigned an occupation zone in the northern half of Korea, could establish a Soviet protectorate over Outer Mongolia, and would be allowed special privileges in Manchuria and other parts of northern China.

Roosevelt's concessions to the Soviet Union at Yalta have since been sharply criticized. Eventually the Soviet Union would establish puppet regimes in Poland and in other eastern European countries and strengthen its position in the Far East. But the Yalta Conference was not to blame for these Soviet gains. By the time the "Big Three" met at Yalta, Soviet troops were already entering Germany in great force. Nothing could have kept the Soviet Union from imposing its will on Poland or the Balkan and Danube regions. As for the concessions in the Far East, the American atomic bomb had not been successfully tested and no one could foresee that by the time Germany surrendered, Japan would be on its knees and Soviet aid not needed. Roosevelt knew that the Russians had driven a hard bargain at Yalta, but he did not see how it could have been avoided. As he told a close adviser shortly after the conference: "I didn't say it was good. . . . I said it was the best I could do."

The Last Days of the Pacific War. Meanwhile, there was still a war to win in the Pacific. From 1943 to 1945 the United States mounted a score of bloody and expensive amphibious operations against the bloated Japanese empire. Moving from the east, American naval task forces, under the command of Admiral Chester Nimitz, thrust deep into Japanese-controlled areas of the central Pacific. Under cover of carrier aircraft and the guns and rockets of battleships and cruisers, waves of marines and army troops landed on enemy island beaches and destroyed resistance. After Midway the Japanese navy no longer controlled the open seas, but it continued to be a danger to amphibious landings, especially as American forces neared Japan itself. On October 25, 1944, the Japanese launched their first *kamikaze* attacks—suicide missions by pilots flying their bomb-loaded planes directly into American invasion ships. Meanwhile, MacArthur's forces, coming from their bases in Australia to the south, made a series of brilliant end runs around Japanese-controlled islands, leaving large pockets of imperial troops behind to be mopped up at leisure. In late 1944 the American and Japanese navies fought a series of battles off the Philippines that virtually eliminated the Imperial Navy as a fighting force. Soon after, American troops, led by MacArthur, landed in the Philippines, fulfilling the general's promise to "return."

The Japanese fought desperately for every scrap of coral reef. Even when overwhelmingly outnumbered they refused to surrender. Whole Japanese garrisons went to their deaths in suicide charges against the Americans. Where the terrain permitted, Japanese troops retreated to interior caves and mountains and fought to the last man. The Pacific fighting was always on a smaller scale than in Europe or North Africa, but it was more vicious and proportionately more costly. At Iwo Jima, 775 miles from the main Japanese island of Honshu, over 4,500 Americans lost their lives early in 1945 in a few days of ferocious battle. Japanese casualties were even greater: Over 21,000 of the emperor's finest troops died defending the small dot of land.

In late February 1945 MacArthur's forces marched into Manila, the wrecked Philippine capital. On April 1 U.S. marines and army units invaded Okinawa, 360 miles from the Japanese main islands. This attack was the largest amphibious operation of the Pacific war and also one of the costliest. *Kamikaze* planes sank or badly damaged 30 American vessels, and Japanese ground troops inflicted almost 40,000 casualties, including over 11,000 deaths, on the American invaders before they could take the island.

Once in American hands, Okinawa was converted into an immense air base in preparation for the invasion of the Japanese home islands. By now Japan was

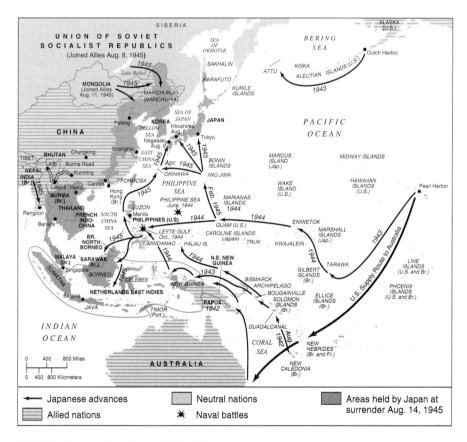

World War II: Assault on Japan, 1942–1945

in desperate straits. Many Japanese cities were in ruins from massive American air raids that incinerated the flimsily built Japanese houses, often with their inhabitants inside. The Imperial Navy rested on the bottom of the Pacific and the surviving parts of the empire that had supplied Japan with vital raw materials were cut off from the home islands by submarine attacks on vital Japanese shipping lanes. Yet the Japanese still had the will and the means to fight. On the main islands 2 million troops and 8,000 kamikaze planes awaited the final American assault. If the experience of Okinawa, Iwo Jima, Guadalcanal, and the other islands occupied by American troops was an accurate foretaste of Japanese determination to resist, the United States, military strategists concluded, could expect hundreds of thousands of casualties in any invasion attempt.

The First Nuclear Attack. The B-29 superfortress air raids on Japanese cities culminated in the destruction of Hiroshima and Nagasaki on Honshu and Kyushu by atomic attack in August 1945. The long road to these devastating events began in 1939 when a group of scientist-exiles from Hitler's Germany, led by Albert Einstein, informed Roosevelt that the Nazis were developing a new bomb of unimaginable destructiveness, based on the newly discovered process of uranium fission. To save the civilized world the United States must beat the Nazis to the punch! In mid-1940 Roosevelt turned the proposal over to a newly formed National Defense Research Committee.

After Pearl Harbor the government created the Manhattan District Project. At three major centers hundreds of scientists and technicians, supervised by physicist J. Robert Oppenheimer, set to work to build an atom bomb. At the cost of almost $2 billion, the engineering problems were gradually solved.

As the war approached its end in 1945, Einstein, Niels Bohr, and other prominent scientists concluded that the bomb would not be needed and, fearing a postwar atomic weapons arms race, they tried to stop the Manhattan Project. By the time the first atomic bomb was exploded experimentally at Alamogordo, New Mexico (July 16, 1945), the decision to use the bomb against Japan had been the subject of much heated debate in high government circles and among atomic scientists. Opponents of the bomb argued that the Japanese were on their last legs and would sue for peace shortly with or without the atomic bomb, especially if the Allies allowed the emperor to remain on the throne. Proponents of dropping the bomb noted that Japan had spurned as "unworthy of public notice" the American warning in July of "prompt and utter destruction" unless it accepted Allied "unconditional surrender" peace terms. If the American invasion casualties had been high in the outlying islands, what would they be when American troops landed on the sacred home islands?

The decision to use the bomb would not be made by FDR. In 1944 Roosevelt had been elected to a fourth term. His running mate was Senator Harry S. Truman of Missouri, who had achieved prominence as Senate investigator of abuses in war production. Roosevelt barely survived two months of his new term. In early April 1945 he died of a cerebral hemorrhage in Warm Springs, Georgia, worn down by twelve years of leadership during some of the nation's most trying and momentous times.

Truman scarcely knew the atomic bomb existed when he took the oath of office. Once he learned of the bomb's power, he decided to use it, convinced that invading Japan could be a colossal bloodbath.

At dawn on August 6, 1945, the superfortress *Enola Gay* and two escorts arrived over southern Honshu. At 8:15 its pilot released his bomb over Hiroshima. Sixty seconds later the *Enola Gay* crew watched in disbelief as an immense fireball rose over the city and slowly turned into a luminous mushroom cloud.

For the bustling Japanese city it was a moment of unspeakable horror. Hundreds of people simply vanished from the face of the earth, incinerated by the intense heat. Others were torn to pieces. Thousands, unshielded from the flash, were severely burned. All told, over 60,000 people died in the first few minutes of the attack. Others, exposed to high radiation levels, sickened and died later. The entire center of the city was flattened except for a few reinforced concrete structures.

Now the war moved swiftly toward a conclusion. Two days after the Hiroshima attack, the Soviet Union declared war on Japan and sent troops across the Manchurian frontier. On August 9 a second atomic bomb killed another 35,000 Japanese in Nagasaki. By this time the Japanese leaders were meeting to consider surrender. The military advised fighting to the bitter end, but the emperor vetoed the idea. Assured at the last minute that Hirohito would not be forced to abdicate, the Japanese accepted Allied surrender terms. On September 2, aboard the battleship *Missouri* anchored in Tokyo Bay, the Japanese signed the capitulation that ended the most devastating war in history. MacArthur presided over the ceremony.

■ CONCLUSIONS ■

During the days of jubilation that marked VJ (Victory-Japan) Day, few people asked themselves why the nation had gone to war. But as the country settled into the comfort, and the problems, of peace, those who had at first opposed the war sought to justify their positions or to even the score with their interventionist opponents.

Those critics believed that the United States had no vital reason to join the anti-Axis coalition. Only Roosevelt's need to escape the political and economic impasse confronting the New Deal or, alternately, his unwarranted and grossly exaggerated fear of Hitler's designs, led him to favor American involvement. Nor was the president honest in his actions, they said. While denying that he wanted war, he was actively turning the United States into the anti-Axis arsenal and maneuvering the Japanese into a position where they had to attack the United States or surrender their vital interests. Pearl Harbor was the result of a dishonest scheme by the administration to overcome antiwar public opinion and force America's hand.

As we have seen, these charges are, at best, partial truths. By 1941 FDR undoubtedly believed that war was unavoidable. But he wanted to fight Hitler, not Tojo; the Japanese could be attended to eventually after Germany's defeat.

The Pacific war was a blunder, but only in the sense that Roosevelt preferred to contain the Japanese while taking care of the Nazis first, and Pearl Harbor forced the United States to fight both simultaneously.

Nor was the president seeking primarily to escape a political impasse. Roosevelt's fear of the dictators predated the New Deal's political and economic difficulties. FDR was a Wilsonian who believed in collective security and detested authoritarian regimes long before the problems of his second term stopped the New Deal in its tracks. It was Hitler's astonishing and frightening successes that awakened his concern after 1937, not political frustration. The president was indeed less than candid in his tactics. While denying that he favored war, he was goading the Nazis into attacking American ships. But however mistaken he was in not taking the voters into his confidence, his purpose was governed by his concern for free American institutions.

And still another qualification is in order. Roosevelt's view of the Axis danger was not his alone; it was shared by a majority of Americans. The president was more eager than many of his fellow citizens to intervene, but the public was treading closely on his heels. In the end it was Germany's utter contempt for humanity and obvious threat to every nation's independence, not Roosevelt's duplicity, that was responsible for America's intervention in World War II. It has, with justice, been called the "good war."

Online Resources

"Rosie Pictures: Select Images Relating to American Women Workers During World War II"
http://lcweb.loc.gov/rr/print/126_rosi.html
See U.S. government-issued posters designed to encourage women to become defense workers. Some feature African-American women and speak to one of the earliest possibilities for women of color to work on production jobs in factories.

"Japanese Internment, Camp Harmony"
http://www.lib.washington.edu/exhibits/harmony/Exhibit/default.htm
This site tells the story of Seattle's "Camp Harmony" Japanese-American community, including information on housing, daily life in the camp, photographs, maps, and excerpts from the camp newsletter.

"Double Victory"
http://www.pbs.org/blackpress/educate_event/treason.html
http://www.pbs.org/blackpress/news_bios/index.html
Read about the "Double V" campaign and the African-American newspaper that started the campaign for freedom abroad and freedom at home from the nation's African-American citizens.

The Rutgers Oral History Archives of World War II
http://fas-history.rutgers.edu/oralhistory/orlhom.htm
This site contains transcripts of almost 150 oral history interviews of men and women who experienced World War II, either on the front lines or on the home front.

Japanese Internment: "War Relocation Authority Camps in Arizona, 1942–1946"
http://dizzy.library.arizona.edu/images/pamer/wraintro.html
On this site read about life for Japanese Americans held in relocation camps during the war. More than 140 photographs are compiled on this site and testify to daily life in the camps.

United States Holocaust Museum
http://www.ushmm.org
Explore virtually every facet of the Holocaust experience for Jews during World War II through online exhibits.

27

POSTWAR AMERICA

Why So Security Conscious?

1944	Bretton Woods Conference; Congress passes the GI Bill of Rights
1945	United Nations charter approved; Potsdam Conference; Roosevelt dies; Truman becomes president
1946	Winston Churchill's Iron Curtain speech; The Chinese civil war resumes; United States gives $3.75 billion in aid to Britain and $11 billion to the United Nations Relief and Rehabilitation Administration
1947	Truman orders the FBI to locate bad security risks in government; Congress endorses the Truman Doctrine, voting $400 million in military and economic aid to Greece and Turkey; Taft-Hartley Act; Congress creates the Central Intelligence Agency (CIA); Cold War begins
1948	Congress approves the Marshall Plan; Berlin Airlift supports West Berlin against Soviet takeover; Executive order desegregates the armed forces; Truman elected president
1949	North Atlantic Treaty Organization (NATO) organized; The Soviet Union explodes its first atomic bomb; People's Republic of China established under Mao Tse-tung; Nationalists retreat to Taiwan
1950	GNP rises above its wartime peak; Alger Hiss convicted of perjury; Senator Joe McCarthy begins campaign against alleged American Communists; McCarran Internal Security Act passed over Truman's veto
1950–53	The Korean War
1952, 1953	The United States and the Soviet Union explode hydrogen bombs
1952	Dwight D. Eisenhower elected president
1954	*Brown v. Board of Education*; Army-McCarthy hearings; Senate condemns McCarthy
1954–59	Housing legislation makes credit available for home buying, accelerating the middle-class move to the suburbs
1955	Montgomery bus boycott; Martin Luther King, Jr., rises to national prominence
1956	Interstate Highway System construction begins; Eisenhower reelected
1957	Federal troops enforce desegregation of Little Rock, Arkansas, Central High School
1960	John F. Kennedy elected president

Sometimes a book expresses the essence of a time so well that it captures the imagination of a wide public. *The Lonely Crowd: A Study of the Changing American Character,* by David Riesman, Reuel Denney, and Nathan Glazer, published in 1950, was one such work.

According to the authors, Americans had once been "inner-directed" people, guided through life by values learned in their youth. But most Americans were now "other-directed." How they acted depended on their peers' behavior; they were anxious to fit in, to conform to a group average. Using the technological imagery of the new postwar era, Riesman described the change as the shift from people with internal gyroscopes to those with internal radar sets.

The Lonely Crowd was interpreted as proof that the spirit of innovation had gone out of American life and conformity now was the prevailing public mood. And there was much truth to the conclusion. Some intellectual naysayers survived from an earlier era. Yet most of the thinkers of the "fifties" (as for convenience's sake we may refer to the decade and a half following VJ Day) were celebrators. Writers and intellectuals had been sharp critics of their society during the 1920s and 1930s and hopeful that it could be improved. Some had been Marxists with unlimited faith in the possibility of constructing a socialist utopia. But during the postwar decade-and-a-half this mood changed. In religious thought beliefs emphasizing humanity's limitations and the inevitability of imperfection and injustice in this world became more common. In political thought a narrow pragmatism became a force for rejecting change and reform. In history, sociology, and political science American scholars ceased to be adversaries and began to praise their society, sometimes uncritically. When former Marxist Daniel Bell published *The End of Ideology* in 1960, he delivered a swan song for the intellectual life of a generation.

And even young people now seemed sedate, committed primarily to security. Theirs was the "silent generation," it was said, aspiring to little more than early marriage, a suburban house, a secure job, and a new car in the garage. Moralists lamented that young people seemed listless and dull.

Why had Americans become so fainthearted? Why had they lost their taste for political change and social reform? Why did they fear bold self-expression? What made this the decade of the safe thought, the safe course, the safe life?

■ THE POLITICS OF DEAD CENTER ■

The public seemingly had little interest in reducing inequalities, expanding opportunities, and erecting further safeguards against life's mischances. Yet liberalism did not die. The trade unions continued to work for higher minimum wages, expanded Social Security, federal health insurance, and racial justice. A liberal press, although a minority voice, survived from the previous decade. And the universities continued to be bastions of liberalism, though some of the more stylish campus intellectuals became conservatives. In 1947 Eleanor Roosevelt and others organized Americans for Democratic Action (ADA), a group dedicated to greater social justice and an expanded social welfare state. But these groups and individuals remained on the defensive through most of the decade.

The Man from Missouri.   Harry S. Truman, who inherited Roosevelt's job, was a throwback to an earlier, more liberal era. Though a protégé of Thomas J. Pendergast, boss of the corrupt Kansas City Democratic machine, he was an honest man who came to the United States Senate in 1934, where he identified himself with the New Deal wing of his party. During the war he achieved national stature by uncovering sensational cases of waste and corruption in defense procurement, and in 1944, to please the party regulars, Roosevelt chose him instead of the erratic and visionary Henry Wallace as his running mate.

Truman was unprepared for his abrupt elevation to the presidency in April 1945. He had not been admitted to the inner war councils of the administration, and FDR's death, he later declared, felt as if "the moon, the stars, and the planets" had landed on his head. Nevertheless the new president moved quickly to take up the reins of domestic policy. Days after the Japanese surrender he submitted to Congress a legislative program that contained the main features of what he would later call the Fair Deal. Truman asked for an extension of unemployment benefits to ward off a new depression; ongoing support of the U.S. Employment Service to help returning veterans get jobs; a permanent Fair Employment Practices law to ensure equal job rights to minorities; retention of price and wage controls to prevent runaway inflation; an increase in the minimum wage from 40 to 65 cents an hour to maintain consumers' purchasing power; a large public works program to build roads, hospitals, and airports to provide jobs; "broad and comprehensive housing legislation" to give returning GIs places to live; government aid for small business; continued agricultural price supports for farmers; an expanded Social Security system; a bill to guarantee full employment; and, down the road, a national health insurance program.

Liberals applauded Truman's agenda, but they deplored his rejection of Roosevelt's New Deal advisers in favor of old cronies from his Kansas City days, men who seemed to one liberal editor "a lot of second-rate guys trying to function in an atom bomb world."

A crucial test of the president's liberalism came with the Employment Act of 1946, a measure mandating "full employment" through federal spending and taxing policies. Truman failed to push Congress hard for votes and the law as finally passed did not commit the government to deficit spending to guarantee full employment. Rather, it merely established a Council of Economic Advisors to inform the president about the state of the economy and recommend economic policies, and set up a Joint Economic Committee of Congress to perform similar functions. As the liberal magazine *The New Republic* wrote: "Alas for Truman, there is no bugle in his voice."

A pressing, immediate problem, in the months after VJ Day, was price controls. Liberals hoped that wartime price regulations would be retained to protect middle- and lower-income consumers against the serious threat of postwar inflation. Conservatives claimed that price controls merely fostered government bureaucracy and guaranteed shortages. When Congress passed a weak price-control bill, the president vetoed it, leaving the country without any price regulation at all. Costs of still-scarce civilian commodities, especially beef, quickly soared. Congress now became more receptive to a stronger bill, but Truman failed to fight effectively for one and signed a measure not much better than the first one. When his control board ordered a roll-back of beef prices, ranchers refused to ship cattle, creating a beef famine that had the public up in arms. Truman held out for a few weeks, then ordered the end of price controls on beef. Meat reappeared in stores, but at prices that shocked consumers. The president once more seemed an ineffectual, confused, and inexperienced man.

The steady and rapid rise in prices in the postwar months injured all consumers, but few expressed their grievances as effectively as trade unionists. During the war the unions had agreed to hold the line on wages. Now union workers felt they deserved to catch up. In January 1946 the steelworkers demanded a wage increase and when industry management refused, they struck. On January 19 some 800,000 workers walked off the job, not to return for eighty crippling days. The following April John L. Lewis of the United Mine Workers led 400,000 coal miners out of the mines to force the coal operators to meet his demands for a miners' welfare fund. Truman ordered the government to take over the mines but then caved in to the union's wage demands, though he considered them inflationary. He was more decisive when, soon afterward, the railroad workers threatened to strike. This time he threatened to seize the rail lines and have the army run them. When this did not work, he went before Congress to announce that he intended to draft the striking railroad workers into the army if they did not return to their jobs. Dramatically, as he was addressing Congress, news reached him that the strike had been settled.

All told, the labor troubles left a bad taste in everyone's mouth. The labor leaders felt Truman had been too hard; the middle-class public felt he had not been hard enough. Many people also resented his public profanity and his tendency to shoot verbally from the hip. In the 1946 off-year congressional elections the Republicans made "Had Enough?" their party's slogan. The voters responded with a resounding "yes," electing a Republican Congress for the first time since 1930.

Election: 1948.   The voters quickly discovered that they had gotten more than they bargained for. The public was undoubtedly more conservative than before the war. But when the Eightieth Congress started to dismantle the New Deal, it provoked the wrath of important blocs of voters.

In June 1947, furious over recent strikes and strike threats, Congress passed the Taft-Hartley Act. This measure made the "closed shop" and secondary boycotts illegal—labor unions were forbidden to force employers to hire only union members, nor could they prevent employers from doing business with other employers on a union hit list. The act permitted states to adopt "right to work" laws forbidding "union shops," that is, agreements where workers, after being hired, had to join the union. The law allowed the government to impose a sixty-day cooling-off period on would-be strikers, legalized injunctions against strikes that threatened national health and safety, ended the practice whereby employers could be forced to collect dues for the unions (the "check-off"), required unions to disclose their financial practices, and imposed an anti-Communist loyalty oath on union officials. The law represented a major check to the power conferred on unions by the New Deal, and organized labor would make its repeal its chief legislative target for the next twenty years.

The same Eightieth Congress frustrated the president on civil rights issues by refusing to abolish racial segregation in the armed forces by statute and rejecting his recommendations for a fair employment practices act to eliminate job discrimination in firms with federal contracts.

Truman improved his liberal credentials by vetoing the Taft-Hartley measure, though Congress easily overrode his veto. He also cheered the liberals by desegregating the armed forces and establishing a fair employment hiring practices commission both by executive order.

The president capitalized brilliantly on the conservative record of the Eightieth Congress in his campaign for a full presidential term in 1948. His major opponent was the governor of New York, Thomas E. Dewey, a member of the northeastern liberal Republican establishment. But he also faced challenges from both ends of the political spectrum. To his right was Senator J. Strom Thurmond of South Carolina, candidate of the States' Rights Democratic party ("Dixiecrats"), a new organization of conservative Southern Democrats strongly opposed to racial equality. To his left was the former vice president, Henry Wallace, running on the Progressive party ticket, supported by left-liberals, Soviet sympathizers, and those who feared that Truman's interventionist foreign policies would lead to war.

Neither Thurmond nor Wallace had a chance, but at the outset Dewey appeared impossible to beat. Fortunately for Truman, Dewey was a stiff, overcontrolled man who reminded one observer of the little spun-sugar groom on top of a wedding cake. The Republican candidate's chief difficulty, however, was the negative record of the Republican Eightieth Congress. Truman took brilliant advantage of that record. Through the late summer and into the fall, he criss-crossed the country by train and spoke 271 times, often to small audiences at whistle stops from the back of his observation car. The president attacked the "do-nothing Congress" and warned that those who had benefited from New Deal programs—farmers, wage earners, ethnic Americans, and blacks—would lose all their gains if Dewey and his party won. The public took heed of his words and came to admire his pluck. Across the country, as the campaign progressed, the crowds began to shout "Give 'em hell, Harry!" at the game little man with the awkward gestures and rough syntax. The result was one of the most remarkable upsets in American presidential history. All the polls had predicted that Truman would lose; he beat Dewey by a popular plurality of 2 million votes.

The Fair Deal.   The American people had announced that they did not want to return to the "bad old days" of Herbert Hoover. It soon became clear that they did not want to go forward very far or very fast, either. The next four years disappointed those who looked for further liberal change. In his State of the

Union Message soon after the election, the president unveiled his agenda for domestic reform, a developed and augmented version of the program he had earlier outlined. Labeled a "Fair Deal," it aimed at rounding out the limited welfare state Roosevelt inaugurated. But Congress, dominated by a coalition of conservative northern Republicans and Dixiecrat Democrats, refused to give him what he wanted. Little of the Fair Deal passed. Congress defeated Truman's farm program (the Brannan Plan), which sought to replace farm price supports with a system of farm income subsidies; rejected the administration's effort to add federal health insurance to the Social Security system; and ignored its scheme to provide federal aid for education. The only concessions that Truman could squeeze from the legislative branch were a higher minimum wage, an extension of Social Security coverage to an additional 9 million citizens, and a Housing Act (1949) for slum clearance and low-cost federal housing. All chance of significant domestic change evaporated when high administration officials, including the president's aide, Harry Vaughan, St. Louis Collector of Internal Revenue James Finnegan, and Assistant Attorney General T. Lamar Caudle, were accused of selling their influence to people who wanted government favors. Truman was innocent of these misdeeds, but in the midterm elections of 1950 the Republicans picked up many additional seats in Congress.

The Republican Decade Begins.   In March 1952 Truman announced that he would not be a candidate for reelection. In the Democratic free-for-all that followed, the nomination went to the one-term governor of Illinois, the articulate, witty, patrician Adlai E. Stevenson, the man favored by the party's liberal northern wing.

Among Republicans the party regulars and conservatives supported Senator Robert A. Taft of Ohio, son of the twenty-seventh president and a man of acute intelligence but little personal warmth. The moderate wing wanted Dwight D. Eisenhower, the hero of the great victory in Europe over the Nazis. Ike was an attractive figure politically. Benevolent in mien, bumbling but reassuring in speech, he seemed to be everyone's kindly uncle. The general had no known party affiliation; but he was clearly a patriot and a moderate, and he seemed certain to prove an irresistible candidate. After adopting a conservative platform, the Republican convention nominated Eisenhower. As its vice presidential candidate it chose an eager young senator from California, Richard M. Nixon, whose reputation as an aggressive campaigner and hard-line anti-Communist had recently brought him to national prominence.

The race that followed had more than its share of surprises. It looked as if the Democrats had a winning issue when it was disclosed that Nixon was the beneficiary of a dubious businessmen's fund to help pay his political expenses. Appearing on nationwide television, he explained that he had not received any personal benefit from the fund. He was not a rich man, he told his viewers. His wife, Pat, unlike the mink-coated wives of Truman administration officials, wore a "Republican cloth coat." He had accepted one gift while in office: a black-and-white cocker spaniel, which one of his two young daughters had named

Checkers. No matter what anyone said about that transaction, he was not going to give Checkers back!

Most voters liked the homey, sentimental quality of the "Checkers" speech, and the public response guaranteed that Nixon would not be dropped from the ticket. In fact, the entire Republican campaign sounded a note of whole-some domesticity and traditionalism that the 1950s public found congenial. By contrast, Stevenson seemed an "egg-head," an intellectual—and a divorced man at that. By the end of the campaign the Republicans were making the Democra-tic candidate and the men around him seem vaguely un-American. The cam-paign clincher came in October, when Eisenhower promised that if elected he would go to the Far East to help end the ongoing Korean War. In the end the Eisenhower–Nixon ticket won with a 7-million-vote margin.

"I Like Ike."   Eisenhower allowed his staff, headed by Sherman Adams, for-mer governor of New Hampshire, to conduct most day-to-day business while he saved himself for the important events. In later years the president declared that he had intended to "create an atmosphere of greater serenity and mutual confi-dence," and he accomplished his end. His opponents attacked him for his indo-lence, but most voters found it soothing. Eisenhower has been described as a hidden hand president who hid behind a passive image to better achieve his ends. Even his sometimes garbled syntax, it has been said, was deliberate, allow-ing him to avoid clarity when he had not yet made up his mind.

Ideologically, "Ike" was moderately conservative. He opposed deficit spend-ing as "fiscal irresponsibility" and once described New Deal–Fair Deal social programs as "creeping socialism." On the other hand he fought off efforts of the ultra-conservatives of his own party to dismantle the welfare state. His cabinet was heavily weighted with businessmen, one of whom, Defense Secretary Charles E. Wilson of General Motors, offended many liberals by his remark that "what is good for the country is good for General Motors, and what's good for General Motors is good for the country."

Eisenhower's domestic policies tended to favor business and the growing suburban middle class over blue-collar wage earners and city dwellers. Between 1954 and 1959 a series of housing acts made credit for home buying more readily available, accelerating the middle-class flight to the suburbs. In 1956 Congress passed the Highway Act, which authorized $32 billion for an immense interstate highway system financed by a federal gasoline tax. The measure, though much needed in an era of fast-growing motor car ownership, further drained the central cities and, by destroying the passenger traffic of the railroads, made Americans still more dependent on the wasteful, polluting private automobile.

In 1956 the general ran for reelection with Stevenson his opponent once more. The team of Eisenhower and Nixon won an even greater victory than in 1952, despite the misgivings many Americans had about Ike's shaky health fol-lowing his heart attack in 1956. During his second term the president spent more time on the golf course. Yet at times Ike could rise above his indolence and natural conservatism. In his parting words to his fellow citizens, he warned against the "military-industrial complex." This close alliance of defense industry

Here "Ike" is making a campaign speech to the Republican National Convention in 1952. The slogan was platform enough for victory in November.

and government was in some ways unavoidable, he noted, but it was also a potential danger to the country's liberties. This was a strange conclusion for a military man, but his warning would be remembered and often praised by dissenting citizens in later years.

■ THE GOOD LIFE ■

Prosperity was a major prop of 1950s conservatism. And its impact was all the greater for being unexpected and hard-won.

Between 1941 and 1945, 12 million GIs had yearned for the day when they could return to the tranquillity and happy pursuits of family, home, and careers. Many women, after months working hard on the "swing shift" and living with parents and in-laws in temporary accommodations, looked forward to starting families and enjoying domestic routines in their own homes.

This vision of private satisfaction left a deep impression on the values of the postwar generation. After 1945 the average age for marriage dropped sharply, birth rates soared, and family sizes swelled. The nation experienced a "baby boom" that lasted until the early 1960s and created a generation of Americans larger than both the one before and the one after. In 1945 the country had 37.5 million households; by 1960 there were almost 53 million. In 1954 *McCall's* magazine would coin the word "togetherness" to describe the new commitment to a close family life revolving about children, one-family suburban houses, and home entertainment.

Avoiding a New Depression. Prosperity made it possible for most GIs to make the difficult adjustment to peace. During the final stages of the war Americans had begun to worry about what the defeat of Germany and Japan would mean for the economy. To avoid disaster, in 1944 Congress passed a measure popularly known as the GI Bill of Rights. This law extended to all honorably discharged veterans generous monthly allowances for education; loans to purchase farms, businesses, or homes; and unemployment compensation of $20 a week for a maximum of fifty-two weeks. Millions of veterans became members of the "fifty-two, twenty club" until they were able to find jobs. Thousands started small businesses financed by government loans. Veterans flocked to the nation's colleges and universities. The "GI Bill" ultimately cost the government $14.5 billion, but it eased the postwar readjustment and, more significantly, created a giant pool of educated, trained people that would serve the economy well in the years to come.

The Rage to Consume. Luck also helped the economy avoid disaster. During the war high wages combined with acute shortages of new homes and consumer durables had forced the public to save. By the end of 1945 the American people had piled up $134 billion in cash, bank accounts, and government bonds. Having gone without the good things of life for so long through the Depression and war, Americans now seemed unwilling to deny themselves anything. In the closing months of the war advertisers reminded their customers that civilian products would shortly become available. "There's a Ford in your future," announced the car manufacturer. A month before Japan's surrender, General Electric advertised its "all-electric kitchen-of-the-future." The breathless copy noted that the dishwasher "washes automatically in less than 10 minutes. And the Disposall disposes of food electrically—completely eliminates garbage."

The immense pent-up demand ensured that there would be no repetition of the collapse of 1929–1933. After an initial period of scarce consumer goods and climbing prices, industry completed its conversion to peacetime production and caught up with demand. During the first full year of peace only a little more than 2 million cars were produced—fewer than in 1934. Two years later output would almost double. Americans soon came to consider many new items also essential for the good life. General Electric's prophecy came true: By the end of the decade the public was buying 225,000 automatic dishwashers and 750,000 electric Disposalls a year. In 1946 the first electric laundry dryers appeared, and housewives began to order them enthusiastically.

Television. One electronic gadget not foreseen by GE would be even more momentous. The first experimental television had begun in the 1920s. In 1939 the Radio Corporation of America had offered for sale the first home television sets. The war stopped further growth in the industry, but after Japan's surrender the market took off. In 1948 RCA and other domestic manufacturers turned out a million sets; in 1956, almost 7.5 million. By 1960 almost half of all American homes had one or more black-and-white television sets.

The new industry had a powerful social and cultural impact. Sports were transformed as lucrative broadcasting contracts converted both the college and the professional variety into immensely profitable big businesses. Hollywood shuddered as families gave up their Saturday nights at the movies to watch TV "sitcoms" or variety shows. Television proved to be more than an entertainment medium, however. It was capable of providing instruction, though parents complained that its reliance on dramas steeped in violence was dangerous to young children, and educators and professors were certain that young TV viewers were losing their capacity to read. Local as well as national and international events came "live" into the living rooms of millions of viewers. Television affected how the public perceived politicians. It made a difference in the 1960 election and also helped bring down Senator Joseph McCarthy, as we shall see.

The drastic increase in the number of families made new housing the nation's most pressing postwar need. At first thousands of returned veterans and their families lived in army surplus Quonset huts or moved in with their parents. Then came William J. Levitt and his imitators. Levitt used standardized

The standard Levittown house with the standard Levittown family (3 children) in 1950. (Courtesy of Time Life Syndication. Photograph by Bernard Hoffman.)

construction components and automatic equipment to create housing "developments" on a giant scale. His houses were virtually all the same, but they had the indispensable modern conveniences and a price tag of $10,000, payable in thirty years on an FHA or GI home mortgage. Levitt's two largest developments were on Long Island and in eastern Pennsylvania, but before long there were "Levittowns" in every part of the country, each boasting the same rows of houses with picture windows, small front lawns, and tree-bordered streets full of playing children.

And so the postwar depression did not materialize. Despite brief recessions—in 1949, 1953–1954, and 1959–1960—the GNP grew at a high average annual rate of 3.2 percent during the fifties. Prices rose at less than 2 percent a year for the remainder of the decade after 1950. The good health of the economy owed little to direct government policy. Far more important, at least at the outset, was the enormous pent-up domestic demand, cheap international raw materials, and America's unique position after 1945 as the only undamaged industrial power, the only nation capable of meeting the needs of war-ravaged Europe and Asia. Over the entire post-1945 period, moreover, the sheer size of the government sector of the economy and the existence of unemployment insurance, old-age pensions, and federal deposit insurance introduced elements of stability that had been absent before 1930.

Suburbia Triumphant.   Economic expansion dramatically altered the quality of American life. As the economy grew, its structure changed. By 1960 occupations such as farming, mining, and even manufacturing had sharply declined in relative importance; more and more Americans worked at service jobs like advertising, technical and clerical services, publishing, accounting, and teaching. Particularly dramatic was the drop in farm workers: from 9 million to 5.2 million between 1940 and 1960. By 1960 there were more white-collar than blue-collar Americans.

The new white-collar class, and many skilled blue-collar workers, developed a characteristic lifestyle centered around suburban living. The pattern was home- and child-oriented. Wives became experts in house decoration, gardening, and meal planning. Husbands took up handicraft hobbies like carpentry and boat building. A "do-it-yourself" craze swept the suburbs as much to accommodate the new domestic interests of men as to help keep down the high cost of home repairs. The doings and problems of children became major new concerns of suburban parents. They worried about their offspring perhaps more than in the recent past, when simple economic survival had overshadowed difficulties about schools, dating patterns, orthodontia, and "cultural advantages." With so many children in the house and some money to spare, many parents discovered the babysitter problem for the first time.

The suburban pattern was often a heavy financial burden. Many married women went to work to help out, especially after 1950. Between 1950 and 1970 the percentage of married women employed went from 23.8 to 40.8. During the 1950s most of these wives took jobs to supplement the family income until husbands completed school on the GI Bill or received a promotion. Such labor seemed unavoidable if the precious new lifestyle was to be maintained.

■ THE OTHER HALF ■

The shift of population from city to suburb was one of the dramatic social developments of the 1950s. Yet millions of people remained in the central cities; many rural or semirural folk moved into the urban neighborhoods emptied by the lure of the suburbs.

Urban Poverty. Some of the newcomers were, as in the past, Europeans—refugees from the war's devastation and disorder. During the decade Congress passed a number of special immigration measures that admitted GI "war brides" and several hundred thousand displaced persons, refugees from Europe's postwar wasteland. Most of the arrivals in the central cities, however, were blacks from the South and people of Hispanic background. Their experiences in some ways repeated those of earlier newcomers to American cities. Largely unskilled, they, too, took the lowest-paying jobs; they, too, moved into housing rejected by the middle class; they, too, were victims of prejudice and discrimination. Like their predecessors, they often found themselves caught in a web of poverty, crime, and family disruption and were blamed for their afflictions.

Most Americans assumed that the latest arrivals, like their predecessors, would move up in society as they acquired skills. It took longer than expected. Mid-twentieth-century America did not offer as many unskilled jobs as in the past. A construction worker now had to know how to operate a bulldozer; he could no longer merely wield a pick and shovel. Thousands of Puerto Rican, Mexican, and black women found jobs as domestics, waitresses, and hospital attendants; but their husbands, brothers, and sons often looked vainly for decent-paying work. And even when newcomers had some skill, they often found that their way up was blocked by unions whose members were hostile to them as a group or who wanted to save the declining number of skilled blue-collar jobs for their own relatives.

Civil Rights. Though poverty continued to afflict minorities, the 1950s did see major advances in civil rights. The war had made a considerable difference for America's racial and religious minorities. By throwing into ghastly relief the fruits of Nazi racism, it shamed many Americans into reconsidering their own behavior and attitudes. Hostility toward Japanese-Americans, whose impressive fighting record in Italy during the war was widely acclaimed, rapidly dissipated. Jews, the Nazis' chief victims, also experienced a new kind of acceptance. And the wartime mingling of Americans of all kinds in a common struggle reduced traditional anti-Catholic prejudice.

Black Americans, the most afflicted by prejudice, benefited the least by the wartime changes. In the South state and local ordinances continued to require hospitals, theaters, buses, trains, playgrounds, parks, and other public accommodations to maintain separate facilities for blacks and whites. Prodded by a new generation of liberal federal judges, southern states by the 1950s were making an effort to upgrade black schools so that they could meet the "separate-but-equal" test of *Plessy* v. *Ferguson*. But almost everywhere they remained both separate and inferior. Nor could blacks vote in most of the South. Intimidation, poll taxes, and rigged registration laws kept most eligible blacks from going to the polls in state and national elections. Worst of all, lynching and other kinds of racial violence survived as a brutal method of social control.

The situation for blacks in the North was better. The movement of thousands of black Americans out of the South, where they were effectively disenfranchised, to northern cities, where they could vote, enormously increased their political influence. In most northern communities there was no legal bar to the schools that black citizens could attend or theaters, hotels, restaurants, or sports events they could patronize. On the other hand, many white northerners continued to believe that blacks were inherently inferior. Their prejudice informally accomplished many of the same ends that statutes did in the South. Whites excluded blacks from private social clubs; restaurant and hotel managers refused to accept black patrons. Landlords' and home owners' prejudice forced blacks to accept inferior housing even when they could afford better. Few blacks, no matter how well qualified, could find skilled professional work. The AFL craft unions, making up the building trades, excluded black workers. Although black talent was often recognized in the arts and in sports, even there bigotry persisted. In baseball, presumably the "national sport," there were no black players in the major leagues until after World War II. In 1947 Branch Rickey, the courageous owner of the Brooklyn Dodgers, signed Jackie Robinson to play second base, finally breaking the major leagues' longtime color bar.

The struggle for black civil rights engaged many white liberals, but blacks carried most of the burden themselves. During the 1940s Walter F. White, secretary of the NAACP, and A. Phillip Randolph, president of the Brotherhood of Sleeping Car Porters, fought for a federal antilynching bill, an end to poll taxes in federal elections, and the outlawing of discrimination in work under government contract. The NAACP initiated a succession of suits aimed at breaking down segregation sanctioned by southern state and local laws.

By 1950 black citizens were growing ever more discontented as they watched the snaillike pace of change in race matters. The political system, however well it responded to the wishes of the white middle class, seemed incapable of meeting blacks' needs. Congress was paralyzed by the resistance of the well-organized southern Democratic bloc to any change in the racial order. The Republicans owed little to black voters and seemed indifferent to their problems.

Brown v. Board of Education.   Into this void stepped the branch of government traditionally the least democratic and the least responsive to public pressures: the federal courts. Beginning in 1953, the Supreme Court was led by Chief Justice Earl Warren, an Eisenhower appointee. A liberal himself, he presided over a court composed of "judicial activists," holdovers from the New Deal who were willing to extend the Court's power into areas hitherto considered legislative concerns or beyond the reach of law. The Warren Court would expand the realm of personal rights as against the state in many areas of life. But its most momentous decisions targeted the legal barriers to racial equality and change.

Even before Warren's appointment, the Court, under NAACP goading, had begun to restrict segregation in housing and in graduate and professional education. Then, in 1954, came its landmark ruling in the case of *Brown v. The Board of Education of Topeka,* brilliantly argued for the NAACP by black attorney Thurgood Marshall. Resting its decision on the findings of sociologists and psychologists that separate schooling inevitably harmed black children, the Warren Court declared that segregation in the public schools was a denial of the Fourteenth Amendment's requirement that the states accord to every person "equal protection of the laws." "We conclude," the chief justice wrote, "that in the field of public education the doctrine of 'separate but equal' has no place. Separate educational facilities are inherently unequal." Hoping to give the Court's words their maximum moral authority, Warren had lobbied his colleagues intensely. The decision had been unanimous.

The road to colorblind schools would be long and difficult. In the southern border states compliance with the Brown decision was generally good. In Washington, D.C., the schools immediately desegragated. In the lower South the decision produced a storm. The more respectable conservatives of the region organized White Citizens' Councils—"uptown Ku Klux Klans," their critics called them—to defeat the Court's order by boycotts and other economic weapons directed against both black and white supporters of desegregation. The Klan itself revived and used violence and threats of violence to prevent compliance with the Brown decision. Everywhere in the lower South school boards dragged their feet in meeting the federal mandate. In 1955, in the so-called *Brown II* decision, the Court ruled that local communities must comply with the desegregation decision with "all deliberate speed," though it left specific timetables to the lower federal courts to decide.

Still "massive resistance" continued. At Little Rock, Arkansas, in 1957 the Klan backed Arkansas Governor Orval Faubus when he defied a court order that black students be admitted to Central High School. Mobs of angry white protesters gathered outside the school, blocking entrance by the black pupils. Faubus refused to remove them. President Eisenhower, though not a civil rights enthusiast, could not allow such blatant disregard of the law of the land and dispatched federal troops to protect the black children seeking admission. Ike was willing to march with the times, but he did not want to lead the parade. He would later call his appointment of Earl Warren as chief justice "the biggest damnfool mistake" he ever made.

Civil Disobedience.   Legal action was the preferred tactic of the NAACP against segregation and denial of voting rights. Other civil rights leaders, however, believed that the white South would only respond to civil disobedience.

This strategy was associated with a new black leadership. There was now a substantial southern black middle class of clergymen, teachers, students, small-business owners, and professionals—men and women better prepared by education and income to defend their race than their predecessors. Such leaders identified their cause with the struggles of oppressed colonial peoples around the world and concluded that the tactics used to evict the European imperialists might be applied to the American South.

The new approach first attracted national attention in December 1955, when Rosa Parks, a black seamstress and activist, weary from her day's work in a downtown department store, refused to give up her seat on a crowded Montgomery, Alabama, bus to a white man as the local Jim Crow law required. Mrs. Parks was arrested and fined $10. Black community leaders, waiting for a case to test Montgomery's segregation ordinances, quickly organized a boycott of the city bus company. The city authorities arrested the boycott leaders, including the twenty-seven-year-old Reverend Martin Luther King, Jr., a Georgia-born, northern-educated Baptist minister. The Klan bombed King's house and burned several black churches.

Yet despite reprisals, day after day, Montgomery's black community refused to patronize the buses; dedicated people got to work on foot or by car-pooling. Some Montgomery blacks were tempted to meet violence with violence, but King, an adherent of *Satyagraha,* Indian leader Mohandas Gandhi's doctrine of nonviolent civil disobedience, headed them off. "We must love our white brothers," he advised, "no matter what they do to us." A year after the boycott began the U.S. Supreme Court ordered the end of segregation on the Montgomery bus system. The black protesters had won.

The Montgomery boycott raised King, whose eloquence and courage had sustained the protesters through difficult times, to the front rank of civil rights leadership. It also made nonviolent civil disobedience the central strategy of the civil rights movement. In 1957 King and his followers established the Southern Christian Leadership Conference (SCLC) in Atlanta as agent of a concerted nonviolent, biracial campaign to challenge the remaining bastions of Jim Crow and restore the voting rights the white South had denied its black citizens for almost a hundred years.

The grass-roots efforts were intended to keep southern race discrimination clearly before the court of public opinion. King and his colleagues on the SCLC never doubted that white support was needed to defeat racism. As the civil rights hymn proclaimed: "White and black together" would "overcome some day." Fortunately the civil rights leaders could at first count on broad white support. By the 1950s many middle-class whites had come to accept the conclusions of social scientists and anthropologists that race differences were culturally derived and that discrimination was costly, irrational, and unjust. With his dazzling eloquence, cultivated mind, and disarming message of Christian love, King was particularly well equipped to capitalize on liberal white attitudes.

Meanwhile, civil rights leaders continued to seek redress on the level of federal law and policy. In September 1957 Congress passed the first of several measures designed to restore voting rights to black southerners. The Civil Rights Act of 1957, the first such legislation since Reconstruction, set up a Civil Rights Commission to investigate complaints that voting rights had been denied, and a Civil Rights Division of the Department of Justice to prosecute authorities found responsible. A relatively modest measure, without much teeth to enforce its goals, it was strengthened by the 1960 Civil Rights Act, which required voting registrars to retain their records for some months following an election so that they could be examined by federal officials. Both laws provided the government with weapons to end black disenfranchisement. But as the 1960s began, the slow and painful process of restoring rights guaranteed to black Americans by the Fourteenth and Fifteenth Amendments almost a century before had just begun.

■ THE COLD WAR ■

The retreat of Americans to private satisfactions during the 1950s can be explained in part by the payoff that fulfilled people's material hopes. Yet as millions surrendered to the pleasures of a consumer society, a great anxiety remained: the threat of nuclear holocaust. This fear, like affluence, would encourage a political and social philosophy that avoided criticism of the nation and its dominant free-market, middle-class values.

The United Nations.　Internationalists had succeeded during World War II in committing the United States to world cooperation. In 1944, at Bretton Woods, New Hampshire, American and other anti-Axis diplomats signed agreements for an international bank and a world monetary fund to stabilize international currencies and rebuild war-torn economies. In November 1945 the Senate endorsed "an international authority to preserve peace," an act, noted the *New York Times,* in a reference to the defeat of the Versailles treaty, that undid "a twenty-four-year-old mistake."

The internationalists achieved their major goal, called for at Yalta, at the conference at San Francisco in April–June 1945. There, by the bay, 282 delegates representing the 50 nations arrayed against the Axis powers created the United Nations, modeled after the League of Nations. The UN charter established a General Assembly composed of all member nations to serve as the ultimate UN policy-making body. An eleven-nation Security Council, consisting of five permanent members—the United States, Great Britain, the Soviet Union, France, and China—and six others elected by the General Assembly for two-year terms—would actually make the major decisions for settling disputes among member nations. Each permanent member was given the power to veto Security Council decisions.

The creation of the UN was a triumph for the old Wilsonian ideal of international cooperation to preserve world peace. But it could not disguise the discord that had long been growing between the Soviet Union and the West or settle all the conflicts brewing in the troubled postwar world.

An Unsettled World.　Clearly, the international balance following VJ Day was very different from the past. Western Europe, long the world's leading power center, emerged after 1945 profoundly enfeebled. France, defeated by the Nazis in 1940, was demoralized and faced with the serious problems of reestablishing national unity and a political consensus. Germany and Italy were shattered societies where children begged on the streets and women sold themselves to American GIs or Soviet soldiers for packs of cigarettes and chocolate bars. Most disruptive of all, victorious Britain was impoverished and incapable of holding its vast empire together. All over the former Nazi-occupied territories misery prevailed. Millions of displaced persons wandered across the continent looking for a place to live and ways to reconstruct their lives. The physical scars of war marked every city and town. Hunger and disease afflicted populations weakened by wartime privations and continuing shortages. Winston Churchill scarcely exaggerated when he described Europe in 1945 as "a rubble heap, a charnel house, a breeding ground of pestilence and hate."

Society in Eastern Europe was even more unsettled than in the West. Millions of Russians, Jews, Poles, and others had lost their lives in combat or been shot, gassed, or starved to death by the Nazi conquerors. Twenty million Soviet citizens had died. The political equilibrium had also been profoundly altered. Before 1939 a group of independent nations, including the Baltic states (Lithuania, Latvia, and Estonia), Finland, Poland, and Romania, had walled the Soviet Union off from the rest of Europe. The regimes in these countries, as well as the next tier west, had been generally unfriendly to the USSR. After 1945 the picture was transformed. Now the Soviets shared occupation zones in Germany and Austria with the Western Allies; had established pro-Soviet "satellite" regimes in Poland, Hungary, Romania, Bulgaria, Albania, and Yugoslavia; had the Baltic states incorporated into the Soviet Union; and had extended the USSR's official borders westward by annexing eastern Poland and compensating the Poles with territory in eastern Germany. Finland and Czechoslovakia remained independent in 1945, but the former did so only at the price of avoiding policies that offended the Soviet Union, while the latter's autonomy would be short-lived.

Meanwhile, the decline of Western Europe had created a power vacuum in Asia and Africa. In the Far East the Japanese military successes of 1941–1943 had stripped away the myth of European invincibility and awakened dormant nationalist feelings in Indonesia, Ceylon (Sri Lanka), Indochina, Burma, India, and Malaysia. In the Middle East and North Africa, Arab nationalism, long held in check by France and Britain, began to seethe. In sub-Saharan black Africa, too, by 1945 Western-educated elites were demanding an end to European colonial rule.

Especially troubling in Asia was the turmoil in China, the world's most populous nation. During the war the United States, Great Britain, and even the Soviet Union had supported the Kuomintang, the Chinese Nationalist government under Chiang Kai-shek. But Chiang's regime had increasingly come under the domination of corrupt bureaucrats, privileged landlords, and rich merchants. It had failed to win the support of the Chinese peasantry and after the war seemed unable to deal with China's economic backwardness and social inequalities.

For many years Chiang's chief adversary had been the Communists led by Mao Tse-tung. In the portion of north China they controlled, the Communists had established an authoritarian, though honest, administration. Hoping to combine the best of both regimes, President Truman sent General George

C. Marshall to China in December 1945 to end the Nationalist–Communist rift. Marshall failed, and by mid-1946 China was entangled in a devastating civil war.

And even in the Americas there were churning discontents. In the Latin countries to the south of the United States, resentment of authoritarian regimes, run by generals, combined with gross inequalities of wealth and power, encouraged radical movements and political restlessness.

Sources of the Cold War.   The postwar instability in Europe, Asia, Africa, and the Americas set the stage for world competition between the only two nations that still possessed international power—the United States and the Soviet Union. Eventually all five major continents would become arenas for unremitting rivalry between the two and their respective allies. Their conflict would become a worldwide struggle waged by diplomacy, propaganda, economic rivalry, and military threat and intimidation. Occasionally the Cold War would erupt in actual combat, though fortunately for humanity, only through surrogates, never between the two superpowers directly.

Both the Soviet Union and the United States undoubtedly contributed to the conflict. The leaders of both nations were certain that they alone represented international justice and a better life for humanity. Both believed that their system must ultimately prevail. Viewed objectively, the Cold War was the attempt of two superpowers to ensure their own safety and protect what they perceived as their vital interests in the dramatically transformed international environment after 1945.

Yet the positions of the two sides were not symmetrical. The Soviet Union was an outsider nation, aggrieved by a sense of exclusion from a central role in world affairs. It resembled, after 1945, a new-made millionaire blackballed from the best private clubs by the established elite and determined to achieve his rightful place at all costs. The belligerence of Soviet leaders was fueled by their sense of inferiority toward America. The United States, on the other hand, felt itself the world's power hub, successor to the European imperialist powers. The relation of outsider to insider was inevitably confrontational. The Soviet Union, to achieve its goals, had to alter the existing world order; the United States need only preserve it.

The asymmetry went beyond strategic locations, however. The two systems were not morally equivalent. America, for all its imperfections, was a democratic society with a functioning multiparty political system and a large private sphere protected by traditions of individual liberty and personal rights incorporated into fundamental law. The Soviet Union was an oppressive, totalitarian society where boundaries between the public and private spheres were weak and political and economic control was centralized at the top in a single, all-powerful Communist party and an unresponsive, rigid bureaucracy.

To make matters worse, during the immediate postwar years the ruler of the sprawling, untidy, monolithic Soviet Union, Josef Stalin, was a ruthless, paranoid dictator who had swept aside or massacred all his domestic enemies and imposed a regime on the Soviet people that made the czars' autocratic reign seem benevolent by comparison. Before, during, and after the war, Stalin's secret police arrested thousands of men and women who were accused, usually on the flimsiest evidence, of being enemies of the state and sent to brutal prison camps or summarily executed. During his last years he became a half-mad recluse who locked himself in the Kremlin and imagined plots against his rule. Even after Stalin's death in 1953, his successors, though never as bad, continued to repress their own people and support the tyrants in the Soviet satellite nations who imitated their masters in Moscow. The USSR continued to be a prison for scores of national groups conquered by the czars and compelled to accept the domination of the Slavic Great Russians who ruled from Moscow.

This moral asymmetry, however, does not mean that the United States was not capable of coercive, arbitrary, and ruthless actions in the pursuit of its interests. At home, the Cold War was fought at times at the expense of civil liberties and repression of dissent. Abroad it often involved self-serving behavior that harmed neutrals and perpetuated injustice and tyranny.

The Emerging Conflict.   As we saw, the leader of the Soviet Union and the Western powers had maintained a show of friendship during the war that papered over serious disagreements. Many ordinary Americans had sincerely admired the brave Soviet people in their fierce struggle with the Nazi invaders. Then, as Soviet troops broke the back of the German army and pushed westward, questions of postwar boundaries, spheres of influence, and relations between the Soviet Union and its immediate neighbors became sources of contention.

By the time of the Big Three's Potsdam Conference in July 1945, the postwar world was already taking shape. Churchill, defeated for reelection by the British voters before Japan surrendered, was replaced at the conference by British Labour Party head, Clement Atlee, the new prime minister. President Harry Truman came in place of the recently deceased Roosevelt. During the conference, Truman received word that the scientists of the Manhattan Project had successfully tested an atomic bomb. Roosevelt had believed he could charm Stalin. Truman, influenced perhaps by the sense of America's awesome new strength, took a more skeptical attitude toward the Soviet dictator. The conferees agreed to little of consequence, and most pending issues between the democracies and the Soviet Union remained unresolved.

Determined to eliminate all unfriendly regimes from the Soviet Union's western borders, Stalin moved rapidly toward establishing political dominion over Eastern Europe and permanent division of conquered Germany. With the Red Army holding all the territory Stalin coveted, his allies had no choice but to concede Soviet gains. The American people, led by Roosevelt to believe that he could handle Stalin, were bitterly disappointed when Truman "lost" Eastern Europe to the Communists.

Most western Europeans and Americans, except those who sympathized with Communist ideology, were alarmed by this shift of Soviet power to the heart of Central Europe, too close to the West for comfort. For their part, the Soviets and their friends argued that they could not allow the "Socialist Motherland" to be surrounded by hostile states as in the past. And, in any event, they said, the new Communist regimes within the Soviet orbit expressed the will of the local people far better than the aristocratic and semifascist ones that had existed in 1939.

The Third World—as the undeveloped countries of Asia, Africa, and the Americas would be called—presented both opportunities and dangers to both superpowers. With France, Britain, Holland, and Japan too weakened to maintain empires, who would benefit from the political changes bound to come in their former colonies? The United States had never been a major colonial power like France or Britain, and during the post-1945 occupation of Japan it had demonstrated a commendable zeal for encouraging free, liberal institutions abroad. Could it now capitalize on the goodwill it possessed to win the emerging Third World nations over to Western-style liberal capitalism? But the Soviet Union also had advantages. It, too, had taken little part in the earlier race for overseas colonies, and so could claim to be free of imperialist taint. The people in almost all these emerging societies were desperately poor and would be attracted by drastic schemes to redistribute land and end the privileged status of local elites. The Soviet Union sought to identify itself with these changes. Communism would be the vehicle for creating juster societies after national independence was achieved. Many Third World intellectuals were strongly influenced by Marxist ideas, which promised quick modernization without the complexities and inconveniences of democratic struggles.

In any struggle over the "nonaligned" world, then, it was not clear who would win. Some Americans, and perhaps some Soviet leaders, did not see the world as a simple polar division of "East" versus "West." But during the immediate postwar period most Americans and Russians found it difficult to imagine that nations could be permanently nonaligned. Either "they were for us, or against us," opinion leaders on both sides seemed to believe.

Containment.   The end of World War II brought rapid international change. The Soviet Union exerted pressure not only to secure its western borders, but also to gain access to warm-water ports to the south. In 1945 it demanded that neighboring Turkey cede to it several frontier districts and concede Soviet control over the Dardanelles, the all-important strait connecting Soviet Black Sea ports with the Mediterranean. In the following year Greece was torn apart by a Communist-led revolt sustained by supplies sent by Stalin and Marshal Josip Broz Tito, the leader of the Yugoslav Communists. Meanwhile, in the months following German surrender, war-damaged, impoverished, and demoralized Western Europe seemed vulnerable to Soviet political inroads. Perhaps the Soviet Union did not anticipate direct conquest and occupation of France, Italy, or Great Britain, but Moscow seemed determined to build pro-Soviet parties within them that would ally these nations with the USSR. Even a neutral Europe would be an enormous defeat for the United States and a corresponding gain for the Soviet Union.

In 1946 Congress authorized a $3.75 billion loan to Great Britain and contributed to the United Nations Relief and Rehabilitation Administration

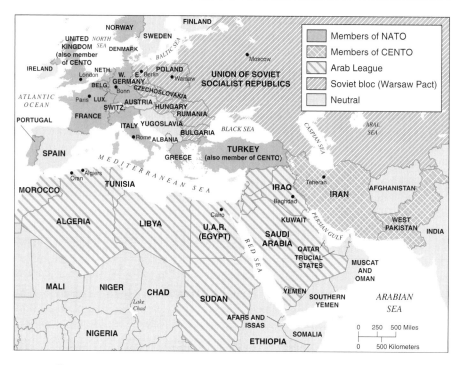

Postwar Alliances in Europe and the Middle East

(UNRRA), an agency formed to funnel money and supplies to starving Europeans. These efforts were not enough, however, and by 1947 Europe seemed on the verge of collapse.

During the first two years of peace a growing chorus of Western leaders warned that something must be done to stop the expansion of Soviet influence. In March 1946 Winston Churchill told an audience at Fulton, Missouri, that an "iron curtain" had "descended across the continent of Europe" behind which Communist tyranny reigned supreme. Elsewhere "Communist fifth columns" were threatening Christian civilization. A little over a year later George F. Kennan, a influential senior American diplomat, told his State Department superiors that the Soviet Union was committed to an "aggressive intransigence with respect to the outside world." American policy, he advised, must be one of "long-term, patient, but firm and vigilant containment of Russian expansive tendencies."

The first significant move to wall in the spreading "red tide" came during the cruel winter of 1946–1947 when Europe seemed in social and economic crisis. In February 1947 the financially besieged British told George Marshall, now Truman's secretary of state, that communist pressure in Greece and Turkey was reaching a climax and Britain could no longer perform its traditional stabilizing role in the eastern Mediterranean. To counter Soviet pressure, on March 12 Truman asked Congress for $400 million in aid for the two beleaguered nations. Under the leadership of Republican Senator Arthur H. Vandenberg of Michigan,

Congress endorsed the Truman Doctrine and made the appropriation. Massive aid to Greece and Turkey, combined with the break in 1948 between Tito and the Soviet Union, blocking Russian arms and supplies to the Greek guerrillas, soon ended the Communist threat in both countries. The Truman Doctrine established a precedent that would inspire American foreign policy for the next forty years.

The Marshall Plan.   The next, and bigger, installment of containment was the Marshall Plan. A joint U.S.–European economic recovery program first broached by Secretary of State Marshall in June 1947 at the Harvard commencement, it sought to restore "the confidence of the European people in the economic future of their own country and of Europe as a whole." That July an all-European conference convened in Paris, formed the Committee for European Economic Cooperation, and agreed on the shape of the program. The American call for a cooperative effort did not exclude the Soviet Union, although the prospect of Soviet participation made American officials uneasy. Suspicious of the United States and wanting no part in any program that would strengthen Western capitalism, the Soviets came to the conference but walked out when they discovered that they could not disrupt the meeting.

Americans did not support containment unanimously. Walter Lippmann, the dean of American journalism, called it a "strategic monstrosity" and feared that it was a blank check for American entanglement in every conflict around the globe. Critics on the left and friends of the Soviet Union considered it a scheme to preserve capitalist injustice and a danger to world peace. Former Vice President Henry Wallace, for one, dubbed it the "Martial Plan." But anti-Communist public opinion, reinforced by farmers' and manufacturers' zeal for enlarged export markets, endorsed the administration proposal. In March 1948 Congress voted to fund the European Recovery Program, and in a few weeks vessels laden with grain and vital manufactures were steaming for Europe.

In all, the United States contributed $12.5 billion to European recovery. It was not pure generosity, of course. Shoring up Western Europe clearly served America's strategic interests and helped bolster the American economy. But however motivated, the Marshall Plan's results were spectacular. By 1950 Western Europe's economic output had outstripped that of 1939, the last prewar year, by 25 percent. Noncommunist Europe was beginning a dramatic economic surge that would carry living standards far beyond anything dreamed of before the war. As poverty receded, so did communism. By 1950 the voters in the fast-recovering West European nations were confident once again and the growth of local communist parties was effectively checked.

The Marshall Plan was accompanied by other moves to stiffen European resistance to Soviet and internal Communist pressures. Britain, France, and the United States were determined to restore an independent German state. In 1948 they stabilized the German currency and soon after created out of their occupation zones a West German Federal Republic with its capital at Bonn. Fearful of a revived and militant Germany, the Russians reacted strongly. In June 1948 they imposed a blockade on all traffic into the western sector of Berlin, a city deep inside Soviet-occupied east Germany. To save Berlin and prevent its complete takeover by the Soviet East German satellite, the United States sent vital supplies into the city by plane. The Berlin Airlift lasted for more than ten months, until the Russians withdrew their barricades and allowed the city to be supplied once more by rail and truck. In October 1949 the Soviets transformed their own German occupation zone into the German Democratic Republic (East Germany) under firm Communist control.

NATO.   During these critical early postwar years the two superpowers played a deadly game across the chessboard of Europe. In February 1948 a Communist coup d'état in Prague, Czechoslovakia, turned the only Eastern European country with a surviving democratic regime into another Soviet satellite. In September 1949 the USSR exploded its first atomic bomb. Knowledge that the Soviets were now capable of waging atomic war sent shock waves through the Western nations.

The Prague coup and the Berlin blockade goaded the Western powers into a defensive alliance. In April 1949 Belgium, Canada, Denmark, France, Great Britain, Iceland, Italy, Luxembourg, the Netherlands, Norway, Portugal, and the United States formed the North Atlantic Treaty Organization (NATO). Each NATO member pledged to go to war if any other member were attacked. Conservative Republican senators fought the NATO treaty, but with the support of Senator Vandenburg, the leading Republican internationalist, it passed. For the first time the United States had committed itself to an international alliance in time of peace. The Soviets soon responded in kind to what they considered a Western provocation. Fearing especially the West's move to include West Germany in NATO, in 1955 they sought to counter the western alliance with the Warsaw Pact, a military alliance of Albania, Bulgaria, Czechoslovakia, East Germany, Hungary, Poland, and Romania with the USSR.

Until 1971 Berlin would remain a Western hostage in Soviet–East German hands, periodically triggering dangerous confrontations. Americans were slow to accept Soviet domination in Eastern Europe. In January 1953 Secretary of State John Foster Dulles declared in a television broadcast that people behind the Iron Curtain, in the Soviet satellite nations, could "count on" the United States. Soon afterward his supporters in Congress introduced the "captive peoples" resolution that suggested that the United States would give military aid to anti-Soviet forces in Eastern Europe. When in 1956, however, the Hungarians rose in revolt and demanded the departure of Soviet troops and an end to Soviet control, the United States refused to intervene and allowed the Hungarian "freedom fighters" to be brutally crushed by Soviet troops and tanks. The tragic failure of the Hungarian uprising clarified the limits of American commitment: The United States would go to war for the NATO countries and West Germany; it would not fight to liberate the "captive peoples" behind the Iron Curtain.

The Arms Race.   Adding to the uncertainties of balance-of-power politics, and coloring almost every international event, was the threat of a direct nuclear exchange between the two superpowers and the possibility of world cataclysm.

Stalin had professed indifference when Truman had alluded to the atom bomb at the Potsdam conference. But the Soviets were actually terrified by their adversary's new weapon. During the war, to help develop their own bomb, they had spied on British and American atomic weapons developments. After 1945 they stepped up their drive to produce atomic weapons. When the United States proposed international control of such weapons in 1946, the USSR rejected it on the grounds that it would freeze the status quo while the Americans were still ahead. The Russians seemed sure to acquire a working bomb sooner or later, but in September 1949 when President Truman announced that the Soviet Union had exploded its first atomic weapon, many Americans were startled.

The Soviet race for the bomb was only the first phase of the great superpower struggle to achieve arms supremacy by every means possible. At first each side sought bigger and better nuclear weapons. In 1950, over the protests of Robert Oppenheimer and other prominent scientists, the American government authorized development of the far more destructive hydrogen bomb. On November 1, 1952, the first of these was exploded at Eniwetok, an atoll in the Marshall Islands. Within ten months the Soviet Union exploded its own H-bomb, thus ending America's brief nuclear advantage.

Over the next few years both sides set off dozens of H-bombs to test their effectiveness and improve their reliability. It soon became obvious that the device was indeed a "hell" bomb that made it theoretically possible to destroy humanity. Each test explosion, moreover, released large amounts of radioactive strontium-90 into the atmosphere, threatening to cause thousands of deaths from cancer in future generations.

Once both superpowers had acquired explosive weapons of unimagined power, the arms race shifted to delivery systems. During the early 1950s the United States maintained a 270,000-person Strategic Air Command, which kept a constant patrol of B-29 bombers in the air, each one carrying H-bombs. The Russians did not try to compete with SAC but sought to outflank the United States by developing guided missiles. Soviet engineers soon succeeded in producing unmanned, radar-guided rockets that could travel great distances and hit their targets within an error of a few miles. To counteract the Russian intercontinental ballistic missiles (ICBMs), the United States established a chain of radar stations, the DEW (distant early warning) line across northern Canada. At the same time American scientists worked furiously to close the "missile gap."

Missiles and H-bombs did not preclude heavy investment in conventional weapons. American budget outlays for planes, tanks, artillery, atomic submarines, and other defense items went from $13 billion in 1950, when it was about one third of the total federal budget, to $46 billion in 1960, when it was half.

Added to the outlays on military hardware were vast disbursements for other Cold War safeguards. In July 1947 Congress passed the National Security Act unifying the army, navy, and air force under a single secretary of defense, establishing the National Security Council (NSC) to advise the president on issues necessary to American safety, and setting up a Central Intelligence Agency (CIA) to gather information deemed essential to American security abroad. Over the next three decades the CIA became the major American spy agency, and its epic battle of wits with its East Bloc counterparts became legendary, reviving the whole genre of spy novels and movies. Along with other Cold War agencies, such as Radio Free Europe and the Voice of America, the CIA cost billions of dollars, though its budgets were hidden in other federal expenditures to conceal the extent of its activities from the Soviet enemy.

A vocal minority of Americans deplored the economic costs of the Cold War. Conservatives believed that it might be possible to achieve economies in military outlays without weakening American defense. During the Eisenhower administration, Secretary of State John Foster Dulles advanced the doctrine of "massive retaliation," including the use of atomic weapons against any Soviet attack, as a way of keeping down costs. Rather than trying to match the Soviet Union man for man, gun for gun, and tank for tank, we should build up an H-bomb arsenal that would deter our adversary from threatening our vital interests. Critics of the secretary's views noted that it would turn every confrontation with the USSR into a possible atomic war. Given another Dulles policy, "brinkmanship"—bringing each crisis with the Soviet Union to the edge of war—the emphasis on atomic weapons seemed a certain prescription for world disaster.

The most determined critics of the arms race went beyond doubts of nuclear strategy. Pacifists, women's civic groups, liberal scientists and academics, and political radicals denounced most arms outlays, nuclear and otherwise, as wasteful and dangerous. Some of the "stop-the-arms-race" groups—including SANE (National Committee for a Sane Nuclear Policy) and the Committee for Nonviolent Action—emphasized the dangers of nuclear fallout and of war from the race itself. Others emphasized the draining effect of armaments expenditures on civic life. Some advocated arms controls; others believed the only way to save the world was for the West to set an example by disarming first ("unilaterally"), even if that entailed risks.

The protests made a deep public impression. Neither the United States nor the Soviet Union abandoned the arms competition, but the peace groups helped induce the superpowers to sign a treaty in 1963 (the Limited Nuclear Test Ban Treaty) forbidding atmospheric testing of nuclear weapons. Their continued pressure, moreover, created a widespread international demand for arms limitations that would eventually bear fruit.

Containment in Asia.   In Asia, meanwhile, the United States found itself facing a new danger. Since the end of World War II Washington had sent $2 billion in aid to Chiang Kai-shek in China with little result. Much of the war matériel was sold off by corrupt Kuomintang officials and ended up in the hands of either profiteers or the Chinese Communists. The Kuomintang soon lost the confidence of the Chinese people. By 1948 Mao Tse-tung's army was advancing triumphantly south, sweeping all before it. In December 1949 Chiang, his entourage, and his remaining troops, fled the mainland to reestablish the "Republic of China" on Taiwan (Formosa), off the south coast of China. Now supreme on the mainland, Mao and his supporters proclaimed the People's Republic of China (PRC) with its capital at Beijing. It now seemed to many Americans that hundreds of millions of Chinese had been added to the Communist side of the scales.

During the Chinese civil war Americans associated with the "China lobby" and an Asia-first policy had supported direct military intervention to prevent the Communist takeover. The Truman administration rejected the idea, convinced that a land war in Asia would be a bottomless quagmire. Even after the Communist victory the American government sought to avoid a direct military role in East Asia as an insupportable position. In January 1950 Secretary of State Dean Acheson declared that the United States did not consider Taiwan, mainland Southeast Asia, or South Korea essential to American security. If any of these places were invaded, the "initial resistance" would have to come from those attacked.

Acheson inadvertently gave the Communists the green light for further expansion. Korea, under the brutal rule of Japan for many years, had been divided after World War II into Soviet and American zones at the thirty-eighth parallel, pending its eventual reunification. By 1948 there were two governments in Korea: a Republic of Korea (ROK) in the South led by Syngman Rhee, elected president under UN supervision, and a People's Republic in the North, closely allied with the Soviet Union. In 1949 the United States withdrew its last remaining troops from the South, leaving the ROK unprotected.

Soon after Acheson's statement the North Koreans—apparently with Soviet approval—concluded that it was time to unite Korea under communist rule by force. On June 25, 1950, 95,000 Soviet-armed North Korean troops pushed across the thirty-eighth parallel in a massive invasion of the Republic of Korea, which was still formally under United Nations control. Reversing his administration's position, Truman acted decisively to stop what he considered a blatant act of aggression. The United States immediately called an emergency session of the UN Security Council, from which the USSR had temporarily withdrawn its representative. On June 27, unimpeded by a Soviet veto, the Security Council asked all members of the United Nations to contribute "such assistance to the Republic of Korea as may be necessary to repel the armed attack and restore international peace and security in the area." By this time American troops under the command of General Douglas MacArthur, Supreme Allied Commander in Japan, had been dispatched to South Korea. The UN resolution made the Korean war a "police action" in which the United States acted technically as agent of the UN.

The initial North Korean attack quickly overwhelmed the small army of the Republic of Korea and the weak and untested force of Americans initially sent from Japan. Seoul, the South Korean capital, fell on June 28 and the ROK and Americans were forced into a tight pocket around the port of Pusan. There they held on desperately until reinforcements began to arrive from the United States and other UN countries. In September the UN forces under MacArthur's overall command made a surprise end run by sea around the North Koreans at Inchon and were soon driving the enemy north, back the they way they had come. By October the UN forces reached the thirty-eighth parallel. Here the American Joint Chiefs of Staff advised MacArthur to stop, but the overconfident general

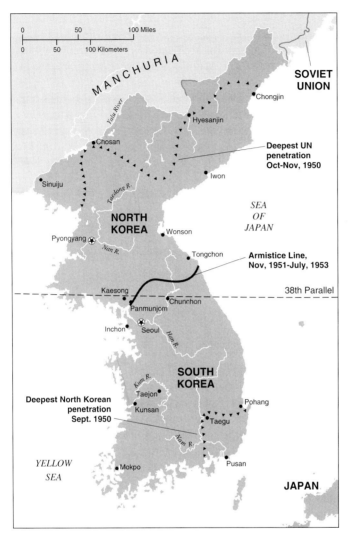

0 | 50 | 100 Miles

0 | 50 | 100 Kilometers

MANCHURIA

Yalu River

SOVIET
UNION

Chongjin

Hyesanjin

Chosan

Deepest UN
penetration
Oct-Nov, 1950

Sinuiju

Taedong R.

Iwon

SEA
OF
JAPAN

NORTH
KOREA

Wonson

Pyongyang

Nan R.

Tongchon

Armistice Line,
Nov, 1951-July, 1953

Kaesong

Panmunjom

Chunchon

38th Parallel

Inchon

Seoul

Han R.

SOUTH
KOREA

Kum R.

Taejon

Deepest North Korean
penetration
Sept. 1950

Kunsan

Pohang

Taegu

Nam R.

YELLOW
SEA

Mokpo

Pusan

JAPAN

The Korean War Arena

believed that the Chinese would not intervene, or if they did, that they would be pushovers. He ordered his troops to advance rapidly toward the Korean–Chinese border at the Yalu River to evict the communists from the whole of Korea.

MacArthur's army drove into a trap. On November 26 masses of communist Chinese troops hit the ROK and UN forces in the Yalu valley. For a time they threatened to capture thousands of South Korea's defenders, and General Walton Walker, MacArthur's field commander, was forced into a headlong retreat south. The Chinese advance was finally checked by General Matthew Ridgeway, who succeeded Walker after he was killed in a jeep accident. Thereafter the two sides settled down to months of cruel and costly trench warfare close to the thirty-eighth parallel, resembling the military stalemate on the Western Front during World War I.

From the moment the Chinese intervened, MacArthur proposed bombing communist bases in Manchuria and "unleashing" Chiang Kai-shek in Taiwan to invade the People's Republic. President Truman warned the general to desist from his bellicose pronouncements, but he refused. When Truman sought to open peace negotiations with the Communists in March 1951, MacArthur publicly threatened to escalate the war against the Chinese, thereby scuttling the talks. Several weeks later the general wrote a public letter to House Republican leader Joseph Martin declaring "there is no substitute for victory," and urging the United States to shift its strategic priorities from Europe to Asia. Truman now concluded that the general had allowed his years as benevolent dictator in Japan to go to his head, and removed him from overall command, replacing him with Ridgeway, a man who obeyed orders.

Many conservative Americans saw MacArthur's dismissal as a sign of weakness in the global struggle against the Communist threat. When the general returned home he was welcomed as a hero. Thousands lined the streets of the cities as he passed through on his way to Washington and Congress invited him to speak to a joint session. The general, a talented actor, made a case in his speech for his policies and bade a tearful farewell to the American people that concluded with the words of an old army song: "Old soldiers never die; they just fade away." Conservative Republicans were soon talking about nominating him for president in 1952. The general's popularity waned after hearings before a congressional committee where the administration made an effective case for prudence in Korea, and he soon retired quietly to private life.

MacArthur's departure cleared the way for peace talks. In July 1951 the United Nations and Communists opened armistice negotiations at Kaesong, soon transferred to Panmunjom. The cease-fire discussions dragged on fruitlessly for two years while hundreds of Americans died in vicious patrol actions along the static front line. At home, frustrations grew. Not until after Stalin's death in March 1953 was a cease-fire agreement reached. On July 26 the fighting finally ceased.

Meanwhile, the American people had paid dearly for the "police action." At home the country had returned to a war footing. Congress revived the draft and expanded the armed forces to more than 3 million men. The decision to rebuild a conventional military force pushed the defense budget to over $50 billion by 1952. The economy, which had been in the doldrums in 1949, quickly revived and then began to overheat. By 1951 the cost of living had risen about 12 percent despite the government's efforts to hold it down by price controls like those of World War II. The total cost in lives and wealth was immense for a struggle that had achieved so little. The United States had suffered 135,000 casualties (including 33,000 killed) and spent an estimated $54 billion.

Yet nothing much of permanence was accomplished. Fifty years later Korea remains divided along a line just a few miles from the June 1950 border. And several thousand American troops still are stationed in South Korea to deter the bellicose communist North from invading once again.

■ A SECOND "RED SCARE" ■

The Cold War sorely tried the patience of Americans. The new enemy was elusive. The danger from Hitler and Tojo had been clear for all to see, and could be directly confronted and defeated. But we could not take direct military action against the chief Cold War enemy, for that threatened nuclear holocaust. Instead, the weapons deployed on both sides were prolonged campaigns of subversion, espionage, and propaganda, all unsuited to the American temperament. And where a military response was possible, we were forced to confront the communist adversary, as in Korea, through distant surrogates in the Third World. Few Americans knew much about the emerging Third World of former colonial states, and most tended to see the Soviet Union behind every social upheaval in Asia, Africa, or Latin America. And indeed, the Soviet Union did use wars of "national liberation" to expand its power and influence. During much of the 1950s, moreover, the Communists appeared to be winning the struggle for world control. Disinclined to make distinctions among Chinese Communists, Yugoslav Communists, and Soviet Communists, many Americans thought the whole world was turning uniformly "red."

The Enemy Within.   Because communism seemed so obviously evil, atheistic, and abhorrently brutal, its Cold War successes awakened suspicions among Americans that along with the visible enemy in China and the Soviet Union must be a disguised and hidden one operating internally to undermine anticommunist resistance. They suspected Communists of hiding behind familiar institutions, secretly supported by respectable people in high places in the United States and Europe. However simplistic this analysis of the Cold War might be, it gained currency among some Americans during the 1950s and beyond.

The distrustful public mood was reinforced by real Soviet espionage operations in the United States. In 1950 the British uncovered the doings of Klaus Fuchs, a German refugee atomic physicist who had been employed at Los Alamos on the Manhattan Project during the war and had transmitted atomic secrets to the Soviet Union. Fuchs's detection led to an enlisted man at the Los Alamos Atomic energy center, who accused his brother-in-law and sister, Julius and Ethel Rosenberg, of passing atomic secrets to the Russians. Although some people believed them innocent, the Rosenbergs were eventually convicted of espionage and executed in what became an international cause célèbre. In March 1950 Judith Coplon and her Soviet agent-lover, Valentin Gubitchev, were convicted of spying. Gubitchev was deported and Coplon sentenced to jail.

Most disturbing of all was the apparent betrayal of the country by a prominent public servant, Alger Hiss. Hiss had served in the State Department during the 1930s and was part of the staff that accompanied Roosevelt to Yalta. In 1948 Whittaker Chambers, an admitted former Communist, told the House Committee on Un-American Activities (HUAC) that he and Hiss had been members of a prewar Soviet spy ring in Washington and that Hiss had given secret government documents to the Russians. Summoned before HUAC and closely questioned by Congressman Richard Nixon, Hiss denied that he had ever known Chambers or stolen official secrets. Because of the statute of limitations, Hiss could no longer be indicted for espionage. He sued Chambers for libel, however, and in the trial Chambers produced documents that he claimed Hiss had stolen. The federal government now tried Hiss for perjury, and in the second of two trials he was found guilty of lying under oath and sentenced to five years in prison.

Conservatives seized on the Hiss case to indict the whole New Deal. Alien to the American way, they said, it represented "twenty years of treason." And the Democrats were still protecting traitors. The Truman administration, charged Congressman Nixon, "was extremely anxious that nothing happen to Mr. Hiss." The left, by contrast, considered Hiss an innocent martyr to Cold War hysteria. Even moderate liberals at times reacted to the charges of Chambers and others as if Soviet espionage against the United States was inconceivable or incapable of posing a threat to the nation.

McCarthyism.   But the public often confused spying with subversion. Many people failed to distinguish between stealing government secrets and merely advocating ideas that were, or seemed to be, "un-American." Before long the country was in the grip of a full-scale panic that endangered the civil liberties of many Americans.

The Truman administration was in part responsible for the hysteria. Afraid to appear "soft on communism," Truman in March 1947 issued Executive Order 9835 establishing a program to eliminate "disloyal" federal employees who, because of their politics or their personal or sexual habits, might pose security risks. As part of the same executive order, he authorized the attorney general to indict eleven top officials of the American Communist party on charges of violating the Smith Act of 1940 by advocating overthrow of the government by force. After a tumultuous trial in New York, in which the communist party sought to indict the government, all the defendants were convicted and sentenced to prison.

Truman did not want the antisubversive drive to go too far, however. In 1950 he vetoed the McCarran Internal Security Act requiring registration of Communist and Communist-front organizations, excluding from the country would-be immigrants who belonged to a totalitarian party, forbidding the employment of Communists in defense work, and providing for the internment of radicals during national emergencies. "In a free country," Truman declared in his veto message, "we punish men for the crimes they commit, but never for the opinions they have." These were stirring words, but Congress overrode his veto. Whether he acted out of conviction or from fear, Truman cannot escape blame for having stimulated the excessive reaction to internal subversion that marked the decade.

It was perhaps inevitable that a demagogue would appear to exploit Americans' fears and suspicions for his own purposes. The man was Joseph R. McCarthy, the Republican junior senator from Wisconsin. Like many demagogues, McCarthy had his attractive side. He genuinely liked people and could never understand why they often despised him. Though he was a scrappy man, willing to take on anyone, he did not make his political foes into personal enemies. But he was also a liar, a petty tyrant, a crude opportunist, and an insensitive boor who could not comprehend that a democratic society required a modicum of civility and political decency to function.

In early 1950 McCarthy was in political trouble. Elected to the Senate over a weak opponent in the 1946 Republican sweep, he had acquired a reputation as an opportunist who exchanged votes and influence for favors from business groups and had even championed the Nazi SS in a case involving the murder of American prisoners-of-war. Clearly, the junior senator had to find an issue that would give him broad exposure and a good press if he wanted to stay in Washington. He quickly found his issue in the country's rising anti-Communist concerns.

In Wheeling, West Virginia, on February 9, McCarthy opened his reelection drive with a speech devoted to the dangers of communism at home and abroad. The United States, he told the local Republican women's club, found itself "in a position of impotency" in international affairs because of "the traitorous actions" of men in high government posts. The State Department, especially, was "thoroughly infested with Communists," bright young men from the privileged classes who had betrayed their country. He could, he said, name 205 members of the State Department whom the secretary of state knew to be members of the Communist party.

McCarthy could do nothing of the sort. His list was based on sources long out of date. But the press began to take notice of his sensational charges, and the country was soon in an excited mood. Soon afterward, while testifying before a Senate subcommittee, McCarthy announced dramatically that the "top Soviet espionage agent" in the United States was Owen Lattimore, a professor of Far Eastern affairs at Johns Hopkins University, who had been a State Department adviser on China policy. The testimony of witnesses failed to support McCarthy's claims, but many Americans, deeply chagrined at the recent "loss" of China, were willing to believe that Lattimore and men like him had betrayed the nation. For days the senator made the headlines. In a few short months the word "McCarthyism" had been added to the language as a term for irresponsible mud-slinging and defamation.

McCarthy and his cause were at first genuinely popular. Opinion polls in 1950 showed that the senator had the approval of 50 percent of the American people. McCarthy's strong political base was confirmed when, in the 1950 congressional election, he helped defeat for reelection Democratic Senator Millard Tydings of Maryland, one of his severest critics. His strength with the voters made McCarthyism an effective weapon for conservative Republicans to use against liberals and Democrats. As such it was sanctioned by many GOP leaders, including Mr. Republican himself, Robert Taft. So pervasive was McCarthy's popularity that even liberal Democrats had to reckon with it. In the early 1950s the young Massachusetts congressman John F. Kennedy noted that "Joe . . . may have something."

McCarthyism became a mood and an attitude that penetrated many layers of American life, with malign consequences. Besides McCarthy's own probes, the

Senator Joseph McCarthy uses "visuals" to show supposed power of communism in the United States as Joseph Welch expresses his skepticism.

House Committee on Un-American Activities and the Senate Internal Security Subcommittee regularly investigated Communist infiltration of American institutions. HUAC's well-publicized public hearings usually focused on very visible areas such as the movies, the universities, the churches, and the unions. The committee forced men and women under subpoena to answer charges, often anonymous, that they had been members of "subversive" organizations. These groups need not be formally Communist; they could be "Communist fronts" included on the "Attorney General's List" of several hundred suspect organizations. HUAC did not punish offenders directly, but many of those called before the committee were injured professionally and lost their jobs.

Private organizations and local officials quickly joined the antisubversive clamor. The broadcasting industry refused to hire anyone for radio or television work who was listed in *Red Channels,* a volume compiled by three former FBI agents that claimed to identify entertainers and media writers with past or existing radical affiliations. In Hollywood there were unofficial blacklists of performers, screenwriters, and directors whom no studio would employ. The theater, too, was rife with accusers and lists of "disloyal" people. Universities imposed loyalty oaths on faculty; states and local governments required clerks, typists, laborers, and officials to swear they had never been members of the communist party.

The prevailing hysteria over Communism and subversion cast a shadow over American life. The fear of attack and the possible consequences for their careers and personal lives undermined creative men and women. Many former political activists retreated to conservatism or became apolitical, a process that reinforced the shift of the political spectrum to the right. Even ordinary citizens were deeply affected. When vigilantes were attacking every dissenting view and every dissenter as Communist, it seemed wise to keep silent and repress opinions that could be considered irreverent. Fear of attack as a dangerous subversive, then, undoubtedly reinforced the 1950s American retreat into privatism.

After Eisenhower's victory and McCarthy's reelection in 1952, observers expected the senator to quiet down. The Republicans were now in office, and attacks on government officials would hurt McCarthy's own party. But he refused to stop. In February 1953 he accused officials of the United States Information Agency, the information arm of the State Department, of attempting to undermine the American propaganda war against the Soviet Union. Panicked, Secretary of State John Foster Dulles ordered hundreds of books by authors of "doubtful loyalty" removed from the agency's shelves.

McCarthy's Downfall. In 1954, with his popularity at its peak, the Wisconsin senator accused Secretary of the Army, Robert T. Stevens, of approving the promotion of Irving Peress, an army dentist who had once been a member of the radical American Labor Party. The promotion was actually a routine reranking of all drafted medical personnel, but in the next few weeks McCarthy made "Who promoted Peress?" a rallying cry for dedicated anti-communists. The army responded by accusing McCarthy of using his influence to gain preferential treatment at Fort Monmouth for G. David Schine, a draftee who had been a member of the senator's staff and a protégé of Roy Cohn, his committee counsel.

Eventually Congress voted to hold an investigation of the charges before McCarthy's own committee with Republican Senator Karl Mundt of South Dakota presiding. On April 22, 1954, the hearings commenced, and when they were over eight weeks later, McCarthy had run his course. Before the glaring lights of the television cameras, the senator seemed like a scowling Hollywood villain. He badgered witnesses and insulted them; he constantly interrupted the proceedings with points of order and irrelevancies. Television viewers in their living rooms and neighborhood bars decided he was a hateful man.

McCarthy's stock quickly plummeted. On December 2, 1954, the Senate passed a resolution condemning him for bringing the Senate into disrepute. The censure motion entailed no legal penalties, but from that day on, his colleagues shunned him, and when he rose to speak, they left the Senate chamber. Worst of all, the media began to ignore him. No matter what he said, he could no longer make the headlines. On May 2, 1957, he died of a liver ailment, unlamented by most Americans.

McCarthy's Legacy. McCarthy was gone, but in various guises the feelings he fed on and the movement he helped launch survived. In 1958 a Massachusetts candy manufacturer named Robert Welch founded the John Birch Society, a far-right anti-communist organization that insisted the entire nation was riddled with secret Communists. Well-supplied with money from southwestern oil, cattle, and electronics magnates, the Birch Society attracted people obsessed with the Communist danger and every opponent of change or novelty. Its local chapters fought against the fluoridation of drinking water, instigated recall elections against liberal school board members, attacked "subversive" college professors, demanded the impeachment of Chief Justice Earl Warren, and resisted efforts to impose gun controls. Even more extreme was George Lincoln Rockwell's American Nazi party and similar neo-Nazi hate groups, and semisecret paramilitary organizations such as the Minute Men, which collected arms and held drills in expectation of an imminent Soviet invasion or an internal Communist takeover.

McCarthyism also affected United States foreign policy. America's refusal to accord diplomatic recognition to Communist China, for example, was in part a response to pressure from the McCarthyite communist hunters. Even more serious, perhaps, fear of being attacked for "losing Indochina," as Truman had "lost China," would help propel Lyndon Johnson into one of the most unfortunate military episodes in American history.

The Election of 1960.   With the popular Ike about to retire, 1960 seemed a promising year for the Democrats, and from the outset they fielded an array of eager and able candidates—liberal Minnesota senator, Hubert Humphrey; the still popular Adlai Stevenson; Lyndon Johnson, the powerful Senate Majority Leader from Texas; and the young senator from Massachusetts, John F. Kennedy.

Kennedy's qualifications for president were not entirely convincing. The oldest surviving son of Wall Street operator Joseph Kennedy, he seemed more interested in wine, women, and song than in public service. He had returned from the war a young navy hero and had been pushed by his ambitious father to run for Congress. As a member of the House and then the Senate, Kennedy had been a mediocre legislator, not generally admired by his colleagues. But his most serious disqualification to many voters was his religion. The Kennedys were Catholics and the last time a Catholic had run for president—Al Smith in 1928—he had been badly beaten. Anti-Catholicism, though it had diminished since 1928, still ran strong in the rural Midwest and the South, and it did not seem likely that a Catholic, even in 1960, could overcome the ingrained religious prejudice of the heartland.

But Kennedy had several things going for him as well. He was handsome, well-spoken, well-educated, and rich. The rich part was important, for money talked eloquently in politics even in 1960. The Kennedys could pay for chartered jets, TV time, and newspaper advertisements far beyond their opponents' means. When Kennedy defeated Hubert Humphrey in the West Virginia primary, the nomination was all but clinched. Kennedy won on the first ballot at the Los Angeles Democratic convention and, in a stunning show of political pragmatism, turned to Texan Lyndon Johnson to balance the ticket.

The Republican candidate was Vice President Richard Nixon. Liberals considered him unprincipled and had long called him "Tricky Dick." But as vice president he had acquired some stature as a foreign-policy expert in part for the "kitchen debate" with Soviet leader Khrushchev, when, at a gleaming model American kitchen on exhibition at a Moscow trade fair, he had scored points for American capitalism. Henry Cabot Lodge, Jr., the UN ambassador, got the Republican vice presidential slot.

The contest was the most exciting in a decade. Nixon plugged his own experience, especially in foreign affairs, and called his opponent a lightweight. The vice president never mentioned Kennedy's Catholicism, but clearly it was on the minds of many traditional Protestants. Kennedy partially neutralized the issue by appearing before the Greater Houston Ministerial Association in September and eloquently endorsing the separation of church and state. The contest may have been decided by a set of TV debates between the two candidates during September and October. In the first one especially, the more telegenic Kennedy, though the younger man, seemed poised and articulate. Nixon, looking unshaven, appeared nervous and tired. The election marked the true onset of the "tube" as the key media instrument in American politics.

The election was one of the closest on record. The Massachusetts senator received only 100,000 more popular votes than Nixon out of almost 69 million cast, and he carried fewer, though larger, states than did his adversary. There is some evidence, moreover, that in both Texas and Illinois the Democratic machines altered the popular votes in favor of the party's candidate. Nixon might have challenged the results but chose to accept them rather than force a major constitutional crisis.

■ CONCLUSIONS ■

During the 1950s Americans sought escape from public problems in private pursuits. Having suffered through the nation's worst depression and its most agonizing war, they could not help regarding the postwar era as an improvement. With all its flaws, prosperity was real, and they turned from politics to revel in the pleasures of growing abundance and domestic life. The pursuit of private goals and satisfactions and the avoidance of controversy after 1945 was to some extent, then, a predictable consequence of the surprising success of the postwar economy.

It was also the result of fear. Communism loomed over half the planet and seemed to be expanding daily. Moreover, for the first time since the Ottoman threat to Christendom in the seventeenth century, the West had to reckon with the competition of non-Europeans with values and cultures different from its own.

It was difficult to deal with this challenge from abroad. An all-out military response, in the era of nuclear weapons, was precluded by considerations of both humanity and self-preservation. The only valid answer, we can now see, was patient diplomatic and intellectual struggle. But Americans are not a patient people, and the resulting frustration and anxiety brought out their worst side as expressed in McCarthyism. McCarthyism in turn engendered further fear and insecurity. Intimidated by public events that seemed to threaten their safety, and exposed to the pleasures of consumerism as never before, Americans turned inward and sought personal, safe satisfactions.

Yet despite the appeal of privatism and prudence, by the mid-1950s acute observers could detect signs of change. In 1956 a popular sociologist, John Keats, wrote *The Crack in the Picture Window,* attacking suburbia as deadening to the mind and spirit. By the end of the decade a new cultural bohemia composed of "Beat" poets and novelists had begun to appear in San Francisco and New York. For bohemians, the Beats were unusually apolitical and "cool," but they took drugs, wore sandals, and were sexually promiscuous. Clearly, the times were beginning to change.

Online Resources

"Readings in the 1950s"
http://www.english.upenn.edu/~afilreis/50s/home.html
This site contains primary sources that reflect the anti-Communist ideology that permeated the cold-war era. Sources on the site include transcripts from testimony from anti-Communist hearings, magazine articles that address the cultural anxiety of nuclear threat, and numerous links to other sites.

"The Truman Doctrine"
http://www.yale.edu/lawweb/avalon/trudoc.htm
Read President Harry Truman's address before a joint session of Congress in which the "Truman Doctrine," or using U.S. economic power to ensure the freedom of all nations, was born.

"Korean War"
http://www.nps.gov/kwvm/war/korea.htm
On this site sponsored by the National Park Service, read about the origins of the Korean War, the conflict year by year, and the context of the homefront. It also features information on the war veterans' memorial.

"Levittown: Documents of an Ideal Suburb"
http://www.uic.edu/~pbhales/Levittown.html
Discover the cultural history of Levittown through contemporary photographs of the suburb and its inhabitants, construction of the houses, family life, and suburb-centered recreation.

"MLK Page"
http://www.umich.edu/politics/mlk
Consult this informative website for timelines of the American civil rights movement and learn more about pivotal events such as *Brown v. Board of Education* and the 1955 Montgomery bus boycott.

"Rebel Poets of the 1950s"
http://www.npg.si.edu/exh/rebels/poets.htm
Part of an exhibit on the beat movement, this site interprets the beats and their impact. Also, see paintings and photographs of beat poets.

"NSC68"
http://www.seattleu.edu/artsci/history/us1945/docs/nsc68-1.htm
This site features a National Security Council report ordered by President

Eisenhower that examines U.S. programs for national defense, the risks of nuclear war, and Soviet preparedness.

Beyond the Playing Field: Jackie Robinson, Civil Rights Advocate
http://www.nara.gov/education/teaching/robinson/robmain.html
Through this Web site, see the activist side of baseball great Jackie Robinson. Through letters written to American presidents and his numerous quotes, these archives record Robinson's quest for racial justice.

The Cold War and Red Scare in Washington State
http://www.washington.edu/uwired/outreach/csph/corcah/main.html#context
Produced by the Center for the Study of the Pacific Northwest, this site explains how McCarthyism played out in Washington State and affected the lives of many of its citizens. The site contains a national overview as well as documents that pertain to statewide anticommunist committees.

The Fifties at Home
http://www.sos.state.mi.us/history/museum/explore/museums/hismus/
1900-75/fifties/50shome.html
Take a virtual tour of a typical 1950s home on the Michigan Historical Museum System Web page. See photos and read about how 1950s consumerism shaped the home and its contents.

History and Politics Out Loud: I Have a Dream Speech
http://database.library.northwestern.edu/hpol/master.asp?=browse&s=
speaker&id=12
Hear the speech of Martin Luther King, Jr., delivered at the March on Washington in 1963. A transcript of this speech and other of King's addresses are also available at this site.

28

THE DISSENTING SIXTIES

Why Protest in the "Great Society"?

1954	French defeated at Dien Bien Phu; Geneva Accords
1957	Russians launch Sputnik into orbit; Martin Luther King, Jr., founds the Southern Christian Leadership Conference (SCLC)
1959	Castro overthrows Batista regime in Cuba; U-2 incident
1960	Student Nonviolent Coordinating Committee (SNCC) founded; Birth-control pill introduced; John F. Kennedy elected president
1961	Peace Corps founded; Kennedy announces the Alliance for Progress; CIA and anti-Castro Cubans launch the Bay of Pigs invasion of Cuba; Berlin Wall built; Kennedy sends American troops to Vietnam
1962	Cuban Missile Crisis
1962, 1963	Attorney General Robert Kennedy enforces integration of state universities in Mississippi and Alabama
1963	Civil rights demonstrators numbering 250,000 march on Washington; Kennedy assassinated; Lyndon Johnson becomes president
1964	Johnson launches the War on Poverty; China explodes its first atom bomb; Congress passes the Civil Rights Act; Tonkin Gulf Resolution
1964–65	Berkeley Free Speech Movement sets precedent for major campus revolts
1965	Johnson orders the bombing of North Vietnam; Great Society Legislation and agencies: Elementary and Secondary Education Act, Medicare, Department of Housing and Urban Development (HUD), Omnibus Housing Act, Voting Rights Act, National Foundations of the Arts and Humanities, Higher Education Act, Metropolitan Area Redevelopment Act, Truth in Lending Act
1965–67	Black riots in Los Angeles, Detroit, Newark
1966	Highway Safety Act; Betty Friedan organizes the National Organization for Women (NOW)
1968	My Lai Massacre; Martin Luther King and Robert Kennedy assassinated; Street riots at Democratic National Convention in Chicago; Richard Nixon elected president
1969	American Indian activists occupy Alcatraz Island; Woodstock and Altamont rock festivals; Americans land on the moon

In April 1968 a group of young actors appeared in a new musical at the Biltmore Theater in New York. The play, *Hair*, glorified every rebellious, nonconformist theme of the decade. *Hair* proclaimed that the Age of Aquarius was at hand, that "harmony and understanding" and "crystal revelation" would soon prevail. A song called "Sodomy" described the delights of oral sex and masturbation; "Air" detailed the horrors of air pollution; and "Walking in Space" was simultaneously about the space program and "tripping" on mind-altering drugs. The musical theme of "Hare Krishna" was borrowed from a Hindu sect whose orange-robed adherents could be seen ringing bells and chanting on the streets of large American cities in these years. The high point of the play's performance came at the end of the first act, when members of the biracial cast removed all their clothes while singing "Beads, Flowers, Freedom and Happiness."

To a Rip Van Winkle of 1948 awakening twenty years later, *Hair* would have been a profound shock. Radical in politics, "liberated" in social vision, ecstatic and orgiastic in cultural texture, it was almost the antithesis of the values Americans had accepted in the years between 1945 and 1960. Only in the darkest corners of American life at the time had there been a hint that such things even existed. But in 1968 the members of the *Hair* cast became culture heroes who, according to theater critic Clive Barnes of the *New York Times*, expressed "the authentic voice of today."

How had this startling transformation come about? America in the 1950s was a prosperous, self-satisfied society. Why did it change so drastically, so quickly? Was it primarily the inexorable swing of the cultural pendulum: having moved so far toward conformity, it could only move toward revolt? Did prosperity, as in the past, breed its special forms of discontent with the status quo? Were outside forces and events responsible?

■ POLITICS IN CAMELOT ■

The decade began with a breath of fresh political air. The thousand days of the Kennedy presidency have been likened to Camelot, the mythical court of King Arthur where, "for one brief shining moment," there flourished an enchanted realm of brave men and beautiful women worthy of the world's admiration. The new president was handsome, articulate, and young, the first chief executive born in the twentieth century. We now know that he was not the personal paragon of the Camelot legend. But for the first time since FDR, the White House became a lively and interesting place, and the public delighted in the change.

Kennedy appealed especially to the idealism of young people. One of his first moves was to propose a Peace Corps of young men and women who would invest their skills and part of their lives in working abroad among the sick and poor of Third World nations. Soon afterward he announced the Alliance for Progress, a foreign aid proposal to pump $20 billion into Latin America to raise economic output and redistribute it among the hemisphere's poor and oppressed.

Kennedy Foreign Policy. However idealistic in tone, Kennedy's Alliance for Progress did not fundamentally alter "containment" as the core of American foreign policy. Yet Kennedy and his advisers brought new ideas to the American conduct of foreign affairs.

In his 1960 campaign Kennedy had warned that his Republican predecessor had allowed the Soviet Union to build more missiles than the United States and that this "missile gap" threatened the nation's security. After taking office he found that the gap did not exist. But the new president had more substantial objections to Eisenhower's weapons policy as well. Ike and his chief foreign-policy adviser, John Foster Dulles, had neglected conventional weapons and built up stockpiles of hydrogen bombs. This meant that in the event of a serious international challenge, America's only credible response was nuclear attack. This might be appropriate for a full-scale Soviet assault on NATO, but would we use "massive deterrence" against Soviet aggression at such pressure points as Berlin, the Middle East, Africa, or Asia? Clearly, the risks of nuclear holocaust were simply too great for the interests at stake. In effect, then, the lack of conventional American military forces only invited Soviet subversion all over the world.

To avoid these unacceptable alternatives of doom or surrender, Kennedy and Secretary of Defense Robert McNamara proposed a "flexible response." The United States must build up its conventional forces and prepare itself to use counterinsurgency tactics to tailor its response to the extent of the threat. To implement the new policy, the administration expanded the army from eleven to sixteen combat divisions and began retraining troops for jungle and guerrilla fighting. This was expensive, and during the Kennedy years the defense budget grew by 25 percent.

Early Tests. The first attempt at counterinsurgency was a humiliating fiasco. In April 1961 Kennedy gave the green light to an operation conceived under Eisenhower to land a small force of armed anti-Castro refugees in Cuba at the Bay of Pigs. According to the CIA, even a small invasion would trigger a general uprising that would topple Fidel Castro, the leader who had overthrown the Cuban dictator Batista in 1959 and installed an anti-American revolutionary regime in Havana. The uprising did not occur; the invaders were quickly pinned down on the beach by Castro's corces. To avoid deeper involvement in an embarrassing enterprise, the president refused to provide American air and military support to rescue them. In a matter of days they were all killed or captured, and the United States found itself condemned as a bully, and an ineffectual one at that.

Kennedy's first direct contact with the Soviets was not much happier. Soviet Premier Nikita Khrushchev, Stalin's successor, though not a paranoid tyrant like his predecessor, was equally suspicious of Western motives and did not intend to surrender any of his nation's interests. His 1955 meeting with Eisenhower at Geneva—the first U.S.–Soviet "summit"—had produced nothing concrete, but its cordial and cooperative tone (the "Spirit of Geneva") cheered the world, uneasy over the superpower rivalry. This quickly dissipated, however, when, in November 1958, Khrushchev escalated Cold War tensions over Berlin.

That city, divided between east and west zones, was a Communist sore point. Between 1949 and 1958 almost 3 million Germans had fled Communist East Germany for West Germany, and to prevent further loss of productive people the Communist authorities had sealed off most of the two Germanies' common frontier. Berlin, however, remained open, and its Western zone continued to be a magnet for disaffected East Germans. Hundreds escaped daily to West Berlin, and each person who fled the German Democratic Republic advertised the superiority of the capitalist over the Communist way of life. Related to the problem of Berlin was the refusal of the Western powers to sign a peace treaty that accepted the division of Germany, and their insistence that they would deal only with the Soviet Union, not the East German authorities, in matters concerned with Berlin. On November 10, 1960, Khrushchev announced that the Soviet Union intended to transfer authority over the eastern zone of Berlin to the East German authorities, thus forcing the Western powers to deal with them. Implied was the possibility of another Berlin blockade.

Fortunately, the Soviet premier withdrew his threat soon after, and for a time the danger of superpower confrontation over Berlin receded. In May 1960 Eisenhower and Khrushchev met in Paris for another summit. It was ill-starred. Just before the meeting the Soviets announced that they had shot down an American U-2 spy plane over the Soviet Union and captured its CIA civilian employee pilot, Francis Gary Powers. On May 17 Khrushchev denounced the spy flight and cancelled the summit. In January the next year he ominously declared his country's "unlimited support" to "peoples fighting for their liberation." The Cold War, in the form of "wars of national liberation," would now be extended around the world.

Kennedy's encounter with Khrushchev at Vienna in June 1961 was an unnerving experience. The Bay of Pigs fiasco led the Soviet leader to conclude that the young American president was weak and inexperienced and could be bullied. At Vienna Khrushchev was abrupt, even insulting. Berlin was a "bone in the throat" of the Soviet Union, he said. If the Western powers failed to sign an agreement that accepted the legitimacy of the communist German Democratic Republic, he would turn over administration of Berlin to its authorities, who might then end free communication between the city and West Germany. If the United States chose to go to war over this, so be it. When Khrushchev returned to Moscow he delivered a number of warlike speeches and raised the Soviet military budget.

Though shaken by Khrushchev's threats, Kennedy refused to be intimidated. He asked Congress for an additional $3.5 billion for defense, announced the call-up of army reserves and National Guard units, and urged Americans to build bomb shelters against a possible nuclear war. Public anxiety soared.

Meanwhile, in Berlin the stream of refugees to the West became a flood. To staunch this hemorrhage, on August 14, 1961, East German authorities began to erect a high wall of brick, concrete blocks, and barbed wire. Anyone caught trying to scale this wall would be shot. For the next twenty-eight years the Berlin Wall would symbolize the barriers separating the two Cold War antagonists.

For a while longer the tension continued. In early September the Soviets defiantly resumed above-ground nuclear testing on a massive scale, releasing enormous quantities of radioactive matter into the atmosphere. In retaliation Kennedy authorized the resumption of American nuclear testing, though only underground. Then Khrushchev backed down. At the end of the month in Moscow he told a visiting diplomat from Belgium, a NATO nation: "I'm not trying to put you in an impossible situation; I know very well that you can't let yourself be stepped on." In mid-October he informed the Communist Party Congress that the Western powers appeared conciliatory and he, accordingly, would defer a peace treaty with East Germany. The second Berlin crisis was over.

The Cuban Missile Crisis.   But Khrushchev recklessly forced one more major confrontation in his war of nerves against the United States and its president. The Soviet leader knew that the United States actually surpassed the Soviet Union in its ability to deliver nuclear weapons. Hoping to equalize the imbalance and to protect Cuba, his new ally, against American attack, a year and a half after the Bay of Pigs invasion he quietly dispatched Soviet troops and missile technicians to Cuba. These Soviet forces brought with them two sorts of missiles: strategic SS-4s of medium range, capable of reaching Washington, D.C., and New York, and short-range tactical missiles that could destroy any American invasion force landing on Cuba's beaches. The strategic missiles remained under Moscow's direct control, but the Soviet commander in Cuba was authorized, without Moscow's approval, to launch the tactical missiles to stop an American invasion if he felt it necessary. As military experts—Soviet, Cuban, and American—concluded thirty years later, after the Cold War had ended, this was a prescription for world nuclear disaster.

Even without full knowledge of the risks, Kennedy and his advisers recognized that the world stood on the edge of catastrophe. From the moment American intelligence revealed the presence of the missiles in mid-October, a special executive committee of the National Security Council (Excom) met in continuous session to debate what course to take. The bellicose Air Force General Curtis LeMay favored an immediate attack on Cuba. Defense Secretary Robert McNamara and the president's brother, Attorney General Robert F. Kennedy, favored a blockade of the island to prevent the missiles still on their way by ship from being landed. The president rejected the aggressive LeMay course. On the evening of October 22, 1962, he appeared on national television to tell the American people about the Soviet missiles and explain that the government had decided to "quarantine" Cuba to prevent delivery of more missiles. If the Soviets tried to run the blockade, the American navy would shoot.

The announcement startled the nation and the world. A wrong move by either of the superpowers might plunge the world into nuclear war. Americans generally supported the president's course, but outside the United States many people thought Kennedy was gambling with the very existence of humanity.

What would the Soviets do when their missile-carrying ships, fast approaching Cuba, encountered the American blockade vessels? For four days the world waited anxiously. In Cuba, Soviet technicians worked feverishly to complete the missile launch pads, and began to assemble crated Soviet bombers. Washington kept NATO leaders informed of minute-by-minute developments. Then the break came. On October 26 Khrushchev sent a long message to the American government admitting for the first time that Soviet missiles were being installed in Cuba. The Soviet Union, Khrushchev stated, would send no more missiles if the United States agreed not to attack Cuba. At the same time he publicly released an offer to remove the missiles from Cuba if the United States removed its missiles from NATO member Turkey, close to the USSR. Overtly ignoring the issue of Turkish bases, Kennedy agreed not to attack Cuba if the Soviet missiles were taken out. Khrushchev did not insist on his initial terms.* Soviet vessels nearing Cuba stopped and reversed course. The crisis was over. The world sighed with collective relief.

Vietnam Intervention Begins.   Even as world attention focused on Cuba and Berlin, a disastrous confrontation was unfolding in Southeast Asia. The setting for the American debacle was Vietnam, Cambodia, and Laos, nations carved out of French Indochina in the years following the Japanese surrender in 1945 and made "associated states" of the French Union—dependent French protectorates. In the northern part of Vietnam, however, Ho Chi Minh, a Communist nationalist, refused to accept continued French rule. Ho established a "Democratic Republic" with its capital in Hanoi and claimed to speak for all Vietnamese, including those in the south. The French attempted to subdue Ho and his Vietminh forces, but in 1954 suffered a major military defeat at Dien Bien Phu. Soon after, they agreed to a division of Vietnam along the seventeenth parallel, pending a 1956 election that would decide the future government for a united country. This decision was ratified by a meeting of the major powers at Geneva, but the election was never held. Fearing that a free ballot might topple his anticommunist regime, South Vietnamese Premier Ngo Dinh Diem, an American client, dithered and delayed and, when the Eisenhower administration failed to exert pressure to coerce him, postponed the election indefinitely.

The French defeat awakened American fears of further Communist expansion in Southeast Asia. As Eisenhower explained in 1954, the countries of the region were like "dominos"; if "you knock over one . . . the last one . . . will go over very quickly." That September the United States negotiated a treaty with Australia, Great Britain, France, New Zealand, Thailand, the Philippines, and Pakistan pledging joint action against Communist aggression in the region. Though designed to emulate NATO, SEATO (the South East Asia Treaty Organization) lacked a unified military command and proved ineffectual in checking East Asian Communist expansion.

Eisenhower refused to send troops to the region, but the United States supplied war matériel and economic aid on a large scale to pro-Western or neutral

---

*We now know that Kennedy promised in private, however, to remove the Turkish missiles at some later time.

regimes in Laos, Cambodia, and South Vietnam to help them resist Communist takeovers. American policy was at best a partial success. In Laos the Pathet Lao, a Communist-led nationalist movement, grew more powerful and threatened to overthrow the neutralist government. In South Vietnam the Diem regime in Saigon failed to pacify the country. Diem and his supporters proved corrupt and unpopular with the country's Buddhists and peasants, and before long the "National Liberation Front" (Vietcong), a Communist guerrilla movement supplied with arms by Ho Chi Minh in North Vietnam, attracted a following among the rural people.

Kennedy, like Eisenhower, accepted a containment policy for Asia and, despite misgivings, for a time continued to help Diem against his Communist enemies. Unlike his predecessor, however, JFK was willing to send American personnel as well as money and supplies. In May 1961 he dispatched 400 Special Forces troops, trained in counterinsurgency tactics, to South Vietnam. By October 1962 over 16,000 Americans, military and civilian, were in South Vietnam advising and assisting the Diem government, and, though none of these were combat troops, the number of Americans injured or killed had reached almost 600.

The Kennedy administration could not refrain from intervening in South Vietnamese affairs in other ways. In late 1963, convinced that Diem had lost the support of his people and could no longer effectively defend South Vietnam against the communists, the president gave the green light for a coup to a group of South Vietnamese generals who had Diem assassinated. Unfortunately the military men who replaced him soon proved no more competent, tolerant, or honest—and no more capable of rallying the South Vietnamese people to the side of the Saigon regime and against the Vietcong.

JFK and Civil Rights.   On civil rights the Kennedy administration's record was mixed. JFK had received his margin of victory in 1960 from blacks in the North. But he also feared driving white southerners out of the Democratic party. Under the aegis of his brother, Robert, the Attorney General, the Justice Department enforced provisions of the 1957 and 1960 Civil Rights Acts and helped get thousands of black southerners on the voting rolls. The administration at times, though reluctantly, was forced to resort to coercion to enforce the law.

In the fall of 1962 the Mississippi authorities refused, despite a federal court order, to admit James Meredith, a black man, to "Old Miss," the state university. Mississippi Governor Ross Barnett had promised to enforce the court order, but Barnett caved in to the threat of force from klansmen and other opponents of desegregation. Kennedy sent federal marshals and federalized national guardsmen. But they could not prevent violence, and in the confrontation that ensued two died and many were injured. In the end Meredith was admitted and graduated the following year. In September 1963 the Governor of Alabama, George C. Wallace, refused to allow the admission of black students to his state university. Wallace declared that he personally would block their entrance by "standing in the schoolhouse door." Wallace backed down when faced with threat of federal enforcement at the point of a military bayonet.

Despite these instances of successful enforcement, many civil rights leaders believed the administration lagged in its commitment to racial justice and was moving too slowly. The administration's caution particularly offended the young activists who were coming to the fore as the sixties unfolded. The new civil rights militancy dated from February 1, 1960, when four black students at North Carolina Agricultural and Technical College at Greensboro took seats at the lunch counter of the local Woolworth. They were denied service. The next day the students returned with friends and resumed their sit-in. Day after day they continued their protest against segregation despite the catcalls and jeers of unfriendly whites. In a few days press reports helped spread the sit-in movement all over the South. The new activism encouraged the formation, with Martin Luther King, Jr.'s sponsorship, of the Student Nonviolent Coordinating Committee (SNCC). SNCC at the outset accepted King's commitment to a nonviolent, biracial approach to civil rights, but it was not clear how long the young militants would agree to the guidance of their elders.

A major test of the administration's civil rights commitment came with the "freedom rides." Seeking to challenge segregation at depots, white and black civil rights activists, under the auspices of the Congress of Racial Equality (CORE), traveled through the South by bus during May 1961. White supremacist threatened the freedom riders wherever they stopped, and in South Carolina and Alabama white toughs beat them severely. The activists appealed to the Justice Department to protect them from their assailants. The government complied, but too slowly to suit the young firebrands. The riders had to cut their plans short.

Yet at times the administration's intervention served the civil rights cause well. In 1963 King and the SCLC launched a campaign in Birmingham to end downtown segregation of eating places and other public facilities and create jobs for qualified blacks. The SCLC leaders shrewdly estimated that to succeed they must arouse the liberal conscience of the nation by showing the brutal face of racism.

Birmingham seemed the ideal setting. The city was thoroughly segregated and racist. At one point Martin Luther King declared that when in Birmingham he felt he was "within a cab ride of being in Johannesburg, South Africa." As anticipated, the city authorities cooperated. The authorities threw King in jail where he composed an eloquent 19-page letter in reply to white ministers who had urged the civil rights leaders to go slow in their demands. King chided the ministers for urging delay, noting that it was easy enough for them but not for people who had "seen vicious mobs lynch [their] mothers at will and drown [their] sisters and brothers at whim," who had seen "hate-filled policemen curse, kick, and even kill [their] brothers and sisters." Smuggled out of jail, the "Letter from a Birmingham Jail" became one of the most effective documents of the civil rights movement.

Even more effective in arousing the conscience of white America was the brutal behavior of Birmingham's police chief, Eugene "Bull" Connor. On May 2, 6,000 black children marched into downtown Birmingham to protest the city's policies. The police arrested a thousand of them. The next day Connor's men used high-pressure water hoses and snarling attack dogs against another group of protesters, including children, in another unauthorized march. The public watched the TV images in horror. The president was appalled and dispatched to the city Justice Department officials who succeeded in negotiating a settlement with the business community and city authorities that gave the SCLC most of what it wanted.

In the summer of 1963 the nonviolent, biracial phase of the civil rights movement reached its culmination when more than 200,000 civil rights supporters, black and white, came to Washington to demonstrate for "jobs and freedom" and to express their support of a pending new federal civil rights bill. At the Lincoln Memorial the enthusiastic and orderly crowd were deeply moved by King's "I Have A Dream" address, a speech that expressed the noblest aspirations of the civil rights movement for a society where skin color would no longer have any significance. Many white Americans would be moved by his vision of a future America that would be "a beautiful sympathy" of "little black boys and girls holding hands with little white boys and girls" and "the sons of former slaves and former slaveholders sitting down together at the table of brotherhood." The president had feared that the march, especially if the militants in the movement were allowed free rein, would hurt the chances of a pending new civil rights bill. Actually the demonstration helped win passage of the measure, but not until after Kennedy was dead.

The 1963 March on Washington was for civil rights, but as several of these signs show, it was also a demonstration for jobs.

The New Frontier. Kennedy's New Frontier, the collective name for his domestic programs, was at best a modest success. At his behest, Congress expanded the number of workers covered by the minimum wage levels, increased those levels and Social Security payments, and passed the Housing Act of 1961, which pumped nearly $5 billion over four years into preserving urban open spaces, developing mass transit, and building middle-income housing. Congress also raised unemployment compensation benefits and provided aid to economically depressed areas.

Yet most of Kennedy's major New Frontier initiatives either died in Congress or were delayed until after his death. He had at best only narrow Democratic majorities in Congress, and the administration was unable to bring to its side the conservative Democrats, primarily from the South, who often neither liked nor respected him and his brash associates. Congress defeated his bill to provide funds for school construction and scholarship aid for college students. It refused to pass a health insurance plan for the aged and to enact measures to help unemployed youth, migrant workers, and commuters. One of the most important Kennedy proposals was a tax cut to stimulate the economy by putting more money into the hands of consumers. A year after its introduction the bill was still wending its way through Congress.

It would be hard to give the Kennedy administration the highest grades for its handling of domestic and foreign affairs. Yet despite his mixed record, Kennedy's popularity grew with the passing months. The public remembered his successes and forgot his failures or blamed them on Congress. Young Americans identified with him and his beautiful wife. In late 1963 Camelot was still untarnished.

The president was not universally loved and admired, however. The far right, particularly strong in the South and Southwest, despised him. The reemerging left saw him as too conservative and a cold warrior. When, in November 1963, the president and his wife set off on a political peacemaking trip to Texas, advisers warned that he might encounter trouble. Shortly before, Adlai Stevenson, then ambassador to the United Nations, had been verbally abused and spat on in Dallas.

Kennedy ignored the advice and went to Texas, accompanied by Vice President Johnson. In Dallas, while his motorcade moved slowly through downtown streets lined with friendly crowds, he was shot through the head by a sniper. Rushed to Parkland Memorial Hospital, he was pronounced dead a half hour later.

His killer, Lee Harvey Oswald, was an unstable leftist who had spent some years in the Soviet Union and had been active in the pro-Castro Fair Play for Cuba organization. Oswald had admitted nothing when, two days later as he was being escorted from jail, before the eyes of millions of horrified television viewers, he was shot by Jack Ruby, a shady Dallas nightclub owner who apparently saw himself as an avenging angel.

Few events in a decade rife with catastrophic shocks so appalled the American people. The assassination in Dallas had not only killed an American

"Jackie" and "Jack," a glamorous couple. Taken during the 1960 presidential campaign. The picture foreshadows "Camelot."

president but had also struck down a young hero who had come to symbolize to many contemporaries all that was best and most worthy in American life. To the young, especially, his death seemed a bitter tragedy. In the somber hours between the murder and the burial at Arlington National Cemetery, television's uninterrupted coverage of the events helped draw the nation together as a family united by a shared grief.

In the months that followed, sorrow over the assassination gave way to uneasiness and frustration. President Lyndon Johnson, hoping to allay public doubts about the murder, appointed a commission headed by Chief Justice Earl Warren to investigate the assassination. In September 1964 the commission reported that Oswald was indisputably the culprit and had acted alone. Most Americans probably accepted the Warren Report, but a large minority suspected that it was incomplete or even a cover-up. There were too many loose ends, they insisted; too many questions unanswered. In the next few years, as the toll of assassinated leaders grew, more and more Americans would conclude that there was an evil plot afoot to kill off the nation's great popular champions.

■ THE AFFLUENT SOCIETY ■

During the 1960s the country enjoyed the longest sustained economic boom in its history, with Gross National Product growing at the average rate of 4 percent annually, well above that for the preceding fifteen-year period. Between 1960 and 1970 average per capita real income increased by 48 percent. Compared to recent years, moreover, the gap between the most affluent and other Americans was relatively modest. The major American industries were still unchallenged at home and still enjoyed large markets abroad. No American worker needed to worry about his or her job going overseas. Unions were strong and regularly bargained successfully for higher pay for their members. Some unemployment persisted, and toward the end of the decade prices began to rise at a fast clip. Yet through most of the 1960s, the public's sense of economic well-being surpassed even that of the previous decade.

The Knowledge Industries. The accumulation and diffusion of knowledge helped fuel the decade's economic boom. In some ways this knowledge explosion was the payoff from years of previous scientific advances. It also owed much to the great postwar outlays for research and higher education. In 1950 Congress had established the National Science Foundation to encourage research, especially in areas related to national defense. By 1957 outlays for research and development (R&D) by public and private organizations had reached almost $10 billion annually. Meanwhile, the country's higher education system surged dramatically. In 1940, the last full peacetime year, there were 1.5 million college students; by 1950 there were 2.6 million. From the mid-1950s on, the country's support of what would later be called the "knowledge industries" was dazzling by any previous standard.

Some Americans complained that the public schools were not teaching children to read or to calculate and blamed it on John Dewey's disciples, the "progressive educators." But most citizens were proud of the job the nation was doing. Their complacency was suddenly shattered when, in October 1957, the Russians put a hollow steel ball called Sputnik into orbit around the earth. Having long considered their nation the world's scientific and technological leader, Americans were dismayed to discover that they had been abruptly pushed off their pinnacle by their chief international rival.

For the next few years Americans subjected themselves to one of their periodic agonizing reappraisals of education. A dozen books were soon echoing the complaints of earlier critics about American educational failings. Public dismay over Sputnik induced Congress in 1958 to pass the National Defense Education Act, providing large federal outlays for scientific and language training for college students. By 1970 federal appropriations for research had almost tripled, and federal funding of higher education was four times as high as it had been ten years earlier. Industrial firms, universities, and foundations also invested billions in basic scientific research and the development of new products.

Booming research and industrial growth made a college education even more valuable than in the past, and with the postwar "baby-boom" generation reaching their late teens, there were also more eligible college-age students. By 1970 some 7 million young men and women were enrolled in colleges and universities, an increase of nearly 500 percent in little more than a generation.

The Impact of Science and Technology.   The scientific and technological advances that flowed from the laboratories were often dramatic. Linus Pauling, James Watson, H. Gobind Khorana, and others discovered how the gene, the basic unit of heredity, was constructed. Besides solving some of nature's great mysteries, genetics bore fruit—literally—in a great surge in the output per acre of rice, corn, and wheat, the so-called Green Revolution that benefited Third World nations especially. During this decade, the electronic computer first became a powerful tool for solving mathematical and scientific problems and controlling

One of the greatest feats of modern technology was the landing of men on the moon in July 1969. This picture of astronaut Edwin "Buzz" Aldrin was taken by fellow moonwalker Neil Armstrong, whose reflection is visible in the visor of Aldrin's helmet.

production processes. The textile industry adopted new high-speed looms and developed new synthetic fibers. A long list of thermoplastics filled needs hitherto met at higher cost by metals and other natural materials. The subsonic passenger jet, first introduced in the early 1950s, replaced the propeller plane in the 1960s and shrank the world to half its former size. Meanwhile, the space program, begun under the auspices of the National Aeronautics and Space Administration (NASA) to challenge the Soviet Union, yielded unexpected scientific dividends. Communications satellites were launched, and new metals and alloys and miniaturized computer elements developed to solve the problems of space travel found surprisingly down-to-earth commercial and technical uses.

Medicine, too, made giant strides in these years. An arsenal of new antibiotic drugs, X-ray techniques, isotope tracers, computerized studies of environmental factors in disease, and other applications of the new science markedly improved the nation's and the world's health. In the 1950s researchers developed vaccines to fight polio. In 1963 they introduced a measles vaccine. Heart disease and cancer remained major killers, and indeed lung-cancer deaths from smoking soared, but the death rate from infectious diseases plummeted.

These medical advances, combined with better nutrition, produced a healthier, longer-lived population than ever before. Life expectancy for a newborn baby rose from 68.2 years in 1950 to 70.9 years in 1970. At the later date it was considerably higher for women (74.8) than for men (67.1) and for whites (71.7) than for blacks (65.3). Still, the improvement was substantial for every segment of the population.

The rapid expansion of the economy and the great surge in technology were not cost-free. American life became increasingly bureaucratized as the federal government expanded its power and size and as ever more private businesses consolidated into giant corporations. Much of the new technology was damaging to the land, to water supplies, and to the air people breathed. By the end of the decade these environmental drawbacks would produce a powerful impulse to protect the public, which came to be called the ecology movement.

■ THE JOHNSON YEARS ■

Lyndon Johnson took office at a time of affluence and optimism when most citizens still trusted government and believed it could make a significant difference in the nation's life. Abundance made the plight of those left out seem especially unacceptable, while the surge in government revenues from a soaring economy made spending for new federal programs relatively easy to bear. The "Great Society" of Lyndon Johnson floated on a sea of prosperity that allowed Americans without too much sacrifice to indulge their periodic yearning for a just and benevolent nation.

The Great Society.   Lyndon B. Johnson was in many ways the antithesis of his predecessor. Middle-aged, rugged, earthy, and self-made rather than young, elegant, and patrician, Johnson lacked the glamour of Kennedy. Yet he was incomparable as a legislative manager. His long years as Senate leader had honed his talent for getting laws enacted. As president his skills were put to good use. A congressman or official who resisted the president's demands was marched into Johnson's office, seated next to the towering Texan, and subjected to a powerful verbal assault of jokes, promises, threats, cajolery, and ego stroking, along with thumps, squeezes, and pokes. Few politicians could hold out against the "Johnson treatment" for very long, and in the course of his five years as president, Johnson initiated more significant domestic legislation than any chief executive since Franklin D. Roosevelt.

Johnson's program was an expression of liberalism's faith in a powerful nurturing and managerial government. The president was a long-time admirer of Franklin Roosevelt and hoped to complete and round out the social welfare state that FDR had launched between 1933 and 1938 and that his Democratic successors, Truman and Kennedy, had been unable to enact.

Johnson wasted no time in pushing his liberal agenda. Invoking the memory of his martyred predecessor, he quickly induced Congress to enact stalled legislation of the Kennedy administration: the tax reduction bill, an Urban Mass Transportation Act, and a Wilderness Preservation Act. In January 1964, following through on a half-developed Kennedy initiative, Congress passed the Economic Opportunity Act establishing an Office of Economic Opportunity (OEO) to reduce illiteracy, find jobs for inner-city youths, improve depressed conditions in the Appalachian area, sharpen skills among the poor, and provide capital to minority businesses. With a mandate to wage a "war on poverty," OEO was authorized to create "community-action" groups to give local-area people a hand in designing and running new antipoverty programs and instill in the poor a new sense of confidence that would enable them to help themselves.

LBJ's impressive early leadership guaranteed his party's 1964 nomination, with Hubert H. Humphrey, Minnesota's liberal senator, as his running mate. The Republicans chose Senator Barry Goldwater of Arizona, who selected an obscure New York congressman, William Miller, as second on the ticket.

Goldwater represented the extreme right wing of his party. His supporters claimed that they were offering the country "a choice, not an echo." The choice, it seemed to many voters, was to dismantle the Social Security system, sell the New Deal's Tennessee Valley Authority to private interests, and return to Hooverism. Given the Republican candidate's bellicose foreign-policy statements and his affection for uniforms and air force bombers, his election also promised an enlarged Vietnam involvement that few Americans wanted. Goldwater made matters worse by inept public statements. When many moderate Americans were still worried about the far right John Birch Society, Goldwater told them, "extremism in the defense of liberty is no vice! And . . . moderation in the pursuit of justice is no virtue!" The Democrats did not play fair. At the very time Johnson was considering escalating the American commitment in Vietnam, he was denouncing Goldwater as a warmonger and promising to "seek no wider war" in Southeast Asia. Johnson won with 61 percent of the popular vote, better even than FDR's 1936 triumph. A year later a bitter joke would make the rounds: "I was told if I voted for Goldwater we would be at war in six months. I did—and we were!"

With a landslide victory to work with, LBJ pushed beyond his predecessor's initiatives. His Great Society sought to do more than just improve material security and well-being. As the president had described it in May 1964 at the University of Michigan, the Great Society was a domain where the "order of plenty" Americans now enjoyed could be used "to enrich and elevate our national life and to advance the quality of our American civilization." In the Great Society every child would find "knowledge to enrich his mind and . . . enlarge his talents." There leisure would be a "welcome chance to build and reflect." It would be a place where "the city of man serves not only the needs of the body but the desire for beauty and the hunger for community," and where people could "renew contact with nature." With the spectacular Democratic majorities in Congress to back him up, he made remarkable progress in fulfilling his promises.

In the spring of 1965, overcoming longstanding Catholic–Protestant disagreements over parochial schools, Congress passed the $1.3 billion Elementary and Secondary Education Act appropriating federal money for the direct support of local public schools for the first time in history. In July, it swept aside the opposition of the organized medical profession and enacted the first federal health insurance programs—Medicare for old-age pensioners and Medicaid for the poor. A month later the Omnibus Housing Act set up a rent supplement program for low-income families. Recognizing the cities' special needs, Congress established the Department of Housing and Urban Development (HUD) in September. The president promptly appointed as its head Robert C. Weaver, who became the nation's first black cabinet member. Soon after the president signed a measure establishing the National Endowments for the Arts and for the Humanities to subsidize artists, writers, composers, painters, and scholars and provide aid to local cultural institutions. Clean air and clean water acts to improve the environment followed soon afterward, as did a Higher Education Act providing the first federal scholarships for college students; the Highway Safety Act to make automobile travel safer; an anti-billboard highway beautification act; and a Truth-in-Lending Act to protect consumers in credit transactions. In October, in the 1965 Immigration Act, Congress replaced the discriminatory national quota system for immigrants (established in the 1920s) with rules to facilitate family reunification and encourage the immigration of skilled workers and professionals.

Some of these laws were hastily drawn; some were ultimately ineffective or even harmful. The OEO programs, critics charged, created unrealistic expectations that only aroused frustration and anger among its anticipated beneficiaries. Federal school aid did not make American children more literate. Nor did the National Endowments produce a golden age of the arts or of scholarship. Medicare and Medicaid, it was claimed, helped fuel a runaway inflation of medical costs and would prove impossibly expensive to a later generation. By the 1990s many Americans would blame the flood of poor, unskilled immigrants on the family reunification provision of the 1965 immigration bill.

But the Great Society had its successes as well. Head Start, a War on Poverty program that paid for educational enrichment of poor preschool children, made a difference in the success of those children in later years. Great Society programs helped low- and moderate-income students pay for college, made automobiles safer, and provided recreation facilities for millions of Americans taking their leisure. Medicare and other programs for the aged and retired virtually ended the serious problem of poverty among older Americans. However costly, federal health programs did make Americans healthier and extended their life spans. Much of the consumer protection and environmental legislation was overdue and produced long-term aesthetic and health benefits.

Space Exploration.   Johnson must also be given credit for major progress in space exploration. In May 1961 Kennedy had set the goal of, within the decade, "landing a man on the moon and returning him safely to earth." Hoping to show the superiority of democratic capitalism to communism by beating the Soviet Union in the space race, Johnson pushed the moon-landing program hard. The competition was attacked by some liberals for starving needed social programs here on earth. Many black Americans considered it a white man's enterprise of no great interest to them. And there were critics among the scientists as well: We could have learned as much about the solar system, they said, by using far cheaper unmanned rockets. But LBJ kept the appropriations coming for the Apollo moon launches. By the end of his presidency, three astronauts had transmitted television Christmas greetings to earth from seventy miles above the moon's forbidding surface. It was now only a matter of months before the first human beings would place their feet on some other part of the universe besides Mother Earth.

Johnson and Civil Rights.   Lyndon Johnson was if anything more committed to racial justice than his predecessor. Though born and raised in a former Confederate state, he had never accepted the racial attitudes of the white South and had distanced himself from his southern colleagues in the Senate when they attacked the Supreme Court's desegregation decisions.

With his incomparable command of parliamentary maneuver, Johnson helped win passage in July of the 1964 Civil Rights Act that Kennedy had originated. The sweeping new law barred discrimination in public accommodations, authorized the Justice Department to initiate suits to force desegregation of schools and other public facilities, outlawed job discrimination based on race, color, religion, national origin, or sex, and reduced the power of local voter registration boards to disqualify black registrants on the basis of literacy. It would change the face of race relations in the nation, especially in the South.

After election in his own right that November, LBJ continued to push for progress on the civil rights front. When, in early 1965, Governor Wallace denied the right of the King and Alabama civil rights protesters to stage a march on the Alabama state capital, Johnson intervened forcefully. The president called Wallace to the White House and subjected him to his standard treatment of cajolery and brow-beating that had worked so well with federal politicians. Wallace yielded to the federal authorities. On March 15 Johnson went before Congress to support a bold new voting rights bill. The civil rights issue, he asserted, was not a black problem or a white problem. "There is only an American problem," and Congress was now assembled to solve it. The whole nation must "overcoming the crippling legacy of bigotry and injustice." The president brought members of Congress to their feet with his ringing peroration that ended with the words of the moving civil rights anthem "And We Shall Overcome."

In August 1965 Johnson signed the Voting Rights Act, the last of the major civil rights bills of the sixties. The measure authorized federal voter registration in districts where local officials had kept the number of registered voters below half the voting-age population. Under its terms the equal franchise promised black southerners a century before was finally fulfilled.

Judicial Activism.   The liberalism of the decade was amplified by the decisions of the Supreme Court under Chief Justice Earl Warren. An exponent of "judicial activism," Warren believed that the federal courts must intervene to defend individual rights against intrusive state control and help guarantee a liberal secular society. In a cascade of decisions the Court took stands on controversial issues that Congress and the state legislatures had long avoided. In *Mapp v. Ohio* (1961) the justices ruled that evidence collected illegally could not be used in court against an accused criminal. In *Gideon v. Wainright* (1963) and *Miranda v. Arizona* (1966), the Court insisted that accused criminals had the right to remain silent when questioned, had the right to consult a lawyer, and had to be provided with a lawyer by the state if they lacked the money to hire one themselves. *Engel v. Vitale* (1962) forbade prayer in the public schools, on the grounds of separation of church and state. *Griswold v. Connecticut* (1964) struck down state laws banning birth control because they violated the right to marital privacy. In *A Book Named . . . "Memoirs of a Woman of Pleasure" v. Attorney General of Massachusetts* (1966), the Court virtually lifted the legal ban on pornography. Hailed by liberals as the great tribune of the disenfranchised and the oppressed, the Warren Court was denounced by conservatives as abettors of crime, pornography, and atheism.

■ THE RISE OF DISSENT ■

By most measures of well-being and social progress the sixties should rank as a golden age. Americans were affluent; government seemed relevant and effective; the lot of the disadvantaged was getting better. And yet no period of the twentieth century would ring with such loud, intemperate cries of protest and dissent as the second half of that momentous decade. Some observers noted that affluence often produced more discontent than poverty.

From Civil Rights to Black Power.   After 1965 the civil rights movement drastically shifted ground. At mid-decade Martin Luther King, Jr., was at the very peak of his career. In January 1964 *Time* had named him Man of the Year. In October he won the Nobel Peace Prize. With passage of the Voting Rights Act, King's formula of black–white cooperation and nonviolent civil disobedience seemed triumphant.

But white participation and the tactic of nonviolence would not last much longer. From the outset black nationalism, or black separatism, which rejected cooperation with whites and what were perceived as white values, had been an undercurrent in the postwar civil rights movement. During the forties and fifties the Black Muslims (the Nation of Islam) had won disciples for a set of beliefs that labeled Christianity a "slave religion," denounced whites as "blue-eyed devils," and proclaimed the superiority and primacy of black people. Led by Elijah Muhammad, the Black Muslims, much like Marcus Garvey before them, sought to foster black racial pride and black separatism. By the early sixties the Black Muslims' most articulate spokesman was Malcolm X, a former convict converted to the Nation of Islam while in prison. Malcolm denied he was a racist, but his rhetoric was often angry and frightened many whites.

Black separatism might have remained a "fringe" if not for the growing frustration of blacks over the slow advance toward racial equality. By 1965 virtually all of the legal barriers to black public access in the South had been swept away. Jim Crow was virtually dead. Blacks, moreover, were voting in record numbers in the South. Nationally, there was also a great surge of black college students and of black workers in retail sales, public services, banking, and other white-collar areas where few had ever served before. But major inequalities remained. Black Americans were still poorer, sicker, less literate, and more badly housed than whites. Thousands of black youths were unemployed and, seemingly, unemployable. The disparity between promise and fulfillment created intense strains. In the ghettos high expectations often coexisted with modest actual achievement. It was an explosive combination.

Five days after Johnson signed the Voting Rights Act a riot exploded in the black Los Angeles suburb of Watts, tripped off by charges of police brutality. During the violence, twenty-eight blacks died; property damage reached $200 million. The fury of Watts shook Martin Luther King and confirmed his resolve to shift his focus from the South to the northern urban ghettos and their problems of jobs and housing. In January 1966 King conducted a series of marches through white Chicago neighborhoods in support of equal housing laws. The Chicago campaign failed. Many white Chicagoans perceived a threat to their neighborhoods and jeered the marchers and pelted them with stones and other missiles. The marchers were forced to retreat. King admitted afterward that he had "never seen anything as hostile and as hateful as I've seen here today." Meanwhile, the ghetto violence seemed to become institutionalized. During the "long, hot summers" of 1966 and 1967 the ghettos of Newark, Cleveland, Detroit, Chicago, and scores of other cities erupted in paroxysms of burning, looting, and attacks on whites and the police. Many of the casualties, however, were black victims of poorly trained, trigger-happy police, national guardsmen, or federal troops.

The ghetto riots helped polarize the civil rights movement. Despite his efforts, King came to be seen by younger activists as too timid and too ineffectual. In 1966 SNCC replaced its moderate head John Lewis with militant Stokely Carmichael; CORE replaced James Farmer with militant Floyd McKissick. Both new leaders endorsed "black power," a position that had first surfaced during a civil rights "walk against fear" from Memphis to Jackson. In mid-1966 SNCC, led by Carmichael, rejected nonviolence and black-and-white-together in favor of black separatism and black self-defense. SNCC and CORE quickly told their white members to leave and continue the fight for racial equality through their own all-white organizations. That same year, in the Oakland, California, ghetto, two students at a local community college, Huey Newton and Bobby Seale, formed the "Black Panther Party for Self-Defense," a paramilitary organization avowedly dedicated to forcing the Oakland police to respect the black community's rights. Dressed in shiny leather jackets and black berets and openly carrying rifles, the Panthers frightened many whites and enraged the police. Their existence attracted national attention when in May 1967 a group of 30 Panthers, carrying rifles, shotguns, and pistols, marched into the California State capitol in Sacramento to protest a bill forbidding the carrying of loaded weapons. Before long the Panthers were engaged in murderous shoot-outs with police in Oakland, Chicago, and other cities.

The Great Insurgency.   The civil rights movement was one sector of a war against the "establishment" of liberal, white middle-class America that erupted in the second half of the sixties. Before the decade ended, the country would experience other insurgent movements—by students, women, gays, Latinos, American Indians, environmentalists, and many other groups.

The revolt had tangled roots. In the political realm it was fed by the decline of repressive McCarthyism and the emergence of a new generation less complacent about good times than their elders and less certain that the Cold War was inevitable. These young people had been raised in the affluence of postwar suburbia and took for granted that America was capable of providing all its people with the means to lead fulfilling and interesting lives. Yet as they looked around them they perceived racism, blight, despair, repression, and international belligerence that seemed to belie the nation's professed values. With so many of these idealistic and dissatisfied young people going to college, the nation's campuses became potentially explosive.

Socially and culturally, too, the nation was ripe for dissent by the mid-1960s. A new, more permissive attitude toward sex was foreshadowed by the investigations in the late 1940s and early 1950s of Dr. Alfred C. Kinsey and his associates, which showed Americans as far less traditional in their sexual behavior than the conventional wisdom taught. Even more important, perhaps, was the advent of oral contraceptives in 1960. Besides reducing the birth rate, "the pill" lowered the chances of unwanted pregnancies and so reduced the dangers and inconveniences of sex outside marriage.

The more permissive sexual values were reflected in the declining power of communities to censor books, movies, and magazines. Beginning with a 1952 decision holding that films were covered by the First Amendment's guarantee of free speech, the Supreme Court extended the principle so that a book, play, or motion picture had to be "utterly without redeeming social value" to be regarded as obscene. Soon long-banned erotic classics were available at bookstores, and before long it became clear that even works with social values no one could detect could be legally published and sold. In 1968, in recognition of the new situation, Hollywood adopted a rating system that placed films in categories ranging from "G" for family movies to "X" for out-and-out pornography.

Meanwhile there appeared a new school of radical social thinkers, such as the sociologist C. Wright Mills, the social psychologist Paul Goodman, and the neo-Marxist philosopher Herbert Marcuse. In their individual ways, each of these men condemned existing society as oppressive, repressive, and rife with inequalities of wealth and power. In 1960 Mills gave currency to the term "New Left" to describe a new radical mood among the young intellectuals and students that he detected emerging in the United States and around the world.

Popular culture, too, especially music, both expressed and encouraged the new dissent. Rock-and-roll, a merger of black rhythm and blues and electronic instruments, burst on the scene in the mid-1950s with Bill Haley's recording "Rock Around the Clock." Soon after, Elvis Presley, a white southerner who borrowed from black musicians, gave rock a strong sexual cast.

Rock was the music of the rebellious young. The most successful rock group of the sixties, the Beatles, wore the long hair and mod clothes of angry English working-class adolescents. The Rolling Stones, also an English group, and various whimsically named American groups wore the "love beads," Indian headbands, and gaudy jeans that soon became trademarks of youthful cultural revolt. Eventually some rock bands began to dabble directly in political matters. Groups like the Grateful Dead, Jefferson Airplane, Country Joe and the Fish became active propagandists for sexual freedom, mind-expanding drugs, and the anti-Vietnam movement. Folk singers like Joan Baez and Bob Dylan also became increasingly political. Dylan's "The Times They Are A-Changin'" would become an anthem of youth rebellion.

Student Activists.   Unlike many other nations, the United States had never had a significant protest movement run primarily by the young. During the sixties this changed when the proportion of young adults reached an all-time record and many of these congregated on college campuses.

Youth is naturally adventurous and rebellious, but the insurgency of the 1960s had its own special roots. Many younger white activists were radicalized by their experiences in the civil rights movement. When excluded by Black Power from direct participation in the militant civil rights movement, they turned their eyes to their home turf. Student militancy, moreover, was encouraged by the campus physical setting. Colleges were crowded and classes were large. To handle the load administrations became more impersonal and bureaucratic. Students soon felt that they were numbers rather than human beings.

But probably the most potent trigger of student radicalism was the accelerating war in Vietnam. At first young men were excused from the military draft merely for attending college. Then they had to pass a test and maintain good grades to be exempt. This system provoked profound anxieties and fed student guilt about evading danger while nonstudents, both black and white, were sent off to Southeast Asia to fight and die. The cast of *Hair* announced the injustice of this arrangement when they sang: "War is white people sending black people to make war on yellow people to defend the land they stole from red people." Some students tried to avoid the war personally by seeking conscientious objector status or wrangling medical disqualifications. Others escaped to Canada. Many channeled their personal dilemma into an angry movement to get the United States out of the Vietnam conflict in any way possible. Broader in its effect than these, the war in Vietnam undermined the nation's leadership and inspired attacks on the whole "system" as unresponsive, corrupt, repressive, and cruel.

The liberal campus of the University of California at Berkeley was the setting for the first of the student rebellions. When, in the fall of 1964, the administration withdrew the right to use university property as a free-speech enclave, student activists, many of whom had worked for civil rights both in the South and in the Bay Area, rebelled. On December 2 a thousand students took over the administration building and refused to leave until the university agreed to cancel its directive. The authorities called in the police, who arrested hundreds of protestors. In the end the Free Speech Movement rebels got the ban rescinded, but for the remainder of the decade Berkeley student activists and the university would struggle over free expression and a wide range of issues including university government, classroom overcrowding, restrictions on students' private lives, ethnic studies, and university–community relations.

Berkeley became the precedent for a wave of campus upheavals that soon spread from coast to coast. Impatient with hierarchies and authority, many students came to see university administrations as prototypes of all oppressive agencies in society and so worthy of assault. The supposed complicity of universities in the Vietnam war effort amplified the sense that they were legitimate targets.

Organized student opposition to the war began in early 1965 with campus "teach-ins," marathon sessions in which students and faculty examined the roots of the American intervention and invariably denounced the administration's policies. Teach-ins were followed by "peace marches" in which students paraded with pacifists, antiwar liberals, radicals, and other concerned citizens to protest U.S. policies. As the antiwar movement accelerated, radical students began to burn draft cards and mob campus recruiters from the armed forces and from businesses, such as Dow Chemical Company, engaged in weapon production.

From 1965 on, many of the campus upheavals were led by Students for a Democratic Society (SDS), an organization that initially condemned both capitalism and Soviet-style communism, proclaimed the need for personal freedom and individual autonomy, and called for a "democracy of participation" to replace the prevailing bureaucratic democracy of the day. SDS became more militant and intolerant as the sixties advanced. By 1968 it had begun to glorify violence toward the oppressive "system" of "Amerika," and had replaced "participatory democracy" by Marxist-Leninism that emphasized a "vanguard party" to lead the inevitable revolution.

The Counterculture. The New Left sought political change primarily, but simultaneously American youth were in revolt against bourgeois behavior, dress, values, and expression. Middle-class conventions, the rebels claimed, were repressive tools by which a timid, hidebound society controlled people's instincts and diminished human potential. Unlike the New Left, the counterculture lacked an organizational center, though at different times the Yippies, the Mayday Tribe, and other colorfully named groups would claim to speak for it.

The counterculture's chief practitioners were called "hippies," from "hip," a jazz musicians' expression meaning knowledgeable or "with it." Hippies displayed their contempt for middle-class values by wearing tattered jeans, sandals, and beads; displaying an abundance of hair; and cultivating an elliptical way of speaking that used such expressions as "like," "groovey," and "dig it." Hippies adopted an aesthetic outlook that emphasized natural things. They wore flowers in their hair and around their necks and referred to themselves as "flower children." They considered material possessions fetishes of the "straight culture" and furnished their own "pads" with a few castoffs.

Old sexual values were already changing when the hippies appeared on the scene. But the counterculture amplified these trends. Gatherings of counterculture people at times included displays of mass nudity and even public sexual intercourse, as at the mammoth rock-and-roll festival near Woodstock, New York, in August 1969. Hippies also experimented with communes where everything, including sexual partners, was shared, and accepted cohabitation without marriage as normal.

As the 1960s unfolded, counterculture values invaded the cultural mainstream. By mid-decade practices that previously were seldom mentioned and mainly relegated to the sexual underground were publicly exhibited. In Tom O'Horgan's play *Futz,* one character has sexual intercourse with a pig. "X-rated" movies, now permitted, brought the depiction of oral sex acts to every large city's downtown theaters. Homosexuality, too, ceased to be a shameful aberration in the eyes of many Americans.

The counterculture was steeped in psychedelic, mood-altering drugs. In the early 1960s two Harvard psychology instructors, Timothy Leary and Richard Alpert, experimented with a new chemical substance, lysergic acid diethylamide (LSD), which they believed capable of "expanding" consciousness and enabling people to conquer their "inner space." Soon LSD and other consciousness-altering drugs were incorporated into the hippie revolt against bourgeois society. As in the case of sexual behavior, the drug culture expanded beyond hippiedom. Large numbers of middle-class white youths were soon experimenting with substances that had only been used in the ghettos or bohemian enclaves before.

The counterculture had its characteristic music, "acid rock." Thousands of young people flocked to mammoth rock concerts where flashing strobe lights and heavy use of "grass" and LSD augmented the music on stage. It also had its characteristic psychedelic art and a host of counterculture, "underground" publications, including *The Berkeley Barb,* the *East Village Other,* and the *Chicago Seed.* Few lasted more than a year or two, but during that time they enjoyed wide readership especially among college students.

The hippie phenomenon was short-lived. During the 1967 "summer of love" hippies flocked to Haight-Ashbury in San Francisco and the East Village in New York, neighborhoods that catered to their special needs. These quickly deteriorated into squalid youth slums. When the larger culture adopted the hippie style of talk, dress, and behavior, it became tainted in the eyes of counter-culture purists. Meanwhile, the great rock music festivals degenerated into sat-urnalias of drugs and violence. The commune movement for a while became the refuge for the more idealistic counterculture people. But then it, too, deflated.

The student political left soon followed the counterculture in a downward spiral. Frustrated by the continuing Vietnam War, infiltrated by rigid, orthodox Marxists, under attack by radical feminists, in June 1969, at its annual conven-tion in Chicago, SDS split in two over who would lead the expected revolution. One faction, the Weathermen, adopted violence and fought with the Chicago police during the "Days of Rage" in October 1969. Thereafter its members became underground terrorists determined to attack "imperialist Amerika" from within. Over the next few years the Weathermen would be responsible for dozens of bombings of government facilities and corporate offices. In February 1970 a Weathermen bomb factory in a Greenwich Village townhouse exploded when someone connected a wrong wire, killing three Weathermen leaders. The resort to violence, the declining economy, and a recognition that revolution was still a long way off combined to finish off what remained of the New Left.

■ LIBERATION ■

The 1960s insurgency spawned a new sense of freedom, of liberation, among ethnic minorities and others who saw themselves as outside the inner circle of privilege.

Chicanos. Mexican-Americans, mostly recent immigrants, were the largest of these minorities, numbering over 6 million in California, the Southwest, and the Chicago area. Called "Chicanos," they worked as domestics and unskilled fac-tory hands, and as migrant farm laborers, picking lettuce, tomatoes, fruit, and other crops in the fertile valleys of California and Texas. They were often the victims of social and economic discrimination by the prevailing "Anglo" culture.

Beginning in the 1960s, a new generation of Chicano leaders began to de-mand better treatment for their people. In New Mexico, Reies Tijerina's Alianza organization demanded that lands in the Southwest that had originally belonged to Mexican-Americans be returned to them. In California, union leader César Chavez sought to compel the grape and lettuce growers to accept unionization of their largely Chicano workforce. In his struggle he was helped by consumer boycotts of nonunion grapes and lettuce by sympathetic liberals and radicals.

Native Americans. The 1960s was a decade of revived self-awareness and assertiveness for American Indians too. Even after passage of the 1934 Wheeler-Howard Act (see Chapter 19) Indians remained a depressed group in America. Whites continued to treat them as second-class citizens; traditional Indian val-ues continued to erode; mortality rates for children on the reservations remained appalling. In 1946 Congress established the Indian Claims Commis-sion to reimburse the Indians for financial injustices against them from the very beginning of the federal government. In 1953, by a joint resolution, it authorized "termination" of all federal benefits and controls over the tribes. Though termination was intended to make Indians equal to other citizens, the National Congress of American Indians protested that it became primarily a way to lower federal costs at the expense of the Indians. The termination process was soon slowed, but not before it had raised up a new class of Indian leaders more militant than any in the recent past.

These leaders were often young urban activists inspired by the civil rights movement of blacks and Chicanos. They demanded that they be called "Native Americans" rather than Indians, a name imposed on them by Europeans. David Edmunds and Vine Deloria, Jr., wrote Native American history from a Native American viewpoint, siding with Sitting Bull against Custer and with the Apaches against the cavalry. In 1969 a group of young activists occupied the abandoned federal prison on Alcatraz in San Francisco Bay and demanded that it be converted into an Indian cultural center. In 1970 the American Indian Movement (AIM) emerged as the center of the young urban militants.

The New Feminism.   The most momentous of the liberation movements was the new feminism. From a feminist perspective, the immediate post-1945 period had been depressing. The ideals of domesticity and togetherness had confined women to the home to a greater degree than at any time since before the first World War. Women who worked seldom had rewarding or well-paid jobs and although many women lacked the training and work experience of men, clearly they were also victims of what would be called sexism. Sex discrimination, feminists would later note, was often indirect and subtle. Female children, they said, were "programmed" from the earliest age to assume that they were emotionally and mentally weaker than men, and came to absorb this view themselves.

As the 1950s drew to a close, perceptions and attitudes began to change. By 1960 millions of women had gone through college, where they had been exposed to psychological, anthropological, and sociological concepts that identified many supposedly feminine characteristics as primarily the result of upbringing. Educated women were confronted with the contrast between their training and the routine lives they led, either as housewives or as "gals Friday" to some male executive. By this time, too, the precedent of black liberation had illuminated the path that the nation's largest "minority" could take.

The new feminism surfaced in 1963 with a report by the Kennedy-appointed President's Commission on the Status of Women urging job equality, day-care centers, and paid maternity leave for women. The intellectual breakthrough came that same year when Betty Friedan, a suburban housewife and mother, published *The Feminine Mystique*. The book described dissatisfaction with the narrow life of the housebound wife and mother as "the problem that has no name." Domesticity was a trap that had diminished women's lives. Like most feminist activists of the past, Friedan, a Smith College graduate and former labor activist, spoke mainly for the educated middle class. But among this group her message reverberated loudly and the book became an immense bestseller. In 1964 the emerging new mood was further encouraged by the Civil Rights Act, which forbade job discrimination based not only on race, but also on sex. The law unleashed a flood of complaints by women to the Equal Employment Opportunity Commission established under the act to monitor compliance with its provisions. When the commission proved resistant to women's complaints, feminists decided to act. In June 1966, they organized NOW, the National Organization for Women, with Friedan as its first president.

NOW was a moderate voice of the new feminism. It worked through the courts and the legislatures to bring "women into full participation in the mainstream of American society" with the right to exercise "all the privileges and responsibilities thereof in truly equal partnership with men. . . ." It did not target men as the enemy or seek to fundamentally restructure the family or society as a whole. To the left of NOW were more militant groups, derived primarily from the student New Left. These "women's liberationists" developed a profoundly radical critique of Western society as hopelessly male-dominated. "Patriarchy," they held, rather than capitalism, was the source not only of female oppression but of all oppression in the world, and its destruction was a prerequisite for the liberation of all humankind.

Radical feminists sometimes seemed to have little respect for conventional women or for the conventional family. A vocal minority were lesbians with an agenda separate from more traditional women. Women's liberationists employed such attention-getting tactics as "guerrilla theater"—street demonstrations in the form of political drama—and disruption of "sexist" rituals. In September 1968 radical feminists picketed the Miss America Pageant in Atlantic City as a woman-degrading event. Though they did not burn their bras, they did toss other supposed symbols of female bondage—corsets, eyelash curlers, high-heeled shoes—into a "freedom ash can."

The radical feminists also introduced "consciousness-raising"—small, intense meetings of women for personal self-examination and disclosure of male oppression. These sessions doubtless helped women to face painful marriages and other unhealthy relationships with men; they also provided a steady stream of recruits for the new women's liberation movements.

Gay Liberation.   The gay rights movement was another late manifestation of the new liberationist mood. Homosexuality had always existed, of course, but gay men and lesbian women had carefully hidden their sexual preferences to avoid "straight" society's stern disapproval and laws that made many homosexual practices criminal offenses. In many large cities homosexuals congregated in their own neighborhoods and developed their own cultural and social institutions where they could be comfortable. Gays often led double lives: one at home, where they felt free; and one at work, where they felt compelled to conform to the straight world's expectations. This enforced concealment, added to the legal hazards, created a deep sense of resentment and the feeling among homosexuals that they, too, constituted an oppressed minority.

By the mid-1960s male and female homosexuals had formed organizations for mutual support and defense such as the Mattachine Society and the Daughters of Bilitis. Then came a crucial event in Gay Liberation. In June 1969 the police raided the Stonewall Inn, a homosexual bar in New York's Greenwich Village. Gays, who usually accepted such raids as a normal part of existence, this time fought back. The battle against the police lasted far into the night and continued the next day. Stonewall marked the end of homosexual acquiescence and the beginning of the Gay Liberation Movement. In its wake militant gays began to "come out of the closet" and demand that the laws against free sexual expression and practice, and those denying gays equal employment and other rights be removed from the statute books.

■ QUAGMIRE IN VIETNAM ■

Lyndon Johnson was a foreign-affairs novice who relied on the advice of better-informed men. He kept on Kennedy's foreign-policy advisers and accepted their view that the United States had no other choice than to support the pro-American regime in Saigon to prevent the communists from conquering the South. Later he would accept his military advisers' views of how to fight the war and their estimates of progress being made in defeating the Vietcong and North Vietnamese forces.

Johnson was also a captive of the past. Like many of his generation, he viewed Vietnam in terms of the "lessons" of the 1930s: If you appeased aggressors, as Chamberlain had appeased Hitler at Munich, they would force you ultimately to fight on more difficult ground. "I knew," Johnson later told his biographer Doris Kearns, "that if the aggression succeeded in South Vietnam, then the aggressors would simply keep on going until all of Southeast Asia fell into their hands, slowly or quickly." However faulty, the formula was convincing to the president and to many other Americans as well. Johnson also feared the precedent of Truman, who had been attacked for "losing" China after the communist takeover in the late 1940s. "I don't want it said of me that I was the president who lost Vietnam," he remarked at one point.

LBJ's first step down the slippery path in Vietnam was the Gulf of Tonkin Resolution he extracted from Congress in August 1964 following a reported attack on American naval vessels off the Vietnam coast. Passed almost unanimously, it authorized the president to "take all necessary measures to repel any armed attack against the forces of the United States." Johnson would treat the resolution as the virtual equivalent of a declaration of war.

During the 1964 presidential campaign, as we saw, Johnson muted the Vietnam issue. Then, early in 1965, following a Vietcong attack on a U.S. airbase at Pleiku, the administration launched "Operation Rolling Thunder," a massive bombing campaign against North Vietnam to induce the Ho Chi Minh government to abandon its effort to overthrow the pro-American regime in South Vietnam. When it proved ineffective, Johnson increased the number of American military advisers to the South Vietnamese army and in April 1965 took the fatal step of dispatching the first American ground combat troops to Vietnam. When asked at a press conference at the time whether the decision represented a sharp change of direction, he denied it vehemently.

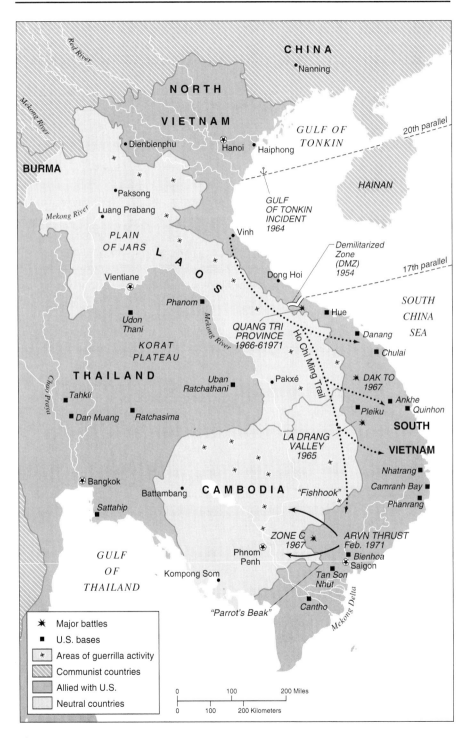

The Vietnam War Arena

All through 1965 and 1966 Johnson increased the pressure on the Vietcong and North Vietnamese in hopes of forcing a settlement that would preserve South Vietnam as an anti-Communist bastion under the pro-American leaders Nguyen Van Thieu and Nguyen Cao Ky. In April 1966 the United States sent B-52s to bomb Hanoi, the North Vietnamese capital, and Haiphong, the major North Vietnamese port of entry for supplies from the Soviet Union. Meanwhile, on the ground, United States marines and army units fought a war in the jungles and rice paddies under terms imposed by Vietcong guerrillas. By the end of 1966 there were 385,000 American troops in Vietnam; by the end of 1967 over 485,000.

While pouring men and material into Vietnam, the administration sought to avoid a total war, such as an actual invasion of North Vietnam the base of communist operations in the south. Such a move might bring the Soviet Union or China in and trip off World War III. It might also reveal that the American people had no heart for the casualties and costs of a full commitment. Confronted with these dangers, the president chose the awkward course of a limited war that many would later say could not be won.

The fighting, nevertheless, was dirty work in every sense of the term. The American military used body counts to chart their progress. The Vietcong, refusing to meet the Americans head-on, chose to hit and run, slipping away into the jungle when confronted by superior forces. South Vietnamese villagers were often caught in the middle and were attacked by both sides. American guerrilla-warfare experts tried to establish secure areas free of "the Cong," but the villages seldom remained secure for long. Too many considered the guerrillas less dangerous than the Americans or the corrupt officials of the Saigon government, or simply could not resist Vietcong threats.

There were atrocities on both sides. The Vietcong set off bombs on the streets of Saigon that killed innocent civilians. They tortured and murdered South Vietnamese villagers, policemen, teachers, and Catholics who opposed them. Americans also committed atrocities, though they were never officially condoned. In March 1968 an American army unit under Lieutenant William L. Calley, Jr., attacked My Lai, a village of 600 people suspected of harboring Vietcong, and massacred virtually every inhabitant. The Defense Department attempted to cover up this crime, but it became known when a former member of Calley's unit informed several high government officials. Calley was eventually tried, but received a light sentence.

By 1968 the United States had sunk deeply into a dirty, divisive, expensive war. As in the Korean conflict, there seemed to be no way to conclude the fighting without surrender. Reassuring government statements were undercut daily by television broadcasts from the battlefields that showed no cause for optimism.

As the war dragged on month after month, it began to damage the economy. Johnson was at first afraid to ask Americans to pay for the war directly, lest economic sacrifice make it even less popular than it was. Yet by 1967 it was costing the country $25 billion a year. This sum, on top of Great Society domestic programs, produced what then seemed large budget deficits: $8.7 billion in 1967 and $25.2 billion in 1968. Finally, the president asked for higher taxes to siphon off excess purchasing power, but by then the harm was done. Until 1966 yearly consumer price increases had remained below 2 percent. In 1966 they rose to 3.4 percent and in 1968 to 4.7 percent. The dollar was becoming one of the war's casualties.

Organized protests against the war by college students, pacifist groups, and various peace organizations began in 1965. In early 1966, the congressional "dove," J. William Fulbright of Arkansas, chairman of the Senate Foreign Relations Committee, conducted televised hearings on the war during which he grilled Secretary of State Dean Rusk remorselessly and exposed many of the weaknesses of the prowar "hawk" position. Fulbright denounced the war as displaying the "arrogance of power." Before long, liberal and radical clergy began to demand an end to the Vietnam slaughter. In early 1967 Martin Luther King, Jr., made a "Declaration of Independence" from the war, announcing that it was "time to break silence." In 1967 Father Daniel Berrigan and his brother, Philip, organized the Catholic Ultra-Resistance.

Most Americans continued to support the war, however. Many considered the protesters traitors to their country. Bumper stickers reading "America: Love it or leave it" began to appear on the streets and highways. Even many anti-Communist liberals continued to believe that abandoning South Vietnam would destroy the credibility of American foreign policy and play into Soviet hands.

After 1967, however, support for the president's Vietnam policies eroded rapidly. The greatest blow to "hawk" confidence came in early 1968 when, during the Vietnamese Lunar New Year (Tet), the Vietcong launched a major offensive against Saigon and scores of other South Vietnamese cities. One squad of Vietcong commandos broke into the American embassy compound in Saigon and threatened to capture the embassy itself. After fierce and bloody fighting, the communist assault was checked. The Vietcong suffered thousands of casualties. But Tet made a mockery of the administration's confident propaganda. Until this point many Americans had found it possible to believe that the war, however protracted, was being won. Tet seemed to show that the enemy was, if anything, growing in strength.

By early 1968 administration leaders were beginning to have doubts themselves. Early in the year a discouraged and disillusioned Robert McNamara left the Pentagon to become head of the World Bank. Johnson himself began to have second thoughts. The war seemed to be getting out of hand and threatening to rip the country apart. The president found himself personally under siege. Whenever he appeared in public he was surrounded by protesters carrying signs denouncing him and chanting "Hey! Hey! LBJ, How Many Kids Did You Kill Today?" On top of his other troubles, as the presidential election of 1968 approached Johnson found himself facing a formidable challenge for renomination from within his own party.

■ THE 1968 ELECTION ■

McCarthy v. Kennedy. The president's challengers were Senators Eugene McCarthy of Minnesota and Robert F. Kennedy of New York. A former Catholic seminarian, McCarthy attracted many students and academics who appreciated his ethical stance. Kennedy could communicate more readily with blue-collar workers and blacks. Wearing the still-shining mantle of Camelot, he projected a warmer image as friend of the masses. McCarthy was first in the field against Johnson. When the "dump Johnson" leaders initially failed to entice Kennedy into running, the Minnesota senator reluctantly announced his candidacy. Few expected that he could make much headway against an incumbent president, but in the New Hampshire Democratic primary in March 1968 thousands of student volunteers turned out to ring doorbells, make phone calls, and stuff envelopes for him. Many "cleaned for Gene," shaving off beards, abandoning jeans and T shirts to avoid offending the state's conservative voters. The results were startling: The challenger received only a few hundred votes less than the president. Having concluded that Johnson was beatable, Kennedy now also entered the race.

By early 1968 Johnson had decided to renounce another full term. His new Defense Secretary, the debonair Clark Clifford, and the informal group of foreign-policy elder statesmen known as the "Wise Men," told him after Tet that the war was unwinnable. He should, they said, gradually reduce the American military commitment. Reluctantly accepting their position, Johnson refused to grant the request of General William Westmoreland, U.S. commander in Vietnam, for an additional 206,000 troops. He also concluded that he could encourage a negotiated peace if he ceased the bombing campaign and withdrew himself from public life. In an address to the nation on March 31 announcing a bombing halt and a major peace initiative, he concluded with the words: "I shall not seek, and will not accept, the nomination of my party for another term as your president." The two Democratic antiwar candidates now began the long struggle through the state primaries to secure the nomination.

Before the campaign's end two tragedies intervened. The first took place in Memphis, where Martin Luther King, Jr., had gone to support a local strike of the predominantly black city garbage collectors. King's nonviolent approach to racial change, as we saw, was under powerful attack by black-power militants, but he was about to open a new phase of his career by leading a "poor people's" campaign to compel the government to revive its flagging effort to end poverty. He never did. On April 4, 1968, he was shot and killed by James Earl Ray, an escaped white convict who may have been in the pay of white supremacists. Black ghettos around the country exploded in rage and despair. From their offices on Capitol Hill congressmen could see the flames and smoke from Washington's burning buildings and stores.

The second tragedy came on June 6 in Los Angeles minutes after Kennedy's victory over McCarthy in the California primary. As he left his cheering supporters in the Embassy Room of the Ambassador Hotel, Kennedy was assassinated by a Palestinian immigrant named Sirhan Bishara Sirhan. These two events confirmed the public's agony over violence and reinforced the sense that the nation must extricate itself from the contaminating brutality of Vietnam. The United States seemed to be at the edge of anarchy.

The forces that converged on Chicago for the Democratic convention in late August represented an explosive mixture. Now that Johnson was out of the running, the hawks had gathered around Vice President Humphrey, who, however much he personally disliked the war, had become Johnson's heir apparent, tied to his policies by loyalty and dependence. On the other side were the combined antiwar groups representing McCarthy and the delegates who had supported Kennedy. On the streets and in the parks of the Windy City were the Yippies (Youth International Party), politicized counterculture protestors led by activists Jerry Rubin and Abbie Hoffman, along with New Left radicals, antiwar students, and pacifists, who were determined to replace the Democrats' "convention of death," with their own "festival of life."

Within the convention hall itself the Humphrey forces triumphed. Supported by the remaining hawks, by union leaders, by party regulars, and by the big-city power brokers, Humphrey overcame the insurgent peace forces and was nominated on the first ballot. In the streets of Chicago, meanwhile, Mayor Richard Daley's police clashed violently with the antiwar activists before the eyes of the delegates and the TV cameras. To many viewers the contrast between political business-as-usual in the convention hall and the images of burly policemen hurling young people and reporters through plate glass windows was final evidence that America was out of control. Many voters blamed the chaos on the Democrats and on Hubert Humphrey; his campaign was in deep trouble from the start.

The Backlash.   The chaotic events in Chicago reinforced the view of many white voters that permissiveness and toleration had gotten out of hand. The ghetto riots, the anti-Americanism of peace protesters, the hippie disregard of public decency, the courts' acceptance of pornography and rejection of school prayer—in fact, the whole thrust of the decade—were sickening, they felt, and should be reversed. Called "backlash" voters, they were disproportionately white males of working-class background who felt left behind by government and a culture they believed was run by elitists who favored society's crazies and extremists over themselves. Many saw a savior in George Wallace, the segregationist governor of Alabama, who had challenged Lyndon Johnson in the Democratic primaries in 1964 and done surprisingly well among blue-collar registered Democrats.

Meanwhile, in Miami, in a convention as bland as the Democrats' was tumultuous, the Republicans nominated Richard M. Nixon. The nomination represented a spectacular comeback for the candidate. In 1962 Nixon had run for governor of California and had been beaten by the incumbent, Edmund Brown. After his defeat, in an intemperate outburst accusing the press of "kicking him around" during the campaign, he had promised never to run for office again. Soon after, he joined a New York law firm to spend his remaining days making money and enjoying the pleasures of private life. He could not stay out of politics, however, and soon started the comeback campaign that finally brought him victory at the Miami convention.

The 1968 presidential contest was a close one. Many observers felt that the Democrats had destroyed themselves in Chicago by their bitter, divisive infighting and the rioting in the streets. The Republicans, on the other hand,

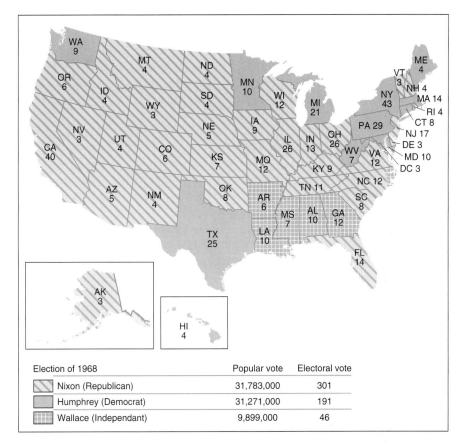

Election of 1968	Popular vote	Electoral vote
Nixon (Republican)	31,783,000	301
Humphrey (Democrat)	31,271,000	191
Wallace (Independant)	9,899,000	46

The Election of 1968

worried about defections in the South and among white blue-collar males to Wallace, running as the American Independent Party candidate on a platform of law and order, total victory in Vietnam, clamping down on dissenters and civil rights activists, and reducing the power of federal bureaucrats over people's lives. To avoid losing the South and the backlash voters to Wallace, Nixon promised Senator Strom Thurmond of South Carolina that if elected he would keep the nation strong militarily, work for a less activist Supreme Court, and slow the pace of desegregation. It was with Thurmond's urging that Nixon selected Spiro T. Agnew, the little-known governor of Maryland, as his running mate.

The Republicans were well in the lead as the campaign opened. Humphrey was handicapped by his association with the administration's Vietnam policy and not until September did he free himself from the onus by proposing a more "dovish" approach to a negotiated peace in Vietnam. He was also in trouble because many blue-collar male Democrats threatened to defect to Wallace. Then, as November approached, the traditional Democratic coalition of ethnics, blacks, eastern liberals, and union members began to rally around Humphrey.

Had the campaign gone on for just a few days longer, the ticket of Humphrey and Senator Edmund S. Muskie of Maine might have pulled ahead. But the surge came too late. On November 5 Nixon won by 31.7 million votes (301 electoral) to Humphrey's 31.2 million (191 electoral) and Wallace's 9.9 million (46 electoral). Richard Nixon would be the thirty-seventh president of the United States.

■ CONCLUSIONS ■

During the 1960s the United States attained a level of material well-being beyond anything dreamed of in the past. Affluence transformed the public mood. The middle class, initially, experienced a new spirit of generosity. Generosity, reinforced perhaps by guilt, and underscored by the sweeping 1964 victory of Lyndon Johnson over Barry Goldwater, in turn unleashed a surge of social reform not equaled since the New Deal.

And, ironically, prosperity also encouraged an unprecedented wave of dissent and social criticism. Minorities, even more keenly than in the past, felt resentment at long-denied basic civil rights and exclusion from the benefits of abundance. To the privileged young, who took America's bounding wealth for granted, American society seemed an ugly place of bureaucratic rigidity, meaningless relationships, racism, manipulation, and aesthetic squalor. With affluence so readily attainable the dissenters could experiment, indulging their yearnings for alternative ways of living their lives.

But there was also the war. The dissenters' disgust with their society was reinforced by a distant and apparently pointless war. Vietnam undermined the legitimacy of many of the nation's established institutions: government, the universities, the mainstream press, the churches.

Thus, some of the chief beneficiaries of prosperity were the very people who despised it the most. Their excesses in turn would outrage those who still held to traditional values and attitudes and force the dissenters on the defensive. The election of Richard Nixon in 1968 expressed that outrage. The sixties were, in effect, over. What would replace it?

Online Resources

"The Cuban Missile Crisis"
http://www.gwu.edu/~nsarchiv/nsa/cuba_mis_cri/cmcchron.html
This site provides an introduction and overview of events of the Cuban Missile Crisis. A glossary of terms includes military jargon and sketches of the key political actors involved. Photos on the site area available from the JFK Library.
"The Great Society Speech"
http://www.tamu.edu/scom/pres/speeches/lbjgreat.html
At this online speech archive, read Lyndon B. Johnson's "Great Society" speech and many others of his presidency.

"The History of NOW"
http://www.now.org/history/history.html
Visit the National Organization of Women's Web site and read about the
group's founding, its involvement in the Equal Rights Amendment drive, and
its advocacy for issues concerning working women. Also, read primary-source
documents addressing woman's liberation at Duke University's online collection
"Documents from the Women's Liberation Movement" at
http://scriptorium.lib.duke.edu/wlm/

"The Wars of Vietnam: An Overview"
http://vietnam.vassar.edu/
Offering an extensive overview of military conflicts in Vietnam from 1945 up
through U.S. engagement, this site offers full text of historical documents
including the Tonkin Gulf Resolution and excerpts from American presidential
speeches.

"The History of GATT and the Structure of the WTO"
http://www.ljx.com/practice/internet.history.html
On this Web site, read more about the fundament policies of the General
Agreement of Tariffs and Trade (GATT), the 1947 economic policy intended to
reduce trade barriers and regulate commerce.

The Psychedelic '60s: Literary Tradition and Social Change
http://www.lib.virginia.edu/exhibits/sixties/index.html
An online exhibit that explores the counterculture of the 1960s addressing
issues such as the war in Vietnam and the civil rights movement through
poetry, literature, and pop art of the day.

29

THE UNCERTAIN SEVENTIES

Why Did the Right Fail?

1960	Organization of Petroleum Exporting Countries (OPEC) is formed
1969	Paris peace talks on Vietnam begin; Nixon orders the secret bombing of Cambodia; Strategic Arms Limitation Talks (SALT) begin in Helsinki; Americans land on the moon; Nuclear Nonproliferation Treaty
1970	United States invades Cambodia; Four students killed by National Guard in antiwar demonstration at Kent State University in Ohio; Congress repeals the Gulf of Tonkin Resolution
1971	The *New York Times* publishes the "Pentagon Papers"; Nixon imposes wage and price controls; Berlin Accord
1972	Nixon visits China; Congress passes the Federal Election Campaign Act; Nixon visits Moscow; The United States and the Soviet Union ratify arms limitation treaties; Watergate break-in; Nixon reelected in landslide
1973	Truce in Vietnam; Senate Select Committee holds public hearing on Watergate; House Judiciary Committee begins hearings on impeachment resolutions; Vice President Agnew resigns in disgrace; Gerald Ford becomes vice president; Israel and Egypt go to war, touching off Arab oil embargo; Abortion legalized by Supreme Court in *Roe* v. *Wade*
1974	Arab oil embargo ends, but OPEC raises oil prices drastically; House Judiciary Committee recommends impeachment of Nixon; Nixon resigns; Ford becomes president; Ford pardons Nixon
1975	North and South Vietnam are reunited
1976	Bicentennial celebrations; Jimmy Carter elected president
1977	SALT II talks collapse; Carter launches moral equivalent of war on United States dependency on foreign oil; Camp David Accords
1978	Panama Canal Treaties
1979	SALT II agreement; Three Mile Island nuclear power plant disaster; Shah of Iran exiled; 66 American hostages taken by Khomeini's followers in Iran; Russia invades Afghanistan
1980	Ronald Reagan elected president

In January 1969 a new administration came to power in Washington apparently determined to dismantle the Great Society, slow the pace of social change, and, more vigorously than ever, push back the tide of world communism. Between that date and the end of the 1970s American public opinion would, by and large, support such a conservative agenda. Yet very little of it would be achieved. Indeed, by the opening of the 1980s the United States, in the eyes of many committed conservatives, had retrogressed: The social welfare state had expanded, the federal courts had pushed into new areas of social change, and the United States was embarked on a course of accommodation to the communist world.

How had such results come about? How had Richard Nixon, the man who seemed to epitomize conservative anti-communism, managed to perpetuate big government and the social welfare state that he and his followers despised and to replace the hard-line anti-communism of recent American policy with a more flexible approach?

■ THE NIXON PRESIDENCY ■

Richard Nixon was one of the most puzzling and inconsistent men to occupy the White House. His father was an angry, abusive man and a financial failure; his mother a sweet-tempered Quaker lady. The contrasting personalities of his parents helped mold the extremes of Nixon's own character: one side self-pitying and vindictive, particularly in the face of frustration; the other generous, even idealistic. Both facets of the new president's nature could be detected in his approach to public issues. He could support welfare reform, environmental protection laws, and reconciliation with Red China and the Soviet Union, for example. But he also sought to weaken civil rights protection, was unscrupulous in confronting his political adversaries, and inspired the illegal political acts we call Watergate.

Nixon's tough, partisan side was reflected in his inner circle of attorney general John Mitchell, White House chief of staff H. R. Haldeman, and chief adviser on domestic affairs John Ehrlichman. Coming from outside the normal American political culture of give-and-take, these men, like the president, believed that winning was all that counted. They also shared with their boss a deep suspicion of the "eastern establishment," a vaguely defined circle of liberal leaders who, they claimed, dominated the press, the universities, and the upper reaches of the professions, and would do anything to malign and frustrate the president if they could.

Nixon also appointed better advisers, however. Daniel Moynihan, assistant for urban affairs, was one of the more imaginative men in American political life. Henry Kissinger, Nixon's national security adviser and later secretary of state, was an unusually adept diplomat with a vision influenced by his deep knowledge of history, though he harbored a streak of deviousness. Other competent Nixon appointees included Treasury Secretary John Connally and Secretary of Defense Melvin Laird. Unfortunately, the inner circle of White House aides under Haldeman and Ehrlichman often exerted disproportionate influence on administration policy.

Détente. Nixon was far more interested in foreign policy than domestic affairs; it was as an international statesman that he hoped to make his mark in history. Foremost, he and Kissinger sought to stabilize relations with the communist world by withdrawing from Vietnam, recognizing the People's Republic of China, and reducing rivalry with the Soviet Union.

However commendable their goals, the Nixon-Kissinger diplomatic style disturbed many observers. Initially the president's national security adviser, Kissinger had little respect for Secretary of State William Rogers, and often employed secret "back channel" negotiations with foreign representatives that bypassed the State Department. This awkward situation was rectified in 1973 when the German-born Kissinger became Rogers's successor. Yet even as Secretary of State, Kissinger continued to rely on what his opponents considered devious stratagems.

Though controversial, the Nixon–Kissinger policy made substantial progress toward reducing world tensions. One source of Soviet–American competition ended during the summer of 1969 when astronaut Neil A. Armstrong took the first steps on the moon while millions around the world watched on television. The United States had undeniably won the "space race," set off by the Soviet launching of Sputnik in 1957. Then, in November 1969, Nixon and Soviet president Nikolai Podgorny signed the Nuclear Nonproliferation Treaty to prevent the spread of dangerous nuclear weapons to nations that did not yet possess them. In 1971 and 1972 the perennial problems of Berlin and the two Germanies (The Federal Republic in the west and the Democratic Republic in the east) were finally settled by the Berlin Accord: Britain, France, the United States, and the Soviet Union agreed to cease threatening communications between the noncommunist zone of Berlin and the Federal Republic, and formally recognized the existence of two separate German nations.

Another step in the process of accommodation with America's chief rival ("détente") came in May 1972 when Nixon visited the Soviet Union, the first American president ever to do so. The visit produced a set of agreements pledging the two nations to facilitate commercial relations and cooperate in the scientific, medical, and environmental realms. More significantly, it led to the signing of the SALT I (Strategic Arms Limitation Treaty) agreements negotiated over several years by the two powers. SALT I confirmed MAD (mutually assured destruction) as superpower policy: The check on nuclear war would be deterrence guaranteed by the ability of either side to massively retaliate against any nuclear attack. The core agreement of SALT I was the Anti-Ballistic Missile (ABM) Treaty forbidding virtually all defensive weapons capable of shooting down hostile incoming ICBMs. It also included agreements to limit the construction and deployment of new offensive missiles.

The People's Republic of China. Even more remarkable in some ways than détente with the Soviet Union was the breakthrough in relations with the People's Republic of China. Until now the United States had refused to recognize the Chinese mainland regime and had vetoed every attempt to admit the People's Republic to the United Nations. In Washington's view, "China" was the Republic of China on Taiwan where Chiang Kai-shek's Nationalists had fled after the Communist mainland victory in 1949. American troops were stationed on Taiwan to provide military support if the Chinese Communists should ever attempt to invade the island across the Strait of Formosa.

There were good reasons to dislike the regime in Beijing. On attaining power, the Communists had executed thousands of people as class enemies and imposed a harsh, authoritarian regime on the Chinese people. To restore flagging revolutionary zeal, in the 1960s they had unleashed a wave of murderous anarchy (the Cultural Revolution) against all traces of the bourgeois past, all Western influences, and all dissenting opinion. Yet, with its 800 million people, China's existence could not be wished away. Not only was America's China Policy unrealistic; it was also not in America's best interests. Nixon perceived that since Stalin's death in the early 1950s, China and the Soviet Union, once closely allied, had become adversaries whose armies at times violently clashed along their common Asian border. It seemed foolish not to take advantage of the Sino–Soviet rift and use one Communist nation to check the goals and ambitions of the other. Indeed, an opening to China seemed an essential ingredient of achieving stable relations with the Soviet Union.

Soon after the 1968 American presidential elections, Beijing indicated its desire to smooth over Sino–American differences. Both countries were soon holding secret meetings in Warsaw. Another signal of friendship came in early 1971 when the Chinese invited an American ping-pong team then visiting Japan to tour the People's Republic and play Chinese teams. In July 1971, after a secret visit by Kissinger to Beijing, Nixon startled the world by announcing that he had been invited to visit the People's Republic of China and would go there sometime in the early part of the following year. In October the United States for the first time abstained from vetoing the admission of Red China to the United Nations. The Beijing government was promptly seated and the Taiwan regime's representatives expelled.

On February 21, 1972, Nixon, his wife, and a large presidential entourage arrived in Beijing by plane. Scores of American reporters and the TV media were present, and millions of viewers in the United States watched the American president shake hands with Premier Chou En-lai. The discussions that followed with Chou and Communist party chairman Mao Tse-tung, China's aging top leader, were largely exploratory; little of a concrete nature was accomplished during the visit except for an agreement to withdraw the American troops from Taiwan. Much of Nixon's time was spent in sightseeing and banqueting. But the meeting was momentous symbolically. Television pictures of Nixon toasting Chou, quoting chairman Mao, and strolling along the Great Wall made clear to the American people that the policy of ignoring the world's most populous nation was finally ended.

The far right considered the settlement with the People's Republic and abandonment of Taiwan a surrender to communism. Most Americans, however, accepted the move as sensible and long overdue. Many of Nixon's liberal critics noted ruefully that only a conservative with a reputation as a militant anti-communist could have gotten away with the abrupt change of policy.

Richard Nixon and Chinese Premier Chou En-lai at a banquet during Nixon's famous 1972 trip to Beijing. Nixon looks dubious about his food.

"Peace with Honor" in Vietnam.   Until the middle of Nixon's second term, however, America remained trapped in the worst of the foreign policy past: Vietnam. In January 1969 serious peace talks between North Vietnam and the United States opened in Paris. They quickly deadlocked, however. North Vietnam had no intention of abandoning its goal of evicting the Saigon regime and reuniting Vietnam under its sole control; the United States did not intend to desert its ally.

The new American administration had little interest in continuing the war. But, like his predecessor, Nixon did not want to be charged with "losing" Vietnam. America must disengage, but it must preserve an independent South Vietnam to keep its reputation and pride intact. Nixon called this "peace with honor"; his critics called it foolish, among other things.

Nixon was willing to use any means to force the Communists to bargain. At one point he spread the story that he was a communist-obsessed nuclear madman capable of blowing up the world if he did not get his way. In March 1969 he secretly ordered the massive bombing of Vietnam's neighbor, Cambodia—a supposedly neutral nation—to hamper Communist operations in South Vietnam. At the same time, however, he announced that the United States would adopt the policy of "Vietnamization": It would gradually shift responsibility for military defense to the South Vietnamese and begin to withdraw American combat troops.

The antiwar forces gave little credit to the president for Vietnamization. Nixon talked peace, they said, but the fighting and dying continued. America should leave Vietnam immediately. "Out Now" was the only valid policy. Then, in late April 1970, Nixon sent American forces on a sweep through Cambodia to attack bases that, he claimed, were refuges for Vietcong guerrillas. A seeming escalation of fighting, this move electrified the antiwar movement. Demonstrations erupted on scores of college campuses. At Kent State University in Ohio, National Guardsmen fired live ammunition at student antiwar demonstrators, killing four and wounding eleven. Hundreds of American campuses shut down to protest the killings and to allow students to mobilize against the detested war. In June Congress reacted to the revived antiwar surge by repealing the 1964 Gulf of Tonkin resolution that Johnson had used as a legal equivalent of a declaration of war.

By now antiwar feeling had spread far beyond the original circle of activists. Seeking to show the war's nefarious roots, in June 1971 Daniel Ellsberg, a former Pentagon official, made public a collection of classified Defense Department documents describing the slow steps to American entrapment in the Vietnam morass and the deception that accompanied the process. The Justice Department indicted Ellsberg for unauthorized use of government material and sought a court injunction to stop publication of the "Pentagon Papers" in the *New York Times* and *Washington Post*. The Supreme Court denied the injunction.* Meanwhile, in Vietnam the morale of American soldiers in the field deteriorated. Determined to avoid danger now that departure was imminent, more and more combat troops disobeyed direct orders or "fragged" officers by rolling live hand grenades into their tents while they slept. Others turned to drugs to make the time till their tour of duty ended pass more quickly. The war, it seemed, was destroying the American military.

In 1972, with only a few thousand American combat troops remaining in South Vietnam, the Communists launched a major offensive to topple the Saigon government. In retaliation, Nixon ordered the resumption of massive bombing of North Vietnam and the mining of Haiphong harbor, the port of entry for most of the arms and supplies from the Soviet Union. It looked as if the escalation pattern of the past would be repeated once more despite Vietnamization. Fortunately, by this time, both the Chinese and the Russians were more anxious for better relations with the United States than for North Vietnamese victory, and they told Hanoi that it must act more reasonably. Meanwhile, the Saigon government, reassured by a billion-dollar gift of American military hardware to help it defend itself against a Communist takeover, also proved more amenable to negotiation.

These events finally broke the peace negotiation logjam in Paris. In January 1973 the United States, South Vietnam, and the Vietcong-North Vietnamese signed an agreement that included (1) a cease-fire between Hanoi and Saigon, (2) the release of all American prisoners of war, (3) the withdrawal of all remaining

---

*As part of the fallout from Watergate, in May 1973 the charges against Ellsberg were dismissed.

U.S. military personnel, (4) massive American economic aid to South Vietnam, and (5) a flock of complicated arrangements intended to reconcile the South Vietnamese government and the Vietcong. Nixon and Kissinger claimed that they had preserved the separate existence of South Vietnam. Whether they truly believed this or merely hoped for "a decent interval" before Saigon fell is not clear. In any event, by April 1975 Communist forces had overwhelmed the South Vietnamese army and occupied all of Vietnam, forcibly uniting North and South under their harsh regime. The Communists had finally achieved their goal of thirty years.

Almost no one could extract satisfaction from the result. Vietnam was devastated—physically, economically, socially. Literally millions of Vietnamese, civilians and soldiers, had died. The United States had paid a high cost. Over 46,000 Americans had lost their lives and the country had squandered over $150 billion. Hawks saw the outcome as a humiliation for the United States. It was the first war that America had lost, and it would weaken the nation's selfconfidence. At first, those who had opposed the war could boast that they had helped end the killing and replaced a corrupt, undemocratic government with a more popular one. It was soon obvious, however, that the communist regime was as benighted as its enemies had long charged. The North Vietnamese conquerors rounded up thousands of the Saigon regime's friends and sent them to forced labor or "reeducation" camps. Over 1.4 million refugees fled the country, many in small boats. Thousands of Vietnamese refugees settled in the United States. For decades Vietnam would remain one of the poorest, most backward nations in all of East Asia, an embarrassment to all who had supported Hanoi's struggle to reunite the country.

The war's outcome would color the debate over future American foreign policy. Some citizens would see it as a lesson in limits: The United States must confine itself to matters that affected its vital interests closer to home. Others would view it as an instance of how defeat would inevitably follow loss of nerve and confidence. For a time the limits group would predominate, and during the mid-1970s American foreign policy would enter a phase that observers called neo-isolationist.

Courting the Backlash Vote.   In domestic affairs Nixon looked two ways. He had based his 1968 election campaign on the existence of a "silent majority," composed mostly of nominal Democrats who were fed up with many of the social trends of the day. Their disgust could be used to forge a new and unbeatable Republican majority. This resembled George Wallace's "backlash" strategy, though it was not as strident or overtly racist.

Nixon and his advisers found many backlash views personally congenial. Administration officials wore American flag pins on their lapels and cultivated a reverent demeanor toward traditional American values. After 1969 the administration set out to woo "Middle Americans," whether Democrats or Republicans, by echoing their views. Nixon described campus radicals as "bums." When it came to crime and disorder, ordinary citizens he said, "have had it up to here." The most hard-line conservative rhetoric came from Vice President Spiro

Agnew, who toured the nation denouncing "rad-libs," the "nattering nabobs of negativism," and "troglodytic leftists." "The disease of our time," he said, "is an artificial and masochistic sophistication—the vague uneasiness that our values are false, and there is something wrong with being patriotic, honest, moral and hard-working."

The campaign to turn back the clock went beyond words. Federal officials eased up on the enforcement of desegregation in the South. In March 1971 Nixon asked Congress to halt "forced busing" of children from neighborhood schools to more distant ones to achieve racial balance. In April he directed veterans' hospitals to cease abortions for ex-servicewomen. The president frequently called for "law and order" and sponsored several bills to strengthen the hand of judges and the police. Nixon and his advisers believed, as had Johnson, that antiwar and New Left dissenters were encouraging the Vietcong and the North Vietnamese to continue their fight. The administration cracked down hard. During a May 1970 antiwar march on Washington, Attorney General Mitchell threw thousands of demonstrators into jail and detention compounds. The Justice Department indicted leading pacifists and student activists, including the Yippies and the baby-doctor, Benjamin Spock, for crimes or conspiracy to commit crimes. The defendants won most of these cases, but the legal defenses depleted the energies and financial resources of the antiwar movement.

Unlike Republicans in the past, Nixon counted on support from the white, formerly solid Democratic South. At the 1968 Republican convention he had promised conservative Dixie leaders to defer to traditional white southern feelings and wishes in regard to administrative and judicial appointments. In early 1969 he nominated to the Supreme Court Judge Clement F. Haynsworth, Jr., of South Carolina, a man suspected of segregationist views. The Democratically controlled Senate used Haynsworth's dubious conflicts of interest on the bench as the basis for rejecting his nomination. Nixon then sent forward the name of Florida federal judge G. Harrold Carswell. Antilabor and racially conservative, the new nominee was a man whose decisions had frequently been reversed by higher courts. The Senate rejected this appointment too. Nixon eventually succeeded in getting confirmed another presumed conservative, Harry Blackmun. Blackmun was a northerner, but the president's efforts on behalf of southerners Haynsworth and Carswell were appreciated by conservative white voters in Dixie.

Nixon undoubtedly helped to slow the movement toward a more turbulent and socially liberal society. On his watch the student revolt subsided; the hippies gradually disappeared; antiwar protest ceased. Still, the results did not satisfy backlash voters. Drug abuse reached into the high schools of suburban America, teenage pregnancies soared, crime and disorder spread, and movies and books continued to deal with sexually explicit themes.

Worst of all was the continued judicial activism of the Supreme Court. Earl Warren retired in 1968 and Nixon appointed as the new Chief Justice Warren Burger, a man opposed to his predecessor's liberal and activist views. Yet the Supreme Court continued to dismay conservatives. In *Swann v. Charlotte-Mecklenburg Board* (1971), the justices condoned busing children to distant schools for the purpose of "racial balance," undermining local control over public schools, in the view of traditionalists.

Far worse to social conservatives was *Roe* v. *Wade* (1973). For many years abortion had been illegal in the United States under state laws. Women got abortions nevertheless, but these were often medically risky or even crudely self-induced. With the rise of feminism in the 1960s public opinion shifted against the prohibition of legal termination of pregnancies and a number of states repealed their anti-abortion laws. Then, in 1973, in the name of expanding the right to privacy, the Supreme Court struck down the remaining state anti-abortion laws and allowed abortion on demand during the first trimester of pregnancy. Conservatives charged the justices with condoning baby murder. The decision would reap a whirlwind of passionate controversy.

Domestic Moderation.   Many of Nixon's conservative constituents, then, remained dissatisfied and would continue to search for ways to restore the nation to old-fashioned virtue. Yet Nixon did not send the American ship of state into full reverse. Those who had hoped that the Republican president would decrease the size and reach of the federal government were disappointed.

In 1969 he proposed a "New Federalism" intended to downsize the federal government by transferring many domestic "entitlement" programs to the states, but in the end, due, he said, to resistance by the Democratic-controlled Congress and liberal federal bureaucrats, he succeeded only modestly. Nixon also left intact most Great Society welfare programs. In fact, during his administration, many received better funding than before. In 1968 federal social welfare expenditures had totaled $142 billion; in 1974 they reached $229 billion. Nixon even added programs to the Johnson roster. He signed into law the Supplementary Security Income Act that guaranteed a check each month for elderly, blind, and disabled Americans who were not otherwise entitled to a federal pension. He also endorsed a drastic welfare reform proposal by Daniel Moynihan to provide a guaranteed $1,600-a-year minimum income to each poor family from federal funds. The measure, many hoped, would end forever the inequalities and indignities that beset the existing "welfare system" and cut through the bureaucratic tangle that encumbered it. The Family Assistance Program never made it through both houses of Congress, in part because liberals felt it was not generous enough, but it was a bold departure for a president marked as a conservative.

Nixon's management of the economy was another surprise to those who expected him to pursue traditional conservative policies. By 1971 inflation was running about 5 percent a year, at the same time the economy was in a slump. On the recommendation of Treasury Secretary John Connally, in August the president announced a ninety-day freeze on all wages and prices, to be enforced by appointed control boards. The United States would also cease making the American dollar convertible into gold in international exchanges. Closing the "gold window" ended the era of fixed international exchange rates that had helped to mend and then stimulate the world economy after 1945. Experts would later say that it accelerated inflation and retarded economic growth.

The New Environmentalism. In some ways the most unexpected of all Nixon's domestic policies was his endorsement of the new environmentalism, if only in a qualified way. Drawing on new scientific insights regarding the interrelatedness of living things, by the 1970s scientists saw humans as part of an "ecosystem," a web of life that extended far beyond our own species. This mandated esteem for all living things and respect for the balances of nature. The public mind was alerted to many of the new ideas by Rachel Carson, a naturalist with the U.S. Fish and Wildlife Service, whose 1962 book, *Silent Spring,* described the long-term lethal effects of the insecticide DDT on wildlife, especially birds, and the dangers of carelessly introducing such potent poisons into the natural environment. For every reader of the bestseller who caught the message of nature's interrelatedness there were many more undoubtedly roused by the threat to human health. *Silent Spring* was followed by a flood of books, magazine articles, and TV reports informing the public of how humans interacted with the natural environment and advertising the dangers of pollution from a host of industrial and agricultural processes.

Many of the new views went on display on Earth Day, April 22, 1970, a one-day nationwide celebration of nature that proclaimed the need to stop the environment-despoiling "development" juggernaut. It is not likely that Nixon personally absorbed much of the advanced new ecological sensibility, but he did respond to growing public fears of environmental hazards. Soon after Earth Day he approved the Clean Air Act of 1970, establishing a billion-dollar air pollution control program and imposing tighter emission standards on automobiles. He also signed the Occupational Safety and Health Act establishing an agency to oversee new standards of health and safety for workers in the job environment. Following a serious tanker oil spill off Santa Barbara, California, he approved the Water Quality Improvement Act of 1970 imposing penalties for pollution of ocean and inland waters. In October of that year he created the Environmental Protection Agency (EPA) to administer the various government antipollution programs. In later years the EPA would be in the thick of the battle to preserve and upgrade the natural environment.

The 1972 Election. Many of Nixon's domestic policies—the price control measures particularly—were driven by short-term political considerations. Nothing, including inflation and a weak dollar, must stand in the way of his reelection in 1972.

In retrospect it is difficult to see why the administration was so politically insecure. The Democrats' choice for president in 1972 was Senator George McGovern of South Dakota who represented the party's most liberal wing. McGovern had won the nomination under new convention rules, adopted in 1968, requiring each state delegation to reflect separate voter blocs—youth, women, minorities, as well as white males—in approximate proportion to their numbers in the general populace. The Democratic delegates at Miami were probably a better cross section of the country's citizens than at past conventions, but traditional Democrats—white southerners, blue-collar Catholics, older people, trade unionists—felt left out. It soon appeared that many of them either would not vote or would vote Republican.

McGovern also proved to be an inept campaigner. He selected Senator Thomas Eagleton of Missouri as his running mate without a careful background check. When Eagleton admitted that he had been hospitalized for mental illness, McGovern first rallied to Eagleton's side and then dropped him for former Peace Corps director Sargent Shriver. The Democratic candidate also stumbled over his welfare reform plan, revealing his own uncertain grasp of a guaranteed annual income scheme that many found extravagant. By early fall the polls were pointing to a Democratic disaster.

With the Democrats obviously fumbling away the election, Nixon could avoid the political rough-and-tumble and act "presidential." By fall the economy was firmly in hand under phase one of Nixon's wage and price control program. The results were predictable. Nixon won 60.8 percent of the popular vote, a tiny fraction below Lyndon Johnson's 1964 landslide, and took all the nation's electoral votes except those of the District of Columbia and Massachusetts.

■ WATERGATE ■

The stunning November victory seemed a mandate for four years of impressive presidential achievement. It was not to be. On June 17, five months before, five men had been arrested at the Washington, D.C., headquarters of the Democratic National Committee in the Watergate housing complex; two accomplices were caught outside. Only later did their probable motives become known: Either they were trying to recover information on an illegal gift by millionaire Howard Hughes to a close Nixon friend; or they were hoping to find some dirt on the Democrats that could be used to prevent disclosure of the Hughes transaction.

Although three of the burglars were connected either to the White House or the Committee to Reelect the President (CRP), no information damaging to the administration came to light before the election. When questioned by reporters in mid-June, White House press secretary Ron Ziegler called the Watergate break-in a "third-rate burglary" that had nothing to do with the administration. McGovern struggled to make a campaign issue of Watergate but could prove little, and it did not affect the outcome. Then, by the time of Nixon's second inauguration, the story behind the break-in began to emerge.

In January 1973 the Watergate burglars came before federal District Court judge John Sirica. Dissatisfied with the unaggressive questioning of the prosecutors, Sirica grilled the defendants himself. After conviction by a jury, to avoid stiff sentences from "Maximum John," James McCord revealed to the court that the break-in had involved others besides the defendants and that perjury had been committed at the trial.

It was unfortunate for the administration that the Democrats were in the majority of both houses of Congress; a Republican House and Senate would undoubtedly have been less aggressive in pursuing the president. In February the Senate established a Select Committee on Presidential Campaign activities under the chairmanship of Senator Sam Ervin, Jr., of North Carolina. In May the Ervin committee began to hear testimony on the Watergate matter from a parade of administration officials including Jeb Stuart Magruder, deputy director of CRP; John Dean, the president's counsel; former Attorney General John Mitchell; and Alexander Butterfield, former deputy presidential assistant.

Both Dean and Magruder had already begun to tell the federal prosecutors all they knew, disclosing that Haldeman, Ehrlichman, and Mitchell had tried to hide the administration's role in the break-in. In effect, three of Nixon's closest associates were seeking to obstruct justice, a clearly indictable crime. On April 30, the president learned that Dean intended to accuse him of attempting to hide the administration's responsibility for Watergate. Nixon announced that he had accepted the resignations of Haldeman, Ehrlichman, and Attorney General Richard Kleindienst, and had fired Dean. He also directed the new attorney general, Elliot Richardson, to appoint a special prosecutor to probe Watergate. Richardson named Archibald Cox of the Harvard Law School to the post.

Further Disclosures.   As the televised Ervin committee hearings proceeded, an appalled and fascinated public watched a steady parade of witnesses reveal the administration's disreputable efforts, through CRP (called CREEP by the unfriendly media), to crush its political opponents and illegally hide its acts. Led by *Washington Post* reporters Bob Woodward and Carl Bernstein, the press exposed other serious misdeeds.

The list of unethical and illegal Watergate actions eventually uncovered was a long one. Though it began as part of a "plumbers" operation to "plug" information leaks damaging to the administration, it soon ballooned far beyond this.

> Administration operatives had broken into the office of Daniel Ellsberg's psychiatrist looking for evidence to use against him in his trial for leaking the classified "Pentagon Papers."

> Ehrlichman had sought to influence the presiding judge in the Ellsberg case by hinting that he might be appointed FBI director if he made the right decision. (The White House effort backfired; when the attempt to suborn the judge came out, charges against Ellsberg were dismissed.)

> White House representatives had paid large sums of cash to the Watergate burglars after they were arrested to keep them silent on the connection between the break-in and CRP. Acting director of the FBI, L. Patrick Gray, under pressure from the White House, had destroyed evidence in the Watergate case. The FBI had also shared information from its Watergate investigation with White House counsel Dean, though the White House itself was clearly the target of the investigation.

> The Nixon reelection committee had engaged in "dirty tricks" to disrupt the campaigns of several Democratic candidates during the 1972 primaries.

> CRP had collected large sums of cash from corporations with promises of favors, or threats of retaliation, in violation of federal law, and had then tried to conceal it.

The White House had drawn up an "enemies list" of adversaries in the media, the universities, and the entertainment world. These people were to be harassed by Internal Revenue Service audits and by other means.

One of the Watergate burglars, E. Howard Hunt, had forged State Department messages to implicate the late President John F. Kennedy in the assassination of Vietnamese leader Ngo Dinh Diem. This was designed to besmirch the reputation of President Kennedy' brother, Ted, a potential Nixon presidential rival.

The administration had engaged in illegal wiretapping, even of its own officials, to ferret out political and national security leaks.

The president himself had taken dubious tax breaks for contributing his personal papers to the Library of Congress and had used federal funds to make improvements on his personal homes in Florida and California.

The most telling testimony before the Ervin committee came from John Dean, who claimed that Nixon had known of the illegal break-in for eight months and had tried to cover it up, even offering executive clemency to the burglars if they would keep quiet. But Dean's testimony could not be corroborated. Then, on July 16 Alexander Butterfield revealed that since 1971 all conversations in the president's Oval Office and in the Executive Office Building had been taped, and all the president's phones had been linked to recording devices. Now, everything that John Dean and others had disclosed could be checked against the actual record. The president immediately tried to block access to the tapes. For a full year his lawyers asserted that "executive privilege," needed to preserve the president's freedom of action, permitted him to keep the tapes of vital White House conversations confidential.

When the Ervin committee hearings concluded, the burden of uncovering the remaining facts about the break-in and the cover-up shifted to special prosecutor Archibald Cox. In July, Cox subpoenaed nine tapes. Nixon refused to surrender them, and Cox went before Judge Sirica to demand that they be produced. In late August, Sirica ordered Nixon to comply. The president's lawyers promptly appealed to the District of Columbia Circuit Court, which upheld Sirica's order.

Nixon Fights Back.   On October 20, 1973, Nixon ordered Richardson to fire Cox. The Attorney General refused, as did his deputy, and both resigned. Solicitor General Robert Bork, as acting attorney general, finally performed the deed.

This "Saturday Night Massacre" produced a storm of criticism. The White House was deluged with telegrams denouncing the president and his actions. *Time* magazine, a conservative journal, in the first formal editorial in its fifty-year history, declared "the President should resign." On October 30 the House Judiciary Committee began to consider impeachment charges against Nixon.

Taken aback by this ferocious reaction, Nixon retreated. On October 23 he agreed to obey Sirica's order to deliver the tapes. On November 1 he appointed a new special prosecutor, Leon Jaworski, a conservative Texas attorney. But then the president's lawyers revealed that two of the tapes requested did not exist and that another, of a crucial June conversation with Dean, contained an 18-minute gap as the result of an "accidental" erasure. By this time few Americans believed anything the president said, and most doubted that the erasure had been unintended.

Meanwhile, Vice President Agnew was having his own troubles with the law. Accused of income tax evasion and of accepting payoffs for favors to contractors when he was governor of Maryland, he resigned from office on October 10, 1973. Under terms of the recently adopted Twenty-fifth Amendment to the Constitution, Nixon nominated House Minority Leader Gerald Ford of Michigan as Agnew's successor. Ford took the oath of office on December 6, 1973, as the new vice president. Now, if Watergate did force Nixon out, the country would at least have an honest man in his place.

Impeachment.   Other bombs soon went off. In late April 1974 Nixon released 1,200 pages of edited transcripts of White House tapes. This was the public's first glimpse of what the president and his advisers had actually been saying and doing about Watergate. The view was appalling. The transcripts revealed Nixon as a profane, confused, and peevish man, willing to use any tack against his nemies and prone to mean-spirited and bigoted remarks. Worse than this, several conversations seemed to confirm his role in abetting a cover-up, though a "smoking gun" was not yet visible.

On May 1 the House Judiciary Committee denied that the release of the edited transcripts constituted full compliance with its subpoena. Jaworski's office had also subpoenaed tapes, and on May 20 Judge Sirica ordered Nixon once more to comply. The president's counsel appealed his decision to the Supreme Court.

That uneasy summer as Americans watched the unfolding drama, matters came to a head. First, the Supreme Court unanimously ruled that Nixon must release all the tapes Jaworski asked for. For reasons that would soon become clear, the president resisted the Court's order, but then relented. The process of transcribing the tapes began. On July 24 the Judiciary Committee opened televised debates on articles of impeachment. A few days later it voted to recommend to the full House of Representatives three articles of impeachment: (1) that Nixon had obstructed justice by his role in the Watergate cover-up; (2) that he had misused federal agencies in violation of the rights of American citizens; and (3) that he had withheld information subpoenaed by the House Judiciary Committee.

On August 5, 1974, Nixon released transcripts of three conversations between himself and Haldeman recorded on June 23, 1972, a scant week after the break-in. They clearly showed that the president had tried to stop the FBI investigation of the burglary; he had in effect conspired to obstruct justice. Here was the "smoking gun" that could not be explained away, and Nixon's remaining congressional supporters now abandoned him. Facing almost certain impeachment by the full House, Nixon resigned as president on August 8 effective at noon the next day. On August 9, 1974, Gerald Ford took the oath of office as the new president.

Causes and Effects.   Observers pondered the roots of Watergate long after the president flew off to retirement in California. Some pointed their fingers at "the imperial presidency." Powers granted FDR and his successors to deal with the Great Depression, World War II, and the Cold War, they said, had raised the chief executive above the other branches of government and tempted the White House inner circle to consider the administration as the American government itself and its political opponents little better than national traitors. Some saw Nixon and his advisers primarily as victims of the paranoid Cold War mentality that at times excused unacceptable activities if done for the sake of "national security." Critics noted that the FBI and CIA had grown into fiefdoms that collected vast files on private citizens considered disloyal, opened private mail, and engaged in dirty tricks operations of their own against suspected subversives. In such an atmosphere it was no wonder that the White House itself should adopt a no-holds-barred attitude toward its opponents.

In the postmortems on Watergate, some Americans saw reasons for optimism in the outcome. The "system had worked," they said; the villains had been caught and punished, and honest, constitutional government had been restored. Others noted that Nixon had, after all, been reelected in a landslide and might easily have gotten away with it all if a few events had happened differently. Overall, Americans could not avoid feeling more cynical than ever about the honesty of politicians and more skeptical about the effectiveness of the nation's political system.

One thing is perfectly clear: Watergate ended whatever hope remained that Nixon would turn back the clock politically. Those voters who had believed that Nixon would return the country to traditional values felt bitterly betrayed. Liberals rejoiced that "Tricky Dick" had got his comeuppance.

The Ford Interlude.   America's only nonelected president, Gerald Ford, assumed office at a time when the nation desperately craved an end to distrust and uncertainty. Ford seemed the right man to start the healing process. A stolid legislator who had served in the House of Representatives for many years without special distinction, he was nevertheless an open, decent, and generous man whom most Americans quickly came to like.

The public's respect for Ford the man was not, however, matched by its view of Ford the president. Ford squandered much of the public's trust at the start of his presidency by granting a pardon to Nixon, thereby cutting off any further legal action against the ex-president. Though in his remarks announcing the pardon he emphasized personal compassion toward the former president and his determination to end the controversy and distrust caused by Watergate, many citizens suspected a secret deal whereby Ford, if chosen as Agnew's successor, would agree to pardon Nixon if he was forced to resign.

In foreign affairs Ford continued the initiatives of the recent past, retaining Kissinger as secretary of state and continuing to push détente. Gradually, however, high hopes for mutually advantageous arrangements with the Soviet Union dissipated. Soviet–American cultural exchanges helped dispel Cold War views that Russians were ogres, but Soviet violations of its own citizens' rights and mistreatment of its Jewish population offset such gains. Besides, the Soviet Union seemed determined to pursue expansionist ends through surrogates. When, for example, the African nation of Angola, newly independent from Portugal, collapsed into civil war, Soviet-armed Cuban troops supported the Angolan Marxists' drive to take control.

In domestic affairs Ford was even less successful. In response to a serious business recession following the spectacular hike in oil prices that accompanied the fourth Arab-Israeli war in 1973, he endorsed a tax cut and sought lower interest rates. By the fall of 1975 national output began once more to rise, but large pockets of unemployment remained.

In his early months as president, Ford had shown little interest in running for a full term. But as he settled into the job, he changed his mind and announced his candidacy for the 1976 election.

The 1976 Election. Ford's supporters believed the president deserved a vote of confidence for having restored Americans' faith in their government. But the bad smell of Watergate lingered on and many Americans were more convinced than ever that Washington was tightly controlled by wheeler-dealers and politicians on the take.

The public's disgust with the "mess in Washington" helped the nomination campaigns of two outsiders, Ronald Reagan of California and Jimmy Carter of Georgia. Reagan, a former Hollywood actor turned conservative politician, had been an effective governor of California. Though a committed conservative, he had often placed ideology aside and compromised with his opponents to get things done. Carter was an Annapolis graduate who had served a single term as his state's governor. Unlike many southern politicians of the past, he had worked to reduce discrimination against blacks. Both candidates could claim to be untouched by the dirt that besmirched Washington insiders.

Despite the Reagan challenge, Ford got the Republican nomination at Kansas City and selected Senator Robert Dole of Kansas as his running mate. Carter won the Democratic nomination on the first ballot in New York and balanced his ticket by choosing as his partner Senator Walter Mondale of Minnesota, a liberal and a close former associate of Hubert Humphrey. In November, the support of black voters and white southerners, along with traditionally Democratic Catholic and Jewish voters, helped carry the Carter-Mondale ticket to victory. At the time many observers saw the Carter-Mondale vote as a reassembly of the old New Deal coalition, and a return of the voters to a more liberal outlook. It is now clear that Northern voters were reacting to Watergate while southerners were determined to elect the only southerner since Zachary Taylor to win a major party nomination (if we except Lyndon Johnson, a Texan).

■ SEVENTIES DISCONTENTS ■

Jimmy Carter had his work cut out for him. The nation he would lead was buffeted by cross-currents, uncertainties, and uncomfortable challenges to its self-confidence and its leading position in the free world.

The celebration of the two-hundredth anniversary of American independence on July 4, 1976, was symbolic of the public's insecurities and hesitations. There had been talk of a major international exposition at Philadelphia to proclaim, as a century before, America's achievements to all the world. It proved impossible to bring off such a celebration. The America of 1976 was far richer than in 1876, but many people lacked the easy confidence in the political and economic future that had prevailed a century earlier. The bitterness of Vietnam lingered, and thousands of antiwar veterans doubted that America had much to boast about. Spokespersons for blacks, Indians, and other minorities insisted that they, the perennial outsiders, had scant reason to celebrate 200 years of nationhood. The country, of course, did not let the day go unmarked. In New York City a fleet of sailing ships from all over the world drew throngs of spectators to the harbor and banks of the Hudson River. In San Antonio a longhorn cattle drive, commemorating the days of the Texas cattle trails, was the celebration centerpiece. In Washington, D.C., half a million people watched a parade down Pennsylvania Avenue. Other communities had their own moving and eye-catching ways of commemorating the great event. Still, to critics, it seemed a party by the white middle class, with millions of skeptics standing on the sidelines.

Blacks and Hispanics.   As the 1970s advanced the predominant mood among black Americans was one of disappointment. The previous decade had promised so much and, in truth, some of it had been achieved. Nowhere could the law be used to bolster exclusion of blacks from public places or services or to enforce separation of the races. Even in the South blacks voted without restraint and were becoming a force to be reckoned with in southern politics. By the early 1980s, the mayors of many big cities—Cleveland, Chicago, Washington, D.C., Los Angeles, Philadelphia, and Atlanta—would be black.

There had also been sweeping economic and social advances for black Americans. The number of black college students had risen from 141,000 in 1960 to 718,000 in 1980. Black median family income had grown from $3,230 in 1960 to $12,674 in 1980. Yet the picture was at best mixed. The gains since 1960 had not ended black poverty; nor had they eliminated the differences between black and white family incomes. At the end of the 1970s the average black family was still only 60 percent as rich as its white counterpart.

A new disturbing feature of the racial picture was the appearance of a two-tier social structure in the black community itself. By 1980 there was a new black middle class of professionals, government workers, skilled white-collar employees, and business managers. But at the same time there was a persistent "underclass" of unemployed ghetto-dwellers who seemed stuck in the groove of poverty, welfare, drug dependence, and—at times—crime.

Many sociologists blamed faulty family structure for this unfortunate result. Successful blacks came primarily from intact, two-parent families; the underclass were primarily mothers without husbands—many mere teenagers—and their children. Since the 1960s, single-parent, female-headed families had grown disproportionately among all social sectors in the United States as a result of soaring divorce rates and teenage pregnancy. But the phenomenon was more severe among blacks than other groups. In such one-parent families—especially those headed by young, poorly educated women—the processes of child nurture and social conditioning needed to produce competent young people were apparently limited.

Unfortunately, it was not certain why the traditional family was becoming less prevalent. Conservative observers often blamed it on the welfare system: By encouraging dependency, the federal welfare system, a heritage of New Deal days, accelerated the breakup of families. They also blamed the cultural excesses of the 1960s, which, they said, had undermined conventional sexual morality and family values and condoned teenage premarital sex and teenage pregnancies. Liberals and black spokespeople often ascribed family failure to persistent racism that made it difficult for young black males to get decent jobs and undermined incentives to remain with the families they had created. Still other analysts believed it derived from structural change in the economy. Factory work and semiskilled labor that had served as ladders upward for wage earners in the past, no longer worked. Now the economy needed men and women who could program computers, sell financial securities, draw up plans for sales campaigns, and design sophisticated machines. Those without the necessary skills were relegated to dead-end jobs that provided neither the income for a reasonable family life nor the psychological and emotional bases it required.

Some observers blamed the freer entry of aliens following the 1965 Immigration and Nationality Act for hurting the black community by depressing the market for unskilled labor. And clearly, immigration of people from poor lands, particularly Latin America, had soared after its passage. During the seventies the number of Hispanics increased enormously, both absolutely and proportionately. By 1980 over 14.5 million Americans identified themselves as of "Hispanic" origins, an increase of 61 percent for the decade. The states with the largest number were California, Texas, New York, Florida, New Jersey, and New Mexico.

Many Hispanics, including all Puerto Ricans, were American citizens by birth. Others were naturalized citizens or legal immigrants. But there was also a very large group of "undocumented" immigrants without visas or immigration clearances who had fled the poverty of their countries for a better life in the United States. Many undocumented Hispanics worked at low-paying jobs in hospitals, restaurants, or offices, and in unskilled construction and factory work. In fact, many of these industries could not survive without them. Though most Hispanic-Americans were poor, there were pockets of notable Latin economic success. In the Miami area, for example, Cuban exiles from Castro's Marxist regime—mostly middle-class people with skills and capital—had reestablished themselves comfortably in their new American homes and were respected if not always liked by their "Anglo" neighbors.

The number of Asians in the United States also increased spectacularly during the 1970s. By 1980 there were 800,000 Chinese, 700,000 Japanese, 774,000 Filipinos, 350,000 Koreans, and 260,000 Vietnamese in the country. As in the case of Hispanics, some of the new arrivals were illegals. Many repeated the experience of early twentieth-century European immigrants by working in ill-paying garment industry "sweat shops" in New York and other cities. But on the whole, Asians did well in their new country. Many opened small businesses—delis, restaurants, dry cleaning establishments; others succeeded as musicians, scientists, and computer experts. Like some white groups before them, Asians benefited from supportive families and respect for education. Asian students worked hard and gained admission in disproportionate numbers to the country's best colleges and universities.

As in past eras, however, the newcomers to America in the sixties and seventies were not integrated into American society without friction. On the Texas Gulf Coast, competing "Anglo" and Vietnamese fishermen clashed in a series of violent incidents. Some middle-class people resented the academic success of Chinese and Japanese students. Hispanics, too, aroused rancor. In Miami blacks often felt bitter about the success of the Cubans. In the Southwest and California some whites feared that Anglo ways would be submerged under a wave of illegal Hispanic immigration. In many communities in the Northeast and Southwest programs to fund the use of Spanish as a language of instruction in the public schools became a divisive issue. Whites feared the displacement of English. Some Hispanic-Americans, on the other hand, worried about their children's loss of the Spanish language and with it their cultural heritage.

During the seventies and eighties public resentment focused especially on illegal immigration. Many Americans demanded tighter controls on immigration, and the Immigration and Naturalization Service deployed massive resources to stem the flood of immigrants crossing the U.S. border, especially from Mexico. Success was limited. In 1986 Congress passed the Simpson-Rodino Act imposing fines on employers who hired undocumented immigrants, but at the same time granting a general amnesty to all illegal immigrants who had arrived in the United States before January 1, 1982. The law was difficult to enforce, however, and did not end the frustration many Americans felt about unregulated immigration.

Women.   In many ways the most revolutionary social issues of the 1970s concerned women. In the 1960s feminists had argued that women should be free to choose roles other than that of "homemaker." By the late 1970s they had entered the labor market in record numbers. In 1965, 37 percent of all women over sixteen were employed; by 1978 the figure was 50 percent. Single women had worked in substantial numbers for many years. The new working woman contingent for the first time, however, included many thousands of married women with children. Only 19 percent of women with children under age six worked in 1960; by 1980 the figure had reached 45 percent.

Many of these women were engaged in serious careers. Educated women flooded into law, medicine, science, college teaching, journalism, computer programming, and other professional fields. By the mid-1980s, the list of women who had attained prominent positions in business, professional life, and government service had grown long: Jeane Kirkpatrick, Ambassador to the United Nations; Ella Grasso, governor of Connecticut; Mayor Jayne Byrne of Chicago; Sandra Day O'Connor, associate justice of the U.S. Supreme Court; Geraldine Ferraro, Democratic vice presidential candidate in 1984; Hannah Gray, president of the University of Chicago; Sherry Lansing, high executive of Twentieth-Century-Fox. Even the military service academies at West Point, Annapolis, and Colorado Springs opened their doors to women in the 1970s, as did the armed services in all their branches, except those involving direct combat.

Yet women did not achieve overall equality with men in the job market. Women's salaries were lower than for equally qualified men, and relatively few women were to be found in top-executive positions. In many businesses there seemed to be a "glass ceiling" beyond which women could not rise. Women activists charged that the major cause of this shortfall was sex discrimination. And clearly "sexism" existed, especially in subtle forms. But others pointed to women's often delayed professional educations, greater job instability, and over-all lower expectations as important factors in slowing their career advance.

The flood of women into the labor market imposed additional strains on the family already reeling from the effects of soaring divorce and illegitimacy. Less and less did the "typical" American family consist of dependent children, a working father, and a mother at home to do the family cooking and cleaning and socializing of young children. By the late 1970s only one in five families followed this pattern, and many conservative observers warned that the change would undermine effective child-rearing practices and damage the health of society as a whole. Feminists and liberals, on the other hand, defended the changes and demanded better and cheaper child-care facilities so that mothers could work without fear that their children's health, safety, and development would suffer.

Families were not only less stable; they were also smaller. By the seventies the baby boom of the 1950s and 1960s was over. In 1960 there had been almost 24 births per thousand Americans. In 1970 they were down to 18.4 and by 1976 had further fallen to 14.8. Social observers speculated on the reasons for the birthrate decline. Some blamed it on a new class of affluent young adults, "baby boomers," who seemed unusually self-centered. Children cost money and interfered with career goals, and female professionals and managers, especially, sought to postpone pregnancies until well into their thirties and then often ex-perienced infertility. Others were less willing to blame individuals. Rather, it was part of a long-term trend, they said, only briefly interrupted by the post-World War II baby boom, and in any case it was worse in other rich industrial nations such as West Germany and Japan than in the United States.

Affirmative Action.   Despite progress toward equality, then, racial minorities and women continued to stand below white males on the economic ladder. Merely leveling the playing field was not enough, argued some activists and social critics. Minorities and women had suffered so much from past bias that even if existing overt discrimination were totally eliminated these groups could not catch up in the foreseeable future. What was needed was not merely equal opportunity, but equal results. This required, at least as a temporary measure, "affirmative action"—that is, preferential treatment to minorities and women in hiring, promotions, admissions to training and apprenticeship programs, and to colleges and professional schools. Such practices would compensate for the past and balance the moral account. Elite groups had long had the deck stacked in their favor. Why not women and minorities now?

Affirmative action was beset by difficulties. Should all employers or institutions be automatically compelled to give preferential treatment to minorities, or only those that were proved to have practiced discrimination in the past? And how could such proof be established? Was it sufficient to show that given employers, for example, had fewer minority employees than their general proportion of the population, or did intent to discriminate have to be demonstrated? And what about assigning definite percentages—quotas—to minority members who must be hired or admitted to comply with the rules?

Many Americans disliked affirmative action. Opponents called it "reverse discrimination." Not only did it disregard "merit" as the key to reward; it also hurt those who, by accident of birth, did not belong to officially designated disadvantaged groups. In some fields, claimed opponents, it was impossible for a qualified white male to get a decent job. Affirmative action was, moreover, inherently sexist and racist because it assumed that members of disadvantaged groups could not make it on their own in America as others had in the past. It effect, it stigmatized those accorded special treatment as people who did not fully deserve their success.

Despite opposition, under Nixon's labor secretary, George Shultz, the government established affirmative action plans for blacks and selected ethnic groups in all firms submitting bids for government contracts (the Revised Philadelphia Plan). These firms, as well as labor unions, would have to seek out minority workers or members aggressively. During the 1970s the policy was further extended by federal court interpretation to women and then applied to a host of additional private firms, to universities, to foundations, and to other employers. Opponents challenged the principle in court with mixed results. In the *Bakke* decision of 1978 the Supreme Court struck down a University of California Medical School affirmative action rule that denied admission to a white applicant—Allan Bakke—while accepting less qualified nonwhites. Yet the Court did not declare affirmative action invalid, only that the university's method of achieving it through a rigid quota system was not permissible. The following year, in the Weber case, the Court ruled that private employers could adopt voluntary affirmative action plans to eliminate "manifest racial imbalance."

ERA and Abortion.   The hottest social issues of the seventies and eighties were the Equal Rights Amendment and abortion. First officially proposed by Alice Paul's National Woman's Party in the 1920s, the ERA stated simply that "equality of rights under the law shall not be denied on account of sex." Introduced into every session of Congress from 1923 onward, it had been rejected many times. In 1972, with the new feminism gathering momentum, Congress finally approved it by the constitutionally required two-thirds' majority and sent it along for ratification to the legislatures of the states.

The ratification process moved swiftly at first. Thirty-two of the necessary thirty-eight states approved the amendment in a little over a year. Then the opposition began to rally. In early 1973 Phyllis Schlafly, a lawyer and mother of six, organized a "Stop ERA" campaign. Schlafly and her allies said the amendment would hurt women's rights in divorce, that it mandated women's military service in the event of war, and that it even precluded separate male and female public bathrooms. The opponents of ERA touched a deep pool of antifeminist feeling in women themselves. Studies would show that wives and mothers not working outside the home, and even many who did solely for the income, often viewed feminists as hostile to the family values and personal relationships that gave their own lives worth.

Under the impact of the counterattack, state ratifications soon ceased and several states even rescinded their earlier approval. By 1979, the original expiration date, ERA had still not gotten the three-fourths' vote it needed. Congress extended the deadline for another three and a half years, but it still failed to get the requisite adoptions. In 1982 ERA was declared dead, though it remained on the feminist agenda for the future.

The abortion issue provoked still stronger reactions. On one side was a "pro-choice" coalition of feminists and liberals who considered the 1973 Supreme Court decision, *Roe* v. *Wade*, legalizing abortion during the first three months of pregnancy, a long overdue confirmation of women's right to "control their own bodies." The "pro-life" opponents of abortion—traditional Catholics,

"Pro-Choice" advocates parading in 1970s.

evangelical Protestants, Orthodox Jews, and political conservatives—considered *Roe* an invitation to infant murder. There were many positions between these extremes, and most Americans probably accepted abortion as necessary under some circumstances but deplored easy recourse to it.

From 1973 on, anti-abortionists sought to limit women's access to abortion in several ways: by requiring that minors obtain prior parental consent to the procedure; by denying welfare recipients the right to federally subsidized abortions; by trying to limit conditions under which abortions could be legally obtained to cases where the pregnancy resulted from rape or incest, or where the birth threatened the life of the mother. By the end of the 1970s pro-lifers were demanding passage of the Human Life Amendment, a constitutional measure to prohibit abortion and place it beyond the jurisdiction of the courts and also to forbid some forms of birth control.

The "Me" Generation.   While some Americans continued to battle over major social and political issues in the 1970s, others turned away from public concerns and issues. Some retreat was probably inevitable given the intense social activism of the previous decade, but it was also encouraged by the unusual difficulty of the problems of the seventies and early eighties. The journalist Tom Wolfe called the mid-1970s the era of the "me generation," a period when people placed personal fulfillment and pleasure before other considerations.

One sign of the new narcissism was the extraordinary interest in personal physical culture. Americans had long allowed their health to suffer through lack of exercise and poor eating habits, and no doubt reformation was long overdue. But the remarkable new interest in "natural" diets, "working out," and jogging that appeared in the late 1970s was closely connected with the new obsession with self. Still another manifestation of this "me" mood was the growth of a multitude of new mental health therapies. Affluent young urbanites flocked to teachers of "primal scream," EST, Rolfing, and other therapeutic programs that promised emotional comfort or personal fulfillment. Others sought satisfaction in one of the new religious cults such as Sun Myung Moon's Unification Church, L. Ron Hubbard's Scientology, the Hari Krishnas, or Jim Jones's People's Temple. Cults provided many young men and women with a sense of purpose and community. They also lent themselves to fraud, manipulation, charlatanism, and fanaticism. Americans would be deeply shocked when, in November 1979, over 900 of Jones's American followers committed mass suicide in their settlement in Guyana at the behest of their unbalanced leader.

Sun Belt versus Snow Belt.   One of the most important social trends of the seventies and early eighties was the shift of population, wealth, and leadership from the long-dominant northeastern quarter of the country—the so-called Snow Belt—to the Sun Belt of the South and West.

For more than a century the region stretching from southern New England to northern Virginia and then through the upper midwest had been the richest, most populous, and most culturally creative part of the United States. It had harbored the nation's most productive industries—clothing, steel, textiles, automobiles, electronics, rubber. Its large cities had been the centers of the nation's cultural life, sheltering its major museums, universities, publishing houses, symphony orchestras, theater, and dance companies. It had been the hub of financial services and insurance.

The balance began to shift during the 1960s and accelerated thereafter. As more and more Americans retired to live on pensions, they chose to leave behind the cold winters of the Northeast and Midwest. Immense retirement communities sprang up in California, Florida, and Arizona. Industry, too, particularly light industry and industry connected with defense, found the warmer climate, abundant land, cheaper nonunionized labor, and lower taxes of the South and West an advantage. Under four presidents from the region—Lyndon Johnson of Texas, Richard Nixon and Ronald Reagan of California, and Jimmy Carter of Georgia—government seemed to favor the Sun Belt through tax and defense-contract policies. Texas, Louisiana, and California, for a time, would also profit from the energy crisis of the late 1970s. With their large reserves of oil and natural gas, these states could offer cheap energy to business and individuals alike. Congress magnified this advantage when it decontrolled most natural gas and petroleum prices in 1978.

Much of this was anticipated by economists as early as the 1960s, but the message was driven home by the figures provided by the twentieth census. The preliminary results, announced on the last day of 1980, showed small increases, or even declines, in the populations of the northeastern and Midwestern states during the previous decade. By contrast, already massive California grew by 17.7 percent; Nevada by almost 64 percent; Texas by 26.4 percent; Arizona by almost 53 percent, and Florida by more than 41 percent. While the population of many older Snow Belt cities stagnated or declined, Phoenix, Albuquerque, Tucson, Houston, Dallas, San Antonio, Miami, Tampa, San Diego, and San Jose leaped ahead. For the first time in history, moreover, the nation's population statistical center had moved west of the Mississippi River, to southeast Missouri.

The figures both confirmed previous trends and foreshadowed new ones. Political power would clearly shift with population. When Congress was reapportioned, New York, Illinois, Ohio, and Pennsylvania would lose seats in the House of Representatives, and Texas, California, Florida, and Arizona would gain several seats each. Because the newer regions were more conservative politically than the older Snow Belt, this obviously meant a rightward trend in the nation's political climate. Besides politics, the nation's cultural life was certain to be affected. Already the Snow Belt's near-monopoly of high culture—painting, music, dance, and theater—had been loosened, partly through the National Endowment for the Arts and its counterpart in scholarship and literature, the National Endowment for the Humanities. Since their founding in 1965 as part of Lyndon Johnson's Great Society, these two federally funded bodies had pumped large sums of money into universities, theatrical and dance companies, and orchestras located outside the old cultural centers. By the early 1980s, universities in the Mountain states, Texas, and the Far West were matching the prestige and creativity of those of the East, while local culture in the Sun Belt was flourishing as never before.

■ THE ENERGY CRISIS AND ECONOMIC MALAISE ■

The growth of the Sun Belt and decline of the Snow Belt were tied to new resource problems facing the United States in the 1970s. For the first time in its history the country faced an acute energy crisis.

Oil and the American Way of Life.   For Americans, the "pursuit of happiness" has traditionally meant the quest for increasing income and wealth. Success has often depended on access to cheap natural resources as well as advanced technology. For a time in the 1970s, however, the world's industrialized nations confronted growing resource dearth. Supplies of such crucial metals as platinum, silver, tin, copper, and nickel—all needed in modern industrial products and processes—seemed to grow scarcer. The real crisis, however, was the oil shortage. To many Americans in the late 1970s, the block-long lines to buy scarce gasoline at prices soaring into the stratosphere seemed to foretell the end of an affluence they had come to accept as their national birthright.

The energy problem had evolved over several decades. By the post-World War II era, the rich industrial nations had become increasingly dependent on oil, and by the 1950s much of the world's supply came from the Middle East. The oil wells themselves were located in places like Saudi Arabia, Kuwait, Iran, and Iraq, but their contents were extracted, refined, and marketed by seven giant Western oil companies, five of them American. These companies had helped finance and develop the oil fields and for many years took the lion's share of the revenues they yielded.

After 1945, under the influence of Arab nationalism, the Middle Eastern rulers of oil-rich countries began to reconsider their agreements with the Western oil companies. At first they demanded increased royalties from the Western oil companies. Then, in 1960, the major oil-producing nations organized a cartel, the Organization of Petroleum Exporting Countries (OPEC), for the purpose of setting world petroleum prices and thereby expanding the profit for themselves.

Political and economic events of the early seventies abetted OPEC's monopoly pricing effort. First, the western nations, including the United States, became ever more reliant on imported energy sources. In the years between 1971 and 1973 alone, America quadrupled its oil imports, mostly from the Middle East. The flood of American demand would help create a world seller's market. Then, in October 1973, two Arab nations, Egypt and Syria, suddenly attacked Israel. The OPEC nations were meeting in Vienna during the "October War," and when the United States backed Israel they responded by boosting the price of oil from $3 to $5 a barrel and announcing an oil embargo against the United States and other nations supporting Israel. Suddenly the United States faced its first peacetime oil shortage since the discovery of petroleum in Pennsylvania more than a century before.

The uncomfortable winter of 1973–1974, with its cold homes and long gas lines, passed. But the embargo made it clear that America now relied for energy on the Arab world. The October War itself had other effects on America's energy situation. After heavy casualties on both the Arab and Israeli sides, the conflict ended with a United Nations-supervised cease-fire but no decrease in the hostility between the enemies and no prospect for a long-term peace settlement. Though the Egyptians and Syrians had not won the war, their limited success had increased Arab unity and buoyed Arab self-confidence. In the years that followed, the OPEC nations promised to be far more effective than in the past at acting in concert to control the oil market.

Energy Alternatives. For a time the energy crisis forced Americans to consider their future as a people of plenty. Some concluded that we must accept "limits." The United States, they said, had been living beyond its means for many years. Now the age of abundance was over. Some of this school of thought predicted that the country would face years of rising social tensions as groups fought over their respective slices of a diminished economic pie. Environmentalists were prominent within the "limits" group. Some seemed almost to welcome the oil crunch, believing it proved the need to keep population growth low, find ways to conserve resources, and generally reduce the human impact on mother nature. By changing our goals from crude expansion of GNP to other, more ecologically sound priorities, we could avoid disappointment and frustration, they promised. Other Americans denied the need for belt-tightening. Some believed that the oil companies had contrived the energy shortage to increase their profits. Others blamed the continuing dearth on the environmentalists, who, they said, resisted every attempt to find alternative energy sources in the name of their precious ideology.

The energy crisis reinforced Americans' sense of malaise brought on by the Vietnam debacle and Watergate. The soaring price of energy drained immense amounts of income and capital from the industrial nations and transferred it to the oil producers. Some of it came back in the form of investments by the OPEC nations in Europe and America and lavish spending on western goods by Saudi sheiks and Kuwaiti businessmen. But it also slowed economic growth rates. For the western world, including the United States, 1973 would be a significant economic watershed marking a division between eras of faster and slower economic growth. Besides impotence abroad and corruption at home, then, it seemed we now had to face for the first time the possibility of long-term material limits. America appeared to have passed its prime; it could no longer achieve all the goals it set for itself.

The nation struggled to contain the energy crisis. Congress clamped a fifty-five-mile-per-hour speed limit on drivers and prescribed minimum gas mileage requirements for car manufacturers. It offered tax credits to homeowners who insulated their houses to conserve fuel. It also passed measures to encourage the development of alternative energy sources, such as geothermal, wind, and solar power. In July 1979, President Carter would ask Congress to fund a synthetic fuels program to free Americans from dependence on foreign energy sources.

The oil shock triggered a major debate over nuclear power. Lauded at one time as the complete solution to the world's energy needs, nuclear power would come under increasing fire on environmental and safety grounds as the seventies advanced. The critics' arguments were given frightening immediacy by an accident at the Three Mile Island nuclear power plant near Harrisburg, Pennsylvania, in March 1979, which for a time threatened to produce a "meltdown" of the reactor's nuclear core. Had that occurred, thousands of lives might have been lost and property in the billions contaminated for decades.

Fortunately, the reaction was contained and no lives and little property lost, but the near disaster intensified the nuclear power debate. Supporters of nuclear energy pointed out that the overall safety record of the industry had been good. Opponents insisted that the accident confirmed the unsuitability of the nuclear solution to the energy problem. Moreover, power from the atom raised difficult issues of nuclear waste disposal. During the next few years environmentalists, organized in various "alliances," conducted a crusade against nuclear power that helped delay construction of new plants and imposed stricter safety standards on old ones. The assault raised the costs of construction so high that by the 1980s the building of new nuclear power plants ceased, and several almost completed plants had to be abandoned. Nuclear power no longer was an energy option in the United States.

Turmoil in the Economy.   The relentless rise in general consumer prices reinforced the public's disquiet and sense of crisis. By mid-1979 the average American family had to earn almost double its 1970 dollar income to achieve the same standard of living. In effect, the value of the dollar had fallen to half its worth from a decade before.

By the end of the decade inflation had become self-perpetuating. Americans rushed to department stores and discount houses to snap up appliances, clothing, sports equipment, and goods of every kind with their credit cards before prices rose further. The buying spree not only aggravated the inflationary surge; it also reduced personal savings. There was little incentive to put dollars into savings accounts when the gain from interest earned was certain to be more than offset by their loss of value. The drop in personal savings made the United States increasingly dependent on foreign sources of capital for financing private industry and to help service the large federal debt.

Experts puzzled over the causes of the inflation. Clearly, skyrocketing energy costs were a factor. But many economists placed even more blame on rising wages not offset by equivalent increases in labor productivity. Labor costs were simply passed along to consumers, they claimed, because in many areas competition was nonexistent. Still others took their cue from the conservative economist Milton Friedman, who insisted that an excess of cheap money and credit, permitted by the Federal Reserve system and reinforced by large federal deficits, explained the powerful inflation surge.

One difficulty in dealing with inflation was that stable prices seemed to depend on keeping unemployment high. Price rises would cease only if the economy flattened. By cutting back government spending and raising interest rates, private investment and consumer spending could be curtailed. This would push up the jobless rate, but at the same time reduce inflation. Conservatives accepted the trade-off as unavoidable. But liberals and organized labor did not. Better higher prices than mass unemployment, they argued.

But the argument soon came to seem pointless. By mid-decade unemployment was accompanied by continued inflation. The combination, called "stagflation" by phrase-makers, could not easily be explained, though some experts believed unemployment figures were exaggerated and others emphasized that millions of Americans, especially minorities, were without the skills needed to find a place in the new "high-tech" economy. No matter what the nation's growth rate, low or high, they would not find work. Whatever the reason, clearly the nation faced a dilemma: It could have full employment, but apparently only at the expense of more severe inflation.

■ THE CARTER YEARS ■

Jimmy Carter would be forced to shoulder much of the blame for the economic troubles of the late 1970s. Yet when he took office in January 1977, many people were optimistic that this ex-peanut farmer, who had come from nowhere to win the presidency, would be an effective leader. They would be disappointed.

Carter as President. Americans at first were impressed by Jimmy Carter. The Carter style seemed refreshingly informal. He broke with precedent by walking in his own inaugural parade with his wife, Rosalynn, and his daughter, Amy, by his side. From the White House he answered citizens' phoned-in questions on TV and wore blue jeans and old sweaters around the Oval Office. Amy went to a Washington public school, like other unpretentious residents of the District of Columbia, rather than a private school. Carter also tried to reduce the number of White House officials, and he cut back on staff limousines and television sets.

The politicians on Capitol Hill found him less enchanting. Having run against the Washington "establishment," Carter had trouble achieving a working relationship with Congress. He also experienced the congressional backlash against presidential leadership following Watergate and the abrasive years of the imperial presidency. Inexperienced in the ways of Washington, he and his staff fumbled badly.

Carter's first mistake was to attack a congressional sacred cow by cutting off federal funding for eighteen dams and other water projects in the West. His arguments that the projects were wasteful were valid, but he had not reckoned with the importance of "pork barrel" to members of Congress and the significance of irrigation in the West. Faced with a storm of protest, he retreated. He did little better in his early relations with key congressional leaders, failing to consult Senate Majority Leader Robert Byrd on which senators to brief on energy policy, and announcing federal appointments in House Speaker Thomas ("Tip") O'Neill's own Massachusetts district without first informing him. Eventually, Carter and his advisers improved relations with Congress, but they were never able to establish an effective partnership with those who enacted the nation's laws.

Domestic Policies.   Carter's gravest challenge was how to end the nation's dependence on foreign oil. The issue aroused all the president's considerable moral fervor. At one point he called the battle to make the United States oil-independent (borrowing from philosopher William James) "the moral equivalent of war."

Unfortunately, his actual recommendations to Congress in February 1977 were disproportionately modest: a federal tax on crude oil imports and on "gas-guzzling" cars. Given the president's dire warnings, this program struck many Americans as ludicrous. Humorist Russell Baker abbreviated the "moral equivalent of war" to MEOW. Congress was similarly unimpressed and acted slowly, though eventually giving the president much of what he asked for.

In the summer of 1979 another grave energy crisis was triggered by the turmoil in Iran. During the confusion of the Islamic fundamentalist revolution that overthrew the Shah, Iranian oil production dropped drastically. The oil-importing nations were soon bidding against one another for the reduced world supply, tripping off a panic that created new gas lines through June and July. By now many Americans had concluded that here, as in other areas, Carter was an ineffectual leader.

The oil crisis of 1979–1980 pushed inflation into high gear. In 1979 consumer prices leaped 13.3 percent in a single year. In early 1980 they began to rise still faster, threatening to reach an astronomical 18 percent per annum if not stopped. The Federal Reserve, under its new head, Paul Volcker, raised interest rates to discourage spending with borrowed money. The president established a Council on Wage and Price Stability to monitor wage and price guidelines. Neither move worked at first. Interest rates were pushed to 20 percent in early 1980, but prices continued to rise. The council proved ineffective. Its orders were unenforceable and its fruitless "jawboning" only made the administration again seem feeble and incompetent.

Carter's Foreign Policy.   Carter was an idealist who hoped to distance the United States from aggressive Vietnam-era policies and make the nation a force for benevolence in the world. The president and many of his advisers believed at the outset that the United States had subordinated too many other considerations to winning the Cold War. A more important destabilizing force than the continuing East–West conflict, they said, was the disparities between the wealthy nations of the world's northern industrial belt and the poor ones of the southern agricultural portion of the globe. In a 1977 speech at Notre Dame the president noted that "an inordinate fear of communism" had "led us to embrace any dictator who joined us in our fear." Reflecting these sunny views, the first two Carter defense budgets, already down from the Vietnam War, fell to the lowest proportion of total federal outlays since 1960. In June 1979 the president signed the SALT II agreement, further limiting U.S. and Soviet nuclear arsenals, and sent the treaty to the Senate for ratification. In 1979 also, going beyond the Nixon initiatives, he established formal American diplomatic relations with the People's Republic of China. Meanwhile, to avoid a confrontation with Panamanian nationalists and to raise American stock in Latin America, he helped push through the Senate a treaty with Panama ending exclusive American control of the Canal Zone. Carter sought to use America's good offices on behalf of victims of government oppression around the world. He called this his "human rights" policy.

Conservatives attacked all these policies for weakening America and encouraging enemies abroad. The "human rights" initiatives, they said, were a slap at many foreign leaders who backed our anticommunist containment policies. The Panama Canal treaties cravenly surrendered American rights in the Canal Zone of seventy years' standing. As for SALT II, it was a Soviet trick. Its predecessor, SALT I, had lulled the United States into a false sense of security while the Soviets had surpassed us in conventional weapons.

There was one foreign-policy area, however—Arab–Israeli relations—where Carter got high marks from everyone. In November 1977 Egyptian president Anwar Sadat had made an unprecedented visit to Jerusalem, the Israeli capital. For the first time the head of an Arab state had made a friendly gesture toward the Jewish nation and it looked as though peace between Egypt and Israel might be at hand. Unfortunately, the peace process soon bogged down over the thorny problem of Palestinian self-rule, and it appeared that Sadat's bold initiative would come to nothing. To break the impasse, in September 1978 Carter induced both Sadat and Israeli Prime Minister Menachem Begin to come to Camp David, the presidential hideaway in the Maryland mountains, to discuss the differences between the two countries. Carter used every means to get these two stubborn men to agree and finally succeeded in squeezing a joint peace statement from them. As a result of the Camp David Accords, in March 1979 Israel and Egypt signed a peace treaty that bound the two nations to full diplomatic relations, to phased-evacuation by Israel of the Sinai Peninsula conquered during the 1967 war, and to some form of autonomy for the Palestinians living in the West Bank and Gaza Strip. The treaty did not bring peace to the Middle East. None of the other Arab nations followed Egypt's lead, and the Palestinian issue continued to fester. But for the first time in its history Israel was at peace with one of its Arab neighbors.

The Hostage Crisis. Whatever credit Carter won from the Camp David accords was squandered by his handling of the hostage crisis with Iran. Iran was a distant, exotic place to most Americans in 1979. Islamic though not Arabic, located on the oil-rich Persian Gulf, it was ruled despotically by Shah Mohammed Riza Pahlevi, a close friend of America. The CIA had helped the Shah gain his throne in 1953 by a coup against his enemies, and the United States considered him a bulwark of anti-Soviet stability in the Middle East. In January 1979 he was ousted by internal enemies who simultaneously despised his repressive methods, his friendship with the West, and his attempts to aggressively modernize his conservative land. The Shah fled to Mexico, leaving behind a nation in turmoil. In October he was admitted to a New York hospital for treatment of cancer. This show of American hospitality outraged the faction now dominant in Iran, the Islamic fundamentalists led by the ultraorthodox religious leader, the Ayatollah Ruhollah Khomeini. On November 4, 1979, a group of pro-Khomeini Iranian students, probably with the Ayatollah's approval, invaded the American Embassy in Teheran and took hostage more than sixty American citizens, mostly embassy employees.

Months of protest, negotiation, and maneuver would follow, but to no avail. Seizing the embassy of a country that one was not at war with was contrary to all civilized practice, and no government could have condoned it. But America found itself dealing with a regime ruled by extremists. The Islamic fundamentalists considered America "the Great Satan" and demanded ransom to release the hostages. The United States must surrender the Shah to his enemies, apologize for supporting him in the past, and agree to turn over to the Iranian government all the assets that he supposedly had taken with him when he fled his homeland. If the United States did not comply, not only would the Americans remain prisoners, they might well be tried for espionage and executed.

The United States refused to accept these conditions. The administration froze billions of dollars of Iranian assets in the United States, cut off all trade with Teheran, and appealed to the United Nations and the World Court to condemn the hostage-taking. Nothing worked. As the weeks passed, outraged Americans became obsessed with the hostage crisis. Public frustration and anger at American impotence grew and voices were soon raised demanding retaliation. Some people called for a declaration of war against Iran and a blockade of the Persian Gulf. Irate citizens attacked Iranian students attending American universities. The administration, too, became consumed with the hostage crisis to the neglect of other important matters. In late April 1980 the president ordered a military rescue operation from U.S. naval vessels in the Persian Gulf against the advice of Secretary of State Cyrus Vance. This maneuver failed dismally and eight men died in the attempt. Vance resigned. The public's level of frustration rose to new heights.

The Cold War Resumes.   Conservative Americans from the outset questioned Carter's optimism about the Cold War. In 1976 a coalition of anti-Soviet hawks from government, business, the universities, and the intellectual community, skeptical of Nixon's détente policy, had organized the Committee on the Present Danger. The committee warned that "the principle threat to our nation and the cause of human freedom" was "the Soviet drive for dominance based on an unparalleled military build-up." The United States must not be lulled into a false sense of security.

Events would shortly confirm the committee's fears. All hope of preserving détente collapsed in late December 1979 when Soviet troops and tanks poured across the border into Afghanistan, the Islamic country bordering Iran, to save a Soviet puppet leader from his domestic enemies. The Soviet invasion substantiated the hard-liners' contentions but shocked Carter. Indignant at what he considered the deception of Soviet premier Leonid Brezhnev, he told the American people that the United States must once more seek to contain Soviet expansionism and be prepared to defend the free flow of oil to the West from the Persian Gulf region. To implement this policy (quickly labeled the "Carter Doctrine"), he cut off sales of wheat and advanced technology to the Soviet Union, withdrew the United States team from the 1980 summer Olympics in Moscow, shelved SALT II for the foreseeable future, and asked Congress to enact legislation requiring all nineteen- and twenty-year-olds to register for the military draft.

The 1980 Election.   Despite this vigorous response, the public came to perceive the Carter administration as feckless and impotent. Americans grew weary of the president's homilies about energy belt-tightening and international morality. Whenever he spoke, it seemed, he sounded the dreary theme of an American "malaise."* Meanwhile, inflation continued; the energy shortage persisted; and, overseas, America seemed to lose force and direction. The voters' gloom about events at home and abroad determined the outcome of the 1980 election.

Though the incumbent, Carter had to fight for his party's renomination against Senator Edward Kennedy of Massachusetts. The youngest of the Kennedy brothers, "Ted" had seriously damaged his reputation for honesty and courage in 1969 when he failed to save the life of a young woman aide when their car went into the water off Chapaquiddick Island. Despite Chapaquiddick, the senator had the support of the party's liberal wing and mounted an energetic campaign to deny Carter the nomination. In the end Carter defeated his challenger and became his party's nominee for the second time.

The Republican nominee was Ronald Reagan, the sixty-nine-year-old spokesman for the new southern and western political right. The former California governor appealed to many of the same backlash voters who had supported George Wallace and Richard Nixon in 1968, with the added backing of business groups associated with the exploding industry and enterprise of Texas, southern California, the Mountain States, and the South.

Though divorced and a former actor, Reagan had been raised in an evangelical Protestant household and endorsed the conservative social agenda of the new religious right. By the mid-1970s this rapidly growing segment of Protestantism had become a formidable challenge to the mainstream liberal Protestant groups. In 1979 Baptist minister Jerry Falwell organized the Moral Majority to bring the nation's evangelicals into the political arena. The Moral Majority favored abortion restriction, traditional family values, heterosexuality, tougher laws against drugs, lower taxes, school prayer, expanded defense spending, and a more aggressive anti-communist foreign policy. Its supporters claimed to favor pluralism and separation of church and state, but their opponents saw them as intolerant and determined to use government to encourage their own religious values. Along with a cluster of secular "New Right" groups, the new religious right operated through political action committees (PACs) funded by money raised through direct-mail appeals.

The Carter administration hoped for a breakthrough in the hostage crisis to give it an electoral boost. But the Iranians toyed with the American negotiators, reinforcing the impression of administration weakness. When election day arrived the hostages were still captive. The result was an impressive Republican victory. Reagan received 43 million popular votes to 35 million for Carter. Going

*In fact, he never used the term, which seems to have been a media creation.

down to defeat along with the president were a flock of liberal Democratic senators and representatives targeted by the New Right and the Moral Majority. Reagan would have a Republican Senate to work with and, though the House of Representatives would remain in Democratic hands, it was doubtful if it could check the new conservative surge.

■ CONCLUSIONS ■

It had taken twelve years for the conservative promise of 1968 to finally be realized. In 1968 the voters had rejected one of its most liberal political leaders and endorsed one of its most conservative. Americans, it seemed, had repudiated the liberal Great Society and all it represented.

But conservatives had been disappointed. Richard Nixon turned out to be a pragmatist and a compromiser. Perhaps, during his second term, Nixon would have taken the conservative agenda more seriously. But the disaster of Watergate kept him from achieving anything after 1973. Gerald Ford, by pardoning the ex-president, kept alive the disgrace of Watergate and damaged his administration. Yet the conservative current continued to run under the surface. In 1976 the public did not endorse an ideological shift; it merely repudiated the party responsible for Watergate. Yet Carter could have reversed the conservative current if he had been adept and likable. He was neither, and in 1980 the voters turned him out of office to try once more to get what they had failed to do in 1968. In the end it was Ronald Reagan, rather than Richard Nixon, who would launch the conservative experiment in Washington.

Online Resources

"May 4 Kent State"
http://www.library.kent.edu/exhibits/4may95/index.html
Through the "May 4" collection, learn more about the Kent State student shootings. The site includes photos, links to various other sites, chronologies, and information on the aftermath of the incident.

Watergate 25
http://www.washingtonpost.com/wp-srv/national/longterm/watergate/front.htm
Read about the Watergate crisis through timelines and biographies of the key players in the affair. Also, the site provides newspaper articles that correspond to the Watergate chronology.

30

THE "REAGAN REVOLUTION"

What Was It? What Did It Accomplish?

1980	Ronald Reagan elected president; Republicans gain control of Senate
1981	Beginning of Reagan era; Conservative agenda put into place; Cutbacks in domestic social programs; Huge increases for defense; Tax cuts seen as stimulus to economic growth; Deregulation of industries; Reagan fires striking air traffic controllers
1982	Budget deficits mount; Breakup of AT&T; Midterm elections see Democrats pick up seats in House while GOP retains Senate control; Contra aid a political issue
1983	Reagan continues to stress military build-up; Adds new missiles in Europe; American marines sent to Lebanon; President pushes Star Wars to counter Soviet missile threat; 241 marines killed in Beirut terrorist attack; Soviets shoot down Korean airliner, killing 269; U.S.–Soviet relations worsen
1984	Reagan reelected in landslide; AIDS crisis grows ever larger
1985	Stock market continues to be bullish
1986	Space shuttle disaster; Trade imbalance worsens; U.S. jets attack Libya; Reagan–Gorbachev summit in Iceland ends on chilly note; Iran-Contra scandal breaks
1987	Congress probes Iran-Contra affair, televised hearings begin; Bork nomination to Supreme Court defeated in Senate; Stock market crash; Reagan and Gorbachev meet in Washington and sign agreement eliminating medium-range missiles from Europe; Scandals beset religious right
1988	Reagan era winds down

Reagan's inaugural address on January 20, 1981, was a display case for the new president's conservative agenda. "Government" was "not the solution to our problem. Government is the problem," he announced. He would "get the government back within its means and . . . lighten our punitive tax burden." He would check runaway inflation and get the economy moving again. His administration would restore America's standing in the world. While we craved peace, we would "maintain sufficient strength to prevail if need be." Finally, in his conclusion, he tipped his hat to his conservative religious constituency. "We are," he declared, "a nation under God," and "God intended for us to be free." He hoped that in future years Inauguration Day would be "declared a day of prayer."

The next eight years have been seen as a major rightward shift in the course the nation was taking, a so-called "Reagan Revolution." Was there a Reagan Revolution? Did the nation reverse its political direction? Did the Reagan victory usher in marked changes in the economy, in America's role in the world, in the nation's predominant cultural and religious values?

■ THE FIRST TERM ■

The American Economy.   Reagan was speaking for millions of voters when he deplored high taxes. In many communities home owners were dismayed by soaring property taxes that had accompanied the inflation of real estate values. Steep income taxes incensed high earners who believed they deserved to keep more of what they made. Business executives were not happy at high state and federal levies on corporations.

These were pragmatic tax cutters; they hoped to avoid the personal burden of taxation. But there was a broader case to be made for tax cuts. "Libertarians," disciples of novelist-social thinker Ayn Rand or of economists Frederick Hayek or Milton Friedman, opposed taxation because they considered virtually all government a denial of personal freedom. During the late 1970s the "supply-side" theories of economist Arthur Laffler became part of the conservative creed. Laffler denounced the dominant Keynesian concepts that emphasized augmented *demand* to achieve growth. Instead, it was essential to augment *supply* by cutting taxes to encourage effort and enterprise now dampened by excessive burdens. There was no need to worry about government deficits, insisted the Lafflerites. As production, profits, and jobs grew the government would be able to cover its expenses even at the lower tax rates since total revenues would rise.

Laffler had made a deep impression on several members of Congress including the young Republicans Jack Kemp of New York and David Stockman of Michigan. In 1976 Kemp, joined by Senator William Roth of Delaware, introduced a bill to reduce income taxes 30 percent across-the-board to restore the economy and encourage growth. During the 1980 presidential campaign Reagan had tentatively embraced the Kemp–Roth, supply-side proposal, believing that the new economics expressed, more truly than the liberals' timid talk of limits and no-growth, the American spirit of enterprise and expansion. Many traditional, no-deficit Republicans disagreed. George Bush, Reagan's chief opponent during the Republican nomination race, called the Laffler theory "Voodoo economics."

As the new president took office in January 1981, the country faced daunting economic problems. Inflation was running at double-digit rates, the steepest since the Civil War. Unemployment was high and overall economic growth rates were down from previous decades. Most shocking of all, the United States seemed to be losing its international competitiveness. In the 1950s the United States had been a towering economic giant. By 1980 Western Europe had recovered, thanks to American aid, and far surpassed its prewar levels. East Asia, moreover—Korea, Taiwan, Singapore, and above all Japan—had become an economic dynamo. Germany and Japan, especially, had become more efficient than the United States in many areas of production, and whole classes of American manufactures—consumer electronics, cameras, even automobiles—were being replaced on the domestic market by foreign imports.

By the opening years of the 1980s the problems of taxation, inflation, and unemployment, and America's international slippage, had convinced many people that the country must try new economic policies.

The Tax Cuts. The administration's first order of business was a tax-cutting bill that expressed the new supply-side theory. Prepared by David Stockman, new head of the Office of Management and Budget, the cuts were the deepest and broadest on record. The Democrats controlled the House of Representatives by a small margin and might have defeated the bill, but many acknowledged the 1980 election as a mandate for change and were willing to go along. Reagan, moreover, proved to be an effective parliamentary leader. His charm, his good humor, his rugged manliness appealed especially to southern Democrats ("Boll Weevils") and many proved willing to support the president. Much of the remaining opposition collapsed when an unbalanced young man shot Reagan on March 30 as he was leaving a Washington hotel. The president's courage and good humor while recovering aroused the admiration of the country and expedited the bill's passage.

The Economic Recovery Act of 1981 mandated a 25 percent cut in the personal income tax over a three-year period and a sharp reduction of the maximum tax on "unearned" income from appreciation of real estate and other investments. It also authorized a drastic cut in corporate taxes—the "largest tax cut in the history of American business," one Reagan official described it—to stimulate investment.

The tax cuts did not produce the quick results that their supporters had predicted. Their passage, in fact, coincided with a sharp recession. By December 1982 unemployment had soared to 10.8 percent of the labor force; 12 million Americans were out of work. This was the highest jobless level since the Great Depression.

In truth, the recession was probably unrelated to the tax cut. The slide had been brought on by the tight money policies adopted by head of the Federal Reserve, Paul Volker, designed to bring down the ruinous inflation of the late seventies. Though wage earners felt considerable pain, the Fed's policies soon began to achieve their intended deflationary effects. By 1983 price rises were down from 13 percent per year in 1980 to a little over 3 percent. Toward the end of Reagan's second term pessimists would warn that inflation was still an untamed dragon, but in fact it would never again become the frightening monster of the late 1970s.

Volcker would be given credit for ending the ruinous inflation of the previous decade. Actually, many forces contributed to the new price stability. By the early 1980s conservation measures had begun to reduce world petroleum demand, while at the same time total world oil output, stimulated by high prices in the 1970s, surged. The world was soon awash in oil capacity. Low energy price removed a major component of the seventies' inflation wave.

Wage pressures also eased. By the later 1980s unions found it difficult to extract wage increases from management. Once powerful bargaining agents for American labor, they lost power as the "smokestack industries"—steel, coal, and automobiles—were downsized under the remorseless pressure of foreign competition. Loss of numbers in industry was offset to some extent by gains in the service trades, especially government employment. But at best union membership, as a percentage of all employees, stagnated. In 1980 it was the same 24 percent as it had been in 1960.

The Reagan administration seriously undercut the remaining power of organized labor. The president himself, though former head of the Screen Actors' Guild, took a tough line on work stoppages. In August 1981, when the Professional Air Traffic Controller Organization (PATCO) called an illegal strike against the government, Reagan fired all 11,000 members and refused to hire them back even when they relented. PATCO disbanded. PATCO was not a large organization, but the attack by a popular president helped undermine the entire trade union movement. Between 1980 and 1984 total membership dropped by over 2.7 million members. By 1988 only 17 percent of American full-time workers were members of trade unions, a 6 percentage-point decline since the beginning of the decade.

The Welfare State.   The administration hoped that cutting domestic social programs would reduce taxpayers' burdens. But Reagan and his advisers also believed that the many welfare "entitlements" from the 1960s and early 1970s had only made poverty and dependency worse. As conservative social thinker Charles Murray would write in 1984, the nation's poverty programs had "tried to provide more for the poor and produced more poor instead." The figures seemed to confirm the view. In 1968, 13 percent of Americans had been classified as poor. After billions of dollars of federal largesse the proportion in 1980 was exactly the same 13 percent!

The president promised that his policies would maintain a "safety net" for the most vulnerable and disadvantaged groups in society. But he would get rid of the "welfare cheats" who received federal money though not eligible under the law; he would eliminate programs that had proved ineffective; he would reduce high administrative costs. Wherever possible he would demand that the able-bodied work rather than receive handouts. Liberals were not reassured and called the proposed cuts in welfare selfish and cruel. Nevertheless, Congress went along with many of the administration's proposals. It cut outlays for food stamps, child nutrition, Aid to Families with Dependent Children, Supplemental Security Income, Low Income Energy Assistance, financial aid for needy students, job training, health block grants, and many other programs. The president and his colleagues claimed that none of these cuts seriously harmed the poor; his critics claimed that their effects were devastating.

The truth is that the combination of tax cuts and welfare cuts amplified American income inequality. By one estimate, between 1983 and 1985 the two together reduced the aggregate income of households earning less than $20,000 a year by $20 billion and increased that of families making more than $80,000 by $35 billion. In 1984 the Census Bureau reported that income distribution in the United States was more unequal than at any time since 1947, when the bureau first began to collect accurate figures on the subject. By 1984, moreover, the proportion of Americans living below the official "poverty line" had grown from the 13 percent of 1980 to 14.3 percent. Nor was the loss felt only by the poorest. In 1986 those people dead center economically were receiving a lower proportion of total national income than at any time since 1947.

But the coin had another side as well. By the late 1980s unemployment had fallen below 6 percent nationally. The administration could also point with pride to job creation in the 1980s. At no time in the past, its friends noted, had the country created jobs for so many people in so short a period as under the Reagan watch. Though the job market had been flooded by the baby-boomers born after 1945 and by women in larger numbers than ever before, it had absorbed them all.

Critics countered that far too many of these were unskilled, minimum-wage positions that forced workers to rely on two or more family wage earners to achieve a reasonable living standard. In many cases their parents had been able to achieve the same standard with only one. All told, critics noted, American real wages were not rising. Many Americans could buy no more with their incomes in 1985 than in 1975. For the first time in memory, they said, adult Americans could not assume that their children would be better off than they were.

Meanwhile, by mid-decade a new class of deprived Americans were to be found living on the streets, under bridges, in parks and public squares, and in municipal shelters in many American cities. Critics of the administration charged that cuts in welfare and housing appropriations explained the surge in homelessness. But the problem was more complex than this. Many of the street people were single men and women afflicted with alcoholism or drug addiction. Others were mentally ill persons who, in a previous period, would have been admitted to state mental hospitals. These institutions, often squalid "snake pits," were now largely shut down, however, and those formerly warehoused in them, out of sight, were now blocking doorways, begging on the streets, using telephone booths and elevators as toilets, and sometimes insulting or assaulting pedestrians.

Yuppies. Meanwhile, a substantial group of well-educated young men and women were forging ahead of the pack. These "Yuppies"—young upwardly mobile professionals—were the social phenomenon of the decade. As depicted by the media, they were brash, materialistic, self-centered, politically and socially insensitive, and greedy. Many were self-indulgent people who used their quick riches for luxury apartments, high-performance cars, imported wines and gourmet foods, class A restaurants, and illegal drugs, especially cocaine. For a time cocaine became a major "recreational drug" in yuppie circles. In some of the more prosperous cities of the Northeast and West Coast by the late 1980s whole neighborhoods catered to yuppie tastes. Food emporia carried quiche and Brie cheese; car dealers sold Mercedes and BMWs; wine merchants offered imported chablis and champagne.

Social Security. One "entitlement" program the Reagan administration found untouchable was Social Security. It was now clear that the aged as a class were no longer underprivileged, as in the past. Thanks to Medicare and Social Security, as well as private savings, people over sixty-five had higher incomes than average Americans. Most of those classified as poor were now families with young children, especially those headed by single parents. Children, in effect, were the new poor. To some conservatives it seemed foolish to coddle the elderly when so many of them were well off. Why not limit the benefits of those over sixty-five in the name of social equity?

Meanwhile the Social Security system was becoming more expensive and fiscally unstable. In the view of some conservatives it should be replaced entirely with a system of private annuities financed by each individual wage earner. Others wanted it drastically downsized. Neither reckoned with the power of the seniors' lobby. When the president proposed revisions to hold down soaring Social Security outlays and help make the system fiscally sound, the outcry from elderly voters forced him to drop the issue like a hot potato. Eventually it required a bipartisan congressional commission to apply some actuarial sense by increasing Social Security taxes, skipping some projected increases in payments, and mandating a gradual rise in the minimum retirement age. The working public was soon complaining that Social Security taxes had become more burdensome than income taxes.

All told, Reagan and his supporters, though they sought drastic changes in the existing welfare system, butted their heads against a stone wall. Congress, fearing public wrath, refused to budge. The overall public mood had become less generous than in the past, but many entitlement beneficiaries, particularly when numerous and well-organized, were able to protect their interests against the budget cutters. A drastic overhaul of the Depression-era welfare system would have to wait for a later day.

Defense Policy. Defense was an even worse budget-buster than the social welfare system. During the 1980 presidential campaign Reagan had described a "window of vulnerability" in nuclear arms as well as deficiencies in conventional arms that had to be corrected if America was to remain strong and safe. He took office pledged to a massive arms build-up that would increase American military power relative to the Soviet Union. Reagan was intensely suspicious of the Soviets and in the first news conference of his administration attacked détente as "a one-way street" that the Soviet Union had "used to pursue its own aims." At a later point in his presidency he would call the Soviet Union an "evil empire" and "the focus of evil in the modern world." The label "evil empire" would dismay the Soviet Union and become a shorthand for a reheated Cold War confrontation.

Among the earliest Reagan proposals as president was a five-year, $1.7 trillion increase in defense spending to catch up with the Soviets. Congress scaled down the administration's military shopping list despite the determined resistance of Secretary of Defense Caspar Weinberger, but defense outlays leaped from $135 billion in 1980 to $210 billion in 1983 and to $231 billion in 1984. All told, the Reagan administration would engineer the largest American military buildup in peacetime history.

Budget Deficits. The explosion in defense spending more than offset the moderate cuts in domestic programs. Combined with the tax cuts lowering federal revenues, it produced the largest budget deficits Americans had ever experienced. The results were ironic. As Democratic critics quickly pointed out, for decades the Republicans had denounced their opponents as wild spenders who had mortgaged the nation's future to gratify their urge to throw money at problems. Now, a Republican president had raised the annual deficit from Carter's $60 billion in 1980 to over $180 billion in 1984. By the final year of his first term, Reagan's shortfalls had increased the national debt by an additional $650 billion. This vast sum was equal to the cumulative total of all the deficits run by every president from Franklin Roosevelt to Jimmy Carter.

Deregulation and the Environment. Deregulation of business was an important part of the president's economic program. Conservatives believed if America was to become more productive, entrepreneurs must be unshackled. Public safety and consumer interests would be taken care of primarily by free market forces.

The process of deregulation had already begun in the Carter administration when, in 1978, Congress passed the Airline Deregulation Act phasing out the regulatory Civil Aeronautics Board, allowing free choice by airlines of routes, and permitting them to set their fares competitively. In 1980 the deregulation process was extended to truckers and, to a more limited extent, to railroads. That same year the Depository Institutions and Monetary Control Act allowed "thrifts," Savings and Loan Associations (S&Ls), to pay market interest rates to depositors and lend on more kinds of security than real estate. Commercial banks too could, under the new rules, pay depositors higher interest to attract savings and could also enter the business of trading in stocks and bonds. In 1982, as a result of an antitrust suit initiated by the Carter administration, the courts ordered the breakup of the American Telephone and Telegraph Company, which had enjoyed a legal near-monopoly on telephone services in many parts of the country. There would now be twenty-two local Bell Companies for local calls plus a scaled-down AT&T, which would retain its long-distance services but would have to compete with special long-distance companies.

Under Reagan, deregulation accelerated. To free business from unnecessary chains, Reagan officials reduced the government's role in consumer protection. The Department of Agriculture stopped printing booklets describing poor dietary habits and detailing good ones. Administration appointees allowed a dubious mixture of fat, meat scraps, gristle, and ground bone to be sold to consumers as ground beef without the warnings previously required. The administration transformed the Occupational Safety and Health Administration from a federal watchdog of the workplace to "a cooperative regulator" of business. Transportation secretary Drew Lewis revoked safety standards mandating automatic seat belts or airbags for automobiles by 1984.

The most controversial change in the regulatory climate was the administration's effort to reduce the government's role in environmental protection. Reagan officials complained that every project to increase the country's energy output, improve its roads and highways, provide new office space, lower the cost of raw materials, or exploit its natural resources inevitably crashed into a wall of environmental regulation or was buried under a wave of environmental lawsuits. The presence of some obscure "endangered species," like the tiny snail-darter fish, could bring to a grinding halt a major dam project; the claim that a new building might cast a shadow over a park could stop a skyscraper from going up. Every major construction scheme was invariably burdened with reams of "environmental impact" statements and other elaborate documentation that added to costs. During the early 1980s a joke went the rounds among Reaganites: "How many Americans did it take to replace a light bulb? Answer: Five—one to change the bulb and four to write an environmental impact statement." The administration claimed, then, that its chief concern was to lower costs and raise productivity. Its critics insisted that its anti-environmentalism was primarily a payoff to the business groups whose support it counted on.

The chief federal agency for safeguarding the public health against pollution and contaminants was the Environmental Protection Agency (EPA), established under Richard Nixon in 1970 and given jurisdiction over a wide range of environmental concerns. During the Reagan administration, the EPA's budget was steadily cut, falling from $5.6 billion in fiscal 1980 to $4.1 billion in fiscal 1984. Reagan's appointee as EPA head was Anne Burford, who administered a $1.4-billion "superfund" to clean up toxic waste dumpsites that dotted the nation. Burford, however, was not an effective guardian of the public's health and she came under attack for delaying the vast task of ridding the environment of dangerous hot spots. In March 1983 she resigned under fire.

Reagan's secretary of the interior, James Watt, also antagonized environmentalists. A Denver lawyer, Watt had been head of the Mountain States Legal Foundation, a public interest law firm financed by the conservative Colorado brewer, Joseph Coors. The foundation was a legal arm of the so-called Sagebrush Rebellion, a movement of western ranchers, mine owners, timber barons, and irrigation farmers who opposed federal control of western resources and favored transferring public lands to state management. Under Watt the firm had initiated lawsuits challenging federal regulation of public land use for the sake of ecological balance, recreational use, and resource conservation.

The environmentalists had opposed his selection to head the Interior Department but, in the wake of the Reagan 1980 election sweep, were unable to stop it. Watt turned out to be just what they feared. Pleading the need to encourage economic growth, he authorized oil drilling in four areas off the Carolina coast that his predecessors had declared off-limits, opened up millions of acres of federal land to prospecting and exploitation by mineral and timber companies, and proposed to sell 35 million acres of federal land to private companies. Environmental pressure groups such as the Wilderness Society, the Sierra Club, the Audubon Society, and the National Wildlife Association denounced Watt, but, despite misgivings, the president kept him. Then, in October 1983, Watt made a remark to a public gathering that managed to offend blacks, Jews, the handicapped, and women simultaneously. Reagan forced him to resign and replaced him with William Clark, a close White House adviser.

First-Term Foreign Policy. Reagan's first term coincided with a gap in the leadership of the Soviet Union. Following the death of Leonid Brezhnev in November 1982 there was a succession of short-term, interim Soviet leaders. Not until Mikhail Gorbachev, a vigorous man of fifty-four, became Communist Party Chairman in March 1985 did the United States have a steady leader to deal with.

In the interim, Soviet–American relations deteriorated. The Soviet invasion of Afghanistan and the hostage-taking episode in Teheran, as we saw, had compelled the Carter administration to assume a more aggressive stance toward America's adversaries. But Reagan went still further. The president and his closest foreign-policy advisers believed the Soviet Union to be the author of virtually all the turmoil and tension in the world. The USSR, they said, had cheated on SALT I and other arms agreements. Either directly, or through surrogates, it was responsible for upheavals in Africa, Latin America, and East Asia. The USSR and its satellites and allies, moreover, were behind the wave of bombings, airplane hijackings, and hostage-taking around the world. They were also the ultimate source of Arab intransigence against Israel in the Middle East. The administration also sought to make a distinction between "authoritarian" regimes, capable of reform, which we should be willing to support if they were anti-communist, and totalitarian societies, like China and the Soviet Union, which were incapable of change and had to be contained.

Shortly after taking office, Reagan found himself forced to deal with a possible Soviet invasion of Poland. In mid-1980 Solidarity, an anti-communist union started by rebellious Polish shipyard workers, challenged the corrupt and repressive puppet regime in Warsaw and its Soviet masters. As Reagan took up the reins of office in early 1981 it looked as if Soviet troops would march once more to put down a popular uprising in one of the satellite nations, as they had in Hungary, Czechoslovakia, and previously in Poland itself. The Soviets avoided an invasion, but in mid-December 1981 they installed a still more repressive regime under Marshall Jeruzelski that imposed martial law and imprisoned Solidarity's leader, Lech Walesa.

Reagan was not prepared to take military action against the Soviets. Yet the president used the occasion to drive home his theme of the Soviet Union as the source of the world's turmoil. During the 1981 Christmas season he ordered lighted candles placed in the White House windows to attest to America's concern for the Polish people and imposed several new economic sanctions on the Soviet Union.

Much of the anti-Soviet campaign was a war of words. A more serious Soviet–American confrontation, however, developed over deploying intermediate-range nuclear missiles in Europe.

At best, neither SALT I nor SALT II had stopped the nuclear arms race. Both sides continued to add to their nuclear delivery systems: long-range ICBMs, bombers, nuclear-carrying submarines, tactical nuclear weapons, and intermediate-range nuclear weapons. In Europe the Warsaw Pact countries and NATO confronted one another with a variety of middle-range nuclear weapons as part of the balance of terror that lay at the heart of the Cold War deterrence policy. In 1980 the Soviets upgraded its Intermediate Nuclear Force (INF) weapons aimed at western Europe with a new, better rocket. On the urging of America's NATO ally, West Germany, Carter promised to send new, upgraded American weapons to restore the balance. But his term ended before he could act, leaving the issue to his successor.

Reagan accepted the commitment to send new "cruise" and Pershing II missiles to Europe. The Soviets reacted with outrage. The Americans, they charged, were threatening the Soviet Union and heating up the Cold War. The issue of the new missiles became the chief concern of the American and Soviet negotiators at Geneva trying to work out a mutual intermediate-range nuclear arms accommodation. The Russians threatened to "walk out in indignation" and hinted at still more dire, if unspecified, consequences if the United States actually deployed the new Pershing II missiles on German soil as scheduled in late 1983. Talks at Geneva on the Pershings soon reached an impasse, and it looked as if Soviet–American relations were once more reaching a crisis point.

The pressure on the Reagan administration to rescind its plans to deploy the Pershings ballooned to enormous proportions in late 1982 and 1983. In Western Europe a new generation of young men and women now feared nuclear war more than the Soviet threat. Marches and rallies to protest the missile deployment and demand the arms race cease once and for all erupted in many cities of America's NATO allies. In the United States, too, the INF crisis fed fears of nuclear holocaust. During 1983 the antiwar and nuclear disarmament movements, in eclipse since the end of the Vietnam War, revived explosively. As in Europe there were demonstrations in major American cities to protest the arms race and demand a "nuclear freeze." Public jitters were amplified by Jonathan Schell's best-selling book *The Fate of the Earth,* which described the likely catastrophic effects of nuclear war. The "no nukes" media campaign culminated in ABC television's "The Day After," a graphic and horrifying depiction of what a nuclear attack would do to one midwestern community.

The administration resisted the pressure to draw back. It also upped the arms race ante. In March 1983 the president had proposed, almost as an afterthought, that the United States abandon MAD (Mutually Assured Destruction) as its sole reliance for nuclear peace. Instead, why not try to find some high-tech defense against enemy missiles, some system to shoot them down before they could reach their targets? Called the Strategic Defense Initiative (SDI) by its friends and "Star Wars" by its enemies, the proposal was unsettling. Many scientists announced that it was simply not possible technically; so why waste billions on such a science fiction scheme? Liberals insisted that SDI would only encourage further Soviet fears and hence further Soviet militancy.

For the Soviet leaders the Star Wars scheme was a shock. We now know how far behind the West the Soviet economy and technological prowess were in the 1980s. To compete with NATO and to maintain its allies abroad, the USSR was already spending as much as 25 percent of its GNP on defense. Even with the Reagan arms build-up of the early 1980s, Americans were spending only one quarter as much proportionately. And nowhere was the Soviet economy so far behind the capitalist nations as in high-tech. Star Wars now threatened the Soviets with another giant round of arms competition with the West—and in the very area where they were most deficient.

In late November 1983 the American Pershing missiles were finally deployed on West German soil. The Soviets now walked out of the ongoing arms talks, declaring that "changes in the global strategic situation" had made it "necessary for the Soviet side to review all problems under discussion." For the first time in many years the United States and the USSR would not be discussing at some forum how to contain the arms race. U.S.–Soviet relations had reached a low point, and many people around the world feared they would get still worse.

Reagan was equally aggressive in other corners of the world, although when real danger appeared, prudence often overcame his hard line. In the Middle East the president maintained close ties with Israel and was rumored to have encouraged the Israeli invasion of Lebanon in 1982. In September 1983, in the hope of pacifying the chronically chaotic country, Reagan sent American Marines to Lebanon. Rather than bringing peace, the Marines became targets of warring Lebanese factions, several of them representing violently anti-American, pro-Iranian terror groups. Earlier in the year a Muslim fanatic had detonated an explosives-laden truck next to the American embassy in Beirut, killing forty-seven people, including sixteen Americans. In October 1983, soon after the Marines arrived, another Islamic terrorist carried out a similar attack against the Marine barracks in Beirut, killing 241 American servicemen. In February 1984 Reagan removed them from the scene of the violence. In later years it was said that this timid response to attack had encouraged terrorists. Meanwhile, ominously, the same militant anti-American groups in Lebanon had begun to take hostages among the Americans residing in Beirut, and the media began to pressure the administration to do something to recover the kidnaped men.

Nicaragua.   The president and his advisers saw the hands of the Soviets and their Western Hemisphere surrogate, Fidel Castro's Cuba, behind much of the social and political unrest in Latin America. Fearing Marxist beachheads in the Western Hemisphere, the administration intervened in El Salvador to help the conservative-to-moderate regime of Napoleon Duarte against a Marxist-led insurgency. In October 1983 American troops invaded the tiny island republic of Grenada, ostensibly to ensure the safety of several hundred American students studying for their medical degrees on the island, but actually to keep the Cubans from getting a toehold.

The most inflamed spot in the Americas was Nicaragua, another small republic in Central America. The country was ruled by the Sandinistas, a leftist group responsible for the overthrow in 1979 of the American-supported strongman, Anastasio Somoza. Since coming to power, the Sandinistas, led by Daniel Ortega, had established a one-party political system governed by increasingly dogmatic and authoritarian Marxist principles. The administration accused the Sandinistas of aiding the Salvadorean rebels and stirring up anti-American discontent in Latin America generally. To undermine the Sandinista regime the United States provided arms, logistical support, and intelligence to the "Contras," made up mostly of Nicaraguan exiles who despised Ortega and his regime.

American public opinion was divided on the civil wars raging in Central America. Most Americans feared another Marxist bridgehead in the Americas, but many worried about a replay of the Vietnam quagmire. In 1983 a Vietnam-shy Congress passed, over the president's protest, the Boland Amendment requiring the chief executive to consult Congress before using any more Defense Department money to supply the Contras. Thereafter, Congress blew hot and cold over the anti-Sandinista rebels, at times refusing them funds of any sort, at other times restricting their use entirely to "humanitarian" aid—food, clothing, medical supplies, and the like. Frustrated by congressional anti-Contra actions, fiercely dedicated anti-communist hardliners within the CIA and the National Security Council soon began to consider ways to evade Congress's intentions. Their schemes would precipitate a political crisis.

Reelection. None of Reagan's missteps affected his standings in the polls. The president's personal charm, his relaxed manner, and his good looks sugar-coated his actions. The "great communicator" seemed tough toward America's enemies while avoiding confrontations. He remained a "good guy" while cutting programs for the poor. A generation raised on images took his words and manner more seriously than his deeds. Exasperated opponents would dub him the "Teflon president," because nothing adverse seemed to stick to his political skin.

In 1982, however, the Republicans had faced, and failed, their first electoral challenge. The 1982 midterm elections found the economy still lagging badly, with unemployment at a frightening 9.7 percent. The Democrats made substantial gains in the House, though they did not regain control in the Senate. By 1984 the economy had sprung back. There remained soft spots in the old Snow Belt industrial areas and—owing to declining world oil prices—the "Oil Patch" of Texas, Oklahoma, and Louisiana began to suffer as well. But on the Pacific Coast and in parts of the Northeast, massive defense spending and the transition to computers pushed the economy to new highs. Middle-class America began to feel flush and confident again.

As the 1984 presidential election approached, the Democrats faced a popular president who could claim he had ended the decade-long inflation surge and brought renewed prosperity. Yet there was no lack of Democratic challengers. In the end, the Democratic race came down to Senator Gary Hart of Colorado and former Vice President Walter Mondale of Minnesota. Hart claimed to speak for the younger voters who were coming of age in the 1980s. Mondale represented a more traditional New Deal, bread-and-butter sort of liberalism. To the left of both was Jesse Jackson, a black minister sprung from the civil rights movement, who sought to create a "Rainbow Coalition" of blacks, Hispanics, feminists, gays, and other minorities and social outsiders. Jackson was the first serious black presidential contender, and his candidacy had special meaning for black voters.

The presidential primaries had become a long, expensive obstacle course and for months the Democrats slugged it out. In the end Mondale won on the first ballot at the Democratic convention in San Francisco. The convention itself was primarily a media event. Jackson gracefully apologized for an anti-Semitic remark he had made in private; the eloquent keynote speaker, governor Mario Cuomo of New York, reiterated the Democrats' social sympathies and asserted their ability to make one "family" of America's diverse strands. Hoping to take advantage of a "gender gap" between the parties, Mondale boldly chose a woman, Representative Geraldine Ferraro of New York, as his running mate. In a fit of rare political honesty, he also promised, if elected, to raise taxes to bring down the escalating budget deficits.

The contest was no contest. By the fall the economy was booming and many Americans felt that Reagan had restored America's standing in the world. Underscoring the new pride was the American sweep at the Summer Olympics in Los Angeles in part because of a Soviet bloc boycott. The Republican campaign slogan, "It's Morning in America," proclaimed in a raft of TV ads, proved effective. As the race reached the home stretch, one Reagan adviser noted that he "almost felt sorry for Mondale, . . . it's like running against America."

It was a Reagan landslide. The Republican presidential ticket won every state except Minnesota, Mondale's home state, and garnered 59 percent of the popular vote. The Republicans had done well in almost every sector of the population. There was one bit of good news for the Democrats, however. Despite the Reagan landslide, the new House of Representatives would remain under Democratic control.

■ THE SECOND FOUR YEARS ■

Few presidents have accomplished as much in their second term as in their first. By the beginning of their fifth year they have achieved most of their agenda and depleted their good will. In Reagan's case the problems would be compounded by the 1986 midterm elections, when the Democrats regained control of the Senate, making it even more difficult for the administration to win congressional cooperation than before.

The administration's second-term problems were aggravated by the president's age and health. Reagan was already seventy when he became president, the oldest man to hold the presidential office. In addition, he had survived an assassination attempt in 1981, and by 1987 he had undergone surgery for colon cancer and an enlarged prostate. At times in his second term he seemed to be tired, distracted, and forgetful. He still read prepared speeches magnificently, but did poorly at extemporaneous press conferences where he had to think on his feet, and so avoided them. Some Americans believed he had lost his grip.

The AIDS Crisis. Troubles and conflicts would come in shoals during Reagan's second four years. In 1981 the calamity of AIDS burst on the scene when scientists discovered that a hitherto unknown agent was attacking the immune systems of thousands of victims and destroying their resistance to cancer and infectious diseases. The afflicted, at first, were predominantly homosexual males, and it was soon learned that the disease was transmitted through infected bodily fluids including semen and blood. In 1984 French and American scientists identified the disease-causing agent as a virus that entered the bloodstream and over time destroyed the body's ability to manufacture antibodies.

AIDS (acquired immunodeficiency syndrome) was not a "gay" disease as such. It infected intravenous drug users, people who received transfusions before blood screening techniques were developed, and some who engaged in heterosexual intercourse. But even five years after the first data became available, over 70 percent of all AIDS victims remained homosexuals.

The disease ravaged the gay community. AIDS ran through New York's Greenwich Village, the Castro district in San Francisco, and other gay neighborhoods, cutting down young men in the thousands and undermining the hard-won self-confidence that gays had acquired since the late 1960s. It also produced a sharp upsurge of antigay feeling. Though the disease obviously afflicted other groups, social conservatives, including many of the Moral Majority, saw it as a sign of God's displeasure at homosexuality.

Although medical experts insisted that the disease could not be transmitted by casual contact, many people initially feared AIDS victims, however they had acquired the disease. People began to avoid contact with gays; they demanded that AIDS-infected children be kept from school. Medical personnel took to wearing masks and gloves when in the presence of AIDS patients. Fear of AIDS also began to affect relations between heterosexual men and women; experts claimed that all sexual contact with infected people created the risk of infection. Combined with a surge of genital herpes and other sexually transmitted diseases, the advent of AIDS took its toll of the permissive sexual revolution of the 1960s and 1970s.

The president was caught in the middle of the controversies that swirled around the AIDS scourge. Gay activists accused him of refusing to mobilize the nation's medical resources against AIDS out of homophobia. The president endorsed mandatory testing of federal and state prisoners, patients admitted to VA hospitals, and marriage-license applicants. These programs fell far short of the mass-testing programs demanded by a few far right advocates, but gays and civil libertarians claimed they would place the jobs and insurance coverage of AIDS patients in jeopardy and were preliminary to an official policy of quarantine. Never highly popular in the homosexual community, the administration probably lost whatever support it had among an emerging self-conscious social minority.

Retreat of the Religious Right. As his second term approached its end Reagan also found his support among the religious right less sustaining. As we saw, he had benefited from the surging political activism of fundamentalist Protestant groups. The Moral Majority coalition and similar groups had applauded the president's pronouncements on abortion, on school prayer, on traditional family values, but they had been less impressed with his actions. Reagan, some said, talked a good game but did little to implement it.

In 1987 the president sought to appease his supporters on the religious and political right by nominating Robert Bork to the Supreme Court. As a federal appeals court judge, Bork had opposed the judicial activism of many of his liberal predecessors on the bench and liberals opposed having him entrenched for life at the nation's judicial center. After widely watched televised hearings, the Senate rejected him. The administration defiantly nominated another far right judge, Douglas Ginsburg. Ginsburg soon confessed to having smoked marijuana while a law professor, and in a matter of days agreed to withdraw his name. The president then nominated Anthony Kennedy of Sacramento, a man closer to the center, whom the Senate finally confirmed. But the ill-conceived initial selections underscored for many social conservatives how little the administration had accomplished in actually reversing the liberal trends of the day.

By 1987 the religious right itself had become a victim of its own excesses. The chief culprit was Jim Bakker, one of a number of fundamentalist "televangelists" who, during the decade, learned to use the electronic media to disseminate their messages of good works, salvation, righteous living, and antimodernism. Bakker, along with his blonde wife, Tammy Faye, sponsored a large resort in Fort Mill, South Carolina, that combined the features of Disneyland, a revival camp, and a country club. There the devout, who paid the requisite sum, could spend their vacations soaking up the sun and God's word at the same time. In March 1987 Bakker resigned as head of his "Praise the Lord" ministry after the media revealed he had made sexual advances to both men and women. In 1989 after investigation of dubious sales practices at Fort Hill, he was tried for fraud and sentenced to forty-five years in prison.

The Jim and Tammy scandal damaged the evangelical movement as a whole. Many sincere followers of fundamentalist preachers became disillusioned. Contributions to TV evangelism dropped; membership growth in fundamentalist churches slowed. Jerry Falwell, discouraged by the un-Christian squabbling and infighting that had erupted over PTL, announced in late 1987 that he was abandoning political activism and would hereafter focus on his pastoral duties as minister at the Thomas Road Baptist church in Lynchburg, Virginia. In 1989 the Moral Majority officially disbanded though other, less visible, groups continued to represent the evangelical voice in the political arena.

The Space Shuttle. Reagan's second term was also marred by a space shuttle disaster that some observers said highlighted the administration's fecklessness and lack of direction in its commitment to space exploration.

Since the dazzling days of the moon landings, the American space program had changed. NASA turned to a shuttle rocket that could place into orbit communication satellites and other devices and perform various scientific tests in a weightless environment, and then return to earth to be reused. The new programs, however valuable, lacked the high drama and adventure of the sixties and early seventies manned moon landings. To keep the interest of the public, NASA invited ordinary civilians to join the shuttle missions. On January 28, 1986, a mission that included Christa McAuliffe, a Concord, New Hampshire, schoolteacher, exploded after liftoff at the Kennedy Space Center.

The tragedy crippled the American space program for a time. The investigation that followed showed that NASA had authorized the launch against expert advice that icing on the rocket might create a problem. With the space shuttle out of service for the foreseeable future, the United States was forced to turn to older rockets to launch needed civilian and military communications satellites. Meanwhile, the Europeans and the Soviets forged ahead in their satellite programs, making America seem a has-been in space. Having promised to restore America's world prestige and pride, the space policy fiasco once again made the administration look bad.

Economic Abuses.   During Reagan's second term the economy's performance continued strong. Unemployment continued to decline, reaching 6 percent in December 1986 and dropping another percentage point by the end of the administration. The inflation rate remained low. Most impressive of all was the stock market boom. In 1985 the Dow Jones Index of leading industrial stocks rose by over 20 percent; in 1986 it leaped by another 15 percent; in the first half of 1987 it soared into the stratosphere.

The bull market in part reflected buoyant corporate profits and earnings. Clearly, certain industries flourished during the decade. In 1983 IBM's personal computer reinforced the movement toward individualizing computing power already begun by Apple, a Silicon Valley firm established by two young inventors, Stephen Wozniak and Steven Jobs. By mid-decade almost every aspect of life was affected by the little box with a keyboard and a screen—the way people banked, wrote letters, kept accounts, and even spent their leisure time. Hundreds of businesses and whole industries—computer magazines, computer retailers, software manufacturers, computer consultants—grew up around the new PC. High-tech stocks were the engine that helped push the stock market to greater highs.

But the bull market also expressed other, less admirable, elements of the 1980s economic culture. The Reagan victory did unleash enterprise, but clearly not all was of the constructive sort. The administration's message that government was there to befriend business, not to restrain it, encouraged a frenzy to get rich without the painful necessity of making a better product or providing a better service.

One aspect of this mood was the resorting by men and women in the securities business to "insider trading," the use of information not available to the general public for private speculative gain. Great fortunes were made during the bull market years by such traders as Ivan Boesky using illegal means of manipulating the stock market. Junk bonds and leveraged buyouts also expressed the new attitude. Junk bonds were risky corporate securities that paid high interest rates. Previously scorned by investors, they gained popularity when a young Los Angeles financier, Michael Milken, convinced the public that they were actually a lucrative investment. Before long Milken's firm, Drexel, Burnham, Lambert, was selling many millions of dollars of junk bonds to private and corporate investors.

Able to tap this new source of funds, other shrewd financiers, with relatively little money of their own, bought up large companies, often engaging in fierce bidding wars with their existing managers and stockholders. The battles for control took on the dimensions of financial epics that resembled the struggles of Gould, Fisk, Vanderbilt, and other robber barons to manipulate Gilded Age corporate finance for their own ends. If successful, the "corporate raiders" were seldom interested in improving the efficiency of the new firm or the quality of its product. Usually, they sold off the profitable pieces of the firm, often receiving more from the sales of the parts than the whole company had cost them. The remaining husk was not only deprived of its money-making subsidiaries; it was also saddled with millions of dollars of high-interest junk-bond debt.

Still another dubious aspect of business during the 1980s was the mismanagement of the nation's savings and loan associations (S&Ls) that hitherto had provided much of the mortgage money for home buyers. As we saw, these institutions had been closely regulated until 1980 when Congress allowed them to pay competitive interest rates and invest in many other ventures besides home mortgages. This helped stem the outflow of deposits. But to pay the higher rates the S&Ls required higher-paying and more liquid investments than the typical twenty-year, 10 percent home mortgage. Many bought the junk bonds that Drexel, Burnham, Lambert and its competitors were offering. Others turned to grandiose commercial construction projects of dubious profitability. Some simply fell into the hands of con artists who made loans to friends, family, or even disguised versions of themselves without real security. Much of this high flying was confined to the fastest-growing sections of the country—California, the Mountain States, Texas, and Florida. When, during the mid-1980s, the economies of some of these places crashed, many S&Ls found themselves with millions of dollars of worthless IOUs, unable to pay their depositors.

The public would have been outraged at such practices in any case, but matters were made much worse by the fact that billions of dollars of S&L deposits were insured by the federal government. This meant that the American taxpayer would have to make good on the troubled thrifts' depositors' claims. By the last months of Reagan's second term, a few experts close to the events warned that a crisis was building. Few took it seriously. It failed to become an issue during the 1988 campaign, but remained a ticking bomb waiting to detonate.

Deficits. The most serious economic worry from the mid-1980s on was America's deteriorating international position. For the previous three quarters of a century the United States had exported huge amounts of farm and manufactured goods, valued at far more than our imports. In 1971, for the first time since 1914, we ran a trade deficit. It was not until the 1980s, however, that this trade gap began to expand at a dangerous rate. By 1984 the American trade shortfall had reached $107 billion a year. In 1986 it had gone to $170 billion, by far the largest in our history.

No nation can continue to run trade deficits for very long unless other nations are willing to lend it money. And so it was now. By 1984, for the first time since World War I, seventy years before, the United States had become a net debtor nation, owing its creditors billions more than they owed us. By 1990, one estimate held, Americans would be paying interest to foreign lenders of over $100 billion a year.

The nation's debtor status had humiliating and unsettling effects. Increasingly foreigners came to own ever larger amounts of American assets—stocks, bonds, factories, and real estate. In 1990 Americans were startled and dismayed when a Japanese company bought Rockefeller Center in New York, long considered an American icon. Bit by bit, worried critics said, we were selling our heritage for a mess of Sonys, Toyotas, and Nikons.

The reasons for the sweeping change in America's international economic position were not simple to diagnose. The quality of American manufactured products relative to their foreign competition had clearly slipped. Through the mid-1980s American industrial and university laboratories continued to lead the world in cutting-edge research. But American companies no longer seemed able to convert this research into attractive, competitively priced consumer goods. Some experts blamed the failure on the excessive focus of American business managers on short-range corporate profit and their own personal financial advantage, versus long-range company growth. Others blamed American workers: They were careless, undisciplined, and ill-educated. Still others blamed the high cost of capital in the United States. Americans were not saving; they were spending a larger proportion of their income than ever before. With little domestic saving, investment capital was higher priced here than overseas.

During the 1980s perceptions like these spawned a flood of self-critical analyses that blamed one aspect or another of American culture or policy: our poor educational system, especially the lower levels; our lack of pride in work and insistence on instant gratification; our excessive spending on defense that protected American industry against the rigors of domestic competition. Toward the decade's close a minor industry of books and articles appeared proclaiming the intellectual and cultural inadequacies of Americans, and especially of the young. The results of various international tests confirmed that Americans ranked behind the citizens of almost all industrial nations in their knowledge of geography, math, science, history, art, and virtually everything needed to excel. How could such a collection of ignoramuses expect to compete with the rest of the world?

But it was also possible to point the finger of blame for America's feeble competitive performance at others. The nation's chief trade rival was Japan, and Japan, many critics said, did not play fair. While the United States remained open to foreign imports, the Japanese refused to buy American goods even when they were indisputably superior to the domestic product. Moreover, said the "Japan bashers," the Japanese government, though professing to favor open markets, actually raised a multitude of phony barriers to foreign goods while at the same time dumping such Japanese products as computer microchips at below cost on foreign markets to destroy the local industry and thereafter become the sole supplier. Japan, in fact, considered international trade a form of warfare and, said some critics, its enormous trading surplus with the United States was a kind of revenge for military defeat in 1945.

Whatever the true facts, the Reagan administration placed strong pressure on the Japanese to import more American goods. The Japanese proved evasive. Agreements were reached but did not accomplish their ends. Somehow American companies could not sell their products in Japan. Japanese trade policies angered many Americans. By the end of the decade many would see Japan as a worse threat to the United States than the Soviet Union. Labor unions and business groups demanded that Congress retaliate with tariffs and other restrictive legislation. And at times the government did. Washington forced the Japanese to limit the number of automobiles exported to America. In March 1987 the administration imposed duties on a wide range of Japanese electronic goods in response to the dumping of microchips. But in the end the Reagan administration, like its successor, would be constrained by the desire to avoid the sort of international trade war that had worsened the effects of the 1930s Great Depression.

And besides the enormous foreign debts, there were the gargantuan domestic debts. As we saw, the tax cuts of 1981 and after, combined with the defense build-up of the early eighties, produced unparalleled annual federal deficits. These continued even after defense spending leveled off. In 1985 Congress passed the Gramm–Rudman Act to force itself to cut the deficit. The law mandated specific yearly target reductions of the federal deficit under penalty of automatic meat-ax, across-the-board cuts in all federal outlays that no one wanted.

Gramm–Rudman did seem to impose some fiscal restraint. By 1988 the annual budget deficit was down to $155 billion from the $221 billion of 1985. Yet Americans still had reason for concern. By that year the deficit had pushed the total national debt to over $2.6 trillion, more than $10,500 for every man, woman, and child. The interest alone on this sum amounted to $214 billion each year. Such an interest payout deprived the private capital markets of an enormous amount of badly needed investment funds. The deficit also thwarted every proposal for additional federal programs, no matter how meritorious or cost-effective. Whether intended or not, Reaganomics had incapacitated the government, the only agency that could tackle many of the problems that faced the American people.

"Irangate." In 1986–1987 Ronald Reagan finally seemed to lose his Teflon coating. The event that changed his luck was a secret deal with Iran instigated, apparently, by CIA director William Casey; National Security Council staffer Lt. Colonel Oliver North; and North's chief at the NSC, Vice Admiral John Poindexter that promised to solve two problems simultaneously: how to fund the Contras and how to win freedom for Americans taken hostage in Lebanon by anti-American Moslem extremists.

All three men were determined to defeat the Nicaraguan Sandinistas. But, as we saw, Congress resisted supplying the Contras with funds and at times had cut these off entirely. At the same time the hostage problem had been blown out of proportion by the media and the public was clamoring for their release. Iran seemed the key to both problems. As they perceived the facts, the Iranians were desperate for weapons to defeat Iraq, with whom they had been at war since 1980. They would pay any price to get American guns, missiles, and aircraft parts, and in gratitude they would use their good offices with the Muslim extremists to release their American prisoners. The profits from the deal did not have to be made public. Why not just transfer them to the Contras, thus getting around Congress's unwillingness to fund the "freedom fighters" struggling to overthrow the Marxist Nicaraguan regime?

The Iran-Contra deals were concocted in mid-1985 when the president uthorized the then-National Security Adviser, Robert McFarlane, to contact Iranian officials and offer to sell them arms. Soon after, he approved sending American owned missiles in Israeli possession to the Iranians, the first of several shipments. In May 1986 North and McFarlane, the latter now a private citizen, flew to Iran to make a deal for further arms sales in exchange for the Lebanon hostages. They were at first unable to secure the release of any of the captives. Finally, on November 2, the day before a Lebanese magazine published details of the arms sales and McFarlane's visit to Teheran, the extremists released the first of a small group of kidnaped Americans. The actual arms deals took place through intermediaries, who took a share of the profits. An uncertain portion of the remainder ended up in the coffers of the Contras, where it paid for arms and supplies in the anti-Sandinista guerrilla war.

Most Americans were shocked when they learned of the Iran-Contra deal at the end of 1986. The public had counted on Ronald Reagan to be tough on terrorists and America's enemies generally. He had repeatedly denounced the Libyans and the Iranians and held them accountable for bombings and hostage-takings. In April 1986, after a number of airplane hijackings, airport bombings, and an attack on an American servicemen's discotheque in West Berlin that implicated the Libyans, Reagan had ordered an air raid against the Libyan cities of Tripoli and Benghasi from aircraft carriers and from air bases in Britain. One of the attacks almost killed Libyan strongman Muammar Qaddafi. Over 77 percent of the American public endorsed the attacks, although they feared the volatile Qaddafi would retaliate and, in droves, cancelled plans to travel in Europe and the Mediterranean during the summer of 1986.

After this bold act, what was the public now to make of the deal with the Iranians, the worst terrorists in the entire Mideast? It seemed hard to believe that the Ronald Reagan who had authorized the arms-for-hostages trade was the same man who had ordered the Libyan and Grenada assaults.

Americans from all parts of the political spectrum were appalled by the Iran-Contra affair. What antiterrorist credibility did America have left now that it had made a deal with Iran to ransom hostages? And who was running American foreign policy? Congress had cut off funds for the Contras. Did the administration or, more accurately, a small cabal within the administration, have the right to ignore the nation's constitutional policy-making processes?

At first the president denied that there had been an arms-for-hostages deal. He acknowledged that the United States had sent "defensive weapons" and spare parts to Iran but refused to concede that the purpose had been to buy the Lebanon hostages' freedom. Few people believed him. A week or so later Attorney General Edward Meese admitted that profits from the arms sales had been diverted to the Contras, and soon thereafter the president announced that he had fired Oliver North and accepted the resignation of Admiral Poindexter.

Through the weeks of new revelations that followed, the president seemed confused and ill-informed about what had been done in his name and under his very nose. Chief of Staff Donald Regan, to save his own reputation, soon disclosed a White House where confusion reigned and where, he said, only his own rearguard actions had prevented open scandal.

Moderates and liberals were especially dismayed. As more information surfaced, it became clear that a rogue operation had been mounted by quite junior officials in the government, in violation of federal law. Once again, as under Nixon, an administration had violated public trust and ridden roughshod over the Constitution. In mid-December Reagan authorized a special prosecutor to investigate the Iran-Contra matter. The president also appointed a commission headed by former Republican Senator John Tower of Texas to uncover what had happened. Meanwhile, Congress established its own investigating committee to look into the affair.

In late February 1987 the Tower Commission issued a report condemning the administration's operations as "chaotic" and "amateurish." It expressed dismay at Reagan's lax "personal management style" and criticized him for allowing his concern for the hostages to get in the way of his good sense. But it absolved him of actual wrongdoing. The chief Tower Commission Report culprit was Donald Regan, who was blamed for not keeping the president informed of White House operations. Regan, now under heavy attack, fought to keep his job, but the First Lady, Nancy Reagan, highly protective of her husband, turned against him and helped force him out. Soon after, Howard Baker, the respected former senator from Tennessee, assumed the role of White House chief of staff. Many people, skeptical of the president's grasp of complexity, applauded the change. At least now the aging chief executive would have a skilled and savvy man to back him up.

The congressional hearings on the Iran-Contra affair began in early May 1987 with a parade of witnesses who told of the complex negotiations and intrigues that constituted the operation. The two chief witnesses were Colonel North and Admiral Poindexter, both of whom appeared under grant of partial immunity from legal prosecution. CIA director Casey could not be examined; he had died of a brain tumor, taking his knowledge of the intrigue to the grave. During the televised hearings the young, crisp, articulate North made a powerful case for his actions and managed to indict his critics as people of dubious patriotism. The public at first ate it up. For a week or two the nation found itself in the grip of "Ollimania," an uncritical acceptance of North as a patriot and a hero.

Meanwhile, the president's reputation and standing slipped badly. A December 1986 poll showed that Reagan's approval rating had dropped from 67 percent to 46 percent in one month. In late April 1987 two thirds of those asked by a *Washington Post*–ABC poll believed the president was not telling the truth about his role in the Iran-Contra fiasco. The Teflon, it seemed, had finally worn off the country's chief executive.

Nicaragua Resolved.   The polls also showed that the public remained unwilling to become deeply involved in Nicaragua. In early 1986, 62 percent opposed giving aid to the Contras. Even among those who considered themselves Reagan partisans, only 35 percent favored Contra assistance. Yet the president and his advisers continued to seek the overthrow of Daniel Ortega and his government. Liberals, as well as activists on the left, meanwhile continued to liken Nicaragua to Vietnam and warned against becoming bogged down in another military and political swamp, this one nearer home.

Toward the end of 1987 it began to look as if a peaceful solution might emerge in Central America after all. Five Central American nations, led by president Oscar Arias-Sanchez of Costa Rica, agreed on a peace plan that would bring the Contras and Sandinistas together, introduce democratic practices into Nicaragua, and end the threat of superpower intervention in that country. The plan was hailed around the world as a model of local self-determination, and President Arias won the 1987 Nobel Peace Prize for his role in its conception. In the United States most Democrats also approved of it as a way out of the Central American impasse, but the administration remained skeptical and for a time it seemed that the peace plan had stalled. Then, in late March 1988, the Sandinistas and the Contras signed a cease-fire. In 1990 an anti-Sandinista coalition led by Violetta Chamorro won a surprise victory over the Sandinistas in a free election. It finally looked as if the Nicaragua problem would be peacefully resolved.

The Soviet Union and Arms Reduction.   For months following emplacement of U.S. Pershing missiles in Germany, the United States and the Soviet Union sniped at one another. But vast changes were underway in the Soviet Union that would soon transform worldwide international relations.

The author of these changes was the new Soviet leader, Mikhail Gorbachev, a communist reformer who sought to revive a society increasingly corrupt, rigid, and inefficient. For a brief time in the 1960s communism had seemed capable of exceeding capitalism in material production. By the 1980s, however, it was clear that the USSR could not provide the consumer products its people craved and the economic strength and technological capacity it needed to compete against the capitalist nations in the world arena. Gorbachev understood the weaknesses of the Soviet system and sought to rectify them by policies of *Glasnost* (openness) and *Perestroika* (economic restructuring).

The Soviet leader was impelled primarily by domestic concerns. But he recognized that the Soviet Union's commitment to expansionist foreign initiatives imposed unbearable economic burdens and must be reduced if Soviet

The two men—President Ronald Reagan and Soviet Premier Mikhail Gorbachev—who arguably ended the Cold War. Gorbachev was on a visit to the United States.

restructuring was to succeed. Perhaps, as some observers believed, the prospect of another arms race with the United States, especially a Star Wars high-tech competition, was a significant factor in his decision to contract Soviet power around the world.

The first fruit of Gorbachev's foreign policy was the resumption of U.S.–Soviet arms talks broken off in 1983. These proved fruitful, and in December 1987 Gorbachev and Reagan signed an agreement in Washington eliminating all medium-range missiles in Europe, thereby accepting the main ingredients of the American position at Geneva three years before. For the first time, a whole class of nuclear missiles would actually be eliminated. During his visit to the United States the affable, balding, Soviet leader delighted the American public. He joked and smiled and stopped his limousine on a Washington street to shake hands with pedestrians. Americans even liked his wife, Raisa, though Nancy Reagan, it seemed, did not. The trim and stylish Raisa Gorbachev was the first Kremlin "First Lady," one wag remarked, who weighed less than her husband.

"Black Monday." In some sense the Reagan era ended on October 19, 1987, when the stock market dropped over 500 points in a few hours. This was the most catastrophic one-day decline in the history of Wall Street. In the estimate of experts, a trillion dollars in paper wealth were wiped out between August 25, when stocks had reached their all-time Dow Jones peak of 2722, and October 20, with most of the loss on Black Monday itself.

For a time there were dire predictions that the nation, and perhaps the world, was staring another Great Depression in the face. This disaster did not happen. Stocks soon recovered and by mid-1990 had risen above their 1987 high. Nor did the nation go into an economic tailspin. Modest growth continued; unemployment remained low; price increases neither slowed nor accelerated.

And yet something significant had happened. Black Monday dissipated the air of cocky economic confidence that surrounded the Reagan era. Thereafter there would be less flaunting of wealth and less facile defense of crude financial wheeling-dealing. For many high-flying Yuppies the stock crash represented a whiff of mortality, and it was sobering.

■ CONCLUSIONS ■

Ronald Reagan and his supporters hoped to launch a "revolution," a conservative revolution. They achieved at least part of what they sought to accomplish.

They wished to limit the size and scope of government, and they succeeded to a point. Domestic programs for the nonworking poor were reduced, restrained, or eliminated. Few new ones were adopted. The federal government reduced its oversight role in many areas of business activity. Federal participation in a wide range of activities was replaced by control by the states instead. More important, however—whether the result was intended or fortuitous—the drastic tax cuts created unprecedented deficits that promised to tie the hands of the federal government for years to come.

Yet the conservative ideologues were never able to make the cut in activist government they really wanted. There were too many constituents for Head Start, water and air pollution controls, resource conservation, health research, and the many other functions and roles that modern government had assumed even in the United States. Federal budget outlays on existing domestic programs continued to grow, though at a slower pace.

The Reaganites had promised to revive the American economy and tap new sources of economic productivity. The United States would once more become the economic locomotive that pulled the free world. And the average American, not just the rich, would benefit, for a booming economy would scatter its blessings over all. The administration could point to some economic successes. Reaganite economic policies helped break the dangerous inflationary cycle of the 1970s. During the 1980s, moreover, the economy absorbed millions of new workers entering the job market. Once past the 1982–1983 slump, the economy began a growth phase that lasted longer than any before it.

Yet the economic downside was undeniable. During the decade there was a shift of income shares from the poorest groups to the richest, with the very richest 1 percent improving their relative standing more than any other sector of the public. Administration policies alone did not explain this outcome; world economic trends were surely in part responsible as well. Still, Reaganite tax policy and deregulation encouraged the unequal result. Nor did the administration's economic policies stem America's relative international decline. Indeed, many experts believed that the massive federal budget deficits imposed severe limitations on any possibility for improving the country's competitiveness. Too much of the nation's savings, they said, was absorbed by the persistent deficits; they prevented needed federal expenditures for education, roads and bridges, research, and many other things required for the United States to catch up to its chief world rivals.

The Reaganites came to office resolved to strengthen old-fashioned family structures. Their immediate success was limited. There was little that any administration in Washington could do in the short run about the drastic changes in American sexual mores and family patterns. Illegitimacy, divorce, and broken families continued to plague the nation.

Reagan pledged to restore world respect for the United States and reduce Soviet power and political influence. He left with America and its allies on the verge of an astonishing victory over their Communist adversaries. Two years into his successor's administration, the Soviet Union had ceased to be a threat to Western Europe or, for that matter, to any nation around the world. Everywhere communism was collapsing; the Cold War was over and it would be hard to refute the claim that the West had won. Obviously the Reagan arms build-up and the stubborn resolve to deploy new nuclear weapons on NATO soil do not by themselves explain the stupefying result. The containment policy went back to the late 1940s and had been supported by half a dozen administrations. Yet it would be difficult to dismiss the influence of 1980s hard-line policies in inducing Kremlin leadership to reconsider aggressive Soviet international commitments.

Was there a Reagan Revolution? Keeping in mind the normal inertia of America's political culture, its resistance to quick shifts, the term may be valid. The years 1981–1989 witnessed more rapid change than most equal intervals of the past. Inevitably, however, Americans would disagree over whether to cheer or to scoff.

Online Resources

"Possible Soviet Responses to the U.S. Strategic Defense Initiative"
http://www.fas.org/spp/starwars/offdocs/m8310017.htm
From the office of the Director of Central Intelligence, this report seeks to ascertain Soviet military strength and intentions during the Reagan era.
"Reagan"
http://www.pbs.org/wgbh/amex/reagan/filmmore/index.html
This comprehensive site contains information on the Iran-Contra affair, a timeline of Reagan's presidency, in-depth coverage of the 1982 recession and the Grenada invasion, and text copies of many of Reagan's presidential speeches. A companion site to a documentary on the president, this site also contains transcripts of interviews with scholars about the Reagan presidency.
"The History of Silicon Valley"
http://www.ocf.berklet.edu/~kenken/svhis.htm

This site details the beginnings of the information age through electronics. Read about the beginnings of Silicon Valley as a research center and how the industry was propelled by the revolutions of the personal computer and the World Wide Web.

"The Intermediate Nuclear Force Agreement (INF)"
http://www.state.gov/www/global/arms/treaties/infl.html
Read the full-text document of the INF agreement between the United States and the Soviet Union, an agreement that was the first true nuclear disarmament treaty.

The Causes of Homelessness in America
http://www.stanford.edu/class/e297c/poverty_prejudice/soc_sec/hcauses.htm
This Web site essay explores the social and economic policies since the 1980s that have contributed to the growing gap between rich and poor and the rise of homelessness in the country.

31

A DIFFERENT AMERICA?

Would Diversity and the Cold War's End Change America?

1988	Presidential race; George Bush defeats Michael Dukakis
1989	Economic slump begins; Bush appoints Anthony Kennedy and Antonin Scalia to Supreme Court; Berlin Wall razed; Communism collapses in Eastern Europe
1990	Bush agrees to raise taxes; Savings and Loan defaults reach over $100 billion; Iraq invades Kuwait; United States sends troops to Persian Gulf
1991	Business bankruptcies reach record high; Clarence Thomas, nominee for Supreme Court, accused of sexual harassment by Anita Hill; Gulf War; American air, naval, and ground forces attack Iraq, win quick victory; In USSR Boris Yeltsin replaces Mikhail Gorbachev; Soviet Union dissolved; Cold War ends
1992	Presidential election; Bill Clinton defeats George Bush; U.S. troops sent to Somalia for humanitarian reasons
1993	Bush pardons Caspar Weinberger of charges he lied to Congress over Iran-Contra; Clinton starts administration with rash of gaffes; Appoints an ethnically diverse set of top advisers; Seeks to legalize gays in the military; Yugoslavia falls apart and ethnic war breaks out among constituent parts; U.S. troops withdrawn from Somalia; Clinton budget, cutting growth of deficits, passed; Also National Service Plan for Youth and Family Leave Bill; Congress passes NAFTA; Administration introduces major federal health care reform bill prepared by First Lady, Hillary Rodham Clinton; Federal agents attack Branch Davidian compound in Waco, Texas, 80 people die
1994	American military forces sent to Haiti to restore democracy; Administration health care bill not passed by Congress; Republicans win majorities in both houses of Congress, claim a mandate for their "Contract with America"
1995	Timothy McVeigh, a right wing militia member, sets bomb at federal building in Oklahoma City, 168 killed; University of California Board of Regents revokes affirmative action at the university
1996	Clinton defeats Bob Dole in presidential election; California voters approve Proposition 209 ending state-mandated affirmative action; Jury acquits O.J. Simpson of murdering his former wife and her friend; Decision divides nation along racial lines

2000	Millennium bug proves less damaging than anticipated; George W. Bush defeats Al Gore and becomes president after a disputed election not decided until a Supreme Court ruling; the stock market "bubble" bursts, economy begins to slump
2001	President Bush succeeds in getting passed a gigantic tax cut bill over Democrats' resistance; Bush seeks to weaken environmental protection policies of Clinton administration; Terrorists linked to Osama bin Laden hijack American commercial airliners and crash them into New York's World Trade Center Towers and the Pentagon in Washington. Over 3,000 die. Bush declares "war" on bin Laden and terrorism; American forces begin campaign to oust bin Laden and his network from Afghanistan

Nineteen eighty-nine was a watershed in global history. In that momentous year the Cold War that had divided the world into two opposing camps for almost half a century and helped define the internal policies of both East and West ended abruptly in what amounted to a Western—and indeed an American—victory. In the United States itself the daily rhythms of life remained the same, but thinking men and women now had reason to assume that a great burden of danger and sacrifice had been lifted from their backs. The decade that followed brought unprecedented prosperity and a sense of American triumphalism. Then, on September 11, 2001, this illusion was destroyed in a matter of minutes when terrorists attacked and killed some 3,000 people on American soil. The world, it became abruptly clear, was still a dangerous place for the United States and for Americans.

In domestic affairs the 1990s were divisive. In politics, the new administration under George Bush (senior) seemed a bland extension of its conservative predecessor. But the eight years in office of Bush's successor, William Jefferson Clinton, generated a wave of vindictive partisanship on the right that startled even savvy observers. Reinforced by moral indignation over Clinton's sexual misdeeds, it provoked the first impeachment trial of a president in 135 years. Meanwhile, outside the political realm, the decade would bring to the surface forces, urges, agendas, and opinions that had been muted before. In the post-Cold War era, the nation would discover within itself deep fissures—ideological, cultural, and social. The decade began with a recession and ended with an extraordinary boom. Although the gains were not enjoyed by all equally, it reduced the unemployment rate to levels not seen since the 1960s. Then, as the new century opened, the economic bubble burst. After the terrorist attack of September 11, 2001 there could be little doubt that the economy plunged into a deep and painful recession.

Faced by the new hazards of the twenty-first century, how would a nation so culturally diverse, so politically at odds, survive and prosper? Would the abrupt end of the boom and the new crisis abroad further divide the country? Or would adversity, as so often in the past, touch and activate reserves of strength that would actually make America a more united, rational, and benevolent society?

■ THE BUSH ADMINISTRATION ■

The 1988 Presidential Election. As the 1988 presidential election approached, Democrats took heart. The "Great Communicator" would soon be off to California and trouble them no more. In the end the Democratic nomination narrowed down to the governor of Massachusetts, Michael Dukakis, a brainy technocrat who claimed to have made his state into a model of high-tech efficiency worthy of emulation by the whole nation. Dukakis chose Senator Lloyd Bentsen of Texas, a conservative Democrat, as his running mate. On the Republican side, Vice President George Bush quickly leaped ahead of his chief adversary, Senator Minority Leader Robert Dole. Winning on the first ballot at New Orleans, he chose a young, rather callow senator from Indiana, Dan Quayle, to share the ticket.

The campaign was no credit to the American political process. Dukakis sought to emphasize "competence" over ideology; he would make America competitive again in the world economy. But the Democrats also harped on the fact that Quayle had ducked active military duty in Vietnam in favor of safe and comfortable National Guard service and had a feeble academic record to boot. The Republican campaign was even more negative. The most effective Republican campaign ad was a TV spot featuring a convicted black murderer, Willie Horton, who, while on furlough under a Massachusetts prison release program during Dukakis's administration, had raped a white woman. The Democrats charged that the Republicans were appealing to racial bigotry. But the spot seemed to be effective with some white voters.

Dukakis proved to be an awkward, wooden campaigner who struck few sparks. Bush, however, was able to shake off his preppie image and take on some of the glow of Ronald Reagan. He also made effective use of the public's deep aversion to taxes. His most memorable campaign line was: "Read my lips; no new taxes." On November 8 the Bush–Quayle ticket won forty states to ten, with a popular vote of 48.8 million to 41.8 million, and an electoral vote of 426 to 112. Dukakis had carried a small group of the most liberal states of the Northeast, the Midwest, and the Pacific Coast, but had lost everywhere else.

The Domestic Scene. As president, George Bush proved to be marginally less conservative than his predecessor. During the campaign he had talked about a "kinder, gentler nation" and a "thousand points of light," phrases that suggested compassion would replace rugged individualism as the administration watchword. As president he made stabs at strengthening environmental safeguards, raising educational standards, and providing help for working mothers. In 1990 he signed the Americans With Disabilities Act, which promised new access for disabled people to mainstream facilities and protected them against discrimination. But he often did not follow through. Bush was a captive of his own antitax promises and the Reagan legacy of enormous federal deficits. There was simply no money for new initiatives even if the president had favored them.

Early on Bush had to deal with the snowballing S&L crisis. Besides the sheer magnitude of the disaster, it soon became obvious that more than incompetence and inattention were involved. Each day brought new revelations of how federal regulators, as well as members of Congress, had abetted the S&L manipulators in exchange for favors and campaign contributions.

Abortion was another prickly domestic problem of the first months of the Bush administration. Social conservatism remained a powerful force in the nation and by the early 1990s it had come to focus most of its energies on reversing the 1973 Supreme Court decision in *Roe* v. *Wade*.

By the end of the 1980s it was clear that the Supreme Court was the key to the pro-life campaign's success. The expectation that a conservative majority would overthrow the liberal abortion rules made each new Supreme Court nomination a battlefield between pro-life and pro-choice proponents. The appointments of Justices Anthony Kennedy and Antonin Scalia had already tipped the balance toward the pro-life side, and in *Webster* v. *Reproductive Health Services* (1989) the court decided by a five-to-four margin that Missouri could limit the right to abortion more strictly than did *Roe* v. *Wade*.

In the summer of 1990 Justice William Brennan, the Court's most liberal member, retired. Bush nominated, and the Senate confirmed, an obscure, but presumably conservative New Hampshire judge, David Souter, to succeed him. Soon after, Thurgood Marshall, the only black justice and an outstanding liberal, joined Brennan in retirement. The overturn of *Roe* v. *Wade*—and much else the liberal Court had made the law of the land—appeared possible.

The Clarence Thomas–Anita Hill Affair. The Court's domination by the political right seemed clinched when Bush nominated Judge Clarence Thomas to succeed Marshall. Thomas was an African American, but he was also a conservative. Bush claimed that Thomas was the person best qualified for the job, but more than a few Americans suspected that as a black man, Thomas could not be "Borked" by the liberals, who would be chary of voting against a man of his race.

But the confirmation process proved to be more than usually rocky. Thomas evaded when asked by senators at the confirmation hearings in October 1991 about his views on abortion. The Bush strategy seemed to be working when, abruptly, a new issue intruded. On October 11 Anita Hill, a black woman law professor at the University of Oklahoma, told the Senate Judiciary Committee that when she worked for Thomas on the Equal Employment Opportunity Commission eight years before he had harassed her by making sexually suggestive remarks and overtures.

Hill's complaints highlighted a long-simmering issue: sexual harassment in the workplace. Many women believed that it was a serious problem all too often ignored. Ardent feminists claimed it was another example of the subordination of women that permeated all of American life. On the other side were those who believed the issue exaggerated. Many men were puzzled about what constituted sexual harassment.

Thomas categorically denied the charges. He was, he said, like so many black males in the past, being "lynched." Most of the senators, recognizing that two of the most delicate subjects in American life—gender and race—were involved, treated the two participants warily. But some feminists saw the all-male inquisitors as insensitive to Anita Hill's concerns. In later months, as they reviewed the confrontation, feminists resolved to make women's views more politically effective. If nothing else, the Thomas confirmation hearings did serve to raise public consciousness of sexual harassment as a problem on the job, on campuses, and in other areas of private life. Revelations of sexual misconduct by public figures were soon making headlines around the country.

The Cold War Ends.   If Bush seemed beleaguered at home, abroad he could glory in the fruits of his predecessors' policies. In Eastern Europe Soviet leader Mikhail Gorbachev was quickly dismantling the communist military alliance, the Warsaw Pact, and discarding the entire repressive political settlement that the Soviets had imposed in Eastern Europe after 1945. The Iron Curtain was soon gone. In 1989 popular movements in Poland, Hungary, Romania, Bulgaria, Czechoslovakia, and the German Democratic Republic replaced corrupt and tyrannical Communist regimes with administrations professing democracy and respect for free market economics. No other episode of the miraculous year would match the razing of the Berlin Wall as a symbol of change. The world watched transfixed as cheering crowds dismantled the wall and Germans on both sides of the line joyously mingled as one people for the first time since 1945. Propelled by Chancellor Helmut Kohl of West Germany, the Communist collapse in East Germany was quickly converted into an economic merger of the two Germanies, soon followed by full political union. For good or ill, Germany would be reunited into one powerful nation for the first time since 1945.

Meanwhile the Soviet leader, bedeviled by a fast sinking economy, was making further cooperative arrangements with the United States. In May 1989 the United States and the Soviets agreed to reopen the START nuclear disarmament talks, and Gorbachev and Bush both proposed substantial cutbacks in the troops and conventional weapons deployed against each other in Europe. By this time the Soviets had withdrawn their military forces from Afghanistan after admitting that the 1979 invasion had been an blunder that had cost the Soviets thousands of lives and enormous resources. The Taliban, a fanatically fundamentalist student-led Islamic party, backed initially by the United States to help fight the Soviet invasion, would soon move into the country's power vacuum. The Russians also began to reduce their support for revolutionary client regimes in Africa, Asia, the Middle East, and Latin America, including Cuba. Deprived of Soviet subsidies and arms, many of the left wing insurrections around the world subsided.

Even the People's Republic of China felt the effects of the freedom wind that began to sweep the world. Mao's successors had jettisoned the hard-line Communist micromanagement of the economy, and foreign capital and technology poured into the country. Though liberalizing the economy, the aging Chinese leaders, Deng Xiaoping and Li Peng, refused to allow a democratic,

444 · Chapter 31

multiparty system and a free press. Among a brave core of students and intellectuals, influenced by Soviet reforms and western values, the mood soon turned bitter.

On May 17, 1989, during a visit to China by Gorbachev, a million protesters camped out in Beijing's Tiananmen Square to demand political change. The protesters, predominantly young men and women, proclaimed their democratic agenda in massive posters and in a large plaster statue that resembled the Statue of Liberty in New York harbor. In early June the hard-line regime ordered the army to clear the square. The brutal operation, caught on tape for the world to see, cost many hundreds of lives and was followed by the trial and conviction of many Tiananmen Square demonstrators.

Americans had applauded the Chinese "Pro-Democracy Movement" as a promise that the world's largest nation was about to be liberated from the Communist yoke. The crackdown outraged westerners and many Americans demanded economic and diplomatic sanctions against the People's Republic. In the end, caution prevailed. The Bush administration condemned the repression and called for liberalization of Chinese political life, but refused to break off the profitable new economic ties with Beijing. Critics accused the administration of putting dollars before democracy.

Chinese backsliding notwithstanding, the Cold War was clearly over. Containment, it seemed, had worked! Few Americans could resist a rush of exhilaration. In the first flush of jubilation, foreign-policy expert Francis Fukuyama published an article entitled "The End of History," proclaiming that the world's dangerous confrontations were finally at an end. The system of liberal capitalism was now universally prized, he asserted, and the bases for world conflict were finally gone. Time would show that the triumph of democratic and free-market values, epitomized by the United States, would scarcely be complete and indeed America would come to seem to some influential groups a lamentable force in the world.

■ THE GULF WAR ■

In the summer of 1990 the euphoria was quickly dissipated by a major international crisis. Suddenly it became clear that the world was still an uncertain and dangerous place, perhaps more unstable than ever, and that Americans could not afford to bury their heads in the sand.

Iraq Invades Kuwait. During the drawn-out Iraq–Iran War of 1980–1988, the United States had tilted toward Iraq. Although it was the aggressor in the war and although its leader, Saddam Hussein, was a brutal tyrant who used terror tactics and poison gas against his own people, Iraq seemed preferable to an Iran controlled by the hostile Shiite Muslim fundamentalists under Ayatollah Khomeini, who had taken American embassy hostages in 1979. American arms support had helped prevent Iraqi defeat, and by 1988 the two Mideast countries had negotiated a cease-fire.

The Iraqi urge to dominate the oil-rich Persian Gulf, which had inspired the attack on Iran, had not subsided with the peace, however. In fact, Iraq's need to pay the billions of debt incurred by the war gave Saddam a new reason for aggression against his Gulf neighbors. Yet it was a complete surprise when, on August 2, 1990, Iraqi troops and tanks thrust across the border into the small, oil-rich kingdom of Kuwait and seized control of the country. Soon after, Saddam announced that Kuwait would be incorporated into Iraq as its nineteenth province. Would Iraq stop at Kuwait? After gobbling up that small kingdom, the world wondered, what would keep him from further conquests in the Persian Gulf including the rich but militarily weak kingdom of Saudi Arabia? Dismay was triggered by abhorrence of naked military aggression. But the Persian Gulf was also the world's richest producer of petroleum, with Saudi Arabia by itself the largest supplier of oil. Could the industrial world tolerate allowing an adventurer like Saddam to have a choke hold on much of the world's petroleum supply? There was also the frightening matter of nuclear arms. Saddam had long sought to acquire nuclear weapons. Set back for years by an Israeli air attack on his nuclear facilities in 1981, he had resumed the quest to make Iraq a nuclear power. Now that Saddam had revealed his aggressive policies, the nuclear issue became urgent. If he succeeded in constructing an atomic arsenal the entire Mideast, even the world, would be destabilized in ways too frightening to contemplate.

Reacting quickly, the United Nations Security Council, with strong American support, passed resolutions condemning the unprovoked aggression against Kuwait and demanding that the Iraqis withdraw their invasion troops. Until they did UN members would embargo all goods and supplies to Iraq and refuse to buy Iraqi oil. But would economic sanctions be enough? If Saddam refused to comply, the UN lacked the military power to force him. In that case, clearly, the United States would have to bear the primary burden of blocking his imperial designs.

Despite public fears, Bush quickly dispatched 125,000 troops to Saudi Arabia. Meanwhile, Secretary of State James Baker and Defense Secretary Richard Cheney criss-crossed the Atlantic to line up military, diplomatic, and financial support for American intervention. Egypt, Syria, and other Arab nations, as well as Britain, France, Italy, and other NATO allies pledged troops and financial help for Operation Desert Shield. Even Russia endorsed the sanctions against Iraq, though the Soviet government remained uneasy about the massive intrusion of the United States into the sensitive Mideast.

During the fall and early winter of 1990 troops, supplies, munitions, and weapons piled up in Saudi Arabia. Most of the troops were American and they reflected the new, revitalized post-Vietnam military. All-volunteer, it included many black and Hispanic troops and, for the first time, a substantial proportion of women, though not generally in combat positions.

Meanwhile, despite the UN embargo and oil sanctions, Saddam's army defiantly dug in along the Kuwait–Saudi border, prepared to fight the kind of defensive war that had served so effectively against Iran. Playing to fears of the American public, Saddam thundered that he was prepared for the "Mother of Battles." He would turn any coalition attack into a bloodbath and would not

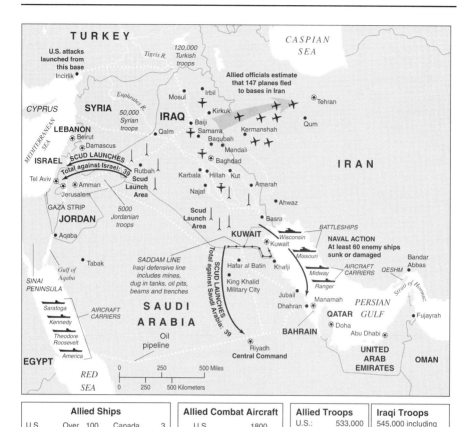

TURKEY

U.S. attacks
launched from
this base
• Incirlik

Tigris R.

120,000
Turkish
troops

*CASPIAN
SEA*

Allied officials estimate
that 147 planes fled
to bases in Iran

⊕ Tehran

CYPRUS   **SYRIA**

Euphrates R.

• Mosul

• Irbil

• Kirkuk

IRAQ   • Baiji

Kermanshah

• Qum

MEDITERRANEAN SEA   **LEBANON**

50,000
Syrian
troops

⊕ Beirut

⊕ Damascus

• Qalm   • Samarra
   • Baqubah
   • Mandali

ISRAEL   SCUD LAUNCHES

Total against Israel: 39

Tel Aviv ⊕   ⊕ Amman
⊕ Jerusalem

⬥ Baghdad

I R A N

⬥ Rutbah

Scud
Launch
Area

Karbala • Hillah • Kut

• Najaf

• Amarah

GAZA STRIP

JORDAN

5000
Jordanian
troops

• Aqaba

• Ahwaz

Scud
Launch
Area

• Basra

BATTLESHIPS

KUWAIT   Wisconsin

⊕ Kuwait

Missouri

NAVAL ACTION
At least 60 enemy ships
sunk or damaged

Bandar
Abbas

• Tabak

*Gulf of
Aqaba*

*SINAI
PENINSULA*

SADDAM LINE
Iraqi defensive line
includes mines,
dug in tanks, oil pits,
beams and trenches

Total against Saudi Arabia: 39

Hafar al Batin   Khafji

King Khalid
Military City

• Jubail

Midway

Ranger

*AIRCRAFT
CARRIERS*

QESHM

Strait of Hormuz

PERSIAN   GULF

Saratoga
Kennedy

*AIRCRAFT
CARRIERS*

**S A U D I
A R A B I A**

SCUD LAUNCHES

Manamah

Dhahran ⊕

QATAR

⊕ Doha

• Fujayrah

Abu Dhabi ⊕

*Theodore
Roosevelt*

Oil
pipeline

• Riyadh

Central Command

BAHRAIN

EGYPT   *America*

*RED
SEA*

0   250   500 Miles

0   250   500 Kilometers

**UNITED
ARAB
EMIRATES**

OMAN

Allied Ships			
U.S.	Over 100	Canada	3
Britain	At least 15	Netherlands	3
France	14	Argentina	2
Italy	10	Turkey	2
Belgium	6	Denmark	1
Germany	5	Greece	1
Spain	4	Norway	1
U.S.S.R.	4	Portugal	1
Australia	3		

Allied Combat Aircraft	
U.S.	1800
Britain	60
France	38
Canada	18
Italy	8
Kuwait	34
Saudi Arabia	300

Allied Troops	
U.S.:	533,000
Coalition:	200,000

Iraqi Troops
545,000 including
110,000 Republican
Guards

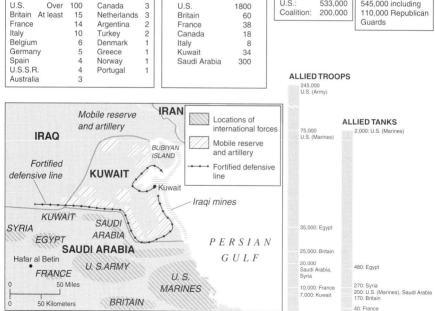

IRAN

Mobile reserve
and artillery

IRAQ

BUBIYAN
ISLAND

Fortified
defensive line   **KUWAIT**

• Kuwait

Locations of
international forces

Mobile reserve
and artillery

Fortified defensive
line

Iraqi mines

KUWAIT   SAUDI

SYRIA

EGYPT   ARABIA

SAUDI ARABIA

Hafar al Betin

FRANCE   U.S. ARMY

0   50 Miles

0   50 Kilometers

BRITAIN

*P E R S I A N
G U L F*

U.S.
MARINES

ALLIED TROOPS

245,000
U.S. (Army)

75,000
U.S. (Marines)

35,000: Egypt

25,000: Britain

20,000
Saudi Arabia,
Syria

10,000: France
7,000: Kuwait

ALLIED TANKS

2,000: U.S. (Marines)

480: Egypt

270: Syria
200: U.S. (Marines), Saudi Arabia
170: Britain

40: France

Gulf War

reject the use of poison gas and germ warfare against his opponents. Appealing to the discontented Arab masses over the heads of their pro-Western leaders, Saddam depicted himself simultaneously as a Robin Hood who would share Gulf oil wealth with the poor and a champion of the Palestinian people in their struggle against Israel.

As a military confrontation approached, the American public debated the Gulf crisis. A majority was convinced from the outset that Saddam was a major threat to world peace and nothing except actual force would deter him. A small minority considered intervention a shameful instance of American imperialism and war-mongering. A much larger bloc of Americans, while deploring Iraqi aggression, favored waiting to see if economic sanctions worked.

War and Victory. The actual shooting war, called Desert Storm, began on January 16 when, on signal from General Norman Schwartzkopf, the commander of the Gulf forces, the United States and its coalition partners launched a massive air offensive against Iraq employing sophisticated new electronically guided weapons. The targets of the initial attacks were Iraqi command headquarters, communications centers, electric power stations, scud missile launchers, chemical weapons factories, and H-bomb development facilities. Though later questioned, the results seemed spectacular at the time. During the next few days the American public saw videos of incredible pinpoint hits on vital Iraqi facilities achieved with few if any coalition losses. A wave of euphoria and relief swept over the nation; the war, it seemed, might be won with air power alone without the need to use ground forces and risk heavy casualties.

Once the fighting started, a wave of patriotism swept the nation and Americans took to wearing red, white, and blue bunting and tying yellow ribbons around curbside trees to indicate support for the troops. In the Middle East, meanwhile, day after day coalition bombers, fighters, and missiles hurtled across the desert to drop their explosives on Iraqi troops, tanks, artillery, bridges, and communications facilities. Much of Iraq's water supply, sewage facilities, and electric generation plants were soon destroyed. Inevitably some Iraqi civilians died.

The Iraqis retaliated by firing off scud missiles, weapons of terror without much military worth. The targets of the scuds were Riyadh, the Saudi capital, and Tel Aviv, Haifa, and other Israeli cities. Israel was not a coalition nation, but Saddam believed that if he could goad the Israelis into retaliation, their response would so offend the Arab world that the hastily forged Gulf coalition would fall apart. Fortunately, powerful pressure from the United States and the loan of American-manned anti-scud Patriot missiles deterred the Israelis from counterattacking. Yet the scuds were more than an annoyance. One disastrous scud missile killed twenty-eight American service troops in Riyadh. The need to take them out tied up many coalition planes and troops.

Americans followed the air war closely as it took its toll of Iraqi strength. The media complained that the government filtered the news from the fighting front and doled it out only through information pools. Most Americans, however, were impressed with the official spokespersons who briefed the reporters and the public daily, particularly Colin Powell, head of the Joint Chiefs of Staff, and Norman Schwartzkopf, commander-in-chief of all the Gulf forces. Both army officers seemed articulate and compassionate men who did not fit the military neanderthal image associated with the commanders in Vietnam.

The long-awaited ground assault came on February 23. General Schwartzkopf had deceived the Iraqis into believing that he would attack across the beaches from the Gulf and head-on from the south across the Saudi–Kuwaiti border. Instead he sent his main armored units in a swing to the west and then north and east around the Iraqi defensive line, cutting off the elite Republican Guards and the bulk of Iraqi armor from retreat to Baghdad. Meanwhile, Saudi, Egyptian, and Kuwaiti troops, bolstered by U.S. marines, crossed directly from Saudi territory into occupied Kuwait.

The armored sweep around their right end smashed the Republican Guard in a brief, one-sided tank battle. In a day or two the vaunted Guard was cut off and forced into a pocket around Basra. Thousands of Iraqis, waving coalition surrender leaflets, gave up without firing a shot. Meanwhile, in sharp fighting south of Kuwait City, the marines and coalition troops forced the main Iraqi army into headlong retreat northward. As they fled, they were mercilessly pounded by coalition planes from the air. Yielding to humanitarian pressure, president Bush ordered a cease-fire rather than continue the slaughter. Before they fled Kuwait, the Iraqis looted the kingdom's capital and ignited thousands of oil wells.

Armored personnel carriers going into battle during Desert Storm.

Only 125 American soldiers died in the fighting in the Gulf in the seven weeks of active air and ground conflict. The Iraqis, however, had suffered thousands of casualties and had lost most of their military equipment. Saddam would be able to repair much of the loss in the months ahead, but the victory was one of the most complete and total in the history of modern warfare.

■ THE ELECTION OF 1992 ■

Victory in the Gulf War did wonders for Bush's popularity, though not everyone felt the war had been perfectly concluded. As the price of ending the coalition attack Saddam was forced to accept UN inspectors to monitor attempts to build weapons of mass destruction and to allow coalition planes to monitor his air space. Some Americans believed that the president should have ordered the coalition troops on to Baghdad, the Iraqi capital, to oust Saddam Hussein from power, a view confirmed by the Iraqi dictator's vengeful treatment after the fighting stopped, of his own nation's Kurdish minority. The Kurds had to be rescued from massacre and starvation by UN forces and relief workers. Still, the public admired the president's overall handling of the Gulf crisis as resolute and effective. A major opinion poll in March 1991 showed that 91 percent of the American people, a truly extraordinary proportion, believed that Bush was doing a good job.

It did not last. The American people had never loved George Herbert Walker Bush as they had Ronnie Reagan. He seemed too much the aloof patrician who tried too hard to affect the common touch. With the onset of the longest recession since the end of World War II his popularity quickly faded.

The Economic Slump. By late 1989 many of the standard economic indicators began to turn down. The real estate boom, fueled by lavish credit from savings and loan associations and by the bounding optimism of the Reagan era, flattened soon after Bush took office. Fear of debt also undermined consumer confidence. Many Americans had gone into hock for cars, boats, VCRs, home computers, second homes, and travel. Once the economic clouds began rolling in, many consumers felt it wiser to save than spend. In short order, the crowds in the shopping malls dwindled and a flock of venerable stores, including the Macy's chain, found themselves in bankruptcy.

The end of the Cold War probably contributed to the recession as well. Congress slashed billions from the budget formerly spent on ships, planes, rockets, tanks, and other weapons. Simultaneously, a congressional Base Closure and Realignment Commission marked military bases for shut down all over the country. Particularly hard hit on both counts were states such as California, Texas, Michigan, and Connecticut where shipyards, gun factories, tank plants, and aircraft companies had flourished or where major air, naval, and army bases had been located. Many communities were economically devastated when the factories and bases closed.

The Bush administration committed a serious political blunder by discounting the severity of the economic downturn and the worries of the voters. The recession would be short and self-righting, the president said. The government must not do anything to worsen the federal deficit, and so should avoid major public works programs or large tax-cuts. Bush endorsed the Federal Reserve's interest rate cuts and pushed minor tax incentives to encourage business investment, but he refused to go further.

The public soon accused the president of obsession with foreign affairs and indifference to domestic problems. By late 1991 the polls revealed a precipitous drop in Bush's popularity. In November, the *New York Times*–CBS poll showed Bush's job performance rating down to 51 percent, a drop of 16 percentage points since October.

The Nomination Battles.   The economic dip formed the background of the 1992 presidential campaign. By the early months of 1992 five Democrats were battling for their party's nomination; three quickly dropped out, leaving former senator Paul Tsongas of Massachusetts, former governor Jerry Brown of California, and Bill Clinton, governor of Arkansas, in the race. The front-runner almost from the beginning, however, was Clinton.

A southerner of working-class origins, William Jefferson Clinton attended Georgetown University and then, in 1968, went to Oxford in England on a prestigious Rhodes Scholarship. These were the turbulent years when many male college students, opposed to the war in Vietnam, resisted being drafted. Clinton was an antiwar activist at Oxford and avoided military service by some dubious maneuvering. Returning from Britain, he entered Yale Law School where he met fellow student Hillary Rodham, a young woman from Illinois. In 1975 they were married.

After teaching and practicing law in Arkansas, Clinton ran for state attorney general. In 1978, at the age of thirty-three, he was elected governor of his home state. In his five terms in the statehouse he won plaudits from his fellow governors for his effective leadership. On the other hand he also made serious enemies, some of whom were appalled by his lax personal morals, others by his moderate policies.

Clinton belonged to the Washington, D.C.-based Democratic Leadership Council (DLC), a group of middle-of-the-road Democrats who opposed the party's left as big spenders and isolationists. The DLC favored cutting federal welfare rolls, encouraging family preservation, holding down deficits, and making the United States strong internationally. Such policies, the DLC leaders believed, would enable the Democrats to recapture the blue-collar voters they had lost to Ronald Reagan and the Republicans. The governor's keynote address to the 1988 Democratic National Convention had put his audience to sleep. But he was an articulate and well-informed man, capable of eloquence and able to project considerable charm and human warmth on public occasions.

Clinton won the nomination on the first ballot in New York and delivered a long-winded "Clinton Special" acceptance speech. He made up for this lapse by choosing the personable young senator from Tennessee, Albert Gore, as his running mate.

Bush, meanwhile, had to fend off Patrick Buchanan, a combative right-wing journalist and TV personality, who claimed to speak for "working people." During the primaries, Buchanan attacked the president as too concerned with overseas problems and at most an ersatz conservative. His most effective jab was that Bush had repudiated his 1988 no-tax pledge, when he had supported the bipartisan 1990 tax bill designed to raise federal revenues by $164 billion over five years. Still, Buchanan could not win more than one third of the vote in any of the Republican state primaries and failed to stop Bush's renomination.

He did force the Republican National Convention in Houston to give him a hearing, however. In a prime-time speech, Buchanan denounced Hillary Clinton as a "radical feminist" and called the coming campaign a religious and cultural war. Moderate Republicans winced at these remarks, and to some voters they seemed strident and divisive. Many observers feared that the Republicans would seek to deflect attention from the slumping economy by stirring up fierce racial and cultural resentments.

The Campaign.   The 1992 presidential campaign marked the political debut of Ross Perot, a self-made Texas billionaire whose chief asset was that he was not a politician. The public had become skeptical of the professional "pols" who seemed incapable of governing. During the previous dozen years a Republican president and a Democratic Congress had been at loggerheads, and few of the country's pressing problems had been addressed. Political life in Washington had also been tarnished by a succession of scandals. In 1990 five United States senators were accused of using their political influence to help the business interests of Charles Keating, head of the Lincoln Savings and Loan Association of California, who was later sent to jail for fraud. Soon after, the public heard that House members had used overdraft checks at the House of Representatives bank, in effect taking interest-free loans for themselves. Public disenchantment with the professional politicians spurred a movement to set term limits on elected officials. By 1992 there was serious talk of a constitutional amendment to keep U.S. senators and representatives from running for reelection more than a prescribed number of times.

Perot profited from the public disgust with politics-as-usual. But in fact, his political views were not easy to define. He favored fiscal restraint and deficit reduction and talked about making America more competitive in the world economy. But he did not seem to possess any core vision. Still, when he announced that if he could get on the ballot in all fifty states he would run for president, many voters responded enthusiastically. As much as a third of the American public initially saw Perot as a real alternative to a corrupt and ineffective party system that had failed the nation. Unfortunately for his followers, Perot was a volatile personality. On July 16, after the Democratic convention, he abruptly announced his withdrawal from the race. Then, on October 1, having sat out much of the campaign, he decided to reenter. He later explained that Bush administration threats to injure his business and disrupt the wedding of his daughter had driven him from the contest. The excuse seemed eerie and many of his followers wondered if the man was not too weird to trust. His candidacy was kept alive, however, by the continuing scorn of many voters for both of the major party nominees.

The job of James Baker, induced to leave the State Department to take over the flagging Republican campaign, was formidable. Week after week the economic indicators reinforced the sense of economic malaise. Everyone knew that the slumping economy was the Republicans' albatross. James Carville, the Democratic campaign manager, had prepared a large sign that he prominently displayed at campaign headquarters—"It's the Economy, Stupid!"—to keep the party contest in clear focus. And generally it remained on target. To contrast with the timid Republican wait-and-see attitude toward the economy, the Democrats promised tax breaks for the middle class, deficit reduction, a more efficient health care system, and heavy investment in education and long-neglected infrastructure to increase America's international competitiveness.

To deflect Democratic attacks, Bush offered one-time economic payoffs to key constituencies. But outbidding the Democrats economically took second place to undermining Clinton's reputation and character. Just before the New Hampshire Democratic primary, a former nightclub singer, Gennifer Flowers, had told a supermarket tabloid that she and Clinton had had a twelve-year romantic affair during his governorship. The accusations almost derailed the Clinton nomination campaign and many voters were left with a sense that Clinton had been less than fully candid. The adultery charge had been contained by the time the presidential race itself began, but the Republicans probed other weak spots in Clinton's personal armor. George Bush had been a navy pilot in World War II and been shot down by the Japanese over the Pacific. Clinton, though the right age for combat in Vietnam, had, as we saw, not served.

But nothing worked for the Republicans. In November Clinton took 32 states with 370 electoral votes and 43 percent of the popular vote (43.7 million). Bush won 168 electoral votes from the remaining 18 states with 38 percent of the popular vote (38 million). Perot did not carry a single state but received 19 percent of the popular vote (19.2 million).

■ CLINTON'S FIRST TERM ■

The American public was initially more than willing to give the young, photogenic president the benefit of the doubt. Perhaps he could revive the economy, improve education and health care, control the burgeoning deficit, and usher in an era of international stability and justice. It did not take long for Clinton to dissipate much of this initial hope and goodwill.

Early Gaffes.   The public gave mixed reviews at best to his choices for cabinet- and subcabinet-level posts. Clinton made no bones about the demographic goals of his appointment agenda. He wanted, he said, to have a cabinet that "looked like America," and, all told, of fourteen people nominated for cabinet positions, two were Hispanic, three were black, and three were women. By his second term half of these appointees had come under legal scrutiny for public or private transgressions.

Clinton seemed inept in his effort to find a female attorney general. Inspired by the First Lady, herself a highly successful lawyer much admired by feminists, his initial choice was Zoe Baird, chief counsel for the Aetna Insurance Company. Unfortunately Baird had employed an illegal alien from Peru to take care of her child, contrary to the immigration laws. He next proposed federal judge Kimba Wood of New York for the Justice Department job. But she, too, had employed an illegal alien as household helper. Not until mid-March did unmarried Florida state attorney Janet Reno, his third choice, make it through to confirmation.

By now many people had begun to question both the administration's political judgment and the president's steadfastness. Polls in late May showed that Clinton's approval rating was the lowest for any president at his stage of office since polling began in the 1930s. At the end of the month, in a major damage-control move, he appointed David Gergen, an ex-Reagan strategist, as White House adviser.

Gergen's steadying presence may explain what many observers considered a very shrewd selection for Supreme Court justice in mid-1993. Clinton's choice settled on Judge Ruth Bader Ginsburg of New York. Ginsburg was a liberal, but not an ideologue. She supported a woman's right to abortion but rejected judicial activism. Her nomination sailed through the Senate without serious demurrer. The appointment helped protect *Roe* v. *Wade* for the foreseeable future, but it did not end the picketing outside abortion clinics and the attempts by pro-life activists to disrupt their operations. In fact, the rancor over abortion seemed to get worse. In March 1993 David Gunn, an abortion clinic doctor, was shot to death in Pensacola, Florida, by a 37-year-old pro-life activist. Pro-choice proponents were soon warning that legal abortion was being nullified by violence and intimidation.

Gays in the Military.   In the midst of the attorney general fiasco, Clinton issued a series of executive orders that offended many conservative Americans, though they clearly pleased liberals. In short order the president lifted the so-called gag rule that forbade federally funded family planning clinic personnel from discussing the abortion option with clients; rescinded restrictions on using fetuses from elective abortions in federally funded medical research; and ordered Secretary of Health and Human Services Donna Shalala to review a Bush-era prohibition on the French-developed RU-486 abortion pill. In the environmental area Clinton ordered the Forest Service to halt clear-cutting by loggers in the Sierra Nevada region to protect the endangered spotted owl. He also cancelled the Bush-created Council on Competitiveness, an agency designed to facilitate business by loosening the restrictions on environmental practices. Meanwhile, Interior Secretary Bruce Babbitt sought to raise the fees paid by ranchers, loggers, and miners for the use and exploitation of federal lands.

The most controversial executive order of all, however, related to homosexuals in the military. For many years gay men and lesbians had quietly served in the nation's armed forces. Few doubted that they had made as good soldiers, sailors, or airmen as heterosexuals. But they could only serve if they hid their sexual identities. Open acknowledgment or discovery of gay preferences had been punished by dismissal from the military. Clinton had made a promise during the campaign to lift the discrimination against gays in the services if elected and had won the support of gay voters. Soon after the inauguration, he sought to follow through on his promise by executive order.

Social conservatives objected to giving homosexuality moral and legal parity with heterosexuality. Many military leaders claimed that acknowledged gays would undermine the esprit de corps of military units and so reduce their combat effectiveness. In Congress, the Senate Republican minority leader, Robert Dole of Kansas, and Democrat Sam Nunn of Georgia, head of the Senate Armed Services Committee, threatened to override Clinton's executive order by statute if he persisted. After much backing and filling, the president arranged a compromise. Called "don't ask, don't tell" by the media, it provided that the military authorities would not question new recruits on their sexual orientation and would not investigate the sexual preferences of military personnel already serving. For their part, gays and lesbians would not make public their sexual preferences and would not engage in sexual activities while on duty on pain of discharge from the service. It seemed a makeshift solution and it pleased few completely. Most Americans, however, polls showed, believed the agreement an acceptable solution to a difficult problem.

Foreign Affairs. Clinton's early unsteadiness in domestic matters was matched by his waffling on foreign policy. By 1993 the former Soviet Union had disappeared as a political entity following an attempted coup by old-line Communists against the reformer Mikhail Gorbachev. Democratic forces, led by Boris Yeltsin, the president of the Russian Federation, rushed to Gorbachev's support and squelched the revolt, but Gorbachev himself did not long remain in power. Yeltsin became head of the Soviet state and moved quickly to establish a market economy, abolish the Communist party, create democratic institutions, a free press, and an independent judiciary. Soviet troops were removed from the non-Russian parts of the old USSR, allowing a flock of nationalities—Ukrainians, Kazakhs, Uzbeks, and others—to create their own independent nation-states. The Soviet Union itself disappeared as a political entity.

During the administration's early months the fate of the former Yugoslavia was a more agonizing issue even than Russia. Located in the chaotic Balkan peninsula, Yugoslavia had been cobbled together after World War I out of a diversity of ethnic and religious groups. Fierce antagonisms among these had been held in check by the Communist regime established in 1946 by Marshal Josip Broz Tito, but after Tito's death in 1980 the country quickly fell apart. The core, Serbia, with its capital in Belgrade, remained under the control of the largest ethnic group, the Orthodox Christian Serbs. Other ethnic groups, however, formed their own independent states. In the midsection of the former Yugoslavia, with their capital in Sarajevo, were the Bosnians, many of whom were Muslims, despised by the Christian Croats and Serbs alike. In 1992 the Bosnians too proclaimed their independence. The European nations and the

United States recognized the independence of all the Yugoslav successor states except Macedonia, to which Greece, a NATO member, objected, fearing designs on its own territory.

Coveting its territory and hostile to Muslims, neither the Serbs nor the Croats were willing to accept an independent Bosnia, at least not with its generous initial boundaries. Serbs and Croats soon launched a campaign to destroy the new Bosnian nation or at least compress it into a mini-state composed almost entirely of Muslims. The Serbs, especially, employed "ethnic cleansing" terror tactics to drive the Muslim population out of regions they coveted. The process reeked of the Nazi Holocaust and sent a shudder through the European and American publics.

But West Europeans and Americans initially refused to become entangled in the age-old hatreds of the Balkans. During the 1992 presidential campaign Clinton scolded the Bush administration for timidity and promised to use American influence and, if needed, its military power, to stop the atrocities in Bosnia. After his inauguration, however, he refused to authorize the use of force until and unless the West European nations, closer than the United States to the killing fields, were willing to intervene directly. They said no, and Clinton threw up his hands in frustration. Some observers depicted the response as another sign of Clinton's weakness and indecisiveness on the foreign-policy front.

Americans did not need to look any further than Somalia to see the dangers of foreign intervention when humanitarian considerations, rather than vital U.S. interests, were the primary concern. The Somalia difficulty was not of Clinton's making. Back in December 1992, just after his election defeat, the lame duck Bush had sent a force of U.S. marines into the East African nation to prevent mass starvation due to a severe drought and political chaos. The mission—Operation Restore Hope—was purely humanitarian, Bush said, and American troops would be back home in two or three months.

The troops restored order and ended the famine. Announcing that the mission had been accomplished, Bush ordered withdrawal of most American armed personnel. In May 1993 the UN took over the job of protecting the relief workers and medical personnel who remained in the country. Some 5,000 Americans were assigned to the UN forces.

After Clinton took office, the picture changed. During the summer Somali warlord Mohammed Farah Aidid, initially cowed, attacked and killed fifty Pakistani UN peacekeepers. The UN forces, including Americans, soon gave chase to capture him and destroy his power. In September Aidid's forces ambushed a group of Americans under UN command, killed fifteen, and dragged their bodies with glee through the streets. The American public, having enthusiastically supported Operation Restore Hope, now screamed with pain. American troops must be brought home immediately! In Congress, Republicans, though hawkish under their own president, now sounded like isolationists. Clinton was risking American lives unnecessarily, they announced, and for a time Congress threatened to limit his power to send troops into dangerous areas or place Americans under UN command.

To many observers, the Somali imbroglio seemed a cautionary tale that must be heeded in the future: The United States could not be the world's emergency rescue squad. Speaking before the United Nations in New York in September 1993 Clinton finally acknowledged the reality by calling for well-defined missions for the world organization and distinct plans for pull-outs when these were accomplished. Unfortunately, we now know, the American retreat in Somalia encouraged terrorists into believing the United States was too cowardly to defend itself.

Domestic Accomplishments.   By the summer of 1993 the administration finally seemed to be moving on the domestic front. On February 17 the president asked Congress for increased long-term government outlays on education, job training, and research in line with Labor Secretary Robert Reich's views that the

Hillary Clinton, the First Lady, and Bill Clinton in a happy moment. Not all moments of his presidency were this sunny.

United States needed a skilled and educated labor force to compete in the globalized economy. He also asked for investment in the nation's dilapidated transportation system and in a high-speed national computer network to make it a leader in "the information age." On this occasion Clinton broached the important issue of national health care. He would soon submit a health plan to Congress developed by a task force headed by his wife, Hillary Rodham Clinton, he announced. The public liked the speech and the plan. But the succession of White House missteps, including the mysterious mass firing of the White House travel office, continued to undermine the public's confidence in the administration.

By this time the administration could count on some solid victories. In early February the president signed into law a Family Leave Bill allowing employees several months of unpaid leave from their jobs to attend to young children or sick relatives. Soon after, Clinton signed the "Motor Voter" bill easing the complicated voter registration process in federal elections by automatically registering voters at the time they applied for auto licenses. Soon after Congress passed the president's National Service Plan for Youth, a scheme to help pay education cost for thousands of young Americans who signed up to serve the elderly, the poor, the homeless, and other disadvantaged groups as part of a domestic Peace Corps.

More significant was passage of the North American Free Trade Agreement (NAFTA), a major addition to the globalization process now underway. This pact merged Canada, the United States, and Mexico into a single economic market of over 350 million consumers and producers unobstructed by tariffs or other barriers. Many Americans feared that it would accelerate the departure of factories and jobs south of the border, and several of the major U.S. industrial unions opposed it bitterly. The treaty had been negotiated by the Bush administration, and at first Clinton seemed reluctant to support it, especially because so many Democrats were beholden to union political support. But by the fall of 1993, he had concluded that he must stand up for freer international trade generally if the United States was to compete in the global economy, and he decided to make NAFTA's passage a test of his leadership. In November, after a major administration show of political muscle, the treaty won by a narrow vote. Though the victory margin included more Republican than Democratic yeas, most informed observers gave Clinton an "A" for presidential leadership.

National Health Insurance. By a wide margin Clinton's most ambitious domestic initiative during his first year was his health insurance scheme. Drawn up by a Health Task Force headed by Hillary Clinton, it was submitted to Congress in late September 1993.

By this time the country's health delivery system seemed in crisis. Health costs as a proportion of total domestic product were already close to 15 percent, about $1 trillion annually, and climbing higher. America's outlays on health care were larger proportionately than any other country's. Whole sectors of the economy would inevitably contract as health care expanded. Already many large American business firms were complaining bitterly that a large part of the cost of their product represented health care outlays for their workers.

But even at these bloated levels the system did not do a consistently good job. Many Americans were indeed adequately insured against illness, and many more at least muddled through under the existing system. The millions of Americans with health insurance or on Medicare received competent medical attention. But there were an estimated 37 million Americans who had no health care coverage at all. Such people, usually the working poor, did without medical attention entirely or were thrown on the dubious resources of public hospitals or of private hospital emergency rooms. The public paid for these services indirectly, either through higher community taxes or through medical charges passed along to insured patients. But even the insured often could not count on health coverage to protect them adequately. Many health plans excluded preexisting conditions or serious chronic disease. People forfeited their coverage when they lost or left their jobs. Retirees on Medicare had to pay for their medicines, often a major cost for people living on pensions.

The Health Task Force under the First Lady held hearings around the country seeking advice from experts. Fearing that leaks would enable the lobbyists and the skeptics to pick apart any plan before it could be officially submitted, the task force kept its meetings and its deliberations private, a procedure that aroused criticism. When the 246-page health plan was finally submitted to Congress in late September 1993, it set off one of the most intense political debates, in Congress and out, since the 1960s.

The plan rejected "single-payer" national health insurance administered by the government and paid for largely by taxes. Instead, the Clinton plan proposed "managed competition." Regional health alliances would represent consumers in striking bargains with drug companies, doctors, and hospitals for the lowest costs. All citizens would be covered whether they worked for large corporations, which normally paid employees' health insurance, or for small firms, which often did not. People would not be denied health insurance for preexisting conditions or dumped from the insurance rolls because they lost their jobs. Employers and patients would pay much of the cost. The self-employed would pay their costs themselves, but could deduct these from their income tax. The remaining funding would come from a tax on cigarettes and perhaps hard liquor, two items that allegedly contributed to poor health in the first place.

Most Americans initially favored the president's proposals. His televised presentation to Congress was agile and convincing. At one point, brandishing a pen, he declared dramatically that if any bill that came from Congress did not include universal coverage, he would veto it. But as the measure worked its way through the legislative process the public began to have doubts. In Congress conservatives attacked it as likely to expand the already excessive federal bureaucracy. Some liberals continued to prefer the single-payer scheme as in Canada. Outside Congress every group with a stake in the nation's health care system weighed in. The insurance companies, certain that they would be deprived of profits, mounted major TV advertising campaigns to convince the public that the bill was unworkable. Small business attacked it as a crippling burden that they could not afford. Physicians groups also took potshots at the administration measure. As the bill wended its way through Congress it was eroded by successive concessions of the White House and the Democratic leadership.

And in the end the bill did not pass. In late September 1994 Senate Majority Leader George Mitchell of Maine declared the health care reform drive dead for the 103rd Congress. He and other administration supporters vowed to take the measure up again the following year but, with Republican gains in the forthcoming elections likely, few believed it possible to achieve major revision of the nation's health care system in the foreseeable future.

In the years that followed more and more Americans, either voluntarily or by compulsion, joined health maintenance organizations (HMOs), private, usually for-profit, health corporations run by hospitals, doctors, or entrepreneurs. These helped check rising health costs for a time but only by providing assembly-line service, stinting on procedures, and refusing to treat special cases. Some Americans wondered if the Clinton plan, for all its unwieldiness, would not have been better. Yet all told, however well intentioned, his effort to reform the health insurance of the American people had hurt the president's standing, reversing the popularity gains of the previous year.

Scandals. By mid-point in his first term the Clinton record was, in fact, a mixed bag. Yet the public had the decided impression that the president was not a strong leader. His partisans argued that the fault was as much the voters' as the president's. The American people did not know what they wanted in either foreign policy or in domestic matters and any initiative was certain to come under fire from all sides. Some of the same people who were attacking the president for weak leadership were also decrying his character. Undoubtedly Clinton was less than a saint. Even after he became president various young women showed up at press conferences and on talk shows to accuse him of sexual indiscretions while he was governor of Arkansas. One of these was Paula Jones, an Arkansas state employee who claimed that Clinton, while governor, had summoned her to a hotel room and then asked her for sex. She claimed she had suffered severe psychological trauma. In May 1994, just before the statute of limitations went into effect, Jones filed a lawsuit for sexual harassment against the president. Clinton's attorney sought to have the suit delayed until after the president left office on the grounds that it would interfere with the vital business of the country's Chief Executive, but in mid-1997 the Supreme Court decided that even the president was not exempt from civil legal action.

More serious, it seemed, were charges that the Clintons had used their powerful position in Arkansas during his governorship to advance their own financial interests. One such claim involved a remarkable gain for Hillary Clinton in a commodities market deal alleged to have involved insider information. Still more serious was "Whitewater," the generic term for a complicated real estate deal by Clinton while governor to develop a tract of land for housing and recreation in the Ozarks. Critics claimed that it involved illegal relations with business groups, including Savings and Loan promoters. The Clintons said that there had been nothing illegal about the Whitewater venture; and they had actually lost money on the deal.

Attorney General Janet Reno, under pressure from the Republicans, finally appointed a special prosecutor to look into Whitewater. He was replaced during the summer of 1994 by Kenneth Starr, a conservative lawyer less friendly to the Clintons. In July Congress began hearings on the role of the Treasury Department and the White House in trying to fend off investigators. If the president and his wife had been more forthcoming, observers said, they might have been believed. Instead, they seemed determined to cover up the details of the scheme and did everything they could to avoid an investigation. At one point Hillary Clinton, some charged, had sought to obstruct justice in a matter concerning her work for Madison Guarantee Savings and Loan, a Whitewater-involved company while she worked for the Rose Law Firm in Little Rock. The files on her work for a time were lost and then, in 1996, mysteriously turned up in the White House.

The 1994 Midterm Elections.   By the midterm congressional elections many voters were disappointed with the president's leadership. The Republicans for their part conducted a vigorous campaign based on a conservative manifesto, "The Contract for America," that pilloried liberalism and promised an "end of government that is too big, too intrusive, and too easy with the public's money." The election produced a major shift rightward in Congress. Twenty-three incumbent House Democrats, including the scandal-ridden Speaker, Tom Foley, were defeated and the Republicans gained some 50 House seats in all, giving them control of the lower house. Many of the new Republican freshmen were conservative firebrands determined to rigorously apply their small-government, balanced-budget, antiwelfare and antientitlement principles. The new House Speaker would be Newt Gingrich of Georgia.

A highly partisan Republican, who in previous Congresses had savaged the Democrats, Gingrich promised to enact the Contract for America. In short order the Republicans introduced a balanced-budget constitutional amendment, a tougher crime bill, a major welfare reform bill, a measure to encourage savings, a proposal to discourage product liability law suits, a law to set term limits for members of Congress, and a capital gains tax cut to encourage business growth. Unfortunately for the conservative agenda, Gingrich proved to be no match for the president in political maneuver. Gingrich lacked the capacity to please and his image as a harsh ideologue was further blackened by charges that he had used tax-deductible donations to fund an American history course he taught at a small Georgia college. Not long after this he was also charged with accepting a $4 million advance from publisher HarperCollins for writing two books while in office, an act that seemed a blatant attempt to capitalize on the power and prestige of his office. (Gingrich cancelled the book contract, but in December 1996 the House Ethics Committee would censure him for the misuse of campaign funds, and in 1997 fine him $300,000 for breaking the House's ethics rules.)

Meanwhile, Clinton moved adroitly toward what he perceived as the vital center. The American public wanted the traditional welfare system altered so that able-bodied adults would be compelled to work rather than subsist on a dole. They also wanted an end to soaring federal deficits. But as usual they did not want change that might reduce their own comfort. Serious funding problems for Social Security and for Medicare and Medicaid loomed, but few Americans wished to reduce benefits, or at least not for their own group.

During 1995 and 1996 the president and the Republican Congress jockeyed over the conservative agenda. Clinton proved remarkably flexible—some liberals called it spineless. He accepted with only minor demurrers the Republican plan to overturn the sixty-year-old federal welfare system instituted during New Deal days. The welfare bill he signed in July 1996 replaced federal cash payments to the poor with block grants to the states to administer welfare programs of their own individual devising. Recipients of food stamps and other aid would have to work and any aid given would be subject to time limits. The bill also ended welfare payments to all immigrants, even legal ones.*

The president got the better of the Republicans on the budget. Clinton accepted the need to achieve a balanced federal budget in the not-too-distant future. But he disagreed with his opponents on how soon the goal should be reached, what programs should be cut to achieve it, and whether any new budget should include tax cuts, especially those like lower estate and capital gains taxes that primarily benefitted the prosperous. Twice during the 1995 session of Congress, the White House and Capitol Hill reached an impasse on the federal budget. To pressure the president the Republican-led Congress refused to enact stopgap spending bills and various offices of the federal government simply closed their doors, causing inconvenience for millions. The Republicans had miscalculated. The public blamed Gingrich and his party in Congress and supported Clinton's refusal to yield. By the summer of 1996 Clinton's dismal approval ratings had recovered. By contrast the polls showed that many moderate Americans had lost patience with the Speaker and the conservative partisans elected to Congress in 1994.

■ RACE, GENDER, AND NATIONALITY ■

As the millennium's end approached, major population changes, long underway, began to alter the texture of American life. The new demographics were reflected in Clinton appointment policy, noted above; they played out even more significantly on the nation's cultural and intellectual stages.

Demographic Change. The social profile of the American people altered rapidly in the 1980s and 1990s. During these decades birth rates fell, health improved, men and women lived longer. As the net effect of these trends, between 1980 and 1997 the median age of the American people rose from 30 years to 34.9, the highest it had ever been, and promised to go much higher in the years ahead as the baby boomers of the post-1945 era moved past middle age.

*Later revised to preserve payments to legal immigrants.

The rise in average age was certain to affect American life in profound ways. An aging population was unavoidably an ailing population. Much of the soaring costs of medicine were incurred at the end of life, as doctors employed heroic methods to delay death by a few weeks or months. In the years ahead, demographers predicted, the flood of people in their eighties and nineties would put intense pressure on the already overloaded health care system.

The problem encouraged new approaches to the last years of life. The "living will" movement sought to guarantee the legal right for victims to reject life support systems when all hope for recovery from serious illness had passed. The euthanasia movement sought to allow people with terminal illnesses to choose suicide—to "die with dignity"—rather than linger hopelessly comatose or in pain. Living wills offended relatively few; legal suicide made many Americans uncomfortable. The activities of Dr. Jack Kervorkian, the "Suicide Doctor," assisting seriously ill patients to end their lives, scandalized many and led the Michigan legislature in 1993 to make assisted suicide a crime.

An aging population raised nonmedical problems as well. As the ratio of retired people to workers rose, the need to support the retired promised to be a drag on the incomes of the economically most productive. Many younger workers feared that the Social Security system would become bankrupt and would simply not be there for them when they were ready to retire. In 1983 a bipartisan revision of the Social Security Act had increased Social Security taxes and raised the age at which future pensioners would receive full benefits. But that measure was only a stopgap and down the road there promised to be further actuarial difficulties. The problem raised the specter of a generational battle between younger workers and retirees that few people welcomed.

And what about the psychology of a geriatric society? How would the country deal with a population with an increasingly foreshortened horizon? "Seniors" could not be faulted for special concern about their own immediate circumstances and the here-and-now. But that was not necessarily the best thing for the country as a whole. An aging population was surely a less innovative and less socially conscious population. Would America, as it grayed, become less creative and less compassionate?

The most significant new demographic trends were changes in the nation's ethnic and racial makeup. Overall, United States birth rates had been dropping for some time. Unlike the citizens of several other advanced industrial countries, Americans still had enough babies each year to offset aggregate mortality. But these birth rates were not equal across the ethnic and racial board. Whites had birth rates of 64.7 per thousand women in 1989; blacks had birth rates of 90.4. Hispanic groups, too, especially Mexican-Americans and Puerto Ricans, had higher birth rates than people of European antecedents. By themselves these differentials meant that the population of both blacks and Hispanics would inevitably increase faster than "Anglo" whites.

Immigration. But there was immigration as well. The growing numbers of Euro-Americans and Afro-Americans derived mostly from natural increase. Much of the Hispanic—as well as the Asian—growth came from immigration, rather than births. America remained a magnet for millions around the world, and during the 1980s immigration was responsible for a third of the country's net population increase.

As we saw, as early as the 1970s, the major sources of immigration had switched from Europe to Latin America and Asia. By 1990 three times as many Asians as Europeans came to America each year, and eight times as many people from Latin America, primarily Mexico, the Caribbean, and Central America. These figures, however, described only legal immigration. Many experts held that the illegal immigration from the newer sources was at least as great. Already the differential birth rates of blacks, European whites, Asians, and Hispanics were changing the overall look of Americans. By the 1990 census almost 25 million Americans were Hispanic, and they were the fastest growing group, with increases during the 1980s of a startling 6.1 percent annually. The continuing wave of immigrants was certain to shift the racial and ethnic balance still further as time passed. In 1993 a Census Bureau report predicted that the Hispanic population of the United States would exceed the black population by the year 2010. It also projected a total population of 392 million in 2050, of which only 53 percent would be "Non-Hispanic White," while 16 percent would be black and 22.5 percent Hispanic. At that date Asians-Chinese, Koreans, Indians, Arabs, Pakistanis—about 3 percent in 1990—would make up 10 percent of the total population.

The magnitude of non-European immigration was in part the result of relaxed American immigration practices. The Immigration Reform and Control Act of 1986, modifying the 1965 immigration law, sought to reduce "illegals" by threatening to punish any employer who offered work to someone without the precious "green card" attesting to lawful residence. The law was not effectively enforced, however, and did little to deter illegal entry. Virtually anyone who set foot on American soil could claim asylum from religious or political persecution and stay in the United States if the claim was valid. Many came on student visas and never registered for college classes. The Immigration and Naturalization Service investigation of claims was slow, and the immigrant was allowed to move into the community at large while waiting. Few if any ever appeared to find out what the INS had determined. Students who used their visas as de facto immigration passes were seldom investigated.

Still another leak in the system allowed illegal immigrants to stay if they had children born in the United States. Under the Constitution these children were American citizens and there was no way to deport their parents. Many immigrant couples, critics said, came to the United States and conceived children before the authorities could expel them. They then remained, courtesy of their American-born offspring. In 1990, reflecting the white public's ethnic and economic anxieties, Congress passed a new measure to encourage immigration of Europeans and trained, educated workers.

Despite what Americans considered low wages, long hours, and the absence of benefits, immigrants sought to reach and stay in the United States in every way possible. In some cases Chinese immigrants offered as much as $30,000 to unscrupulous entrepreneurs to smuggle them in and were kept in near-slavery, toiling at menial jobs or even working as prostitutes, until they repaid their debt. This deplorable traffic was highlighted in June 1993 when a small freighter, the *Golden Venture,* carrying 300 ill-fed, sick Chinese aliens, grounded on a New York beach and the illegals and their exploiters were taken into custody.

The loose immigration policies of the United States were thrown into still more vivid relief by the events of early 1993 in lower Manhattan. Suddenly, on February 26, 1993, an explosion ripped through the lower floors of one of the twin towers of the World Trade Center, the second tallest buildings in the nation. Six people died in the explosion in the underground parking garage and thousands had to be hurriedly evacuated by stairs to escape the deadly smoke. No one guessed that the event foreshadowed a far worse catastrophe in the same place eight and a half years later.

In a matter of days combined federal and local police forces discovered the culprits, a group of Muslim immigrants from North Africa and the Middle East who worshiped at mosques in Brooklyn and New Jersey under the spiritual guidance of Sheik Omar Abdel-Rahman, a fundamentalist Egyptian cleric who despised the secular Arab government of his homeland and preached violence against the perceived enemies of Islam, including America. He had been carelessly allowed to enter the United States, even though his extreme views were well documented by the Egyptian authorities. In the next months the FBI uncovered plots among the Sheik's other adherents to blow up the UN, plant bombs in the major tunnels and bridges connecting New York and New Jersey, and assassinate American politicians and American Jewish leaders considered unfriendly to Islamic causes. Four of the defendants in the World Trade Center bombing were convicted in May 1994 and sentenced to long terms in prison. In the summer of 1993 the conspirators in the larger plot were indicted. Ten, including Sheik Rahman, were convicted in October 1995 and sentenced to long prison terms. In late 1997 Ramzi Ahmed Yousef, an admitted terrorist, captured in Pakistan two years before, was convicted of masterminding the World Trade Center bombing.

Without doubt the feelings of native-born Americans toward the newest immigrants were, as in the past, tainted by prejudice. Arab-Americans, for example, clearly suffered from the anti-Muslim attitudes of some Westerners, intolerance reinforced by the World Trade Center bombing and the activities of Sheik Rahman; crude racism obviously played a part in biases against people from Asia and Latin America. But the swelling immigration tide raised reasoned concerns as well. What was the net economic impact, for example, of the flood of immigrants? Did the newcomers take more from the economy in the way of free public education, medical services, and "welfare" than they contributed in taxes and needed skills? Did they displace poor, but striving, native-born Americans from necessary entry-level jobs? Did they depress the wages of the unskilled? The answers were not clear, but the governor of California, a state hard-hit by defense cutbacks and soaring unemployment rates in the early 1990s, concluded that they did. The United States must tighten its immigration laws, declared Governor Pete Wilson, even if this meant repealing the existing citizenship provision of the Fourteenth Amendment.

Nor was Governor Wilson the only one concerned about the costs of uncontrolled immigration. Many black leaders complained that foreigners were undermining the wages of, and stealing jobs from, black American citizens. Some American-born Hispanic citizens also thought that the deluge from Latin America and the Caribbean hurt them economically. Middle-class white Americans seldom competed directly with foreign-born workers from Latin America, but Asians were another case. Many, it seemed, were nosing out white Americans for top professional jobs and elite college admissions. At the prestigious University of California, Asians in turn complained that university officials had put a lid on their admission in order to guarantee blacks, Hispanics, and whites a prescribed proportion of new freshman admissions. When criticized by Asian spokespersons, the Berkeley administration noted that the university "must provide effective leadership in an increasingly multiethnic society. . . ." In effect, "diversity" took precedence over "merit."

The Struggle over Culture.   The changing profile of the American population promised shifts in values and culture. What would these be when a majority of Americans were no longer of European ancestry?

Some effects already seemed apparent. At colleges and universities around the country nonwhite students and faculty, often led by blacks, demanded curricula changes to refocus courses on the achievements, values, and history of non-European peoples. Ever since the 1960s, colleges had offered black history, Asian culture, Latin American studies, and the like. But the Western tradition continued to be the core of the cultural and intellectual curriculum. The new "multicultural" mood on campuses, especially the more cosmopolitan ones, sought to replace this emphasis. At Stanford, for example, the administration dropped the long-term required course "Western Culture" in 1988 in favor of a three-course sequence "Cultures, Ideas, Values," that pared down the European component of the core. Defending the decision, President Donald Kennedy of Stanford announced: "We confirm that many minority issues and concerns are not the special pleadings of interest groups, but are Stanford issues—ones that engage all of us."

Curriculum revisions like Stanford's assumed the idea of a common core for all Americans to share, though a somewhat different one from the past. Some multiculturalists, however, rejected the idea of a shared tradition entirely. Americans had no truly common experience, they seemed to say, and each component of the country's population needed to understand only its own cultural heritage.

The new cultural offensive on campus was directed not only against Euro-centered education. There was a parallel feminist drive to change the campus intellectual and cultural environment. If the usual curriculum gave excessive attention to Europe and its traditions, feminists declared, it was also dominated by the male view of the world.

Feminist scholarship and thought had been evolving ever since the late 1960s toward a view of culture, history, science, and politics that broke with traditional approaches to several of the disciplines. Some feminist scientists claimed that "male" science ignored the intuitive nature of much knowledge; feminist literary critics denounced the exclusion of talented women and their insights from the standard literary "canon"; feminist historians noted that half the world's population had been ignored by the male-led discipline. Feminist social scientists and psychologists also sought to change basic perspectives on the nature of men and women. They distinguished "sex," a biological category, from "gender," a "socially" and historically "constructed" entity. The observable differences between the way men and women thought and behaved, they said, derived predominantly from the cultural environment of a particular time and place, not from body parts and hormones.

The new perspectives of race, ethnicity, and gender were strongest in the academic world, where they were particularly influential in the humanities departments. There, they appealed not just to black and female faculty and students but also to younger men and women who had been influenced by the ideological shifts of the late 1960s and 1970s. In the field of American history, a woman's perspective, an ecological perspective, and a Native American perspective were added to the previously adopted black perspective, to alter the traditional emphases.

One effect of these new currents was to polarize student bodies. Observers of campus life noted that, increasingly, black and white students ate separately, partied separately, and studied separately. On some campuses, black students demanded their own residences and student centers, and university administrations often obliged. Defenders of the self-segregation tendency claimed that it was necessary to protect black students, many from poor inner-city backgrounds, against a hostile, predominantly white university environment. Critics said that it created resentment and encouraged the ghettos it was designed to prevent.

There were also growing tensions on campus between men and women as feminists redefined rape and sexual harassment to include long-tolerated male practices. Some observers felt that the new concern was long overdue. For far too long men had imposed their wills on women in the guise of "boys will be boys." Now men must be made to accept "no" for an answer. Traditionalists often questioned the new attitudes. The evils were exaggerated, they said. Some of the practices proscribed were inevitable parts of the "mating game" and not offenses at all. The university's attempts to protect women, some critics insisted, treated them as children. More than a few men professed to be thoroughly confused about what they could or could not do.

It is hard to say what was cause and what effect, but the new multiculturalism, feminist sensibility, and "political correctness" made some campuses acrimonious places during the early 1990s. At Dartmouth, where an off-campus, student-run, conservative paper frequently attacked "politically correct" views of the college's faculty and students, there were frequent clashes over the whole range of cultural issues. At the University of Pennsylvania nine black students, offended by a *Daily Pennsylvanian* editorial attacking affirmative action, destroyed 14,000 copies of the student newspaper. Modern campuses, one Ivy League professor remarked, had "the cultural diversity of Beirut. There are separate armed camps. The black kids don't mix with the white kids. The Asians are off by themselves. Oppression is the great status symbol."

The new cultural and ideological styles and tensions went beyond the universities. A gay sensibility began to alter the tone and content of the performance and visual arts. One manifestation was a flock of moving plays about the devastation wrought by AIDS on the homosexual community. There was also a growing irreverence toward mainstream "square" values and culture informed by a gay perspective. At times the influence was subtle and nuanced. At other times, however, it challenged "square" moral and aesthetic values by flaunting extreme aspects of the gay sensibility. The photographs of Robert Mapplethorpe, for example, showed men engaged in undisguised sado-masochistic homosexual acts. Even more extreme was an occasional "in your face" confrontational quality apparently designed to offend and provoke. One of the works of Andres Serrano, called "Piss Christ," was a photograph of a crucifix immersed in Serrano's own urine.

Race Relations.   Academe and the intellectual and artistic worlds are rather remote from the lives of most Americans. But the widening national divisions both affected and reflected the way many Americans regarded their fellow citizens.

Race relations during the late 1980s and 1990s in many ways became more tense. Following the successes of the civil rights movement, racial reconciliation and mutual acceptance seemed to spread widely across groups, sections, and classes. The process soon reversed. Economic stagnation and even retreat in the inner cities created a degree of hopelessness and frustration that fed black racial resentments. In some ghetto communities these feelings were directed not just at whites but also at Asian storekeepers, who were accused of treating black customers with suspicion and discourtesy. In New York, Los Angeles, and other cities Korean grocers and black customers engaged in feuds that led to boycotts and picketing.

The late 1980s and 1990s also witnessed an eruption of white racism that frightened many moderate Americans. White supremacist and anti-Semitic groups—"skinheads" and neo-Nazis—proliferated in the Northwest, Mountain States, and the South. In 1991 David Duke, former Grand Wizard of the Louisiana Ku Klux Klan, placed second in the state gubernatorial primary and, in the general election, came frighteningly close to defeating the Democratic candidate.

Serious violence would mar the nation's record of racial tolerance through the period. In 1986, in New York's Howard Beach, a group of white youths attacked some young black men whose presence in their neighborhood they resented, leading to the death of one. The black community demanded and got a special prosecutor to push the case. Violence was narrowly averted when the jury convicted three of the youths of second-degree murder. In another New York neighborhood, where a close-knit community of orthodox Hassidic Jews lived close by a black community, the death of a young black boy in an automobile accident led to several days of racial violence aimed at Jewish residents of Crown Heights, in Brooklyn. A visiting Australian Jewish scholar died during the disturbances, and a black youth was tried but acquitted by a predominantly black and Hispanic jury. In Miami, the shooting of two black motorcyclists in 1989 by a Hispanic policeman set off three days of riots in the black Overtown and Liberty City districts. Six people were shot, 27 stores burned, and 400 people arrested.

Los Angeles, however, was the setting of the most serious racial explosion of all. The city had never solved the problems that triggered the Watts riots of 1965. In the South-Central district poverty remained as ingrained as ever; crack-cocaine had brought wholesale gang violence and murder; family disintegration and out-of-wedlock births had become the norm for thousands of residents. Relations between the black community and the Los Angeles police, never very good, had worsened under police chief Daryl Gates, a man who seemed to have little respect for the city's minority population.

The trigger for massive community violence was the arrest of black motorist Rodney King in early March 1991, after a high-speed freeway chase. The cops kicked and beat King mercilessly for fifteen minutes. The brutal attack on a single unarmed civilian was recorded by a citizen on his video recorder. Played over and over on the local and national airwaves, the tape outraged millions of Americans of all races. The authorities indicted four Los Angeles Police Department members for using excessive force.

The trial, in April 1992, was not held in Los Angeles where the jury was apt to be multiracial but in predominantly white and conservative Simi Valley. On April 29, to the amazement of many Americans, the jury of ten whites, one Asian, and one Hispanic acquitted three of the officers completely and convicted one on a minor charge.

South-Central Los Angeles erupted within minutes in a fountain of rage and violence. White truckers and motorists passing through the community were pulled from their vehicles and beaten and stomped. Hundreds of stores, offices, and shops were torched and looted, with Korean-owned businesses particular targets, though even black establishments were not spared. Latinos and others joined the riots, which spread beyond South-Central and threatened to spill over into affluent white neighborhoods. Not all the destruction was politically motivated. Many of the rioters were obviously taking advantage of group outrage to steal and destroy. The violence spread to several other cities including San Francisco, Atlanta, Seattle, Miami, and Las Vegas. As they watched the TV images of smoke, flame, broken glass, looting, and tear gas, many Americans feared a reprise of the sixties' "Long Hot Summers." After five days, physical and emotional exhaustion, the voices of responsible community leaders, and National Guard and federal troops put a stop to the disorders. Rodney King appeared on TV to ask for calm. "I mean, please, we can get along here," he pleaded. "We can all get along. We've just got to." A final tally listed 58 lives lost and $1 billion of property damage. More than 11,900 people were arrested, mostly for burglary and for receiving stolen goods, a few for beating innocent bystanders.

In the wake of the catastrophe, the presidential candidates visited Los Angeles and made promises that something would be done to improve conditions.

The explosion of violence in South Central Los Angeles following the acquittal of white police officers for a brutal attack on a black driver shocked the country. The rioters beat whites and Hispanics and destroyed property—especially white- or Korean-owned stores.

Los Angeles replaced Police Chief Gates with a man more sensitive to the feelings of the inner city community. In early 1993 the Justice Department indicted the acquitted police on federal charges that they had violated Rodney King's civil rights. This time the trial was held in Los Angeles before a less racially uniform jury, and this time the jury voted to convict two of the four officers. Black Americans by and large felt satisfied by the verdict and there was no eruption.

O. J. Simpson and the Racial Divide.   But concern over the differing black and white perception of justice was revived by the jury decision in the trial of O. J. Simpson for murder of his ex-wife, Nicole Brown and a companion, Ronald Goldman, in June 1994. The case of *The People* v. *O. J. Simpson* riveted the attention of Americans, and millions around the world, as no other criminal trial in recent history.

An African American, Simpson was a former football hero who had a spectacular career playing for the University of California and then for the Buffalo Bills professional team. After football, the handsome, charming "OJ" had become a film actor and a celebrity endorser for the Hertz auto rental agency. Rich and famous, in 1985 he had married a pretty blond "trophy wife" with whom he had two children. But OJ and Nicole were not happy. Some eight times during the 1980s the Los Angeles police had been summoned to their home by Nicole to keep her husband from beating her. In 1992, the two were divorced and Nicole went to live with her children at an apartment not far from OJ's house.

In the late evening of June 12, 1994, a dog walker found the brutally slashed, bloody bodies of Nicole and Ronald Goldman, an employee of the restaurant where she had recently dined. After determining that the dead woman was the ex-wife of Simpson, the police went to his house. He was not home, but according to the detectives' story, outside the house they found a bloody glove similar to the one at the crime scene and detected blood on Simpson's white Ford Bronco parked nearby on the street. (They later found a bloody sock in Simpson's house.) Simpson, however, was in Chicago on a business trip and when informed of the crime returned quickly to Los Angeles.

The case against Simpson was "circumstantial"; no one had seen him commit the two murders. But it was powerful. His blood was found at the scene of the crime; the bloody right-hand glove the police said they had found on OJ's grounds matched the one at the crime scene; Simpson had a deep cut on his hand that explained how his own blood had mixed with the victims' at the crime scene; hair at the crime scene matched Simpson's; carpet fibers from his Ford Bronco matched fibers on a cap at the crime scene; Simpson could not account for his time during the period when the crime was probably committed. There was also believable motivation: Simpson was a ferociously jealous man and a confessed wife beater.

However convincing by the usual measures, not all Americans accepted his guilt. The public divided along racial lines. White Americans as a group were certain that Simpson was a brutal murderer. But a large majority of African Americans rejected this view. Though his connection to the black community was actually tenuous, OJ became a hero of African Americans, an example of a famous "brother" whom white America wanted to destroy as it had so many others before. In the charged atmosphere of suspicion of the police in the wake of the Rodney King beating, it was easy for blacks, especially in Los Angeles, to doubt the evidence the police had gathered and even to believe the LAPD was determined to frame OJ for a crime he did not commit.

The televised trial played to high ratings for 11 months. The prosecution, conducted by Marsha Clark and Christopher Darden, the first white, the second black, made many mistakes including failing to monitor the jury selection process carefully enough. In the end a majority of the jurors were black women, a group that, as a whole, were natural partisans of OJ. The defense, on the other hand, proved immensely skilled in shifting the focus of the trial from the defendant to the supposed misdeeds of the LAPD, who were accused of an elaborate conspiracy to frame OJ for racist reasons. The so-called "dream-team," led by talented black criminal lawyer Johnny Cochrane, was able to nail detective Mark Fuhrman as a blatant bigot who probably planted the second bloody glove simply to destroy the black hero.

The trial concluded on September 29, 1996, and the jurors began their deliberations three days later. After two hours of discussion, they declared O. J. Simpson "not guilty." Black Americans from all walks of life cheered the verdict. Most white Americans were amazed and appalled. Given the makeup of the jury, many were certain that OJ's acquittal was proof that race, rather than innocence, had decided the outcome. The social pundits wondered whether this was a glimpse of a future when white and black perceptions of reality would have little in common.

The Attack on Affirmative Action.   One sore spot in black–white relations was affirmative action. As we saw, this effort to ensure more equal results in hiring, promotion, college and professional school admissions, and other areas, provoked resentment among whites who felt it was "discrimination in reverse." Even some black Americans felt it placed a stigma on their achievements and created a permanent dependence among blacks. Beginning in the early 1990s, opponents of affirmative action launched a major drive to replace it with "color-blind" selection based on "merit" alone.

The issue came to a head in the nation's two largest states, California and Texas. In July 1995 the University of California's Board of Regents dropped affirmative action for admissions to university programs. In March 1996 a federal appeals court declared illegal University of Texas Law School admissions policies favoring black and Hispanic applicants over others. Later that year, California voters approved Proposition 209 forbidding the state government to establish race or gender preferences in educational admissions, public hiring, and public contracting. In August 1997, after an unsuccessful court challenge, it went into effect.

President Clinton joined the affirmative action discussion in the spring of 1997. Clinton himself, as we saw, was a firm believer in diversity and seeking out talent in every group. He endorsed affirmative action though he agreed it might be improved. At the graduation ceremony of the University of California at San Diego he challenged the Regents' decision to drop ethnic and racial preferences at the University and proposed a long, frank dialogue on the subject of race among Americans. He also appointed an advisory board on race relations which, when it refused to hear opponents of affirmative action, was accused of bias against "color-blind" methods of deciding merit.

By this time the results of dropping affirmative action recruitment at the law schools of the Universities of California and Texas had become known. Black enrollments plummeted at both institutions; the number of new Hispanic students also dropped drastically. The outcome was so disappointing that even opponents of affirmative action were dismayed. The two schools trained only a fraction of the nation's lawyers, but was this a portent of what would follow if racial policies changed? Virtually no one wanted to see a return to the days when professional schools had no black students, but it was not clear how the system could be "fixed" to produce results that most Americans would judge "fair."

Meanwhile, in a further blow against the preferential policies of the recent past, the Supreme Court in mid-1995 struck down federal rulings that mandated Congressional redistricting in the states to guarantee one or more predominantly black districts. By a 5-to-4 decision the Court ruled that race could not be used as a decisive factor in laying out the boundaries of Congressional districts. At virtually the same time, in *Adar and Constructors* v. *Pena*, it restricted the federal government's right to confer preferences in the awarding of contracts to minority businesses.

Balkanization.   In fact, there were many disturbing signs during the early 1990s that Americans were losing their sense of common identity and beginning to define themselves primarily as part of some smaller, more cohesive, quasi-tribal group. Some Americans felt that the federal mandate of bilingual education aided and abetted the process. However benign in its intentions, it discouraged foreign-born children from acquiring English and perpetuated group separateness. In Milwaukee, the school board sought to establish a publicly financed high school just for black males. The curriculum would emphasize the black experience and so, it was said, raise the self-esteem of the young black men, a group who often failed in the regular schools. Critics said it was divisive and should not be paid for out of public taxes.

The multicultural trend disturbed many Americans who prized what they perceived as the civic unity of the past. In 1992 Arthur Schlesinger, Jr., a distinguished liberal historian, published *The Disuniting of America,* deploring the divisive effects of the new sensibility. Schlesinger lauded the discovery of ethnic and racial "roots" by Americans and credited it with giving neglected groups their proper due. But he also praised, with qualification, the assimilationist ethic of the past. Noting the growing tribalism around the world and its often murderous effects, he warned that denial of common values and sense of the past might well propel the United States along the same dangerous, discordant path as Yugoslavia, the former Soviet Union, and language-torn Canada. Americans should be wary of replacing the focus on the individual that had long been central to the country's tradition with the concept of group identity so common elsewhere in the world. "Watching ethnic conflict tear one nation after another apart, one cannot look with complacency at proposals to divide the United States into distinct and immutable ethnic and racial communities, each taught to cherish its apartness from the rest."

Yet other intellectuals praised the new trends. Ronald Takaki, an American historian of Japanese ancestry, in *A Different Mirror,* described how Americans "have been constantly redefining their identity" and lauded the retention of strong ties with ancestral cultural and intellectual roots. As if to overcome the assimilationist forces, Takaki, like other multiculturalists, emphasized the victimization through history of ethnic and nonwhite Americans by the old-stock, Anglo-Saxon elite.

Cults and Militias.   The new cultural divisions brought to the surface a pool of resentment and paranoia among some white Americans that resembled the reactions to social change by the Ku Klux Klan in the 1920s and by backlash voters in the 1960s. At its most extreme these feelings transmuted into the "Militias," paramilitary organizations dedicated to resisting the supposed seizure of the federal government by nonwhites, led in many cases, by Jews or some other "alien" group. The bible of the militia groups was a science fiction novel, *The Turner Diaries,* by William Pierce, a neo-Nazi. The book advocated guerrilla war against blacks, Jews, and the federal government in the name of personal freedom.

The militia groups demonized the federal government and its agents as tyrannical and inimical to the exercise of unfettered personal rights. The most sacred of these, it seemed, were the rights to bear arms in defiance of gun control laws and to abstain from paying taxes. Several militia groups denied all legitimacy to the government and claimed the rights to establish their own sovereign states beholden to no other. They refused to obey local laws, denied the legality of commercial contracts, and threatened state, local, and federal officials.

At times federal law enforcement agencies were grossly heavyhanded in their response to those who defied federal weapons laws and denied the sovereignty of the United States government. In August 1992, the wife of Randall Weaver, a white supremacist and militia sympathizer who had refused to appear for trial on illegal weapons charges, was killed by an FBI sharpshooter during a standoff with federal agents at their cabin in Idaho. The FBI tried to cover up the details of the Ruby Ridge assault, but the facts that came out during Weaver's trial and at congressional hearings confirmed government high-handedness and mismanagement. Weaver was acquitted and the FBI official who was responsible for the siege was fired.

The consequences of government ineptitude were even more lamentable at Waco, Texas, where a religious sect calling itself the Branch Davidians, led by a zealot, David Koresh, had established a community, Mt. Carmel, housed in a cluster of wooden structures. The Davidians believed Koresh was a prophet who could point the way of repentance to society and so hasten the return of Jesus. The Davidians helped pay their expenses by buying and selling guns, and were rumored to have accumulated an arsenal of weapons in their compound. They were also said to be devotees of dissolute sexual behavior and Koresh, it was believed, had created a virtual harem of young women who catered to his pleasures.

In February 1993 federal agents, trying to arrest Koresh on charges of illegal weapons and explosives possession, engaged in a shoot-out with the Branch Davidians in which four agents were killed. The FBI surrounded Mt. Carmel and tried to negotiate a peaceful surrender of the perpetrators. After 51 days the authorities lost patience and stormed the compound. Tear gas canisters lobbed into the buildings may have ignited the wooden structures, burning to death 80 people, including women and children.

The government defended its actions. Attorney General Janet Reno said she had ordered the attack only when she heard that children were being abused by Koresh. Though many Americans supported the government, others believed federal agents should not have launched the assault. To members of the militias the disaster at Waco was proof of the government's arbitrary, despotic behavior.

The loathing for the federal government took murderous form in the bombing of the federal office building in Oklahoma City in April 1995. The instigator was Timothy McVeigh, a veteran of the Gulf War who sought revenge against the federal government for Waco by exploding an enormous truck bomb in front of the building. The most ghastly terrorist attack in American history till then, the blast killed 168 people, many of them children and visitors to the building, rather than federal employees. Just minutes after the explosion the state police intercepted McVeigh fleeing the city and arrested him. McVeigh, it turned out, was a fringe member of the militia movement and had long talked with friends and his family of avenging Waco. Tried in Denver in the spring of 1997, he was convicted and sentenced to death. He was finally executed in the summer of 2001.

Election 1996.   As the 1996 presidential election year approached Clinton's position had greatly improved. The budget impasse with the Republicans had worked in his favor. The Democrats also had good times on their side. By mid-1996 the economy had recovered from the slump of 1989–1990 and was booming. There was never any question that Clinton would be renominated; he had no opponents within his party. The Republicans turned to Senate Majority Leader Bob Dole, who chose as his running mate former Congressman and cabinet officer Jack Kemp.

The campaign was a walkover. Many Americans had doubts about "Slick Willy," as his enemies labeled the president. He could charm the birds out of the trees, but he seemed such an unprincipled manipulator. Liberals were dismayed by his collaboration with the Congressional Republicans on welfare reform and a balanced budget, which seemed to repudiate the Democratic party's New Deal legacy. Moreover, the Whitewater scandal and related financial misdeeds, and Paula Jones's accusations of sexual harassment, remained unresolved. Yet the public liked Clinton personally and, more important, the economy was making unprecedented gains. And there were also Dole's negatives. He was 73, the oldest man ever to run for president, and at times it showed. The Republican candidate ran a lackluster campaign and was badly behind from the beginning.

Campaign finance was a worse scandal than ever. Both parties tapped foreign sources to pay their bills, but the Democrats did so on a more massive scale. Particularly disturbing was the money that flowed to the Democrats from the Chinese government, clearly intended by the Chinese to influence American policies toward their country. In July 1997 the Senate began a major investigation into the finances of the 1996 election that promised some serious effort at campaign finance reform.

In the end Clinton won by a vote of 45.6 million (379 electoral) to Dole's 37.9 million (159 electoral). Perot, who ran again in a lackluster campaign, got almost 8 million popular votes. The Republicans retained control of both houses of Congress by about the same margins as in 1994.

Second Term.   After his second inauguration Clinton continued to face challenges in foreign policy. In the Middle East, Saddam Hussein, chaffing under the UN cease-fire terms imposed by the victors at the Gulf War's end, sought to defy UN inspectors monitoring his programs to develop nuclear, chemical, and biological weapons. Saddam refused to let the inspectors visit suspicious sites and sought to single out the Americans on the inspection teams as unacceptable observers. The United States launched a massive buildup of military might on Iraq's borders, forcing the Iraqis to back down initially. In the end, however,

Saddam succeeded in ousting the UN inspectors and, almost certainly, resuming his quest for military prowess.

The former Yugoslavia also remained a trouble spot. In November 1995 Clinton had brokered an agreement among the contending parties to solve the Bosnian problem that included the dispatch of NATO troops, Americans among them, to serve as peacekeepers in the tumultuous former Yugoslav province. In deference to the American public's reluctance to become entangled in Balkan problems, Clinton had promised to remove the Americans in a year. The continuing tensions in the region forced him to renege; American troops stayed on. Fortunately, through mid-1998, no American service personnel had died from enemy action, but meanwhile a new danger appeared in the Serbian province of Kosovo. There, ethnic Albanians, a majority, were demanding autonomy from the oppressive Serbs and a new round of violence and guerrilla war was soon looming. Americans wondered again if the United States would be able to avoid becoming entangled in a shooting war against the Serbs to prevent another round of atrocities as in Bosnia.

In early 1998 Clinton faced a challenge on the world financial front as the economies of the hitherto booming East Asian nations—stressed by bad debts and corrupt mismanagement—stumbled and threatened to collapse. As head of the world's largest economy, the president had to help organize some sort of bailout to stop the turmoil in Asia lest it precipitate a worldwide economic meltdown like that of the 1930s. Many Americans balked at having to accept financial burdens to save other nations from their misdeeds and it seemed that, if the International Monetary Fund's loans and other help did not prove sufficient, growing demands from economic isolationists at home might force the United States to adopt an every-nation-for-itself policy.

On the domestic front, legislative war continued between the president and the Republican leadership in Congress during Clinton's second term. With the economy booming, the Treasury faced, for the first time in many decades, a budget surplus. The president proposed that the surplus be used to strengthen Social Security so that future retirees would not be shortchanged. The Republicans in Congress preferred that the public benefit in the shortrun by a tax cut.

Monica Lewinsky. By this time Bill Clinton had come under sharp personal attack as an obsessive womanizer. Clinton's behavior was certainly both immoral and reckless. There can be no excuse for the president of the United States betraying his marriage vows in the West Wing of the White House with a love-smitten woman half his age. As the Monica Lewinsky scandal intensified, evidence turned up that as president Clinton may have made sexual overtures to other women as well. To make his behavior still more lamentable, Clinton could not bring himself to confess his errors. Instead, over the course of the scandal, he evaded the truth and took refuge in semantical nitpicking that dismayed many Americans.

In November 1995 Lewinsky, a young White House aide, began a sexual liaison with Clinton in a back room of the Presidential Mansion. In April 1996 a protective White House official had her removed from her job. Monica did not leave government. Instead, the White House staff found a place for her in the Pentagon. Clinton terminated the relationship completely in late March 1997 when even he judged it too risky to continue. Unreconciled, Lewinsky sought without success to return to the White House from the Pentagon and the president, seeking to appease her, asked his friend Vernon Jordan, an influential black lawyer, to find her a job in New York. Jordan failed, but his efforts seemed to be a thinly disguised attempt to keep Lewinsky from blabbing about her affair with the president.

In any event, the move did not work. Lewinsky told her story to Linda Tripp, a new friend at the Pentagon. A former White House aide herself, Tripp despised the entire Clinton circle and encouraged Monica to confide in her while she secretly taped her words. By now the writing of articles and books about the Clintons' supposedly unethical doings had became a profitable minor industry and Tripp, apparently, saw no reason why she should not cash in by publishing Monica's juicy story.

When he learned of the Lewinsky affair, special prosecutor Kenneth Starr, hired to investigate Whitewater, leaped at the chance to nail the president on a new count. Some of his aides believed the liaison was too far afield for their investigation, but to the hard core anti-Clintonites in the independent counsel's office the chief executive seemed an evil man and the Lewinsky affair looked like the perfect way to bring him down. On January 18, 1998, members of Starr's staff waylaid Lewinsky and hustled her off to a room at the Ritz-Carlton hotel in Washington where they pressured her to testify as to what she knew of Clinton's sexual peccadillos. Only when promised immunity from prosecution did she agree to tell her story. On July 19 she turned over to Starr a semen-stained dress from one of her meetings with the president. Now the special prosecutor had a sample of Clinton's DNA to refute him if he should deny his liaison with the former White House aide.

Meanwhile, on January 17 Clinton was deposed by Paula Jones's attorneys in Washington. The president was asked about his contacts with Jones, with Gennifer Flowers, with a White House volunteer Kathleen Willey, and with Monica Lewinsky. Clinton denied categorically that he and Lewinsky ever had sexual relations. "I have never had sexual relations with Monica Lewinsky," he declared. "I have never had an affair with her."

Americans were both shocked and dismayed when they learned about the Lewinsky affair. Clinton bashers saw it as confirmation that he was a debauched and unprincipled man. Religious conservatives judged his behavior proof of every charge ever made against the moral laxity of the 1960s, the decade when Clinton had reached manhood. But even many of his supporters thought his conduct egregiously reckless. Loyalists, however, defended the president. Appearing on the "Today" show, First Lady Hillary Clinton repeated the president's denial of the Lewinsky affair and called the Kenneth Starr investigation part of a "vast right-wing conspiracy" against her husband that had begun "since the day he announced for president." The First Lady's charge ignored Clinton's actual wrong-doing. It also suggested a degree of close coordination among Clinton's enemies that did not exist. Yet it was not an incorrect description of the unusual array of ferociously partisan and dogged forces, predominantly regional, determined to demolish Clinton politically. Clinton's defenders would claim that his enemies, unable to accept his popularity, were in fact seeking to nullify the elections of 1992 and 1996 through litigation. It seemed another sign of the deep divisions within the country.

Impeachment.   During the months that followed, the Lewinsky scandal and its meaning for Clinton's presidency dominated the nation's domestic news. The independent counsel's office considered the Lewinsky affair a godsend. After expending three years of labor and $30 million of public money on Whitewater and ancillary issues, Starr and his colleagues had come up with very little they could legally use to impugn the president. Now they thought they had finally caught Clinton in an indictable offense—obstructing justice.

On August 17, 1998, the president was forced to testify to the grand jury in the Lewinsky affair. Never before had a sitting president been called before such a body. He now admitted he had "engaged in conduct that was wrong." On the other hand, he stated, neither he nor Vernon Jordan had sought to keep Monica Lewinsky from telling the truth. Shortly after his testimony he confessed on TV to his relations with Lewinsky. They had been "inappropriate" and he had misled his wife. But he attacked the independent counsel and noted that it was "time to stop the pursuit of personal destruction and prying into private lives and get on with our national life." A portion of the press treated his failure to provide a full apology to the American people as a serious moral lapse. The public did not share the journalists' outrage. By this time there was a distinct gap between the views of the press and the general public. To the chagrin of Clinton's opponents, the polls continued to show the president with a high public approval rating.

But neither Starr nor partisan Republicans were willing to desist. Starr's September 9 report to Congress on the results of his long investigation described Clinton's sexual adventures at distasteful length and pilloried the president mercilessly. It accused Clinton of lying under oath and called for his impeachment and removal from office.

House Republicans heartily concurred; Democrats as solidly demurred. The public as a whole agreed with the Democrats. A clear majority of Americans refused to believe that the president should be removed for a failing that involved no major public policy concerns and that hurt his wife and daughter rather than the nation. Many Republicans in Congress probably agreed that Clinton's misdeeds did not warrant impeachment, but the intensely partisan party leadership was determined to push the proceedings to completion. On the other hand, the Democrats as a whole were equally determined to defeat their opponents, though many in fact deplored the president's egregious personal behavior. Efforts to replace the full impeachment process with some form of censure failed and on December 19, 1998, the House voted to impeach on the first count, perjury before the grand jury, by a vote of 228 to 206. The ballot was highly partisan: only five Democrats voted for the motion; only five Republicans opposed it.

The trial of the president before the Senate for "High Crimes and Misdemeanors," the first such event since 1868, began on January 7, 1999. The president's attorney defended him eloquently from charges of obstructing justice. Another of the president's lawyers, respected former Arkansas senator, Dale Bumpers, insisted that the president's misdeeds were entirely of a personal nature and that impeachment represented "a total lack of balance" in dealing with them. The House managers subpoenaed to testify Monica Lewinsky; Vernon Jordan; Betty Currie, Clinton's personal secretary; and Sidney Blumenthal, a White House aide close to the First Lady. Since a two-thirds majority was required to convict in an impeachment trial, a proportion the Republicans could not muster, the results were a forgone conclusion. But in the end even some Republican Senators defected. The final vote on the crucial first count of lying to the grand jury was 45 guilty, 55 not guilty. Five moderate Republicans had voted with the president. Conviction had failed as in 1868, but by a much wider margin.

■ THE NEW ECONOMY ■

The Lewinsky scandal played out against a background of unprecedented prosperity for America and the world. In less than a year, helped by loans from the International Monetary Fund, the economies of Asia began to rebound. Disaster, anticipated by many experts, was averted. Meanwhile, at home, the economy soared. Between 1993 and 1998 Gross Domestic Product leaped from $6.6 trillion to $8.5 trillion.* Real growth rates in the last years of the 1990s averaged well over 3.5 percent annually, a high figure by historical terms. The revival that began in 1993, continued through Clinton's second term, and by 2000 the economic expansion had lasted longer than any in the past, even exceeding the surge of the 1960s. One feature of the boom was the apparently remarkable rebound of American productivity. As the nineties progressed the output per capita of American workers, so long stagnant, finally spurted ahead, helping to reduce inflationary pressures.

Overall the expanding economy fostered rapid job growth. Between 1993 and 1997 it generated 13.5 million new jobs. By the last quarter of 1998 the unemployment rate touched 4.4 percent, the lowest since the 1960s and the lowest for any large industrial country in the world. By early 2000 it was below 4 percent. The surge was a boon to many, even those who, in the past, seemed to belong to the "hard core" unemployed group. Though new federal legislation slashing welfare eligibility clearly played a role, the buoyant job market was probably the most important reason for the sharply reduced welfare rolls by the end of the century.

Sources of 1990s Prosperity. The sources of the sustained boom were, as usual, controversial. Many observers emphasized the restructuring of the

---

*In standard 1992 dollars, which discount for inflation, the increase was from $6.4 trillion to $7.6 trillion, a smaller figure but impressive nonetheless.

American and world economy through "globalization" that reduced the economic importance of national boundaries. An important component of the globalization process was technological advance. During these last years of the twentieth century the costs of information transfer through the internet and cable systems dropped, new electronic networks appeared for transferring money, new international exchanges for stock and commodity transaction were created. At the same time international trade was transformed through the General Agreement on Tariff and Trade (GATT), the World Trade Organization (WTO), the World Bank, the European Economic Union, and NAFTA—the North American Free Trade Agreement. These pacts and agencies expedited the free movement across borders of technical knowledge, skilled management, and technical personnel and drastically reduced protective duties and regulations that impeded free transfer of products between countries. Not since before World War I had people, goods, services, and ideas moved so freely without regard to borders. Taken together, these worked to create global markets for goods and services.

Few economists doubted that the overall effect of globalization was to raise international living standards. For "developing" nations, particularly, it was a boon, triggering the transition to manufacturing and facilitating the shift to modernity. At home it compelled American firms to become more efficient and innovative to confront increasing competition abroad. The proof of the benign domestic effects ultimately registered in the declining American unemployment rate and the nation's GDP surge of the period.

Other observers saw the key to the boom in the breakthrough in the innovative technologies of the 1990s. First of these was the Internet, the "information superhighway," as president Clinton and others had quaintly called it early in the decade. By the end of the century millions of Americans, especially more prosperous and educated ones, were able to access from their computers, connected to the telephone or cable systems, vast pools of useful information and engage in buying and selling without leaving their homes or offices. Internet service providers like America Online, CompuServe, and Yahoo had acquired millions of clients and become multibillion dollar companies. Meanwhile, "e-mail" provided a new way for individuals and family members to keep in touch and companies to knit together their operations. By the end of the century "dot-com" companies such as Amazon, eBay, Priceline, and others had established Internet systems for the purchase of books, toys, computers, even groceries. Though in fact traditional marketing remained far larger in volume, in part it was the investing public's expectation that "e-commerce" was the wave of the future that led to the extraordinary boom in the NASDAQ stock index, measuring the value primarily of high-tech securities.

And other electronic wonders contributed to the boom. Especially important were cell phones, devices that enabled people on the move or away from standard telephone connections to call anyone, anywhere, from anyplace. By the end of the decade one could observe many people walking on busy sidewalks talking to friends and colleagues on little phones pressed to their ears, completely indifferent to all around them.

Another promising technical innovation of the so-called New Economy was biotechnology based on the structure of DNA, the building blocks of life. By the end of the century, "bio-tech" promised to provide breakthroughs in medicine, agriculture, and even psychology. Among its many appeals, its practitioners declared, was its potential for producing hardier and more productive food plants and animals, thereby making cheaper food and fiber available to the world's consumers. One amazing bio-tech development of the 1990s was animal cloning, a form of asexual reproduction that produced living organisms identical genetically with their parents. The advances in the new field were encouraged by the federal government, which, beginning in the early 1990s, began to subsidize a major scientific project, the Human Genome Project, to decipher the genetic "code" that defined human beings physically, and perhaps behaviorally as well. Meanwhile, a private firm, Celera, led by J. Craig Venter, set out on the same quest using different techniques. In June 2000 the two competitors announced completion of the first "rough draft" of the human genome. The media reported it as one of the greatest scientific breakthroughs in history. And perhaps it was, though practical applications in the form of new drugs and new medical knowledge remained years away.

But if globalization and the new technology were boons, they also created stresses. In much of the developing world they produced social and cultural turmoil that governments and institutions found difficult to deal with. Some societies were able to use the innovations to modernize and raise living standards; others rejected them and fell further behind. The changes also created strains at home. American businesses now competed with the best that the world had to offer, with bankruptcy the price of failure. Firms felt compelled to become "lean and mean" by cutting out layers of management and reducing workers' fringe benefits. (It did not apparently reduce the compensation of top executives, whose salaries often seemed to rise despite mediocre company performance.) Many companies transferred their operations to cheap-labor countries in Latin America or Asia. Over and over, during the early 1990s the public would be dismayed with yet another headline announcing that a major firm—TWA, AT&T, Sears, Eastman Kodak, IBM, American Airlines, GM—was "downsizing," shucking off thousands of workers, white-collar as well as blue-, and closing less efficient plants or abandoning less profitable routes, to remain competitive. Even workers not directly affected wondered how long they would continue to draw a paycheck. Clearly, if the American economy overall benefited from globalization and the new technology that sustained and reinforced it, particular segments were injured.

The Bubble Economy.   One component of the economic surge, said many experts, was the "irrational exuberance" (to quote Alan Greenspan, Chair of the Federal Reserve Board) that pumped up the financial markets, especially the stock markets, to unprecedented heights. Based on the hype of a world transformed by computers and the Internet, the public poured its savings into stocks, especially the issues of firms expected to profit from the new high-tech devices and the new high-tech way of doing things. The stock markets had quickly rebounded from the frightening 1987 sell-off, and by 1990 the Dow Jones index of industrial stocks was at about 2700. By mid-1999 it reached 11,000, a quadrupling in less than ten years. The NASDAQ, a new securities market, primarily for technical stocks, reached a spectacular peak in mid-2000.

With almost half of American households invested in "the market" by the end of the decade, either through pension funds or through individual accounts, the extraordinary performance of the stock market made many Americans feel rich. So did the soaring market value of private and commercial houses and land. The "wealth effects" on consumers of soaring stocks and real estate translated into lively business at the department stores, the malls, the automobile showrooms, the travel agencies, the restaurants, and the theaters. The bubble of the late 1990s also floated on a sea of rising credit. Millions of Americans "maxed out" their credit cards, borrowed on their homes, took out bank loans. Why not? they asked; the booming economy would provide the means to repay these debts when they came due.

Many savvy observers considered the prosperity of these years dangerously shaky. It represented a "Bubble Economy" that soon must collapse. And when it did, they warned, trillions in paper wealth would evaporate, jobs would disappear, and millions of people would find themselves in deep debt. Yet other observers refused to accept the gloomy analyses and predictions. The old rules no longer applied. A truly New Economy had come into being, they said. The promise of computers was finally being realized and for the first time in a generation, they noted, the productivity of American workers was rising, conferring benefits on many. The gains were not temporary; they were permanent. This economy was not a bubble, then; it reflected, said the optimists, a real structural change that promised to revolutionize American material life.

Winners. Some Americans profited exorbitantly from the New Economy. Programmers, mathematicians, electrical engineers, and geneticists found employers bidding competitively for their skills and services. Labor shortages developed in these areas, and American firms welcomed with open arms a flood of foreign-born and trained technicians, mostly from India, Taiwan, Korea, China, and other parts of Asia. Men and women working as high-level technicians for successful high-tech firms frequently took modest salaries in exchange for stock options. Often, during the high-flying late 1990s, when the companies made their "initial public offering," their stock was snapped up by the public and these young men and women found themselves rich overnight. In 1997 an extraordinary 21,000 employees of Microsoft Corporation in Seattle, two thirds of its personnel, had become millionaires through such a process. Silicon Valley, the region south of San Francisco Bay in California, where many of the most successful software firms were located, probably had more millionaires per square yard than any other spot on earth. Elsewhere around the country—in Austin, Boston, New York—were pocket versions of Silicon Valley with thousands of established and would-be high-tech millionaires.

Even greater rewards went to those who had entrepreneurial, as well as technical, skills. During the 1990s boom, individuals who could take new high-tech ideas and approaches and convert them into saleable products or services were able to become millionaires many times over. The outstanding example was Microsoft's Bill Gates, who became the richest man in America, worth almost half a trillion dollars, through developing DOS and then Windows, the dominant operating systems for personal computers. But there were scores of others, including Jeff Bezos of Amazon, Larry Ellison of Oracle, Steve Case of AOL, and Michael Dell of Dell Computer, who became billionaires.

And there were many other beneficiaries of the boom, especially those who provided services to the New Economy. Lawyers were in great demand and well paid in the 1990s. It was they who helped organize new corporations and new mergers of existing corporations into larger ones and helped protect the "intellectual property" of firms against the many who sought to use it without paying tolls. Attorneys in this last decade of the century also benefited from the extraordinary proliferation of personal liability litigation growing out of supposedly defective products produced by the expanding economy. As the century ended, the United States had almost a million lawyers, far more proportionately than any other country in the world. Bankers, stock brokers, and financial experts also prospered mightily in the late 1990s, buying and selling stocks for clients and helping to raise capital to start new enterprises.

Losers.   Yet however impressive the economy's performance, many Americans were left behind in these boom years. The native-born unskilled and undereducated, recent immigrants from less developed nations, the physically and mentally handicapped, as well as the unambitious and the unlucky, were left in the rear. In fact, for those whose incomes fell in the bottom percentiles, life scarcely improved materially over the 1960s. Until the very end of the decade, when the growth of labor productivity and the tight job market finally changed the picture, "real wages," which measured actual buying power, remained stuck, scarcely rising at all for many categories of wage earners. In 1998 almost 13 percent of American families were considered below the poverty level, scarcely better than in 1970.*

Resisters.   Inevitably some Americans fought against the forces that fueled the New Economy. Many resisters found globalization a particularly attractive target. Labor unions complained bitterly about having to compete with cheaper labor abroad and employers' moving jobs offshore. Some politicians, especially Democrats with ties to the labor unions, sought to impose restrictions on goods made with foreign labor to protect American workers. House Minority leader, Richard Gephart of Missouri, was an instance of this. At least one right winger, however, Pat Buchanan, also sought to capitalize on the globalization insecurities and discontents of American blue-collar workers. A perennial gadfly within

---

*Admittedly, the poverty criteria are arbitrary. In fact, the late 1990s dollar figures defining poverty were higher than those for 1970, but in part this reflects price rises since the 1970s and also the greater overall family income of the 1990s.

the Republican party during the 1990s, Buchanan worked to mold a right-wing populist response to the globalization process.

By the new century a broader, international movement to resist the disruptive and often frightening new forces behind the New Economy began to attract younger, activist Americans, whose attitudes often resembled those of 1960s rebels. In early 2000 opponents of free international trade and economic globalization targeted the meeting in Seattle of the World Trade Organization to express their opposition. WTO was the successor to GATT, the General Agreement on Trade and Tariffs formed in 1945 to implement freer international trade. Most economists considered it a major source of the enormous post-World War II economic expansion. Despite its successes, WTO came under fire for failing to protect the environment and for neglecting the working conditions of industrial workers in undeveloped parts of the world. More important, perhaps, it had become the symbol of those forces, cultural as well as economic, that were changing the world at speeds that many found upsetting. To the surprise of the delegates and Seattle officials, the representatives of WTO were greeted by hostile demonstrations of trade unionists and anti-capitalist anarchists and other radicals. Protesters prevented the delegates from going to their meetings. In places, radical anti-establishment activists rampaged through the city, smashing store windows, setting fires, and looting. An even more violent confrontation between the pro- and anti-globalization forces occurred in 2001 at an economic summit meeting at Genoa, where at least one protester was killed by the police and many other manhandled brutally.

Nor did everyone admire the new technology that accompanied globalization. The dangers of bio-technology seemed potentially even more serious than the drawbacks of the electronic revolution. Most people were spooked by the thought of human cloning; in March 1997 President Clinton, noting the "troubling prospect" of making humans through cloning processes, banned the use of federal funds for experiments in the field. But more significant was the growing fear that genetic alteration of plants and animals would create grave health dangers or cause unforeseen hazards to the environment. Environmentalists, led by such activists as Jeremy Rifkin and Ralph Nader, pressured the American government to bar genetically altered seeds and plants. Since the United States was the leader in genetic alteration, European environmentalists were able to insulate their consumers from the supposed dangers of the new technology by import barriers on genetically altered foods and seeds. The pressure of the environmentalists, domestic and foreign, induced a number of seed companies and major bio-tech firms to limit or abandon their plans to market genetically engineered products. Defenders of the new technology called the nay-sayers "Luddites," backward-looking people whose exaggerated fears would abort benefits to mankind, especially to the poor in the Third World. But enough Americans, displaying a growing fear of modern "Frankenstein monsters," were skeptical of the new bio-technology and it appeared that their concerns might well establish serious roadblocks to the success of many commercial genetic engineering ventures.

■ ELECTION 2000 ■

It seemed likely that the surge of economic growth since 1992 must redound to the Democrats' advantage in the 2000 presidential election, especially since the frontrunner for the Democratic nomination was Al Gore, Clinton's vice president, a man closely associated with the administration that had presided over the recent gains. On the other side of the Democrats' ledger, however, was Clinton's personal disgrace. Although the public, by and large, had opposed the impeachment drive, it had not absolved Clinton for his personal transgressions. And Gore himself carried some dubious ethical baggage. No one accused him of sexual immorality, but there was evidence that he had violated the election laws in raising money for the 1996 campaign by soliciting funds from the White House. Also dubious was his solicitation of money in that election year from various Buddhist groups.

In early 2000 the vice president was challenged in the state Democratic primaries by former New Jersey senator Bill Bradley, a former star basketball player for the New York Knicks. But Bradley in the end failed to ignite a large enough segment of the party voters. By the early spring he had suffered a set of primary defeats and been eliminated from the race.

A more interesting primary contest developed on the Republican side. As the campaign season began the Republican frontrunner was George W. Bush, the governor of Texas, oldest son of former president Bush. Called "W," to distinguish him from his father, he called himself a "compassionate conservative." Despite his moderate image, he appealed to conservative Republican contributors and power brokers who, long exiled from power, were anxious for a winner. Through their efforts Bush accumulated what quickly became the largest campaign war chest on record. Bush's chief opponent for the party nomination was Senator John McCain of Arizona who emerged from a large field of challengers during the primaries and for a time gave the Bush forces a scare. McCain, a former navy pilot, had been a prisoner-of-war during Vietnam and had survived five years of brutal captivity. Although a conservative, he deplored the power of money in politics, attacked his rival's apparent willingness to smother his opponents in greenbacks, and made campaign finance reform his chief plank. He drew heavily on independents and, where crossover votes were allowed, on Democrats as well. But he could not overcome the size of the loyal straight Republican cohort, and by the early spring of 2000 he, too, had been eliminated from the nomination race.

With the respective presidential candidates in effect already chosen, the national conventions themselves were uninteresting. The major TV networks, which had traditionally covered the two major party conventions from "gavel to gavel," now chose only to break into their regular schedules with occasional convention reportage. There was little of the usual squabbling over the respective platforms. Only the vice presidential nominations aroused much attention. Gore made the unusual choice of Senator Joseph Lieberman of Connecticut, an orthodox Jew. Given the age-old affliction of antisemitism, this seemed a bold, if not reckless, departure. It could be explained by Lieberman's sincere piety and his criticism of Bill Clinton for his moral transgressions. These seemed likely to inoculate the Democrats against the stigma of the president's shoddy personal behavior. Bush's selection of Richard Cheney, the Secretary of Defense under Bush's father during the Gulf War period, seemed motivated by Bush's own inexperience with national issues and his need for veteran guidance around Washington if elected.

The campaign was not notable for new ideas. But it was the most expensive on record by far. Together the two parties spent a billion dollars to get their messages across to the public. These costs confirmed for many Americans the worrisome reality of money's critical role in American political life. One problem for the Democrats was the candidacy of Ralph Nader on the Green Party ticket. The hero since the 1960s of environmentalists and anti-establishment activists, Nader accepted the nomination though many liberals warned that he would draw votes from Al Gore and help assure the election of Bush, the more conservative and less environmentally sensitive major candidate. One notable feature of the final push was the enormously successful effort by the Democrats to get out the African-American vote, a constituency that could be counted on to give the Democratic candidates over 90 percent of their votes. An interesting lesser race during the fall election was the Senatorial contest in New York in which the Democratic candidate was Hillary Clinton, the First Lady. Never before had a president's wife run for national office, and the contest attracted attention all over the country.*

The Disputed Election of 2000. The outcome of the voting was a "statistical tie." When all the ballots were counted Al Gore had won a popular majority of a half-million votes out of more than 100 million cast. But as we know, it is the electoral college that is legally decisive in choosing a president. And this time—the first occasion since 1876—the electoral college outcome was unclear. Gore carried most of the Northeast, the upper Midwest, and the Pacific Coast. Bush swept the South, the Mountain states, and the farm belt. In many states, however, the results were very close. On election eve, as important contested states like Pennsylvania, Michigan, Wisconsin, and Florida seesawed back and forth, the TV networks often made "too close to call" announcements based on exit polls.

One key state, Florida, where Jeb Bush, George W's younger brother was governor, was called for Gore by the networks early in the evening count. As the tally continued, however, and most of the undecideds fell into place, Florida seemed to move into the Bush column. A large state with 25 electoral votes, this seemed to guarantee a Bush majority in the electoral college and make the Texas governor president-elect. Assuming he had lost Florida, Vice President Gore phoned his rival from Nashville and congratulated him on his victory. But then, unexpectedly, the vote counters changed their minds. Florida, it seemed, was too close to call after all. Gore now called the Texas governor and withdrew his concession.

*In November Hillary Clinton won the Senate race in New York.

For the next month the Florida count, and with it the choice of the next president of the United States, remained in doubt. Early unofficial results showed that Bush had a 1,700 vote majority, out of over six million cast. A machine recount soon reduced this to fewer than 400. In Florida, Nader's 97,000 votes, many of which the experts assumed would have gone for Gore, were far more than enough to have put the vice president over the top. In some sense, as many Democrats had feared, the Nader candidacy had kept the vice president from a clean victory.

But even more disturbing to loyal Democrats were what they considered "irregularities" in the overall Florida count. In populous and heavily Democratic Palm Beach county, for example, a confusing "butterfly" paper ballot had possibly led several thousand voters to mark their ballots for Pat Buchanan, the far right candidate of the Reform Party. Even Buchanan thought this result an error. In other counties, several thousand punch-card ballots failed to register a choice for president since the small paper "chad" had not been completely detached. The presidential totals for these ballots had been set aside by the machines that counted the totals. If the vote had not been so close these imperfect results would not have meant much. The United States has a chaotic system of thousands of electoral districts with many different procedures for voting, and in every American national election there are undoubtedly irregularities of some sort. They seldom affect the final result. But with the choice of president dependent on so few votes, the Florida aberrations promised momentous consequences.

Who would decide the final popular vote in the Sunshine State and so determine Florida's slate of electors? Both sides sent teams of lawyers and spokespersons to Tallahassee and other Florida cities to oversee the final tabulations. The Republicans insisted that the Florida Secretary of State, Katherine Harris, was the person legally charged with certifying the official results. The Democrats pointed out that she was a Republican as well as a zealous worker in the Bush presidential campaign. The Democrats insisted that before certifying the results that there be a hand recount in selected counties where, they claimed, many de facto Gore votes had been disregarded by the voting machines. Such recounts were ordered by local election officials in several counties, and the unofficial results threatened to wipe out the tiny Bush lead. The Republicans, for their part, claimed that hand recounts were subjective and inevitably biased. There were no uniform standards, they said, to judge the "intention" of voters in the rejected ballots. The Bush legal team, obviously concerned that if these recounts continued Gore would forge ahead, responded by asking the U.S. Supreme Court to stop all hand counts. Meanwhile, Ms. Harris asked the Florida Supreme Court to suspend hand counts. Controlled by judges appointed by Democratic governors, the court refused. Soon after it ordered Harris to postpone formal certification of the state vote until the recounts had been completed.

While the nation and the world looked on aghast, both the legal struggles and the contest in the court of public opinion, seesawed back and forth. On November 26, refusing to accept the results of ongoing hand recounts in several

counties, Harris declared Bush the winner in Florida by 537 votes. Bush announced that he had been legally elected and called on Gore to concede. The
vice president refused and, in a televised speech to the country, declared that
every vote must be counted. "A vote is not just a piece of paper," he noted.
"A vote is a human voice. We must let those voices count." The Gore legal team
asked the courts to force Harris to wait for further hand counts.

As the battle continued with no resolution, many observers worried that the
deadline for the electors in Florida to transmit their votes to Washington for
the official electoral tally would come and pass. In that event, Florida's vote
would not count and Gore would receive a majority in the electoral college. To
keep this from happening, the Florida legislature, with a two-to-one Republican
majority, prepared to choose the electors itself. This raised the issue of de facto
nullification of the public vote and, if carried out, promised to reduce still further the legitimacy of Bush's presidency, already in doubt.

The contest was finally resolved on December 12 when the United States
Supreme Court ordered the Florida Supreme Court to reverse an earlier
additional decision authorizing a resumption of hand counts. The U.S. Supreme
Court decision was by a narrow five-to-four vote with all the most conservative
justices, in effect, on the side favoring Bush, and the liberal minority on
the other. As observers pointed out, the decision was ironic. Though the
grounds for overruling the Florida court was that time was running out, and
that the hand recounts, lacking standards, in effect deprived some voters of their
equal protection under the law, the justices who most strongly advocated state
over federal power had in effect nullified a decision of a state court. They had
done an ideological flip flop. Politically savvy Americans understood that the
Supreme Court was not composed of non-partisan sages, but the Court retained
the respect for its decisions among the general public by a show of objectivity. It
now seemed to some that it had forfeited that respect.

However flawed the decision, Gore now withdrew his challenge and acknowledged his defeat. In a brief nationally televised speech he announced that
"now that the U.S. Supreme Court has spoken, let there be no doubt, while I
strongly disagree with the court's decision I accept it. And for the sake of the
unity of the people and our democracy, I concede." "We will," he continued,
"stand together behind our new president." It was considered by all who listened a gracious act. An hour later Bush, now president-elect, appeared on the
same forum. He thanked his rival for his concession and promised to be the
president of all Americans, not just his supporters.

■   BUSH AND WAR AGAINST TERRORISM   ■

Early Bush Policies.   Bush dismayed the liberals and the moderates of his
own party by his early policies. He quickly rolled back Clinton's environmental-
friendly resource decisions, many made at the last moment just before he
left office. Citing rising petroleum prices, he and Vice President Cheney, both
previously connected to the oil and gas industry, recommended that the oil

reserves of Alaska's pristine Arctic Slope be opened to oil drilling and commercial exploitation. In later months, the administration's affiliations with the energy producers and distributors would became major political disadvantages.

But the keystone of his early agenda was a massive cut in federal taxes. Like his conservative predecessor, Ronald Reagan, Bush justified the cut of over $1.5 trillion on the grounds of encouraging economic growth. By now the economy was slumping badly. The stock market had reached its peak in the summer of 2000. Then the bubble burst. Between then and inauguration day in January 2001 the Dow index plummeted hundred of points. The NASDAQ, which measured the economy's high-tech component, was even more precipitous than the blue-chip-connected Dow. The country turned for salvation to Alan Greenspan, head of the Federal Reserve system, a man virtually idolized when the New Economy was in full flower. The Fed cut short-term interest rates steadily by quarter- and half-point increments. By the fall the rediscount rate was down to $2\frac{1}{2}$ percent, a forty-year low. But the economy did not respond. Consumer spending for a time held up, but business investment went into a nose dive since, during the Bubble period, many firms had already over-invested in new products and technologies and much slack remained. By late summer 2001 many companies, especially in the Internet area ("dot-coms" they called them), were shedding workers by the thousands or closing their doors. The newspapers during the summer of 2001 carried many stories of dot-com bankruptcy parties where the erstwhile high-tech millionaires ironically celebrated the collapse of their high hopes. The unemployment rate, extraordinarily low during the bubble period, began to rise. It looked as if the economy, after the longest expansion on record, was about to fall into full recession.

Bush claimed that his tax cuts would stimulate the economy. But many critics, mostly Democrats, believed they were an excuse by conservatives to scale down government programs including drug benefits to seniors and education improvements. They also seemed designed to benefit disproportionately the rich, the Republican party's chief benefactors, a conclusion seemingly confirmed by a parallel Republican push to repeal the inheritance tax, or, as its critics preferred to call it, the "death tax." This levy applied only to a tiny fraction of estates—the very largest—though its repeal promised to cost the treasury billions. Critics of the president's tax cut proposals also charged that they were so large that they threatened the treasury surplus and the money set aside to sustain the social security system in later years. Despite the criticism the disciplined Republican majorities in Congress gave the president what he asked. Congress passed the Tax Relief Act of 2001, though reducing the president's total cuts to $1.35 trillion in lowered levies. The touted stimulating effects did not materialize but, combined with lowered revenues from recession and increased defense spending, the budget surplus quickly disappeared and once again the national debt began to soar.

September 11, 2001. The world changed abruptly for Bush and millions of other Americans on the morning of September 11, 2001. At 9:50 a.m. EST a

Boeing jet liner carrying over a hundred passengers from Boston, crashed into Tower One of New York's World Trade center skyscrapers on the southern tip of Manhattan island. Minutes later another passenger-filled jet hit Tower Two. Both planes were carrying thousands of gallons of aviation fuel which instantly ignited. Many died in the initial impact; almost 3,000 others perished when the huge buildings, after an hour or so, collapsed into piles of rubble. Several hundred New York City firefighters and police, engaged in rescue efforts, died in the collapse. At almost the same time another civilian jet slammed into the Pentagon, seat of the U.S. Defense department, slicing a large wedge from the building and killing 186 civilians and military personnel. Meanwhile still another hijacked civilian jet, apparently aimed at some target in Washington, crashed into an open field in Pennsylvania. The authorities immediately grounded all civilian planes to prevent further hijackings and put the FBI, the CIA, federal marshals, and the military on high alert.

The perpetrators' modus operandi soon became apparent. The hijackers, all of Middle East background, had boarded commercial flights in Boston, Washington, and Newark. Brandishing knives and box cutters, they had taken over control from the pilots and aimed the planes into their targets as giant flying bombs. The case of the Pennsylvania misfire, deduced from cell phone calls by frightened passengers who had just heard of the World Trade Center attacks, suggested a brave failed effort by some of the passengers to disarm the suicide bombers.

The country, though in shock, responded vigorously. The security agencies quickly identified many of the culprits and ferreted out and detained scores of people suspected of being part of the plot or helping those involved. Others were arrested in France, Germany, and Britain. As more and more was learned, it became clear that the terrorists had long planned the blow. Many had hidden in the country for many months living seemingly quiet, normal lives while taking flying lessons and maturing their plans. All were from Middle Eastern countries including Egypt, Saudi Arabia, Lebanon, and the United Arab Emirates. The trail led back, it seemed, to Osama bin Laden, a violently anti-American Saudi, who for years had promoted terrorist attacks on America and the West. bin Laden, and his followers in the terror network called al Qaeda, despised the United States for many reasons. They considered it a Godless land and the source of the immorality and corrosive, hedonistic values of the modern world. They deplored what they considered its pro-Israel tilt. They saw it as a sponsor of a new Crusade of Christendom against Islam. They perceived it as an exemplar of democracy and unfettered capitalism. bin Laden had been implicated in attacks on American military bases in Saudi Arabia in 1995 and 1996 and in the August 1998 bombing of two American embassies in East Africa which had caused the death of more than 200 people, including many Americans. He had probably planned the attack on an American destroyer *Cole* in Aden harbor in October 2000 in which 17 American sailors died.

In the late 1990s bin Laden had transferred his operations to Afghanistan, where he was given refuge by the Taliban, a brutal, repressive regime of ultra-fundamentalist Moslems that had seized control of the country after the expulsion of the Soviets in 1989. One of the ironies of the bin Laden case, and of Islamic terrorism in general, was that many of the perpetrators had been originally armed and trained by the United States to defeat the Soviet intrusion into Afghanistan during the 1980s. After the embassy bombings the United States had fired missiles at suspected bin Laden bases in Afghanistan, but had failed to destroy him or impede his operations.

For many days after September 11, the nation mourned its losses. Although most of the dead or missing were from the New York area they represented an enormous range of nationalities and races, attesting to the diversity of the nation. Hearts went out particularly to New York's firefighters and police many of whom had rushed to the damaged buildings to help in rescue efforts and had died as they collapsed. Americans from all over identified with the tragedy that overwhelmed New York City and its environs and thousands came to personally help or contributed blood, food, medical supplies, or money. Many who followed the tragedy hour by hour came to admire New York's mayor Rudy Giuliani whose management and ability to calm fears seemed masterful. The giant smoking hole where the buildings had came down became almost a place of pilgrimage. For months the media followed the progress of the elaborate cleanup of the site and the thousands came to view it. The tragedy awakened a great wave of patriotism. Millions put American flags on their houses and cars. Others wore red, white, and blue ribbons on their lapels. Quick polls showed that an overwhelming majority of Americans wanted vigorous action taken to punish the guilty, not just the immediate perpetrators, bin Laden and his associates, but all those that gave them safe-haven as well. Meanwhile abroad, the European nations, particularly Britain, pledged to back the United States in its efforts to punish the culprits and eradicate terrorism. In the Muslim world the response was guarded. Pakistan's ruler Perez Mushareff, defied the views of his own Islamic extremists and pledged to help the United States. Pakistan's strategic location made its aid vital. The government's of other friendly Muslim countries offered support. Congress voted several billion dollars as compensation for the victims of the catastrophe and appropriated other billions for the City of New York and for the airlines which suffered extraordinary losses in the post "nine-eleven" period when passenger traffic plummeted.

The War Against Terrorism. To the surprise of some Americans, President Bush rose to the occasion. His first pronouncements seemed to confirm fears that he intended a shoot-from-the-hip response. bin Laden, he declared, was wanted "dead or alive," like in the old western posters. The United States was now engaged in a "war" against terrorism that would be carried through to the bitter end. This attitude probably reflected the views of many angry Americans, but shrewder minds pointed out that such an approach was not appropriate. Unlike most previous wars, the enemy in this case had no capital city, no organized military force, no industrial infrastructure—"assets" that could be destroyed. There would be no set battles, no clean victory. When located, bin Laden and his associates would undoubtedly be attacked, but the war would be fought as much through diplomacy, financial maneuvers, and intelligence as through guns. It would resemble the Cold War more than World War II.

One problem was how to keep the war from appearing to be an assault by the Christian West on Islam. Indeed, there were Americans who considered it just that. The September 11 attack aroused fierce resentments against Muslims in America and abroad and, despite stern warnings from federal and local officials, some hotheads in the United States vandalized Islamic symbols and beat people who were identified, often mistakenly, as Arabs or Muslims. The anti-Muslim feelings among Americans were clearly reciprocated. Abroad some Muslims cheered the attack on America and threatened to invoke a holy war against the United States and any country that sought to attack bin Laden. In the wake of September 11 the media showed tapes of Palestinians dancing joyfully in the streets when they heard of the Trade Center attack. On the other hand the administration was able to forge a coalition of moderate Muslim states in the Mideast to support the United States and, in varying degrees, help with the offensive against bin Laden and the terrorist networks. As for Muslim-Americans, overwhelmingly they pledged loyalty to their adopted country. For their part most non-Muslim Americans proved tolerant rather than bigoted. Meanwhile, experts on Islam assured Americans that Islam was a peaceful and compassionate religion that did not condone the murder of innocent people.

For a time, at least, the terrorist attacks brought Americans together. It was impossible, in the wake of the World Trade Center and Pentagon attacks, not to be impressed with the expressions of loyalty from Americans from every conceivable background. The victims, the people who sought to help with the rescue operations at the World Trade Center site, the "men-in-the-street" who appeared regularly on TV to declare their horror of the assault and their solidarity with the nation, reflected the new diversity of the times. They came from every part of the nation. It almost seemed as if many of the divisions that had erupted during the previous decade had been assuaged. Politicians, too, rallied around the flag. Partisanship was suspended, for a time, as Congress joined to provide the president with the legislation he needed to pursue the "war" on terrorism. Undoubtedly much of the unity was temporary. Once the acute crisis was past some of the seams were sure to open again, but perhaps there would remain a sense that Americans shared a love of country that had been obscured before.

Congress would need its new found unity. The economy was in bad shape. Barely avoiding recession in August, it seemed sure to plunge into full recession after September 11. During the days following the catastrophic event the airlines were grounded to prevent further terrorist acts and, already losing passengers and money, they hovered on the edge of bankruptcy. To prevent their collapse Congress quickly voted $15 billion in relief. It also approved large-scale grants to New York City to pay for the tremendous cost of rescue and rebuilding at the World Trade Center. Soon after, the president announced that he favored pumping between $60 and $75 billion into the economy as an economic stimulus to offset weak consumer demand and even weaker new business investment.

Congress and federal agencies also needed legislation to help protect the country against further terrorism and to pursue the antiterrorist war. Many Americans had been shocked at the lax measures against hijacking at the nation's airports on September 11. Immediately after the attacks airport security was tightened and new measures were proposed to overhaul the entire program of airport security to make it as rigorous as in Europe and elsewhere. Meanwhile the CIA and the FBI—and indeed the nation's whole security apparatus—came under scrutiny. President Bush soon announced the appointment of Governor Tom Ridge of Pennsylvania to a new cabinet level post on "homeland security" to tighten safety for Americans and provide coordination for counter measures against terrorism. At the same time Attorney General John Ashcroft proposed major changes in laws to permit more rigorous federal surveillance of people suspected of endangering national security.

Despite the rally-round-the-flag effect, the president's economic package and the Attorney General's new security proposals did not please all Americans. Many Democrats believed the stimulus package too meager and disliked the sort of tax breaks the president favored. Some conservative Republicans, on the other hand, considered the program a return of big government policies that they deplored. Had George Bush become a convert to an activist federal government? they asked. If anything, Ashcroft's proposals proved even more controversial. Civil libertarians, liberals and conservatives alike, thought they went too far in allowing government agencies to violate privacy rights and breach constitutional protections against arbitrary arrest and detention.

The Anthrax Scare. The worst of the "nine-eleven" shock was scarcely past when the American public suffered another blow to their sense of security. In mid-October a series of letters arrived at the offices of several broadcast studios and newspaper offices and at the Senate office building in Washington containing especially deadly forms of Anthrax spores. Before the rash of mailing had run their course a half dozen people had died of Anthrax at several targeted offices and in the post offices that had delivered the envelopes. Millions of dollars were expended on cleanups of post offices and Washington buildings.

The authorities and the frightened public at first assumed that the Anthrax mailings were connected with the 9/11 terrorism attacks, but as the weeks passed the most intensive investigations failed to show a connection with foreign enemies of the United States. By the summer of 2002 no perpetrators had been identified but the best guess seemed to be that they were probably instigated by a domestic terrorist, perhaps by a disgruntled scientist.

War in Afghanistan. Bush warned the American people soon after the attacks of 9/11 that the campaign against terrorism would be unlike any other war the United States had fought. Much of it would be covert, out of sight, and would take place as much on the diplomatic, financial, judicial and international law enforcement fronts as in the military arena. And so it was. The United States succeeded in rallying other nations to the support of the American campaign, over 46 countries around the world, including most of the moderate Moslem countries expressed support for the war against terrorism. Several, including Britain, Canada, Turkey, actually contributed military assistance and even troops to the American anti-terrorist effort. The United States also cut off sources of funds for al Qaeda, Hamas, Islamic Jehad, and other terrorist groups by closing down fake Islamic charities and other front organizations. It and its allies abroad rounded up and arrested as many as 1,000 al Qaeda operatives residing in Europe, Africa, and Asia.

But in the opening months of the anti-terrorist war, the chief arena was Afghanistan, an undeveloped Muslim nation north of India where, as we saw, the repressive Taliban regime had provided refuge for bin Laden and his al Qaeda group. The United States, Britain, and several other countries sent ground troops to Afghanistan, but the "coalition" forces relied for manpower primarily on the Taliban's domestic enemies among the Afghans themselves. The United States, meanwhile, as in the Gulf War, deployed its airpower against the Taliban and al Qaeda, this time using even more sophisticated weapons than those deployed against Saddam Hussein and Iraq. The Taliban regime quickly collapsed and the coalition installed a new, democratic government pledged to renounce terrorism. Meanwhile, the Qaeda went into hiding in remote areas of Afghanistan and coalition forces attacked them in their lairs by precision bombing and by ground action. Unfortunately, many al Qaeda probably escaped to neighboring Pakistan or dispersed across the countryside. One of the refugees may well have been Osama bin Laden himself though, for all the coalition intelligence forces knew, he might also have been killed along with many of his associates. In their operations, the coalition forces captured several hundred al Qaeda and Taliban fighters and shipped many of them to the U.S. military prison at Guantanimo Bay in Cuba where they were subject to intense grilling about the terrorists' plans and future targets. Unfortunately, in the course of the bombings, several hundred Afghan civilians lost their lives.

As of the summer of 2002 it was widely believed that, although al Qaeda's ability to mount terrorist attacks against the United States had been impaired, it had not been ended. Many Americans expected further attacks and indeed, in the first half of 2002, a number of Americans abroad became targets for extremist Islamic groups. One notable instance was the kidnapping and murder of *Wall Street Journal* reporter Daniel Pearl by a militant anti-American group in Karachi, Pakistan. Meanwhile, Governor Ridge, secretary of defense Rumsfeld and other authorities warned of possible further large scale terrorist attacks at home using biological, chemical, or even nuclear weapons. Clearly, from evidence found in Afghanistan, the terrorist groups were seeking weapons of mass destruction to use against the United States and Americans, with reason, worried that they might succeed.

After 9/11 Americans remained on a state of high alert. Congress and the Transportation Department hired new security agents and services at the airports and deployed new bomb detection machines. The various immigration agencies clamped down on immigrants who had overstayed their visas and foreign students who had failed to register at the colleges they had applied for admission to attend. The Justice Department rounded up suspects, primarily in the American Islamic community, for questioning on terrorist activities, often without careful regard to civil liberties protections. During the country's 2002 Fourth of July celebrations, the first since 9/11, security was exceptionally tight at the many large fireworks displays. Civil Libertarians complained that the government was violating the constitutional rights of many detained for questioning or deported from the country. But most Americans apparently agreed that the danger of another attack warranted risks to traditional civil liberties.

Israel and the Palestinians. The administration viewed the war against terrorism as broader than the destruction of al Qaeda. Bush announce in the spring of 2002 that the United States would seek to end terrorism in other places where nations sponsored it. He included Iran, North Korea and Iraq in his "Axis of Evil."

The most serious of these enemies was Saddam Hussein's Iraq which had expelled the arms inspectors who had been deployed there after the Gulf War to detect Iraqi development of nuclear, biological, and chemical weapons. Without their presence, who knew what horrible weapons of mass destruction the Iraqi dictator was cooking up to provide them, for all we knew, to terrorists? Bush seemed determined to topple the dangerous Iraqi regime, though most of America's friends abroad believed that an actual military attack would be a mistake.

In any event, the likelihood of winning support in the Middle East seemed virtually nil so long as the Israeli-Palestinian conflict remained unresolved. The Bush administration, which initially had avoided intervention into that thorny issue, now found itself compelled to seek a solution if only to clear the path to dealing with Saddam Hussein.

Unfortunately, the problem of competing Israeli-Palestinian interests and aspirations was dauntingly intractable. President Clinton, as we saw, had tried to forge a compromise that would satisfy Palestinian statehood aspirations while assuring Israel that its security needs would be met. Some observers believed that the two parties had come close to agreement at that time, but soon after, the Second Intifada, this time employing the tactic of suicide bombing against Israeli civilians, had begun. The Israeli public's response was to throw out the moderate prime minister Ehud Barak and replace him with the hard-liner Ariel Sharon. Sharon used harsh tactics against Yasser Arafat and his Palestinian Authority as well as against groups suspected of sponsoring suicide bombers. In the spring of 2002 he sent the Israeli army into West Bank Palestinian communities, previously granted autonomy under the Oslo Accords, and destroyed much property and killed suspected supporters of terrorism. Many observers around the world were dismayed by the military occupation, and the attack, though suspended after a few weeks, aroused a wave of anti-Israeli feeling.

Worst of all the Israeli operation did not stop the suicide bombings against civilians in Tel Aviv, Jerusalem, and other Israeli cities. Israel sought to associate its struggle with America's post-9/11 war against terrorism. The campaign met with some success among Americans. President Bush, for one, seemed to tilt strongly against Arafat and in favor of Israel. But in the Islamic world, the United States' position, and its apparent pro-Israel bias, aroused anger and further encouraged anti-American feelings. Several moderate Arab states, including Saudi Arabia, proposed a formula of Palestinian statehood joined with Arab recognition of Israel's legitimacy, but this went nowhere. Meanwhile, both sides seemed to become more intransigent. More and more Israelis concluded that a Palestinian state would be dedicated from the outset to Israel's destruction. The Palestinians in turn became convinced that the Israelis intended to continue indefinitely their harsh occupation of the West Bank and had no intention of ever allowing them to achieve national statehood. In any case, so long as the Palestine-Israel conflict remained unresolved, any effort to keep Iraq from developing and disseminating weapons of mass destruction against the United States seemed remote.

Enron and End of the "New Economy" Era. For some months after September 11, stimulated by federal spending and the remarkable resilience of consumer confidence, the economy rebounded. Then, in the first half of 2002, it plunged again. By mid-July 2002 the Dow-Jones Average fell below 8,000, almost a third below its peak two years before. With as much as sixty percent of the American public invested in stocks, the bear market promised to hurt millions.

The trigger for the downturn was not bad news regarding output, profits, and employment, but rather revelations that one of the largest American energy conglomerates, the Enron Corporation, had falsified its earnings reports to inflate its stock value and was on the verge of bankruptcy. Enron executives, including CEO Kenneth Lay and Jeffrey Skilling, with the connivance of the company's auditor, the Arthur Andersen accounting firm, had allegedly manipulated its financial statements to show profits where there were really losses. The high executives of Houston-based Enron managed to dump their stock holdings before they plummeted. Skilling, for example, had sold off some $20 million in Enron stock shortly before its collapse. Enron soon declared bankruptcy of over $60 billion. Many Enron employees, with their pensions invested in the company's stock, lost most of their life savings. The Enron collapsed awakened bitter feelings among its employees and aroused resentful populistic responses among many Americans generally.

Public outrage goaded Congressional investigations of Enron. When questioned Lay and Skilling pleaded the Fifth Amendment right against self-incrimination. Congressional committees began to consider new regulatory legislation to strengthen the Securities and Exchange Commission. The administration seemed implicated in the Enron debacle. At least one member of the Bush administration, secretary of the army, Thomas White had close ties to Enron. Critics charged that he had sought to help the firm through dubious use of his influence. And he too had somehow managed to cash out his investment before the collapse.

The Enron collapse brought down the major accounting firm, Arthur Andersen of Chicago. Andersen was supposed to supply judicious accounting oversight for Enron and the other firms it audited. But Andersen had financial reasons to accept Enron's dubious accounting practices and failed its duties.

Indeed, when Enron's malpractices began to emerge, Andersen officials destroyed mountains of documents to avoid implicating themselves and their company in the scandal. In mid-2002 a Houston jury found Andersen guilty of obstructing justice and imposed a large fine. The Enron-Anderson affair raised serious doubts of the honesty of the nation's corporate accounting methods. It seemed to make a mockery of the "transparency" of American business methods that, during the New Economy era, was held to be one of the sterling merits of the American economy.

The Enron scandal proved to be the first of a series. In subsequent months during 2002 huge firms like TYCO, QWEST, and WorldCom, all emblems of the 1990s New Economy, were found to have used various tricks to inflate their profit statements. WorldCom, a conglomerate that included the telecommunications giant MCI, admitted that it had inflated its profits of 2001–2002 by $3.8 billion. In late July 2002 the company declared bankruptcy. At $107 billion it was the largest business failure in American history. In the summer of 2002 even General Electric, the poster boy of New Economy corporate management, fell under suspicion that its success was due as much to accounting manipulation as to the genius of its long-time CEO, Jack Welch.

The scandals of 2001–2002 undermined the faith of many Americans in the business system that had been so triumphant in the 1990s. Though into mid-2002 basic economic indicators continued to look fairly good, the stockmarket refused to respond. Unable to tell whether a company was making money, when so many were "cooking the books," how could investors be expected to buy or hold their stock? By mid-July hundreds of billions of dollars of private and institutional wealth had evaporated and the media circulated stories of retirees being forced to return to work because their pensions had been drastically undercut, or men and women, counting on early retirement, being forced to postpone it indefinitely, or parents losing the savings they had put away for their children's college tuition.

The pressure for Congress and the administration to restore public trust and to prevent a repetition of the post-1929 economic debacle, grew urgent. President Bush sought to get ahead of the curve by recommending a strengthened SEC and greater legal accountability of CEOs. His critics said his proposals were feeble. The stockmarkets refused to respond favorably. Some critics suggested that the administration and Bush himself were too close to business to accomplish the drastic reforms needed. During the summer of 2002 the media uncovered a dubious business deal involving Bush when he was a Texas oil executive back in the 1980s. The president noted that he had been cleared of all wrongdoing by the SEC. Still, as the 2002 midterm election season approached, Republicans feared that the public would blame the GOP for the business scandals and punish the party at the polls, especially if Congress failed to enact rigorous new regulatory legislation. The Democrats, of course, hoping to counter the president's still high approval ratings for his conduct of the war on terrorism, sought to take advantage of the scandals. But they moved cautiously, fearing to make the plight of the investors too partisan and thus incurring the wrath of the voters themselves.

■ CONCLUSIONS ■

It is difficult, of course, to reach firm conclusions about events that are still unfolding. Historians properly deal with the past, not the present; they need perspective. Yet it is obvious that in the new twenty-first century the United States and the American people face immense challenges unforseen in the immediate euphoria that followed the end of the Cold War.

The years that began with Bill Clinton's taking office were a rollercoaster ride. In 1992 the United States economy was still in the doldrums. The experts worried that the country had lost its talent for creating wealth, and they looked to Japan for lessons on how to succeed in manufacturing and trade. By 2000 Japan had lost its economic luster, and the United States once more seemed to lead the world in innovation and economic efficiency. Then the bubble burst. In the fall of 2001 the economy was already retreating when terrorists destroyed the World Trade Towers and damaged the Pentagon. The country began an economic dive that threatened to pull down with it the entire world economy. Then, in the first half of 2002, as one disclosure of business malfeasance after another made the headlines, the whole concept of a breakthough New Economy, and the inherent superiority of the American business model, was called into question.

The country also faced a new enemy. This enemy seemed more insidious and elusive than enemies in the past. As unchallenged leader in the post-Cold War era the United States had become the target of forces that deplored all that it seemed to represent in the modern world. Its enemies, however, could not be confronted directly and it was unclear whether the trials ahead would not exceed the nation's patience and resolve.

The outcome of the new "war" against terrorism remains uncertain as these lines are written. It promises to be a conflict unlike any other, a shadow war without visible enemies and obvious military targets. Will the American people have the patience, the fortitude, and the will to fight it? How will such a conflict end? And will the economy quickly revive? Or did the events of 2001 mark the start of another Great Depression like that of the 1930s?

Meanwhile the country faced internal stresses as well. During the 1990s, demographic change, racial antagonisms, feminist activism—all churning for two decades—broke through the surface. The America that appeared to be emerging—rancorous, exasperated, bigoted, at times violent—was not a pretty picture. But then on September 11, 2001 the terrorists struck America, jarring awake the nation's buried sense of itself. Suddenly the rancor and the divisions receded. An overwhelming majority of Americans pledged anew their allegiance to the United States. Abruptly it became clear that, except for a few, many of the nation's newcomers and supposed outsiders considered themselves patriotic Americans. The heartland got a glimpse of the nation's patriotic diversity. On the other side, many who formerly saw themselves as marginal to the country in which they lived now expressed sincerely their love for America. No one could tell how long this mood would last. Adversity often produces temporary unity. Would it this time leave behind a lasting residue?

Online Resources

"The Gulf War"
http://www.pbs.org/wgbh/pages/frontline/gulf/
Read about the Gulf War commanders, read testimonies of American soldiers in combat, and learn about the events leading up to the invasion by consulting the timeline of events.

APPENDIX

In Congress, July 4, 1776

The Declaration of Independence
The Unanimous Declaration of the Thirteen United States of America

When in the Course of human events, it becomes necessary for one people to dissolve the political bands which have connected them with another, and to assume among the powers of the earth, the separate and equal station to which the Laws of Nature and of Nature's God entitle them, a decent respect to the opinions of mankind requires that they should declare the causes which impel them to the separation.

We hold these truths to be self-evident, that all men are created equal, that they are endowed by their Creator with certain unalienable Rights, that among these are Life, Liberty, and the pursuit of Happiness.

That to secure these rights, Governments are instituted among Men, deriving their just powers from the consent of the governed.

That whenever any Form of Government becomes destructive of these ends, it is the Right of the People to alter or to abolish it, and to institute new Government, laying its foundation on such principles and organizing its powers in such form, as to them shall seem most likely to effect their Safety and Happiness. Prudence, indeed, will dictate that Governments long established should not be changed for light and transient causes; and accordingly all experience hath shewn, that mankind are more disposed to suffer, while evils are sufferable, than to right themselves by abolishing the forms to which they are accustomed. But when a long train of abuses and usurpations, pursuing invariably the same Object evinces a design to reduce them under absolute Despotism, it is their right, it is their duty, to throw off such Government, and to provide new Guards for their future security.

Such has been the patient sufferance of these Colonies; and such is now the necessity which constrains them to alter their former Systems of Government. The history of the present King of Great Britain is a history of repeated injuries and usurpations, all having in direct object the establishment of an absolute Tyranny over these States. To prove this, let Facts be submitted to a candid world.

He has refused his Asset to Laws, the most wholesome and necessary for the public good.

He has forbidden his Governors to pass Laws of immediate and pressing importance, unless suspended in their operation till his Assent should be obtained; and when so suspended, he has utterly neglected to attend the them.

He has refused to pass other Laws for the accommodation of large districts of people, unless those people would relinquish the right of Representation in the Legislature, a right inestimable to them and formidable to tyrants only.

He has called together legislative bodies at places unusual, uncomfortable, and distant from the depository of their public Records, for the sole purpose of fatiguing them into compliance with his measures.

He has dissolved Representative Houses repeatedly, for opposing with manly firmness his invasions on the rights of the people.

He has refused for a long time, after such dissolutions, to cause others to be elected; whereby the Legislative powers, incapable of Annihilation, have returned to the People at large for their exercise; the State remaining in the mean time exposed to all the dangers of invasion from without, and convulsions within.

He has endeavoured to prevent the population of these States; for that purpose obstructing the Laws for Naturalization of Foreigners; refusing to pass others to encourage their migrations hither, and raising the conditions of new Appropriations of Lands.

He has obstructed the Administration of Justice, by refusing his Assent to Laws for establishing Judiciary powers.

He has made judges dependent on his Will alone, for the tenure of their offices, and the amount and payment of their salaries.

He has erected a multitude of New Offices, and sent hither swarms of Officers to harass our people, and eat out their substance.

He has kept among us, in times of peace, Standing Armies without the Consent of our legislatures.

He has affected to render the Military independent of and superior to the Civil power.

He has combined with others to subject us to a jurisdiction foreign to our constitution, and unacknowledged by our laws; giving his Assent to their Acts of pretended Legislation:

For quartering large bodies of armed troops among us:

For protecting them, by a mock Trial, from punishment for any Murders which they should commit on the Inhabitants of these States:

For cutting off our Trade with all parts of the world:

For imposing Taxes on us without our Consent:

For depriving us in many cases, of the benefits of Trial by Jury:

For transporting us beyond Seas to be tried for pretended offences:

For abolishing the free System of English Laws in a neighbouring Province, establishing therein an Arbitrary government, and enlarging its Boundaries so as to render it at once an example and fit instrument for introducing the same absolute rule into these Colonies:

For taking away our Charters, abolishing our most valuable Laws, and altering fundamentally the Forms of our Governments:

For suspending our own Legislatures, and declaring themselves invested with power to legislate for us in all cases whatsoever.

He has abdicated Government here, by declaring us out of his Protection and waging War against us.

He has plundered our seas, ravaged our Coasts, burnt our towns, and destroyed the Lives of our people.

He is at this time transporting large Armies of foreign Mercenaries to compleat the works of death, desolation and tyranny, already begun with circumstances of Cruelty & perfidy scarcely paralleled in the most barbarous ages, and totally unworthy the Head of a civilized nation.

He has constrained our fellow Citizens taken Captive on the high Seas to bear Arms against their Country, to become the executioners of their friends and Brethren, or to fall themselves by their Hands.

He has excited domestic insurrections amongst us, and has endeavoured to bring on the inhabitants of our frontiers, the merciless Indian Savages, whose known rule of warfare, is an undistinguished destruction of all ages, sexes and conditions.

In every stage of these Oppressions We have Petitioned for Redress in the most humble terms: Our repeated Petitions have been answered only by repeated injury. A Prince, whose character is thus marked by every act which may define a Tyrant, is unfit to be the ruler of a free people.

Nor have We been wanting in attentions to our British brethren. We have warned them from time to time of attempts by their legislature to extend an unwarrantable jurisdiction over us. We have reminded them of the circumstances of our emigration and settlement here. We have appealed to their native justice and magnanimity, and we have conjured them by the ties of our common kindred to disavow these usurpations, which, would inevitably interrupt our connections and correspondence. They too have been deaf to the voice of justice and of consanguinity. We must, therefore, acquiesce in the necessity, which denounces our Separation, and hold them, as we hold the rest of mankind, Enemies in War, in Peace Friends.

We, therefore, the Representatives of the United States of America, in General Congress, Assembled, appealing to the Supreme Judge of the world for the rectitude of our intentions, do, in the Name, and by Authority of the good People of these Colonies, solemnly publish and declare, That these United Colonies are, and of Right ought to be Free and Independent States; that they are Absolved from all Allegiance to the British Crown, and that all political connection between them and the State of Great Britain, is and ought to be totally dissolved; and that as Free and Independent States, they have full Power to levy War, conclude Peace, contract Alliances, establish Commerce, and to do all other Acts and Things which Independent States may of right do.

And for the support of this Declaration, with a firm reliance on the protection of divine Providence, we mutually pledge to each other our Lives, our Fortunes and our sacred Honor.

John Hancock

NEW HAMPSHIRE
Josiah Bartlett
William Whipple
Matthew Thorton

MASSACHUSETTS BAY
Samuel Adams
John Adams
Robert Treat Paine
Elbridge Gerry

RHODE ISLAND
Stephen Hopkins
William Ellery

CONNECTICUT
Roger Sherman
Samuel Huntington
William Williams
Oliver Wolcott

NEW YORK
William Floyd
Philip Livingston
Francis Lewis
Lewis Morris

NEW JERSEY
Richard Stockton
John Witherspoon
Francis Hopkinson
John Hart
Abraham Clark

PENNSYLVANIA
Robert Morris
Benjamin Rush
Benjamin Franklin
John Morton
George Clymer
James Smith
George Taylor
James Wilson
George Ross

DELAWARE
Caesar Rodney
George Read
Thomas M'Kean

MARYLAND
Samuel Chase
William Paca
Thomas Stone
Charles Carroll, of Carrollton

VIRGINIA
George Wythe
Richard Henry Lee
Thomas Jefferson
Benjamin Harrison
Thomas Nelson, Jr.
Francis Lightfoot Lee
Carter Braxton

NORTH CAROLINA
William Hooper
Joseph Hewes
John Penn

SOUTH CAROLINA
Edward Rutledge
Thomas Heyward, Jr.
Thomas Lynch, Jr.
Arthur Middleton

GEORGIA
Button Gwinnett
Lyman Hall
George Walton

Resolved. *That copies of the Declaration be sent to the several assemblies, conventions, and committees or councils of safety, and to the several commanding officers of the continental troops; that it be proclaimed in each of the United States, at the head of the army.*

The Constitution of the United States of America

Preamble

We the People of the United States, in Order to form a more perfect Union, establish Justice, insure domestic Tranquility, provide for the common defence, promote the general Welfare, and secure the Blessings of Liberty to ourselves and our Posterity, do ordain and establish this Constitution for the United States of America.

Article I

Section 1. All legislative Powers herein granted shall be vested in a Congress of the United States, which shall consist of a Senate and House of Representatives.

Section 2. The House of Representatives shall be composed of Members chosen every second Year by the People of the several States, and the Electors in each State shall have the Qualifications requisite for Electors of the most numerous Branch of the State Legislature.

No Person shall be a Representative who shall not have attained to the Age of twenty-five Years, and been seven years a Citizen of the United States, and who shall not, when elected, be an Inhabitant of that State in which he shall be chosen.

Representatives and direct Taxes shall be apportioned among the several States which may be included within this Union, according to their respective Numbers. [which shall be determined by adding to the whole Number of free Persons, including those bound to Service for a Term of Years, and excluding Indians not taxed, three fifths of all other Persons.][1] The actual Enumeration shall be made within three Years after the first Meeting of the Congress of the United States, and within every subsequent Term of ten Years, in such Manner as they shall by Law direct. The Number of Representatives shall not exceed one for every thirty Thousand, but each State shall have at Least one Representative; and until such enumeration shall be made, the State of New Hampshire shall be entitled to chuse three; Massachusetts eight; Rhode Island and Providence Plantations one; Connecticut five; New York six; New Jersey four; Pennsylvania eight; Delaware one; Maryland six; Virginia ten; North Carolina five; South Carolina five; and Georgia three.

When vacancies happen in the Representation from any State, the Executive Authority thereof shall issue Writs of Election to fill such Vacancies.

The House of Representatives shall chuse their Speaker and other Officers; and shall have the sole Power of Impeachment.

Section 3. The Senate of the United States, shall be composed of two Senators from each state, [chosen by the Legislature thereof,][2] for six Years; and each Senator shall have one Vote.

Immediately after they shall be assembled in Consequence of the first Election, they shall be divided as equally as may be into three Classes. The Seats of the Senators of the first Class shall be vacated at the Expiration of the second year, of the second Class at the Expiration of the fourth Year, and of the third Class at the Expiration of the sixth Year, so that one third may be chosen every second Year; [and if Vacancies happen by Resignation, or otherwise, during the Recess of the Legislature of any State, the Executive thereof may make temporary Appointments until the next Meeting of the Legislature, which shall then fill such Vacancies.][3]

---

[1]Bracketed material superseded by Section 2 of the Fourteenth Amendment.

[2]Bracketed material superseded by Clause 1 of the Seventeenth Amendment.

[3]Bracketed material modified by Clause 2 of the Seventeenth Amendment.

No Person shall be a Senator who shall not have attained to the Age of thirty Years, and been nine Years a Citizen of the United States, and who shall not, when elected, be an Inhabitant of that State for which he shall be chosen.

The Vice President of the United States shall be President of the Senate, but shall have no Vote, unless they be equally divided.

The Senate shall chuse their other Officers, and also a President pro tempore, in the Absence of the Vice President, or when he shall exercise the Office of President of the United States.

The Senate shall have the sole Power to try all Impeachments. When sitting for that Purpose, they shall be on Oath or Affirmation. When the President of the United States is tried, the Chief Justice shall preside: And no Person shall be convicted without the Concurrence of two thirds of the Members present.

Judgment in Cases of Impeachment shall not extend further than to removal from Office, and disqualification to hold and enjoy any Office of honor, Trust or Profit under the United States: but the Party convicted shall nevertheless be liable and subject to Indictment, Trial, Judgment and Punishment, according to Law.

Section 4. The Times, Places and Manner of holding Elections for Senators and Representatives, shall be prescribed in each State by the legislature thereof; but the Congress may at any time by Law make or alter such Regulations, except as to the Places of chusing Senators.

[The Congress shall assemble at least once in every Year, and such Meeting shall be on the first Monday in December, unless they shall by Law appoint a different Day.][4]

Section 5. Each House shall be the Judge of the Elections, Returns and Qualifications of its own Members, and a Majority of each shall constitute a Quorum to do Business; but a smaller Number may adjourn from day to day, and may be authorized to compel the Attendance of absent Members, in such Manner, and under such Penalties as each House may provide.

Each House may determine the Rules of its Proceedings, punish its Members for disorderly Behaviour, and, with the Concurrence of two thirds, expel a Member.

Each House shall keep a Journal of its Proceedings, and from time to time publish the same, excepting such Parts as may in their Judgment require Secrecy; and the Yeas and Nays of the Members of either House on any questions shall, at the Desire of one fifth of those Present, be entered on the Journal.

Neither House, during the Session of Congress, shall, without the Consent of the other, adjourn for more than three days, nor to any other Place than that in which the two Houses shall be sitting.

Section 6. The Senators and Representatives shall receive a Compensation for their Services, to be ascertained by Law, and paid out of the Treasury of the United States. They shall in all Cases, except Treason, Felony and Breach of the Peace, be privileged from Arrest during their Attendance at the Session of their respective Houses, and in going to and returning from the same; and for any Speech or Debate in either House, they shall not be questioned in any other Place.

No Senator or Representative shall, during the Time for which he was elected, be appointed to any civil Office under the Authority of the United States, which shall have been created, or the Emoluments whereof shall have been encreased during such time; and no Person holding any Office under the United States, shall be a Member of either House during his Continuance in Office.

Section 7. All Bills for raising Revenue shall Originate in the House of Representatives; but the Senate may propose or concur with Amendments as on other Bills.

Every Bill which shall have passed the House of Representatives and the Senate, shall, before it becomes a Law, be presented to the President of the United States; If he

[4]Bracketed material superseded by Section 2 of the Twentieth Amendment.

approve he shall sign it, but if not he shall return it, with his Objections to that House in which it shall have originated, who shall enter the Objections at large on their Journal, and proceed to reconsider it. If after such Reconsideration two thirds of that House shall agree to pass the Bill, it shall be sent, together with the Objections, to the other House, by which it shall likewise be reconsidered, and if approved by two thirds of that House, it shall become a Law. But in all such Cases the Votes of both Houses shall be determined by Yeas and Nays, and the Names of the Persons voting for and against the Bill shall be entered on the Journal of each House respectively. If any Bill shall not be returned by the President within Ten Days (Sundays excepted) after it shall have been presented to him, the Same shall be a Law, in like Manner as if he had signed it, unless the Congress by their Adjournment prevents its Return, in which Case it shall not be a Law.

Every Order, Resolution, or Vote to which the Concurrence of the Senate and House of Representatives may be necessary (except on a question of Adjournment) shall be presented to the President of the United States; and before the Same shall take effect, shall be approved by him, or being disapproved by him, shall be repassed by two thirds of the Senate and House of Representatives, according to the Rules and Limitations prescribed in the Case of Bill.

Section 8. The Congress shall have Power To lay and collect Taxes, Duties, Imposts, and Excises, to pay the Debts and provide for the common Defence and general Welfare of the United States; but all Duties, Imposts and Excises shall be uniform throughout the United States;

To borrow Money on the credit of the United States;

To regulate Commerce with foreign Nations, and among the several States, and with the Indian Tribes;

To establish an uniform Rule of Naturalization, and uniform Laws on the subject of Bankruptcies throughout the United States;

To coin Money, regulate the Value thereof, and of foreign Coin, and fix the Standard of Weights and Measures;

To provide for the Punishment of counterfeiting the Securities and current Coin of the United States;

To establish Post Offices and post Roads;

To promote the Progress of Science and useful Arts, by securing for limited Times to Authors and Inventors the exclusive Right to their respective Writings and Discoveries;

To constitute Tribunals inferior to the supreme Court;

To define and punish Piracies and Felonies committed on the high Seas, and Offences against the Law of Nations;

To declare War, grant Letters of Marque and Reprisal, and make Rules concerning Captures on Land and Water;

To raise and support Armies; but no Appropriation of Money to that Use shall be for a longer Term than two years;

To provide and maintain a Navy;

To make Rules for the Government and Regulation of the land and naval Forces;

To provide for calling forth the Militia to execute the laws of the Union, suppress Insurrections and repel Invasions;

To provide for organizing, arming, and disciplining, the Militia, and for governing such Part of them as may be employed in the Service of the United States, reserving to the States respectively, the Appointment of the Officers, and the Authority of training the Militia according to the discipline prescribed by Congress;

To exercise exclusive Legislation in all Cases whatsoever, over such District (not exceeding ten Miles square) as may, by Cession of particular States, and the Acceptance of Congress, become the Seat of the Government of the United States, and to exercise like Authority over all Places purchased by the Consent of the Legislature of the State in which the Same shall be, for the Erection of Forts, Magazines, Arsenals, dock-Yards, and other needful Buildings;—And

To make all Laws which shall be necessary and proper for carrying into Execution the foregoing Powers, and all other Powers vested by this Constitution in the Government of the United States, or in any Department or Officer thereof.

Section 9. The Migration or Importation of such Persons as any of the States now existing shall think proper to admit, shall not be prohibited by the Congress prior to the year one thousand eight hundred and eight, but a Tax or duty may be imposed on such Importation, not exceeding ten dollars for each Person.

The Privilege of the Writ of Habeas Corpus shall not be suspended, unless when in Cases of Rebellion or Invasion the public Safety may require it.

No Bill of Attainder or ex post facto Law shall be passed.

No Capitation, or other direct, Tax shall be laid, unless in Proportion to the Census or Enumeration herein before directed to be taken.[5]

No Tax or Duty shall be laid on Articles exported from any State.

No Preferences shall be given by any Regulation of Commerce or Revenue to the Ports of one State over those of another; nor shall Vessels bound to, or from, one State, be obliged to enter, clear, or pay Duties in another.

No Money shall be drawn from the Treasury, but in Consequence of Appropriations made by Law; and a regular Statement and Account of the Receipts and Expenditures of all public Money shall be published from time to time.

No Title of Nobility shall be grated by the United States: And no person holding any office of Profit or Trust under them, shall, without the Consent of the Congress, accept of any present, Emolument, Office, or Title, of any kind whatever, from any King, Prince, or foreign State.

Section 10. No State shall enter into any Treaty, Alliance, or Confederation; grant Letters of Marque and Reprisal; coin Money; emit Bills of Credit; make any Thing but gold and silver Coin a Tender in Payment of Debts; pass any Bill of Attainder, ex post facto Law, or Law impairing the Obligation of Contracts, or grant any Title of Nobility.

No State shall, without the Consent of the Congress, lay any Imposts or Duties on Imports or Exports, except what may be absolutely necessary for executing its inspection Laws: and the net Produce of all Duties and Imposts, laid by any State on Imports or Exports, shall be for the Use of the Treasury of the United States; and all such Laws shall be subject to the Revision and Control of the Congress.

No State shall, without the Consent of Congress, lay any Duty of Tonnage, keep Troops, or Ships of War in time of Peace, enter into any Agreement or Compact with another State, or with a foreign Power, or engage in War, unless actually invaded, or in such imminent Danger as will not admit of delay.

Article II

Section 1. The executive Power shall be vested in a President of the United States of America. He shall hold his Office during the Term of four Years, and, together with the Vice President, chosen for the same Term, be elected, as follows.

Each State shall appoint, in such Manner as the Legislature thereof may direct, a Number of Electors, equal to the whole Number of Senators and Representative to which the State may be entitled in the Congress; but no Senator or Representative, or Person holding an Office of Trust or Profit under the United States, shall be appointed an Elector.

[The Electors shall meet in their respective States, and vote by Ballot for two Persons, of whom one at least shall not be an Inhabitant of the same State with themselves. And they shall make a List of all the Persons voted for, and of the Number of Votes for each; which List they shall sign and certify, and transmit sealed to the Seat of the Government of the United States, directed to the President of the Senate. The President of the Senate shall, in the Presence

---

[5]Modified by the Sixteenth Amendment.

of the Senate and House of Representatives, open all the Certificates, and the Votes shall then be counted. The Person having the greatest Number of Votes shall be the President, if such Number be a Majority of the whole Number of Electors appointed; and if there be more than one who have such Majority, and have an equal Number of Votes, then the House of Representatives shall immediately chuse by Ballot one of them for President; and if no Person have a Majority, then from the five highest on the List the said House shall in like Manner chuse the President. But in chusing the President, the Votes shall be taken by States, the Representation from each State having one Vote; A quorum for this Purpose shall consist of a Member or Members from two thirds of the States, and a Majority of all the States shall be necessary to a Choice. In every Case, after the Choice of the President, the Person having the greatest Number of Votes of the Electors shall be the Vice President. But if there should remain two or more who have equal Votes, the Senate shall chuse from them by Ballot the Vice President.][6]

The Congress may determine the Time of chusing the Electors, and the Day on which they shall give their Votes; which Day shall be the same throughout the United States.

No Person except a natural born Citizen, or a Citizen of the United States, at the time of the Adoption of this Constitution, shall be eligible to the Office of President; neither shall any Person be eligible to that Office who shall not have attained to the Age of thirty-five Years, and been fourteen Years a Resident within the United States.

[In Case of Removal of the President from Office, or of this Death, Resignation, or Inability to discharge the Powers and Duties of the said Office, the Same shall devolve on the Vice President, and the Congress may by law provide for the Case of Removal, Death, Resignation or Inability, both of the President and Vice President, declaring what Officer shall then act as President, and such Officer shall act accordingly, until the Disability be removed, or a President shall be elected.[7]

The President shall, at stated Times, receive for his Services, a Compensation, which shall neither be encreased nor diminished during the Period for which he shall have been elected, and he shall not receive within that Period any other Emolument from the United States, or any of them.

Before he enter on the Execution of his Office; he shall take the following Oath or Affirmation—"I do solemnly swear (or affirm) that I will faithfully execute the Office of the President of the United States, and will to the best of my Ability, preserve, protect and defend the Constitution of the United States."

Section 2. The President shall be Commander in Chief of the Army and Navy of the United States, and of the Militia of the several States, when called into the actual Service of the United States; he may require the Opinion, in writing, of the principal Office in each of the executive Departments upon any Subject relating to the Duties of their respective Offices, and he shall have Power to grant Reprieves and Pardons for Offences against the United States, except in Cases of Impeachment.

He shall have Power, by and with the Advice and Consent of the Senate, to make Treaties, provided two thirds of the Senators present concur, and he shall nominate, and by and with the Advice and Consent of the Senate, shall appoint Ambassadors, other public Ministers and Consuls Judges of the supreme Court, and all other Officers of the United States, whose Appointments are not herein otherwise provided for, and which shall be established by Law; but the Congress may by Law vest the Appointment of such inferior Officers, as they think proper, in the Presidents alone, in the Courts of Law, or in the Heads of Departments.

---

[6]Bracketed material superseded by the Twelfth Amendment.

[7]Bracketed material modified by the Twenty-fifth Amendment.

The President shall have Power to fill up all Vacancies that may happen during the Recess of the Senate, by granting Commissions which shall expire at the End of their next Session.

Section 3. He shall from time to time give to the Congress Information of the State of the Union, and recommend to their Consideration such Measures as he shall judge necessary and expedient; he may, on extraordinary Occasions, convene both Houses, or either of them, and in Case of Disagreement between them, with Respect to the Time of Adjournment, he may adjourn them to such Time as he shall think proper; he shall receive Ambassadors and other public Ministers; he shall take Care that the Laws be faithfully executed, and shall Commission all the Officers of the United States.

Section 4. The President, Vice President and all civil Officers of the United States, shall be removed from Office on Impeachment for, and Conviction of, Treason, Bribery, or other high Crimes and Misdemeanors.

ARTICLE III

Section 1. The judicial Power of the United States, shall be vested in one supreme Court, and in such inferior Courts as the Congress may from time to time ordain and establish. The Judges, both of the supreme and inferior Courts, shall hold their Offices during good Behaviour, and shall, at stated Times, receive for their Services, a Compensation, which shall not be diminished during their Continuance in Office.

Section 2. The judicial Power shall extend to all Cases, in Law and Equity, arising under this Constitution, the Laws of the United States, and Treaties made, or which shall be made, under their Authority;—to all Cases affecting Ambassadors, other public Ministers and Consuls;—to all Cases of admiralty and maritime Jurisdiction;—To Controversies to which the United States shall be a Party;—to Controversies between two or more States;—between a State and Citizens of another State;—between Citizens of different States;—between Citizens of the same State claiming Lands under Grants of different States, and between a State, or the Citizens thereof, and foreign States, Citizens or Subjects.[8]

In all Cases affecting Ambassadors, other public Ministers and Consuls, and those in which a State shall be Party, the supreme Court shall have original Jurisdiction. In all the other Cases before mentioned the supreme Court shall have appellate Jurisdiction, both as to Law and Fact, with such Exceptions, and under such Regulations as the Congress shall make.

The Trial of all Crimes, except in Cases of Impeachment, shall be by Jury; and such Trial shall be held in the State where the said Crimes shall have been committed; but when not committed within any State, the Trial shall be at such Place or Places as the Congress may by Law have directed.

Section 3. Treason against the United States, shall consist only in levying War against them, or in adhering to their Enemies, giving them Aid and Comfort. No Person shall be convicted of Treason unless on the Testimony of two Witnesses to the same overt Act, or on Confession in open Court.

The Congress shall have Power to declare the Punishment of Treason, but no Attainder of Treason shall work Corruption of Blood, or Forfeiture except during the Life of the person attained.

ARTICLE IV

Section 1. Full Faith and Credit shall be given in each State to the public Acts, Records, and judicial Proceedings of every other State. And the Congress may be general Laws prescribe the Manner in which such Acts, Records and Proceedings shall be proved, and the Effect thereof.

Section 2. The Citizens of each State shall be entitled to all Privileges and Immunities of Citizens in the several States.

A Person charged in any State with Treason, Felony, or other Crime, who shall

---

[8]This paragraph modified in part by the Eleventh Amendment.

flee from Justice, and be found in another State, shall on Demand of the executive Authority of the State of which he fled, be delivered up, to be removed to the State having Jurisdiction of the Crime.

[No Person held to Service or Labour in one State, under the Laws thereof, escaping into another, shall, in Consequence of any Law or Regulation therein, be discharged from such Service or Labour, but shall be delivered up on Claim of the Party to whom such Service or Labour may be due.][9]

Section 3. New States may be admitted by the Congress into this Union; but no new State shall be formed or erected within the Jurisdiction of any other State; nor any State be formed by the Junction of two or more States, or Parts of States, without the Consent of the Legislatures of the States concerned as well as of the Congress.

The Congress shall have Power to dispose of and make all needful Rules and Regulations respecting the Territory or other property belonging to the United States; and nothing in this Constitution shall be so construed as to Prejudice any Claims of the United States, or of any particular State.

Section 4. The United States shall guarantee to every State in this Union a Republican Form of Government, and shall protect each of them against Invasion; and on Application of the Legislature, or of the Executive (when the Legislative cannot be convened) against domestic Violence.

Article V

The Congress, whenever two thirds of both Houses shall deem it necessary, shall proposed Amendments to this Constitution, or, on the Application of the legislatures of two thirds of the several States, shall call a Convention for proposing Amendments, which, in either Case, shall be valid to all Intents and Purposes, as Part of this Constitution, when ratified by the Legislatures of three fourths of the several States, or by Conventions in three fourths thereof, as the one or the other Mode of Ratification may be proposed by the Congress; Provided that no Amendment which may be made prior to the Year One thousand eight hundred and eight shall in any Manner affect the first and fourth Clauses in the Ninth Section of the first Article; and that no State, without its Consent, shall be deprived of its equal Suffrage in the Senate.

Article VI

All Debts contracted and Engagements entered into, before the Adoption of this Constitution, shall be as valid against the United States under this Constitution, as under the Confederation.

This Constitution, and the Laws of the United States which shall be made in Pursuance thereof; and all Treaties made, or which shall be made, under the Authority of the United States, shall be the supreme Law of the Land; and the Judges in every State shall be bound thereby, any Thing in the Constitution or Laws of any State to the Contrary notwithstanding.

The Senators and Representatives before mentioned, and the members of the several State Legislatures, and all executive and judicial Officers, both of the United States and of the several States, shall be bound by Oath or Affirmation, to support this Constitution; but no religious Test shall ever be required as a Qualification to any Office or public Trust under the United States.

Article VII

The Ratification of the Conventions of nine States, shall be sufficient for the Establishment of this Constitution between the States so ratifying the Same.

DONE in Convention by the Unanimous Consent of the States present the Seventeenth Day of September in the Year of our Lord one thousand seven hundred and eighty seven and of the Independence of the United States of America the Twelfth. IN WITNESS whereof We have hereunto subscribed our Names.

[9]Bracketed material superseded by the Thirteenth Amendment.

George Washington—*President and deputy from Virginia*

NEW HAMPSHIRE
John Langdon
Nicholas Gilman

CONNECTICUT
William Samuel
 Johnson
Roger Sherman

NEW YORK
Alexander Hamilton

NEW JERSEY
William Livingston
David Brearley
William Paterson
Jonathan Dayton

PENNSYLVANIA
Benjamin Franklin
Thomas Mifflin
Robert Morris
George Clymer
Thomas FitzSimons
Jared Ingersoll
James Wilson
Gouverneur Morris

DELAWARE
George Read
Gunning Bedford, Jr.
John Dickinson
Richard Bassett
Jacob Broom

MASSACHUSETTS
Nathaniel Gorham
Rufus King

MARYLAND
James McHenry
Daniel of St. Thomas
 Jenifer
Daniel Carroll

VIRGINIA
John Blair
James Madison, Jr.

NORTH CAROLINA
William Blount
Richard Dobbs
 Spaight
Hugh Williamson

SOUTH CAROLINA
John Rutledge
Charles Cotesworth
 Pickney
Charles Pinckney
Pierce Butler

GEORGIA
William Few
Abraham Baldwin

Attest: William
 Jackson, *Secretary*

The Amendments

ARTICLES in addition to, and Amendment of the Constitution of the United States of America, proposed by Congress, and ratified by the Legislatures of the several States, pursuant to the fifth Article of the original Constitution.

Article I

[*Articles I through X, now known as the Bill of Rights, were proposed on September 25,* 1789, *and declared in force on December 15,* 1791.]

Congress shall make no law respecting an establishment of religion, or prohibiting the free exercise thereof; or abridging the freedom of speech, or of the press; or the right of the people peaceably to assemble, and to petition the Government for a redress of grievances.

Article II

A well regulated Militia, being necessary to the security of a free State, the right of the people to keep and bear Arms, shall not be infringed.

Article III

No Soldier shall, in time of peace be quartered in any house, without the consent of the Owner, nor in time of war, but in manner to be prescribed by law.

Article IV

The right of the people to be secure in their persons, houses, papers, and effects, against unreasonable searches and seizures, shall not be violated, and no Warrants shall issue, but upon probable cause, supported by Oath or affirmation, and particularly describing the place to be searched, and the persons or things to be seized.

Article V

No person shall be held to answer for a capital, or otherwise infamous crime, unless on a presentment or indictment of a Grand Jury, except in cases arising in the land or naval forces, or in the Militia, when in actual service in time of War or public danger; nor shall any person be subject for the same offence to be twice put in jeopardy of life or limb; nor shall be compelled in any criminal case to be a witness against himself, nor be deprived of life, liberty, or property, without due process of law; nor shall private property be taken for public use, without just compensation.

ARTICLE VI

In all criminal prosecutions, the accused shall enjoy the right to a speedy and public trial, by an impartial jury of the State and district wherein the crime shall have been committed, which district shall have been previously ascertained by law, and to be informed of the nature and cause of the accusation; to be confronted with the witnesses against him; to have compulsory process for obtaining witnesses in his favor, and to have the Assistance of Counsel for his defence.

ARTICLE VII

In Suits at common law, where the value in controversy shall exceed twenty dollars, the right of trial by jury shall be preserved, and no fact tried by a jury shall be otherwise reexamined in any Court of the United States, than according to the rules of the common law.

ARTICLE VIII

Excessive bail shall not be required, nor excessive fines imposed, nor cruel and unusual punishments inflicted.

ARTICLE IX

The enumeration in the Constitution, of certain rights, shall not be construed to deny or disparage others retained by the people.

ARTICLE X

The powers not delegated to the United States by the Constitution, nor prohibited by it to the States, are reserved to the States respectively, or to the people.

ARTICLE XI

[Proposed March 4, 1794; declared ratified January 8, 1798]

The Judicial power of the United States shall not be construed to extend to any suit in law or equity, commenced or prosecuted against one of the United States by Citizens of another State, or by Citizens or Subjects of any Foreign State.

ARTICLE XII

[Proposed December 9, 1803; declared ratified September 25, 1804]

The Electors shall meet in their respective states and vote by ballot for President and Vice-President, one of whom, at least, shall not be an inhabitant of the same state with themselves; they shall name in their ballots the person voted for as President, and in distinct ballots the person voted for as Vice-President, and they shall make distinct lists of all persons voted for as President, and of all persons voted for as Vice-President, and of the number of votes for each, which lists they shall sign and certify, and transmit sealed to the seat of the government of the United States, directed to the President of the Senate;—The President of the Senate shall, in the presence of the Senate and House of Representatives, open all the certificates and the votes shall then be counted;—The person having the greatest number of votes for President, shall be the President, if such number be a majority of the whole number of Electors appointed; and if no person have such majority, then from the persons having the highest numbers not exceeding three on the list of those voted for as President, the House of Representatives shall choose immediately, by ballot, the President. But in choosing the President, the votes shall be taken by states, the representation from each state having one vote; a quorum for this purpose shall consist of a member or members from two-thirds of the states, and a majority of all the states shall be necessary to a choice. [And if the House of Representatives shall not choose a President whenever the right of choice shall devolve upon them, before the fourth day of March next following, then the Vice-President shall act as President, as in the case of the death or other constitutional disability of the President.][10]—The person

---

[10]Bracketed material superseded by Section 3 of the Twentieth Amendment.

having the greatest number of votes as Vice-President, shall be the Vice-President, if such number be a majority of the whole number of Electors appointed and if no person have a majority; then from the two highest numbers on the list, the Senate shall choose the Vice-President; a quorum for the purpose shall consist of two-thirds of the whole number of Senators, and a majority of the whole number shall be necessary to a choice. But no person constitutionally ineligible to the office of President shall be eligible to that of Vice-President of the United States.

ARTICLE XIII

[*Proposed January 31, 1865; declared ratified December 18, 1865*]

Section 1. Neither slavery nor involuntary servitude, except as a punishment for crime whereof the party shall have been duly convicted, shall exist within the United States, or any place subject to their jurisdiction.

Section 2. Congress shall have power to enforce this article by appropriate legislation.

ARTICLE XIV

[*Proposed June 13, 1866; declared ratified July 28, 1868*]

Section 1. All persons born or naturalized in the United States, and subject to the jurisdiction thereof, are citizens of the United States and of the State wherein they reside. No State shall make or enforce any law which shall abridge the privileges or immunities of citizens of the United States; nor shall any State deprive any person of life, liberty, or property, without due process of law; nor deny to any person within its jurisdiction the equal protection of the laws.

Section 2. Representatives shall be apportioned among the several States according to their respective numbers, counting the whole number of persons in each State, excluding Indians not taxed. But when the right to vote at any election for the choice of electors for President and Vice President of the United States, Representatives in Congress, the Executive and Judicial officers of a State or the members of the Legislature thereof, is denied to any of the male inhabitants of such State, being twenty-one years of age, and citizens of the United States, or in any way abridged, except for participation in rebellion, or other crime, the basis of representation therein shall be reduced in the proportion which the number of such male citizens shall bear to the whole number of male citizens twenty-one years of age in such State.

Section 3. No person shall be a Senator or Representative in Congress, or elector of President and Vice President, or hold any office, civil or military, under the United States, or under any State, who, having previously taken an oath as a member of Congress, or as an officer of the United States, or as a member of any State legislature, or as an executive or judicial officer of any state, to support the Constitution of the United States, shall have engaged in insurrection or rebellion against the same, or given aid or comfort to the enemies thereof. But Congress may by a vote of two-thirds of each House, remove such disability.

Section 4. The validity of the public debt of the United States, authorized by law, including debts incurred for payments of pensions and bounties for services in suppressing insurrection or rebellion, shall not be questioned. But neither the United States nor any State shall assume or pay any debt or obligation incurred in aid of insurrection or rebellion against the United States, or any claim for the loss or emancipation of any slave; but all such debts, obligations and claims shall be held illegal and void.

Section 5. The Congress shall have power to enforce, by appropriate legislations, the provisions of this article.

ARTICLE XV

[*Proposed February 26, 1869; declared ratified March 30, 1870*]

Section 1. The right of citizens of the United States to vote shall not be denied or abridged by the United States or by any State on account of race, color, or previous condition of servitude.

Section 2. The Congress shall have power to enforce this article by appropriate legislation.

Article XVI

[Proposed July 12, 1909; declared ratified February 25, 1913]

The Congress shall have power to lay and collect taxes on incomes, from whatever source derived, without apportionment among the several States, and without regard to any census or enumeration.

Article XVII

[Proposed May 13, 1912; declared ratified May 31, 1913]

The Senate of the United States shall be composed of two Senators from each State, elected by the people thereof, for six years; and each Senator shall have one vote. The electors in each State shall have the qualifications requisite for electors of the most numerous branch of the State legislatures.

When vacancies happen in the representation of any State in the Senate, the executive authority of such State shall issue writs of election to fill such vacancies: *Provided,* That the legislature of any State may empower the executive thereof to make temporary appointments until the people fill the vacancies by election as the legislature may direct.

This amendment shall not be so construed as to affect the election or term of any Senator chosen before it becomes valid as part of the Constitution.

Article XVIII

[Proposed December 18, 1917; declared ratified January 29, 1919; repealed by the Twenty-first Amendment December 5, 1933]

Section 1. After one year from the ratification of this article the manufacture, sale, or transportation of intoxicating liquors within, the importation thereof into, or the exportation thereof from the United States and all territory subject to the jurisdiction thereof for beverage purposes is hereby prohibited.

Section 2. The Congress and the several States shall have concurrent power to enforce this article by appropriate legislation.

Section 3. This article shall be inoperative unless it shall have been ratified as an amendment to the Constitution by the legislatures of the several States, as provided in the Constitution, within seven years from the date of the submission hereof to the States by the Congress.

Article XIX

[Proposed June 4, 1919; declared ratified August 26, 1920]

The right of citizens of the United States to vote shall not be denied or abridged by the United States or by any State on account of sex.

Congress shall have power to enforce this article by appropriate legislation.

Article XX

[Proposed March 2, 1932; declared ratified February 6, 1933]

Section 1. The terms of the President and Vice President shall end at noon on the 20th day of January, and the terms of Senators and Representatives at noon on the 3d day of January, of the years in which such terms would have ended if this article had not been ratified; and the terms of their successors shall then begin.

Section 2. The Congress shall assemble at least once in every year, and such meeting shall begin at noon on the 3d day of January, unless they shall by law appoint a different day.

Section 3. If, at the time fixed for the beginning of the term of the President, the President elect shall have died, the Vice President elect shall become President. If a President shall not have been chosen before the time fixed for the beginning of his term, or if the President elect shall have failed to qualify, then the Vice President elect shall act as President until a President shall have qualified; and the Congress may by law provide for the case wherein neither a President elect nor a Vice President elect shall have qualified, declaring who shall then act as President, or the manner in which one who is to act shall be elected, and such person shall act accordingly until a President or Vice President shall have qualified.

Section 4. The Congress may by law provide for the case of the death of any of the persons from whom the House of Representatives may choose a President whenever the right of choice shall have devolved upon them, and for the case of the death of any of the persons from whom the Senate may choose a Vice President whenever the right of choice shall have devolved upon them.

Section 5. Sections 1 and 2 shall take effect on the 15th day of October following the ratification of this article.

Section 6. This article shall be inoperative unless it shall have been ratified as an amendment to the Constitution by the legislatures of three-fourths of the several States within seven years from the date of its submission.

Article XXI

[*Proposed February 20, 1933; declared ratified December 5, 1933*]

Section 1. The eighteenth article of amendment to the Constitution of the United States is hereby repealed.

Section 2. The transportation or importation into any State, Territory, or possession of the United States for delivery or use therein of intoxicating liquors, in violation of the laws thereof, is hereby prohibited.

Section 3. This article shall be inoperative unless it shall have been ratified as an amendment to the Constitution by conventions in the several States, as provided in the Constitution, within seven years from the date of the submission hereof to the States by the Congress.

Article XXII

[*Proposed March 24, 1947; declared ratified March 1, 1951*]

Section 1. No person shall be elected to the office of the President more than twice, and no person who has held the office of

President, or acted as President, for more than two years of a term to which some other person was elected President shall be elected to the office of the President more than once. But this Article shall not apply to any person holding the office of President when this Article was proposed by the Congress, and shall not prevent any person who may be holding the office of President, or acting as President, during the term within which this Article becomes operative from holding the office of President or acting as President during the remainder of such term.

Section 2. This article shall be inoperative unless it shall have been ratified as an amendment to the Constitution by the legislatures of three-fourths of the several States within seven years from the date of its submission to the States by the Congress.

Article XXIII

[*Proposed June 16, 1960; declared ratified April 3, 1961*]

Section 1. The District constituting the seat of Government of the United States shall appoint in such manner as the Congress may direct:

A number of electors of President and Vice President equal to the whole number of Senators and Representatives in Congress to which the District would be entitled if it were a State, but in no event more than the least populous state; they shall be in addition to those appointed by the States, but they shall be considered, for the purposes of the election of President and Vice President, to be electors appointed by a State; and they shall meet in the District and perform such duties as provided by the twelfth article of amendment.

Section 2. The Congress shall have power to enforce this article by appropriate legislation.

Article XXIV

[*Proposed August 27, 1962; declared ratified February 4, 1964*]

Section 1. The right of citizens of the United States to vote in any primary or other election for President or Vice President, for electors for President or Vice President, or for Senator or Representative in Congress, shall not be denied or abridged by the United States or any State by reason of failure to pay any poll tax or other tax.

Section 2. The Congress shall have power to enforce this article by appropriate legislation.

ARTICLE XXV

[Proposed July 6, 1965; declared ratified February 23, 1967]

Section 1. In case of removal of the President from office or of his death or resignation, the Vice President shall become President.

Section 2. Whenever there is a vacancy in the office of the Vice President, the President shall nominate a Vice President who shall take office upon confirmation by a majority vote of both Houses of Congress.

Section 3. Whenever the President transmits to the President pro tempore of the Senate and the Speaker of the House of Representatives his written declaration that he is unable to discharge the powers and duties of his office, and until he transmits to them a written declaration to the contrary, such powers and duties shall be discharged by the Vice President as Acting President.

Section 4. Whenever the Vice President and a majority of either the principal officers of the executive departments or of such other body as Congress may by law provide, transmit to the President pro tempore of the Senate and the Speaker of the House of Representatives their written declaration that the President is unable to discharge the powers and duties of his office, the Vice President shall immediately assume the powers and duties of the office as Acting President.

Thereafter, when the President transmits to the President pro tempore of the Senate and the Speaker of the House of Representatives his written declaration that no inability exists, he shall resume the powers and duties of his office unless the Vice President and a majority of either the principal officers of the executive department or of such other body as Congress may by law provide, transmit within four days to the President pro tempore of the Senate and the Speaker of the House of Representatives their written declaration that the President is unable to discharge the powers and duties of his office. Thereupon Congress shall decide the issue, assembling within forty-eight hours for that purpose if not in session. If the Congress, within twenty-one days after receipt of the latter written declaration, or, if Congress is not in session, within twenty-one days after Congress is required to assemble, determines by two-thirds vote of both Houses that the President is unable to discharge the power and duties of his office, the Vice President shall continue to discharge the same as Acting President; otherwise, the President shall resume the powers and duties of his office.

ARTICLE XXVI

[Proposed March 23, 1971; declared ratified July 5, 1971]

Section 1. The right of citizens of the United States, who are eighteen years of age or older, to vote shall not be denied or abridged by the United States or by any State on account of age.

Section 2. The Congress shall have power to enforce this article by appropriate legislation.

Presidential Elections

Year	Candidates Receiving More than One Percent of the Vote (Parties)	Popular Vote	Electoral Vote
1789	GEORGE WASHINGTON (No party designations)		69
	John Adams		34
	Other Candidates		35
1792	GEORGE WASHINGTON (No party designations)		132
	John Adams		77
	George Clinton		50
	Other Candidates		5
1796	JOHN ADAMS (Federalist)		71
	Thomas Jefferson (Democratic-Republican)		68
	Thomas Pinckney (Federalist)		59
	Aaron Burr (Democratic-Republican)		30
	Other Candidates		48
1800	THOMAS JEFFERSON (Democratic-Republican)		73
	Aaon Burr (Democratic-Republican)		73
	John Adams (Federalist)		65
	Charles C. Pinckney (Federalist)		64
	John Jay (Federalist)		1
1800	THOMAS JEFFERSON (Democratic-Republican)		162
	Aaon Burr (Democratic-Republican)		14
1808	JAMES MADISON (Democratic-Republican)		122
	Charles C. Pinckney (Federalist)		47
	George Clinton (Democratic-Republican)		6
1812	JAMES MADISON (Democratic-Republican)		128
	De Witt Clinton (Federalist)		89
1816	JAMES MONROE (Democratic-Republican)		183
	Rufus King (Federalist)		34
1820	JAMES MONROE (Democratic-Republican)		231
	John Quincy Adams (Independent-Republican)		1
1824	JOHN QUINCY ADAMS (Democratic-Republican)	108,740	84
	Andrew Jackson (Democratic-Republican)	153,544	99
	William H. Crawford (Democratic-Republican)	46,618	41
	Henry Clay (Democratic-Republican)	47,136	37
1828	ANDREW JACKSON (Democratic)	647,286	178
	John Quincy Adams (National Republican)	508,064	83
1832	ANDREW JACKSON (Democratic)	687,502	219
	Henry Clay (National Republican)	530,189	49
	William Wirt (Anti-Masonic)	33,108	7
	John Floyd (National Republican)		

Year	Candidates Receiving More than One Percent of the Vote (Parties)	Popular Vote	Electoral Vote
1836	MARTIN VAN BUREN (Democratic)	765,483	170
	William H. Harrison (Whig)		73
	Hugh L. White (Whig)	739,795	26
	Daniel Webster (Whig)		14
	W. P. Mangum (Anti-Jackson)		11
1840	WILLIAM H. HARRISON (Whig)	1,274,624	234
	Martin Van Buren (Democratic)	1,127,781	60
1844	JAMES K. POLK (Democratic)	1,338,464	170
	Henry Clay (Whig)	1,300,097	105
	James G. Birney (Liberty)	62,300	0
1848	ZACHARY TAYLOR (Whig)	1,360,967	163
	Lewis Cass (Democratic)	1,222,342	127
	Martin Van Buren (Free Soil)	291,263	0
1852	FRANKLIN PIERCE (Democratic)	1,601,117	254
	Winfield Scott (Whig)	1,385,453	42
	John P. Hale (Free Soil)	155,825	0
1856	JAMES BUCHANAN (Democratic)	1,832,955	174
	John C. Fremont (Republican)	1,339,932	114
	Millard Fillmore (American)	871,731	8
1860	ABRAHAM LINCOLN (Republican)	1,865,593	180
	Stephen A. Doublas (Democratic)	1,382,713	12
	John C. Breckinridge (Democratic)	848,356	72
	John Bell (Constitutional Union)	592,906	39
1864	ABRAHAM LINCOLN (Republican)	2,206,938	212
	George B. McClellan (Democratic)	1,803,787	21
1868	ULYSSES S. GRANT (Republican)	3,013,421	214
	Horatio Seymour (Democratic)	2,706,829	80
1872	ULYSSES S. GRANT (Republican)	3,596,747	286
	Horace Greeley (Democratic)	2,843,446	—*
	Other Candidates		63
1876	RUTHERFORD B. HAYES (Republican)	4,036,572	185
	Samuel J. Tilden (Democratic)	4,284,020	184
1880	JAMES A. GARFIELD (Republican)	4,453,295	214
	Winfield S. Hancock (Democratic)	4,414,082	155
	James B. Weaver (Greenback-Labor)	308,579	0
1884	GROVER CLEVELAND (Democratic)	4,879,507	219
	James G. Blaine (Republican)	4,850,293	182
	Benjamin F. Butler (Greenback-Labor)	175,370	0
	John P. St. John (Prohibition)	150,869	0

*Greeley died shortly after the election: the electors supporting him then divided their votes among other candidates.

Year	Candidates Receiving More than One Percent of the Vote (Parties)	Popular Vote	Electoral Vote
1888	BENJAMIN HARRISON (Republican)	5,447,129	233
	Grover Cleveland (Democratic)	5,537,857	168
	Clinton B. Fisk (Prohibition)	249,506	0
	Anson J. Streeter (Union Labor)	146,935	0
1892	GROVER CLEVELAND (Democratic)	5,555,426	277
	Benjamin Harrison (Republican)	5,182,690	145
	James B. Weaver (People's)	1,029,846	22
	John Bidwell (Prohibition)	264,133	0
1896	WILLIAM McKINLEY (Republican)	7,102,216	271
	William J. Bryan (Democratic)	6,492,559	176
1900	WILLIAM McKINLEY (Republican)	7,218,491	292
	William J. Bryan (Democratic; Populist)	6,356,734	155
	John C. Wooley (Prohibition)	208,914	0
1904	THEODORE ROOSEVELT (Republican)	7,628,461	336
	Alton B. Parker (Democratic)	5,084,223	140
	Eugene V. Debs (Socialist)	402,283	0
	Silas C. Swallow (Prohibition)	258,536	0
1908	WILLIAM H. TAFT (Republican)	7,675,320	321
	William J. Bryan (Democratic)	6,412,294	162
	Eugene V. Debs (Socialist)	420,793	0
	Eugene W. Chafin (Prohibition)	253,840	0
1912	WOODROW WILSON (Democratic)	6,296,547	435
	Theodore Roosevelt (Progressive)	4,118,571	88
	William H. Taft (Republican)	3,186,720	8
	Eugene V. Debs (Socialist)	900,672	0
	Eugene W. Chafin (Prohibition)	206,275	0
1916	WOODROW WILSON (Democratic)	9,127,695	277
	Charles E. Hughes (Republican)	8,533,507	254
	A. L. Benson (Socialist)	585,113	0
	J. Frank Hanly (Prohibition)	220,506	0
1920	WARREN G. HARDING (Republican)	16,143,407	404
	James M. Cox (Democratic)	9,130,328	127
	Eugene V. Debs (Socialist)	919,799	0
	P. P. Christensen (Farmer-Labor)	265,411	0
1924	CALVIN COOLDIGE (Republican)	15,718,211	382
	John W. Davis (Democratic)	8,385,283	136
	Robert M. La Follette (Progressive)	4,831,289	13
1928	HERBERT C. HOOVER (Republican)	21,391,993	444
	Alfred E. Smith (Democratic)	15,016,169	87
1932	FRANKLIN D. ROOSEVELT (Democratic)	22,809,638	472
	Herbert C. Hoover (Republican)	15,758,904	59
	Norman Thomas (Socialist)	881,954	0

Year	Candidates Receiving More than One Percent of the Vote (Parties)	Popular Vote	Electoral Vote
1936	FRANKLIN D. ROOSEVELT (Democratic)	27,752,869	523
	Alfred M. Landon (Republican)	16,674,665	8
	William Lemke (Union)	882,479	0
1940	FRANKLIN D. ROOSEVELT (Democratic)	27,307,819	449
	Wendell L. Willkie (Republican)	22,321,018	82
1944	FRANKLIN D. ROOSEVELT (Democratic)	25,606,585	432
	Thomas E. Dewey (Republican)	22,014,745	99
1948	HARRY S. TRUMAN (Democratic)	24,179,345	303
	Thomas E. Dewey (Republican)	21,991,291	189
	J. Strom Thurmond (States' Rights)	1,176,125	39
	Henry Wallace (Progressive)	1,157,326	0
1952	DWIGHT D. EISENHOWER (Republican)	33,936,234	442
	Adlai E. Stevenson (Democratic)	27,314,992	89
1956	DWIGHT D. EISENHOWER (Republican)	35,590,472	457
	Adlai E. Stevenson (Democratic)	26,022,752	73
1960	JOHN F. KENNEDY (Democratic)	34,226,731	303
	Richard M. Nixon (Republican)	34,108,157	219
1964	LYNDON B. JOHNSON (Democratic)	43,129,566	486
	Barry M. Goldwater (Republican)	27,127,188	52
1968	RICHARD M. NIXON (Republican)	31,785,480	301
	Hubert H. Humphrey (Democratic)	31,275,166	191
	George C. Wallace (American Independent)	9,906,473	46
1972	RICHARD M. NIXON (Republican)	45,631,189	521
	George S. McGovern (Democratic)	28,422,015	17
	John Schmitz (American Independent)	1,080,670	0
1976	JAMES E. CARTER, JR. (Democratic)	40,274,975	297
	Gerald R. Ford (Republican)	38,530,614	241
1980	RONALD W. REAGAN (Republican)	42,968,326	489
	James E. Carter, Jr. (Democratic)	34,731,139	49
	John B. Anderson (Independent)	5,552,349	0
1984	RONALD W. REAGAN (Republican)	53,428,357	525
	Walter F. Mondale (Democratic)	36,930,923	13
1988	GEORGE H. BUSH (Republican)	48,881,221	426
	Michael Dukakis (Democratic)	41,805,422	112
1992	WILLIAM J. B. CLINTON (Democratic)	44,908,254	370
	George H. Bush (Republican)	39,102,343	168
	H. Ross Perot (Independent)	19,741,065	—

Chief Justices of the Supreme Court

Term	Chief Justice
1789–1795	John Jay
1795	John Rutledge
1795–1799	Oliver Ellsworth
1801–1835	John Marshall
1836–1864	Roger B. Taney
1864–1873	Salmon P. Chase
1874–1888	Morrison R. Waite
1888–1910	Melville W. Fuller
1910–1921	Edward D. White
1921–1930	William H. Taft
1930–1941	Charles E. Hughes
1941–1946	Harlan F. Stone
1946–1953	Fred M. Vinson
1953–1969	Earl Warren
1969–1986	Warren E. Burger
1986–	William Rehnquist

Presidents, Vice Presidents, and Cabinet Members

President and Vice President	Secretary of State	Secretary of Treasury	Secretary of War	Secretary of Navy	Postmaster General	Attorney General	Secretary of Interior
1. George Washington (1789) John Adams (1789)	Thomas Jefferson (1789) Edmund Randolph (1794) Thomas Pickering (1795)	Alexander Hamilton (1789) Oliver Wolcott (1795)	Henry Knox (1789) Timothy Pickering (1795) James McHenry (1796)		Samuel Osgood (1789) Timothy Pickering (1791) Joseph Habersham (1795)	Edmund Randolph (1789) William Bradford (1794) Charles Lee (1795)	
2. John Adams (1797) Thomas Jefferson (1797)	Timothy Pickering (1797) John Marshall (1800)	Oliver Wolcott (1797) Samuel Dexter (1801)	James McHenry (1797) John Marshall (1800) Samuel Dexter (1800) Roger Griswold (1801)	Benjamin Stoddert (1798)	Joseph Habersham (1797)	Charles Lee (1797) Theophilus Parsons (1801)	
3. Thomas Jefferson (1801) Aaron Burr (1801) George Clinton (1805)	James Madison (1801)	Samuel Dexter (1801) Albert Gallatin (1801)	Henry Dearborn (1801)	Benjamin Stoddert (1801) Robert Smith (1801) J. Crowninshield (1805)	Joseph Habersham (1801) Gideon Granger (1801)	Levi Lincoln (1801) Robert Smith (1805) John Breckinridge (1805) Cesar Rodney (1807)	
4. James Madison (1809) George Clinton (1809) Elbridge Gerry (1813)	Robert Smith (1809) James Monroe (1811)	Albert Gallatin (1809) George Campbell (1814) Alexander Dallas (1814) William Crawford (1816)	William Eustis (1809) John Armstrong (1813) James Monroe (1814) William Crawford (1815)	Paul Hamilton (1809) William Jones (1813) Benjamin Crowninshield (1814)	Gideon Granger (1809) Return Meigs (1814)	Caesar Rodney (1809) William Pinckney (1811) Richard Rush (1814)	
5. James Monroe (1817) Daniel D. Thompkins (1817)	John Quincy Adams (1817)	William Crawford (1817)	Isaac Shelby (1817) George Graham (1817) John C. Calhoun (1817)	Benjamin Crowninshield (1817) Smith Thompson (1818) Samuel Southard (1823)	Return Meigs (1817) John McLean (1823)	Richard Rush (1817) William Wirt (1817)	
6. John Quincy Adams (1825) John C. Calhoun (1825)	Henry Clay (1825)	Richard Rush (1825)	James Barbour (1825) Peter B. Porter (1828)	Samuel Southard (1825)	John McLean (1825)	William Wirt (1825)	

Presidents, Vice Presidents, and Cabinet Members (continued)

President and Vice President	Secretary of State	Secretary of Treasury	Secretary of War	Secretary of Navy	Postmaster General	Attorney General	Secretary of Interior
7. Andrew Jackson (1829) John C. Calhoun (1829) Martin Van Buren (1833)	Martin Van Buren (1829) Edward Livingston (1831) Louis McLane (1833) John Forsyth (1834)	Samuel Ingham (1829) Louis McLane (1831) William Duane (1833) Roger B. Taoney (1833) Levi Woodbury (1834)	John H. Eaton (1829) Lewis Cass (1831) Benjamin Butler (1837)	John Branch (1829) Levi Woodbury (1831) Mahlon Dickerson (1834)	William Barry (1829) Amos Kendall (1835)	John M. Berrien (1829) Rober B. Taney (1831) Benjamin Butler (1833)	
8. Martin Van Buren (1837) Richard M. Johnson (1837)	Louis McLane (1833)	Levi Woodbury (1837)	Joel L. Poinsett (1837)	Mahlon Dickerson (1837) James K. Paulding (1838)	Amos Kendall (1837) John M. Niles (1840)	Benjamin Butler (1837) Felix Grundy (1838) Henry D. Gilpin (1840)	
9. William H. Harrison (1841) John Tyler (1841)	Daniel Webster (1841)	Thomas Ewing (1841)	John Bell (1841)	George E. Badger (1841)	Francis Granger (1841)	John J. Crittenden (1841)	
10. John Tyler (1841)	Daniel Webster (1841) Hugh S. Legaré (1843) Abel P. Upshur (1843) John C. Calhoun (1844)	Tomas Ewing (1841) Walter Forward (1841) John C. Spencer (1843) George M. Bibb (1844)	John Bell (1841) John McLean (1841) John C. Spencer (1841) James M. Porter (1843) William Wilkins (1844)	George E. Badger (1841) Abel P. Upshur (1841) David Henshaw (1843) Thomas Gilmer (1844) John Y. Mason (1844)	Francis Granger (1841) Charles A. Wickliffe (1841)	John J. Crittenden (1841) Hugh S. Legaré (1841) John Nelson (1843)	
11. James K. Polk (1845) George M. Dallas (1845)	James Buchanan (1845)	Robert J. Walker (1845)	William L. Marcy (1845)	George Bancroft (1845) John Y. Mason (1846)	Cave Johnson (1845)	John Y. Mason (1845) Nathan Clifford (1846) Isaac Toucey (1848)	
12. Zchary Taylor (1849) Millard Fillmore (1849)	John M. Clayton (1849)	William M. Meredith (1849)	George W. Crawford (1849)	William B. Preston (1849)	Jacob Collamer (1849)	Reverdy Johnson (1849)	Thomas Ewing (1849)

President (Vice President)							
13. Millard Fillmore (1850)	Daniel Webster (1850) Edward Everett (1852)	Thomas Corwin (1850)	Charles M. Conrad (1850)	John J. Crittenden (1850)	Nathan K. Hall (1850) Sam D. Hubbard (1852)	William A. Graham (1850) John P. Kennedy (1852)	Thomas McKennan (1850) A. H. H. Stuart (1850)
14. Franklin Pierce (1853) William R. King (1853)	William L. Marcy (1853)	James Guthrie (1853)	Jefferson Davis (1853)	Caleb Cushing (1853)	James Campbell (1853)	James C. Dobbin (1853)	Robert McClelland (1853)
15. James Buchanan (1857) John C. Breckinridge (1857)	Lewis Cass (1857) Jeremiah S. Black (1860)	Howell Cobb (1857) Philip F. Thomas (1860) John A. Dix (1861)	John B. Floyd (1857) Joseph Holt (1861)	Jeremiah S. Black (1857) Edwin M. Stanton (1860)	Aaron V. Brown (1857) Joseph Holt (1859)	Isaac Toucey (1857)	Jacob Thompson (1857)
16. Abraham Lincoln (1861) Hannibal Hamlin (1861) Andrew Johnson (1865)	William H. Seward (1861)	Salmon P. Chase (1861) William P. Fessenden (1864) Hugh McCulloch (1865)	Simon Cameron (1861) Edwin Stanton (1862)	Edward Bates (1861) Titian J. Coffey (1863) James Speed (1864)	Horatio King (1861) Montgomery Blair (1861) William Dennison (1864)	Gideon Welles (1861)	Caleb B. Smith (1861) John P. Usher (1863)
17. Andrew Johnson (1865)	William H. Seward (1865)	Hugh McCulloch (1865)	Edwin M. Stanton (1865) Ulysses S. Grant (1867) Lorenzo Thomas (1868) John M. Schofield (1868)	James Speed (1865) Henry Stanbery (1866) William M. Evarts (1868)	William Dennison (1865) Alexander Randall (1866)	Gideon Welles (1865)	John P. Usher (1965) James Harlan (1865) O. H. Browning (1866)
18. Ulysses S. Grant (1869) Schuyler Colfax (1869) Henry Wilson (1873)	Elihu B. Washburne (1869) Hamilton Fish (1869)	George S. Boutwell (1869) William A. Richardson (1873) Benjamin H. Bristow (1874) Lot M. Morrill (1876)	John A. Rawlins (1869) William T. Sherman (1869) William W. Belknap (1869) Alphonso Taft (1876) James Cameron (1876)	Ebenzer R. Hoar (1869) Amos T. Akerman (1870) G. H. Williams (1871) Edwards Pierrepont (1875) Alphonso Taft (1876)	John A. J. Creswell (1869) James W. Marshall (1874) Marshall Jewell (1874) James N. Tyner (1876)	Adolph E. Bone (1869) George M. Robeson (1969)	Jacob D. Cox (1869) Columbus Delano (1870) Zachariah Chandler (1875)

Presidents, Vice Presidents, and Cabinet Members (continued)

President and Vice President	Secretary of State	Secretary of Treasury	Secretary of War	Secretary of Navy	Postmaster General	Attorney General	Secretary of Interior
19. Rutherford B. Hayes (1877) William A. Wheeler (1877)	William M. Evarts (1877)	John Sherman (1877)	George W. McCrary (1877) Alexander Ramsey (1879)	R. W. Thompson (1877) Nathan Golf, Jr. (1881)	David M. Key (1877) Horace Maynard (1880)	Charles Devens (1877)	Carl Schurz (1877)
20. James A. Garfield (1881) Chester A. Arthur (1881)	James G. Blaine (1881)	William Windom (1881)	Robert T. Lincoln (1881)	William H. Hunt (1881)	Thomas I. James (1881)	Wayne MacVeagh (1881)	S. I. Kirkwood (1881)
21. Chester A. Arthur (1881)	E. T. Frelinghuysen (1881)	Charles J. Folger (1881) Walter Q. Gresham (1884) Hugh McCulloch (1884)	Robert T. Lincoln (1881)	William E. Chandler (1881)	Timothy O. Howe (1881) Walter Q. Gresham (1883) Frank Hatton (1884)	B. H. Brewster (1881)	Henry M. Teller (1881)
22. Grover Cleveland (1885) T. A. Hendricks (1885)	Thomas E. Bayard (1885)	Daniel Manning (1885) Charles S. Fairchild (1887)	William C. Endicott (1885)	William C. Whitney (1885)	William F. Vilas (1885) Don M. Dickinson (1888)	A. H. Garland (1885)	L. Q. C. Lamar (1885) William F. Vilas (1888)
23. Benjamin Harrison (1880) Levi P. Morgan (1889)	James G. Blaine (1889) John W. Foster (1892)	William Windom (1889) Charles Foster (1891)	Redfield Procter (1889) Stephen B. Elkins (1891)	Benjamin F. Tracy (1889)	John Wanamaker (1889)	W. H. H. Miller (1889)	Jon W. Noble (1889)
24. Grover Cleveland (1893) Adlai E. Stevenson (1893)	Walter Q. Gresham (1893) Richard Olney (1895)	John G. Carlisle (1893)	Daniel S. Lamont (1893)	Hilary A. Herbert (1983)	Wilson S. Bissel (1893) William L. Wilson (1895)	Richard Olney (1893) Judson Harmon (1895)	Hoke Smith (1893) David R. Francis (1896)

President / Vice President	State	Treasury	War	Navy	Postmaster General	Attorney General	Interior
25. **William McKinley** (1897) **Garret A. Hobart** (1897) **Theodore Roosevelt** (1901)	John Sherman (1897) William R. Day (1897) John Hay (1898)	Lyman J. Gage (1897)	Russell A. Alger (1897) Elihu Root (1899)	John D. Long (1897)	James A. Gary (1897) Charles E. Smith (1898)	Joseph McKenna (1897) John W. Griggs (1897) Philander C. Knox (1901)	Cornelius N. Bliss (1897) E. A. Hitchcock (1899)
26. **Theodore Roosevelt** (1901) **Charles Fairbanks** (1905)	John Hay (1901) Elihu Root (1905) Robert Bacon (1909)	Lyman J Gage (1901) Leslie M. Shaw (1902) George B. Cortelyou (1907)	Elihu Root (1901) William H. Taft (1904) Luke E. Wright (1908)	John D. Long (1901) William H. Moody (1902) Paul Morton (1904) Charles J. Bonaparte (1905) V. H. Metcalf (1906) T. H. Newberry (1908)	Charlese E. Smith (1901) Henry Payne (1902) Robert J. Wynne (1904) George B. Cortelyou (1905) George von L. Meyer (1907)	Philander C. Knox (1901) William H. Moody (1904) Charles J. Bonapart (1907)	E. A. Hitchcock (1901) James R. Garfield (1907)
27. **William H. Taft** (1909) **James S. Sherman** (1909)	Philander C. Knox (1909)	Franklin McVeagh (1909)	Jacob M. Dickinson (1909) Henry Stimson (1911)	George von L. Meyer (1909)	Frank H. Hitchcock (1909)	G. W. Wickersham (1909)	R. A. Ballinger (1909) Walter L. Fisher (1911)
28. **Woodrow Wilson** (1913) **Thomas R. Marshall** (1913)	William J. Bryan (1913) Robert Lansing (1915) Bainbridge Colby (1920)	William G. McAdoo (1913) Carter Glass (1918) David F. Houston (1920)	Lindley M. Garrison (1913) Newton D. Baker (1916)	Josephus Daniels (1913)	Albert S. Burleson (1913)	J. C. McReynolds (1913) T. W. Gregory (1914) A. Mitchell Palmer (1919)	Franklin K. Lane (1913) John B. Payne (1920)
29. **Warren G. Harding** (1921) **Calvin Coolidge** (1921)	Charles E. Hughes (1921)	Andrew W. Mellon (1921)	John W. Weeks (1921)	Edwin Denby (1921)	Will H. Hays (1921) Hubert Work (1922) Harry S. New (1923)	H. M. Daugherty (1921)	Albert B. Fall (1921) Hubert Work (1923)
30. **Calvin Coolidge** (1923) **Charles G. Dawes** (1925)	Charles E. Hughes (1923) Frank B. Kellogg (1925)	Andrew W. Mellon (1923)	John W. Weeks (1923) Dwight F. Davis (1925)	Edwin Denby (1923) Curtis D. Wilbur (1924)	Harry S. New (1923)	H. M. Daugherty (1923) Harlan F. Stone (1924) John G. Sargent (1925)	Hubert Work (1923) Roy O. West (1928)

Presidents, Vice Presidents, and Cabinet Members (continued)

President and Vice President	Secretary of State	Secretary of Treasury	Secretary of War	Secretary of Navy	Postmaster General	Attorney General	Secretary of Interior
31. Herbert C. Hoover (1929) Charles Curtis (1929)	Henry L. Stimson (1929)	Andrew W. Mellon (1929) Ogden L. Mills (1932)	James W. Good (1929) Patrick J. Hurley (1929)	Charles F. Adams (1929)	Walter F. Brown (1929)	W. D. Mitchell (1929)	Ray L. Wilbur (1929)
32. Franklin D. Roosevelt (1933) John Nance Garner (1933) Henry A. Wallace (1941) Harry S. Truman (1945)	Cordell Hull (1933) E. R. Stettinius, Jr. (1944)	William H. Woodin (1933) Henry Morgenthau, Jr. (1934)	George H. Dern (1933) Harry H. Woodring (1936) Henry L. Stimson (1940)	Claude A. Swanson (1933) Charles Edison (1940) Frank Knox (1940) James V. Forrestal (1944)	James A. Farley (1933) Frank C. Walker (1940)	H. S. Cummings (1933) Frank Murphy (1939) Robert Jackson (1940) Francis Biddle (1941)	Harold L. Ickes (1933)
33. Harry S. Truman (1945) Alben W. Barkley (1949)	James F. Byrnes (1945) George C. Marshall (1947) Dean G. Acheson (1949)	Fred M. Vinson (1945) John W. Snyder (1946)	Robert P. Patterson (1945) Kenneth C. Royal (1947) *Secretary of Defense* James V. Forrestal (1947) Louis A. Johnson (1949) George G. Marshall (1950) Robert A. Lovett (1951)	James V. Forrestal (1945)	R. E. Hannegan (1945) Jesse M. Donaldson (1947)	Tom C. Clark (1945) J. H. McGrath (1949) James P. McGranery (1952)	Harold L. Ickes (1945) Julis A. Krog (1946) Oscar L. Chapman (1949)
34. Dwight D. Eisenhower (1953) Richard M. Nixon (1953)	John Foster Dulles (1953) Christian A. Herter (1959)	George M. Humphrey (1953) Robert B. Anderson (1957)	Charles E. Wilson (1953) Neil H. McElroy (1957) Thomas S. Gates (1959)		A. E. Summerfield (1953)	H. Brownell Jr. (1953) William P. Rogers (1957)	Douglas McKay (1953) Fred Seaton (1950)
35. John F. Kennedy (1961) Lyndon B. Johnson (1961)	Dean Rusk (1961)	C. Douglas Dillon (1961)	Robert S. McNamara (1961)		J. Edward Day (1961) John A. Gronouski (1963)	Robert F. Kennedy (1961)	Stewart L. Udall (1961)

President / Vice President	Secretary of State	Secretary of Treasury	Secretary of Defense	Postmaster General	Attorney General	Secretary of Interior
36. **Lyndon B. Johnson** (1963) Hubert H. Humphrey (1965)	Dean Rusk (1963)	C. Douglas Dillon (1963) Henry H. Fowler (1965) Joseph W. Barr (1968)	Robert S. McNamara (1963) Clark M. Clifford (1968)	John A. Gronouski (1963) Lawrence F. O'Brien (1965) W. Marvin Watson (1968)	Robert F. Kennedy (1963) N. deB. Katzenbach (1965) Ramsey Clark (1967)	Stewart L. Udall (1963)
37. **Richard M. Nixon** (1969) Spiro T. Agnew (1969) Gerald R. Ford (1973)	William P. Rogers (1969) Henry A. Kissinger (1973)	David M. Kennedy (1969) John B. Connally (1970) George P. Schultz (1972) William E. Simon (1974)	Melvin R. Laird (1969) Elliot L. Richardson (1973) James R. Schlesinger (1973)	Winton M. Blount (1969)	John M. Mitchell (1969) Richard G. Kleindienst (1972) Elliot L. Richardson (1973) William B. Saxbe (1974)	Walter J. Hickel (1969) Rogers C. B. Morton (1971)
38. **Gerald R. Ford** (1974) Nelson A. Rockefeller (1974)	Henry A. Kissinger (1974)	William E. Simon (1974)	James R. Schlesinger (1974) Donald H. Rumsfeld (1975)		William B. Saxbe (1974) Edward H. Levi (1975)	Rogers C. B. Morton (1974) Stanley K. Hathaway (1975) Thomas D. Kleppe (1975)
39. **James E. Carter, Jr.** (1977) Walter F. Mondale (1977)	Cyrus R. Vance (1977) Edmund S. Muskie (1980)	W. Michael Blumenthal (1977) G. William Miller (1979)	Harold Brown (1977)		Griffin B. Bell (1977) Benjamin R. Civiletti (1979)	Cecil D. Andrus (1977)
40. **Ronald W. Reagan** (1981) George H. Bush (1981)	Alexander M. Haig, Jr. (1981) George P. Schultz (1982)	Donald T. Regan (1981)	Caspar W. Weinberger (1981)		William French Smith (1981)	James G. Watt (1981) William Clark (1983)
41. **Ronald W. Reagan** (1985) George H. Bush (1985)	George P. Schultz (1985)	James A. Baker III (1985)	Caspar W. Weinberger (1985)		Edwin Meese III (1985)	Donald P. Hodel (1985)
42. **George H. Bush** (1988) James D. Quayle Ii (1988)	James A. Baker III (1988)	Nicholas Brady (1988)	Richard B. Cheney (1988)		Richard L. Thornburgh (1988)	Manuel Lujan, Jr. (1988)
43. **William J. B. Clinton** (1993) Albert Gore, Jr. (1993)	Warren Christopher (1993)	Lloyd Bentsen (1993)	Les Aspin (1993)		Janet Reno (1993)	Bruce Babbit (1993)

BIBLIOGRAPHIES

CHAPTER 16 *Reconstruction*

Eric L. McKitrick. *Andrew Johnson and Reconstruction* (1960). Andrew Johnson, says the author, failed to see that the North needed evidence of southern contrition before it could forgive and allow a return to normal relations between the two regions.

Clement Eaton. *The Waning of the Old South Civilization, 1860–1880* (1968). Eaton concludes that the New South retained much of the old, especially its devotion to states' rights, white supremacy, and the cult of southern womanhood.

Albion W. Tourgée. *A Fool's Errand: A Novel of the South During Reconstruction* (1879). Edited by George M. Frederickson (1966). An autobiographical novel by a "carpetbagger" lawyer from Ohio who settled in North Carolina after the Civil War and became a Radical superior court judge.

Allen W. Trelease. *White Terror: The Ku Klux Klan Conspiracy and Southern Reconstruction* (1971). The definitive study of the first Klan after the Civil War and a potent indictment of all its doings.

Joel Williamson. *After Slavery: The Negro in South Carolina During Reconstruction, 1861–1877* (1965). Williamson concludes in this detailed study of race relations in one key Reconstruction state that racial segregation was not wholly a product of "redemption."

Willie Lee Rose. *Rehearsal for Reconstruction: The Port Royal Experiment* (1964). Though the ex-slaves ultimately lost the rich cotton lands to their former owners, the temporary success of the Port Royal experiment tells us what might have been if the northern commitment to black freedom and racial justice had been stronger.

Roger Ransom and Richard Sutch. *One Kind of Freedom: The Economic Consequences of Emancipation* (1977). An important book by two "cliometricians" about how emancipation affected the economic well-being of the freedmen and the South as a whole.

LaWanda Cox and John Cox. *Politics, Principles, and Prejudice, 1865–1866: Dilemma of Reconstruction America* (1963). A study of presidential Reconstruction that gives the Radicals much credit for idealism and suggests how much personal political advantage actually entered into Andrew Johnson's decisions.

Leon Litwack. *Been in the Storm So Long: The Aftermath of Slavery* (1980). Professor Litwack tells us what black men and women felt about the new world of freedom after 1863.

Herbert Gutman. *The Black Family in Slavery and Freedom, 1750–1925* (1976). Excellent social history, not only of the slavery period but also of the post-slavery experience of black families.

Kenneth Stampp. *The Era of Reconstruction, 1865–1877* (1965). An excellent overall view of the "new" Reconstruction history by a man who helped pioneer it.

C. Vann Woodward. *Reunion and Reaction: The Compromise of 1877 and the End of Reconstruction* (1951). Concludes that the agreement to end the presidential election dispute of

1876–1877 was a behind-the-scenes agreement to exchange continued Republican supremacy for major economic favors to southern business groups.

Jonathan Wiener. *Social Origins of the New South, 1860–1885* (1978). A Marxist-oriented study of post-bellum southern society that emphasizes the continued domination of the planter class and the near-slavery of the freedmen.

Eric Foner. *Reconstruction, America's Unfinished Revolution, 1863–1877* (1988). A long history of Reconstruction that reflects the revisionist research of the past generation as well as the political and cultural perceptions of today. (The reader could substitute Foner's briefer version, *A Short History of Reconstruction* (1990)).

CHAPTER 17 *The Triumph of Industrialism*

Edward C. Kirkland. *Dream and Thought in the Business Community, 1860–1900* (1956). This intellectual history of Gilded Age businessmen is based on their private correspondence, congressional testimony, and published writings.

Matthew Josephson. *Edison* (1959). According to Josephson, Edison's Menlo Park laboratory was his greatest invention: It was the first industrial research laboratory, applying scientific theory and technical knowledge to practical problems.

Harold C. Livesay. *Andrew Carnegie and the Rise of Big Business* (1975). This brief book—not a full biography—makes Carnegie's role in the post-Civil War economic surge clear.

Frederick Lewis Allen. *The Great Pierpont Morgan* (1949). A breezy, entertaining biography of Morgan that succeeds in defining his place in American economic life.

Irvin G. Wyllie. *The Self-Made Man in America: The Myth of Rags to Riches* (1954). Wyllie follows the myth of the self-made individual from colonial times to 1929.

Theodore Dreiser. *The Financier* (1912). The hero of this novel is modeled after the Gilded Age streetcar magnate Charles Yerkes.

Herbert Gutman. *Work, Culture, and Society in Industrializing America* (1976). A collection of essays by a leading social historian emphasizing the experience of working-class life in the half century following 1865.

Stephen Thernstrom. *Progress and Poverty: Social Mobility in a Nineteenth-Century City* (1964); and *The Other Bostonians: Poverty and Progress in the American Metropolis* (1973). Both books deal with social mobility for working people and the middle class in nineteenth-century America. The results were mixed: In Newburyport movement up the social and occupational ladder for wage earners was modest and difficult; in Boston it was remarkably easy, especially for native-born Americans, Northern Europeans, Protestant immigrants, and Jews.

Stanley Buder. *Pullman: An Experiment in Industrial Order and Community Planning, 1880–1930* (1967). As much urban as labor history, this book tells the story of the town of Pullman and views it as an example of unsuccessful paternalism.

David Montgomery. *Beyond Equality: Labor and the Radical Republicans, 1862–1872* (1967). An interesting attempt to connect the Gilded Age labor movement to the egalitarian ideas of the 1860s Radical Republicans.

Daniel Walkowitz. *Worker City, Company Town: Iron and Cotton Worker Protest in Troy and Cahoes, New York, 1855–1884* (1978). A study of two New York industrial towns with different ethnic mixes and with different property distribution patterns.

David Brody. *Steelworkers in America: The Nonunion Era* (1960). Brody shows not only what produced discontent among American steelworkers before 1919, but also what encouraged labor's stability and acquiescence.

Harold C. Livesay. *Samuel Gompers and Organized Labor in America* (1978). Goes beyond biography and tells us much of the evolving labor movement, particularly the AFL, during the years 1890 to 1920.

Daniel T. Rogers. *The Work Ethic in Industrial America, 1850–1920* (1975). Examines the intellectual defense of hard work and steady application that accompanied industrialization in the United States.

Daniel Bell. *Marxian Socialism in the United States* (1962). Bell, a former Marxist, is critical of socialism in this short history.

Nick Salvatore. *Eugene V. Debs: Citizen and Socialist* (1982). Written by a scholar sympathetic to, but not uncritical of, the Socialist leader.

Charles Francis Adams, Jr., and Henry Adams. *Chapters of Erie* (1866). The classic account of the chicanery of Jay Gould and his confederates. The work of patrician descendants of Presidents John Adams and John Quincy Adams.

Maury Klein. *The Life and Legend of Jay Gould* (1986). Professor Klein attempts the difficult here: rehabilitating the reputation of Jay Gould.

Ron Chernow. *Titan: The Life of John D. Rockefeller, Sr.* (1998). A new, first rate biography of the man who parlayed business acumen and rigid, puritan morals into the country's largest fortune.

CHAPTER 18   *Age of the City*

Maury Klein and Harvey A. Kantor. *Prisoners of Progress* (1976). The authors briskly describe American industrialization and the growth of cities between 1850 and 1920.

Sam B. Warner. *Streetcar Suburbs: The Process of Growth in Boston, 1870–1900* (1962). Warner describes the developing economic and social segregation of city and suburbs as the middle and upper classes left Boston, spurred on by the "rural ideal."

Thomas Kessner. *The Golden Door: Italian and Jewish Immigrant Mobility in New York City, 1880–1915* (1977). A case study of urban social mobility for two important New Immigrant groups.

Philip Taylor. *The Distant Magnet: European Immigration to the U.S.A.* (1971). This volume by an English scholar deals with European immigration to the United States for the whole period from 1830 to 1930.

Stanford Lyman. *Chinese Americans* (1974). Tells of the constant tension in Chinese-Americans between desires for community and ethnic integrity and acceptance in the wider world of Caucasian America.

Matt S. Meier and Feliciano Rivera. *The Chicanos: A History of Mexican Americans* (1972). A brief survey of the whole sweep of Mexican-American history.

John Higham. *Strangers in the Land: Patterns of American Nativism, 1860–1925* (1955). Higham demonstrates how the post-Civil War European immigrant often became a scapegoat when Americans suffered a loss of confidence as a result of depression, war, or some other crisis.

Abraham Cahan. *The Rise of David Levinsky* (1917). Written by a Jewish immigrant journalist and editor who settled in New York's Lower East Side, it vividly describes sweatshops, problems between the established German Jews and the newer arrivals from eastern Europe, and conflicts between generations in immigrant families.

Seymour Mandelbaum. *Boss Tweed's New York* (1965). Tweed was not a good man, but he was a useful one—as Professor Mandelbaum shows in this study of Thomas Nast's favorite villain.

Zane Miller. *Boss Cox's Cincinnati* (1968). Cox, too, was useful, but more enlightened and honest than Tweed.

Humbert Nelli. *The Italians in Chicago, 1880–1930* (1970). A model study of an urban ethnic group of the New Immigration following 1880.

Melvin Holli. *Reform in Detroit: Hazen Pingree and Urban Politics* (1969). Pingree was the "potato-patch mayor" of Detroit who fought the transit magnates and brought reform with a heart to his city.

Theodore Dreiser. *Sister Carrie* (1900). Recounts the experiences of a young rural woman who comes to Chicago to make her fortune and succeeds primarily by choosing, and using, the right lovers.

Gunther Barth. *City People: The Rise of Modern City Culture in Nineteenth-Century America* (1980). A fine treatment of the culture of Gilded Age American cities.

CHAPTER 19 *The Trans-Missouri West*

Walter P. Webb. *The Great Plains* (1931). The classic study of the Great Plains. Webb shows the important ways in which geography and climate modified transplanted institutions.

Fred A. Shannon. *The Farmer's Last Frontier: Agriculture, 1860–1897* (1945). This older work is still the indispensable study of agriculture in the generation following the Civil War.

Allan G. Bogue. *Money at Interest: The Farm Mortgage on the Middle Border* (1955); and *From Prairie to Corn Belt* (1963). Bogue denies that eastern moneylenders made excessive profits from western farmers. He also claims that corn belt farmers did very well for themselves in the late nineteenth century.

Everett Dick. *The Sod-House Frontier, 1854–1890* (1954). The subtitle of this book is: "A Social History of the Northern Plains from the Creation of Kansas & Nebraska to the Admission of the Dakotas."

Rodman W. Paul. *Mining Frontiers of the Far West, 1848–1880* (1963). Combines excellent scholarship with a sense of the romantic aspect of the great western mining bonanzas.

R. K. Andrist. *The Long Death: The Last Days of the Plains Indians* (1964). A skillful overview of the tragic destruction of the Plains tribes by the encroachment of "civilization."

Robert W. Mardock. *Reformers and the American Indian* (1970). Surveys the Indian reformers through to the Dawes Act of 1887 and sees them as sincere but limited and culture-bound.

Ernest Staples Osgood. *The Day of the Cattlemen* (1929). A brief classic study of the range cattle industry of the northern Plains.

Robert Utley. *The Lance and the Shield: The Life and Times of Sitting Bull* (1993). An impressive new scholarly treatment of Sitting Bull and his tribe and also, along the way, a reexamination of Indian–white relations after the Civil War.

Robert Dykstra. *The Cattle Towns* (1968). A study of the cattle towns between 1876 and 1885 that emphasizes the nature of town life in the cattle communities and talks as much of drygoods merchants as of cowboys and dance-hall girls.

Gene M. Gressley. *Bankers and Cattlemen* (1966). The subtitle of this book is "The Stocks-and-Bonds, Havana-Cigar, Mahogany-and-Leather Side of the Cowboy Era."

Hamlin Garland. *Main-Travelled Roads* (1891). Garland, who settled with his parents on the Iowa prairie, learned early that "farming is not entirely made up of berrying, tossing the new-mown hay, and singing 'The Old Oaken Bucket' on the porch by moonlight."

Frank Norris. *The Octopus* (1901). In this description of California wheat growers in the Central Valley, the Southern Pacific Railroad is depicted as "a giant parasite fattening upon the lifeblood of an entire commonwealth."

Robert Utley. *The Last Days of the Sioux Nation* (1963). The best, most complete treatment we have of the Ghost Dance uprising and the Wounded Knee massacre.

CHAPTER 20   *The Gilded Age*

H. Wayne Morgan, (editor). *The Gilded Age: A Reappraisal* (1970). Twelve contributors write on civil service reform, labor, the robber barons, science, the currency question, the party system, Populism, foreign policy, popular culture, and the arts.

Richard Jensen. *The Winning of the Midwest: Social and Political Conflict, 1888–1896* (1971). Using statistical data, Jensen demonstrates how political affiliations during the Gilded Age were often determined by social and religious values rather than by pocketbook issues.

John G. Sprout. *"The Best Men": Liberal Reformers in the Gilded Age* (1968). A fine study of Gilded Age reform focusing on the Liberal Republican movement of 1872 and the later Mugwumps.

Irwin Unger. *The Greenback Era: A Social and Political History of American Finance, 1865–1879* (1964). Deals with post-Civil War finance as an example of who controlled political power in the Gilded Age. The author of *These United States* tends to be partial to this work.

Morton Keller. *Affairs of State: Public Life in Late-Nineteenth-Century America* (1977). Shows how the social and economic transformation of the nation between 1865 and 1900 was reflected in its political life.

Matthew Josephson. *The Politicos, 1865–1896* (1938). The classic older treatment of Gilded Age politics. According to Josephson, the political leadership of the period was thoroughly unprincipled.

Allan Nevins. *Grover Cleveland: A Study in Courage* (1932). One of the best political biographies for the era remains this older work by a master of narrative history, Allan Nevins.

Ari Hoogenboom, *Rutherford B. Hayes* (1996). Another fine biography of a Gilded Age political leader.

Mark Twain and Charles Dudley Warner. *The Gilded Age* (1873). This satire on the "all-pervading speculativeness" in business life and corruption in politics gave the Gilded Age its name.

Mary R. Dearing. *Veterans in Politics: The Story of the G. A. R.* (1952). A study of the Civil War Union veterans' organization, the Grand Army of the Republic, as a political pressure group and a bulwark of the Republican party after 1865.

John D. Hicks. *The Populist Revolt: A History of the Farmers' Alliance and the People's Party* (1931). This is the standard older treatment of late-nineteenth-century agrarian insurgency. Hicks sees the Populists as the forerunners of twentieth-century American liberalism.

O. Gene Clanton. *Populism: The Humane Preference in America, 1890–1990* (1991). A strong defense of Populism as a humane alternative to mainstream politics of the 1890s.

Lawrence Goodwyn. *Democratic Promise: The Populist Movement in America* (1976). An impassioned defense of the Populists against their detractors.

Louis W. Koenig. *Bryan: A Political Biography of William Jennings Bryan* (1971). The best one-volume biography of Bryan. Fair without being enthusiastic.

Paul Kleppner. *The Cross of Culture: A Social Analysis of Midwestern Politics 1850–1900* (1970). Kleppner's book is the pioneer study of Gilded Age cultural politics.

Morton White. *Social Thought in America: The Revolt Against Formalism* (1957). Written by a Harvard philosopher who has made American thought his province, it is by far the best study of the changes in social thought as molded by Darwinism in these years.

Richard Hofstadter. *Social Darwinism in American Thought* (1944). This work deals not only with the conservatives who used Darwin to defend the social and economic status quo, but also with those who used evolutionary ideas to defend reform.

Lawrence Vesey. *The Emergence of the American University* (1965). The best one-volume study of the new currents in graduate and professional training that arose during this period.

Lawrence A. Cremin. *The Transformation of the School: Progressivism in American Education, 1876–1957* (1961). Examines the roots, the course, and the eventual transformation of the "progressive movement" in education that John Dewey helped to launch.

Arthur M. Schlesinger. *The Rise of the City, 1878–1898* (1933). This older book is still one of the few good treatments of popular culture as a whole during the Gilded Age.

Oliver W. Larkin. *Art and Life in America* (1949). This work covers far more than the period of this chapter, and so can be consulted selectively by the student of the Gilded Age.

John Burchard and Albert Bush-Brown. *The Architecture of America: A Social and Cultural History* (1966). What applies to Larkin's book also applies to this work.

Lewis Mumford. *The Brown Decades: A Study of the Arts in America, 1865–1895* (1931). This still readable and useful book was a ground-breaking attack on Victorian architecture and a defense of the "modern" trend.

W. A. Swanberg. *Citizen Hearst* (1961). A colorful, critical biography of William Randolph Hearst, one of the creators of yellow journalism, by an outstanding popular biographer.

Sidney Hook. *John Dewey* (1939). An intellectual biography of Dewey by one of his most articulate disciples.

Burton Bledstein. *The Culture of Professionalism: The Middle Class and the Development of Higher Education in America* (1976). Bledstein makes a linkage between the ambition of the mid-nineteenth-century American middle class, the development of the professions, and the rise of the university.

Justin Kaplan. *Mr. Clemens and Mark Twain* (1966). As the title suggests, Kaplan sees Mark Twain as a deeply divided personality, a man who wanted both wealth and success and yet despised all they represented.

Gunther Schuller. *Early Jazz* (1968). The best discussion of jazz from its origins to the early 1930s—by a fine modern composer.

CHAPTER 21   *The American Empire*

Walter LaFeber.   *The New Empire: An Interpretation of American Expansion, 1860–1898* (1963). A study of late-nineteenth-century American expansionism by a scholar who believes that "economic forces [were] the most important causes" of the expansionist impulse.

Ernest R. May.   *American Imperialism* (1968). May ascribes American expansionism at the end of the nineteenth century to the appearance of a foreign policy elite inspired by the example of Britain, France, and Germany.

Walter Millis.   *The Martial Spirit: A Study of Our War with Spain* (1931). Sees the war's origins in the gradual development of a warlike spirit that derived from a mixture of boredom, greed, politics, and the yearning for glory.

Julius W. Pratt.   *Expansionists of 1898: The Acquisition of Hawaii and the Spanish Islands* (1936). Pratt criticizes the view, common in his day, that the Spanish-American War was the work of business groups anxious to acquire markets.

Graham A. Cosmas.   *An Army for Empire: The United States Army in the Spanish-American War* (1971). This study of the army and the War Department during the war with Spain seeks to refute the usual picture of bungling and general incompetence.

Kenton J. Clymer.   *John Hay: The Gentleman as Diplomat* (1975). A study of Secretary of State John Hay's thought about such matters as race, expansion, England, and China.

Howard K. Beale.   *Theodore Roosevelt and the Rise of America to World Power* (1956). An effective, if not always fair, attack on TR for his jingoism and imperialistic arrogance.

Joseph Wisan.   *The Cuban Crisis as Reflected in the New York Press* (1934). Wisan probably exaggerates the significance of the Hearst–Pulitzer circulation battle in New York as a cause of the Spanish-American War, but this study does tell us much about American values and prejudices, and how prowar groups played on them.

Frank A. Freidel.   *Splendid Little War* (1958). The words and pictures of news correspondents, artists, and photographers tell the story of the war in Cuba.

Robert Beisner.   *Twelve Against Empire: The Anti-Imperialists, 1898–1900* (1968). Beisner studies twelve prominent Americans who opposed the Spanish-American War. All upper-class Republicans or former Mugwumps, they believed that acquiring unwilling colonies ran counter to American principles and would threaten democracy at home.

Leon Wolff.   *Little Brown Brother* (1961). War in the Philippines lasted from 1898 to 1902, but after 1898 the United States, as explained in this work, fought not Spain but Filipino guerrillas.

Thomas J. McCormick.   *China Market: America's Quest for Informal Empire, 1893–1901* (1967). Informed by Vietnam era views, this book claims America's China policies were intended to solve the problems of domestic economic overproduction through an Open Door agreement to assure American domination of the China market.

David C. McCulloch.   *The Path Between the Seas: The Creation of the Panama Canal, 1870–1914* (1977). A lively account of the building of the great isthmian canal, from the early French effort to the final success under the auspices of the United States.

CHAPTER 22   *Progressivism*

Richard Hofstadter.   *Age of Reform: From Bryan to F.D.R.* (1955). Urban and middle-class in origin, according to Hofstadter, the progressive movement failed to achieve real reform because its members distrusted organized labor and immigrants and were obsessed with threats to their own status from both the left and the right.

Lincoln Steffens. *Autobiography* (1931). The famous muckraker eventually became disillusioned with the liberal values that motivated progressivism, concluding that capitalism itself was responsible for political corruption and social oppression.

James Harvey Young. *The Toadstool Millionaires: A Social History of Patent Medicines in America Before Federal Regulation* (1962). This funny and tragic tale of the gullible, hypochondriacal public and the patent-medicine manufacturers will tell you something about modern advertising.

Allen F. Davis. *Spearheads for Reform: The Social Settlements and the Progressive Movement, 1890–1914* (1967). Shows the frustration of settlement workers' efforts for social justice in the wards. Davis evaluates their success in citywide and national politics, especially their influence on education, housing, unions, and female and child labor.

David Thelen. *The New Citizenship: Origins of Progressivism in Wisconsin, 1885–1900* (1972). This well-written monograph on progressivism in Wisconsin emphasizes the role consumer anger and frustration played in launching the new reform movement.

August Meier. *Negro Thought in America, 1880–1915* (1963). Analyzes what Booker T. Washington, W. E. B. Du Bois, and other black leaders' thought about contemporary politics, economics, migration, colonization, racial solidarity, and industrial and elite education.

James Weldon Johnson. *Autobiography of an Ex-Coloured Man* (1912). This is a fictional composite autobiography of blacks before World War I by a real black composer and lyricist, lawyer, a founder of the NAACP, and chronicler of Harlem.

Henry F. Pringle. *Theodore Roosevelt* (1931). Pringle's long and graceful biography follows the many TRs: sickly boy, university dude, reformer in New York City, Dakota rancher, Washington office seeker, Rough Rider in Cuba, president, Bull Mooser, and anti-Wilsonite.

Upton Sinclair. *The Jungle* (1906). Sinclair, a socialist, intended this novel to arouse the nation's indignation about the meatpackers' working conditions. Instead, his nauseatingly detailed descriptions of the meat prepared for public consumption turned the nation's stomach.

Roy Lubove. *The Progressives and the Slums* (1962). Focusing on New York City, Lubove has written a fine study of how the progressives dealt with one of the key social problems of the day—the slums.

William Harbaugh. *The Life and Times of Theodore Roosevelt* (1975). Harbaugh's, biography of TR is more up-to-date and more in tune with recent scholarship than Pringle's.

Samuel P. Hays. *Conservation and the Gospel of Efficiency: The Progressive Conservation Movement, 1890–1920* (1959). This was a ground-breaking book when it appeared and is still important for the serious student of progressivism. Emphasizes the progressives' obsession with efficiency.

John D. Buenker. *Urban Liberalism and Progressive Reform* (1973). Buenker believes that we must not ignore the interest in, and support of, progressivism by urban working people and their political spokespersons in Congress and the state legislatures.

George Mowry. *The California Progressives* (1951). This study of progressivism in a banner progressive state helped introduce the thesis that the progressives were middle-class citizens suffering from acute social anxiety as a result of threats to their status.

Arthur Link. *Woodrow Wilson and the Progressive Era* (1954). Still the best study of the Wilsonian phase of progressivism. Link admires his subject, but he can also see his flaws.

Aileen Kraditor. *The Ideas of the Woman Suffrage Movement, 1890–1920* (1965). A study of the thought of the women's suffrage movement leaders during the final drive that brought success.

William O'Neill. *Everyone Was Brave: A History of Feminism in America* (1971). A lively, intelligent discussion of feminism with an especially good section on feminist politics in the Progressive Era.

CHAPTER 23   *World War I*

N. Gordon Levin. *Woodrow Wilson and World Politics: America's Response to War and Revolution* (1968). Levin maintains that the "effort to construct a stable world order of liberal–capitalist internationalism"—safe from "imperialism of the Right" and "revolution of the Left"—was basic to Wilson's foreign policy and all subsequent American policy-making.

Robert E. Quirk. *An Affair of Honor: Woodrow Wilson and the Occupation of Veracruz* (1962). Quirk's treatment of the Tampico incident and the shelling and occupation of Veracruz by American marines is brief and well written.

Walter Millis. *Road to War: America, 1914–1917* (1935). Writing when most citizens believed that America's entry into World War I was a mistake, Millis blames Allied propaganda, American businessmen, and anti-German prejudice for dragging the nation into an unnecessary conflict.

Arthur S. Link. *Woodrow Wilson and the Progressive Era, 1910–1917* (1954). Half of this book is devoted to Wilson's foreign policy and the advent of war with the Central Powers. Link sees the president as motivated by idealism and a sincere desire to stop brutal aggression.

Frederick Luebke. *Bonds of Loyalty: German-Americans and World War I* (1974). Luebke describes the unfair treatment of German-Americans during 1917–1918.

Ralph Stone. *The Irreconcilibles: The Fight Against the League of Nations* (1970). This is the best study of Lodge and his anti-League colleagues.

Randolph S. Bourne. *War and the Intellectuals: Collected Essays, 1915–1919.* Edited and introduced by Carl Resek (1964). Bourne, a brilliant political commentator, ridicules the tendency of many of his fellow intellectuals to justify American intervention in progressive and moral terms. Why did the United States fight? Because, Bourne says, "War is the health of the State."

John Dos Passos. *Three Soldiers* (1921). Three young men of very different temperaments and backgrounds meet in an army training camp and go to war. Dos Passos traces their spiritual destruction in this novel.

Erich Maria Remarque. *All Quiet on the Western Front* (1929) The author of this novel was a German private serving in the trenches of the Western Front. He recounts the death of spirit and passion in living men under the extreme conditions of trench warfare.

Florette Henri. *Black Migration: Movement North, 1900–1920* (1975). A sympathetic survey of the migration of 1.25 million blacks from the South, the "hard-luck place," to northern cities, where wages were higher and jobs more plentiful.

Ernest May. *The World War and American Isolation, 1914–1917* (1959). A balanced study of American entrance into World War I that uses the German as well as the Allied archives.

Robert Ferrell. *Woodrow Wilson and World War I, 1917–1921* (1985). Ferrell celebrates Wilson's soaring idealism but also criticizes his stubbornness and racial bigotry.

CHAPTER 24   *The Twenties*

Frederick Lewis Allen. *Only Yesterday: An Informal History of the 1920s* (1931). This 1932 bestseller vividly sketches the politics, morals, fashions, heroes, business, and arts of the "bally-hoo" twenties.

Irving Bernstein. *The Lean Years* (1960). Bernstein describes the very different responses of organized and unorganized 1920s workers to change, the role played by employer associations, and the courts' use of injunctions to break strikes.

Ray Ginger. *Six Days or Forever? Tennessee v. John Thomas Scopes* (1958). Ginger's sharp, witty portraits of Darrow and Bryan are entertaining, and quotations from the court proceedings make this book valuable for research as well as good general reading.

William E. Leuchtenburg. *The Perils of Prosperity, 1914–1932* (1958). Leuchtenburg treats the cultural conflicts of the 1920s, industrial development, labor, morals, and the nature and limits of the decade's prosperity. He emphasizes the confrontation of the city and the small town.

Robert S. Lynd and Helen M. Lynd. *Middletown: A Study in Modern American Culture* (1929). In this classic sociological study of Muncie, Indiana, during the 1920s, the Lynds examine the effects of mass production, the car, electricity, and advertising on attitudes toward work, leisure, education, the family, and the community.

Robert K. Murray. *Red Scare: A Study in National Hysteria, 1919–1920* (1955). A fine study of the post-World War I Palmer raids. Murray is highly critical of the attorney general's brutal disregard of civil liberties.

William Manchester. *Disturber of the Peace: The Life of H. L. Mencken* (1951). Superpatriots, public officials, intellectuals, reformers, and "homo boobiens"—none were safe from Mencken's gibes.

Roderick Nash. *The Nervous Generation: American Thought, 1917–1930* (1970). Nash writes of the uncertainty and contradiction in American thinking about war, democracy, the nation, aesthetics, nature, humanity, and ethics during the 1920s.

Andrew Sinclair. *Prohibition: Era of Excess* (1962). Sinclair explores the social and psychological forces behind the enactment and repeal of Prohibition.

Edmund Moore. *A Catholic Runs for President, 1928* (1956). A good treatment of the Smith-Hoover battle.

Joan Hoff Wilson. *Herbert Hoover, Forgotten Progressive* (1975). Portrays Hoover as a progressive, rather than the reactionary New Dealers believed him to be.

Norman Furniss. *The Fundamentalist Controversy, 1918–1931* (1954). Discusses the Scopes trial and much else regarding the conservative Protestant surge of the twenties.

Paula Fass. *The Damned and the Beautiful: American Youth in the 1920s* (1977). The title is misleading; this is really a book about college youth in the twenties. But on that subject it is the last word.

Geoffrey Perrett. *America in the Twenties: A History* (1982) A brilliant account of a period that has often inspired brilliant writing.

Ann Douglas. *A Terrible Honesty: Mongrel Manhattan in the 1920s* (1995). The book's thesis is that during the 1920s the nation's metropolis profited from a rare blend of blacks and whites, Jews and Christians, men and women who joined together to create a tolerant, sophisticated, culture that quickly conquered the western world.

CHAPTER 25 *The New Deal*

John Kenneth Galbraith. *The Great Crash, 1929* (1955). This account of the great Wall Street panic of 1929 explains its causes and effects without resorting to technical jargon.

Peter Temin. *Did Monetary Forces Cause the Great Depression?* (1976). Tackles the question: Was it money mismanagement that produced the Depression? Author says no, and accepts instead the Keynesian view that weak investment was the culprit.

William E. Leuchtenburg. *Franklin D. Roosevelt and the New Deal, 1932–1940* (1963). In this excellent short history of Roosevelt and the New Deal, Leuchtenburg maintains that Roosevelt assumed "that a just society could be secured by imposing a welfare state on a capitalist foundation."

Richard H. Pells. *Radical Visions and American Dreams: Culture and Social Thought in the Depression Years* (1973). In a well-written analysis of articles, books, novels, plays, and films of the 1930s, Pells seeks to demonstrate an underlying conservatism in the thought of the intellectual elite.

Studs Terkel. *Hard Times: An Oral History of the Great Depression* (1970). Terkel interviews miners, farmers, migrant farm workers, corporation presidents, a "Share Our Wealth" organizer, hobos, and teachers. Depression poverty created feelings of confusion, shame, and guilt in many of these people.

Robert S. Lynd and Helen M. Lynd. *Middletown in Transition: A Study in Cultural Conflict* (1937). Returning to Muncie, Indiana in the 1930s, the Lynds found that its citizens believed the Depression to be a temporary problem that did not require radical changes.

James Agee and Walker Evans. *Let Us Now Praise Famous Men* (1941). Evans's photography complements Agee's sensitive, compassionate record of the daily lives of three white tenant cotton farmers in Alabama during the hard years of the 1930s.

Theodore Rosengarten. *All God's Dangers: The Life of Nate Shaw* (1974). An aged black Alabama cotton farmer tells of his years as a sharecropper in a world dominated by white landlords, bankers, fertilizer agents, gin operators, sheriffs, and judges.

Robert E. Sherwood. *Roosevelt and Hopkins: An Intimate History* (1948). Only about a third of this dual biography concerns the New Deal years, but that third is one of the best brief histories of political leadership during the Depression.

James M. Burns. *Roosevelt: The Lion and the Fox* (1956). The best discussion of Roosevelt as a domestic leader. Burns describes FDR's early life and his preparation for ultimate greatness.

Paul Conkin. *The New Deal* (1967). Conkin sees the New Deal as a lost opportunity to equalize wealth and power in the United States.

John Steinbeck. *The Grapes of Wrath* (1939). Recounts the story of midwestern farmers fleeing the Depression by heading west to California, and their reception there.

Michael Bernstein. *The Great Depression: Delayed Recovery and Economic Change in America, 1929–1939* (1989). The most recent discussion of the causes of the Great Depression. Rather technical at times.

Frank Freidel. *Franklin D. Roosevelt: A Rendezvous with Destiny* (1990). A one-volume distillation of decades-long research and writing on Roosevelt by the dean of Roosevelt scholars.

Lizabeth Cohen. *Making a New Deal: Industrial Workers in Chicago, 1919–1939* (1990). A first-rate study of ethnic life and ethnic politics in Chicago during the New Deal era and the decade immediately preceding.

CHAPTER 26   *World War II*

William Langer and S. Everett Gleason. *Challenge to Isolation, 1937–40* (1952); and *Undeclared War, 1940–41* (1953). These weighty studies are defenses of Roosevelt's foreign policy and support the view that war between Germany and the United States was inevitable.

James M. Burns. *Roosevelt: The Soldier of Freedom* (1970). Also sees foreign policy before and during the war through Roosevelt's eyes.

Robert Dallek. *Franklin D. Roosevelt and American Foreign Policy, 1932–1945* (1979). A monumental study (540 pages) covering all of Roosevelt's foreign policy.

Charles A. Beard. *President Roosevelt and the Coming of the War, 1941* (1948). Written by the dean of American progressive historians just before his death, this book indicts Roosevelt for bringing on an unnecessary war in 1941 to revive the flagging fortunes of his party and the New Deal.

Samuel Eliot Morison. *The Two-Ocean War: A Short History of the United States Navy in the Second World War* (1963). Morison had the good fortune to witness much actual sea action in both the Atlantic and Pacific, so this well-written account is based on some firsthand knowledge.

Barbara Tuchman. *Stilwell and the American Experience in China, 1911–1945* (1971). General "Vinegar Joe" Stilwell brilliantly commanded American forces in China until 1944, when Chiang Kai-shek had him recalled for advocating increased aid to Chinese Communist forces.

Dwight D. Eisenhower. *Crusade in Europe* (1948). An account in Eisenhower's own words of the American war effort in Europe that led to the final defeat of the Germans.

John Morton Blum. *V Was for Victory: Politics and American Culture During World War II* (1976). Shows the greed, bigotry, dishonesty, and stupidity as well as the selflessness, goodwill, patriotism, and intelligence of Americans "back home" during the war.

Richard Lingeman. *Don't You Know There's a War On? The American Home Front, 1941–45* (1970). Lingeman's book is lighter fare than Blum's and better at catching the flavor of American civilian life during the war.

Audrie Gardner and Anne Loftis. *The Great Betrayal: The Evacuation of the Japanese-Americans During World War II* (1969). A critical account of an event that weakened the moral position of the United States in a war against the enemies of freedom.

James P. Baxter. *Scientists Against Time* (1946). This popular history of the Office of Scientific Research and Development tells how industrial and university scientists worked with the military to develop improved radar, antisubmarine devices, rockets, blood substitutes, and medicines.

John Hersey. *Hiroshima* (1946). A gripping account of how the first atomic bombing affected six survivors: a clerk, two doctors, a poor widow with three children, a German missionary priest, and the pastor of a Japanese Methodist church.

John Toland. *The Rising Sun: The Decline and Fall of the Japanese Empire, 1936–1945* (1970). An American journalist-scholar tells the story of Japan's tragic try for world greatness. Rather sympathetic to Japan.

Robert Leckie. *Delivered from Evil: The Saga of World War II* (1987). A vivid, well-written journalistic history of the war on all fighting fronts.

CHAPTER 27   *Postwar America*

Dean Acheson. *Present at the Creation* (1969). Acheson's own account of his State Department experiences from 1941 to 1953, it is, not surprisingly, a strong defense of the Truman Doctrine, the Marshall Plan, NATO, and the Korean intervention.

Athan Theoharis. *Seeds of Repression: Harry Truman and the Origins of McCarthyism* (1971). Theoharis blames the liberals, rather than the political right, for McCarthyism.

Thomas C. Reeves. *The Life and Times of Joe McCarthy: A Biography* (1982). A masterly and unfailingly interesting biography by a careful scholar.

William F. Buckley, Jr., and L. B. Bozell. *McCarthy and His Enemies* (1954). A favorable view of Joe McCarthy by two conservatives associated with the *National Review*.

Alan Weinstein. *Perjury: The Hiss-Chambers Case* (1978). A definitive study that concludes that Hiss was guilty as charged.

Walter LaFeber. *America, Russia, and the Cold War* (1975); and David Horowitz, editor, *Containment and Revolution* (1967). "Revisionist" studies of the Cold War that strongly endorse the view that American policy was the predominant, and avoidable, cause of the confrontation with the Soviet Union.

Daniel Yergin. *Shattered Peace: The Origins of the Cold War and the National Security State* (1977). The United States after 1945, says Yergin, vacillated between the position that it could accommodate to the Soviet Union and that it was impossibile to compromise with an aggressive, expansionist power.

Alonzo Hamby. *Beyond the New Deal: Harry S Truman and American Liberalism* (1973). This solid volume is a defense of Truman and Truman liberalism.

Charles C. Alexander. *Holding the Line: The Eisenhower Era, 1952–1959* (1975). The title suggests the author's view of the Eisenhower administration.

Douglas T. Miller and Marion Nowak. *The Fifties: The Way We Really Were* (1977). The authors see the firties as a time of real but neglected problems.

David Riesman, Reuel Denney, and Nathan Glazer. *The Lonely Crowd: A Study of the Changing American Character* (1950). The influential study that made Americans worry about the loss of "inner direction." An important cultural document.

Scott Donaldson. *The Suburban Myth* (1969). Suburbs, Donaldson believes, were the most realistic solution of the mid-twentieth-century housing problem—the negative attitudes of American intellectuals notwithstanding.

Richard O. Davies. *The Age of Asphalt: The Automobile, the Freeway, and the Condition of Metropolitan America* (1975). Davis describes the reason for the 1956 Highway Act and discusses the neglected alternatives that might have eased our energy and urban crises.

Richard Kluger. *Simple Justice: The History of Brown v. Board of Education and Black America's Struggle for Equality* (1975). The best single volume on the civil rights movement in the 1950s. Focuses on the famous 1954 school desegregation decision of the Supreme Court.

Bruce Cook. *The Beat Generation* (1971). Cook's thesis is that the Beat movement of the 1950s anticipated much of the cultural and political radicalism of the 1960s.

Jack Kerouac. *On the Road* (1957). A Beat novel of characters frantically moving across the American landscape of the 1950s.

Ralph Ellison. *Invisible Man* (1952). A beautifully written, convincing, and often amusing novel of the coming of age of a young black man who is caught up in—and then dumped by—the Communist party.

Max Hastings. *The Korean War* (1987). This lively review of the Korean "police action" depicts the conflict as a dress rehearsal for Vietnam, with many of the same frustrations and confusions as the later war.

J. Ronald Oakley. *God's Country: America in the Fifties* (1986). Oakley shows that all was not necessarily well in the Garden of Eden, what with racism, the Cold War, and Joe McCarthy.

CHAPTER 28   *The Dissenting Sixties*

William O'Neill. *Coming Apart: An Informal History of America in the 1960s* (1971). A witty, highly readable, and opinionated overview of the mores, politics, culture, and thought of the 1960s.

Irwin Unger and Debi Unger. *1968: Turning Point* (1988). A panorama of the 1960s from the perspective of its culminating year. Strongly recommended.

Allen Matusow. *The Unraveling of America: A History of Liberalism in the 1960s* (1984). A critical examination of 1960s political liberalism as seen from the moderate left.

Arthur M. Schlesinger, Jr. *A Thousand Days: John F. Kennedy in the White House* (1965). A highly sympathetic portrait of the Kennedy presidency by a professorial participant in it.

Herbert Parmet. *Jack: The Struggles of John F. Kennedy* (1980); and *JFK: The Presidency of John F. Kennedy* (1983). A more balanced assessment of Kennedy and his administration than Schlesinger's.

Lyndon B. Johnson. *The Vantage Point: Perspectives of the Presidency, 1963–69* (1971). Johnson defends his administration's policies—not only the Great Society programs, but also the intervention in Vietnam.

Michael Harrington. *The Other America: Poverty in the United States* (1962). In this influential book, Harrington rediscovered poverty in America after the experts had said it no longer existed.

Irving Bernstein. *Guns Or Butter: The Presidency of Lyndon Johnson* (1996). A compendious survey of the Johnson presidency with particularly good sections on the Great Society.

Irwin Unger. *The Best of Intentions: The Triumph and Failure of the Great Society Under Kennedy, Johnson, and Nixon* (1996). Reviews the origins of the Great Society programs of the Sixties and gives them mixed reviews.

Doris Kearns. *Lyndon Johnson and the American Dream* (1976). A fascinating combination of psychological study, biography, and memoir, written by a scholar who enjoyed Johnson's trust and confidence from 1967 to his death in 1973.

Eric Goldman. *The Tragedy of Lyndon Johnson* (1969). Written by the White House "intellectual in residence," this critical book catches the tragic downfall of Lyndon Johnson.

Norman Podhoretz. *Why We Were in Vietnam* (1982). The author, a leading neoconservative intellectual, makes the best case possible for American involvement in Vietnam.

George Herring. *America's Longest War: The United States and Vietnam, 1950–1975* (1986). Herring was a dove who believed that America's containment policy, as displayed in Vietnam, was "fundamentally flawed in its assumptions."

Frances Fitzgerald. *Fire in the Lake: The Vietnamese and the Americans in Vietnam* (1972). Discusses the Vietnamese people and their history to provide the setting for the Vietnam War.

David Halberstam. *The Best and the Brightest* (1972). A sharply critical account of the foreign policy "establishment" under Kennedy and Johnson and how its members entangled the United States in the Vietnam War.

Nancy Zaroulis and Gerald Sullivan. *Who Spoke Up? American Protest Against the War In Vietnam, 1963–1975* (1984). A blow-by-blow account of the anti-Vietnam War movement. Encyclopedic.

Betty Friedan. *The Feminine Mystique* (1963). Friedan devastatingly attacks the 1950s cult of female domesticity and leaves it a shambles among most intellectuals and a large proportion of college-educated women. Helped launch the Sixties New Feminism.

Alice Echols. *Daring to Be Bad: Radical Feminism in America, 1967–1975* (1989). The author considers radical feminism "the most vital and imaginative force within the women's liberation movement."

David Garrow. *Bearing the Cross: Martin Luther King, Jr., and the Southern Christian Leadership Conference* (1986). Not so eloquent as Stephen Oats's *Let the Trumpet Sound* (1982), but better balanced on King.

Taylor Branch. *Parting the Waters: America in the King Years, 1954–63* (1988). An effective invocation of the early, more successful years of the civil rights movement.

Morris Dickstein. *Gates of Eden: American Culture in the Sixties* (1977). Written by a professor of literature who is young enough to have been at the center of things himself during the 1968 student uprising at Columbia University.

Theodore Roszak. *The Making of a Counter Culture: Reflections on the Technocratic Society and Its Youthful Opposition* (1969). Both a description of the 1960s counterculture phenomenon and an influential force in its emergence.

Charles Perry. *The Haight-Ashbury: A History* (1984). A depiction of "hippie heaven" during its brief glory period.

W. J. Rorabaugh. *Berkeley at War: The 1960s* (1989). The best treatment of the free speech movement as well as the later struggles in Berkeley between the young radicals and the university and political authorities.

James Miller. *Democracy Is in the Streets: From Port Huron to the Siege of Chicago* (1987). A sympathetic treatment of the student New Left during its heyday.

Todd Gitlin. *The Sixties* (1987). A positive, and nostalgic, treatment of the Sixties' insurgencies by a founder of SDS who became a journalism professor.

CHAPTER 29 *The Uncertain Seventies*

Richard Nixon. *Six Crises* (1962). Tells Nixon's own version of major early crises in his life, including the Hiss case, the Checkers Speech, Eisenhower's heart attack, his near-catastrophic visit to Caracas, the "kitchen debate" with Khrushchev, and the 1960 presidential contest with Kennedy.

Gary Wills. *Nixon Agonistes: The Crisis of the Self-Made Man* (1970). One of the best analyses of Richard Nixon and his place in American political history.

Theodore White. *Breach of Faith: The Fall of Richard Nixon* (1975). An excellent summary of Watergate by a master of political journalism who once admired Nixon.

Richard Nixon. *Memoirs* (1978). Not ultimately convincing, perhaps, but it does make it clear that Nixon was a fallible human being, not some inhuman monster. Written after Watergate.

Joan Hoff Wilson. *Nixon Reconsidered* (1994). Seeks to rehabilitate Nixon as a kind of liberal who expanded the Great Society programs of his predecessor.

Henry Kissinger. *The White House Years* (1979). A fascinating inside report on the making of American foreign policy during Nixon's first four years, by his national security adviser at the time.

John Osborne. *White House Watch: The Ford Years* (1977). A moderate appreciation of the Ford administration by a liberal journalist.

Robert Shogan. *Promises to Keep: Carter's First Hundred Days* (1977). A journalist's favorable report on the Carter administration's first three months in office.

Haynes Johnson. *In the Absence of Power: Governing America* (1980). An indictment of the Carter administration for its feebleness and lack of competence.

Studs Terkel. *Working People Talk About What They Do All Day and How They Feel About What They Do* (1974). Here 130 people from a wide range of American types talk about the frustrations and gratifications of earning a living in the 1970s while maintaining their sense of individual worth.

Barry Commoner. *The Politics of Energy* (1979). An indictment of American energy policy by a man who believes that most of the nation's energy difficulties have been caused by big-business groups greedy for profits.

Robert B. Stobaugh and Daniel Yergin, editors. *Energy Future: Report of the Energy Project at the Harvard Business School* (1978). The authors of these essays consider the 1970s energy crisis real and urge strict conservation as the way to deal with it.

William Quandt. *Decade of Decision: American Policy Toward the Arab-Israeli Conflict* (1977). The single best volume on this important subject.

Christopher Lasch. *The Culture of Narcissism: American Life in an Age of Diminishing Expectations* (1979). A pessimistic and somewhat carping book about what has gone wrong with American culture in the 1970s.

Ralph E. Smith, editor. *The Subtle Revolution: Women at Work* (1979). A survey of the enormous changes that have taken place in women's roles in the American economy since 1945, with special emphasis in the 1970s.

Kirkpatrick Sale. *Power Shift: The Rise of the Southern Rim and Its Challenge to the Eastern Establishment* (1975). A good analysis of the political rise of the Sun Belt and its significance for national affairs.

CHAPTER 30　*The "Reagan Revolution"*

Ronnie Dugger. *On Reagan: The Man and His Presidency* (1983). A highly critical view of Reagan and his administration by the publisher of the *Texas Observer*, a liberal magazine.

Elizabeth Drew. *Campaign Journal: The Political Events of 1983–1984* (1985). This volume is not as readable as Theodore White's *The Making of the President* series, but it is probably better reportage.

Charles Murray. *Losing Ground: American Social Policy, 1950–1980* (1984). Though this work deals with the years before Reagan's presidency, it conveys many of the conservative attitudes toward social policy that characterized the Reagan administration.

Sidney Blumenthal. *The Rise of the Counter-Establishment: From Conservative Ideology to Political Power* (1986). A critical, liberal-oriented analysis of the conservative surge of the 1970s and 1980.

Thomas Ferguson and Joel Rogers. *Right Turn: The Decline of the Democrats and the Future of American Politics* (1986). The authors conclude that Reaganism triumphed, not because public opinion shifted right, but because a new elite, composed of rich businesspeople, manipulated the electoral process successfully to achieve their conservative ends.

Robert S. McElvaine. *The End of the Conservative Era: Liberalism After Reagan* (1987). Placing his faith in a theory of conservative–liberal cycles, McElvaine believes the impetus behind the Reagan Revolution had waned by the mid-1980s.

Randy Shilts. *And the Band Played On: Politics, People, and the AIDS Epidemic* (1987). A San Francisco reporter chronicles the AIDS plague, both as an unfolding human tragedy and as a story of folly and error.

Garry Wills. *Reagan's America* (1988). An impressionistic, skeptical view of Ronald Reagan's life and career by a liberal scholar of the American presidency.

Jack W. Germond and Jules Witcover. *Wake Us When It's Over: Presidential Politics of 1984* (1985). This description of the 1984 election emphasizes the work of professional media and campaign advisers who packaged the candidates and brainwashed, misled, and deceived the voting public in the process.

David Stockman. *The Triumph of Politics: The Inside Story of the Reagan Revolution* (1986). The Reagan budget director's account of how he sold the president and his advisers an economic policy that he himself was unsure of and how, in his estimate, it failed.

Martin Anderson. *Revolution* (1988). A "supply-side," true-believer's view of the Reagan Revolution.

Donald Regan. *For the Record: From Wall Street to Washington* (1988). Bitter at being made the scapegoat for the Iran-Contra fiasco, Reagan chief-of-staff Don Regan reveals the confusion in the White House, Nancy Reagan's influence on the president, and various astrologers' influence on her.

Peggy Noonan. *What I Saw at the Revolution* (1990). A witty and wry account of what it was like to be a speechwriter for Ronald Reagan.

Nancy Reagan. *My Turn: The Memoirs of Nancy Reagan* (1989). The former First Lady gets her licks in in this volume—after taking it on the chin herself.

Clyde Prestowitz. *Trading Places: How We Allowed Japan to Take the Lead* (1988). Japan-bashing at its most convincing by a former U.S. trade official who had to negotiate with the Japanese.

Laurence Tribe. *Abortion: The Clash of Absolutes* (1990). A sophisticated history and analysis of the abortion war by a strong pro-choice constitutional lawyer at Harvard Law School.

Kevin Phillips. *The Politics of Rich and Poor: Wealth and the American Electorate in the Reagan Aftermath* (1990). Phillips, a conservative political analyst, is disillusioned by Reaganomics and foresees a new populist uprising based on class resentment just down the road.

Paul Freiberger and Michael Swaine. *Fire in the Valley: The Making of the Personal Computer* (1984). The best single-volume history of a subject so new that the ancient past is 1975.

CHAPTER 31   *A Different America?*

Arthur M. Schlesinger, Jr. *The Disuniting of America* (1992). A noted liberal expresses fear that recent tribalism will undermine a shared history and set of values among Americans.

Ronald Takaki. *A Different Mirror: A History of Multicultural America* (1992). Himself a Japanese-American, Takaki celebrates the diversity of America and emphasizes the plight of ethnics and people of non-European ancestry in a society dominated mostly by people of North European background.

Robert Hughes. *The Culture of Complaint: The Fraying of America* (1992). A prominent Australian-born art critic who finds both the purveyors of political correctness and many of their shriller conservative critics rather foolish people.

Katherine Roiphe. *The Morning After: Fear, Sex and Feminism* (1993). A young Ivy League graduate who condemns what she considers the excesses of feminist responses on campus to male behavior toward women.

Catherine MacKinnon. *Only Words* (1993). A leading feminist attorney attacks pornography as demeaning to women and calls for strict laws against it.

Dinesh D'Souza. *Illiberal Education: The Politics of Race and Sex on Campus* (1991). A sharp indictment of "politically correct" attitudes and teachings on American campuses by a young conservative, Asian by birth, who rejects the philosophy behind affirmative action and other forms of ethnic preference.

Joe Klein. *Primary Colors* (1996). An amusing novel about a presidential campaign, featuring a thinly disguised Bill Clinton, by "Anonymous," a thinly disguised political reporter, Joe Klein.

David Maraniss. *First in His Class: A Biography of Bill Clinton* (1995). A critical review of Clinton's early life. Shows the talents and the failings.

■ PHOTO CREDITS ■

INDEX